WORKING DRAFT

REVISING

New! Chapter 14 "The Form of Nonfiction Prose" emphasizes how form in writing embodies writers' purposes. It includes instruction on the following writing strategies.

- **Patterns of essay organization**
  Top down order
  Culminating order
  Open form

- **Connecting the parts**
  Introductions
  Endings
  Keeping your purposes visible
  Use reasons to explain
  Create topic chains
  Use transitions

- **Designing paragraphs**
  Seeing paragraphs: the visual dimension

  Unity and coherence:
    the psychological dimension
  Topic sentences
  Paragraph development

- **Making patterns of organization easy to recognize**
  Narration
  Description
  Definition
  Classificationv
  Comparison and contrast

A NOTE ABOUT THE ART IN *THE CALL TO WRITE*

The illustrations on the cover and pages of *The Call to Write* come from the murals painted in 1934 on the interior walls of the Coit Tower in San Francisco, an architectural landmark that offers visitors sweeping panoramas of the city and surrounding Bay Area.

The Coit Tower murals are the collaborative effort of twenty-six artists and their nineteen assistants. Funded by the Public Works of Art Project, the 3,691 square feet of murals in Coit Tower is one of the finest examples of public art commissioned by Franklin Delano Roosevelt's New Deal. The murals depict various scenes of life in California over half a century ago—the bustle of city streets, agricultural and industrial labor, the stock exchange, banking and law, department stores, libraries, newspaper work, college sports, and children at play.

Inspired by the muralists of the Mexican Revolution—Diego Rivera, David Alfaro Siqueiros, and José Clemente Orozco—the artists who painted the Coit Tower murals sought to capture the social and political concerns of the Great Depression. Their visual testimony to the resilience and hopes of ordinary people provides a fitting accompaniment to the goal of *The Call to Write*. Writing should belong to everyone in all aspects of their lives, as private individuals, as students, as workers, and as participants in public life. *The Call to Write* presents writing not just as a skill to master but as a means to participate meaningfully in the common life and to influence its direction.

THE CALL TO WRITE
Brief Edition

SECOND EDITION

John Trimbur
Worcester Polytechnic Institute

New York San Francisco Boston
London Toronto Sydney Tokyo Singapore Madrid
Mexico City Munich Paris Cape Town Hong Kong Montreal

Senior Vice President and Publisher: Joseph Opiela
Acquisitions Editor: Lynn M. Huddon
Development Manager: Janet Lanphier
Development Editor: Leslie Taggart
Executive Marketing Manager: Carlise Paulson
Supplements Editor: Donna Campion
Senior Production Manager: Valerie Zaborski
Project Coordination, Text Design, and Electronic Page Makeup: Electronic
    Publishing Services Inc., NYC
Cover Designer/Manager: John Callahan
Cover Illustration/Photo: Don Beatty Photo ©1981
Photo Researcher: Photosearch, Inc.
Manufacturing Buyer: Lucy Hebard
Printer and Binder: R.R. Donnelley & Sons
Cover Printer: Coral Graphic Services

Library of Congress Cataloging-in-Publication Data

Trimbur, John.
    The call to write / John Trimbur.--2nd ed.
        p. cm
    Includes bibliographical references and index.
    ISBN 0-321-08497-7 (pbk.)
    1. English language--Rhetoric. 2. Report writing--Problems, exercises, etc. 3. College
readers.   I. Title.

PE1408 .T694 2001
808'.0427--dc21

2001036685

Please visit our website at http://www.ablongman.com

ISBN 0-321-08497-7 (Brief, paperback)

1 2 3 4 5 6 7 8 9 10—DOC—04 03 02 01

Brief Contents

Detailed Contents

PART 2 WRITING PROJECTS 107

CHAPTER 4 LETTERS: ESTABLISHING AND MAINTAINING RELATIONSHIPS 111

Guide to Visuals

Writing is increasingly becoming a matter of designing documents that integrate written text with visual elements. The persuasiveness of many types of writing today relies on effective page layout and the appropriate incorporation of graphics. Desktop publishing systems, the hypermedia capabilities of the World Wide Web, and the availability of other new writing technologies enable writers to do the kind of work formerly reserved for print shops and graphic design professionals. To help you understand the options writers now have, *The Call to Write* contains many examples of visual design. The following list shows the range of visuals and documents that integrate text and graphics.

ADVERTISEMENTS AND PUBLICITY

BROCHURES

INFORMATIONAL GRAPHICS

FLYERS

LOGOS

MURALS AND GRAFFITI

POSTCARD

POSTER

REVIEWS AND RATING SYSTEMS

WEB PAGES

Preface

The Call to Write, Second Edition, offers students a broad introduction to writing so that they can learn to write with flexibility and influence in a variety of settings. Many of the assignments in the following chapters are typical of the writing college students are called on to do. A central aim of this book, after all, is to help students become effective writers in their college coursework. At the same time, The Call to Write takes as its starting point the view that writing is much more than a school subject. Writing is an activity individuals and groups rely on to communicate with others, organize their social lives, get work done, entertain themselves, and voice their needs and aspirations. Accordingly, this book presents a wide range of situations that call on people to write—in everyday life, in school, in the workplace, and in the public sphere.

Just as the situations that give rise to writing differ, so do the tools available to writers. Technologies of writing range from the handwritten note to the typed or word-processed essay to the new means of composing e-mail and hypertext in cyberspace. Writing can no longer refer simply to the traditional forms of print literacy. It also involves the visual design of the page and screen and the electronic communication media that enable the integration of text, graphics, sound, and video. While The Call to Write cannot teach many of the skills needed to operate the new writing technologies, it takes into account how writers use these new means of communication and how many forms of writing combine words and graphics to present a message.

One of the main premises of this book is that writing should belong to everyone in the various roles people play—as private individuals, as students, as workers, and as participants in public life. The Call to Write offers students an education in writing, with the goal of enabling them to see how writing connects individuals to others and to the cultural practices and social institutions that shape their lives. In this regard, the call to write—the felt sense that something needs to be said—presents writing not just as a skill to master but as a means to participate meaningfully in the common life and to influence its direction.

DISTINCTIVE FEATURES OF *THE CALL TO WRITE*

The goal of this book is to offer teachers and students a range of activities grounded in rhetorical traditions and the accumulated experience of successful writing instruction. It has been enormously gratifying that teachers and students who used the first edition of this book have confirmed the practical value of its approach. This second edition builds on—and seeks to refine—the basic features that give *The Call to Write* its distinctive character:

- **An emphasis on the rhetorical situation:** *The Call to Write* begins with the idea that writing doesn't just happen but instead takes place in particular social contexts. Throughout the book, students are provided with opportunities to analyze how rhetorical situations give rise to the call to write. A wide array of writing—from speeches, letters, Web sites, op-ed pieces, proposals, and reviews to comic strips, graffiti, listservs, ads, flyers, and newsletters, as well as academic articles, literary essays, and student work—illustrates the range and richness of situations that call on people to write.

- **Genre-based writing assignments:** To help students understand the choices available to them when they respond to the call to write, the "Writing Projects" in Part Two use the notion of genre as the basis for guided writing assignments. Each chapter in Part Two includes individual and collaborative writing assignments based on familiar genres; extensive treatment of invention, planning, peer commentary, and revision; samples of student writing; and an opportunity for students to reflect on the process of writing.

- **An emphasis on collaborative learning:** *The Call to Write* includes many opportunities for working together, as well as a collaborative project and guidelines for peer commentaries in each of the chapters in Part Two. Chapter 12, "Case Study of a Writing Assignment," traces a student's use of peer response to write an academic paper, and Chapter 13, "Working Together: Collaborative Writing Projects," offers information and advice about group writing projects.

- **Integration of reading and writing:** Chapter 2, "Reading Strategies: Analyzing the Rhetorical Situation," has been revised to help students learn how to analyze the situations that call on people to write, the choices writers make, and the effects of those choices on readers. Throughout the book, questions entitled "For Critical Inquiry" ask students to read closely and carefully, to understand their response as readers and the decisions writers make when they take up the call to write.

- **A focus on visual design:** *The Call to Write* emphasizes not only how many types of writing integrate text and graphics but also that writing itself is a form of visible language. Each chapter in Part Two includes a "Visual Design" reading that asks students to evaluate critically how a particular example of visual communication works. Chapter 19, "Visual Design," has been extensively revised to explore how visual design is used for purposes of identification, information, and persuasion and to provide instruction in effective page design.

■ **Online activities:** Throughout *The Call to Write* are many samples of online writing—e-mail messages, listservs, newsgroups, and Web sites. Each chapter in Part Two includes a "Going Online" activity that invites students to explore and evaluate the new electronic communication media; and the revised Chapter 15 "Communicating Online: Writing in the Age of Digital Literacy," presents information on how writers use the new writing technologies, as well as readings about the emerging cyberculture.

■ **An emphasis on ethics and the writer's responsibilities:** *The Call to Write* presents boxes on the "Ethics of Writing" that raise issues concerning writers' responsibilities toward their readers and their subjects. Chapter 3, "Persuasion and Responsibility: Analyzing Arguments," includes extensive coverage of how writers can deal responsibly with disagreements and negotiate their differences with others.

NEW TO THE SECOND EDITION

This second edition includes new and revised features to help students understand and respond to the call to write. These additions come in large part from discussions with writing teachers who used the first edition of *The Call to Write*.

■ **New writing assignments in Part One:** Each chapter in Part One now culminates with a writing assignment—to analyze a literacy event, to analyze a rhetorical situation, and to analyze an argument. Accompanied by a sample analysis, these assignments are meant to help students deepen their understanding of how writing works in the world.

■ **A new chapter, "Fact Sheets and FAQs, Brochures, and Web Sites," in Part Two:** This new chapter provides students with the opportunity to work with print and online informative genres of writing. On the page or on the screen, these three genres call on students to present ideas and information in forms that are easy for their intended audiences to read and use.

■ **New features in Part Two:** Each chapter in Part Two now includes "Exploring Your Experience," to tap into students' existing genre knowledge; "Rhetorical Analysis," to build on the analytical strategies in Part One; and "Genre Choices," to consider how writers decide which genre to use in a given situation.

■ **A new chapter, "The Form of Nonfiction Prose," in Part Three:** This new chapter (Chapter 14) emphasizes how the forms of writing embody writers' purposes. It includes sections on organization, beginnings and endings, transitions, and paragraphing.

- **A new section "The Ethics of Fieldwork" in Part Four:** This new section extends the treatment of the writer's responsibilities to consider relations between researchers and subjects.

- **Redesign of *The Call to Write*:** The new design makes the book more accessible and easier to use. Particularly in Part Two, we have streamlined the chapter structure to help students identify key points and stay focused on the various genres of writing.

USING *THE CALL TO WRITE*

This book is meant to be used flexibly to fit the goals and local needs of teachers, courses, and writing programs.

While there is no single path to follow in teaching *The Call to Write*, for most teachers the core of the book will be the writing projects in Part Two— the guided writing assignments based on common genres. Teachers can choose from among these genres and assign them in the order that best suits their course design.

A rich array of material appears in the other sections of *The Call to Write*, and teachers may draw on the various chapters to introduce key concepts and deepen students' understanding of reading and writing. It can be helpful to think of the organization of the book as a modular one that enables teachers to combine chapters in ways that emphasize their own interests and priorities.

The following overview of the organization of *The Call to Write* describes the six main parts of the book.

- **Part One, "Writing and Reading,"** introduces students to the notion of the call to write, offers strategies for critical reading and rhetorical analysis, and presents methods for identifying disputed issues, planning responsible arguments, and negotiating differences with others. These chapters can serve to introduce central themes at the beginning of a course, or they can be integrated throughout the course.

- **Part Two, "Writing Projects,"** presents familiar genres of writing, with examples, questions "For Critical Inquiry," and individual and collaborative writing assignments. Assignments call on students to write for a number of different audiences and in a number of different settings, ranging from everyday life to the academic world to public forums. These chapters form the core of *The Call to Write*.

- **Part Three, "Writers at Work,"** presents a case study of a student using peer commentary to complete an academic writing assignment, looks at how writers work together on collaborative writing projects, explores the meaning and purpose of form in writing, and considers the new electronic writing technologies. The chapters in Part Three can be integrated into a course at a number of points—to initiate discussion of how writers manage individual writing projects, to enhance student understanding of peer commentary, to prepare students for collaborative writing projects, to deepen students' understanding of form, and to highlight issues in electronic communication.

- **Part Four,** "Doing Research," explores what calls on people to do research, how they formulate meaningful questions, and what sources they typically use. Part Four provides an overview of the research process and introduces students to library, online, and field research. This section is particularly appropriate for writing courses that emphasize research-based writing.

- **Part Five,** "Presenting Your Work," looks at how writers communicate the results of their work to readers. It includes information on research papers and documentation, visual design, essay exams, and portfolios. The chapters in this part can be integrated into a course at many points, depending on the teacher's goals.

ADDITIONAL RESOURCES FOR *THE CALL TO WRITE*

The Call to Write, Second Edition, is accompanied by many helpful supplements, for both teachers and students.

For Instructors

The Instructor's Resource Manual, by Stephen Ruffus and Lisa Bickmore, both of Salt Lake Community College, provides background on the genre approach of *The Call to Write,* as well as practical teaching approaches to public writing, the ethics of writing, literacy narratives, portfolios, and collaboration. Sample syllabi and teaching tips for the Second Edition are also included.

An Introduction to Teaching Composition in an Electronic Environment, by Eric Hoffman and Carol Scheidenhelm of Northern Illinois University, offers a wealth of computer-related classroom activities. It also provides guidance for both experienced and inexperienced instructors who wish to make creative use of technology in a composition course.

The Allyn & Bacon Sourcebook for College Writing Teachers, Second Edition, edited by James McDonald of the University of Louisiana at Lafayette, provides instructors with a varied selection of readings written by composition and rhetoric scholars on both theoretical and practical subjects.

"Longman Resources for Instructors" also includes these other helpful texts: *Using Portfolios,* by Kathleen McClelland of Auburn University; *Comp Tales,* a collection of writing teachers' accounts of their teaching experiences, edited by Richard Haswell and Min-Zhan Lu; and the videos *Writing, Teaching, and Learning,* by David Jolliffe, and *Writing Across the Curriculum: Making It Work,* produced by Robert Morris College and the Public Broadcasting System.

For Students

The Literacy Library Series (*Public Literacy,* by Elizabeth Ervin of the University of North Carolina at Wilmington; *Workplace Literacy,* by Rachel Spilka of the University of Wisconsin, Milwaukee; and *Academic Literacy,* by Stacia Neeley of Texas Christian University offers additional models and instruction for writing for each of these three different contexts.

Visual Communication: A Writer's Guide, Second Edition, by Susan Hilligoss and Tharon Howard, both of Clemson University, examines the rhetoric and principles of visual design, with an emphasis throughout on audience and genre. Practical guidelines for incorporating graphics and visuals are featured along with sample planning worksheets and design samples and exercises.

Analyzing Literature: A Guide for Students, Second Edition, by Sharon James McGee of Southern Illinois University at Edwardsville, provides advice and sample student papers to help students interpret and discuss works from a variety of literary genres.

Researching Online, Fifth Edition, by David Munger and Shireen Campbell of Davidson College, gives students detailed, step-by-step instructions for performing electronic searches; for using e-mail, listservs, Usenet newsgroups, IRC, and MUDs and MOOs to do research; and for assessing the validity of electronic sources.

The Longman Writer's Journal, by Mimi Markus of Broward Community College, provides students with their own personal space for writing. It contains journal writing strategies, sample journal entries by other students, and many writing prompts and topics to help get students writing.

The Call to Write may also be packaged with other books at a discount. Two dictionaries are available: *Merriam-Webster's Collegiate Dictionary,* Tenth Edition, a hardcover desk dictionary, and *The New American Webster Handy College Dictionary,* Third Edition, a briefer paperback dictionary. Also, in conjunction with Penguin Putnam, Longman is proud to offer a variety of Penguin titles, such as Mike Rose's *Lives on the Boundary* and Julia Alvarez's *How the Garcia Girls Lost Their Accents.*

The Mercury Reader offers a database of nearly 500 classic and contemporary reading selections, with accompanying pedagogical elements, from which an instructor can create a customized book tailored to their course. An optional genre-based Table of Contents is available for *The Mercury Reader,* thus allowing instructors to create a custom reader that complements the approach of *The Call to Write.* For more information, please visit <http://www.pearsoncustom.com/database/merc.html>

Take Note! is a complete research information-management tool for students working on projects that require the use of outside sources. This cross-platform CD-ROM integrates note taking, outlining, and bibliography management into one easy-to-use package.

For Instructors and Students

A Companion Web site, *The Call to Write Online* (at <http://www.ablongman.com/trimbur>), also developed by Stephen Ruffus and Lisa Bickmore, includes interactive material for both the student and the instructor. For students, the site features two kinds of exercises: 1) writing and critical thinking activities, and 2) exercises to accompany online readings, that demonstrate the different genres highlighted in the text. The Web site also features "Going Online" sections that offer links to numerous other Web sites of interest, and "In the News" sections that highlight particular headline events in the news and provide a writing activity and annotated links for further inquiry. Finally, a collection of sample student documents is included on the site, annotated with marginal notes that discuss the strengths of each sample.

For instructors, this companion website also features the following materials:

■ sample course syllabi

■ a practical guide to "Communicating Online" that includes information on electronic portfolios, links to samples online, and sample assignments

■ a discussion of multimedia and visual rhetoric, with sample assignments

■ annotated links of interest to instructors

■ a brief discussion of the approach of The Call to Write and how it fits with the objectives described in the WPA Outcomes Statement.

CourseCompass is a nationally hosted, interactive online course management system powered by BlackBoard. This easy-to-use and customizable program enables professors to tailor content and functionality to meet individual course needs. Every CourseCompass course includes a range of preloaded content such as testing and assessment questions, chapter-level objectives, chapter summaries, illustrations, web activities and the complete text in electronic form—all designed to help students master core course objectives. For more information, or to see a demo, visit <www.coursecompass.com>.

Acknowledgments

Preparing *The Call to Write,* Second Edition, has made me acutely aware of the intellectual, professional, and personal debts I have accumulated over the years teaching writing, training writing teachers and peer tutors, and administering writing programs and writing centers. I want to acknowledge the contributions so many rhetoricians and composition specialists have made to my thinking about the study and teaching of writing, and I hope they will recognize—and perhaps approve of—the way their work has influenced the design of this book.

The unifying theme of the "call to write," as many will note immediately, comes from Lloyd Bitzer's notion of "exigence" and the "rhetorical situation." My treatment of argument and persuasion is informed by Aristotle's appeals (by way of Wayne Booth's sense of "rhetorical stance") and stasis theory (as articulated recently in Dick Fulkerson's *Teaching Argument in Writing*), and my understanding of reasoning in argument is altogether indebted to Stephen Toulmin (though the terminology I use differs somewhat). The influence of Carolyn Miller's seminal work on genre as "social action" should be apparent at every turn.

I learned to teach writing from two great mentors, Ken Bruffee and Peter Elbow, and their mark is everywhere in the book. My interest in visual design grows in part out of an ongoing collaboration with Diana George. Lester Faigley got me to pay attention to electronic communication and cyberspace. Bob Schwegler listened and offered key advice at many points.

I am happy to feature so much writing from students I have taught at Worcester Polytechnic Institute, where I developed and taught the bulk of the material that now appears in *The Call to Write.* Some of the student writing, I should note, has been edited for this book.

Leslie Taggart was the development editor for *The Call to Write,* and Lynn Huddon provided the in-house editorial support at Longman. I want to acknowledge their hard work, careful attention, good sense of humor, and loyalty to this project.

To the many reviewers who provided valuable feedback at many points, my thanks:

Jim Addison, Western Carolina University
Cathryn Amdahl, Harrisburg Area Community College

Jeff Andelora, Mesa Community College
Virginia Anderson, Indiana University Southeast

Chris Anson, North Carolina State University

Janet Atwill, University of Tennessee

Margaret Batschelet, University of Texas at San Antonio

Michelle Bellavia, Southeastern Louisiana University

Linda Bensel-Meyers, University of Tennessee

David Blakesley, Purdue University

Louise Bown, Salt Lake Community College

Barbara Boyd, California State University at Northridge

Patrick Bruch, University of Minnesota at Twin Cities

Rich Bullock, Wright State University

Vicki Byard, Northeastern Illinois University

Rich Caccavale, University of Denver

Tara Carter-Miller, Hawkeye Community College

Vincent Cassaregola, St. Louis University

Virginia Chappell, Marquette University

John Clark, Bowling Green State University

Lauren Coulter, University of Tennessee at Chattanooga

Avon Crismore, Indiana University-Purdue University

Meoghan Cronin, St. Anselm College

Helen Dale, University of Wisconsin

Beth Daniell, Clemson University

Susan DeRosa, Eastern Connecticut University

Tom Fox, California State University, Chico

Christy Friend, University of South Carolina

Ed Fryzel, Henry Ford Community College

Patrick Scott Geisel, Wright State University

Greg Glau, Arizona State University

Paula Guetschow, University of Alaska

Kay Heath, Louisiana State University

Marsha Lee Holmes, Western Carolina University

Rebecca Moore Howard, Syracuse University

Dollie Hudspeth, St. Philip's College

Christina Hult, Utah State University

Maurice Hunt, Baylor University

Jennifer Huth, University of Texas, Austin

Ted Johnston, El Paso Community College

Debra Jacobs, University of South Florida

Peggy Jolly, University of Alabama, Birmingham

Bonnie L. Kyburz, Utah Valley State College

Bill Lamb, Johnson County Community College

Elmer Lange, Northern Kentucky University

Madeline Lanza, Kansas State University

Sarah Liggett, Louisiana State University

Billie Luckie, Tidewater Community College

Michael Mackie, Community College of Denver

Barry Maid, University of Arizona, East

David Mair, University of Oklahoma

Rita Malenczyk, Eastern Connecticut State University

Marcia Mani, St. Louis Community College of Meramac

Miles McCrimmon, J.S. Reynolds Community College

Rick McDonald, University of South Florida

Sharon James McGee, Southern Illinois University at Edwardsville

Carolyn R. Miller, North Carolina State University

Lynn Meeks, Utah State University

Elizabeth Metzger, University of South Florida

Chrys Mitchell, Kirkwood Community College

Kate Mohler, Arizona State University

John David Moore, Eastern Illinois University

Marti Mundell, Washington State University

Gary Olson, University of South Florida

David Owens, Purdue University

Anne-Marie Paulin, Owens Community College

Jean Pickering, Fresno State University

Linda Polley, Indiana University/Purdue University

Nancy Prosenjak, Metropolitan State College

Kathryn Raigh, University of North Texas

Alison Regan, University of Utah

Duane Roen, Arizona State University

Stephen Ruffus, Salt Lake Community College

John Ruszkiewicz, University of Texas, Austin

Lucy Schultz, University of Cincinnati

Charles Schuster, University of Wisconsin, Milwaukee

Bob Schwegler, University of Rhode Island

Sally Shigley, Weber State University

John Shilb, Indiana University at Bloomington

Marsha Shively, Indiana University-Purdue University, Fort Wayne

James Simmons, University of North Dakota, Lake Region

Phil Sipiora, University of South Florida

David Smit, Kansas State University

Lee Smith, University of Houston

Rachelle Smith, Emporia State University

Joyce Stauffer, Indiana University/Purdue University

Bruce Stevenson, Mira Costa College

Margaret Syverson, University of Texas, Austin

Richard Taylor, East Carolina University

Peter Telep, University of Central Florida

Jeff Todd, West Texas A & M University

Mary Trautman, University of Rhode Island

Pauline Uchmanowicz, State University of New York, New Paltz

Victor Villanueva, Washington State University

Tony Viola, Ohio University-Athens

Irene Ward, Kansas State University

Jackie Wheeler, Arizona State University

Joe Williams, University of Chicago

Donna Winchell, Clemson University

Wendy Wright, El Camino Community College

Finally I want to acknowledge the contributions made by members of my family—Lundy Braun and Clare, Lucia, and Martha Catherine Trimbur. They not only provided emotional support; they were coworkers, contributing samples of their writing, suggesting readings and assignments, and locating listservs, newsgroups, and Web sites. This has been, in many respects, a joint venture, and I am gratified by their presence in the book.

John Trimbur

Cranston, RI

August 2001

PART ONE

Writing and Reading

INTRODUCTION: THE CALL TO WRITE

People write in response to situations that call on them to put their thoughts and feelings into words. The call to write may come from a teacher who assigns a paper, or from within yourself when you have ideas and experiences you want to write down. In any case, as you will see throughout this book, people who write typically experience some sense of need that can be met by writing. And, accordingly, what a person writes will be shaped by the situation that gave rise to the need.

The situations that call on people to write are as various as social life itself. Here are a few examples:

- Someone you know dies, and you want to write a letter of sympathy to the family.

- A friend transfers to another college, and you decide to stay in touch through e-mail.

- Your boss asks you to write a report on how to market a new product line.

- Your company wants to have a home page on the World Wide Web, and you offer to help design it.

- You belong to a campus organization and need to publicize your group's activities.

- You belong to an advocacy group (such as Amnesty International or the Sierra Club), and you need to inform the public about the issues—and to call on your readers to write to government officials.

- As a college student you are assigned book reviews, critical analyses, research papers, case studies, and lab reports.

As you can see, writing takes place in many different settings and for many purposes. By thinking about these various occasions for writing, you can deepen your understanding of your own and other people's writing and develop a set of strategies that will help you become a more effective writer. The three chapters in Part One of this textbook offer a way of looking at why and how people respond to the call to write. In Chapter 1, we'll look more closely at four contexts in which writing occurs—everyday life, the workplace, the public sphere, and school. In Chapter 2, we focus on how writers read in order to analyze the rhetorical situation. In Chapter 3, we consider what makes writing persuasive and how you can build a responsible and persuasive argument.

But first we look at how writers identify the call to write and determine whether and how to respond to it.

IDENTIFYING AND RESPONDING TO THE CALL TO WRITE

See Chapter 20, "Writing Portfolios," for more on integrating Reflecting on Your Writing exercises into a portfolio.

In some situations, identifying the call to write is straightforward. For example, your instructor assigns a term paper for a history class or a lab report for biology. In other situations, however, the call to write is far less direct. Suppose, for example, that you've just heard that there will be major cuts in student financial aid next year. Is this a situation you feel a need to respond to? Should your response take the form of writing?

In the case of the financial aid cuts, you'll have to analyze and interpret the situation. By doing so, you'll know whether you want to respond and will begin to see how you can do so effectively. Your analysis will involve asking questions about the situation: What's going on? What has happened? Who is involved? What seems to be at stake? What needs to be done?

Just because a situation seems to call for writing doesn't necessarily mean that you will respond in writing, however. You can probably think of times when you could have written something but, for one reason or another, let the occasion go by. Maybe you thought of writing to a friend who was going through hard times, but you decided to make a phone call instead. Or maybe you thought of writing a letter to the editor of your local newspaper, but never quite got around to it. Situations that seem to call for writing, after all, don't automatically put writers in motion.

If, however, you do respond to a situation by writing, your response should grow out of your analysis of the situation, whether it is relatively straightforward or complicated. For example, if you decide to send written invitations to a party (instead of phoning), your writing task is easy to identify: You need to buy invitations (or design one on your computer), include the pertinent information (for example, date, time, and place), and ask people to RSVP.

In contrast, if you decide to express your concern about cuts in financial aid, a range of writing tasks may be appropriate: You could write a leaflet proposing that students take action to stop the cuts, write a letter of protest to the officials who made the cuts, write a letter to the editor of the local newspaper explaining the significance of the cuts, or send a fact sheet to public officials to inform them about the cuts.

The fact that student financial aid will be cut, then, doesn't in itself determine your writing task or the form your response will take. In this and many other situations, responding effectively to the call to write means thinking about several crucial factors: your purpose, your readers and the relationship you want to establish with them, the appropriate voice or tone, and the larger social context. Taking these factors into account will enable you to choose the type (or *genre*) of writing—leaflet, letter, or fact sheet—that best suits the situation.

FACTORS THAT WRITERS TAKE INTO ACCOUNT

Let's look more closely at each of the factors writers typically take into account when they identify a call to write and turn it into a writing task:

- **Purpose:** Writers need to clarify what they are trying to accomplish with their writing. How do they want to influence the situation that gave rise to the call to write? What effect do they intend to have, and how will the writing achieve this effect?

  Let's return to the cuts in student financial aid. If you decide to respond to this situation, what kind of change will you try to bring about? Is it your purpose to call for a total reversal of the decision or only to propose a reduction of cuts? How will you try to bring about this change? Is it your purpose to rally students to oppose the cuts or to call on the decision makers directly? Depending on your purpose, what genre can best accomplish your goals?

- **Relationship to readers:** Closely related to decisions about purpose are decisions about your readers. As you can see, part of clarifying your purpose involves clarifying who your primary readers will be. How you construct a writing task depends in part on whom you choose as your intended readers and on what you know about them, their familiarity with the situation, and their interests and opinions.

  As you determine who your readers will be, you will also make decisions about your relationship to them. For example, if you are trying to convince students to demonstrate against the financial aid cuts, you can appeal to your relationship as peers and emphasize your common interests. On the other hand, if you are writing to decision makers in positions of authority, you are probably addressing readers who have more power than you do. Do you want to approach these readers as a humble petitioner, as a concerned student, as a morally outraged victim, as a threat, or as something else?

- **Voice:** The tone of voice in a piece of writing will vary depending on the purpose and the kind of relationship you want to establish with your readers. Voice is basically the attitude writers want to project to readers. Should your tone be formal or informal, intimate or distanced? Is it appropriate to express concern, sarcasm, or anger? These decisions hinge on what you want to achieve and whom you are addressing.

  In the case of the financial aid cuts, a tone that's appropriate for a piece of writing intended to call on students to take action may not be appropriate when intended to persuade decision makers or to inform the public. An important part of responding to the call to write is knowing how to modulate your voice to take on the right tone for the situation.

- **The social context:** Writing takes place in a social context. In the example of the financial aid cuts, the social context is a college or university, which is itself part of the larger system of higher education in the United States. To shape their writing tasks, writers draw on their knowledge of the social context by considering the people who are part of that context, what roles and relationships they have with one another, what they can and can't do in that context, and what kinds of writing are typically used in that context.

At the same time, the act of writing not only draws on what you know about the social context but connects you to it in various ways, depending on your situation and purposes. Writing answers to an exam, for instance, is very different from writing flyers to rally students against cuts in financial aid. And both forms differ from doodling in the margins of your notebook during a dull lecture. The social context in which each piece of writing takes place is the same, namely an American college or university. Nonetheless, each instance of writing puts you in a different relationship to the institutional context—whether as an academic performer trying to get a good grade, as an activist trying to change the direction of the institution, or as a bored student trying to make class time pass more easily.

- **Genre of writing:** Genres are the different types of writing people draw on to respond to the call to write. If you think about the genres listed in the discussion of financial aid cuts—leaflets, letters of protest, letters to the editor, and fact sheets—you can see that each one has characteristics that enable readers to recognize the writer's purpose and to understand the type of relationship the writer wants to establish with them. Accordingly, your choice of genre is always a key factor, because different genres approach readers in different ways and express different strategies to influence the situation at hand.

There are, of course, many genres of writing. In Part Two we treat some of the most familiar ones—letters, memoirs, public documents, profiles, fact sheets, brochures, websites, commentary, proposals, and reviews. Each genre offers a distinct strategy for dealing with typical writing situations.

Reflecting On Your Writing

1. Choose a piece of writing you've done at some time in the past. It could be a writing assignment in school, a note to a friend, something you wrote at work, a diary entry, a letter, an article for a student newspaper or community newsletter, a petition, a flyer, or a leaflet for an organization you belong to. Whatever the writing happens to be, write a page or two in which you describe the call that prompted you to write.

   - Describe the situation that made you feel a need to respond in writing.
   - Why did you decide to respond in writing instead of taking some other action or not responding at all?

■ How did you construct your writing task? Describe your purpose, the relationship you wanted to establish with your readers, and the tone of voice you decided to use in your writing. How did you make these decisions? What knowledge of the social context did you draw on to make those decisions? What type or genre of writing did you use to communicate your purpose?

2. With two or three other students, take turns reading aloud what you have written. Compare the situations that gave rise to the call to write and the way each of you responded. What, if anything, is similar about the way you identified and responded to the call to write? What was different? How would you account for the differences and similarities?

Note: You will find further exercises for Reflecting on Your Writing in Chapter 1 and at the end of each chapter in Parts One and Two. These activities can be used for various purposes:

■ for classroom discussion

■ as short writing assignments

■ to incorporate into a portfolio to submit at the end of the term

CHAPTER ONE

What Is Writing? Analyzing Literacy Events

Learning to write involves an understanding of your own experience as a writer—seeing how various situations have called on you to write, how you have shaped your writing tasks accordingly, and how your writing has involved you in relationships with people in various social contexts. In this chapter we look at how people respond to the call to write in four contexts:

1. writing in everyday life
2. writing in the workplace
3. writing in the public sphere
4. writing in school

In this chapter we present a wide range of writing samples to illustrate how writing is an integral part of our lives as private individuals, as workers, as citizens, and as students. The writing samples and assignments in this chapter ask you to come up with your own answer to the question, What is writing? by looking at how writing works in these contexts and how it can differ in purpose, intended readers, tone, and genre.

The goal of this chapter is to enable you to analyze how writing actually takes place in the world and how you and others make sense of the writing you encounter and produce. The writing assignment at the end of the chapter "Analyzing a Literacy Event" calls on you to examine an occasion in which writing played an important role in people's interactions and the social context in which the writing took place.

Analyzing such "literacy events" can help you understand the role writing plays in your life. And it can help you become a more flexible writer who understands the effects writing has in the wider social world. In this way, you can learn to fit what you want to say to the occasions that call on you to write.

REFLECTING ON YOUR WRITING

Before you read further in this chapter, write a page or two that gives a preliminary answer to the question, "What is writing?" How would you define the term *literacy*? What does it mean to be able to read and write? Save your writing to return to later.

WRITING IN EVERYDAY LIFE

The writing we do in everyday life is tied to our daily routines and private purposes. For this reason, in much of the writing that takes place in everyday life, it is up to the individual to decide whether, why, and how to write.

The call to write in everyday life emerges from a range of situations. People respond by drawing on various genres to carry out their purposes: they write lists to remember things and notes for friends or family members. People write to maintain social relationships—for example, by a letter of condolence, a thank-you card for a birthday present, or a note to a friend in class. Some people keep personal diaries to record their experiences—and to let off steam, put their feelings in perspective, and cope with the stresses of life. Others write poetry or fiction for similar purposes and for the pleasure of using language to create imaginary worlds.

The purposes mentioned so far have in common a tendency to be personal rather than public. Intended readers are generally limited to people we know well, like friends and family—or even to just ourselves. Not surprisingly, the tone is characteristically informal and familiar. And although these writings are personal, they are, like everyday life itself, tied to the larger social context.

Analyzing Writing In Everyday Life: A Shopping List

Nothing could be more ordinary than a shopping list. Shopping lists reveal one of the most powerful aspects of writing: It frees us from having to commit everything to memory. It's easier and more efficient to list items on paper and let the list remind us of what we want.

A typical shopping list might look something like this:

apples	butter	rice
spaghetti	meat for Sunday dinner	hot dog rolls
bananas	milk	cat food
eggs	bread	paper towels
chicken	two cans of tomatoes	salad stuff

Notice that only the writer could actually bring home exactly what he or she wants. Someone else wouldn't know, for example, how many apples or what kind of meat to buy. This type of writing is a kind of private code that works

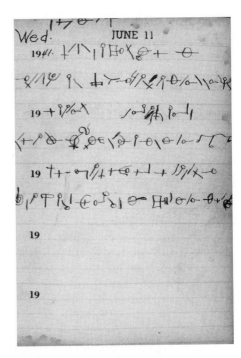

The first piece of writing, an invitation to an anniversary party, is easy enough to recognize. Less recognizable may be the second piece of writing, a secret code invented by Noah John Rondeau, who lived as a hermit in the Adirondack mountains in upstate New York on and off from the 1930s until 1950, hunting and trapping, reading philosophy and astronomy, and writing his diary in code. Consider the purpose each piece of writing serves and what it expresses about the writer's relationship to the social context.

when you want to talk to yourself. How would this list have to be rewritten if someone other than the writer were going to do the shopping?

With some small changes, the shopping list could be written to be an organizing tool as well as a memory aid. You could compose the list so that it corresponds to the aisles in the grocery store:

apples	bananas	salad stuff
chicken	meat for Sunday dinner	
two cans of tomatoes		
spaghetti	rice	
paper towels		
butter	milk	eggs
bread	hot dog rolls	
cat food		

Even as simple and straightforward a piece of writing as a shopping list shows how writing occurs within—and connects the writer to—the larger social context. Consider, for example, how the act of writing a shopping list reveals the shopper's relationship to the everyday work of preparing meals and managing a household. What might the role of the shopping list be in maintaining social relationships? Think of the relationship between you as a consumer and the larger economic order of food production and distribution, as well as your relationship to others in the domestic economy of cooking and cleaning.

WRITING IN THE WORKPLACE

In many respects, the world of work is organized by acts of writing. Government agencies, for example, cannot exist without enabling legislation and funding, nor can corporations exist without articles of incorporation.

The call to write emerges repeatedly in the workplace. For financial and legal reasons, companies need to keep careful records of all their transactions, their inventory and sales, the contracts they enter into, and their dealings with unions and federal and state regulatory agencies.

Equally important is written communication among the members of an organization. Such writing serves to establish a sense of shared purpose, a clear chain of command, and procedures to evaluate performance. Writing helps manage the flow of work and the progress of individual projects.

Companies, moreover, need to make their goods and services known to potential customers and clients, and advertising and public relations have become major industries in their own right.

Today writing in the workplace is undergoing great change as a result of computerization. Inventory, sales figures, and other records are now immediately available on line. E-mail has replaced the traditional memo and letter. In addition, companies and agencies can communicate with customers and clients through the Internet, and the World Wide Web is increasingly becoming a means of advertising and sales.

Writing in the workplace is often specialized. Many professions have their own genres of writing—for example, legal briefs of lawyers, diagnostic reports of doctors and psychologists, case reports of social workers, and proposals and surveys of engineering and architectural firms. So crucial has specialized writing become that our ability to master the genre of a profession largely determines our success in the world of work.

Analyzing Writing in the Workplace: Nike Code of Conduct

Nike is one of the most visible companies in the world today. Its ads feature such prominent athletes as Michael Jordan and Marion Jones, and its trademark slogan "just do it!" has helped make the company famous. Concerns have been raised, however, about the working conditions in its manufacturing plants in

ETHICS OF WRITING

We sometimes think that learning to write means acquiring a skill—to get our point across clearly and correctly. While this is true, learning to write also involves a consideration of the writer's responsibilities and the ethics of communication—not just what works but what is right and wrong.

Some of the ethical principles responsible writers take into account can be summarized briefly: Writers should be trustworthy, using the best information available and presenting it accurately; they should be honest, acknowledging the sources of their information; they should be fair, treating opposing views seriously; they should keep in mind the best interests of the individuals and groups they write about; and they should be reasonable, approaching their readers to persuade rather than manipulate them.

Listing these principles, however, does not fully describe the ethical issues raised by situations that call on us to write. The ethics of writing is always a matter of applying such principles in actual writing situations where ethical conflicts can arise. We may find, for example, that some of the evidence we have uncovered challenges a social or political belief we share with others and value deeply (for example, an advocate of the death penalty might find data suggesting that capital punishment does not deter violent crimes). Would ignoring the evidence be dishonest, or would presenting it be disloyal to others and a shared cause?

Because ethical issues are so embedded in particular writing situations, they are treated throughout this book. As you will see, the ethics of writing can be complex, especially when you encounter conflicts of interest, loyalty, and values.

Graffiti is a good example of writing that raises ethical issues. As you've no doubt seen, graffiti has become an omnipresent feature of contemporary urban life. Spray-painted on

(continued)

ETHICS OF WRITING

(continued)

walls and subway cars, graffiti can perform a number of functions: marking a gang's turf, putting forth political messages, expressing the individual writer's identity, expressing grief for someone killed or anger at an enemy. Our reactions to graffiti differ dramatically. Some see it simply as a crime—an antisocial act of vandalism—while others see it as a form of artistic expression and political statement by the disenfranchised. What ethical issues are raised for you by such examples of graffiti as the two printed here? Do you consider graffiti a justified form of writing even though it is illegal? Why or why not?

China, Vietnam, and Indonesia. Critics have called Nike's labor practices into question, charging that its plants are in effect sweatshops. Students have organized campaigns calling upon their colleges to support workplace standards and effective monitoring of the labor practices of apparel manufacturers such as Nike that make sweatshirts and other items bearing their school's logo. The Nike Code of Conduct lays out general principles for contractors who run Nike plants. Compare Nike's version of its labor practices to the versions given by such organizations as Sweatshop Watch <www.sweatshopwatch.org> and Vietnam Labor Watch <www.saigon.com/~nike/>. Do you find the criticisms of Nike persuasive? Why or why not? For more on labor practices and labor codes in the apparel industry, visit the Dutch Web site Cleanclothes <www.cleanclothers.org>.

Nike Code of Conduct

1   Nike, Inc. was founded on a handshake.

2   Implicit in that act was the determination that we would build our business with all of our partners based on trust, teamwork, honesty, and mutual respect. We expect all of our business partners to operate on the same principles.

3   At the core of the Nike corporate ethic is the belief that we are a company comprised of many different kinds of people, appreciating individual diversity, and dedicated to equal opportunity for each individual.

4   Nike designs, manufactures and markets products for sports and fitness consumers. At every step in that process, we are driven to do not only what is required, but what is expected of a leader. We expect our business partners to do the same. Specifically, Nike seeks partners that share our commitment to the promotion of best practices and continuous improvement in:

1. Occupational health and safety, compensation, hours of work and benefits.
2. Minimizing our impact on the environment.
3. Management practices that recognize the dignity of the individual, the rights of free association and collective bargaining, and the right to a workplace free of harassment, abuse or corporal punishment.
4. The principle that decisions on hiring, salary, benefits, advancement, termination or retirement are based solely on the ability of an individual to do the job.

5   Wherever Nike operates around the globe, we are guided by this Code of Conduct. We bind our business partners to these principles. While these principles establish the spirit of our partnerships, we also bind these partners to specific standards of conduct. These are set forth below:

1. **Forced Labor.** (Contractor) certifies that it does not use any forced labor—prison, indentured, bonded or otherwise.
2. **Child Labor.** (Contractor) certifies that it does not employ any person under the age of 15 (or 14 where the law of the country of manufacturing allows), or the age at which compulsory schooling has ended, whichever is greater.
3. **Compensation.** (Contractor) certifies that it pays at least the minimum wage, or the prevailing industry wage, whichever is higher.
4. **Benefits.** (Contractor) certifies that it complies with all provisions for legally mandated benefits, including but not limited to housing; meals; transportation and other allowances; health care; child care; sick leave; emergency leave; pregnancy and menstrual leave; vacation, religious, bereavement and holiday leave; and contributions for social security, life, health, worker's compensation and other insurance.
5. **Hours of Work/Overtime.** (Contractor) certifies that it complies with legally mandated work hours; uses overtime only when employees are fully compensated according to local law; informs the employee at the time of hiring if mandatory overtime is a condition of employment; and, on a regularly scheduled basis, provides one day off in seven, and requires no more than 60 hours of work per week, or complies with local limits if they are lower.
6. **Health and Safety.** (Contractor) certifies that it has written health and safety guidelines, including those applying to employee residential facilities, where applicable, and that it has agreed in writing to comply with Nike's factory/vendor health and safety standards.
7. **Environment.** (Contractor) certifies that it complies with applicable country environmental regulations; and that it has agreed in writing to comply with Nike's specific vendor/factory environmental policies and procedures, which

are based on the concept of continuous improvement in processes and pro-grams to reduce the impact on the environment.

8. **Documentation and Inspection.** (Contractor) agrees to maintain on file such documentation as may be needed to demonstrate compliance with this Code of Conduct, and further agrees to make these documents available for Nike or its designated auditor's inspection upon request.

MEMORANDUM

TO: The thief that has been stealing pens from the IBM.

FROM: A very angry phone receptionist who is constantly putting more pens near the IBM and who is perpetually frustrated with the fact that when-ever he/she goes to use them they are missing

RE: A way to remedy this situation.

DATE: The summer

Over the course of the summer it has come to my attention that pens were myste-riously vanishing from the IBM computer. This action causes significant trouble when one tries to take a PHONE MESSAGE or attempts to take a START and com-mit it to memory. Instead of philosophizing about the possible criminals who insist on making my life harder (I know who you are!), I simply ask that if you, per chance, notice the absence of a pen or pencil near the IBM that you take it upon yourself to correct this mishap and replace one immediately.

I thank you for your time and efforts in this matter.

HAZARDOUS WASTE STORAGE AREA

ALL CONTAINERS:

1) Must be marked with the words **"HAZARDOUS WASTE"**.
   Please call X3353 for labels.

2) Must be labeled with the **FULL** chemical name (NO ABBREVIATIONS) and the appropriate characteristic identifier:
   Corrosive/Ignitable/Toxic/Carcinogen/Reactive.

3) Must be capped at **ALL** times except when actively adding waste.

4) Must be compatible with the material it is holding.

5) Must be in secondary containment.

6) WHEN FULL; must be dated and brought to the central storage area within 3 days.

ORM 98 For more information or training, please contact Risk Management at 863-3353

Compare the flyer "Hazardous Waste Storage Area" to the memo written by one individual to her coworkers. In each case, what seems to have been the call to write? What does the tone of voice indicate about the relationship the writer seeks to establish with readers? Do you think these pieces are effective for their purpose?

WRITING IN THE PUBLIC SPHERE

In the broadest sense, writing in the public sphere refers to all the writing we encounter in public places—official signs (for example, street names, building names and addresses, and parking signs), notices put out by companies and groups (for example, posters announcing meetings and concerts, billboards advertising movies and products, and leaflets seeking support for causes), books, newspapers and magazines, and even the graffiti spray-painted on the sides of buildings and subway cars.

This section focuses on a particular use of writing in the public sphere—namely, writing intended to inform and influence members of the public on matters of concern to all. Here, the public sphere can be understood as the context in which people deliberate on the important issues of the day and seek to shape the direction of society.

Material produced and disseminated by the mass media—books, newspapers, magazines, journals of opinion, radio, and television—is an important element of writing in the public sphere. The media, after all, links us to others in society, provides information, and helps shape opinions and attitudes.

Also important contributors to writing in the public sphere are the many advocacy groups. These include environmental groups, animal rights groups, labor unions, business groups, political parties, groups that oppose abortion and groups that support abortion rights, groups for and against gun control—the list goes on and on. Some of these advocacy groups are concerned with a single issue; others have a broad agenda. Some are active at the local level, others at the national level. What these diverse groups share is a concern with social issues that leads them to writing and other actions that can shape public opinion and change society.

People can also contribute as individuals to writing in the public sphere. For example, you may feel moved to write a letter to the editor of a newspaper or to a senator or member of congress. Electronic communication is greatly increasing our access to the public sphere. With newsgroups and Web sites devoted to social and political issues, it is now possible for individuals to exchange views with people in other parts of the country or the world.

Writing in the public sphere poses special challenges. Its broad purpose is to influence opinion—often precisely on the issues that most divide society. Moreover, in contrast to writing in other contexts, writing in the public sphere is often addressed to a large and unknown audience. You need to imagine this audience in your mind in order to figure out what relationship to establish with readers, how to establish this relationship, what voice to use, and what genre. These challenges, of course, are inseparable from the considerable benefits of writing in the public sphere: You have the opportunity to inform and influence your readers on issues they truly care about.

Analyzing Writing in the Public Sphere: Newsletter

Bits & Pieces is the quarterly newsletter of the South Providence Neighborhood Ministries, a nonprofit social agency in Providence, Rhode Island, that provides

SOUTH PROVIDENCE NEIGHBORHOOD MINISTRIES

Bits & Pieces

747 Broad Street Providence, RI 02907   (401)461-7509   Fax 785-8277

SPRING 1998

You are invited

South Providence
Neighborhood Ministries

ANNUAL MEETING

TUESDAY MAY 12, 1998
747 BROAD STREET DOWNSTAIRS
6:00 - 8:00 P.M.

ETHNIC POT - LUCK
Bring a dish somehow related
to your background

Program Highlights from children, teens
and adults
Election of Board of Directors

VOLUNTEER RECOGNITION

We shall begin dinner with a prayer promptly at 6:00 p.m.
and begin clean-up promptly with a prayer at 8:00 p.m.

SHARE has become SERVE

Grace Wilcox, our Direct Services Coordinator, also manages the host site at SPNM for this successful program which encourages volunteerism. As of January 1, the regional organization changed its name from SHARE to SERVE. To be a part of this quality food cooperative you need only register during the first week of a month, prepay $14 to purchase your food and then perform two hours of community service. The food is picked up here at SPNM on Distribution Day, usually the last Saturday of the month.
    Have you tried this program yet?

It will really **stretch** your food dollar, and the food is of excellent quality.

    To qualify you need only be willing to contribute your efforts and two hours to any community service. This can be at your church, school, library or even here at SPNM.

Our mission is to meet essential needs, enhance the quality of life for children and adults, encourage self-worth and self-sufficiency, and foster community pride in a neighborhood of diverse ethnic, racial and social backgrounds.

adult literacy classes, children's programs, a food pantry, and other social services in a racially and ethnically diverse neighborhood. South Providence Neighborhood Ministries is typical of many nonprofit organizations that operate in the public sphere. Formed to address particular social needs, it works with government agencies and other nonprofit community organizations. It has a paid staff but also relies extensively on volunteers—including high school and college students—and its own fund raising.

As you can see, the cover of the newsletter contains two announcements—one inviting readers to the annual meeting and the second explaining the name change of a food cooperative. *Bits & Pieces* is performing its basic function of communicating information to all those interested in the work of South Providence Neighborhood Ministries. Notice, however, that this information serves a different purpose, depending on who reads it. As is true of community organizations in general, South Providence Neighborhood Ministries has multiple audiences to address in its newsletter.

Consider, for example, how the newsletter provides information to people in the community about the services available through the food cooperative and how to qualify to participate. What purpose does this information serve for other audiences? Take into account, for example, volunteers and staff who work at South Providence Neighborhood Ministries, as well as government agencies, nonprofit organizations, and individual donors who provide funding. How are each of these audiences likely to use the newsletter?

Consider the two samples of writing in the public sphere. One is a flyer protesting a business that buys nonunion products. The other is a wall mural from East Los Angeles in the Chicano mural tradition of California and the Southwest. Notice key differences in how these two examples of public writing are disseminated: the flyer was handed to individuals, while the mural is painted on a wall for all passersby to see. Taking this important difference into account, consider how each writing responds to a call to write. Who are the intended readers? What sort of relationship do the writers establish with readers?

CONSUMER ALERT

This business purchases scab products from F. DiZoglio & Sons Paper Company

Recycle Paper— *Not People!*

**You have a choice of where you spend your money
Send them a message...
Stand up fpr the American Family**

 Teamsters Local 251
East Providence, RI

GOING ONLINE

ORGANIZING WORLDWIDE NETWORKS

The Zapatista uprising began on New Year's Day in 1994, when the Zapatista National Liberation Army (EZLN) seized four small towns in Chiapas, Mexico. Though isolated geographically in the jungles and forests of southeastern Mexico, the Zapatistas, unlike any rebel movement before, have used the Internet extensively to communicate their struggle for social justice to the world. In response, as you can see from the home page of the Irish Mexico Group, international networks have formed to disseminate information about the situation in Mexico and to publicize the Zapatistas' goals. To learn more about these networks, visit the Irish Mexico Group <flag.blackened.net/revolt/mexico/html> and the Zapatista Network—A Clearinghouse of Zapatista Information and Support Worldwide <www.zapatistas.org>. What are the main types of information provided? How do the sites seek to shape public opinion about the Zapatista uprising? What opportunities do they offer visitors to get involved?

For other examples of organizing international networks, see Amnesty International <www.amnesty.org>, Greenpeace <www.green peace.org>, Global Exchange <www.global exchange.org>, and the Rain Forest Action Network <www.ran.org>.

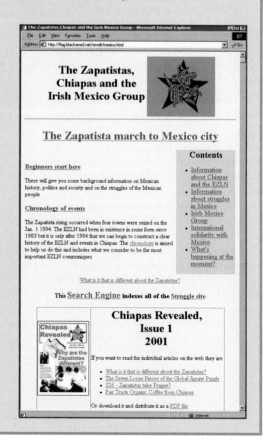

WRITING IN SCHOOL

At first glance it may appear that writing in school is relatively uncomplicated—a call to write, from a teacher who is also the audience, with the purpose of showing how well the student understands the material. From this perspective, school writing fits into the social context of schooling, in which students are in the role of performers, teachers are in the role of evaluators, and writing serves as the basis for ranking students according to the prevailing reward system of grades.

Writing in school, however, is more complex than this description allows us to see. First, students do lots of writing for their own purposes that is not directly evaluated by teachers—taking notes in lectures, for example, or writing summaries of textbook chapters to study for tests. And papers that students turn in to teachers for grades may not include all the writing—for example, research notes, outlines, first drafts, and false starts—a student has done to complete the assignment.

Second, even when students are writing for grades, they are not just displaying knowledge of the material. They must also take into account how the different academic fields call for different genres of writing—a lab report in chemistry, a critical essay on a poem for English, or a case study in psychology. For this reason, learning a subject is in part learning how chemists, literary critics, psychologists, and others use writing to communicate in their respective fields.

Analyzing Writing in School: Samples from Grade 3

Before we look at the kind of writing college teachers ask students to write, let's stop for a moment and think about whether writing as a display of learning is the only kind of writing you have been called on to do in school.

Here are two samples of writing drawn from a student in a third-grade class:

SAMPLE 1

I will not forget my name and number.
I will not forget my name and number.
I will not forget my name and number.
I will not forget my name and number.
I will not forget my name and number.

SAMPLE 2

Dear Dad,
I had to stand in the lunch room today. I am very, very sorry. Mrs. Bailey is horrified. I love you.

Love,
Martha

Consider the purpose of these two writings. What is the relationship in each case between the student and the teacher? In the second sample, how does the student's relationship to her father play a role in the writing?

The same student also wrote the following piece:

SAMPLE 3

My Big and Small Dream

One morning when I woke up I was a monster with pink eyes, purple faded hair, a green body, and a fluorescent yellow face. I went downstairs and ate the stove, the fridg, and all the food. I started shrinking. I was so surprised, then for the next five days I stopped eating. Then to my surprise I was as big and as high as the sky. Since I was big I bumped into a tree that was smaller than me. Also, by mistake, I stepped on a house with people having a party. Then I went to bed and the next morning I woke up and was myself again.

Consider how this sample of writing differs from the first two. What does the student's purpose seem to be? How does this purpose compare to her purposes in the first two samples? What is she learning in the three samples about school and her relationship to teachers?

Samples of Writing in School

The following two pieces were both written by the same student, the first in the first year of high school and the second in the first year of college. As you read, compare the two pieces.

■ How does the writer seem to understand the assignments? What does her purpose seem to be in each instance?

■ What kind of relationship does she establish with her reader and her subject?

■ What features distinguish the college writing from the high school writing? Does the college writing seem to be more "mature" or "advanced" than the high school writing?

SAMPLE 1: HIGH SCHOOL RESEARCH PAPER

The revival of the modern Olympic Games was influenced by the politics of the late nineteenth century. The Baron de Coubertin had two motives in reviving the Olympic Games. After France lost the Franco-Prussian War, a gloom set over all of France. The Baron wanted to revive the games to inspire the youth of France. In the lycees of France, the intellectual aspects dominated the school. There were no physical education classes and very little, if any, athletic training. The Baron wanted both athletics and education in the schools. When creating these perfect schools of France he used the ephebes of ancient Greece and the public schools of England as examples when education and athletics played a major role in the young boy's lives; there would be a perfect school. The Baron's other purpose in recreating the Olympics was to promote world peace by gathering all the countries together.

Though the Baron's intentions were to produce world amity he did the opposite. Instead of peaceful relations the games created many conflicts. In 1936, for example, there was much conflict at the summer games in Berlin. The problem of the games was racism. Adolf Hitler wrote the following in Mein Kampf, while in prison in 1924. "Americans ought to be ashamed of themselves for letting their medals be won by Negroes. I myself would never even shake hands with one of them." Adolf Hitler, the leader of Germany at the time was clearly very racist. When Jesse Owens, a black American won the gold medal in the 100 meter dash, Hitler was infuriated. Hitler refused to congratulate him. Political incidents like these increased over the course of the Olympic Games.

In 1968 the politics shifted from racism to protests against racism. Before the games sprinter Tommie Smith and other students suggested to boycott the Olympics because of the racial conditions in the United States. Although Tommie Smith went to Mexico City, he expressed his feelings on racism there as well. During the ceremony for the two hundred meter dash the "Star Spangled Banner" was played. At that time, both Tommie Smith and John Carlos staged a protest by giving the black power salute. They were suspended by the International Olympic Committee and ordered to leave the country.

Another incident that politics played a major role in was the boycott of the Moscow Olympics in 1980. After Russian troops were sent into Afghanistan in 1979, President Jimmy Carter proposed that the games be rescheduled and moved to another location. The response of the International Olympic Committee was that "politics should be of no influence in the Olympic Games." After failing to reschedule and move the games to another location, the President and sixty-four other countries boycotted. Of the one-hundred and forty-five nations that were invited to take part in the games, only eighty-one entered. Some nations that boycotted the games were West Germany, China, Japan, Canada, Kenya, Australia, New Zealand, Great Britain, France, and Italy. Though many athletes within the United States protested that politics should be of no factor in the games, Carter refused to reconsider. By boycotting the Olympics, Carter did not get the troops out of Afghanistan, but simply increased the tension between the United States and the Soviet Union.

In 1984, in response to the boycott four years earlier, Russia, along with East Germany, Czechoslovakia, Poland, Hungary, Bulgaria, and Cuba, declined the invitation to participate in the summer games in Los Angeles. The Soviets denied the boycott was revenge, but argued that the publicity and ten billion dollar cost of the games were outrageous. They also argued that the security in Los Angeles was not sufficient.

In the most recent games, politics as usual, influenced the games. The games were held in South Korea. Though the bid was won fairly by South Korea, North Korea felt they deserved to be the co-hosts. Fearing what North Korea might do out of jealousy, South Korea had 120,000 specially trained antiterrorist fighters, 700,000 men of the Republic of Korea's armed forces, 40,000 permanently stationed United States soldiers and marines, and 100,000 United States sailors aboard aircraft carriers patrolling the Korean shores. In addition, there was 63 armed personnel for each of the 13,000 athletes. Both the United States and South Korea had to take drastic measures to secure the safety of the athletes. If politics played no role in the Olympics none of those measures would be necessary.

When Baron de Coubertin revived the Olympic Games he had nothing but good intentions. His hope was that the Olympics could be a place where people from all over the world could gather together in peace doing what they all had in common. Though his intentions were good, politicians took advantage of the Olympics. They used the games as chances to boycott what they thought was wrong and, in other cases, as revenge. Jesse Owens and all the athletes that were not able to go to the 1980 and 1984 Olympics suffered from politics. The purpose of the Olympics has changed into something that is not right. Let's leave the politics to the politicians and competition to the athletes.

SAMPLE 2: COLLEGE RESPONSE PAPER

Assignment: *What is the role of popular religion—as portrayed through the worship of the Madonna—in defining the ethnic identity of the Italian community of East Harlem?*

As I read through the *Madonna of 115th Street: Faith and Community in Italian Harlem, 1880–1950,* and the important role that popular religion played in the role of defining ethnic identity in the Italian community of East Harlem, I could not help but to think of my hometown, Cranston and the similarities that popular religion played there as well. As I read about the feasts of the Madonna of 115th Street I was reminded of the Feast of St. Mary in Cranston and the almost identical origins of the feasts. In Cranston, the feast of St. Mary was started to honor La Madonna della Citta or the Madonna of the city, who was from a small village in southern Italy where many of the first Cranstonians originated. It also served as a distinguishing feature from other Catholics in the area and a marker of ethnic identity. Both of the creations of the Madonnas and the feasts in their honor were popular religion. Popular religion was an important role in shaping ethnic identities in Italian communities.

Both of the feasts in Cranston and East Harlem's purpose were to honor the Madonnas, each from a specific place in Italy, where many of the honorees were from. The Madonna served as a shared history in the new world and gave immigrants something to serve as a reference point. Each immigrant could relate to the Madonna and trusted her with their most sacred prayers. The Madonna listened to the needs of the newly arrived immigrants. As quoted from the work, *The Madonna of 115th Street,* the author says of immigrant Italians, "the Italian feels safer when he plays homage to the patron saint of his hometown or village who in the past was considerate to the people."

The feast of the Madonna of 115th Street began in the summer of 1881 when immigrants from the town of Polla formed a mutual aid society. One of the functions of the mutual aid society was to give unemployment and burial benefits to immigrants. But a larger function of the mutual aid societies and the feasts that it started was to gather immigrants and preserve as well as observe traditional customs in the new world. Because mutual aid societies were unique to Italian Roman Catholics they served as a model for ethnic identity. Furthermore, Catholics of other ethnic backgrounds such as Irish Catholics, were hostile to feasts of the Madonna of 115th Street. Orsi speaks of an attack published in the *Catholic World* in 1888. The attack criticized the shrines, holy cards and pagan superstitions and "devotions" of the Italian Roman Catholic and the ignorance for "great faith of religion." These attacks on Italian Catholics served to further separate Italians from other Catholics and create a stronger ethnic identity.

In addition the building of certain specifically Italian churches, (chiesa), which again, is popular religion, in East Harlem served as another ethnic identity. Italians as a group gathered to build their own churches. The building was a gathering of everyone, of an ethnic group to create something that they could call their own. As the book noted, junkmen and icemen donated their carts and horses to help manage the burden of building materials as people prepared refreshments for the workers. This act was substantial in the creation of ethnic identity.

During the late nineteenth century, popular religion served as an ethnic identity for Italians in East Harlem, Cranston, RI, as well as in other parts of the eastern seaboard. The creation of Madonnas from hometowns as well as feasts for their honor were the most unique feature and distinguishing characteristic. The separation of Italian Catholics from other Catholics such as Irish Catholics provided further ethnic identity in America.

REFLECTING ON YOUR WRITING

Make a separate list of writing you've done or are doing in each of the four contexts—everyday life, the workplace, the public sphere, and school. Include even the simplest forms of writing, such as e-mail, lists of things to do, forms you've filled out, leaflets or posters you've designed, and the notes you take in class or while reading.

Look at the lists you've created:

1. How much variety do you see—more or less than you would have expected?

2. Describe some of the purposes for writing. How do your purposes vary?

3. What relationships does your writing put you into with other people and with social contexts?

4. Compare the writing you have done in school with the writing you have done in everyday life, the workplace, and the public sphere. How would you explain differences and similarities?

Analyzing a Literacy Event

The term *literacy event* gives us a way to think about how reading and writing enter our lives and shape our interactions with others. All the samples of writing in this chapter, for example, can be considered literacy events, because they focus our attention on the role that particular moments of reading and writing play in our experience. These literacy events take place in different social contexts, but each of them, in one way or another, reveals an aspect of what writing does in the world.

When analyzing a literacy event you are asked to examine how people make sense of their encounters with reading and writing—how they understand what writing is and what it does. You will need to focus on a particular moment in which writing takes on a meaningful role in your life or in the lives of others. The three reading selections that follow provide further examples of literacy events. As you will see, each example concentrates on a specific encounter with writing and the social relationships involved. These examples can give you some practice in analyzing literacy events before you do an analysis of your own.

1. The first selection is a passage from *Narrative of the Life of Frederick Douglass,* the account of Douglass's life as a slave and his escape from slavery. In this passage, you can see how Douglass's master forbade him as a slave to learn reading and writing—and how Douglass made sense of this encounter with literacy.

2. The second selection is a passage that appears in the memoir *One Writer's Beginnings* by the Pulitzer Prize-winning fiction writer Eudora Welty. This literacy event is drawn from Welty's childhood in Jackson, Mississippi, in the early twentieth century.

3. The third selection comes from Margaret J. Finders' book-length study *Just Girls: Hidden Literacies and Life in Junior High.* These passages were written by a literacy researcher who spent a year in a midwestern junior high observing how girls used reading and writing to establish personal identities and social networks.

From *Narative of the Life of Frederick Douglass*
FREDERICK DOUGLASS

Very soon after I went to live with Mr. and Mrs. Auld, she very kindly commenced to teach me the A, B, C. After I had learned this, she assisted me in learning to spell words of three or four letters. Just at this point of my progress, Mr. Auld found out what was going on, and at once forbade Mrs. Auld to instruct me further, telling her, among other things, that it was unlawful, as well as unsafe, to teach a slave to read. To use his own words, further, he said, "If you give a nigger an inch, he will take an ell. A nigger should know nothing but to obey his master—to do as he is told to do. Learning would spoil the best nigger in the world. Now," said he, "if you teach that nigger (speaking of myself) how to read, there would be no keeping him. It would forever unfit him to be a slave. He would at once become unmanageable, and of no value to his master. As to himself, it could do him no good, but a great deal of harm. It would make him discontented and unhappy." These words sank deep into my heart, stirred up sentiments within that lay slumbering, and called into existence an entirely new train of thought. It was a new and special revelation, explaining dark and mysterious things, with which my youthful understanding had struggled, but struggled in vain. I now understood what had been to me a most perplexing difficulty—to wit, the white man's power to enslave the black man. It was a grand achievement, and I prized it highly. From that moment, I understood the pathway from slavery to freedom. It was just what I wanted, and I got it at a time when I the least expected it. Whilst I was saddened by the thought of losing the aid of my kind mistress, I was gladdened by the invaluable instruction which, by the merest accident, I had gained from my master. Though conscious of the difficulty of learning without a teacher, I set out with high hope, and a fixed purpose, at whatever cost of trouble, to learn how to read. The very decided manner with which he spoke, and strove to impress his wife with the evil consequences of giving me instruction, served to convince me that he was deeply sensible of the truths he was uttering. It gave me the best assurance that I might rely with the utmost confidence on the results which, he said, would flow from teaching me to read. What he most dreaded, that I most desired. What he most loved, that I most hated. That which to him was a great evil, to be carefully shunned, was to me a great good, to be diligently sought; and the argument which he so warmly urged, against my learning to read, only served to inspire me with a desire and determination to learn. In learning to read, I owe almost as much to the bitter opposition of my master, as to the kindly aid of my mistress. I acknowledge the benefit of both.

From *One Writer's Beginnings*
EUDORA WELTY

1   Jackson's Carnegie Library was on the same street where our house was, on the other side of the State Capitol. "Through the Capitol" was the way to go to the Library. You could glide through it on your bicycle or even coast through on roller skates, though without family permission.

2   I never knew anyone who'd grown up in Jackson without being afraid of Mrs. Calloway, our librarian. She ran the Library absolutely by herself, from the desk where she sat with her back to the books and facing the stairs, her dragon eye on the front door, where who knew what kind of person might come in from the public? SILENCE in big black letters was on signs tacked up everywhere. She herself spoke in her normally commanding voice; every word could be heard all over the Library above a steady seething sound coming from her electric fan; it was the only fan in the Library and stood on her desk, turned directly onto her streaming face.

3   As you came in from the bright outside, if you were a girl, she sent her strong eyes down the stairway to test you; if she could see through your skirt she sent you straight back home; you could just put on another petticoat if you wanted a book that badly from the public library. I was willing; I would do anything to read.

4   My mother was not afraid of Mrs. Calloway. She wished me to have my own library card to check out books for myself. She took me in to introduce me and I saw I had met a witch. "Eudora is nine years old and has my permission to read any book she wants from the shelves, children or adult," Mother said. "With the exception of *Elsie Dinsmore*," she added. Later she explained to me that she'd made this rule because Elsie the heroine, being made by her father to practice too long and hard at the piano, fainted and fell off the piano stool. "You're too impressionable, dear," she told me. "You'd read that and the very first thing you'd do, you'd fall off the piano stool." "Impressionable" was a new word. I never hear it yet without the image that comes with it of falling straight off the piano stool.

5   Mrs. Calloway made her own rules about books. You could not take back a book to the Library on the same day you'd taken it out; it made no difference to her that you'd read every word in it and needed another to start. You could take out two books at a time and two only; this applied as long as you were a child and also for the rest of your life, to my mother as severely as to me. So, two by two, I read library books as fast as I could go, rushing them home in the basket of my bicycle. From the minute I reached our house, I started to read. Every book I seized on, from *Bunny Brown and His Sister Sue at Camp Rest-a-While* to *Twenty Thousand Leagues under the Sea*, stood for the devouring wish to read being instantly granted. I knew this was bliss, I knew it at the time. Taste isn't nearly so important; it comes

in its own time. I wanted to read *immediately*. The only fear was that of books coming to an end.

From *Just Girls: Hidden Literacies and Life in Junior High*
MARGARET J. FINDERS

1   As school years draw to a close, students across the nation anticipate the biggest school-sanctioned literacy event of the year: the sale and distribution of the school yearbook. Like students elsewhere, Northern Hills Junior High students anxiously awaited its arrival.

2   Produced by 65 students working together with the help of two staff advisors, the yearbook, a 48-page soft-bound document, captured the year through photographs, student-produced artwork, and captions. Sports held a prominent place in the pages of the yearbook: Photos of football, track, basketball, and wrestling events for the boys and track, tennis, volleyball, and basketball for the girls filled the pages. The book also contained photos of Soda—a drug and alcohol awareness club—and drama club.

3   I believe that most teachers would agree with one of the yearbook's faculty advisors, the media specialist, who described the importance of the yearbook this way:

4   If you can find your mug in here [yearbook], it gives you a tremendous sense of belonging. We tried to cover all the major events, and it's important to find yourself. We took a lot of pictures. If you and your mom can find yourself in here, then everything is just A-OK.

5   At Northern Hills Junior High, the yearbook had become a central part of the end-of-the-year curriculum…. For the most part, teachers described the yearbook as a celebration and well-earned reward for hard work. They allocated class time for signing and sharing yearbooks. Perceived as a way to control the behavior of the 531 seventh and eighth graders who in late May may not be eager to participate in discussions or complete end-of-semester projects, signing time was a tool for negotiating with students, often appearing as a bribe. Teachers told students: "If we get all our work done…" "If you are all good…" "If you cooperate, and we can hurry through this…" The following teacher comment received several nods and "me-toos" from staff in the teacher's lounge: "I give them the last five to ten minutes to write depending on how the class goes. It's a reward. It's a privilege. It's their reward for good behavior."

6   The yearbook played such a large role in the end-of-school activities because the teachers and administrators all believed, as the media specialist articulated, that it gave a tremendous sense of belonging. The discourse of adolescence that privileges peer-group allegiances constructed filters, it seems, that prevented school personnel from seeing the yearbook as exclusionary. Although the yearbook was viewed as a symbol of solidarity for all students, only a particular

population of students was made to feel as if they belonged to this club. Other students remained outsiders.

7   Constant comments from Northern Hills staff that "Everybody gets one" and "Everyone loves them" reveal that Cleo and Dottie [social outsiders from poor families who did not buy yearbooks] and many others were invisible to school personnel. Current enrollment was 531; 425 books were ordered. Eight were sold to adults, 10 distributed as complimentary copies, 10 were mailed to students who no longer lived in the district, and 5 remained unsold. 397 copies were sold to students, which left 134 students without yearbooks. That figure represents 25% of the total student population. While students may not have purchased a yearbook for a variety of reasons, the socioeconomic status of families may have been a critical issue. For whatever reason, when teachers rewarded students with "signing time," one out of four students was not able to participate.

Katie: Can I sign your yearbook?
Barb: No.

8   A quick glance at the yearbooks shows row after row of white faces ordered by alphabetical arrangement. The seeming homogeneity conceals diversity: Invisible barriers such as attitudes, beliefs, economics, and experiences separate these young people into at least two camps. The girls created markers to maintain the borders between them. Allegiances became visible in both the act of writing and in the messages themselves. What is written and to whom is controlled by one's social status. Yearbooks circulated across social boundaries, yet those with the greatest social status stood in judgment of those less powerful. Students carefully monitored who could sign their yearbooks. To allow one of lesser status to mark one's book appeared to lower the status of the book owner. Students often asked for and were denied signing privileges.... Some students were in fact told "No," after asking, "Can I sign your yearbook?" In the same way, some students refused to sign yearbooks of those perceived to be outside the circle of significance. Who had the right to write was clearly an issue of entitlement.... If one was perceived as an outsider, then one was not entitled to write. Likewise, one might or might not be entitled to even view the message. Students guarded their written texts and controlled who had the right to see them.

9   Students with the greatest status were freed from judgment, and their written comments became models for others to copy. As I watched, one student carefully moved her finger across the page, working cautiously to transfer a phrase exactly from one yearbook to another. Because a particular phrase was perceived as carrying more currency in this arena, this teen appropriated the words of another student as her own in order for her voice to contain that power. Students shared texts and at times took another person's message for her own, copying the same phrase from one yearbook to the next to the next. In such borrowing of texts, one, in a sense, borrowed the social status of another. In taking another's message as her own, each girl had to be careful not to overstep her boundaries and write...what she was not entitled to write.

10   In the act of writing, students inadvertently may mark themselves as outsiders by writing a message judged inappropriate by others. If one was not savvy enough to create an appropriate text or powerful enough to forgo judgment, often, out of fear of marking oneself as an outsider, one just scribbled safe messages such as "Have a good summer" or "See ya next year."

11   Some students, in order to preserve their social position, asked a friend, "What should I write? What do you want me to say?" Students took this opportunity to exert their position of authority and made such playful comments as "Say I'm 'just too cool'" or "Say 'she's always got a taco'" (a current description for shorts or jeans that were considered too tight across the seat of the pants) or "Write, 'BFF ASS'" (a code for best friends forever and always stay sweet or sexy). Many comments were so highly coded that only those few insiders could translate them.

12   In order for students to demonstrate that they were with it, comments carrying the current pop jargon taken from movies, television, and local sources become etched into this school-sanctioned document, creating an unusual juxtaposition of sanctioned and out-of-bounds literacies. Dark, graffiti-like messages boldly cut across the white-bordered layout and quite literally "defaced" students and teachers alike. With big pink erasers, students rubbed out the faces of outsiders.

13   In all of this signing, the [social] queens [a group of the most popular girls] demonstrated a tremendous sense of play. Signing yearbooks had the feeling of recess, providing playtime away from the institutional demands of schooling, away from adult supervision. Similar to the playground, who could play was controlled by the peer dynamic. The yearbook was used to stake out territory and control social interactions.

14   Conceived as an opportunity for all to celebrate the completion of another successful academic year, the yearbook provided much more. For Tiffany and all the other social queens it reaffirmed their position in the school arena and in the larger community. They measured their status by the number and size of their pictures and by the number of requests to sign books: "Everybody wants me to sign their book." For Cleo and her friends, it also reaffirmed their position: "None of my friends are in there anyway."

15   The role of the yearbook in the institutional context remains central to the closing of the school year. The yearbook stands as an icon. Unknowingly, some are allowed to speak while others are silenced, some to write while others are written upon.

For Critical Inquiry

1. The literacy event Frederick Douglass recounts involved a "new and special revelation, explaining dark and mysterious things." What is the literacy event to which Douglass refers? What exactly is this revelation?

2. What insights does Eudora Welty gain from getting a library card and access to books? What roles do her mother and the librarian, Mrs. Calloway, play

in this literacy event? Explain how each makes sense of Welty's encounter with literacy and how their interactions shape the literacy event. What role, if any, does Welty's gender play?

3. Margaret J. Finders begins by describing the end-of-school ritual of the junior high yearbook from the perspective of teachers and staff. How do school personnel make sense of the yearbook? How do their views differ from the way students' do? How does Finders analyze and explain the interactions among students that take place around signing yearbooks?

WRITING ASSIGNMENT: ANALYZING A LITERACY EVENT

Now it's your turn to analyze a literacy event. Your task is to identify a particularly meaningful encounter with writing—whether those involved are in the role of a writer, a reader, or both. Then you need to explain how the people involved made sense of the event and the role that writing played in their interactions.

DIRECTIONS

1. Select a particular encounter with writing in which you were directly involved or that you observed. For possibilities, review the lists you wrote in response to "Reflecting on Your Writing."

   Look for encounters with writing that reveal powerful feelings or strong responses on the part of the people involved. Look for misunderstandings, conflicts, resolutions, or alliances in which writing plays a key role. Look for instances of writing that had an effect on people's sense of themselves as individuals or as part of a group. If you have time, discuss with a partner three or four literacy events that you are considering for this assignment. See what seems most interesting to another person. Use this information to help you make a decision about the literacy event you want to analyze.

2. Analyze the literacy event. Here are some questions to take into account:

   - Describe what happened. What is the social context of the encounter with writing? Who was involved? What did they do?
   - What type of writing did the encounter center on? What were the specific features of the writing? What was its purpose?
   - How did the participants make sense of the literacy event? Did they share the same perspective or differ? How would you account for these differences or similarities?
   - What were the relationships among the participants? What role did writing play in their interactions? What were the results or consequences of these interactions?

3. Write an analysis of the literacy event. You will need to describe what happened and to explain how the participants made sense of the literacy event and how this particular encounter with writing shaped their interactions.

REFLECTING ON YOUR WRITING

Return to the writing you did at the beginning of this chapter and at the end of the section on writing in school. How would you now answer the question, "What is writing?" Have your views on what it means to read and write changed, expanded, or been confirmed by the work you've done in this chapter? Explain.

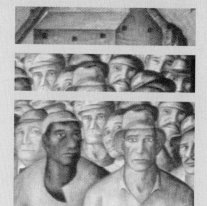

CHAPTER TWO

Reading Strategies: Analyzing the Rhetorical Situation

There are many purposes for reading—enjoyment, as when you read a novel; learning how to do something, as when you consult a user's manual to program a VCR; or obtaining information, as when you check the newspaper for today's weather report or last night's basketball scores. The reading strategies presented in this chapter are typical of those writers use when the purpose of reading is to gather information, assess what others have said about a topic, and understand how other writers have responded to the call to write. Whether you are working on a research paper in a history class, preparing a marketing strategy for a new product, or writing a flyer for or against a controversial law, the reading strategies in this chapter can help you do the kind of reading needed to handle these and many other kinds of writing tasks.

The chapter is arranged sequentially to look at three related sets of reading strategies:

1. strategies such as underlining, annotation, and summarizing to help you get a clear understanding of what you're reading

2. strategies of analysis such as outlining, identifying facts and claims, and evaluating evidence to help you understand how the material you're reading presents its ideas and conveys its meaning

3. strategies such as using background information, analyzing the writer's relationship to readers, and analyzing the writer's language to help you understand how the writer identified and responded to the call to write

Which of these strategies you decide to use—and in what combination—will depend, of course, on your purpose for reading and the writing task you're working on. If you're reading to acquire information, the first set of reading strategies may be all you need to understand, say, how acid rain affects the environment or the basic features in Freud's theory of instincts. In other cases, however, especially when there are a range of views on a topic, you may need to understand not only the information in what you're reading but also how the writer has constructed an argument and how the reading fits into its social context. For example, if you're researching the influence of video games on young people, the second set of reading strategies can help you understand how a piece of writing establishes and supports its main points. The third set of reading strategies is useful in developing an understanding of how that particular piece of writing relates to the larger discussion of video games and youth culture.

No doubt you're familiar with and have been using some of the reading strategies in this chapter. The goal of this chapter is to build on reading strategies you already know in order to deepen your understanding of what you're reading. By developing a heightened awareness of familiar reading strategies such as underlining, summarizing, and outlining, you can lay the groundwork for reading in a way that analyzes a piece of writing in greater depth.

In the main writing assignment at the end of this chapter, "Analyzing the Rhetorical Situation," we ask you to use the reading strategies already given to look closely at a particular piece of writing and to analyze its rhetorical situation. The *rhetorical situation* refers to the factors and circumstances that writers take into account when they respond to the call to write. By analyzing the rhetorical situation, you will see how writers develop a sense of purpose, establish a relationship with their readers, adopt a particular tone of voice, and choose a genre of writing that fits their context. You will then understand the decisions that writers make—and the choices you will face when you respond to the call to write.

BASIC READING STRATEGIES

The strategies in this section will help you read any type of writing. In the discussion of the first strategy, we offer suggestions on how to approach what you're reading—to decide on your purpose for reading, the genre of the writing, and what reading strategies to use. Underlining, annotation, summarizing, and exploratory writing can be particularly useful when you want to make sure you understand key concepts in what you are reading. You have probably used some or all of these strategies reading textbooks, but they are helpful with other readings as well. When you are doing research, for example, these basic reading strategies can help you compare and contrast the main ideas from diverse sources. And they can provide the groundwork for the analytical reading strategies you'll find later in this chapter.

Previewing

A first step toward knowing what reading strategies to use is to identify your own purpose for reading and the genre of the writing you are about to read. As we have already mentioned, the reading strategies you choose will depend on your purposes for reading—whether you're trying to find out how many Latinos

Part Two contains discussion of various genres of writing and their characteristic features.

currently live in the United States or to understand how various writers have explained the growing political influence of Latinos in that country. Identifying the genre of writing can also be useful in determining your reading strategies. Reading census data on Latinos differs considerably from reading a commentary about their political clout in a newspaper or magazine—and your reading strategies are likely to differ accordingly.

To preview a piece of writing, read the title, headings, and the first sentence of each paragraph. Also examine the captions under any photos or graphic displays of information. Then answer these questions:

1. What is your purpose for reading? What use are you planning to make of your reading? What do you expect to find?

2. What does the writer's purpose seem to be? What does the title convey to you? Is there a statement that describes the writer's purpose explicitly? Or is it implied?

3. What does the genre of writing seem to be? Can you put the reading into a category of writing you are familiar with? What other writings does it remind you of?

4. If the reading seems unfamiliar, how can you get a handle on it? Do editorial comments, prefaces, author notes, or blurbs on book jackets provide background information for your reading? Is there someone you can talk to for more information—for example, another student, your teacher, or a librarian?

5. Who is the intended audience? What are their purposes likely to be in reading the writing?

6. What reading strategies best fit the piece of writing?

Underlining

Underlining the writer's key points helps you identify and keep track of main ideas and important information. It also enables you to return to the marked phrases to reconstruct the writing's meaning quickly.

Underlining should be done selectively. If you underline everything, you will not be able to use your underlinings to recall the overall meaning of the writing. Selective underlining enables you to identify where the writer presents important information, claims, evidence, interpretations, and conclusions.

See how the underlinings of "Alfred Binet and the Original Purpose of the Binet Scale" focus on Stephen Jay Gould's main ideas.

Annotation

Annotations are comments that readers write in the margins of a piece of writing. The purposes of annotation are to help you to actively engage in what you are reading and to create a record of your experience as you come to grips with its meaning.

There are no rules about annotation, but here are some suggestions:

1. Write brief notes on what you see as major points.
2. Agree or disagree with what the writer is saying.
3. Refer to what the writer is doing at a particular point (for example, making a claim, giving an example, presenting statistical evidence, or refuting an opposing view).
4. Raise questions on voice confusion about something you need to clarify.
5. Draw connections to other things you have read or know about.

The following selection is taken from Stephen Jay Gould's book *The Mismeasure of Man,* an acclaimed study of the history of psychometrics, the science of measuring intelligence. As you will see, the passage describes how the French psychologist Alfred Binet developed IQ testing in the early 1900s.

Notice that although the passage is part of the larger argument Gould makes about the theoretical inconsistencies and misuse of data in psychometrics, his purpose in the two paragraphs is largely informative. The reading strategies of underlining and annotation are good choices to clarify your understanding of the passage's meaning.

IQ test developed for specific purpose of identifying special ed students.

In 1904 Binet was commissioned by the minister of public education to perform a study for a specific, practical purpose: to develop techniques for identifying those children whose lack of success in normal classrooms suggested the need for some form of special education. Binet chose a purely pragmatic course. He decided to bring together a large series of short tasks, related to everyday problems of life (counting coins, or assessing which face is "prettier," for example), but supposedly involving such basic processes of reasoning as "direction (ordering), comprehension, invention and censure (correction)" (Binet, 1909). Learned skills like reading would not be treated explicitly. The tests were administered individually by trained examiners who led subjects through the series of tasks, graded in their order of difficulty. Unlike previous tests designed to measure specific and independent "faculties" of mind, Binet's scale was a hodgepodge of diverse activities.

How did it become standard measure of intelligence?

He hoped that by mixing together enough tests of different abilities he would be able to abstract a child's general potential with a single score. Binet emphasized the empirical nature of his work with a famous dictum (1911, p. 329): "One might almost say, 'It matters very little what the tests are so long as they are numerous.'"

(continued)

3 stages in scale:
1905-order of difficulty
1908-age level
1912-IQ
quotient
emerges

Binet published three versions of the scale before his death in 1911. The original 1905 edition simply arranged the tasks in an ascending order of difficulty. The 1908 version established the criterion used in measuring the so-called IQ ever since. Binet decided to assign an age level to each task, defined as the youngest age at which a child of normal intelligence should be able to complete the task successfully. A child began the Binet test with tasks for the youngest age and proceeded in sequence until he could no longer complete the tasks. The age associated with the last tasks he could perform became his "mental age," and his general intellectual level was calculated by subtracting this mental age from his true chronological age. Children whose mental ages were sufficiently behind their chronological ages could then be identified for special educational programs, thus fulfilling Binet's charge from the ministry. In 1912 the German psychologist W. Stern argued that mental age should be divided by chronological age, not subtracted from it, and the intelligence *quotient,* or IQ, was born.

Summarizing

A summary condenses clearly and accurately what you have read. Like underlining, a good summary identifies the main idea and important supporting material. But it also calls on you to explain the connections between points.

To write an effective summary, follow these steps:

1. Read the text carefully, underlining and annotating it. Identify the writer's purpose and the main point of the reading (this main point might or might not be explicitly stated). Underline and, where relevant, annotate the ideas that support the main point and the key details that support these ideas.

2. Review your underlinings and annotations. Think about what questions you may have. If the writer didn't explicitly state his or her main point, write the main point as you see it. (The main point is often tied to the writer's purpose, so thinking about purpose might help in stating the main point.)

3. Start your summary with a statement in your own words that identifies the writer's purpose and expresses the main point.

4. Consult your underlinings and annotations to identify the most important supporting details. Rewrite these details in your own words, combining ideas when you can.

5. Check your summary to see if it holds together as a coherent piece of writing and is not simply a series of unconnected statements. Add transitions where needed to make connections between parts of the summary.

Look at the following sample summary, and notice how it starts by explaining the author's purpose and then provides selected details on key developments in the test, using a series of parallel phrases—"In the original edition," "In the second edition," and "In 1912"—to order the information.

SAMPLE SUMMARY OF "ALFRED BINET AND THE ORIGINAL PURPOSE OF THE BINET SCALE"

In *The Mismeasure of Man*, Stephen Jay Gould traces the origins of the IQ test to 1904, when the French psychologist Alfred Binet was asked to identify children in need of special education. To measure children's reasoning abilities, Binet developed a series of intelligence tests based on practical problems instead of learned skills. Binet believed that numerous short tasks could provide a single score to represent children's intellectual potential. In the original edition of the test (1905), Binet used a scoring scale that ranked the tasks in order of difficulty. In the second edition (1908), Binet gave each task an age level at which a normally intelligent child could perform it. Binet then used these age levels to determine a child's general intelligence by subtracting mental age (or the most difficult task a child could do) from chronological age. In 1912, the idea of an intelligence quotient or IQ appeared when Stern suggested mental age be divided by chronological age instead of subtracted from it.

Exploratory Writing

Exploratory writing offers you a chance to explore your thoughts and feelings about the ideas in a piece of writing. You can use what you have read as a springboard to see where your thoughts lead you.

The only direction is that you begin with what you have just read and write nonstop for a predetermined amount of time, say five or ten minutes. The idea is to build up momentum, so don't stop to revise, edit, or correct anything you have written. Don't worry about whether your ideas are consistent or contradictory. Just see where your writing takes you.

SAMPLE EXPLORATORY WRITING:

IQ tests have this mystique about measuring people's intelligence and finding out who is a genius. You hear kids in school talking about who has a high IQ and who doesn't. So I was interested to read that the origins of the IQ test had a much more modest purpose, namely to identify students in need of special education. It seems that Alfred Binet just put together these tasks in a kind of scattergun way to get some insight about children's potential. This seems to me very different than the way IQ tests are being used today, as if they were this standard, objective measure of intelligence.

ETHICS OF READING

BOREDOM AND PERSISTENCE

Going to college means that you will encounter a wide range of academic and professional writing, some of which may be specialized and technical. You may find at times that the reading you're assigned is intimidating and hard to follow. You may wonder what the writer is trying to prove or feel that he or she is splitting hairs. The writing may seem abstract, detached from the real world.

These are all symptoms of boredom, and the danger is that you will give up at this point and say you weren't really interested in the first place. What is often the case, though, is not that you aren't interested but rather that you are unfamiliar with the particular type of writing, its forms, specialized vocabularies, and ways of reasoning.

To act responsibly in college, the workplace, and the public domain, you need to read writing that is pertinent and carries weight. An ethics of reading holds that readers need to give difficult material a chance. It's not simply a matter of being fair to the writer. By working on new and difficult material, you also, in effect, refuse to be alienated from it. And in this regard, you avoid the threat of boredom leading to the premature closure of communication.

WORKING TOGETHER

Practicing Basic Reading Strategies

Working with two or three other students, select a short passage of two or three paragraphs. (You can find your own reading, or use any of the reading selections in this book.) Follow these directions:

1. On your own, read the paragraphs you've chosen. Underline and annotate. Then write a one-paragraph summary. Finally write one or two paragraphs of exploratory writing in response to the reading.

2. Compare your underlinings, annotations, summary, and exploratory writing to what others in your group have done. What are the main similarities and differences? Don't argue about who is right or wrong. Instead, notice what each person's work on the reading has brought to light.

STRATEGIES FOR ANALYZING WRITING

The strategies in this section offer ways to do a close reading of a piece of writing when you want not only to understand the information presented but also to analyze how the writer presents the main ideas and the evidence he or she uses to support those ideas. The reading strategies that follow are particularly useful in cases where the writer is making an argument.

To see how these strategies work, let's look at a passage from Jonathan Kozol's essay "Distancing the Homeless." Kozol begins with the commonly held view that homelessness results from the release of mental patients from state hospitals in the 1970s. Then he counters this view with an alternative explanation of the cause of homelessness, as well as an explanation of why the "deinstitutionalization" view is so widespread.

Because Kozol is asking us to reconsider our ideas about the cause of homelessness, we need to do more than just understand the information he presents. Although the basic reading strategies from the previous section are good ways to start a close reading of Kozol's argument, you'll also need other strategies to weigh the alternative explanations of homelessness, consider the evidence Kozol presents to support his explanation of homelessness, and to assess his conclusions. Outlining, describing the writer's strategy, analyzing facts and claims, and evaluating the writer's evidence are good tools for doing this work.

From "Distancing the Homeless"
JONATHAN KOZOL

1. It is commonly believed by many journalists and politicians that the homeless of America are, in large part, former patients of large mental hospitals who were deinstitutionalized in the 1970s—the consequence, it is sometimes said, of misguided liberal opinion that favored the treatment of such persons in community-based centers. It is argued that this policy, and the subsequent failure of society to build such centers or to provide them in sufficient number, is the primary cause of homelessness in the United States.

2. Those who work among the homeless do not find that explanation satisfactory. While conceding that a certain number of the homeless are or have been mentally unwell, they believe that, in the case of most unsheltered people, the primary reason is economic rather than clinical. The cause of homelessness, they say with disarming logic, is the lack of homes and of income with which to rent or acquire them.

3. They point to the loss of traditional jobs in industry (2 million every year since 1980) and to the fact that half of those who are laid off end up in work that pays a poverty-level wage. They point out that since 1968 the number of children living in poverty has grown by 3 million, while welfare benefits to families with children have declined by 35 percent.

4. And they note, too, that these developments have occurred during a time in which the shortage of low-income housing has intensified as the gentrification of our major cities has accelerated. Half a million units of low-income housing are lost each year to condominium conversion as well as to arson, demolition, or abandonment. Between 1978 and 1980, median rents climbed 30 percent for people in the lowest income sector, driving many of these families into the streets. Since 1980, rents have risen at even faster rates.

5. Hard numbers, in this instance, would appear to be of greater help than psychiatric labels in telling us why so many people become homeless. Eight million American families now use half or more of their income to pay their rent or

mortgage. At the same time, federal support for low-income housing dropped from $30 billion (1980) to $7.5 billion (1988). Under Presidents Ford and Carter, 500,000 subsidized private housing units were constructed. By President Reagan's second term, the number had dropped to 25,000.

6   In our rush to explain the homeless as a psychiatric problem, even the words of medical practitioners who care for homeless people have been curiously ignored. A study published by the Massachusetts Medical Society, for instance, has noted that, with the exceptions of alcohol and drug use, the most frequent illnesses among a sample of the homeless population were trauma (31 percent), upper-respiratory disorders (28 percent), limb disorders (19 percent), mental illness (16 percent), skin diseases (15 percent), hypertension (14 percent), and neurological illnesses (12 percent). Why, we may ask, of all these calamities, does mental illness command so much political and press attention? The answer may be that the label of mental illness places the destitute outside the sphere of ordinary life. It personalizes an anguish that is public in its genesis; it individualizes a misery that is both general in cause and general in application.

7   There is another reason to assign labels to the destitute and single out mental illness from among their many afflictions. All these other problems—tuberculosis, asthma, scabies, diarrhea, bleeding gums, impacted teeth, etc.—bear no stigma, and mental illness does. It conveys a stigma in the United States. It conveys a stigma in the Soviet Union as well. In both nations the label is used, whether as a matter of deliberate policy or not, to isolate and treat as special cases those who, by deed or word or by sheer presence, represent a threat to national complacence. The two situations are obviously not identical, but they are enough alike to give Americans reason for concern.

8   The notion that the homeless are largely psychotics who belong in institutions, rather than victims of displacement at the hands of enterprising realtors, spares us from the need to offer realistic solutions to the deep and widening extremes of wealth and poverty in the United States. It also enables us to tell ourselves that the despair of homeless people bears no intimate connection to the privileged existence we enjoy—when, for example, we rent or purchase one of those restored town houses that once provided shelter for people now huddled in the street.

Outlining

Outlining can help you analyze how writers arrange their material—what the parts are and how they are organized.

There are various ways to set up an outline. A standard way, like the outline below, is to divide the writing into three main sections—the introduction, the body, and the conclusion. The outline states the main point at the beginning, uses roman numerals to mark off the main sections, uses capital letters to identify important ideas within each section, and uses arabic numerals to note details that support these ideas.

The benefit of such an outline is that it gives you a clear, concise record of what the piece of writing says. In this way, it is similar to a summary. However, it also goes beyond a summary by helping you visualize the relationships among the parts of the writing so that you can analyze the writer's strategy, as discussed in the next section.

The following outline shows how Kozol has organized his argument.

SAMPLE OUTLINE

Main point: The cause of homelessness is not mental illness but rather the lack of homes and of income with which to rent or acquire them.

    I.   *Introduction:* Two views of the cause of homelessness
        A. Common view: Deinstitutionalizing the mentally ill
        B. Kozol's view: The lack of homes and income
   II.   *Body:* Supporting evidence for Kozol's view
        A. Lack of income
            1. Loss of traditional jobs in industry
            2. Increase in numbers of people working for poverty-level wages
            3. Increase in children living in poverty
            4. Decrease in welfare benefits
        B. Shortage of low-cost housing
            1. Loss of public housing to condominium conversion and to arson, demolition, and abandonment
            2. Increase in rents
        C. Other revealing statistics
            1. Eight million families using half or more of their incomes for rent or mortgage
            2. Drop in federal support for low-income housing
            3. Decrease in construction of subsidized private housing
        D. Statistics on most frequent illnesses among homeless
  III.   *Conclusion:* Reasons for labeling homeless as mentally ill
        A. Treating problem as individual rather than public
        B. Stigma of mental illness isolating homeless as special cases
        C. Way of not dealing with real problems
        D. Distancing ourselves from plight of homeless

Describing the Writer's Strategy

As you have seen, an outline helps you identify how a writer organizes his or her ideas to support a main point. The next step is to analyze the organization by describing the strategy the writer uses to connect these parts.

This reading strategy asks you to identify the main sections in a piece of writing and to explain how each section functions (instead of just recording what the writing says, as in an outline). By focusing on what the writer is doing—comparing and contrasting, supporting with evidence, explaining causes and effects—you can see the strategies the writer uses to connect the sections and thereby accomplish his or her overall purpose. (See the box on page 43 for a fuller listing of such strategies). Describing the writer's strategy can give you insight into the writer's purposes and how the sections in a piece of writing function together.

To describe a writer's strategy:

1. Write a statement that describes the writer's overall purpose. What is the writer trying to accomplish—provide information (as Gould does), challenge a common view (as Kozol does), or do something else? You can probably think of a number of other purposes writers have: for example, profiling a person or place, rendering personal experience, endorsing a policy, reviewing a book or movie, interpreting an event, or explaining a concept.

2. Divide the writing into what appear to be the main sections, grouping paragraphs that seem to go together. (This step is similar to marking the main sections with roman numerals in an outline.) Look for an opening section that introduces the topic or main idea, a middle section or sections that develop the writer's subject, and an ending.

3. Label the function each major section performs. Your label should explain how the section fits into the writing as a whole. Consider how the opening section introduces the topic or main idea, how a middle section or sections develop it, and how the writing ends.

4. Label the parts within each main section according to the function they perform. (Notice that you are analyzing here the parts marked by A, B, C,... and 1, 2, 3,... on an outline.) Explain how each part develops the main idea of the section in which it appears.

To label the parts in steps 3 and 4, you may find it useful to consult the box of strategies. Since the box only gives some of the most common, however, be prepared to invent your own terms.

Sample Description of the Writer's Strategy

Notice how the following sample divides the writing into three main sections by grouping paragraphs together according to the function they perform—introducing the argument, providing supporting evidence, and explaining the consequences of the argument.

As you can see, these sections correspond to the introduction, body, and conclusion in the outline. But instead of referring to the content of the writing, the sample description of the writer's strategy uses labels that explain how the main sections build Kozol's argument and how the parts of each section develop its main idea.

Overall purpose: To challenge a common view about the causes of homelessness

¶1–2: Introduces the main idea.

Replaces a common belief about the cause of homelessness with an alternative view.

¶3–6: Provides supporting evidence for the main idea.

Offers the testimony of experts, statistical evidence, and a medical study to refute the common view.

Raises a question about why the common view commands attention and offers an answer.

¶7–8: Explains the implications of the argument.

Offers a second reason for the common view.

Compares how the common view operates in the United States and the Soviet Union.

Explains important consequences of the common view.

Analyzing Facts and Claims

Readers justifiably expect that when writers make arguments they will back up their claims with factual evidence. This makes sense because facts have tremendous authority. But the facts do not speak for themselves. Instead, readers need to analyze how facts are used and whether they actually support the writer's claims. For this reason, an important reading strategy is to distinguish between facts and claims. By doing this, you can identify how writers link the use of factual information to the arguable positions they take.

Facts are basically statements that no one calls into question. Facts have to be established to acquire such authority, and journalists, scientists, legal experts, historians, economists, engineers, and others have developed methods to certify what counts as a fact and what remains in doubt. Some facts are

---

WRITING STRATEGIES

- Narrates, tells a story, relates an anecdote or incident.
- Describes things, people, places, processes.
- Illustrates by using examples, details, data.
- Defines key terms, problems, issues, trends.
- Compares and/or contrasts one thing, idea, person, place to another.
- Classifies things, ideas, people, places, processes into categories.
- Explains causes and effects.
- Gives reasons.
- Offers evidence (for example, statistics, established facts, expert testimony).
- Cites other writers.
- Makes concessions.
- Refutes opposing views.

expressed in the form of numbers, statistics, or other units of measurement (the number of industrial jobs lost since 1980, the percentage of millionaires who pay no income taxes, or the length of the Mississippi River). Others describe in words what is known (DNA has a double-helical structure, Morocco is located in North Africa, the Soviet Union collapsed in 1989). In either case, the facts can be verified by reliable sources.

The facts, however, don't necessarily tell us what to do with the information they contain. For example, the fact that John F. Kennedy was killed on November 22, 1963, doesn't tell us much about the meaning of his death, why it happened, or whether the assassin Lee Harvey Oswald acted alone or with others. These are questions that fall into the domain of interpretation, and as you may know, there are hundreds of books and articles that offer more or less plausible claims about the Kennedy assassination.

See Chapter 3 for a fuller discussion of how writers connect facts and claims.

As a reading strategy, analyzing facts and claims can help you identify what the writer assumes readers will accept as the available information and whether these facts do indeed support the claim (an issue we'll look at further in the following section).

Sample Analysis of Facts and Claims

Jonathan Kozol's essay "Distancing the Homeless" offers a good opportunity to analyze how facts and claims are connected. Here are some examples:

Fact	Claim
Loss of jobs (2 million a year since 1980) and poverty-level wages	Homelessness caused by lack of income
35 percent decline in welfare benefits to families with children since 1968	Homelessness caused by lack of income
Loss of low-income affordable housing	Homelessness caused by lack of half a million units each year
Rents increased 30 percent between 1978 and 1980	Homelessness caused by lack of affordable housing
Mental illness accounts for only 16 percent of illness among homeless	Homelessness not caused by mental illness

As you can see, while the facts Kozol presents do not automatically lead to the claims he makes, the connections are arguable ones. In other instances, however, the connection is less clear. What, for example, are we to make of the fact that since 1968 the number of children living in poverty has increased by 3 million? This may indeed point to a deplorable situation that requires action, but whether this fact supports Kozol's central claim is another matter.

Evaluating the Writer's Evidence

The value of a writer's argument depends in many respects on the sources of information the writer uses to provide evidence for his or her argument. The following list includes the most common forms of evidence and criteria for evaluating how writers use their sources:

Statistics

Statistics have taken on an unquestioned authority, in part because they seem to provide hard and incontestable evidence. Nonetheless, there are some good reasons to be skeptical about the use of statistics and to have some questions at hand to evaluate them. In advertisements, for example, you may read that nine out of ten successful runners wear a certain brand of running shoe, but to evaluate these statistics, you need to ask what the numbers actually mean. If the person who designed the ad talked to only ten runners, that is hardly a large enough sample to suggest that 90 percent of all successful runners wear that brand of shoe.

You should ask, too, whether the statistics are complete. For example, a writer calling for a get-tough approach to crime may cite the statistic that the city you live in had 182 homicides last year—a chilling figure that averages one murder every other day. Suppose, however, last year's number of murders actually represents a 15 percent decline over the previous year and a 30 percent decline over a five-year period. Any claim that ignores this larger pattern must be considered dubious. As a reader, stay alert to such possible distortions in the writer's use of sources.

Research

Colleges and universities, the federal government, professional societies, independent research institutes, and corporations all conduct research in a range of fields. Citing such published studies from reputable sources adds credibility to the writer's case.

A key question for you as a reader, though, is which published studies do in fact provide reputable evidence. Let's say you are investigating the published literature on the addictive properties of nicotine, whether for academic purposes or to develop policies on cigarette advertising. One of the things you should pay attention to is who sponsored the research studies—the tobacco companies? the National Institutes of Health? the American Cancer Society? The fact that the tobacco companies have sponsored research on the properties of nicotine should not automatically disqualify their findings. At the same time, you should note that the tobacco companies can hardly be considered impartial sponsors, and you should look for possible biases in the studies.

A second question to ask about research studies is how up-to-date they are. In general, the most recent studies are more authoritative than older ones.

Expert Testimony

Writers often cite experts to support their arguments. The experience and professional credentials of people who are close to the issue at hand can certainly lend credibility to the writer's case. To evaluate the use of expert testimony as evidence, you can ask what experience and background make these people experts. What reason is there to believe that they will offer informed accounts? What political, cultural, social, or other commitments are likely to influence what they have to say?

Examples

Examples generally serve the purpose of illustrating a point the writer wants to make. Examples can be drawn from a number of sources: anecdotal accounts of personal experience, observations in field research and case studies, or readings on the topic.

To evaluate a writer's use of examples, ask yourself whether the example is truly representative of the point the writer wants to establish. Imagine that the writer of a letter to the editor of your local newspaper calls for the establishment of a civilian police review board, using the example of a bad encounter the writer recently had with the police. In this case, as a reader you need to determine whether the writer's personal experience really furnishes evidence of the need for the review board. Is the example truly representative? Does the writer fit it into a pattern of police abuse? Or does the example stand as an isolated instance leading to a hasty and unjustifiable conclusion?

WORKING TOGETHER

Practicing Strategies for Analyzing Writing

Working with two or three other students, pick a short piece of writing that makes an argument. A good source for this assignment is the editorial page of a newspaper—whether it's a student, local, or national newspaper (such as *The New York Times* or *USA Today*). Look for a piece of writing that is five to ten paragraphs long. Then follow these steps:

1. Working together, compose an outline of the writing.
2. Now use the outline you have written to describe the writer's strategy.
3. Identify the facts the writer presents. What claims does the writer make based on these facts?
4. Evaluate the writer's evidence. What sources are used? Do these sources seem reliable?

STRATEGIES FOR ANALYZING THE RHETORICAL SITUATION

Analyzing the rhetorical situation of a piece of writing is a matter of building on the reading strategies already presented to examine how and why a particular piece of writing got written in the first place, who its intended readers are, and what its writer is trying to accomplish. In other words, the goal of analyzing the rhetorical situation is not just to understand the content of a piece of writing or how the writer put it together but to understand its context. Analyzing the rhetorical situation involves asking questions like these: Who is the writer? What called on the writer to put his or her views down on the page? What kind of relationship is the writer trying to establish with readers? How does the writer's work relate to the larger context of discussion about an issue?

Certainly the following set of reading strategies will not be needed when you read sports scores, recipes, weather reports, or gossip columns. But there are occasions when analyzing the rhetorical situation is important because you want to get a fuller picture of what you're reading. For example, if you are reading arguments about ballot measures in a coming election, the more you know about the writers and their purposes, the better you will be able to interpret their writings and decide if and how they should influence your own position. The same is true in any kind of discussion where the issues are disputed—whether the dispute is about advocacy of a living wage for all workers at your college or about how literary critics differ in their interpretations of Mary Shelley's *Frankenstein*.

This section presents three strategies for analyzing the rhetorical situation—using background information about the context of issues, the writer, and the place of publication; analyzing the writer's relationship to readers; and analyzing the writer's use of language as clues about the rhetorical situation.

Using Background Information

Background information about the context of issues, the writer, and the publication where the writer's work appears can be useful in understanding the rhetorical situation and how the writer identifies the call to write.

As you will see, the information you turn up about the context, the writer, and the place of publication does not speak for itself. You need to interpret this information in order to determine what it means for your analysis.

The Context of Issues

One of the main themes of this book is that writing doesn't just happen. It is called up when writers are moved by some sense of urgency that makes them want to be heard. This means that there is often a debate, discussion, or controversy already under way, which for one reason or another, the writer feels compelled to enter. This certainly seems to be the case with Jonathan Kozol, who sees the dominant explanations of homelessness as inadequate and misleading. In other cases, dramatic events, such as the impeachment hearings against Bill Clinton or the shootings at Columbine High in Littleton, Colorado, moved writers to try to make sense of these incidents. But even in these situations, there was already a larger discussion going on—about Clinton's character or about teens and the media—that formed the context of the issues.

To understand the context of issues for the writing you're analyzing, you'll need to fill in some background information. Here are some questions to help you do so:

1. What do you know about the particular topic the writer is treating? If your knowledge is limited, where can you get reliable background information? You might do some library research—the *Readers' Guide to Periodical Literature* is a good place to start for contemporary issues—or a search on the Web. You can also talk to friends, older students, parents, teachers, librarians, or other adults.

2. What have people been saying about the topic? What do they think the main issues are? What seems to be at stake in these discussions?

3. Do people seem to be divided over these issues? If so, what positions have various people taken? What proposals or interpretations have they offered?

The Writer

Information about the writer—his or her education, credentials, experience, politics, prior publications, awards, institutional affiliations, reputation —is often summarized briefly in an author note following an article or on a book's dust jacket. You may also find the writer listed in the standard reference source *Contemporary Authors.*

This background information can give you some clues about the writer's authority to speak on the topic and the perspective he or she is likely to bring to it. Such background information can also make you aware of the assumptions readers might make about the writer. In the case of Jonathan Kozol, for example, many readers will recognize him as an award-winning nonfiction writer, radical educator, and social activist whose publications include *Death at an Early Age* (his account of teaching in Boston's inner-city schools in the

1960s), *Illiterate America,* and *Savage Inequalities* (a study of underfunded inner-city schools). For those familiar with Kozol's work, his turn from education to the problem of homelessness may well seem a natural one. And, of course, readers' background information about Kozol will also call up their own expectations about his purposes and point of view.

Here are some questions you may find useful:

1. Based on what you know about his or her background, how much authority and credibility can you attribute to the writer? Is there reason to believe that the writer will provide informed accounts and responsible arguments, whether you agree with them or not?

2. Does the information you've found offer suggestions about why the writer was moved to write on the topic? What political, cultural, social, or other commitments is the writer known for? How are these commitments likely to influence the writer's argument?

3. How do these commitments relate to your own views? How is this relationship likely to influence your evaluation of the writer's argument?

The Publication

Type of publication can also provide you with some useful background information. Readers are likely to form very different impressions based on the type of publication in which a writer's work appears. You can find background information on the intended audience and editorial slant of many magazines in the standard reference source *Magazines for Libraries.*

In the case of Jonathan Kozol's "Distancing the Homeless," readers, whether they agree with his analysis or not, will acknowledge that his work appears in reputable publications. "Distancing the Homeless" first appeared in the *Yale Review* (a well-regarded journal that publishes social commentary, literary criticism, fiction, and poetry) and then was incorporated into Kozol's book-length study *Rachel and Her Children: Homeless Families in America,* published by one of the leading publishing houses.

Here are some questions to ask about the type of publication:

1. What do you know about the publication? Who is the publisher? Is it a commercial publication? Does it have an institutional affiliation—to a college or university, an academic field of study, a professional organization, a church? Does it espouse an identifiable political, social, cultural, economic, or religious ideology?

2. If the publication is a periodical, what other writers—and types of writing and topics—appear in the issue?

3. Who would be likely to read the publication?

Even when you don't know much about a publication, you can make informed guesses about its point of view and intended audience. One factor to consider is the look of the publication. Notice how the Globe has a very different appearance than the Wall Street Journal. List features about each front page that give you clues to the degree of sensationalism of each publication.

Analyzing the Writer's Relationship to Readers

The purpose of analyzing the writer's relationship to readers is to understand where the writer is coming from, on whose behalf he or she is speaking, and the common ground the writer is asking readers to share. In some instances, the writer will address one particular audience, while in others the writer will try to appeal to many different audiences. In either case, the writer will have to make some key assumptions about readers' knowledge of the topic and their point of view on the issues it raises.

In the case of "Distancing the Homeless," notice how Kozol quickly locates himself in opposition to the common belief of journalists and politicians that the homeless are mainly former mental patients. Instead, he aligns himself with those "who work among the homeless" and believe that the cause of homelessness is the lack of homes and income. In that sense, he hopes to speak on behalf of the homeless, who, he believes, have been unfairly represented in the media and politics. And Kozol is probably anticipating that some of his readers already share or will be predisposed to accept his perspective and social allegiances.

After presenting evidence for his counterinterpretation of the causes of homelessness, Kozol shifts in the sixth paragraph to speak in the collective voice of first-person plural ("we may ask"). At this point, Kozol seems to assume that he has offered enough compelling evidence about the actual causes of homelessness to expect readers who did not originally side with him to join with him on common ground to ask why the mental illness label has been persistently applied to the homeless.

As you can see in the passage from "Distancing the Homeless," writers' relationships to their readers seek points of identification—to establish the common ground that joins individuals together as "we." And, as the passage illustrates, forming a "we" can often imply the existence of a "they" from whom "we" are somehow distinguished, different, perhaps antagonistic. For these reasons, analyzing the writer's relationship to readers is an especially important reading strategy where the issues under consideration are contested and the writer is attempting to line them up on one side or another. It can help you figure out where you stand on the issues and where your own allegiances reside.

Here are some questions to help you identify the writer's allegiances and relationship to readers:

1. Based on what you have read and the available background information on the writer, can you identify on whose behalf the writer is speaking? Whose interests does the writer seem to represent? Where do her loyalties seem to reside?

2. What assumptions does the writer seem to make about readers? Is the writer trying to establish common ground with a particular audience or with many different audiences? Does she seem to assume that some readers are already predisposed to share her perspective and social allegiances?

3. What would it mean to agree with the writer? How would agreement position readers in relation to what the writer and others have said about the topic? Would agreement align readers with certain groups, individuals, points of view, institutions, values—and put them into opposition with others? What would readers have to believe to agree with the writer?

GOING ONLINE

EVALUATING WEB SITES

Evaluating information on the Web poses special problems for the reader. Unlike printed material such as newspapers, magazines, government documents, academic journals, and books, Web sites do not necessarily go through a process of editing and peer review that filters out unreliable and unsubstantiated information. Instead, what appears on the Web is largely unregulated and sometimes of questionable credibility. After all, anyone can put up a Web site and include in it whatever they wish. That is, of course, part of the Web's attraction, but it is also the primary reason that readers need to approach Web sites with care. Here are some basic suggestions for evaluating the reliability and authority of information found on the Web.

Reading a Web Document

Web documents contain three main elements: header, body, and footer. (See the diagram of the Historical Collections at the New York Academy of Medicine, Scholarly Seminars Web site.) Knowing where to look in the document should enable you to answer the following questions as a starting point for evaluating the Web site:

1. Who is the author or contact person? This is usually located in the footer.

2. What institution or Internet provider supports the Web site? This is usually located in the header or footer. (*.edu* indicates an educational institution; *.org,* a nonprofit organization; *.gov,* a government institution; and *.com,* a commercial source.)

3. When was the Web site created or updated? This is usually located in the footer.

4. What is the purpose of the information contained in the Web site? This is determined by examining the body.

5. Who is the intended audience? This is determined by examining the body.

Evaluating Web sites

You can use the information you have gathered to ask the following questions. Your answers should enable you to evaluate the reliability of the information at the Web site:

1. What do you know about the author? Does he or she list an occupation, institutional affiliation, years of experience, or other information or qualifications? Does the author seem to be qualified to write and present information on the topic at hand?

2. What do you know about the institution or Internet provider that supports the Web site? What influence, if any, is the author's affiliation to this particular organization, institution, or provider likely to have on the information presented at the Web site?

3. What seems to be the purpose of the Web site—to inform, explain, persuade, or some combination? Who is the site's audience likely to be? What uses are visitors likely to make of the site?

4. How much of the information at the Web site has the author created? How much is already existing material that the author has organized? Where does such information come from? Do these sources seem reliable? Is the Web site linked to other sites? Do linked sites seem to be reliable and authoritative? How can you tell?

Exercise

Use the questions to visit and evaluate the two Web sites shown on page 54—the Schol-
(continued)

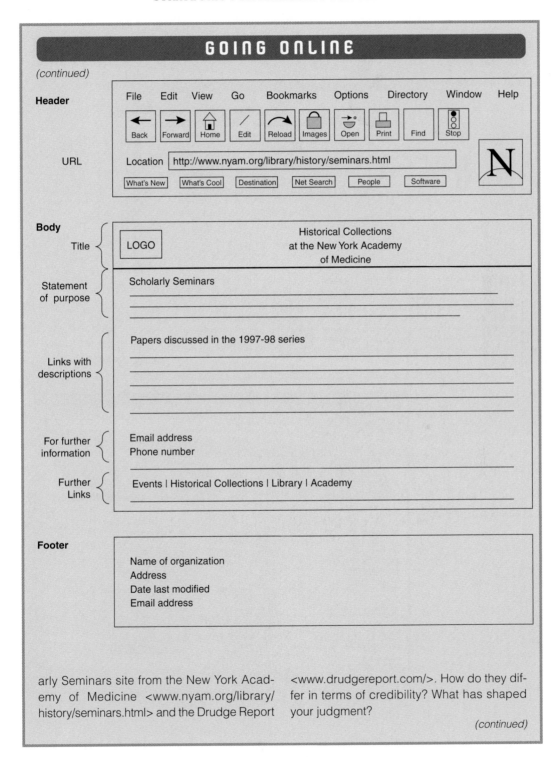

GOING ONLINE

(continued)

Header

File   Edit   View   Go   Bookmarks   Options   Directory   Window   Help

← Back   → Forward   🏠 Home   ✏ Edit   ↻ Reload   🛍 Images   Open   🖨 Print   Find   🚦 Stop

URL

Location   http://www.nyam.org/library/history/seminars.html

N

| What's New | What's Cool | Destination | Net Search | People | Software |

Body

Title

LOGO

Historical Collections
at the New York Academy
of Medicine

Statement
of purpose

Scholarly Seminars

Links with
descriptions

Papers discussed in the 1997-98 series

For further
information

Email address
Phone number

Further
Links

Events | Historical Collections | Library | Academy

Footer

Name of organization
Address
Date last modified
Email address

arly Seminars site from the New York Academy of Medicine <www.nyam.org/library/history/seminars.html> and the Drudge Report <www.drudgereport.com/>. How do they differ in terms of credibility? What has shaped your judgment?

(continued)

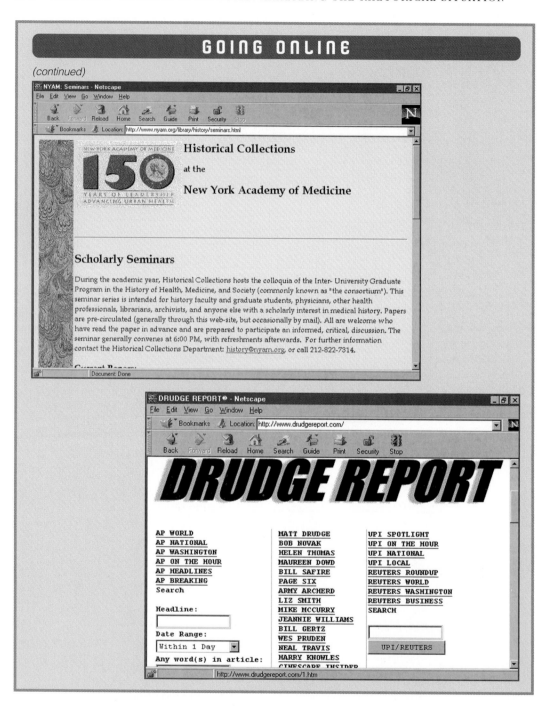

Analyzing the Writer's Language

Words and phrases carry powerful associations that can sway readers to share or reject what a writer is saying. It is one thing, after all, to refer to business executives as "corporate leaders" or "entrepreneurial visionaries" and quite another to call them "fat cats" or "robber barons." The choice of terms reveals the writer's attitude and the perspective the writer is inviting readers to share. For this reason, it is useful to look at some of the ways writers use language to influence their readers. Reading closely the actual words that writers use can give you some clues to understanding where they are coming from and what they are trying to accomplish.

Tone

The tone in a writer's voice is one of the first things readers respond to because tone projects the writer's attitude and a sense of the writing's intended effect. In some cases, such as the passage from Stephen Jay Gould's *Mismeasure of Man,* the tone of voice is serious, objective, and authoritative. Readers are likely to feel that they are reading the work of someone who knows what he is talking about and that the purpose of the passage is basically informative. Jonathan Kozol's "Distancing the Homeless" is likewise serious in tone, but readers will also detect a sense of urgency and engagement that is not present in the passage from Gould. Kozol wants to inform his readers, but in order for them to do something—to see that "the despair of homeless people" does bear an "intimate connection to the privileged existence we enjoy."

The complete text of Patinkin's column appears in Chapter 4.

A writer's tone can be serious or lighthearted, formal or informal, stuffy or down-to-earth, distanced or intimate. Sometimes readers can hear sarcasm, anger, self-importance, flippancy, and many other attitudes in a writer's tone. Notice, for example, how the informal, conversational tone of the newspaper columnist Mark Patinkin creates a commonsense, man-on-the-street attitude.

> Yes, I know caning is harsh, but am I the only one who's tired of Michael Fay's whining? Am I the only one who feels President Clinton has better things to do than write letters appealing for leniency?

Denotation/Connotation

Words have precise meanings, which you can find in the dictionary. These are their *denotative* meanings. For example, the denotative meaning of *virus* is "a microscopic organism that can replicate only within the cells of a living host," and nationalism means "a feeling of loyalty to a particular country."

Nonetheless, the meaning of these terms is not exhausted by their denotation. They also conjure up connotative meanings, depending on the circumstances in which they are used. *Connotation* means that words take on a certain coloring and emotional force based on how writers use them.

Nationalism, for example, might call up images of unity and belongingness, but it can also release fears of war and ethnic antagonisms. *Virus* may lead the reader to think of new and mysterious "killer diseases" invading the country from the Third World.

Notice, for example, how denotation and connotation work in Kozol's comparison of the United States and the Soviet Union, particularly in regard to the latter. At the level of denotation, the Soviet Union simply refers to the government system that resulted from the Russian Revolution in 1917—and one that collapsed in 1989, just after Kozol published "Distancing the Homeless." At a connotative level, however, the term *Soviet Union* has negative associations for many Americans, conjuring up images of a totalitarian police state. Kozol, of course, is quite aware of these negative connotations, and he uses them to indict the United States by way of comparison.

Figures of Speech

Figures of speech compare one thing to another. You have probably learned that similes use the words *like* or *as* to make a comparison. ("My love is like a red, red rose." "He is as happy as a clam.") Metaphors make an implicit comparison, as though one thing is actually another. ("She was a thin reed of a girl." "The long arm of the law grabbed him and brought him to trial.") Often figures of speech are used to describe—to set a scene or create a mood—as in the following instance:

> If buildings could shiver, this Camden, N.J., tenement would have the shakes.
> *(Jason DeParle, "Learning Poverty Firsthand")*

Figures of speech, however, are not simply decorative. They also provide ways of thinking, and carry judgments on the writer's part. In "Distancing the Homeless," for example, Kozol writes:

> Hard numbers, in this instance, would be of greater help than psychiatric labels in telling us why so many people become homeless.

Numbers, of course, are neither hard nor soft, but their "hardness" here is meant to invest authority in the evidence Kozol presents, in contrast to "psychiatric labels."

> The notion that the homeless are largely psychotics who belong in institutions, rather than victims of displacement at the hands of enterprising realtors....

Literally this sentence says that "enterprising realtors" used their own hands to displace the homeless. Kozol, of course, does not believe that realtors ejected people in person from their homes. But to say that the homeless were displaced "at the hands of enterprising realtors" accentuates the sense of responsibility Kozol assigns to gentrification in causing homelessness.

Stereotypes

Stereotypes are oversimplified representations that fit people into unvarying categories. These broad generalizations break down under careful scrutiny but appear to carry powerful (and often self-serving) explanations.

"Women are more emotional than men" is a classic stereotypical statement that justifies why women won't do well under the stress of positions of authority (and therefore shouldn't be promoted over men). Along the same line, stereotypes of poor and working-class people and racial and ethnic minorities have created popular images (of "white trash," "drunken Indians," "welfare queens") that make subordination of one group to another seem necessary and inevitable. They are used to shame people who fall under the stereotype.

In this sense, stereotyping people, events, and behaviors can, as Kozol says concerning the stereotype of homeless people as mentally ill, stigmatize others and thereby distance us from their fates.

SAMPLE ANALYSIS OF A RHETORICAL SITUATION

The following analysis draws on a number of reading strategies presented in this chapter to examine how the writer Kevin Powell identifies and responds to the call to write in his commentary "My Culture at the Crossroads."

"My Culture at the Crossroads" appeared in the October 9, 2000, issue of *Newsweek* (along with *Time* and *US News & World Report,* one of the three leading news magazines in the United States) as part of its special feature cover story "The Rap on Rap." As you will see, Powell establishes his own credentials for speaking on hip-hop culture in the opening paragraph. *Newsweek* provides further useful background information in the author blurb at the end of Powell's commentary.

> [Kevin] Powell is the editor of *Step Into a World: A Global Anthology of New Black Literature,* to be published in November [2000] (Wiley), and is guest curator of the Brooklyn Museum of Art's "Hip-Hop Nation: Roots, Rhymes and Rage."

First we present the commentary. Then a sample rhetorical analysis with annotations.

My Culture at the Crossroads

A rap devotee watches corporate control and apolitical times encroach on the music he has loved all his life. BY KEVIN POWELL

I AM A HIP-HOP HEAD FOR LIFE. I HAVE TAGGED MY moniker—"kepo1"—on walls; break-danced on cardboard; bumped elbows with fellow hip-hoppers at legendary clubs like The Rooftop, Union Square and Latin Quarter in New York City, and done everything from organizing rap shows to working as a hip-hop journalist and managing music producers. This culture has not only rescued the lives of countless masses who look like me, but it has empowered more young, working-class black and Latino cats than the civil-rights movement.

Yet something peculiar erupts when you've been around hip-hop for a while. Although you still love it, you look at its culture from a more critical perspective, particularly if you have studied other music genres, traveled widely and reflected intensely. You realize that what began as party music has come to be the soundtrack for post-civil-rights America. You realize that hip-hop is urban folk art, and as much an indication of the conditions in impoverished areas as bluesman Robert Johnson's laments in the 1930s. Naturally, you see a connection between the lives of Johnson and Tupac Shakur, not to mention a not-so-funny link between the mainstream hyping of Elvis and Eminem as innovators of black music forms. And, for sure, you wonder, loudly, if what happened to rock and roll will happen to hip-hop, if it hasn't already.

That is the external battle for hip-hop today: corporate control and cooptation. But there is also a civil war going on within the hip-hop nation. Part of it, unquestionably, has to do with this corporate stranglehold. Part of it has to do with the incredibly apolitical times in which we live: for some white Americans the current economic boom has created the myth that things are swell for all Americans. Not the case; 20 years after the Reagan backlash on civil rights, the influx of crack and guns and the acceleration of a disturbing class divide in black America, hip-hop has come to symbolize a generation fragmented by integration, migration, abandonment, alienation and, yes, self-hatred. Thus, hip-hop, once vibrant, edgy, fresh and def, is now as materialis-

Urban art: '80s graffiti, D.M.C. of Run-D.M.C.'s glasses, Powell

tic, hedonistic, misogynistic, shallow and violent as some of the films and TV shows launched from Hollywood.

It wasn't always that way. But, unfortunately, the golden era of hip-hop—that period in the late '80s and early '90s when such diverse artists as Public Enemy, N.W.A, Queen Latifah, MC Hammer, LL Cool J and De La Soul coexisted and there was no such thing as "positive" or "negative" rap—has long been dead.

Gone as well is an embrace of hip-hop's four elements: graffiti writing, the dance element (or what some call break-dancing), DJing and MCing. The MC or "rapper" has been singled out to be his own man in this very male-centered arena, and the formula for a hit record is simple: fancy yourself a thug, pimp or gangster; rhyme about jewelry, clothing and alcohol; denigrate women in every conceivable way, and party and b.s. ad nauseam.

None of this would matter much to me if videos didn't pump visual crack into the minds of young people across the planet. Or if "urban radio" actually played something other than the same 10-12 songs every day. Or if some of our fabulous hip-hop magazines didn't make constant references to marijuana, liquor and "niggas" under the guise of keeping things real. The above notwithstanding, I am not a hater, or someone who disses for the sake of dissing. Nor do I feel hip-hop has created urban misery, racism, sexism, homophobia or classism. That said, what I do believe is that hip-hop is at a crossroads, struggling for control over its creativity, while truly creative artists like Mos Def, Bahamadia and Common wonder when they will get the attention they deserve.

In other words, Jay-Z's "Big Pimpin'" would not bother me so much if Dead Prez's "Mind Sex" received as much notice. Perhaps Chuck D is correct in stating that the Internet is the great equalizer for would-be artists. But what does it matter if homeboys are still screaming "nigga" or "bitch" for global consumption, with no regard for who is inhaling those sentiments?

POWELL *is the editor of "Step Into a World: A Global Anthology of the New Black Literature,"* to be published in November (Wiley), and is guest curator of the Brooklyn Museum of Art's "Hip-Hop Nation: Roots, Rhymes & Rage."

Rhetorical Analysis of "My Culture at the Crossroads"

Indentifies publication

"My Culture at the Crossroads" by Kevin Powell appeared in the *Newsweek* issue of October 9, 2000, as part of a special feature in the Arts and Entertainment section on the current crisis in rap music and hip-hop culture. In Powell's view, there is a "civil war going on within the hip-hop nation," caused in part by corporate control of the music and in part by an apolitical climate in post-civil rights America. The result, as Powell sees it, is that hip-hop is now as "materialistic, hedonistic, misogynistic, shallow, and violent" as Hollywood movies and TV shows. Powell points out that hip-hop was not always this way. In the "golden age" of the late 1980s and early 1990s, hip-hop was a vital "urban folk art" that included graffiti writing, breakdancing, DJing, and MCing. Since that time, however, the single focus on the MC or rapper as a thug, pimp, or gangster has brought hip-hop culture to a crossroads. The issue for Powell is whether the most creative artists can gain control of the music and take it in a positive direction.

Summarizes the commentary

Explains the context of issues

Powell's commentary is part of a larger debate about the current status of rap. Hip-hop culture has always been controversial, but for many people, black and white, inside and outside the hip-hop nation, rap music now seems to focus exclusively on money, sex, and violence. The murders of Tupac Shakur and Biggie Smalls have heightened concerns about rap's "gangsta" image, and the constant preoccupation with guns, expensive jewelry, fancy cars, drugs, and partying worry many that rap is feeding racist stereotypes and has turned the music away from its original promise to tell the truth about black America. As Michael Eric Dyson is quoted in another article in *Newsweek*'s coverage of rap, "There's a war going on for the soul of hip-hop."

Identifies the call to write

Describes writer's credentials

Describes purpose

The term "war" that both Dyson and Powell use gives the commentary its sense of urgency and enables readers to see what was calling on Powell to write. He appears to have excellent credentials to speak on the topic. As he notes in the opening paragraph, Powell has a lot of experience in the hip-hop world and, despite recent trends that bother him, he is a "hip-hop head for life." In fact, it is his devotion to hip-hop culture as creative and empowering that defines his purposes in this commentary. He wants first to explain what has gone wrong and then to call for change within the hip-hop nation. It would not make much sense to call for reform unless there was something worth preserving, and Powell describes rap as an "urban folk art" and discusses the "golden age of hip-hop" to establish the positive possibilities.

Analyzes relationship to one intended audience

Powell's relationship to his readers is a complicated one because he has a number of intended audiences. One audience is the broad readership of Newsweek and includes many people who know very

(continued)

(continued)

little about rap and may have negative feelings about it. For these readers, it might come as a surprise that someone within hip-hop is so critical of it, and Powell seems to use this fact to explain the power of hip-hop for "young, working-class black and Latino cats" and to provide readers with a way of understanding how corporate control and an apolitical times have brought out the worst in hip-hop culture. Powell's criticism of hip-hop may well increase his credibility with these readers and encourage them to see that hip-hop did not create "urban misery, racism, sexism, homophobia, or classism" and that its glorification of money, sex, and violence is no different from what Hollywood and the TV networks put out.

Analyzes relationship to second intended audience

These mainstream readers, however, are not the people who can change the hip-hop nation. If Powell's goal is to educate *Newsweek* readers about the crisis in rap (and perhaps to neutralize feelings of hostility toward it), he has another goal in addressing intended readers within hip-hop culture, namely to acknowledge the crisis and do something about it. Powell must have been aware (and maybe worried) that these readers might be skeptical about his publishing criticisms of hip-hop in a mainstream magazine. This perhaps accounts for the way Powell lists his own roots in hip-hop and proclaims his devotion to it. He also tries to make it clear that he is not "someone who disses for dissing sake." But he must also know that he is unlikely to convince those MCs who are making millions rapping about pimps, "niggas," and "bitches." Instead, his commentary seems to seek out those readers within hip-hop who might join with him to turn things around.

Analyzes language use

Tone

Denotation/ connotation

Figure of Speech

Powell's language is one technique he uses to establish his allegiances to hip-hop and a common ground where progressive forces can join together. The commentary has an informal, conversational tone that emphasizes Powell's sincerity and makes it seem he is speaking directly to his readers. Powell sprinkles his commentary with rap terms such as "tagged," "def," and "DJing" and the names of rap artists, not so many that mainstream readers will lose the train of thought but enough to ensure Powell's authenticity for his hip-hop readers. The use of the term "fresh," for example, will probably just go by many readers as denoting something new, while hip-hop readers will recognize its connotative use as a key term in rap vocabulary. Finally, Powell's most powerful figure of speech—the phrase describing videos that "pump visual crack into the minds of young people"—provides all readers with a striking image of what he sees as wrong with the current rap scene.

My analysis suggests that Powell's commentary is rhetorically effective, given the constraints of space and the fact that we cannot assume that Powell's argument will actually rally progressive rappers

Evaluates rhetorical effectivenenss

and produce genuine change. The commentary does, however, make available to many readers what may well be a new and more complicated understanding of hip-hop, and it clearly offers points of identification for "positive" rappers. For some readers, Powell's argument that "the current economic boom has created the myth that things are swell for all Americans" may be too brief and lacking in evidence, but this in part is a problem of space. Those predisposed to share Powell's view that there is an accelerating class divide may just be glad to see this idea put forward in a major mainstream publication like *Newsweek*. In all, Powell has done a skillful job of conveying the sense of urgency that called on him to write this commentary and a skillful balancing act in establishing the authority to address two very different audiences.

WRITING ASSIGNMENT: RHETORICAL ANALYSIS

Your task is to select a piece of writing that argues a position and analyze its rhetorical situation. Use the sample rhetorical analysis as a flexible guide—not as a rigid model. How you organize your analysis will depend in part on the writing you choose and in part on the decisions you make about how to arrange the parts of your analysis.

DIRECTIONS

1. Select a short (five to ten paragraphs) piece of written text that takes a position on an issue. Newspaper editorials and op-ed pieces, featured columnists published in newspapers and magazines, magazine commentary, political ads, and ads from advocacy groups are all good sources for this assignment. It helps if you know something about the topic and the issues involved. Make sure you are interested.

2. To prepare for your analysis, use the reading strategies presented in this chapter to do a careful preliminary reading of the writing you've chosen.
   - Do a first reading that uses strategies such as underlining, annotation, summarizing, and exploratory writing to make sure you understand what the writer is saying. Go back to any sections that need clarification.
   - On a second reading, start to pay attention to what the writer is doing. You may want to outline the writing and describe the writer's strategy. Notice how the writer uses facts to support claims and the types of evidence.

3. Once you've completed these preliminary readings and feel you have a good grasp of the writing, you can now turn to analyzing the rhetorical situation. Here are some questions to guide your analysis:
   - What is the context of issues? What do you know about the topic? What issues does the topic raise? Is there a larger debate, discussion, or controversy already going on? What seems to be at stake?

- Who is the writer? What do you know about the writer's background, credibility, knowledge of the topic, beliefs, and social allegiances?
- What is the publication? What do you know about its intended readers, reputability, political slant, and the topics it covers?
- What is the call to write? Why is the writer addressing the issue and taking a position at this particular time? Is there some sense of urgency involved? How does the writer identify the significance of the issues involved?
- What is the writer's purpose? What is he trying to accomplish? Is his purpose stated explicitly or implicitly?
- Who is the intended audience? Is the writer addressing one group of readers or more than one? What kind of relationship is he trying to establish with readers? What assumptions about readers does he seem to make?
- How does the writer use language? What is the writer's tone? What does his word choice show about his assumptions about readers? Does he use specialized terms or slang? Are there memorable figures of speech? Does the writer stereotype?
- What is your evaluation of the rhetorical effectiveness? Does he accomplish his purposes? What constraints, if any, qualify the writing's effectiveness?

4. Write an essay that analyzes the writing you've chosen. Begin by summarizing the main line of reasoning. Use your answers to the questions just listed to help you develop your essay, but remember: Your essay should be an integrated analysis and not just a list of answers. Conclude with your evaluation of the writing's rhetorical effectiveness.

REFLECTING ON YOUR WRITING

The main emphasis in this chapter has been on reading and rhetorical analysis. Think back over all you've done in this chapter. How does the work relate to your writing? What have you learned that can help you develop as a writer?

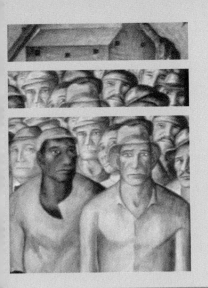

CHAPTER THREE

Persuasion and Responsibility: Analyzing Arguments

Imagine you are taking a walk and encounter an elderly man whose car has broken down in the middle of the street. His request "Can you give me a hand?" requires no explanation. What makes his request persuasive is the shared belief that people should help each other in times of need. Persuasion seems to occur spontaneously, based largely on a mutual understanding that goes without saying.

You can probably think of other occasions when persuasion takes place as a spontaneous meeting of the minds. A friend suggests that you go to the basketball game together on Friday night, and you agree. Neighbors ask if you can feed their cat when they are away for the weekend. You laugh when a family member tells a story about your uncle's eccentricities. Woven into the fabric of social life, persuasion refers to moments when people reach agreements and join together to accomplish a wide range of purposes and activities.

Moments such as these require no elaborate explanation. You don't need an explicit argument to convince you to go to the basketball game or to feed your neighbors' cat. And everybody knows your uncle is one strange guy. The reasons are implied in the situation and the shared understandings of the people involved.

In many other instances, however, we do need to make explicit arguments—to give reasons and explanations—to persuade others. Here are some situations that call on people to make explicit arguments:

- A Jewish man and a Catholic woman want to get married. Both families are very devout and always imagined that their children would marry someone of their faith in a religious ceremony. Grandchildren, of course, would be raised in the family religion. The couple, however, decide that the best way to handle their different religious backgrounds is to get married in a civil ceremony and let their children make their own decisions about religion. Since the couple are of legal age, they could just go ahead and get married, but they want their parents' blessing. Clearly, they have a problem of persuasion and need to come up with some good arguments.

63

■ Persuasion poses a problem for a public relations executive assigned to write a news release explaining why her company has decided to lay off a quarter of the workforce. She knows her audience consists of different interests—stockholders concerned with the company's profit margin, company executives responsible for the layoffs, the individuals who have lost their jobs, the public and its low opinion of downsizing and corporate restructuring. What reasons can she give that will present the public image of the company in the best way?

■ As part of a campaign to increase childhood immunization, a group of health workers has been commissioned to develop public service announcements for television. They have some decisions to make about the pitch of their publicity. What is the most persuasive approach? Should they emphasize the health risks and what can happen if children are not inoculated? Or should they appeal instead to positive images of good parents taking care of their children? Should they target mothers as the primary audience?

■ As a student you know from experience that essay exams amount to exercises in persuasion. The point is to convince the teacher you have mastered the material and can intelligently answer questions about it. Part of learning in any course involves knowing what counts as a good answer, what kinds of statements teachers find persuasive, and the supporting evidence they expect. How can you use this understanding to prepare for tests and perform well on them?

As you can see, situations that call for explicit arguments to persuade others can be complicated. Part of learning to write is learning how to deal with such situations. And that is precisely the purpose of this chapter.

This chapter is arranged to help you:

■ understand the nature of argument,

■ analyze issues to write about,

■ develop a persuasive position,

■ plan convincing arguments, and

■ negotiate differences with others.

WORKING TOGETHER

Successful Persuasion

Work with two or three other students. Before you meet, write a short description of three occasions when someone or something persuaded someone else. Then follow these directions:

1. Take turns reading the descriptions aloud. Working together, choose one example from each group member. As much as possible, select examples

that differ so that you wind up with three or four instances that describe different situations, interactions, and types of persuasion.

2. Working together, analyze the examples you have chosen. In each case, what calls on someone to persuade someone else? Who is trying to influence whom? For what purpose? By what means (written, spoken, visual)? Does the persuasion rely on an explicit argument or on something else? What makes the persuasion successful? What common ground, shared values, mutual understandings are involved?

3. Prepare a report, written or oral depending on your teacher's directions, to present to the class. Use the group reports to identify similarities and differences in the acts of persuasion.

UNDERSTANDING ARGUMENT

People often think of arguments as heated moments when tempers flare and discussion degenerates into a shouting match. There is no question such arguments can be seen frequently on television, whether on daytime talk shows like *Ricki Lake* and *Sally Jessy Raphael* or on political commentaries like *Crossfire* and *Firing Line.*

For our purposes, however, such images of argument are not very useful. We want to think of argument instead as a particular type of persuasion that writers and speakers turn to when people have reasonable differences about the issues that face them. This definition may sound obvious. If people didn't disagree, there would be nothing to argue about. Still, the idea that argument occurs when people have reasonable disagreements is worth examining.

What Is Argument? Dealing with Reasonable Differences

There are disagreements among people that are not, properly speaking, reasonable ones. Two people might disagree, for example, about the driving distance between New York City and Buffalo, New York, or about the chemical composition of dioxin. These are not altogether reasonable disagreements because they can be resolved by consulting a road atlas or a chemistry book. There are sources available to settle the matter, so there's really no point in arguing.

On the other hand, people might reasonably disagree about the best route to drive to Buffalo or about the best policy concerning the production and use of dioxin. In disagreements such as these, there are no final, definitive answers available. One person may prefer a certain route to Buffalo because of the scenery, while another wants only the fastest way possible. By the same token, some may argue that policy on dioxin needs above all to take risks to the environment and public health into account, while for others the effect of policy on the economy and workers' jobs must also be a prime consideration.

ETHICS OF ARGUMENT

THE WRITER'S RESPONSIBILITY

The recognition that argument is a reasonable disagreement is not simply a technical definition of the term. It also carries important ethical implications about the writer's responsibilities in making arguments.

Genuine argument (as opposed to a shouting match) is devoted to understanding the reasonable differences that divide people and using this understanding to clarify the issues. Arguing is not just a matter of stating your position and scoring points. To argue responsibly means responding to others.

Whether you are arguing about public policy on dioxin, how to reform the welfare system, or the long-term consequences of the Vietnam War, the most persuasive argument is likely to be one that takes into account conflicting interests and differing views. Treating differing views as reasonable (instead of malicious, ignorant, or deviant) makes the goal of argument that of expanding your readers' understanding of the issues so that they can see exactly how and why your position fits into a controversy and what the merits of your thinking are.

This view of argument does not mean that you can't hold strong positions or find weaknesses in the views of people who differ with you. It means that you need to take such people seriously—to see them not as obstacles to your views but as reasonable human beings. Arguments often polarize all too quickly into "us" arguing against "them." However, to think of arguing responsibly as responding to others can help you see that when you argue you are entering a relationship with others that seeks mutual understanding, even if agreement is not possible. In this sense, arguments involve working with as much as against others. Reasonable disagreements amount to a collective effort to understand what is at stake and what the best course of action may be.

Darcy Peters and Marcus Boldt: Exchange of Letters

Following is an exchange of letters between Darcy Peters, a homemaker from Camas, Washington, and her representative in the state legislature, Marcus Boldt, a recently elected Republican. As you will see, Peters wrote to Boldt asking him to oppose a plan to eliminate the state's Readiness to Learn program, which supported the Family Learning Center, an adult education and preschool program that Peters and her three sons attended in Camas. Included here are Peters's letter and the response from Representative Boldt.

Representative Marcus Boldt:

1   Please do not cancel funding for the Readiness to Learn Family Learning Center.

2   Our family came to the learning center frustrated. Barely self-supportive, we were struggling but living with no outside assistance. My husband was frequently laid off from work, and I was a full-time mother, not working outside the home. With four-year-old twins and another child, age three, we couldn't afford to pay for a preschool program. When I went to the Head Start program, I was told that we were ineligible because we made too much money. I felt like a victim of the system.

3   I was thrilled to find out we were eligible for the Readiness to Learn program. My children could all attend, and so could I. My sons, Caleb, Zachary, and Nathan, have learned so much at the center. They constantly surprise me with skills I didn't even know they had. I am so proud of their success. I myself have learned a great deal as well. Being challenged academically has sparked a thirst for learning that I never knew existed in me. I have seen the world open up before me, and I feel capable of meeting any academic challenge. Furthermore, using one of the agencies I learned of at the center, my husband is making a career change, having decided to leave the construction business to become an electrician.

4   This has been such a valuable experience that I hope many other families are able to attend the center. Abolishing Readiness to Learn might rob another family of the chance to improve itself and reach its long-term goals. We need this program in our area.

Sincerely,
Darcy Peters

Dear Ms. Peters:

1   Thank you for writing to me about your concerns regarding funding for the Family Learning Center. Your letter goes to the heart of the matter in the area of budgetary reform. My positions on budget expenditures are well-known, and served in large measure to assure my election to this office.

2   I see that you have three children, ages three and four. You wrote that your husband is subject to frequent layoffs. You indicate that you are a "full-time mother, not working outside the home."

3   The concerns expressed by the taxpayers over your situation are as follows:

a. If your situation was subject to so much financial instability, then why did you have three children?

b. Why is your husband in a line of work that subjects him to "frequent layoffs"?

c. Why, in the face of your husband's ability to parent as a result of his frequent layoffs, are you refusing to work outside the home?

d. Since there is no state or federally mandated requirement that children attend these programs, why should the taxpayer foot the bill for them?

e. Since your family apparently makes too much money for assistance, why should you receive subsidies of any kind?

f. How much of the situation outlined in your letter should be the responsibility of the people of this state?

g. What arrangements have you made to repay this program at some future date?

4   I do not necessarily agree with all of these perspectives. But I must contend with the expectations of a constituency that is tired of paying for so many programs without any discernible return.

5   The voters have made it clear that, in this era of personal responsibility, life must become a more "pay-as-you-go" proposition. To put it bluntly, the taxpayers' perspective says, "This program is something that Darcy wants to have, and not something that she must have."

Thank you for your time.

Marcus Boldt
State Representative

FOR CRITICAL INQUIRY

1. What argument is Darcy Peters making? What differences are at issue in the two letters? Do they seem to be reasonable ones? On whose behalf is she writing? How does she seem to imagine her relationship to Representative Boldt? How can you tell?

2. How does Boldt seem to identify differences? On whose behalf is he writing? How does he seem to imagine his relationship to Peters? How can you tell?

3. Peters's letter, clearly, did not persuade Boldt or lead to a meeting of the minds. By the same token, it is not likely that Boldt's letter persuaded Peters either. Here, then, is a situation in which arguments have failed to achieve their intended aims. How would you explain this failure? Does the exchange clarify the differences that divide the two? Can you imagine some common ground on which agreement might take place? Why or why not?

WORKING TOGETHER

Looking at Differences

Work with two or three other students. Watch a television talk program such as *Nightline* or *Crossfire* that presents opposing views. Prepare a report that analyzes the speakers' presentations and interactions. On whose behalf did they seem to be speaking? How did they define the issues and make their arguments? What perspectives and alternatives, if any, did they ignore? Did the opposing speakers seek a clarification of their differences? What did each try to accomplish? Prepare an oral or written report depending on your instructor's direction. If you are presenting an oral report and your instructor agrees, tape the program and show in class short clips to illustrate your points.

What Do Readers Expect from Arguments?

In high school and college courses, you've probably been assigned papers that call on you to take a position and back it up. Thesis and support, after all, are common features of written academic work. This is also true of persuasive writing in everyday life, in the workplace, and in the public sphere. But whether the writing is for a class assignment or a petition circulated to increase state funding for the arts, readers expect successful arguments to have a number of features in common.

Readers justifiably expect that the writer's line of thinking will be easy to identify and to follow. Otherwise, they will have a hard time evaluating the writer's argument, and that defeats the whole purpose of taking a position on matters where there are reasonable differences. Accordingly, arguments typically provide the following things:

- A clear statement of the writer's position on the issue at hand. This statement is the writer's central claim (or *thesis*) in the argument.

- Evidence that supports the claim. As noted in Chapter 2, the main types of evidence are statistics, research, expert testimony, and examples.

- Clear explanations of how this evidence actually supports the main claim. These explanations are the reasons in the argument—the statements that show how the writer's evidence is linked to the claim.

- A sense of the larger implications of the main claim.

The following annotated student essay offers a good illustration of how Krista Guglielmetti makes a claim, explains how her evidence supports the claim, and points out one major consequence of the claim. As you will see, because of the nature of the topic, the evidence in this case is a series of examples. (You will find a fuller treatment of how Kris wrote this essay in Chapter 12 "Case Study of a Writing Assignment.")

Family Life and Television

It's 8:00 on a Monday night, and I am sitting at home in my bedroom peacefully reading a novel. Suddenly, the dreaded call comes, "Kris, you been in that room for two hours. Come on out here and be with the family for awhile. *Cosby* is going to start in five minutes. Don't you want to watch it with us?" This predictable Monday night call from my Dad reveals one of the ways families use television viewing. It is supposed to be "quality" time, where real families gather together to watch fictional families in sitcoms like *Cosby*. Now it may be true that in some families people actually interact while they are watching television, discussing the meaning of recent news or sharing in the victory or defeat of their

(continued)

(continued)

States main claim

favorite team. But in families like mine, television viewing too often means evading each other by replacing real families with fictional ones.

Explanation of how examples that follow support the main claim

When my family watches television together, what we share is not the experience of actual family members but episodes in the fictional lives of television families. One of the effects of watching these television families is that we use the actors and actresses to do our work for us. The fictional families offer television viewers vicarious experiences that can substitute for real experience. People, for example, remember it is Thursday and at 5:00 they can watch the heartwarming merger of the blended family *Full House*. Yet, without a calendar, they have a difficult time remembering that this particular Monday is their stepmother's or stepfather's birthday and they should get a card or gift on

Example

Example

Example

the way home from work or school. Television viewers can tell you that the hot couple on *Melrose Place* is headed for divorce more easily than they can see the status of their own marriages. People may not have noticed, but fiction has become stronger than reality.

Explanation of how examples support the main claim

Perhaps the greatest attraction to fictional television families is that, unlike real families, they can solve their problems in hour or half hour segments. On TV, blended families always work out, drug addicts are always treated, and no one is ever hurt permanently. It's easy. Just follow the script and everything will be fine. After all, if you're watching TV, you won't fight (except over who has the remote). If you don't fight, no one can get hurt and everyone will be happy. So we let the TV characters do our fighting for us because they always make up on the half hour.

Examples

Points out consequences of main claim

In my family, watching television families work things out doesn't bring us closer together. Instead of being shared quality time, our experience as television viewers brings about a sense of failure and demoralization. Even though no one says so, we all know we'll never measure up to the television families. Our lives are messier, and our problems seem to persist no matter how much we watch *Cosby*.

To present her argument, Kris uses the short four- or five-paragraph theme so familiar in school writing assignments. As teachers often expect, her thesis appears at the end of the first paragraph. And in paragraphs 2 and 3, she provides plenty of examples to support the claim. Now you may have been told to provide examples in your writing. This is good advice, but the real question, as the essay shows, is not how many examples there are but how Guglielmetti makes clear to readers what these are examples of. The opening sentences of paragraphs 2 and 3 are certainly topic sentences because they alert readers to what's going to be discussed. Just as important—and this is what makes Guglielmetti's argument work well—is the fact that these sentences explain to readers how the examples that follow offer evidence for the essay's main claim. These sentences provide strong links in the writer's chain of reasoning.

This sense of how the ideas in an essay relate to each other is what makes the essay easy to follow. And because the essay meets readers' expectations about the presentation of ideas, readers don't have to spend a lot of time trying to figure out what the writer is saying. Instead, readers can engage with the writer's ideas to see if they make sense and offer a persuasive point of view.

In the rest of this chapter, we'll be looking at how writers develop the kinds of arguments that meet readers' expectations.

ENTERING A CONTROVERSY

The idea that argument takes place when there are reasonable disagreements among people means that writers do not just start arguments from scratch. Rather, they enter a field of debate—or a controversy—where some positions have already been staked out and people are already arguing. For example, Krista Guglielmetti (whose essay you just read) has entered a discussion that has now been going on for years: the influence of television on life in the United States.

Entering a controversy is like coming into a room where a heated conversation is taking place. You may know some of the people talking, but not all of them. You need to listen for a while to find out what the various speakers are saying and what the issues seem to be. You may find yourself drawn toward some of the views argued, and skeptical about others. Some speakers may be throwing out facts and figures, but you may not be quite sure what they are trying to prove. Some may be taking jabs at other speakers' reasoning.

Gradually, as you listen, you find you agree with some of the speakers' views but oppose others. The controversy begins to make sense to you, and you start to speak.

Entering a controversy, as this scenario reveals, is a matter of coming into the middle of something, and it takes some time to learn your way around and figure out what is going on. It might well be considered rude or presumptuous if you started arguing the moment you entered the room. You need to listen first to see how you can fit your own views into the stream of debate.

A second point this scenario illustrates is that people enter controversies through their relations to others. As the scenario reveals, your sense of what the debate is about depends on what others have said, what they value, what they propose to do. For this reason, when you do step forward to speak, you are also articulating your relationship to others—whether it is agreement, qualified support, or counterargument. Entering a controversy inevitably draws a person into alliances with some people and differences with others.

Analyzing Issues

Listening to and reflecting on the heated conversation going on around you amounts to analyzing the issues. To take part in a controversy—to have your say—you need to first understand why speakers disagree and what they have at stake. This can be complicated—and sometimes confusing—because people do not always agree on what they are arguing about.

Take the following argument about the meaning of Bill Clinton's presidency:

- One person claims that the main achievement of the Clinton presidency has been widespread prosperity for the nation. In his view, the Clinton administration's free trade economic policies have made Americans much better off economically than they were at the start of his two terms.

- A second person responds that the Monica Lewinsky affair has tarnished the office of the presidency. According to her, the fact that the American people supported Clinton through the impeachment hearings only shows how Clinton's indiscretions have lowered public standards of conduct for elected officials and for the culture in general.

- A third person chimes in, claiming that the Clinton administration blew an opportunity to reform the health care system. The crisis we're facing now, he says, is the direct result of Clinton's failed policies in his first term.

These people might argue all night long, but their argument will be fruitless and unproductive unless they can agree on what they are arguing about. In fact, one person could hold all three of these views and agree with each of the speakers, though we sense that some real differences divide them. The problem is they have not sufficiently clarified the nature of the disagreement.

To enter a controversy and argue responsibly, your arguments (unlike those of the speakers in this example) must in fact respond to the issues already posed in dispute. Otherwise, you cannot possibly engage with others. You will simply be left with a sequence of claims but little productive debate about how and why people differ in their assessment of Clinton.

But let's not give up on the three people in our example. They may still be able to engage each other and find out where and how they differ. But first they need to agree on what the issues are. They need to do some work, some sorting out, to understand what is at stake in the various claims they have made.

Types of Issues

Issues are arguable points that people make when reasonable differences exist. For example, the statement "William Jefferson Clinton was elected president in 1992" isn't an issue because no one would dispute it. Instead, most people would agree that the statement is an established fact. On the other hand, the statement "Americans are better off than they were at the start of Clinton's two terms as president" raises an issue because in this case the facts are disputed. Some will say that the unprecedented bull market on Wall Street during Clinton's presidency shows the vitality of the economy, while others will argue that only a limited number of Americans actually made out economically during the Clinton administration.

To return to our three speakers, we can see that there are three different and distinct types of issues in their argument about the Clinton presidency. Each of these issues offers a place to begin a productive argument.

Issues of Substantiation

Issues of substantiation are questions of disputed facts, definitions, causes, and consequences. They involve asking whether something actually happened, what it is, what brought it about, and what its effects are. The first speaker raises an issue that can be substantiated by asserting that Clinton's economic policies caused certain things to happen. This is an issue that asks us to look at the available evidence.

As it turns out, the claim that Clinton's free trade policies have led to widespread prosperity is an issue of substantiation because it actually contains two other issues that call for substantiation. To make his case, the first speaker has to show first that all Americans in fact profited from the "new prosperity." Second, he would also have to show that Clinton's economic policies were responsible.

Issues that call for substantiation occur regularly in ongoing arguments:

- Did Microsoft violate antitrust laws by pressuring PC manufacturers to include its Web navigator (question of disputed fact)?

- What kinds of actions amount to sexual harassment (question of definition)?

- Are environmental carcinogenics responsible for the increase in breast cancer (question of cause)?

- Has expansion of pro football into new cities increased teams' profits (question of consequences)?

Issues of Evaluation

Issues of evaluation are questions about whether something is good or bad, right or wrong, desirable or undesirable, effective or ineffective, valuable or worthless. The second speaker addresses an issue of evaluation when she says that Clinton's presidency contributed to a lowering of public standards. In this case, support or refutation of her claim will necessarily rely on a value judgment.

Issues of evaluation appear routinely in all spheres of life:

- Is a Macintosh or a DOS-based computer system best suited to your computing needs?

- Are daytime talk TV programs such as Jenny Jones and Sally Jessy Raphael a national scandal or do they provide a needed public forum for controversial issues?

- Is affirmative action unfair to white males?

- What novels should be included in an American literature course?

Issues of Policy

Issues of policy are questions about what we should do and how we should implement our aims. The third speaker takes on a policy issue when he finds fault with Clinton's attempt to reform the health care system. Support or refutation of policy issues typically focus on how well the policy solves an existing problem or addresses a demonstrable need.

Issues about policy are pervasive in public discussions. Typically, they use the terms *should, ought,* or *must* to signal the courses of action they recommend:

- Should the federal government implement a single income tax for all people, or should it substitute a national sales tax?

- Must all students be required to take a first-year writing course?

- Should there be a moratorium on capital punishment?

Identifying what type of issue is at stake in a speaker's claim offers a way to cut into an ongoing controversy and get oriented. This does not mean, however, that controversies come neatly packaged according to type of issue. The three types of issues are tools of analysis to help you identify how and why people disagree. As you prepare to enter an ongoing controversy, you are likely to find that the three types of issues are connected and lead from one to the next.

Here is an example of how the three types of issues can be used to explore a controversy and invent arguments.

Controversy: Should High Schools Abolish Tracking and Assign Students to Mixed-Ability Classrooms Instead?

1. **Issues that can be substantiated:** How widespread is the practice of tracking? When did it begin? Why was tracking instituted in the first place? What purposes was it designed for? What are the effects of tracking on students? What experiments have taken place to use mixed-ability groupings instead of tracking? What are the results?

2. **Issues of evaluation:** What educational values are put into practice in tracking? Are these values worthy? Is tracking fair to all students? Does it benefit some students more than others? What values are embodied in mixed-ability classrooms? How do these compare to the values of tracking?

3. **Issues of policy:** What should we do? What are the reasons for maintaining tracking? What are the reasons for implementing mixed-ability groupings? Can mixed-ability classrooms succeed? What changes would be required? What would the long-term consequences be?

TAKING A POSITION: FROM ISSUES TO CLAIMS

The point of analyzing the issues in any ongoing controversy is to clarify your own thinking and determine where you stand. Taking a position amounts to entering into the debate to have your own say. Determining your position means you have an arguable claim to make—an informed opinion, belief, recommendation, or call to action you want your readers to consider.

Look at the following two statements:

Tracking was recently dismantled in a local school district.

Tracking has become a very heated issue.

As you can see, these sentences simply describe a situation. They aren't really arguable claims because no one would reasonably disagree with them. They don't tell readers what the writer believes or thinks should be done. Now take a look at these two statements:

For the dismantling of tracking to be successful, our local school district should provide teachers with in-service training in working with mixed-ability groups.

Tracking has become such a heated issue because parents of honors students worry unnecessarily that their children won't get into the best colleges.

Notice that in each statement you can see the writer's stand on the issue right away. The first writer treats an issue of policy, while the second is trying to substantiate the cause of the tracking controversy. What makes each claim arguable is that there can be differing views regarding the issue. Readers could respond that in-service training is a waste of money because teachers already know how to teach different levels of students or that the real reason tracking is so controversial is because it holds back the brightest students. To make sure a claim is arguable, ask yourself whether someone could reasonably disagree with it—whether there could be at least two differing views on the issue on which you've taken a position.

Both writers have successfully cued readers to their positions, in part by using key words that typically appear in position statements. Notice that in the first sentence, the writer uses *should* (but could have used similar terms such as *must, ought to, needs to,* or *has to*) to signal a proposed solution. In the second, the writer uses a *because* statement to indicate to readers that there is evidence available to back up the claim. Writers also use terms such as *therefore, consequently, thus, it follows that, the point is* to signal their positions.

EXERCISE

Steps Toward A Tentative Position

Take a current controversy you know something about, where reasonable differences divide people. It could be the death penalty, drug testing for high school or college athletes, censorship of lyrics, curfews for adolescents under eighteen. The main consideration is that the controversy interests you and that you believe it is important.

1. State the controversy in its most general terms in the form of a question: "Should colleges routinely conduct drug tests on varsity athletes?" "Do we need a rating system for television shows similar to the one used for movies?"

2. Then use the three types of issues—substantiation, evaluation, and policy—to generate a list of more specific questions: "How do drug tests work?" "Why were drug tests developed in the first place, and what are their consequences?" "Do drug tests violate constitutional freedoms?" "Is drug testing sound policy?"

3. Pick one set of questions from your list of types of issues. For example, you might pick the interrelated questions "Do drug tests actually work?" "Are they reliable?" "Can they be circumvented?" Develop a tentative position that responds to the question or questions. Make sure it presents an arguable claim.

4. Consider whether your tentative position is an informed claim. At this point, you may need more information to analyze the issues responsibly and develop an arguable claim with sufficient evidence.

DEVELOPING A PERSUASIVE POSITION

What Are the Rhetorical Appeals?

Once you have a tentative position in mind, you can begin to think about how to present it to your readers in the most persuasive way possible. One powerful set of persuasive strategies is known in classical rhetoric as *the appeals*. The three appeals—ethos, pathos, and logos—offer three different but interrelated ways to influence your readers by appealing to their ideas and values, sympathies, and beliefs.

- **Ethos:** *Ethos* refers to the writer's character as it is projected to readers through the written text. The modern terms *personality* and *attitude* capture some of the meaning of ethos and how readers build an impression of the writer's character—how credible, fair, and authoritative.

- **Pathos:** *Pathos* refers to the readers' emotions and the responses a piece of writing arouses in them. Pathos should not be associated simply with emotional appeals to readers' fears and prejudices. Instead, it offers a way to analyze their state of mind and the intensity with which they hold various beliefs and values.

- **Logos:** *Logos* refers to what is said or written. Its original meaning was "voice" or "speech," though the term later took on association with logic and reasoning. For our purposes, the term offers a way to focus on the writer's message and the line of reasoning the writer develops.

The term *rhetorical stance* refers to the way writers coordinate ethos, pathos, and logos as interrelated components in persuasive writing. To see how this coordination of the three appeals works in practice, let's look at a passage from one of Malcolm X's most famous speeches, "The Ballot or the Bullet," delivered to a largely black audience in 1964. At the time Malcolm X gave his speech, the Senate was debating the Civil Rights Act of 1964, which passed later in the year, following a filibuster by its opponents.

From "The Ballot or the Bullet"
MALCOLM X

1   I'm not a politician, not even a student of politics; in fact, I'm not a student of much of anything. I'm not a Democrat, I'm not a Republican, and I don't even consider myself an American. If you and I were Americans, there'd be no problem. Those Hunkies that just got off the boat, they're already Americans; Polacks are already Americans; the Italian refugees are already Americans. Everything that came out of Europe, every blue-eyed thing, is already an American. And as long as you and I have been over here, we aren't Americans yet.

2   Well, I am one who doesn't believe in deluding myself. I'm not going to sit at your table and watch you eat, with nothing on my plate, and call myself a diner. Sitting at the table doesn't make you a diner, unless you eat some of what's on that plate. Being here in America doesn't make you an American. Why, if birth made you American, you wouldn't need any legislation, you wouldn't need any amendments to the Constitution, you wouldn't be faced with civil-rights filibustering in Washington, D.C. right now. They don't have to pass civil-rights legislation to make a Polack an American.

3   No, I'm not an American. I'm one of the 22 million black people who are the victims of Americanism. One of the 22 million black people who are the victims of democracy, nothing but disguised hypocrisy. So, I'm not standing here speaking to you as an American, or a patriot, or a flag-saluter, or a flag-waver—no, not I. I'm speaking as a victim of this American system. And I see America through the eyes of the victim. I don't see any American dream; I see an American nightmare.

Notice in this passage how ethos, pathos, and logos are not separate aspects of the speech but rather work together in fashioning Malcolm X's rhetorical stance.

Analysis of Persuasive Appeals in "The Ballot or The Bullet"

- **Ethos:** Malcolm X identifies himself first by explaining what he is not—a politician, a student of politics, a Democrat, or a Republican. In fact, he does not even consider himself an American. Instead, he identifies himself as "one of the 22 million black people who are victims of Americanism."

  Malcolm X presents himself as someone who is willing to look at the racial situation in America without illusions. "I am one," he says, "who doesn't believe in deluding myself." Just being in America, he argues, doesn't make black people Americans. Otherwise, black people would not need Civil Rights legislation to achieve equality.

  The tone and attitude Malcolm X projects are militant and unrelenting, chosen in part to distinguish his appeal from the appeals of Civil Rights leaders such as Dr. Martin Luther King, Jr., who emphasized racial reconciliation and working through the system. For Malcolm X, there is no point in appealing to American democratic values, as King often did, because the system has always been hypocritical—not a dream but a nightmare.

- **Pathos:** By locating a stance outside the system, Malcolm X invites his audience to join him in rejecting the moderation of Civil Rights leaders and to share a new, more militant politics.

  He seeks, on one hand, to mobilize his black listeners' feelings about what it means to be an American. By offering an explanation of how blacks have been systematically excluded from the American dream, Malcolm X seeks to redirect the intensity of his black listeners' emotions—away from the hope of racial integration and toward a new identity based on the power and self-reliance of black people united in struggle. He is offering them a way to see themselves not as humble petitioners to the white power structure but as a power in their own right.

  On the other hand, it may well appear that Malcolm X has written off white listeners. For some, his use of ethnic slurs such as *Hunkies* and *Polacks* are offensive and can hardly have endeared him to his white audience (many whites did indeed reject his message as antiwhite and potentially dangerous). But for others, Malcolm X's unflinching analysis of race relations in America brought with it the shock of recognition that white-skin privilege is a pervasive feature of American life. In fact, Malcolm X did gain a wide audience of whites who came to admire his unyielding insistence on "telling it like it is" and who were thereby led to rethink the consequences of racism in America.

■ **Logos:** As you have just seen, Malcolm X established a relationship with his listeners by projecting an attitude and a message that elicited powerful responses. If anything, the way he presents himself (ethos) and his listeners' responses (pathos) are inseparable from the form and content of his message (logos). Still, it is worth noting how cogently reasoned this message is.

Malcolm X's reasoning is simple yet devastating. It all revolves around the issue of how people get to be considered Americans. According to Malcolm X, people who came from Europe are already considered Americans. They don't need Civil Rights legislation. At the same time, the fact of being born in America is not necessarily enough for a person to be considered an American; otherwise black people born in America would not need Civil Rights legislation. Put these two propositions together and you get the unavoidable conclusion: The fact that black people need Civil Rights legislation proves in effect that they are not considered Americans, and the implication is that they are therefore something else—not the inheritors of the American dream but the victims of an American nightmare.

Constructing an Appropriate Rhetorical Stance

Experienced writers know that to make persuasive arguments they need to construct an appropriate rhetorical stance. Whether the rhetorical stance you construct is appropriate will, of course, depend on the situation that calls for writing, your purposes, and the beliefs of your readers. Arguments that are appropriate and persuasive in one situation may not necessarily be appropriate and persuasive in another.

Two Letters of Application

The following letters were written by a student applying for a summer internship at a cable television station—Greater Worcester Media Cable Company. As you read, notice that the student is making an arguable claim, namely, "you should hire me as an intern." The question is whether the rhetorical stance he develops is appropriate to the occasion.

Letter 1

Dear _____,

I would like to apply for a summer internship at Greater Worcester Media Cable Company. I've just switched my major from pre-med to mass communication, and I'm really excited about getting out of those boring science classes and into something that interests me. I just finished this great video production class and made a short documentary called "Road Kill," about all the animals that get run over on Highway 61. It was pretty arty and punk, with a sound track dubbed from Sonic Youth.

2   I want to learn everything I can about television. I'd love to eventually be an anchorman on the national news, like Dan Rather or Peter Jennings or Tom Brokaw. I've always known that television is one of the most influential parts of American life, and I think it would be awesome to be seen nightly by millions of viewers. Think of all the influence—and fun—you could have, with everyone watching you.

3   Of course, if I do get the internship, I won't be able to go home this summer, and that will be kind of a bummer because my parents and girlfriend are pretty much expecting I'll be around. But still, it would be worth it to get into television because that's where I see myself going long-term.

Letter 2

Dear _____ :

1   I would like to apply for a summer internship at Greater Worcester Media Cable Company. As my réumé indicates, I am a Mass Communication major in my sophomore year, with course work in video production, mass communication theory, and the history of television. In addition, I have a strong background in the natural sciences.

2   I believe that my studies in Mass Communication have given me skills and experience that would be valuable in a summer internship. In my video production class, I filmed and edited a short documentary, and I am eager to gain more experience in production and editing.

3   A summer internship would be a wonderful opportunity for me to learn how the day-to-day world of cable television works. This kind of practical experience would be an invaluable complement to my coursework in the history and theory of the media.

WORKING TOGETHER

Rhetorical Stance

You have probably concluded that the first letter is inappropriate as a letter of application to Greater Worcester Media Cable Company and that the second letter has a greater chance of success. Your task now is to explain why. Work together with two or three other students. Follow these directions:

1. Compare the two letters in terms of the rhetorical stance the writer has constructed in each case. Be specific here and point to words, phrases, and passages that reveal how the writer coordinates ethos, logos, and pathos.

2. Think of a situation in which the first letter would be appropriate to the writer's purposes and the interests of readers. It may be inappropriate when applying for a summer internship, but that doesn't mean it is not as well-written as the second. Notice that in certain respects it has more

life, more telling details, and more of a sense of the writer's personality than the second letter.

EXERCISE

Crafting an Argument

Use the information in the two letters to write a third letter addressed to either the writer's parents or his girlfriend. The letter should explain why you want to apply for the summer internship and should persuade your reader that this is a good idea, even though it would mean not being able to come home for the summer. Consider how an appropriate and persuasive rhetorical stance would coordinate the three appeals—ethos, pathos, and logos.

MAKING AN ARGUMENT

Good arguments aren't found ready to use. They have to be made. To make a persuasive argument, you need to develop an effective line of reasoning. To do that, it is helpful to look at the parts that go into making an argument. In this section, we draw on a model of argument developed by the philosopher Stephen Toulmin, although we use somewhat different terms.

What Are the Parts of an Argument?

Here is a quick sketch of the parts of an argument we'll be considering in more detail in this section:

Claim:	Your position, the basic point you want readers to accept
Evidence:	The supporting material for the claim
Enabling assumption:	The line of reasoning that explains how the evidence supports the claim
Backing:	Reasons that show that the enabling assumption is valid
Differing views:	Disagreements with all or part of your argument
Qualifiers:	Words that modify or limit the claim

Claims, Evidence, and Enabling Assumptions

As you have seen, you can't have a responsible argument unless you have an arguable claim, and you've looked at some ways to develop claims by analyzing issues and constructing an appropriate rhetorical stance. In this section, we look in detail at the three basic parts of an argument—claims, evidence, and enabling assumptions. Taken together, these terms give us a way to think about the line of reasoning in an argument. Readers justifiably expect writers to provide evidence for the claims they make. Moreover, they expect the evidence a writer offers to have a clear connection to the claim. As you will see, enabling assumptions are explanations of how the evidence supports a writer's claim.

To see how these connections work, take a look at the following two evaluations students wrote of their composition instructor:

1. Ms. Smith is probably the worst teacher I've had so far in college. I've never been so frustrated. I could never figure out what the teacher wanted us to do. She didn't grade the papers we turned in but instead just wrote comments on them. Then we had to evaluate each others' writings. How are students qualified to judge each others' writing? This is the teacher's job. We had to revise some of our writing to put in a portfolio at the end of the term. How were we supposed to know which papers were any good?

2. Ms. Smith is probably the best teacher I've had so far in college. I really liked how she organized the work. By not grading our papers, she gave us the opportunity to select our best writing and revise it for a portfolio at the end of the term. The comments she offered on drafts and the evaluations we did of each others' papers really helped. I found this freed me to experiment with my writing in new ways and not worry about getting low grades. This system made me realize how important revision is.

In one sense, both evaluations are persuasive. It's hard not to be convinced, at the level of lived experience, that the first student did not like the class, while the second student did. But what are we to make of these differences? What do they tell us about the teacher and her way of teaching writing?

In this case, to understand why the two students differ, it will help to see *how* they differ. Each has made an argument, and we can analyze how the arguments have been made. Each consists of the same basic parts.

Claims

In the two student evaluations, the competing claims are easy to find: Ms. Smith is either the best or the worst teacher in the student's experience. Each claim, moreover, meets the test for writing arguable claims.

> **Reasonable differences:** Both claims are matters of judgment that can't be decided by referring to an established, authoritative source. The question of whether Ms. Smith is a good teacher is worth arguing about.

Chapter 2 has information about the main types of evidence and how to evaluate the way writers use them.

> **Plausibility:** Both claims could be true. Each has a certain credibility that a claim like "An invasion of flying saucers will take place next week" doesn't have.

> **Sharable claims:** Both claims can be argued on terms that can be shared by others. In contrast, there's no reason to argue that blue is your favorite color or that you love the feel of velvet. Such a claim refers to a personal preference based on subjective experience and can't really be shared by others.

Evidence

Evidence is all the information available in a particular situation. Like detectives in the investigation of a crime, writers begin with the available evidence—data, information, facts, observations, personal testimony, statistics, common knowledge, or any other relevant material.

Writers use this evidence to construct a sense of what happened and what the unresolved issues are. Notice in the two evaluations of Ms. Smith that the students do not seem to differ about what happened in class. Both describe the same teaching strategies: Students wrote papers that were not graded; they received comments from the teacher and from other students; they were required to revise a number of the papers for a final portfolio. The difference is in how each uses this evidence.

Enabling Assumptions

Consider how the two students move from the available evidence—the facts that neither disputes—to their differing claims. This is a crucial move that each argument relies on. For an argument to be persuasive, readers need to know how and why the evidence cited by the writer entitles him or her to make a claim. This link—the connection in an argument between the evidence and the writer's claim—is called the *enabling assumption* because it refers to the line of reasoning that explains how the evidence supports the claim. Such assumptions are often implied rather than stated explicitly.

Notice that the enabling assumptions in the two student evaluations are implied but not directly stated. To find out how the two students connect the evidence to their claims, let's imagine we could interview them, to push them to articulate this missing link in their arguments:

Student 1

Q. How was your writing teacher?

A. She was the worst teacher I've had so far [*claim*].

Q. What makes you say that?

A. The teacher never graded our papers. We had to evaluate each others' papers and then revise a few and put them in a portfolio [*evidence*].

Q. So why was that so bad?

A. Well, because good teachers give you lots of graded evaluations so you know exactly where you stand in a class [*enabling assumption*].

Student 2

Q. How was your writing teacher?

A. She was great, best I've had so far [*claim*].

Q. What makes you say that?

A. The teacher never graded our papers. We had to evaluate each others' papers and then revise a few and put them in a portfolio [*evidence*].

Q. So why was that so good?

A. Well, because good teachers help you develop your own judgment by experimenting without worrying about grades [enabling assumption].

QUESTIONS TO ASK ABOUT EVIDENCE

To make a persuasive argument, you need evidence for your claim—and you also need some guidelines to evaluate whether the evidence you turn up will work for your argument. Here are some questions to ask yourself:

1. **Is the evidence clearly related to the claim?** As you plan an argument, you are likely to come up with lots of interesting material. Not all of it, however, will necessarily be relevant to the claim you want to support. For example, if you are arguing about how Darwin's theory of evolution influenced fiction writers in the nineteenth century, it doesn't make sense to give a lot of biographical details on Darwin. They may be interesting, but it's unlikely that they will help you explain the influence of his theory.

2. **Do you have enough evidence?** Basing a claim on one or two facts is hardly likely to persuade your readers. They are likely to dismiss your argument as hasty and unjustifiable because of insufficient evidence. The fact that two people in your neighborhood were laid off recently from their construction jobs is not enough evidence for claiming that the construction industry is in crisis. You would need to establish a pattern by showing, say, a decline in housing starts, the postponement of many major building projects, layoffs across the country, or bankruptcies of construction companies.

3. **Is your evidence verifiable?** Readers are likely to be suspicious of your argument unless they can check out the evidence for themselves. For instance, to support an argument for campaign finance reform you use examples of how corporate donations influenced politicians' voting. If you don't tell readers who the politicians and corporations are, they will have no way to verify your evidence.

4. **Is your evidence up-to-date?** Readers expect you to do your homework and provide them with the latest information available. If your evidence is dated, readers may well suspect that newer information has supplanted it, and may therefore find your argument unpersuasive. If you are arguing for gender equity in medical education, citing figures on the enrollment of women in medical schools in the 1960s (around 10 percent) will be quickly dismissed because women currently represent around 50 percent of students entering medical school classes. (You might build a better case for gender equity by looking at possible patterns of discrimination in residency assignments or at the specializations women go into.)

5. **Does your evidence come from reliable sources?** You would probably not make an argument based on *The Weekly World News*'s latest Elvis sighting. As mentioned in Chapter 2, evidence needs to be evaluated and interpreted in light of its sources. Scientific studies, government reports, and research by academics, professional associations, and independent research institutes are likely to carry considerable authority for readers. Partisan sources—magazines such as the conservative *National Review* or the left-liberal *Nation*—often contain important evidence you can use persuasively, especially if you acknowledge the bias and ask readers to consider the merits of the information in the context of your argument.

Of course, we could push each writer further to explore the assumptions that underlie the one he or she has articulated. If we push far enough, we are likely to find fundamental beliefs that each holds about the nature of education and learning. For example, in the case of the second student, an exploration of assumptions might look like this:

- **Assumption 1:** Good teaching helps students develop judgment by experimenting and not having to worry about grades.

- **Assumption 2:** Too much emphasis on grades can get in the way of developing judgment through trial and error.

- **Assumption 3:** Education should emphasize the development of individual judgment as much or more than the learning of subject material.

- **Assumption 4:** Students naturally want to learn, and will do so if given the chance.

This process could continue indefinitely, and exploring the assumptions underlying assumptions can be a useful exercise. The practical question in making an argument is to decide which of these assumptions—or some combination of them—are likely to be shared by your readers and which ones can best clarify differences you have with others.

WORKING TOGETHER

Analyzing Claims, Evidence, and Enabling Assumptions

To work with the terms introduced here, analyze the statements that appear below. Identify the claim each statement makes. Identify the evidence that each statement relies on. Finally, explain how an enabling assumption, which may or may not be stated explicitly, connects the evidence to the claim.

- Ultraviolent video games will inevitably lead to more school shootings.

- Since Kobe Bryant and Shaquille O'Neal started playing together, the Los Angeles Lakers have been virtually unbeatable.

- The current increase in cases of tuberculosis can be attributed to new strains of the disease that are resistant to treatment by antibiotics.

- The fact that both parents have to work just to make ends meet is destroying the American family.

- It is reasonable that the CEOs of American corporations make over one hundred times in salary and bonuses what the average worker in the company earns.

Backing

Backing refers to evidence and explanations showing that an argument's enabling assumption is valid and reliable. If your readers accept your enabling assumption, whether explicit or implied, there is probably no reason to provide backing for it. But, as in the case of the two student evaluations, where enabling assumptions differ, you need to explain why your enabling assumptions are preferable or more important than competing ones.

As you have seen, the differences that divide the two student evaluations of Ms. Smith hinge on the different enabling assumption each uses to connect the evidence to the claim. Only by identifying these unstated assumptions can we really understand what is at stake. To construct responsible arguments that can clarify their differences, the two writers need to make their enabling assumptions explicit. Here is what the opening of the first student's evaluation might look like if he made the enabling assumption explicit:

> One of the marks of good teaching is giving students frequent graded evaluations of their work so that they understand the teacher's expectations and know where they stand in the class. I just had a composition teacher who demonstrates the disaster that can happen when teachers don't take this basic principle of teaching into account.

This is certainly a clearer version of what the writer is trying to argue, but it still leaves open the question of whether giving frequent grades is a "mark of good teaching" and a "basic principle." Is this a safe assumption to make, one that readers will find a reliable measure of good teaching? We may or may not be persuaded, depending on our own assumptions about teaching. In fact, as you can see, the enabling assumption itself is arguable and therefore needs support if the student hopes to persuade readers.

For this reason, the writer could strengthen the argument further by adding backing to the enabling assumption. To bolster the persuasiveness of the enabling assumption, he could provide supporting evidence and explanations: research studies about the level of student anxiety in classes where there is little graded work; expert testimony on the subject of what constitutes good teaching; statistics showing how students learn more in classes where the teacher frequently hands out grades; personal accounts from other students about how they slack off when their work isn't graded.

WORKING TOGETHER

Backing an Argument

Work together in groups of two or three. What kind of backing can you think of that would support the following enabling assumptions? What sources would you turn to?

1. In the final analysis, the state of the economy determines presidential elections.

2. To win in the NBA, a team needs an intimidating power forward.

3. In time, we will see that most diseases are hereditary.

4. We must strengthen the American family.

5. Big business is greedy.

Differing Views

To argue responsibly, you can't pretend that no one disagrees with you or that there are no alternative perspectives. To note these differences does not, as students sometimes think, undermine your own argument. In fact, it can strengthen it by showing that you are willing to take all sides into account, that you can refute objections to your argument, and, when necessary, that you can concede the validity of differing views.

Summarize Differing Views Fairly and Accurately

Readers often detect when writers handle differing views in a distorted way. In fact, their impressions of a writer's credibility and good character—the writer's ethos—depend in part on how reasonably the writer deals with differences. For that reason, the ability to summarize fairly and accurately is quite important to the success of your argument. By summarizing fairly and accurately, you can show readers that you have anticipated reasonable differences and intend to deal with them responsibly.

This can help avoid having your readers jump into your argument with objections you've overlooked—"Sure, the government creating jobs for people on welfare sounds like a good idea, but what about the cost? And what about personal responsibility? Doesn't this just make people dependent in a different way?"—or rushing to the defense of objections you have characterized unfairly—"Not all conservative Christians believe women should be barefoot and pregnant."

Refuting Differing Views

For views that differ from yours, summarize them briefly, fairly, and accurately. Then explain what's wrong with them. Your best chance of persuading readers that your position is preferable to others is to clarify the differences that divide you and explain what you see as the weaknesses in other lines of reasoning.

To return to the student evaluations, the first student could strengthen his argument about what good teaching is by anticipating, summarizing, and refuting elements in the second student's argument. He might argue, for example, that while peer response to the written work of others may sound like a good idea, in fact it doesn't really help students improve their writing; he would then explain why. It would enhance the persuasiveness of the argument, of course, if the explanation consisted of more than personal anecdotes ("why peer review didn't help me")—for example, references to research studies on the effects of peer review.

Note: The author of this book does not endorse the view that peer review doesn't work, but does recognize it as an arguable claim.

Conceding Differing Views

When differing views have merit, don't avoid them. Remember that your readers will likely think of these objections, so you're better off taking them head on. Summarize the view and explain what you concede. Such concessions are often signaled by words and phrases such as *admittedly, granted, while it may be true, despite the fact,* and *of course she is right to say.*

The purpose of concession is not to give up on your argument but to explain how it relates to differing views. In this sense, it's another means of clarifying differences and explaining your position in the fullest possible way. To concede effectively, follow it up right away with an explanation of how your position relates to the point you have conceded. Otherwise, you may give readers the impression that you endorse the point.

In the case of the student evaluations, the first student could make good use of concession. For example, he might concede the second student's point that an important goal of education is developing independent judgment. And then he could go on to show that in practice the teacher's methods don't really lead to independent judgment but instead leave students to flounder on their own. In fact, conceding the point offers the student a line of reasoning he could pursue to strengthen his argument by explaining how the development of independent judgment depends on constant interaction with and regular evaluation from a more experienced and knowledgeable person.

Negotiating Differing Views

For more on this strategy, see "Negotiating Differences" later in this chapter.

Negotiating differences means finding points of agreement in differing views. Once again, your purpose is not to abandon your views but to see if you can find any common ground with those who hold differing positions. Negotiating differences may sound like unnecessarily compromising what you believe or giving in just to make other people happy, but it doesn't have to lead to such results. Think of it as combining elements in reasonable differences in order to come up with new solutions and perspectives. Sometimes this is possible, but not always. Still, it's worth trying because negotiated differences can strengthen your argument by broadening its appeal and demonstrating your desire to take into account as many views as possible.

Back to the student evaluations. The first student might concede that the teacher's portfolio system of evaluation has some merit because it bases grades on student improvement. But from his perspective, it still has the problem of not providing enough evaluation and information on the teacher's expectations. To negotiate these differences, he might propose that the teacher grade but not count the first writing assignment so that students can see the teacher's evaluative standards in practice. He might also suggest that the teacher give students a midterm progress report on where they stand in the class, and again grade but not count one paper between midterm and the end of class.

Such a solution may not satisfy everyone, but it is likely to enhance the reader's impression of the student as someone who doesn't just criticize but tries to deal with differences constructively.

Qualifiers

Qualifiers modify or limit the claim in an argument by making it less sweeping, global, and categorical. For most claims, after all, there are exceptions that don't necessarily disprove the claim but need to be noted. Otherwise, you will needlessly open your claim to attack and disbelief. In many instances, a qualifier is as simple as saying "Many students at Ellroy State drink to excess" instead of "The students at my school get drunk all the time." Qualifiers admit exceptions without undermining your point, and they make statements harder to refute with a counterexample—"I know students who never drink" or "Some students drink only occasionally" or "My friends drink moderately."

You can qualify your claim with words and phrases such as *in many cases, often, frequently, probably, perhaps, may* or *might, maybe, likely,* or *usually.* In some instances, you will want to use a qualifying clause that begins with *unless* to limit the conditions in which the claim will hold true: "Unless the DNA evidence proves negative, everything points to the accused as the murderer."

Putting the Parts Together

To see how the various parts of argument we've just discussed can help you make an argument, let's look at the notes a student wrote to plan an argument opposing a recent proposal to the local school committee that would require students to wear uniforms at Middlebrook High School. No one contests the fact that there are some real problems at Middlebrook—declining test scores, drug use, racial tensions, lack of school spirit, a growing sense of student alienation. But, as you will see, the student doesn't think school uniforms can really address these problems.

- **Claim:** Middlebrook High School should not require students to wear uniforms.

- **Evidence:** School uniforms don't have the intended effects. I could use examples from schools that require uniforms to show they don't increase discipline, improve self-esteem, or alleviate social tensions.

    Teachers oppose requiring uniforms because it would make them into cops. I could get some good quotes from teachers.

    Even if they are required to wear uniforms, students will figure out other ways to show what group they are in. Jewelry, hairstyles, shoes, jackets, body piercing, tattoos, and so on will just become all the more important.

Uniforms violate students' right to self-expression. I could call the American Civil Liberties Union to see if they have any information I could use.

Requiring uniforms will make students hate school. I could get more on this by talking to students.

- **Enabling assumption:** A uniform requirement doesn't really address the problems at Middlebrook. Instead, it would make things worse.

- **Backing:** The uniform proposal is based on a faulty view of what influences student behavior. More rules will just lead to more alienation from school.

  To address Middlebrook's problems, students must be given more responsibility, instead of given regulations from above. They need to be brought into the decision-making process so they can develop a stake in what happens at school.

  The proposal to require uniforms is based on the desire to return to some mythic age in Middlebrook's past when students were orderly, disciplined, filled with school spirit—namely, all the same kind of white, middle-class students. Middlebrook has changed, and the proposal doesn't deal with these changes.

- **Differing views:** Some uniform supporters claim that the success of Catholic and private schools is based on the fact students are required to wear uniforms. I need to show the causes of success are not uniforms but other factors.

  I'll concede that there are real problems at Middlebrook but maintain my position that uniforms aren't the way to deal with them.

  I could also concede that what students wear sometimes gets out of hand but argue that the best way to deal with this is to get students involved, along with teachers and parents, in writing a new dress code. In fact, I could extend this argument to say that the way to deal with some of the problems is for the school to get the different groups— whites, Latinos, blacks, and Cambodians—together to look at the problems and propose some solutions.

- **Qualifiers:** My position is set. I'm against uniforms, period. But maybe I should state my claim in a way that takes uniform supporters' views into account. For example, I could say, "Admittedly there are a number of problems at Middlebrook that need attention, but requiring uniforms will not solve these problems."

As you can see, using the parts of argument has given this students a lot of material to work with and some leads about where to get more. Just as important, using the parts of argument offers a way to see the connections among the available material and how they might fit together in developing the writer's line of reasoning. Not all of this material will necessarily turn up in the final version of the student's argument, of course. This can only be determined through the process of drafting and revising. In fact, she might turn up new material and new arguments as she composes.

WORKING TOGETHER

Analyzing the Making of an Argument
The ad on page 92 from the International Ladies' Garment Workers Union (ILGWU) seeks to influence public opinion about the "corporate greed" of Leslie Fay and to persuade people to join in a boycott of their products.

"The Price Of Corporate Greed At Leslie Fay"
As you read, notice the evidence presented and how it is connected to the ad's central claim.

FOR CRITICAL INQUIRY

1. The central claim of the ILGWU ad comes across clearly in boldface type: **Don't buy Leslie Fay.** What evidence does it present to support this claim? What are the enabling assumptions that connect this evidence to the claim?

2. Does the ad present any backing to explain and support the enabling assumptions? What backing can you imagine that would be persuasive?

3. How does the ad use concession and refutation to bolster its argument?

4. What qualifiers, if any, does the ad use?

5. The ad refers to Leslie Fay's search for sources of cheap labor as a "formula for disaster—for all of us." Who is the "we" in this phrase? Who does the term include? Who does it exclude?

NEGOTIATING DIFFERENCES

Newspapers, talk shows, and political debates often treat disagreements as arguments that have two sides—pro and con, for and against. You are either prochoice or antiabortion, for or against the death penalty, a tax-and-spend liberal or a budget-slashing conservative.

Knowing how to argue persuasively and responsibly for your side is an important skill. Without it, people would be powerless in many situations. Unless you can make an effective argument, there may well be occasions when

The price of corporate greed at Leslie Fay

MARIE WHITT is fighting to keep the job she has held for 17 years at a Leslie Fay plant in Wilkes-Barre. Marie earns $7.80 and hour—hardly a fortune. On June 1st, she and 1,800 coworkers were forced to strike because Leslie Fay plans to dump them. Ninety percent are women whose average age is 50. They have

given their whole working lives to the company and losing their jobs would be a disaster. Marie knows she will never find a comparable job in today's economy. Without her union benefits, she and her husband won't be able to pay for his anti-cancer medication. "What Leslie Fay wants to do is so rotten," she says. "You've got to draw the line somewhere and fight."

Marie Whitt, 56, Wilkes-Barre, Pennsylvania

DORKA DIAZ worked for Leslie Fay in Honduras, alongside 12- and 13-year-old girls locked inside a factory where the temperature often hits 100° and where there is no clean drinking water. For a 54-hour week, including forced overtime, Dorka was paid a little over $20. With food prices high—a quart of milk costs 44 cents—Dorka and her three-year-old son live at the edge of starvation. In April, Dorka was fired for trying to organize a union. "We need jobs desperately, " she says," but not under such terrible conditions."

Dorka Diaz, 20
Choloma, Honduras

—From Ms. Diaz's testimony before a Hearing of the Subcommittee on Labor-Management Relations, Committee on Education and Labor, U.S. House of Representatives, Wilkes-Barre, PA, June 7, 1994

LESLIE FAY EXECUTIVES claim they can only "compete" by producing in factories like Dorka's. But identical skirts—one made by Dorka, the other by Marie—were recently purchased at a big retail chain here. Both cost $40. Searching the world for ever-cheaper sources of labor is not the kind of competition America needs. Leslie Fay already does 75% of its production overseas. If it really wants to compete successfully in the global economy, it would modernize its facilities here in the U.S. as many of its competitors have done. But Leslie Fay wants to make a fast buck by squeezing every last drop of sweat and blood out of its workers. Marie Whitt and Dorka Diaz don't think that's right. And they know it's a formula for disaster—for **all** of us.

You can help by not buying Leslie Fay products—
until Leslie Fay lives up to its corporate responsibilities at home and overseas.

Don't buy Leslie Fay!

Boycott all clothing made by Leslie Fay and sold under these labels:

▶ LESLIE FAY ▶ JOAN LESLIE ▶ ALBERT NIPON ▶ THEO MILES ▶ KASPER
▶ LE SUIT ▶ NOLAN MILLER ▶ CASTLEBERRY ▶ CASTLEBROOK

INTERNATIONAL LADIES' GARMENT WORKERS' UNION 1710 Broadway, New York, NY 10019 • 212-265-7000

your perspective will go unheard and your views unrepresented. Moreover, if you do not argue for what you and others with shared values hold in common, someone else is likely to do your talking for you.

There is little question, then, that arguing for your side is a crucial means of participating in public life and influencing public opinion. Still, as important as argument is, you need to look carefully at how arguments are conducted and what happens to the character and quality of public discussions when issues are polarized into pro-and-con, for-and-against positions.

Consider, for example, the following three ways pro-and-con, for-and-against arguments can limit discussion.

- **Adversarial stance:** One of the limits of pro-and-con arguments is that they put people in an adversarial stance toward those with whom they disagree. Instead of clarifying the issues and reaching mutual understandings, the goal of the argument may turn into defeating your opponent.

- **Limited perspectives:** By polarizing issues along adversarial lines, pro-and-con arguments frequently limit the perspectives available in public debate to two—and only two—sides: those for and those against. This may well restrict who is entitled to be heard to the members of rival camps and thereby limit the alternatives considered in making decisions.

- **Lack of common ground:** The pro-and-con, winner-take-all style of adversarial argument makes it nearly impossible for participants to identify the points of agreement and common ground they might share with others. The search for common ground does not assume that everyone is going to drop their differences and harmonize their interests. Instead, trying to find common ground can establish areas of agreement, large or small, that people can use as a basis to talk about their differences.

EXERCISE

Looking at Polarized Arguments

Write an account or prepare an oral presentation of an argument you witnessed or took part in that polarized into opposing sides. Describe what happened, and explain why the polarization took place. The point of this exercise is not to condemn the people involved but to understand what happened and why. Remember, polarization is not necessarily a bad thing. It may be unavoidable as people begin to identify their differences or involve a matter of principle, where a person finds no alternative but to make a counterargument and take a stand. Your task here is to analyze what took place and to consider whether the polarization was inevitable or could have been avoided.

Beyond Pro and Con

The following strategies offer approaches to reasonable differences that divide people. These strategies enable writers to remain committed to their own goals and values but at the same time to avoid some of the limitations of simply arguing for or against, pro and con, in an adversarial relation to others.

These strategies seek to engage people with whom you may differ—to enter into a dialogue that seeks not a victory in debate but a clarification of the issues that may ultimately make it easier for you and others to live together and perhaps to locate common ground.

As you will see, these strategies do not deny differences in the name of having everyone get along for the common good. Nor do they assume that people can easily reconcile their differences or harmonize conflicting interests. Too often, some members of society—women, minorities, working people, seniors, teenagers, and children—have been asked to keep quiet and sacrifice their interests to create what is in fact a false unity. Instead of setting aside differences, these strategies seek to use them constructively in order to take more interests and perspectives into account.

The strategies that follow seek to bring differences out into the open—but not in an adversarial way. Instead of imagining issues in terms of warring camps, you can use these strategies to negotiate—to understand how others feel about the issues, why people might be divided in their views, and what is thereby at stake for all involved. Negotiating differences does not mean abandoning the goal of influencing others, but it does recognize that we need to be open to influence from others—if not to change our minds, at least to deepen our understanding of other views and ways of thinking.

Dialogue With Others

It is difficult to think of people negotiating their differences unless they recognize one another as reasonable beings in the first place. To recognize another person does not mean to see him or her as an opponent to be defeated in debate or as someone to overwhelm with convincing arguments or manipulate with emotional appeals. It means to start by listening to what that person has to say—to put yourself in his or her shoes and imagine how the world looks from his or her perspective. It is presumptuous, of course, to think that you can be totally successful in understanding those with whom you differ. (Just assuming you can understand them, after all, may well imply a sense of your own superiority.) But it is the engagement with others that counts—to keep talking and trying to understand.

The reading selection that follows illustrates how recognizing others can lead people into dialogue and open the possibility of mutual understanding. As you read, notice that the strategy of recognizing others differs in important respects from the standard moves of adversarial argument—refuting opposing views or making concessions to them.

An Electronic Exchange of Views

The following correspondence brings together two people who are strangers, a gay teacher and a Vietnam vet, joined in conversation on an electronic bulletin board by the technology of the Internet. While the two correspondents do not know each other personally, they are nonetheless engaged, as you will see, in a deeply personal dialogue.

1   Do you have any idea what it is like to be gay? I have to hide the most important thing about yourself, even though you had no choice about it? To live in terror of discovery? To be laughed at, isolated and beaten up? To live around people who hide their children from you? Who wouldn't let you teach them if they knew? Because I am a teacher who dreads every call to the principal's office. I always wonder if it will be my last. How can you love a country that finds you too disgusting to serve? That permits people to attack you and your friends, throw things at them from car windows, deny them the right to be married, have families? Can you conceive of that? Does this get through to you on any level at all?

2   Two years ago, my lover and I walked through the French Quarter of New Orleans. We vacationed there because we knew it to be a tolerant place. We left a restaurant just off Bourbon Street, and three men jumped out of their cars. They knocked my lover and me down. They kicked us in the face, in the kidneys, in the groin. They knocked four of my teeth out, broke my jaw. Then they urinated on us. They laughed and said they were soldiers. That they'd love to have us in the military. I couldn't tell the police what happened. I was afraid the school district might find out back home.

And a reply:

1   I was very touched by your message, buddy. What happened to you was horrible, unsupportable. That's not what I lost three toes for in Vietnam, for scum to beat up on people like you and your friend. I fought so you could do whatever you wanted so long as you didn't hurt anybody or break the law. You and I have no quarrel. But we do have these problems, and I'll be straight with you about it, just like you were with me. Do you have any idea what it's like to be in a field or jungle or valley with bullets and shells blowing up all around you? With your friends being cut down, ripped apart, bleeding, dying right next to you screaming for their moms or kids or wives? Do you know how much trust and communication it takes to get through that? Do you have any idea what it's like to go through that if there's tension among you?

2   I'm not saying this can't be worked out. I'm saying, go slow. Don't come in here with executive orders and try to change things in a day that should take longer. Don't make me into a bigot because I know it takes an unbelievable amount of feeling to crawl down there into a valley of death. It takes love of your buddy. And that's something both of us can understand, right? But if you hate him, or fear him or don't understand him—how can you do it?

Source: From the computer bulletin board on CompuServe.

FOR CRITICAL INQUIRY

1. Describe the gay teacher's posting. What does his purpose seem to be? What kind of relationship is he trying to establish with his readers? How can you tell? What cues does he give readers about how he would like them to respond?

2. Consider the Vietnam vet's reply. What does he see as at stake in the gay teacher's posting? To what extent is he able to see things from the teacher's perspective? What is he getting at when he says, "You and I have no quarrel. But we do have these problems." What, if anything, does the writer offer to work these problems out? To what extent does the Vietnam vet seem committed to a dialogue with the teacher?

3. Imagine that the gay teacher had replied to the Vietnam vet. What kind of response would help keep the dialogue open? What kind of response would tend to close it or turn it into a polarized argument?

4. The teacher and the vet are strangers. They do not know each other personally. What is the effect of such anonymity on this exchange of views?

5. Find someone who holds a position or represents a point of view that you don't share. Arrange an interview with the person. The point of the interview is to engage in a dialogue that can help you understand where the person is coming from and why. You will need to explain your own position or point of view, but your goal is not to argue with the other person. Instead, try to reach some understanding of how and why you differ. If you can, tape and transcribe the interview. Follow a presentation of the

GOING ONLINE

HANDLING DIFFERENCES

To see how people handle differences online, find a bulletin board, chat room, or other electronic discussion group where controversial issues are raised. Your college newspaper, for example, may have an electronic forum, or there may be other online student discussion groups on your campus. You can also find electronic discussion such as "Welcome to MSNBC Chat," at the news network's Web site <www.msnbc.com/chat/default.asp>. Visit one of these discussions. Consider to what extent people are trying to engage in dialogue with others, to make points, to win arguments, to flame, or do something else. Notice, too, whether people identify themselves or remain anonymous. Some have claimed that anonymity in electronic discussion groups promotes irresponsible and sometimes anti-social postings. What effect does a writer's anonymity seem to have? Do you think people should be required to sign their posts—as is the case with letters to the editor in a newspaper or magazine?

interview with your own account of what you learned about the differences that divide you and the other person. Indicate how or whether you changed your mind in any respect.

Recognizing Ambiguities and Contradictions

To negotiate differences is to recognize ambiguities and contradictions. Recognizing ambiguities and contradictions goes beyond acknowledging that there are differing sides, perspectives, and interests that divide people over particular issues. It further suggests that the positions people hold may themselves contain internal differences—that things may not be as simple as they seem at first glance, with views neatly arranged for and against.

Recognizing the ambiguities or contradictions in your position does not mean that you are abandoning what you believe in. It means that you maintain your views but are willing to talk about gray areas, troubling aspects, and conflicting loyalties.

The following reading illustrates how the ambiguities and contradictions writers recognize may be both internal—in the writer's own thinking—and a result of the contradictory character of the world and how it repeatedly resists being organized into neat categories.

Abortion Is Too Complex To Feel All One Way About

ANNA QUINDLEN

Anna Quindlen is a newspaper columnist and fiction writer. The following essay was first published in her column for *The New York Times*. As you read, notice how Quindlen writes about the abortion debate by expressing a range of contradictory feelings.

1   It was always the look on their faces that told me first. I was the freshman dormitory counselor and they were the freshmen at a women's college where everyone was smart. One of them could come into my room, a golden girl, a valedictorian, an 800 verbal score on the SATs, and her eyes would be empty, seeing only a busted future, the devastation of her life as she knew it. She had failed biology, messed up the math; she was pregnant.

2   That was when I became pro-choice.

3   It was the look in his eyes that I will always remember, too. They were as black as the bottom of a well, and in them for a few minutes I thought I saw myself the way I had always wished to be—clear, simple, elemental, at peace. My child looked at me and I looked back at him in the delivery room, and I realized that out of a sea of infinite possibilities it had come down to this: a specific person born on the hottest day of the year, conceived on a Christmas Eve, made by his father and me miraculously from scratch.

4   Once I believed that there was a little blob of formless protoplasm in there and a gynecologist went after it with a surgical instrument, and that was that. Then I got pregnant myself—eagerly, intentionally, by the right man, at the right time—and I began to doubt. My abdomen still flat, my stomach roiling with morning sickness, I felt not that I had protoplasm inside but instead a complete human being in miniature to whom I could talk, sing, make promises. Neither of these views was accurate; instead, I think, the reality is something in the middle. And there is where I find myself now, in the middle, hating the idea of abortions, hating the idea of having them outlawed.

5   For I know it is the right thing in some times and places. I remember sitting in a shabby clinic far uptown with one of those freshmen, only three months after the Supreme Court had made what we were doing possible, and watching with wonder as the lovely first love she had had with a nice boy unraveled over the space of an hour as they waited for her to be called, degenerated into snipping and silences. I remember a year or two later seeing them pass on campus and not even acknowledge one another because their conjoining had caused them so much pain, and I shuddered to think of them married, with a small psyche in their unready and unwilling hands.

6   I've met 14-year-olds who were pregnant and said they could not have abortions because of their religion, and I see in their eyes the shadows of 22-year-olds I've talked to who lost their kids to foster care because they hit them or used drugs or simply had no money for food and shelter. I read not long ago about a teenager who said she meant to have an abortion but she spent the money on clothes instead; now she has a baby who turns out to be a lot more trouble than a toy. The people who hand out those execrable little pictures of dismembered fetuses at abortion clinics seem to forget the extraordinary pain children may endure after they are born when they are unwanted, even hated or simply tolerated.

7   I believe that in a contest between the living and the almost living, the latter must, if necessary, give way to the will of the former. That is what the fetus is to me, the almost living. Yet these questions began to plague me—and, I've discovered, a good many other women—after I became pregnant. But they became even more acute after I had my second child, mainly because he is so different from his brother. On two random nights 18 months apart the same two people managed to conceive, and on one occasion the tumult within turned itself into a curly-haired brunet with merry black eyes who walked and talked late and loved the whole world, and on another it became a blond with hazel Asian eyes and a pug nose who tried to conquer the world almost as soon as he entered it.

8   If we were to have an abortion next time for some reason or another, which infinite possibility becomes, not a reality, but a nullity? The girl with the blue eyes? The improbable redhead? The natural athlete? The thinker? My husband, ever at the heart of the matter, put it another way. Knowing that he is finding two children

somewhat more overwhelming than he expected, I asked if he would want me to have an abortion if I accidentally became pregnant again right away. "And waste a perfectly good human being?" he said.

9 Coming to this quandary has been difficult for me. In fact, I believe the issue of abortion is difficult for all thoughtful people. I don't know anyone who has had an abortion who has not been haunted by it. If there is one thing I find intolerable about most of the so-called right-to-lifers, it is that they try to portray abortion rights as something that feminists thought up on a slow Saturday over a light lunch. That is nonsense. I also know that some people who support abortion rights are most comfortable with a monolithic position because it seems the strongest front against the smug and sometimes violent opposition.

10 But I don't feel all one way about abortion anymore, and I don't think it serves a just cause to pretend that many of us do. For years I believed that a woman's right to choose was absolute, but now I wonder. Do I, with a stable home and marriage and sufficient stamina and money, have the right to choose abortion because a pregnancy is inconvenient right now? Legally I do have that right; legally I want always to have that right. It is the morality of exercising it under those circumstances that makes me wonder.

11 Technology has foiled us. The second trimester has become a time of resurrection; a fetus at six months can be one woman's late abortion, another's premature, viable child. Photographers now have film of embryos the size of a grape, oddly human, flexing their fingers, sucking their thumbs. Women have amniocentesis to find out whether they are carrying a child with birth defects that they may choose to abort. Before the procedure, they must have a sonogram, one of those fuzzy black-and-white photos like a love song heard through static on the radio, which shows someone is in there.

12 I have taped on my VCR a public-television program in which somehow, inexplicably, a film is shown of a fetus in utero scratching its face, seemingly putting up a tiny hand to shield itself from the camera's eye. It would make a potent weapon in the arsenal of the antiabortionists. I grow sentimental about it as it floats in the salt water, part fish, part human being. It is almost living, but not quite. It has almost turned my heart around, but not quite turned my head.

FOR CRITICAL INQUIRY

1. Although Quindlen characterizes the abortion debate as a "quandary," she nonetheless takes a position. What is it? What evidence does she use to support her position?

2. How does Quindlen describe the two sides in the debate? What does her attitude toward them seem to be? How does Quindlen locate her own position in relation to the two sides? How can you tell?

3. What do you think Quindlen is trying to accomplish by exploring the "quandary" of the abortion debate? How are readers likely to respond?

4. Think of an issue about which you have ambiguous or contradictory feelings. How could you plan an essay that explains your thinking?

Locating Common Ground

Locating common ground is built on the strategies we have just looked at but seeks to go one step further by identifying how people can join together, in spite of their differences, to address an issue of mutual concern.

Locating common ground is a strategy for looking for ways out of the impasse of polarized debate. Instead of focusing on the arguments that divide people, it tries to establish basic points of agreement in order to get people talking to each other about what can be done. In this sense, locating common ground amounts to consensus building—forming alliances and coalitions with others.

As you can see, the following Call for a Moratorium on Executions seeks to unite individuals and organizations, whether they support or oppose the death penalty.

"Call for a Moratorium on Executions"

No one would doubt that capital punishment has been one of the most divisive and volatile issues in American political life. Recently, however, there has been a growing dialogue among people who are worried that the death penalty is not being applied fairly, whether they support executions on principle or not. The following letter seeking support for an ad in *The New York Times* shows how people who differ in fundamental beliefs about capital punishment can nonetheless find common ground and identify issues of shared concern.

FOR CRITICAL INQUIRY

1. Analyze the argument presented here. What is the main claim? What evidence is offered to support it? What enabling assumptions link the claim and evidence?

2. Explain what you see as the common ground this letter seeks to establish. What line of reasoning might lead someone who supports the death penalty to support the Call for a Moratorium On Executions?

3. How do you think people who oppose the death penalty would respond to this letter?

4. Take up an issue that has divided your campus, your community, or the nation. Imagine ways to offer common ground on which people with polarized views might nonetheless join together in a shared undertaking such as the Call for a Moratorium on Executions. What arguments would be needed to establish such a common ground?

New York Times Ad Campaign

September 1999

Dear Friend,

Later this fall, the United Nations General Assembly is expected to vote on a resolution calling for a moratorium on executions worldwide. This vote will prove pivotal to the international community's vision of human rights as we enter the next millennium.

The reasons for a moratorium on executions *here in the US* are particularly compelling:

▶ Legal representation for most capital defendants – the vast majority of whom are indigent – is grossly inadequate. Poor people are most likely to be sentenced to death, and innocent people are inevitably going to be executed.

▶ Race continues to play a primary role in determining who lives and who dies.

▶ Juvenile offenders and the mentally disabled continue to be subject to executions despite international condemnation.

This reality led the American Bar Association, which has never taken a position for or against the death penalty, to call for an immediate halt on executions in 1997. The ABA has concluded that inequities in our system are so pervasive that they undermine confidence in the outcome of capital trials *and* appeals.

In 1998, the United Nations Commission on Human Rights issued a condemnatory report on the US death penalty, urging the US government to halt all executions while it brings the states into compliance with international standards and law.

Yet our nation's use of the death penalty is increasing. Already, 66 people have been executed this year. At this pace, the number of executions in 1999 could top 100, approaching rates last seen during the Great Depression.

The UN vote presents an international moment for citizens of the US to raise our voices for a moratorium.

We urge you to join us in signing an ad urging a moratorium to run in *The New York Times* in the weeks preceding the General Assembly's vote.

The ad statement is on the reverse side. Your name can be added for a gift $35. Organizational signatures are $50. Consider becoming a endorser for $100 or a co-sponsor for $1,000. We will send a copy of the final ad to all signers, and it will be published on our website, www.quixote.org/ej. *The deadline for signatures is November 4.*

Whether you support or oppose the death penalty, please stand with us publicly in this call for simple justice. We need to hear from you soon!

Sincerely,

Bianca Jagger
Human Rights Activist

Bud Welch
father of Oklahoma City
bombing victim, Julie Welch

Noam Chomsky
Professor of Linguistics, M.I.T.

Arthur Schlesinger, Jr.
Historian

Bishop Thomas J. Gumbleton
(Roman Catholic)

Susan Sarandon
Actress

The Very Rev. James Parks Morton
The Interfaith Center of New York

QUIXOTE CENTER
PURSUING JUSTICE, PEACE & EQUALITY
P.O. BOX 5206, HYATTSVILLE, MD 20782
301-699-0042 / [FAX] 301-864-2182 / WWW.QUIXOTE.ORG / EJUSA@QUIXOTE.ORG

(Ad Statement)

Call for a Moratorium on Executions

Signature Deadline: November 4

A Story from Death Row

Anthony Porter was to be executed by the State of Illinois on September 23, 1998. Just 48 hours before his scheduled death, the Illinois Supreme Court granted a stay to consider last-minute questions about whether Porter, whose IQ is 51, should be legally barred from execution because he could not understand what was happening to him.

The delay gave four Northwestern University journalism students time to conduct an independent investigation of the case. No physical evidence tied Porter to the 1982 double murder in Chicago. His conviction was based solely on eyewitness testimony. After visiting the crime scene, the students found that this testimony did not add up. With the aid of a private investigator, they began questioning witnesses. Thanks to the students' efforts, another man confessed to the murders for which Porter was almost executed. Porter was freed in February 1999 after 17 years on death row.

We, the undersigned, are US citizens and organizations. Some of us support the death penalty and some oppose it. Yet we *all* join together today to call for an immediate moratorium on executions because of the way capital punishment is applied in our country.

We support a moratorium because of the increasing risk of executing innocent people like Anthony Porter. Nationwide, 82* innocent death row prisoners have been released since 1973 – six in 1999 alone. Some were saved only days before their scheduled execution. The average time these prisoners spent on death row was seven years.[1] Efforts by courts and legislatures to speed up the time between conviction and execution mean that other prisoners likely have been and will be executed before their innocence is discovered. Porter's story is a painful reminder that all too often, a prisoner's innocence is discovered only because of the extraordinary and fortuitous efforts of people *outside* the system.

We support a moratorium because – as the American Bar Association (ABA) has concluded – "fundamental due process is now systematically lacking in capital cases."[2] Porter's case is symptomatic of this crisis in death penalty jurisprudence. Like *90 percent* of those facing capital charges, Porter was too poor to hire his own attorney.

Most indigent defendants suffer from grossly inadequate legal representation.[3] Furthermore, the US General Accounting Office has found "a pattern of evidence indicating racial disparities in charging, sentencing and imposition of the death penalty."[4] Many states continue to execute people who are mentally retarded or who were under age 18 at the time of their crimes or both – even in the face of nearly unanimous international condemnation.

Unfairness and mistakes in the application of the death penalty are undermining public confidence in the criminal justice system and fueling the call for a moratorium. **More than 600* groups and tens of thousands of people across the US are now calling for an immediate halt to executions.** Among them is the ABA, which led the way in early 1997. Opinion polls show that many people in the US embrace alternatives to a death sentence if other means are taken to ensure that the guilty do not further endanger the innocent.[5]

In the coming weeks, the United Nations General Assembly will vote on a resolution urging an international moratorium on executions. We note that many governments of the world are already observing a moratorium, while 105 countries have abandoned capital punishment in law or practice. We urge our government to join in the proposed UN resolution.

We also urge President Clinton, all members of the US Congress, our respective governors and state legislators and members of our state and federal judiciary to enact an immediate moratorium on executions.

Numbers will be updated at publication of ad as necessary.

---

[1] *Innocence and the Death Penalty: The Increasing Danger of Executing the Innocent*, Death Penalty Information Center, 1320 18th St. NW, 5th Floor, Washington, DC 20036, 202-293-6970, July 1997. See also www.essential.org/dpic.

[2] Report accompanying ABA Death Penalty Moratorium Resolution (107) adopted by the ABA House of Delegates in February 1997.

[3] Same as note 2. To date, no state has met *all* of the American Bar Association (ABA) policies for administration of the death penalty, including standards for representation for indigent defendants.

[4] *Death Penalty Sentencing: Research Indicates a Pattern of Racial Disparities,* General Accounting Office report, February 1990.

[5] See Death Penalty Information Center website at www.essential.org/dpic/po.html.

SAMPLE RHETORICAL ANALYSIS OF AN ARGUMENT

The annotations on the sample analysis of the argument in the Call for a Moratorium on Executions point out some of the things you can do in your own analysis of an argument.

Sample Rhetorical Analysis of the Argument in "Call for a Moratorium on Executions"

Indentifies the timing and purpose of the call

"The Call for a Moratorium on Executions," along with an accompanying letter, was sent out in September 1999 to solicit signatures and contributions for an ad in the *New York Times,* just before the United Nations General Assembly voted on a resolution calling for a moratorium on the death penalty. The Call focuses on the issue of capital punishment in the United States. It does not argue against the death

Summarizes the argument

penalty in principle. Instead, the Call argues that "[u]nfairness and mistakes in the application of the death penalty" are "undermining public confidence in the criminal justice system." In particular, the Call notes the lack of due process in capital cases, the inadequate legal representation of poor people charged with capital crimes, the racial disparities in the use of the death penalty, and the fact that juveniles and the mentally retarded are executed in the U.S. Since 1973, 82 innocent death row prisoners were released, due largely to efforts of people outside the criminal justice system, such as the Northwestern University journalism students who succeeded in freeing Anthony Porter in 1999, after another man confessed to the crime for which Porter was to be executed.

Describes the context of issues

The debate over the death penalty, of course, has long divided the American people. As the Call says the number of executions has been increasing in recent years. In general the American public supports capital punishment, although support has dropped from 80% in 1997 to 66% today. The Call, however, includes both supporters and opponents of the death penalty as its intended readers. By focusing on whether the death penalty is being applied fairly, the Call reaches out to both sides in the death penalty debate on the basis of people's shared beliefs in due process and justice.

(continued)

(continued)

Analyzes the rhetorical stance

The Call establishes its rhetorical stance by saying that some of us "support the death penalty and some oppose it." The ethos it projects is

Ethos

that of reasonable, concerned citizens and groups who are troubled by the current flaws in capital punishment. The tone is serious, and the Call seeks to enhance its authority and credibility by drawing on the conclusions of such reputable organizations as the American Bar Association and the General Accounting Office of the federal government. In terms of

Pathos

pathos, the Call appeals to readers who will be worried by unfairness in the current system and do not want to see innocent people executed. The inclusion of the Story from Death Row personalizes the policy issue of capital punishment and gives it a sense of urgency and immediacy for read-

Logos

ers. The logos of the Call sends the message that readers do not have to be against the death penalty to recognize that the system is not working the way it is supposed to.

Analyzes the parts of the argument

The argument in the Call begins with the claim that executions should be suspended because of the unfairness of the system. The evidence includes the story about Anthony Porter, the number of innocent death row

Claim

prisoners released since 1973, the American Bar Association's report that

Evidence

poor defendants lack adequate legal representation, and the General Accounting Office's finding of racial disparities in charging and sentencing in capital cases. The enabling assumptions that link this evidence to

Enabling Assumptions

the Call's claim are beliefs in due process and the right to competent legal counsel. These assumptions are backed up by the U.S. Constitution and the American legal tradition that everyone (rich or poor, black or white) is equal in the eyes of the law. The Call does not include either differing views or qualifiers in regard to its argument for a moratorium on executions.

Examines strategy for negotiating differences

The major purpose of the Call is to provide a common ground on which both opponents and supporters of the death penalty can join together to deal with inequities in the present system. This emphasis on an issue of policy helps both to clarify the current situation of the death penalty and

Indentifies type of issue

to allow the broadest group of readers to join the call for a moratorium. Some supporters of the death penalty might argue that a moratorium

(continued)

(continued)

would permit guilty death row prisoners to evade capital punishment. Nonetheless, one of the enabling assumptions in the Call is that the concern for fairness and the public good is worth the risk. It is always difficult to know whether individual readers will be persuaded, but the Call's overall strategy of reaching out on the basis of fairness is certainly a reasonable one in the circumstances.

Evaluation of overall effectiveness

WRITING ASSIGNMENT: ANALYZING AN ARGUMENT

Your task is to write an analysis of a short argument. Use the sample analysis as a guideline, but be flexible in the way you approach the argument you're analyzing. What you emphasize will depend in large part on the nature of the argument you're analyzing.

DIRECTIONS

1. Select a short argument (five to ten paragraphs is a good length). You can use one of the readings in this chapter or elsewhere in this book, a newspaper editorial or op-ed piece, a featured column in a newspaper or magazine, magazine commentary, political ads, and ads for advocacy groups as sources for your analysis.
2. Analyze the argument. Here are some guidelines for your analysis:
   - Summarize the argument. What is the main claim?
   - Identify the type of issue—substantiation, evaluation, policy.
   - Describe the context of issues. Is the argument part of an ongoing debate, discussion, or controversy? What positions have people taken in the past?
   - Describe the intended readers and explain how the argument seeks to influence them (to take action, support or oppose a policy, reconsider an established fact or belief, make a value judgment).
   - Analyze the rhetorical stance. How does the writer integrate ethos, pathos, and logos?
   - Analyze the parts of the argument—claim, evidence, enabling assumptions, backing, differing views, qualifiers—and how the writer puts them together.
   - Examine any strategies used to negotiate differences.
   - Evaluate the overall effectiveness of the argument. Keep in mind that the goal of argument is to clarify reasonable differences as well as to convince others.

3. Use your analysis to write your essay. Begin by summarizing the argument. Then provide an analysis in the order that best suits your material. End with your evaluation of the argument's effectiveness.

REFLECTING ON YOUR WRITING

Reread any of the writing you have done for this chapter. Consider what your understanding of argument was when you began the chapter and what it is now. How would you account for any changes in your views? What role, if any, did your writing play in these changes?

PART TWO

Writing Projects

INTRODUCTION: GENRES OF WRITING

The mail has just arrived, and you glance through it, putting letters in one pile, magazines in another, and junk mail in still another. You may do this automatically, but your ability to sort the mail is based on some very real experience with the written materials of print culture. That is why people can distinguish immediately between, say, an L. L. Bean catalog and the recent issue of *Newsweek*—identifying one as advertising and the other as journalism. The same is true of the letters they receive—a personal letter from a friend, a fund-raising appeal from Amnesty International, a library overdue notice, and junk mail advertising storm windows or aluminum siding.

Each type of writing is likely to have a different appearance—a four-color catalog, a slick newsmagazine, handwritten stationery, a form letter with profiles of human rights abuse, a computer printout, and a promotional flyer addressed to "Resident." People use such visual cues to make sense of the written material they receive and what they should do with it.

People are likely to notice, for example, how the different types of writing address them in different ways. A personal letter may call for a reply, whether by letter, phone call, or e-mail message. A library notice calls for prompt action if you want to avoid running up a fine. A fund-raising letter may lead to a financial contribution to support a particular cause. A catalog from L. L. Bean may lead to placing an order or just to fantasy reading about the lifestyles of the outdoorsy middle classes.

This example of sorting the mail is meant to illustrate how people classify different types of writing into categories in order to get a handle on what they are reading—to know what to expect from it and how to respond. Based on their past experience with written texts, people fit what they read into patterns. For example, when you read (or hear) the phrase "Once upon a time," you are likely to recognize right away that you are in the realm of fairy tales. The familiar opening line is an immediate giveaway that prepares you for the story that follows, whether it's about Cinderella, Snow White, or Jack and the Beanstalk.

The same is true for many other types—or genres—of writing. Based on their familiarity with various genres of writing, people browsing at a bookstore can easily distinguish, say, science fiction from Westerns, cookbooks from dictionaries, or poetry from biography. This is the same kind of knowledge that enables you to distinguish between different types—or genres—of movies. You probably know that you can expect something very different from a Jackie Chan kung fu action adventure, a Disney cartoon version of Hercules or Pocahontas, and a romantic comedy starring Julia Roberts—and you are likely to make your viewing choices accordingly.

Genre Choices

Just as knowing about various movie genres can help you make informed decisions about what you want to see, understanding the various genres of writing can help you make sense of situations that call on you to write. As writers identify a call to write, they typically draw on past experience to help them determine the genre best suited to the current occasion. To do this, they look for recurring patterns: How is this writing situation similar to ones I've encountered in the past? How well do genres of writing I've used in the past match the demands of the present? What genre best fits my purposes, given the situation and the intended readers?

In the following chapters, you'll see how writers use various genres to respond to recurring writing situations. You'll see how writers' choice of genre takes into account the occasion that calls for writing, the writer's purposes, and the relationship the writer seeks to establish with readers.

Understanding Genres of Writing

While writing teachers do not always agree on how best to classify genres of writing, the eight chapters in Part Two offer practical examples of how writers use some of the most familiar genres:

- letters

- memoirs

- public documents

- profiles

- fact sheets/FAQs, brochures, and Web sites

- commentaries

- proposals

- reviews

This, of course, is by no means a comprehensive list of all genres of writing. Nor are the genres of writing fixed once and for all. New genres are always emerging in response to new conditions. Witness, for example, the proliferation of e-mail messages, newsgroups, and Web sites with the appearance of new electronic communications technologies. In the following chapters, we have selected some of the most common genres to illustrate how writers respond to the call to write—genres you will find helpful when you are called on to write in college, in the workplace, and in public life.

As you will see, some genres are broader than others. The genre of letters, for example, can be further divided into personal letters, business letters, letters to the editor, letters of appeal, and so on. Nonetheless, each genre has distinctive features that readers will recognize—whether, for example, the re-creation of personal experience in a memoir or the evaluative judgment of a review. Studying and experimenting with a range of genres will help you expand your repertoire of writing strategies so that you can respond flexibly and creatively to situations that call on you to write.

The Arrangement of the Chapters

The chapters are arranged according to the purpose writers bring to their writing tasks and the focus of attention they thereby establish for their readers.

In the first three chapters—"Letters," "Memoirs," and "Public Documents"—the dominant purpose is to express individual and group identities, whether by rendering personal experience or codifying communal beliefs and norms of conduct. In the next two chapters—"Profiles" and "Fact Sheets/FAQs, Brochures, and Web Sites"—the focus of attention shifts from presentation of self and community to the subject matter being investigated and analyzed; here the writers' main purposes are to inform and explain. In the final three chapters—"Commentary," "Proposals," and "Reviews"—the main focus shifts once again, this time from an emphasis on the topic under consideration to an emphasis on the writer's own interpretations and judgments; here the writers explicitly seek to persuade readers to take a particular point of view.

It is important to understand that the differences in purpose and focus are matters of emphasis rather than absolute ones. All writing, after all, involves a presentation of the writer's identity, even if it is subordinated to another purpose, such as informing readers. By the same token, a convincing commentary, proposal, or review often relies on extensive background information and analysis, so it's best to understand the arrangement of the chapters as a continuum in which the emphasis shifts depending on the writer's purpose and focus of attention.

Your instructor may ask you to read some or all of the chapters. You may want to consult chapters you haven't been assigned for advice about writing tasks you face in and out of school.

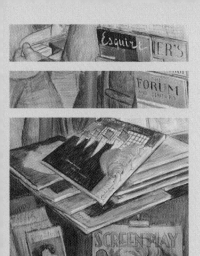

CHAPTER FOUR

Letters: Establishing and Maintaining Relationships

THINKING ABOUT THE GENRE

Letters are easy to recognize. Whether handwritten, typed, word-processed, or composed as e-mail, letters have a predictable format that usually includes the date of writing, a salutation that addresses the reader directly ("Dear Jim"), a message, a closing (such as "Sincerely" or "Yours truly"), and a signature. There are many different occasions for and purposes of letter writing, and the genre of letters can be divided into a number of subgenres, such as personal letters, business letters, letters to the editor, or letters of appeal. Nonetheless, letters are easy to identify because of the way they appear on the page or computer screen.

But it's not only the visual form of the writing that makes letters a distinct genre. Just as important is the way letters address their readers and establish a relationship between the writer and the reader. In part because of two elements of their form—the salutation and the closing and signature—the letter is the genre that comes closest in feeling to conversations between people. The letters you receive—whether a postcard from a friend on vacation, an invitation to a party, a notice from an organization you belong to, or a grade report from your college—are addressed to you and come from someone.

This relationship established between writer and reader is one of the main attractions of the genre of letters. It's also one of its most basic functions: letters are important links that help you maintain your networks of personal and social relations.

When you read a letter, you can almost hear the voice and feel the presence of the person writing to you. This is particularly true of personal letters, which often convey the immediacy and intimacy of face-to-face conversation, but it is also true of other letters as well. Think, for example, of the correspondence you have received from your college. Such letters address you directly, but in your role as a student. The voice you hear sounds official and institutional—not entirely unlike the voice you would hear if you spoke to a school administrator you didn't know about some official business.

Letters are also like conversation in that the writer seeks to engage the reader in an ongoing interaction. They often call for a response from their readers—whether it's to RSVP to a party invitation, attend a meeting, donate to a worthy cause, pay an overdue bill, or just write back.

One way that letters differ from conversation is that the person you're writing to can't talk back, at least not immediately. As a writer with something to say, you therefore have certain advantages. In a letter, you can talk directly to someone without being interrupted. And you know that the reader can return several times to your letter and reflect on its message before responding to you.

Thus, permanence is also a difference between letters and conversation. Once you've sent a letter, you can't take your words back as easily as you can in conversation. By expressing thoughts and feelings in a letter and sending it to someone, the letter writer may be taking a greater risk than by talking face to face or on the phone.

Although from one perspective a disadvantage, permanence—and the greater risk it entails—is actually another attraction of letters. G. K. Chesterton once described the mailbox as "a sanctuary of the human heart" and the letter as "one of the few things left entirely romantic, for to be entirely romantic, a thing must be irrevocable." Many people save the letters they receive from relatives, friends, lovers, and other correspondents as a personal record of what their life was like at a particular time. There is a long tradition of letters in which writers reveal their deepest, most intimate thoughts to readers in a language that would be unimaginable in conversation—love letters, letters of advice, letters of friendship, letters of condolence, letters of despair, and letters written on the eve of death.

Other kinds of letters play just as important a role as personal letters in maintaining the social networks that link people together. Business letters serve a wide range of indispensable functions for businesses and government, going to clients and customers, suppliers and contractors, employees, and the general public in order to advertise products and services, discuss policy changes, request payment, and negotiate agreements.

Letters written for the public realm are equally wide ranging in their functions and, taken together, are crucial to a democratic society. For example, individuals and groups write to politicians to influence the direction of public policy. Letters to the editor, which are included in most newspapers and magazines, give readers a chance to respond to news stories, feature articles, editorials, and other letters, as well as to raise neglected issues.

Letters of appeal have several different purposes. For example, advocacy groups such as the Sierra Club or the National Rifle Association, historical restoration groups, arts groups, and community groups write fund-raising letters appealing for memberships and donations. Another kind of letter of appeal, often called an open letter because it is circulated widely, is a political tradition in democratic cultures. Sent out through the mail or Internet and sometimes appearing as a paid advertisement in a magazine or newspaper, the letter of appeal calls on its readers to support a cause, protest a policy, or otherwise take action.

The readings in this chapter include personal letters, letters to the editor, an exchange of letters, and an open letter. As you read these letters, look at what calls on people to write letters and at the particular relationships that the letters establish between writers and readers.

EXPLORING YOUR EXPERIENCE

List the kinds of letters you write and receive, including e-mail correspondence. Classify the letters according to the relationship they are based on—letters to and from family, letters to and from friends, love letters, letters to you as a consumer or a potential donor, letters from your college, and so on. Are there particular letters you wrote or received that are especially important to you? What makes these letters important? Do you save letters? If so, what kinds of letters, and why? Compare your answers to those of your classmates.

READINGS: LETTERS HOME

The following two personal letters were written against the backdrop of larger public events—the Vietnam War in the case of the first letter and the coming-out episode on the television show *Ellen* in the second. The letter from Richard Marks, who saw combat duty in Vietnam as a marine, was published in the book *Dear America,* which became the basis for a PBS special. The second letter was published, with the writer's name omitted, in *Letters of the Century: America 1900–1999,* a collection documenting social and political life through letters.

Richard Marks, Dear Mom

Last Will & Testament of
PFC Richard E. Marks
December 12, 1965

Dear Mom,

1 I am writing this in the event that I am killed during my remaining tour of duty in Vietnam.

2 First of all I want to say that I am here as a result of my own desire—I was offered the chance to go into 2nd Marine Division when I was first assigned to the 4th Marines, but I turned it down. I am here because I have always wanted to be a Marine and because I always wanted to see combat.

3 I don't like being over here, but I am doing a job that must be done—I am fighting an inevitable enemy that must be fought—now or later.

4   I am fighting to protect and maintain what I believe in and what I want to live in—a democratic society. If I am killed while carrying out this mission, I want no one to cry or mourn for me. I want people to hold their heads high and be proud of me for the job I did.

5   There are some details I want taken care of. First of all, any money that you receive as a result of my death I want distributed in the following fashion.

6   If you are single, I want you and Sue to split it down the middle. But if you are married and your husband can support you, I want Sue and Lennie to get 75% of the money, and I want you to keep only 25%—I feel Sue and Lennie will need the money a lot more.

7   I also want to be buried in my Marine Corps uniform with all the decorations, medals, and badges I rate. I also want Rabbi Hirschberg to officiate, and I want to be buried in the same cemetery as Dad and Gramps, but I do not want to be buried in the plot next to Dad that I bought in mind of you.

8   That is about all, except I hope I never have to use this letter.

9   I love you, Mom, and Sue, and Nan, and I want you all to carry on and be very happy, and above all be proud—

Love & much more love,
Rick

An *Ellen* Viewer to Her Mother

May 1997

Dear Mom,

1   With all the Ellen stuff that's been happening lately, I figured that this would be a good time to tell you that I'm attracted to women too. The main reason I haven't told you is because I was afraid that you would treat me differently. You and _____ are the two people I love the most, and I've been worried that you wouldn't love me anymore if I told you.

2   This whole thing seems SO ridiculous because I have no idea who the heck decided that being gay is a bad thing in the first place! I don't even think it's a big deal at all! And I certainly don't think it's a bad thing. When two humans love each other, no matter what gender the two of them are, why should it be wrong? It shouldn't matter who we love—all that matters is that we love! I wish more people would realize this.

3   One of the reasons Ellen's coming out was so amazing for me is because it's the first time a t.v. character depicted my own feelings and experiences about this "issue." It doesn't surprise me that so many gay/bisexual people grow up thinking they are "abnormal" or "wrong." I mean, how many gay or lesbian characters have there been on t.v. and in movies? We've been brainwashed into thinking that the only valid (and "normal") relationships are heterosexual ones.

4   I totally understand that this will probably freak you out—especially because we've all been taught that being attracted to the same sex is a "bad" thing. I really

have no expectations about how you will react. Most families (and friends) have trouble accepting this news, especially when it is their own daughter or son, sister, or brother. I bet that most families try to deny/ignore it—hoping they will change (that it's "just a phase," etc.). I can imagine the kinds of feelings that you might have about this, and I don't want you to think that you "shouldn't" have any negative feelings or thoughts, etc. Know that however you react or feel will not change how I feel about you.

5   It's SO hard to describe, but I've often said that it's as though my heart (emotion) doesn't "activate" with men the way it does when I am with a woman. As Ellen described, that "click" just doesn't occur. A lot of people think that the "reason" people are gay is because they have had bad experiences with the opposite sex, or because they had a bad childhood. But it's not like being with men is some horrible experience for me—because it is not like that at all. I have lots of fun with them. I feel comfortable with men, enjoy their company, etc. It's just that when I am in a relationships with a man, there is always a sense that something is missing. I enjoy being with women so much more. I can relate to them on a much deeper level, and can therefore really love and care about them. Being able to feel such deep love and connection with another person, whatever their gender (or race, ethnicity, etc.) is such a wonderful thing. It makes me really sad (and angry) that we've been taught the complete opposite, and I know that if I continue to hide who I am out of fear of what other people will think, I will only be contributing to the false (and harmful) belief that being gay or bisexual is wrong or bad. And I don't want to do that. That's pretty much why I'm telling you this.

6   I thought that writing you a letter would be easier—I've always been able to express myself better in writing anyway.

I love and miss you!!

xoxox

Analysis: Private Purposes and Public Events

Letters home offer a good example of how people use writing to maintain family ties. Part of this is simply the responsibility family members feel to stay in touch, to use the available means of communication (telephone and e-mail as well as letters), when someone is away from home. But while the two letters certainly reaffirm the importance of family to the writers, they also reveal how private lives intersect—and are caught up in—public events.

Notice how the occasions that seem to be calling on the two individuals to write their letters come from their involvement in the larger social context. As Richard Marks says, "I am writing this in the event I am killed during my remaining tour of duty in Vietnam." In turn, the second writer says that with "all this Ellen stuff that's been happening lately, I figured this would be a good time to tell you that I'm attracted to women too."

Both of these occasions—the Vietnam War and the coming-out episode on *Ellen*—were marked by public controversy. The Vietnam War was undoubtedly the most divisive in American history, and the *Ellen* episode was greeted by protests from conservative groups, praise from gay-rights groups, and a heated discussion nationwide. In this sense, the two writers are not only staying in touch but explaining and justifying their own relationship to the two occasions.

FOR CRITICAL INQUIRY

1. Both letters, as just noted, involve justifications of decisions the two writers have made—to become a marine and to come out as a lesbian. Analyze the reasons each writer offers to explain this decision.
2. What kind of relationship do these letters establish between the writers and their readers at home? How do you imagine the readers responded?
3. Describe the tone of each letter. Give examples of specific words and phrases that convey the tone, and explain how these words and phrases project a particular attitude or personality.

READINGS: LETTERS TO THE EDITOR

The newspaper column and letters to the editor presented in this section follow a cycle of writing that is common in newspapers—a pattern of call and response where the writers respond to the views of those who wrote before them. First, newspaper columnist Mark Patinkin of the *Providence Journal Bulletin* wrote a column on an item in the news: The authorities in Singapore had sentenced Michael Fay, an American teenager who lived there, to be caned as a punishment for spray-painting cars. (As you'll see on page 117, Patinkin's column was actually itself inspired by a column.) Patinkin's column, which supported the caning, led to a round of letters, many of them condemning him for taking that position. The letter from Kristin Tardiff, which starts below, was among those published at this point. There followed a second round of letters, responding to Patinkin and the first round of letters. Many of these supported Patinkin, including the letter from John N. Taylor.

Kristin Tardiff, Letter to the Editor

To the Editor,

1   I wonder why I continue to read Mark Patinkin's columns. At best they bore me, at worst they anger me. I've thought before of responding to his maudlin whining or self-righteous hypocrisy, but this time I really had to put pen to paper.

2   Mr. Patinkin has chosen this time to attack Michael Fay, the 18-year-old boy who has been accused of spray-painting some cars in Singapore. Mark, jury of one,

THE COLUMN

Commit a crime, suffer the consequences

Mark Patinkin

At their best, columnists are supposed to leave people thinking, "That's just how I feel and didn't know it until reading that." Well, it took reading a column by an 18-year-old student to crystallize my own feelings about an issue I've been perusing day to day.

The Singapore caning case: The American teenager who's about to be flogged because he spray-painted several cars. From the start, I'd viewed it as a barbaric punishment for a poor kid who just did a little mischief. Then I read a column by an 18-year-old telling Michael Fay, the convicted American, to take it like a man, and learn from it.

Something in me instantly said, "She's right."

Yes, I know caning is harsh, but am I the only one who's tired of Michael Fay's whining? Am I the only one who feels President Clinton has better things to do than to write letters appealing for leniency?

Singaporeans get caned all the time for vandalism. Are we Americans supposed to be exempt when we break their laws? What are we — princes?

I'll tell you what else I'm tired of: Michael Fay's father — his biological father here in America — traveling the country insisting his precious boy didn't do it.

It's a setup, the father says. Supposedly, he says, Michael only pleaded guilty as a bargain with the police — after the local cops leaned on him — with the promise of little punishment.

But suddenly the judge sentenced him to six strikes with a cane.

Not once have I read Michael's parents saying their child was out of line. They just make excuses. Gee, I wonder if a life of such excuse-making is part of why he's so troubled.

See, that's the other line here. First, the father says he didn't do it. Then he says, well, Michael also has personal problems, like Attention Deficit Disorder. I happen to think that's a legitimate syndrome, but not for excusing crimes like vandalizing cars.

All this is just part of the new American game of always saying, "It's not my fault." No one, when caught, seems ready to admit having done wrong anymore. They just whine and appeal. As in: "Your honor, the stabbing was not my client's fault. He had a bad childhood. And was caught up in a riot at the time. In fact, he's not a criminal at all, he's one of society's victims."

That's Michael Fay. All those cars he spray-painted? Not his fault. He's had a hard life.

I might have had sympathy for him if he'd only said, "I admit it. I did a dumb thing. I was with the wrong crowd and crossed the line into criminality. I deserve to pay. And I'm truly sorry for the victims."

But we're not hearing that.

There's another thing. Many articles on this — including a paragraph in a column I wrote — have referred to what Michael Fay did as "mischief."

Well, it's not. It's hardcore vandalism. He spray-painted a bunch of cars.

Michael Fay might want to think about what it feels like to the car owners. Anyone whose car has been vandalized knows. Personally, I've had about four car stereos stolen. I still remember the shock — each time — of seeing the broken window and the damage. I remember having to take a good half day out of work to deal with it. And during the times I had little money, I remember how badly it pinched to have to pay the deductible on the insurance.

Finally, I remember how creepy and unnerving it was. It took weeks before I could approach my car again without feeling nervous. It erodes your trust in the world. And it's worse for women, I think, who feel a heightened vulnerability to crime in the first place.

In short, it's beyond mischief, beyond obnoxious — it's vandalism. A violation. And it's downright mean-spirited.

But after he was caught, Michael Fay and his family have been telling the world that he — not the car owners but HE — is the victim.

Sorry, Michael, you're not the victim. You're the criminal. Caning may well be rough.

But if you do the crime, you've got to pay the price.

Mark Patinkin is a Journal-Bulletin columnist. His column appears in Lifebeat each Tuesday and Thursday, and in the Metro section each Sunday.

has decided that Fay is unequivocally guilty, and that his sentence of jail term, fine, and caning is fitting punishment. "Stop whining, take it like a man," he says.

3   I find it interesting that Mr. Patinkin has completely ignored the statements of those who may have a little more experience with the Singaporean police than he does. What about the Navy officer who said that our military police were under order to immediately take into custody any American soldier who was going to be arrested by the Singaporean police to protect them? Did he make that up? What

about those who have had the experience of being detained in Singapore and tell of torture and forced confessions? Are they just wimpy bleeding hearts in Mark's eyes?

4   Perhaps as a teenager Mr. Patinkin never made a mistake, never did anything considered wrong in the eyes of the law. Hard to believe, but I'll give him the benefit of the doubt. Had he, however, ever been caught and punished for some infraction, that punishment certainly would not have involved being tied up with his pants around his ankles while someone split his cheeks the opposite way with a water-soaked cane. Nor do I think he would have considered that just. The punishment should fit the crime.

5   Michael Fay is willing to serve his time in jail and make restitution. He has already suffered physically and psychologically, and has, I'm sure, seen the error of his ways. Is this not enough punishment? Have we become so warped by the violence of our society that we now see justice as incomplete without the imposition of physical pain? Do we really want to see the young graffiti artist in our neighborhood caned? (I hear some saying yes, but what if it turns out to be your child? Think about it.) Is this really the way we want society to turn? What comes next? Amputation for thieves and maybe prolonged torture and death for drug dealers? Should we just kill all the "bad" people? Why can't we for once work on the causes instead of lashing out blindly at the symptoms?

6   Just one more thing. Regarding Mr. Patinkin's criticism of Fay's parents' pleas for leniency for their son, as a parent he should have more empathy. What else can parents do when they truly feel that their child is being unjustly treated?

7   I hope Mark's children all turn out as perfect as their dad. Maybe he should send to Singapore for a cane. Just in case.

Kristin Tardiff
Providence

John N. Taylor, Letter to the Editor

To the Editor,

1   The letters...denouncing Mark Patinkin's support for caning Michael Fay ("Patinkin should know better than to advocate caning," 5/3) are no different from any of the other whiny, moralizing claptrap we hear from those mawkish people who fear more for Mr. Fay's buttocks than for those who are victimized everyday by the crimes of young punks like Fay. The arguments...are laden with the rancid, canting self-righteousness common to all opposing Fay's caning, and evince concern only for the criminal while telling crime victims to go eat cake.

2   From Ms. Tardiff, we get a lot of sarcasm, a lot of questions, and no answers. If she can't propose any semblance of an idea for controlling crime, then neither she (nor anyone else) has the moral authority to condemn a nation which has come up with its own means of dealing with criminals....

3   Singapore has in recent years carried out canings of 14 of its own citizens who were convicted of offenses similar in nature to those of Mr. Fay. Why should Fay be treated any differently from these people? Just because Fay is an affluent white American with many powerful supporters in America (like President Clinton) doesn't mean he should be above the law of the nation where he resides. To let Fay out of the caning simply because he has the support of powerful leaders is an affront to the people of Singapore, who have abided by the law or taken their lumps for violating same. Clemency for Fay would effectively divide Americans and Singaporeans into separate, unequal classes, whereby the former avoid punishment because of America's political and economic clout while the latter, who do not enjoy such powerful connections, suffer the consequences.

4   The caning of Fay is simply an affirmation of the principle that all people, whether they are wealthy white Americans or poor Chinese Singaporeans, are equal in the eyes of the law.... It has much to do with upholding Singaporean mores and nothing to do with Fay being American or U.S. political traditions; these sanctions, as applied to crimes like vandalism and other non-political offenses, are designed to discourage repetition of criminal behavior. And they succeed in this goal. How many drive-by shootings go down in Singapore?

5   Like American authorities, the Singaporeans perceive crimes to be the individual act and choice of the perpetrator.

6   There is no doubt Singapore is a non-democratic nation which punishes even peaceable political dissent, and there is no doubt that Singapore's criminal laws are harsh. But Michael Fay knew what the laws were like and freely assumed the risks of getting punished when he engaged in his spree of vandalism. It is the height of arrogance and folly for Americans living or traveling abroad to expect to be protected by the Bill of Rights when they break other nations' laws.

7   Americans have no right demanding a blanket exemption from foreign laws they violate, or that foreign governments give them easier treatment than they would give their own people under similar circumstances.

8   And if caning is immoral, is not the American criminal justice system itself laden with unfairness? Where is the morality in releasing quadruple murderer Craig Price into the community after only four years? Is it right that in the U. S., a murderer draws an average sentence of only about six years? Is it right that dangerous criminals are dumped onto communities simply because the prisons don't meet the standards of some soft-headed judge? We in America sacrifice the lives of innocent people in the name of criminals' civil rights, and then have the gall to denounce Singapore as harsh and oppressive! If anyone's justice is extremist, it is America's.

9   America's approach to crime is to do nothing and let the community be damned, while Singapore has opted to let the offender be damned. What the Michael Fay fan club here in America conveniently forgets while moaning about Singaporean tyranny is the everyday tyranny of violence and fear imposed on millions of Americans by violent criminals in our inner cities and suburbs. These people are

oppressed by a dictatorship of criminals and their rights are violated on a massive scale every day. Yet I see more concern for Michael Fay's rear end than I do for people who bear the scars of bullets and knives of criminals.

10   My heart will not bleed if Fay's rear end does. Given the carnage on America's streets, and in Rwanda, Bosnia and Haiti, the supporters of Michael Fay will just have to excuse me if I fail to shed a tear.

John N. Taylor Jr.
North Providence

Analysis: A Public Forum

Like a lot of newspaper columnists, Mark Patinkin uses short paragraphs, an informal, conversational tone, and a commonsense man-in-the-street approach to his readers. Notice that he speaks to his readers as an equal, not as someone who is more knowledgeable or somehow above them. This approach in effect positions the column as something that readers can and should respond to. The controversial nature of the topic—and of some of Patinkin's comments about the topic—make it all the more likely that readers will respond.

In the letters to the editor, the writers argue a position in response to what they've read. The letters to the editor reveal an intensity of feeling, and at times they resort to logical fallacies and other questionable tactics. These tactics include name-calling: Kristin Tardiff refers to Patinkin's "maudlin whining" and "self-righteous hypocrisy." By the same token, John N. Taylor says Tardiff's letter contains the "whiny, moralizing claptrap" of "mawkish people." The writers use exaggeration: "What comes next? Amputation for thieves and maybe prolonged torture and death for drug dealers [Tardiff]?" They are not always completely accurate: "in the U.S., a murderer draws an average sentence of only about six years [Taylor]." At times, they beg the question instead of explaining the point: "What else can parents do [Tardiff]?" and make questionable comparisons: "If caning is immoral, is not the American justice system laden with unfairness [Taylor]?" The letters are definitely opinionated, and finally that is the point: Letters to the editor give people the chance to talk back, to take strong positions, to have their say in a public forum.

FOR CRITICAL INQUIRY

1. Reread Tardiff's letter to the editor. What is it about Patinkin's column that seems to call on her to respond? How does she define her own position in relation to what Patinkin has written? To what extent does her letter respond directly to Patinkin's column? To what extent does it introduce other issues?

2. Reread the letter from Taylor. How would you describe his response to the call to write? How does he define his own position in relation to Patinkin and Tardiff?

3. What is this exchange of letters really about? Although the letters are ostensibly about Michael Fay, his punishment doesn't exactly seem to be the main issue. Try to distill the main issues that emerge and explain how the letters relate to these issues and to each other. What is at stake for these writers?

READINGS: AN EXCHANGE OF LETTERS

The two letters that follow present an exchange of views between Galen Sherwin, president of the New York chapter of the National Organization of Women (NOW), and Ingrid Newkirk, president of People for the Ethical Treatment of Animals (PETA), concerning a particular ad for PETA.

Galen Sherwin, "To Whom It May Concern"

To Whom It May Concern:

1 I am outraged by the most recent advertisement by PETA featuring a woman's unshaven panty line with the tag line "Fur Trim. Unattractive." This is a gratuitous and insulting image that makes its point at the expense of women.

2 It is ironic that PETA, an organization that seeks to counter mainstream notions about what makes women beautiful (i.e., wearing fur), would choose to do so with an image that reinforces oppressive beauty standards. This ad basically says that women's natural state is unattractive—hardly an original point, as that is what women are told in one form or another by countless ads for beauty products, accessories, and clothing lines. It also resorts to a crotch shot to make its point—a cheap shock tactic with a twist that adds insult to injury.

3 Enough already! Why don't you try protecting animals without objectifying women! I think you'll find that this approach is much less likely to alienate those who might be inclined to support the work you do.

Sincerely,
Galen Sherwin

Dear Ms. Sherwin:

4 I was dismayed to read your snotty letter about our panty ads.

5 I would be surprised if you don't shave your legs or underarms. I also bet that if you have ever worn a bikini you made sure not to have hairs poking out. If you

didn't, you would have been the only woman at the pool or the beach not to be so particular.

6   PETA's ad speaks to something the overwhelming majority of women—not men, women—worry about: grooming. Since we left the '60s style of unshaven leg hair and bushes behind, most people like the groomed look better. It's not sexist, it's just a fact.

7   The depiction of a woman's waxed legs or crotch isn't automatically exploitative. Do you picket Montgomery Ward or Bloomingdale's when you open the paper and see the underwear ads? I'd bet not. In fact, if you're like the majority of women, you have probably thought, "That's a nice push-up bra," and cut out the sales ad for panties. If women didn't do and think those things, the stores would stop running the ads. They aren't for men. And what if they were? If the women in the NOW office see a picture of a cool-looking man in BVDs do you all pitch a fit or do the heterosexual staff linger over it? If you're a lesbian, substitute some hot chick for the guy and tell me the harm in enjoying the scenery.

8   Do you not wear pantyhose because it creates an exploitative look? What about skirts? Or are you only threatened by the sight of women's "naughty bits" used as a political statement? Frankly, I'd be amused to see Christian women "Jigglin' for Jesus," or how about relief workers using their sexuality for their cause by showing their buttocks? Think of it: "Fannies Against Famine!" Please stop this knee-jerk, reactionary rubbish. There are a lot of women out there—including longtime feminists like me—who don't appreciate being spoken for in this repressive way. We can use our bodies for pleasure, profit, and politics if we want. Please stop playing the role of an outraged father, brother or boyfriend!

Best wishes,
Ingrid Newkirk

Analysis: Protest and Defense

This exchange amounts to a letter of protest from Galen Sherwin ("I am outraged") about a PETA ad and a defense of the ad from Ingrid Newkirk ("Please stop this knee-jerk, reactionary rubbish"). One of the things that makes this exchange so interesting is that the facts are not in dispute. PETA did run an ad featuring a woman's unshaven panty line, accompanied by the tag-line "Fur Trim. Unattractive." What's at issue is how the correspondents make sense of the ad— as reinforcing sexist beauty standards or as using women's sexuality for a worthy cause. These differences in interpretation, moreover, are complicated by the fact that both writers claim to speak on behalf of women. As you can see, what's at stake in this exchange is not simply whether PETA should or should not have run the ad but also differences about representations of women's bodies.

FOR CRITICAL INQUIRY

1. What is the nature of Galen Sherwin's protest? What reasons does she give for objecting to the PETA ad?

2. How does Ingrid Newkirk defend the ad? What reasons does she give?

3. The exchange brings up issues that seem to go beyond just a disagreement about the ad. What are these issues? What assumptions underlie the writers' differences?

4. Describe the tone of each letter. Notice those points in the letters where the writer's tone heats up. What attitude does each writer project? Do you think these attitudes are justifiable, given the circumstances and the issues that divide the correspondents?

READINGS: OPEN LETTER

This letter from the writer James Baldwin to his nephew was published as part of the book-length essay *The Fire Next Time,* which appeared in 1962. *The Fire Next Time* is an extended analysis of black-white relations in the United States, written with the passion and eloquence characteristic of Baldwin's prose. In this letter, Baldwin speaks directly to his nephew in what appears to be a traditional letter of advice from an older family member to a younger one. At the same time, he is using the intimacy of family relations to instill a personal intensity into an open letter on race relations.

My Dungeon Shook: Letter to My Nephew

JAMES BALDWIN

Dear James:

1　　I have begun this letter five times and torn it up five times. I keep seeing your face, which is also the face of your father and my brother. Like him, you are tough, dark, vulnerable, moody—with a very definite tendency to sound truculent because you want no one to think you are soft. You may be like your grandfather in this, I don't know, but certainly both you and your father resemble him very much physically. Well, he is dead, he never saw you, and he had a terrible life; he was defeated long before he died because, at the bottom of his heart, he really believed what white people said about him. This is one of the reasons that he became so holy. I am sure that your father has told you something about all that. Neither you nor your father exhibit any tendency towards holiness: you really are of another era, part of what happened when the Negro left the land and came into what the late E. Franklin Frazier called "the cities of destruction." You can only be destroyed by believing that you really are what the white world calls a *nigger.* I tell you this because I love you, and please don't you forget it.

2　　I have known both of you all your lives, have carried your Daddy in my arms and on my shoulders, kissed and spanked him and watched him learn to walk. I don't know if you've known anybody from that far back; if you've loved anybody

that long, first as an infant, then as a child, then as a man, you gain a strange perspective on time and human pain and effort. Other people cannot see what I see
whenever I look into your father's face, for behind your father's face as it is today
are all those other faces which were his. Let him laugh and I see a cellar your father
does not remember and a house he does not remember and I hear in his present
laughter his laughter as a child. Let him curse and I remember him falling down
the cellar steps, and howling, and I remember, with pain, his tears, which my hand
or your grandmother's so easily wiped away. But no one's hand can wipe away
those tears he sheds invisibly today, which one hears in his laughter and in his
speech and in his songs. I know what the world has done to my brother and how
narrowly he has survived it. And I know, which is much worse, and this is the crime
of which I accuse my country and my countrymen, and for which neither I nor time
nor history will ever forgive them, that they have destroyed and are destroying hundreds of thousands of lives and do not know it and do not want to know it. One
can be, indeed one must strive to become, tough and philosophical concerning
destruction and death, for this is what most of mankind has been best at since we
have heard of man. (But remember: most of mankind is not all of mankind.) But it
is not permissible that the authors of devastation should also be innocent. It is the
innocence which constitutes the crime.

3   Now, my dear namesake, these innocent and well-meaning people, your countrymen, have caused you to be born under conditions not very far removed from
those described for us by Charles Dickens in the London of more than a hundred
years ago. (I hear the chorus of the innocents screaming, "No! This is not true!
How *bitter* you are!"—but I am writing this letter to *you,* to try to tell you something
about how to handle *them,* for most of them do not really know that you exist. I
know the conditions under which you were born, for I was there. Your countrymen
were *not* there, and haven't made it yet. Your grandmother was also there, and no
one has ever accused her of being bitter. I suggest that the innocents check with
her. She isn't hard to find. Your countrymen don't know that *she* exists, either,
though she has been working for them all their lives.)

4   Well, you were born, here you came, something like fourteen years ago; and
though your father and mother and grandmother, looking about the streets through
which they were carrying you, staring at the walls into which they brought you, had
every reason to be heavy-hearted, yet they were not. For here you were, Big James,
named for me—you were a big baby. I was not—here you were: to be loved. To be
loved, baby, hard, at once, and forever, to strengthen you against the loveless world.
Remember that: I know how black it looks today, for you. It looked bad that day,
too, yes, we were trembling. We have not stopped trembling yet, but if we had not
loved each other none of us would have survived. And now you must survive
because we love you, and for the sake of your children and your children's children.

5   This innocent country set you down in a ghetto in which, in fact, it intended that
you should perish. Let me spell out precisely what I mean by that, for the heart of
the matter is here, and the root of my dispute with my country. You were born where
you were born and faced the future that you faced because you were black and *for*

no other reason. The limits of your ambition were, thus, expected to be set forever. You were born into a society which spelled out with brutal clarity, and in as many ways as possible, that you were a worthless human being. You were not expected to aspire to excellence: you were expected to make peace with mediocrity. Wherever you have turned, James, in your short time on this earth, you have been told where you could go and what you could do (and *how* you could do it) and where you could live and whom you could marry. I know your countrymen do not agree with me about this, and I hear them saying, "You exaggerate." They do not know Harlem, and I do. So do you. Take no one's word for anything, including mine—but trust your experience. Know whence you came. If you know whence you came, there is really no limit to where you can go. The details and symbols of your life have been deliberately constructed to make you believe what white people say about you. Please try to remember that what they believe, as well as what they do and cause you to endure, does not testify to your inferiority but to their inhumanity and fear. Please try to be clear, dear James, through the storm which rages about your youthful head today, about the reality which lies behind the words *acceptance* and *integration.* There is no reason for you to try to become like white people and there is no basis whatever for their impertinent assumption that *they* must accept *you.* The really terrible thing, old buddy, is that *you* must accept *them.* And I mean that very seriously. You must accept them and accept them with love. For these innocent people have no other hope. They are, in effect, still trapped in a history which they do not understand; and until they understand it, they cannot be released from it. They have had to believe for many years, and for innumerable reasons, that black men are inferior to white men. Many of them, indeed, know better, but, as you will discover, people find it very difficult to act on what they know. To act is to be committed, and to be committed is to be in danger. In this case, the danger, in the minds of most white Americans, is the loss of their identity. Try to imagine how you would feel if you woke up one morning to find the sun shining and all the stars aflame. You would be frightened because it is out of the order of nature. Any upheaval in the universe is terrifying because it so profoundly attacks one's sense of one's own reality. Well, the black man has functioned in the white man's world as a fixed star, as an immovable pillar: and as he moves out of his place, heaven and earth are shaken to their foundations. You, don't be afraid. I said that it was intended that you should perish in the ghetto, perish by never being allowed to go behind the white man's definitions, by never being allowed to spell your proper name. You have, and many of us have, defeated this intention; and, by a terrible law, a terrible paradox, those innocents who believed that your imprisonment made them safe are losing their grasp of reality. But these men are your brothers—your lost, younger brothers. And if the word *integration* means anything, that is what it means: that we, with love, shall force our brothers to see themselves as they are, to cease fleeing from reality and begin to change it. For this is your home, my friend, do not be driven from it, great men have done great things here, and will again, and we can make America what America must become. It will be hard, James, but you come from sturdy, peasant stock, men who picked cotton and dammed rivers and built railroads, and, in the teeth of the most terrifying odds, achieved an unassailable and monumental dignity. You come from a long line of great poets, some of the greatest poets since Homer. One of them said, *The very time I thought I was lost, My dungeon shook and my chains fell off.*

6   You know, and I know, that the country is celebrating one hundred years of freedom one hundred years too soon. We cannot be free until they are free. God bless you, James, and Godspeed.

Your Uncle,
James

Analysis: Private and Public Audiences

Of all the genres of writing gathered in this book, letter writing may appear to be the most personal and the most intimate. As James Baldwin writes to his nephew, "I keep seeing your face."

But as the opening lines of Baldwin's letter indicate—"I have begun this letter five times and torn it up five times"—writing on such intimate terms can bring with it certain complications, especially in this case, because Baldwin actually has two audiences, his nephew and a public audience of readers.

On the one hand, Baldwin represents himself as a concerned and loving uncle writing a letter of advice to his namesake nephew, thereby invoking the sacred institution of the family as the ground to speak. On the other hand, the advice he offers his nephew—to accept white people without accepting their definitions of him—is meant to be overheard by Baldwin's other audience.

When Baldwin explains to his nephew that white people are trapped in a history of race relations they don't understand and can't escape, he is also explaining to his white readers how their own identities have been based on a belief in the inferiority of African-Americans. By using the form of a letter of advice from one family member to another, Baldwin is simultaneously offering his white readers a way to reposition themselves in relation to their own history and identities.

FOR CRITICAL INQUIRY

1. Where in the letter does Baldwin first indicate his main point and reason for writing to his nephew? Mark this passage and explain why you think he locates his main point here. How does this passage connect what comes before and what follows?

2. A good deal of the long fifth paragraph involves Baldwin's admonition to his nephew "to be clear...about the reality that lies behind the words *acceptance* and *integration*." What is the reality Baldwin alludes to here? What does he see as the relation between "acceptance" and "integration"? What assumptions have led him to this view?

3. Baldwin wrote a number of essays concerning race relations in the United States. In this instance, however, he has chosen the more personal form of a family letter addressed directly to his nephew but published for all to read.

How does this traditional letter of advice from an older family member to a younger one influence the way you read the letter? What advantages do you see in Baldwin's strategy of addressing his nephew instead of the more anonymous audience of people who read *The Fire Next Time,* in which "My Dungeon Shook: Letter to My Nephew" appeared? Are there things Baldwin can say to his nephew that he can't say directly to this audience?

READINGS: VISUAL DESIGN — LETTER OF APPEAL FROM DOCTORS WITHOUT BORDERS

Doctors Without Borders is an international organization that sends volunteer nurses, doctors, and other health care workers to war-torn countries such as Bosnia, Rwanda, Afghanistan, and Liberia. The organization was awarded the Nobel Peace Prize in 1999. The following is a letter publicizing the work of Doctors Without Borders and appealing for donations.

Analysis: The Visual Design of Letters of Appeal

The letter from Doctors Without Borders is typical of the letters of appeal that humanitarian and advocacy groups rely on to bring their work to public attention. Notice these key design features:

- **Organization name and logo:** The organization's name and logo appear at the top left in the letterhead. Logos are symbols or icons that companies, organizations, and institutions use to identify themselves visually. (Think, for example, of the Nike swoosh or the CBS eye.) Logos are meant to stick in the mind as a graphic representation of an organization and to suggest something about the ethos of the organization.

- **Listing of the board of directors and advisory board:** Running down the left side of the page are the names of Doctors Without Borders board of directors and advisory board, along with identifying titles and affiliations. Because board members are often prominent people, such listings give a letter of appeal legitimacy and authority in the reader's eye.

- **Focusing quote:** A quote from surgeon and volunteer Angie Saridakis appears centered above the text of the letter—to focus the reader's attention by establishing a sense of urgency and the main theme of the letter.

- **Selective underlining:** To reinforce the central theme of the letter, one sentence in the body of the letter has been underlined, as well as two single words, *your* and *urgently.*

- **Clinching P.S.:** You will notice that the letter does not end with Joelle Tanguy's signature but contains a final P.S. to underscore the urgency of its appeal.

DOCTORS WITHOUT BORDERS
MEDECINS SANS FRONTIERES

*"Over here, there is no such thing
as minor surgery..."*

*— American surgeon Angie Saridakis
Doctors Without Borders Rwanda volunteer*

Dear Friend:

You have read the horrifying stories. You have seen the gruesome pictures. You have heard of the unspeakable atrocities. By now, the wars in Bosnia, Rwanda, Afghanistan, Liberia and other tortured regions may seem sadly familiar.

Yet every day, men, women and children are fighting to stay alive. Thousands of them are being saved by volunteer physicians of Doctors Without Borders: the surgeons of war.

Who are these incredibly skilled men and women who freely give up time from their secure practices to work at the center of the violence, often in abhorrent conditions? Why do they do it?

They are people like you. And they do it because they care.

Like you, they have been moved by the immeasurable pain of the victims of war. They feel they must act to help save lives, restore hope and dignity and bear witness to an often indifferent world about genocide, torture and other atrocities that must be stopped.

The surgeons of war often work at the front lines, under deplorable conditions. They repair the devastating injuries of war: the bullet wounds, the missing limbs from mine explosions, the bodies hacked by hand-held knives.

I know how crucial their work is. I have seen them myself, working in Somalia and Bosnia. Arriving promptly at the site of a medical emergency, they may start operating in a local hospital, then perhaps move to a makeshift operating room in the basement if the shells and bombs begin to fall. Or they may work in a temporary tent hospital set up by Doctors Without Borders, under lights provided by our emergency generators and with clean water supplied by a system we rushed to the battlefield.

You should be proud of their successes. Because in part, your support makes it possible for them to be there.

Today, we need your support more than ever to keep the volunteer surgeons of war working where they are needed most, saving lives.

Please help us.

⊛ H495

(continued)

(continued)

Your continued support helps make possible Doctors Without Borders outreach to more than 70 countries in crisis.

Every surgeon, anesthetist, doctor and nurse that we can send, every surgical kit we can provide, every antibiotic we will administer increases the odds that more lives will be saved.

$35 can provide a basic suture kit. $50 brings infection-fighting antibiotics to treat more than 20 wounded children in Bosnia. $120 supplies a volunteer surgeon with a basic surgery kit for an unlimited number of operations. $175 provides anesthesia for 25 patients. $220 supplies a specialized surgical kit to perform six lifesaving amputations a day for the length of an entire mission. $600 gives a doctor the necessary tools to perform emergency abdominal surgery.

As you can see, your contributions have a direct, positive effect. You help save lives through your generosity.

Please, won't you continue to help Doctors Without Borders bring desperately needed medical aid—and hope—to the victims of violence and disease? On behalf of our surgeons of the war and our other volunteers, I thank you so much for your support!

Most gratefully,

Joelle Tanguy
Executive Director

P.S. If you are following the news, you know that now, more than ever, your help is urgently needed!

FOR CRITICAL INQUIRY

1. Discuss how the design features contribute to the overall effect of the Doctors Without Borders letter:

    a. What does the logo seem to represent? What does it suggest about the organization? What is the effect of including the organization's name in both English and French on the letterhead?

    b. What credentials do the people on these boards have? Why might this combination of people impress potential donors?

    c. How does the initial quote establish the theme and tone of the letter?

    d. How does the selective underlining work?

    e. How would the letter be different without the P.S. and why is this particular content used in it?

2. Notice that the actual appeal for contributions appears on the bottom of the first page of the letter. Why do you think it is located at the bottom

of that page? Explain how the writing that precedes it sets up the appeal and the function of the writing that follows it.

3. What sort of relationship does this letter want to establish with readers? What assumptions about intended readers does the letter seem to make?

4. Design the letterhead for a club, organization, or institution that you belong to or know about. You can use the Doctors Without Borders letter as a model, modifying the design to fit your organization. The letterhead should include the name and a logo that represents the spirit and aims of the organization. If appropriate, list the names of board members (or officers or sponsors).

FOR DISCUSSION AND ANALYTICAL WRITING

RHETORICAL ANALYSIS

Analyze the writer's argument in one of the letters (or, if you wish, one of the exchanges). Pay particular attention to how the writer establishes a rhetorical stance that combines the persuasive appeals of ethos, pathos, and logos. See guidelines and a sample rhetorical analysis of an argument in Chapter 3.

GENRE CHOICES

Like letters, e-mail, chat rooms, newsgroups, and listservs are forms of correspondence that enable writers to stay in touch and exchange views. Despite this similarity, there are also significant differences between letters and these new electronic genres. Draw on your own experience or the examples of electronic genres in Chapter 14 to examine the similarities and differences between letters and one of the new forms of correspondence. Take into account the occasions when it makes sense to use one or the other. When, for example, is it better to write a letter than e-mail? Or, given you have something urgent to say, when would you write a letter to the editor, to a politician, or to an organization and when would you post your views online?

GOING ONLINE

Instant Messages

Instant messages—or Internet Relay Chat (IRC)—represent a new wrinkle on e-mail. They combine the written character of letters with the immediacy of spoken conversation. In this sense, it's not really clear whether instant messages are a form of writing that takes place in real time or are more like a phone call that takes place in writing instead of speech. Or maybe the real problem is trying to fit instant messages into old distinctions between writing and speaking. In any case, we know from personal experience that the medium of communication influences the way people engage each other—that letters are different from e-mail and that both differ from telephone conversations. If you already write and receive instant messages, pay attention to how you use this medium and how it affects the way you communicate with others. If you haven't used instant messenger, get someone to help you learn how. Use your experience to draw some conclusions about how instant messages affect the process of communication and how they are similar to and different from letter writing and phone calls.

WORKING TOGETHER

Designing a Letter of Appeal

Use the letter from Doctors Without Borders as a model to write a letter of appeal. As a group, you will need first to identify an issue, a cause, or an organization you want your readers to support. Then you need to decide exactly what you will ask your readers to do. Here are some possibilities:

1. You could write a fund-raising letter for a worthy organization or a particular cause (such as a fund for victims of a recent flood, hurricane or earthquake).

2. You could call on your readers to write to government, business, or education officials asking them to change a policy or implement a new one, to release a prisoner who has been unjustly jailed (as appeals from Amnesty International do), or to support or oppose impending legislation.

3. You could call on readers to donate their time to a project worth supporting (such as mentoring at-risk teenagers, volunteering in a soup kitchen or food pantry, or attending a demonstration or rally).

Once you have determined the purpose of your letter, consider to whom you will send the letter. Who is most likely to respond to your appeal? Based on your sense of who your readers will be, consider what arguments are most likely to persuade them to take the action you call for. What information will prove persuasive? What appeals to shared values? Use this information to design the letter of appeal. Part of the letter's persuasiveness, of course, will depend on its design. How do you want the letter to look? What features of document design will make it more likely that the letter will get a sympathetic reading?

WRITING ASSIGNMENT

For this writing assignment, compose a letter. In the pages that follow, you will find exercises and ideas for deciding the kind of letter you'll write, what the letter will be about, to whom you will send it, and how your letter should be presented. There are many possibilities. You can write to someone you know, to the editor of a newspaper, to a politician, to a college officiator, or to a local community group concerning an issue of public concern. Here are some other letters you might find yourself called to write:

- A letter to your parents explaining the impact of a public event on you personally, how you make sense of it, and, if appropriate, what you have done or plan to do.

- A letter to the editor of a newspaper or magazine responding to a news story, feature article, editorial, or column that particularly moved you. Or you might raise an issue that's important to you but hasn't yet appeared in the press.

- A letter to a company or an organization protesting an advertisement or a policy.

- An open letter to a younger relative or student. You might use James Baldwin's letter to his nephew as a model here. That is, speak directly to the younger person but include a public audience as your intended readers. You might explain what it takes to survive in college or how to handle particular kinds of peer group pressures such as drinking, drugs, and sex. Or you might explain what it's like to be a scholarship athlete, a woman, an African-American, a gay or lesbian, a Latino, or a working-class student in a middle-class college.

- A letter of appeal, calling on readers to support a cause, take an action, or make a contribution. You can identify an organization or cause that you believe deserves support, and design a letter that presents the aims and activities of the organization and that calls on readers to do something—to become a member, to send a donation, to write a letter. You may want to design this letter of appeal for the Internet.

- A posting to an electronic discussion group. To do this, you will need first, of course, to follow the discussion for a week or so to catch on to the concerns and tone of the group. For information on finding discussion groups, see "Going Online: Finding Newsgroups and Listservs" in Chapter 15.

Invention

Identifying the Call to Write

Because this assignment is relatively open-ended, the first thing you'll need to do is identify something that moves you to write. Obviously, one thing that is calling on you to write is the fact that you've just been given a writing assignment in a composition course. But to write a letter that you can be proud of, you'll need to find your own reasons and your own motivation to write. Make this assignment work for you. After all, here's a chance to use the familiar form of the letter to do something you've been wanting to do anyway.

ETHICS OF WRITING

USING THE INTERNET

One of the most exciting aspects of the Internet is its capacity to open up new public forums for the exchange of ideas. A posting from an individual to a mailing list or newsgroup can connect him or her to people all over the world with an immediacy that promotes rapid feedback and response. But precisely because e-mail offers such exciting possibilities for transmitting information and ideas, it is important to use it properly—to understand what can be sent to whom under what conditions.

- **Author's permission:** Communicating on the Internet requires the same attention to copyright and intellectual property as print communication. In other words, you need to cite your sources, and if you want to forward a message written by someone else, you need to secure permission first.

- **Reader's permission:** Don't just assume that people will want to be added to a regular mailing list or newsgroup. You need to secure people's permission before adding their names. Readers are likely to resent unsolicited e-mail and feel imposed upon. Be careful not to flood cyberspace with junk e-mail.

Carnegie Mellon University's Internet site offers a collection of articles on Internet issues such as copyright, access, and politics, as well as Internet protocols. The address is <eng.hss.cmu.edu/internet/>.

If nothing immediately springs to mind, work through the following exercise. In this way, you can identify a topic you feel strongly about or find a person you've been wanting to write to.

EXERCISE

Follow as many of the steps below as you like.

1. Is there a particular subject that has been making you curious or angry? If so, you can use this letter as a way to express your opinions, or to learn more about the subject, or to respond to something someone else has written about that subject.

2. Is there something that you are learning in one of your courses that you want to tell someone about?

3. Is there something you've read recently in a newspaper or magazine that you'd like to respond to?

4. Is there a public issue in your community, either on campus, at home, or in the national or international scene that has captured your interest and made you want to participate? If so, you can become involved in that issue by participating in online conversations, by talking with local agencies about writing something for them, or by starting a conversation in any of the forums you have open to you.

Throughout this chapter there have been examples of different kinds of letters people have written. As you can see, there is a broad range of types of letters that are possible. Is there a subgenre of letters that you would like to try writing? Do any of those subgenres make you think of something you have been meaning to do? If so, you can choose to do it now.

Once you have worked through these exercises, go back through them and note those calls to write that you find most compelling. Which interest you the most?

EXERCISE

Write a statement of purpose, using these questions to guide you:

- To whom are you writing?

- What calls on you to write?

- What are you going to say?

- What do you want to accomplish in your letter?

- How do you want your reader to respond?

Understanding Your Readers

How successful you will be in eliciting the response you want from your readers depends in part on how well you understand them and your relationship to them. If you are appealing for something—whether it's money from your parents or donations to a cause you believe in—you need to figure out what might persuade your readers. If you want to irritate them or get under their skin, you need to know what buttons to push. To influence a politician, you need to know his or her interests and how you can tap into them.

EXERCISE

To gather ideas about how you can most effectively address your reader, respond to these questions:

1. On what terms do you know your reader—family, personal, institutional? Describe your relationship to the person. Is it formal or informal? How does this relationship affect what you can and cannot say in your letter? If you are writing online, how does the electronic forum of the Internet affect your relationship to your reader?

2. What is an effective way to present yourself to your reader? What will it take to establish the credibility and authority of what you have to say? What kind of personality or attitude is your reader likely to respond to?

3. What attitude is your reader likely to have toward your letter? What is your reader's interest in what you have to say? Will your reader care personally or read your letter as part of work?

4. What is your reader likely to know about the message you are sending? How much shared information is involved? How much do you need to explain?

5. What values and beliefs do you think your reader might hold about the subject of your letter? What common ground can you establish? What shared values can you appeal to?

EXERCISE

Another step in understanding your readers is to understand the forum in which your readers communicate with one another. After all, readers do bring certain expectations with them when they open a letter in the mail, read a newsletter, or log on to read their e-mails. Find some models that you can use to guide your decisions as you write your letter. Think about the following issues:

1. How long do these types of letters tend to be?

2. How do readers address one another? Do they use first names only, last names only, or some other way?

3. Do paragraphs tend to be short or long? Or do they vary greatly?

4. What level of formality do these writers tend to use?

5. If the writers are giving someone else credit for a quote or an idea, how do they handle the citation (if there is one)?

Planning

Establishing the Occasion

Letters often begin by establishing their timeliness: why they're written at that moment, in response to what call to write, to what person or people, on the basis of what relationship. Notice the ways in which writers establish the occasion in the reading selections:

■ Providing instructions in case of death [Richard Marks]

■ Explaining the timing of the letter [*Ellen* viewer]

■ Establishing authority to speak and familiarity with the topic [Kristin Tardiff, regular reader of Mark Patinkin's column]

■ Characterizing an opponent's position, expressing sense of outrage [John N. Taylor, "whiny, moralizing claptrap"]

- Making a complaint [Galen Sherwin]

- Invoking family ties as the right to speak [James Baldwin]

The need to establish the occasion of a letter—the grounds for writing it in the first place—is also true of business letters, job application letters ("I am interested in applying for the position you have advertised…"), letters to politicians and public officials ("I write to urge you to…"), letters of sympathy and condolence ("I know this is a difficult time, and I wanted you to know…"), letters of congratulations ("Congratulations, you really deserve…"), and letters of gratitude ("Thanks for the birthday present…"). In some instances, writers will make explicit their relationship to the reader—as in letters to politicians ("I have been a registered Democrat in the Third Ward for thirty years, and like my neighbors I am concerned about…") or letters of complaint ("I bought one of your [name of product] and…"). In letters where the reader knows you personally, relationships are often implied rather than stated.

In your letter, you need to design an opening that treats the occasion of the letter and your relationship to the reader. How explicitly you do this will depend on what your reader needs to hear. Politicians, businesspeople, government officials, and newspaper editors all appreciate letters that get right to the point. In letters home and other personal letters, staying in touch (as much or more than the letter's content) may be the main point of writing.

Arranging Your Material

List the points you want to make and the information you want to include in your letter. Arrange the material in an outline that consists of three sections:

- **Opening:** To establish occasion, relationship, point of letter

- **Main body:** To explain and develop the point of the letter, whether that means concentrating on one main topic or including a number of separate topics

- **Closing:** To reiterate the main point of the letter, whether that involves calling for action, firing a final salvo, reaffirming your relationship to the reader, sending regards, or thanking the reader for his or her time.

Notice the discernible pattern in Galen Sherwin's letter to PETA:

- **Opening:** Marks the occasion of the letter ("I am outraged" at the PETA ad) and says why ("insulting image").

- **Main body:** Explains why the ad is objectionable (it "reinforces oppressive beauty standards" and uses a "cheap shock tactic.")

- **Closing:** Announces the ending ("Enough already!") and points out the consequences of alienating potential supporters.

Working Draft

Once you have a list of the main points you want to make, the next step is to write a working draft. As you write, new ideas may occur to you. That's only natural. Don't censor them out by trying rigidly to follow your list of points. Instead, try to incorporate new points by connecting them to the ones you have already listed. If you can connect them, the new points probably belong in the letter. If you can't, then you'll need to think carefully about whether they really fit your letter. As you write your working draft, keep in mind the overall movement you want in your letter—from an opening that sets the occasion to a main body that explains your key points to a closing that wraps things up for the reader.

Beginnings and Endings: Using an Echo Effect

One effective way to begin and end your letter may be to use an echo effect by looping back in the ending to issues raised in your opening. This echo effect can provide a satisfying sense of closure because it reminds readers of the major themes you introduced earlier.

Joelle Tanguy uses an echo effect in her letter on behalf of Doctors Without Borders. In the opening paragraph she addresses readers directly. She assumes that her intended readers will already know about the wars in Bosnia, Rwanda, Afghanistan, Liberia, and elsewhere and will be concerned:

> You have read the horrifying stories. You have seen the gruesome pictures. You have heard of the unspeakable atrocities.

Then, after detailing the work of Doctors Without Borders in these war zones and making an appeal to readers, Tanguy closes with a P.S. that echoes the theme established in the first paragraph by referring again to her intended readers' knowledge of events in the news. This echo effect gives the ending a sense of timeliness and urgency:

> P.S. If you are following the news, you know that now, more than ever, your help is urgently needed.

You may want to try this echo effect in your own writing. Take a look at your opening and see if you find a theme that you would like to have recur in your closing. Or think about adding the suggestion of a theme to your introduction and return to it at the end of your letter.

Using Topic Sentences

Topic sentences help to guide readers by establishing a paragraph's focus of attention and by explaining how the paragraph is linked to earlier ones. The most common type of topic sentence appears at the beginning of a paragraph and thereby enables readers to anticipate what is to come in the rest of the paragraph. When writers stick to the topic they've announced in the opening topic sentence, paragraphs are easier to follow. They unify the letter, since they don't digress or run off the point. Notice how Mark Patinkin uses a topic in the following paragraph in his column about the Micheal Fay caning. The underlined first sentence (the topic sentence) establishes the focus of the paragraph, and then the rest of the sentences explain it more fully:

> *All of this is just part of the new American game of always saying, "It's not my fault."* No one, when caught, seems ready to admit having done anything wrong anymore. They just whine and appeal. As in: "Your honor, the stabbing was not my client's fault. He had a bad childhood. And was caught up in a riot at the time. In fact, he's not a criminal at all, he's one of society's victims."

Topic sentences also link paragraphs together. To keep readers oriented to the train of thought as it moves from paragraph to paragraph, writers often show how a particular paragraph's focus of attention is linked to the paragraphs that precede and follow. Richard Marks's letter to his mother, for example, uses the topic sentence in one paragraph to set up the expectation that the following paragraphs will contain specific instructions for dealing with his death. The next several paragraphs then do just that.

> There are some details I want taken care of. First of all, any money that you receive as a result of my death I want distributed in the following fashion.
>
> If you are single…
>
> I also want to be buried…
>
> That is about all, except I hope I never have to use this letter—

Sometimes topic sentences appear at the end of the paragraph instead of the beginning—as the point the writer is leading to in the rest of the paragraph. Building toward the topic sentence can give a paragraph a powerful dramatic structure. James Baldwin uses this type of dramatic structure in the second paragraph by moving from the personal—what he knows about his nephew and "your Daddy"—toward a general point about the "crime of which I accuse my country and my countrymen":

> I have known both of you all your lives, have carried your Daddy in my arms and on my shoulders, kissed and spanked him and watched him learn to walk. I don't know if you've loved anybody from that far back; if you've loved anybody that long, first as an infant, then as a child, then as a man, you gain a strange perspective on time and human pain and effort….and this is the crime of which I accuse my country and my countrymen, and for which neither I nor time nor history will ever forgive them, that they have destroyed and are destroying hundreds of thousands of lives and do not know it and do not want to know it. One can be, indeed one must strive to become, tough and philosophical concerning destruction and death, for this is what most of mankind has been best at since we have heard about man. (But remember: most of mankind is not all of mankind.) But it is not permissible that the authors of destruction should also be innocent. *It is the innocence which constitutes the crime.*

By the end of this paragraph, Baldwin has worked his way from a loving tribute about his brother to a painful critique of society's destruction. In turn, the topic sentence at the end of this paragraph sets Baldwin up to make a transition that links his "countrymen's" crime of innocence to the next paragraph:

> Now, my dear namesake, these innocent and well-meaning people, your countrymen, have caused you to be born under conditions....

Peer Commentary

Exchange working drafts with a classmate. Depending on your teacher's direction, you can do this peer commentary electronically via e-mail or a class listserv. In classes without computer access, however, you will probably want to write your comments either on your classmate's paper itself or on a separate sheet of paper. Comment on your partner's draft by responding to these questions:

1. Who is the writer addressing? What is the occasion of the letter? Where in the letter did you become aware of the writer's purpose? Be specific— is there a particular phrase, sentence, or passage that alerted you to the writer's purpose? If not, where would you like this information to be?

2. What kind of relationship does the writer seem to want to establish with the reader? How does the writer seem to want the reader to respond? How can you tell? Are there places where you think the writer should make the relationship or the desired response more explicit?

3. Does the writer address the reader in a way that makes a positive response likely or possible? Explain your answer. What could the writer do to improve the chances of making the impression he or she wants?

4. Describe the tone of the letter. What kind of personality seems to come through in the letter? What identity does the writer take on in the letter? Do you think the intended reader will respond well to it? If not, what might you change?

Revising

Review the peer commentary. Based on the response to your working draft, consider the following points to plan a revision:

1. Have you clearly defined the occasion and your purpose?

2. Does the letter establish the kind of relationship with your reader or readers that you want?

3. Do you think your readers will respond well to the way you present yourself?

4. Do you think you accomplished your purpose with your letter?

Once you are satisfied with the overall appeal of your letter, you can fine-tune your writing. You might look, for example, at your topic sentences to see if they establish focus and help readers see how ideas are linked in your letter.

Strengthening Topic Sentences for Focus and Transition

The following two paragraphs show how Michael Brody worked on his letter to the editor (the final version appears below in Writers' Workshop). Notice how he clarifies the focus of the third paragraph by rewriting the topic sentence so that it emphasizes what "readers need to understand" about the Singapore government's use of the Michael Fay case. Clarifying the focus in paragraph 3's topic sentence also strengthens the transition between paragraphs and makes it easier for readers to see how the ideas in the two paragraphs are linked:

¶2 . . . As readers point out, the crime rate in Singapore is low, the streets are safe, and there are no drive-by shootings. While this picture of Singapore may appear to be reassuring to some readers, it hides the fact that beneath a polished, secure, and business-like facade Singapore is ruled by a brutal dictatorship that keeps its people in fear by punishing not only vandalism and spraypainting but chewing gum as antisocial crimes.

Readers need to understand how the

¶3 . . . ~~Michael Fay's actions were~~ admittedly immature and illegal, ~~call~~
Michael Fay case is being used by the Singapore
~~ing for some official response. But this should not blind us to the~~
government as a lesson to its own people about the decadence of American ways
~~problems in Singapore and how the government is using the Michael~~

~~Fay case.~~ The leaders of Singapore are portraying Michael Fay as a living illustration of all that's flawed about American values of freedom and individual rights, *and his admittedly immature and illegal actions are held up as a direct consequence of the American way of life.*

Mark Patinkin and his supporters have failed to see . . . .

WRITERS' WORKSHOP

Michael Brody wrote the following letter to the editor in a first-year writing class after he read Mark Patinkin's column "Commit a Crime, Suffer the Consequences" that appeared in the *Providence Journal-Bulletin* on April 19, 1994 (he then followed with two more letters to the editor on May 3 and May 9, 1994). As you will see, entering the caning debate at this point enables Brody to summarize positions people have already taken as a way to set up his own main point. The letter to the editor is followed by a commentary Brody wrote to explain his approach to the issue.

MICHAEL BRODY, LETTER TO THE EDITOR

May w, 1994

To the Editor:

Mark Patinkin's column "Commit a crime, suffer the consequences" (4/19) has generated heated responses from readers and understandably so. For some, the sentence of six strokes of the cane, at least by American standards, does indeed seem to be "cruel and unusual punishment," no matter what Patinkin writes about Michael Fay's "whining." On the other hand, Patinkin and those readers who side with him are right that Michael Fay is the criminal in this case, not the victim, and that he deserves to suffer the consequences of his actions.

I happen to agree with readers who argue for leniency. Let Michael Fay pay for his crime by fines and a jail sentence. It worries me that some readers are willing to tolerate or even endorse caning. Obviously, these sentiments show how fed up Americans are with the problem of crime in our society. But there is a tendency in some of the pro-Patinkin letters to idealize Singapore's strong measures as a successful get-tough solution to crime. As readers point out, the crime rate in Singapore is low, the streets are safe, and there are no drive-by shootings. While this picture of Singapore may appear to be reassuring to some readers, it hides the fact that beneath a polished, secure, and business-like facade Singapore is ruled by a brutal dictatorship that keeps its people in fear by punishing not only vandalism and spraypainting but chewing gum as antisocial crimes.

Readers need to understand how the Michael Fay case is being used by the Singapore government as a lesson to its own people about the decadence of American ways. The leaders of Singapore are portraying Michael Fay as a living illustration of all that's flawed about American values of freedom and individual rights, and his admittedly immature and illegal actions are held up as direct consequences of the American way of life. Mark Patinkin and his supporters have failed to see how the Michael Fay incident is more than a matter of whether America, unlike Singapore, is soft on crime, coddles law breakers, and ignores the true victims. For the

Singapore government, the caning of Michael Fay is a stern warning to the people of Singapore against the dangers of American democracy.

What is ironic about this attempt to use Michael Fay for anti-American purposes is the fact that caning is itself not a traditional Singapore means of punishment. It's tempting to think of caning as the barbaric practice of cruel Asian despots, but in reality Singapore learned about caning from the British colonial powers who once ruled the country. The British Empire, as I'm sure Mark Patinkin is well aware, took a tough stand on law and order in the colonies and routinely crushed native movements for freedom and independence. I wish Mark Patinkin and others who are properly concerned about crime would consider the lessons Singapore leaders learned from their former masters about how to control and intimidate those they rule. Caning is not a matter of different national customs, as some people make it out to be. Nor is it an extreme but understandable response to crime in the streets. In Singapore, caning is part of both a repressive judicial system and a calculated propaganda campaign to discredit democratic countries and silence dissent.

Michael Brody
Worcester, MA

MICHAEL BRODY'S COMMENTARY

When I read Mark Patinkin's column, I got angry and wanted to denounce him as a fascist. Then I read the letters readers had written opposing or supporting Patinkin's point of view, and they made me realize that I didn't want to follow them because they all seemed to be too emotional, just gut responses. I wanted to find a different approach to the whole caning incident so that I could raise an issue that was different or had been overlooked.

Now I must admit that when I first heard about the sentence of caning, I thought it was barbaric, probably something typical of Asian dictatorships. I thought of the massacre at Tienamien Square, and I dimly recalled what I had heard when I was young about how the Chinese Communists tortured Catholic missionaries, stuff like bamboo slivers under the fingernails. Then I read somewhere that caning was brought to Singapore by the British in colonial days, and I started to think along new lines. It occurred to me that maybe the caning wasn't just about crime but had something to do with how governments ruled their people.

As I read more in the newspapers, *Time,* and *Newsweek* about the incident, I was shocked to discover how Michael Fay was being used by Singapore leaders to build up anti-American sentiment, to paint America as a permissive society that coddled its criminals. I decided that I'd try to write something that looked at how the case was being used by

Singapore's rulers. The more I thought about it, this seemed to give me an angle to go beyond agreeing or disagreeing with Patinkin's column and still have something interesting to say.

When I was getting ready to write, I made a quick outline of my points. I wanted to sound reasonable so I decided to concede that both sides, for or against caning, had some valid points. I decided to show this in my opening and wait until the second paragraph to indicate where I was coming from. I wanted to create the effect that there's this debate going on, which I figured readers would know about and already have their own opinions about, but that I had an angle people maybe hadn't thought about. So I tried to get this point to emerge in the second paragraph and then drive it home at the beginning of the third paragraph with the sentence that starts "Readers need to understand..."

That sentence set me up to give my own analysis of the incident and of how Patinkin and the pro-caning people failed to see the full political picture. I decided to leave the idea that caning came from British colonial powers until the end as my clincher. I figured this would do two things. First, it would surprise people, who like me thought caning was a barbaric Asian punishment. Second, it would have an emotional charge because I assumed most people would be against colonialism, especially British colonialism, given that America had to fight England for our independence. Besides I'm Irish, and I know a lot of people where I live are against the British in Ireland, and I knew they'd be against anything associated with the British empire.

I'm not totally sure the irony I talk about in the opening line of the last paragraph works. I remember learning about irony in English class in high school, and how funny or odd it is when things don't turn out the way you expected. So I wanted to throw that in, to make readers feel, well I thought it was one way but when you look at it again, it's another way. I thought this might work in the very end to show that caning is not just this (a barbaric national custom) or that (an extreme form of punishment) but also a form of political intimidation.

WORKSHOP QUESTIONS

1. When you first read Michael Brody's letter to the editor, at what point did you become aware of his perspective on the caning debate? Is it just a matter of being for or against caning? Note the sentence or passage that enabled you to see where Brody is coming from.

2. Brody devotes considerable space in the first two paragraphs to presenting positions people have already taken on the caning debate. What kind of relationship does he seem to want to establish with his readers by doing so?

3. Describe the tone Brody uses in the letter. How does it compare to the tone in Mark Patinkin's column and in the letters to the editor from Kristin Tardiff and John N. Taylor? Do you think Brody's tone works well? Explain your response.

4. Reread Brody's commentary. If you could talk to him, how would you respond to what he says about composing his letter?

REFLECTING ON YOUR WRITING

Use the commentary Michael Brody wrote as a model for writing your own account of how you planned and composed the letter you wrote. Explain how you defined the call to write and how you positioned yourself in relation to your readers, your topic, and what others had already said about your topic (if that applies to your letter). Notice that Brody explains how he developed his own position by considering what others had said and reading newspapers and magazines on the Michael Fay incident. Explain, as Brody does, in a step-by-step way how you composed your letter, what effects you were trying to achieve, and what problems or issues emerged for you along the way. Indicate any aspects of the letter that you're not certain about. Add anything else you'd like to say.

A CLOSING NOTE

The point of writing a letter is to communicate with someone. While your instructor and classmates can be helpful readers, they may not be the real readership for the letter you have written. This audience may be located outside of your writing classroom. If this is the case, send your letter to the audience it is intended for.

CHAPTER FIVE

Memoirs: Recalling Personal Experience

THINKING ABOUT THE GENRE

Writing a *memoir,* as the word itself suggests, involves memory work. Memoirists draw on their pasts, looking back at events, people, and places that are important to them, in order to re-create, in written language, moments or episodes of lived experience. This re-creation of particular experiences distinguishes memoirs from the genre of autobiographies, which seek to encompass an entire life. But memoirists don't just re-create moments of experience—they seek to imbue them with a significance readers will understand.

The call to write memoirs comes in part from the desire people have to keep track of the past and to see how their lives have intersected with public events. This impulse to remember is what leads people to take photographs, compile scrapbooks, and save letters and keepsakes of all sorts. Long after a particular experience is over, these objects help remind us of how things were at that moment. They also help remind us of how we were. You may have experienced how objects you've saved give you a sense of connection to your past.

This sense of connection between present and past is at the center of memoir writing. By re-creating experiences from the past and exploring their significance, memoirists can begin to identify the continuities and discontinuities in their own lives. Writing memoirs is at least in part an act of self-discovery, of clarifying where the writer has come from and what he or she has become. The memoir writer is both participant and observer: On the one hand, the writer often appears as a character in the memoir, a participant in the events that unfold. On the other hand, the writer is also an observer who comments on and interprets these unfolding events, giving them a shape and meaning for the present. Writing memoirs thereby puts the writer in a complicated relationship to his or her own experience.

Because memoirs are not simply reports from the past in which the events speak for themselves, writing memoirs also puts the writer in a complicated relationship to readers, a relationship that carries certain risks. For one thing, self-disclosure leaves the writer vulnerable to the judgments of readers. For another, there is the risk of seeming self-indulgent or sentimental. The memoir writer, after all, is asking readers to devote time and attention to his or her reminiscences.

The solution to this last potential problem lies in an aspect of memoirs already mentioned: Successful memoirs make personal experiences significant to others. Thus, the reader of the memoir isn't peering at intimate details of the writer's past as a mere voyeur but rather is gaining insights into other times and places, as well as into the writer's personality. A memoir aims for understanding—to help readers come to terms with the writer's experience of the past and its meanings for the present.

One strategy memoir writers often use to this end is to focus on details that reveal deeper meanings to themselves and to readers. For memoirist Patricia Hampl, details such as a "black boxy Ford" in a photograph, a "hat worn in 1952," an aunt polishing her toenails, and the "booths of the Gopher Grill" at the University of Minnesota can move writers to recover and convey to readers what might otherwise be overlooked in their pasts—the "intimate fragments…that bind even obscure lives to history." Memoir writers can take an immediately recognizable incident from, say, childhood or adolescence—such as visiting grandparents, going on a first date, moving to a new town, or going away to college—and bring out meanings that readers may not have suspected were there. Writers may focus on moments of revelation, showing how crises and insights have challenged and changed their perceptions, expectations, and values.

Another strategy that writers typically use in memoirs is to put their experiences into a larger historical or cultural context. That is, they present their pasts in part as exemplifying and shedding light on something larger—what it meant, say, to grow up in the Great Depression or during the 1960s. Thus, as you'll see, Henry Louis Gates, Jr., begins "In the Kitchen" with a personal scene from childhood that anchors a larger discussion and comes to evoke a whole way of life in African-American communities.

The point here is that as detailed, specific, and filled with sensory impressions as successful memoirs typically are, it is the larger context that gives these details their significance. To put it another way, memoirs offer writers a way to show how the details of everyday life take on wider meanings when located in a wider framework.

Ultimately, people are called on to write memoirs not only to establish a connection to the past and to inform and entertain readers about the past but also from a sense of responsibility to the past, from a desire to bear witness to things that might otherwise be overlooked or forgotten. In many respects, memoirs derive their unique power to move readers from the way writers position themselves in the present in order to bear witness to the past, thus revealing the secrets and unsuspected meanings of ordinary lives that turn out to be not so ordinary after all.

Consider Patricia Hampl's point that memories are stored in the details of photos, a particular hat, and the booths at a campus hangout. Write a list of things that somehow capture an important moment or period in your life—such as photos, popular songs, hairstyles, articles of clothing, movies, posters, stuffed animals, toys, letters, cards, newspaper clippings, school or team uniforms, art objects, or souvenirs. Compare your list to your classmates' lists. What generalizations can you make about the capacity of things to hold and evoke memories?

READINGS

Gary Soto, "Black Hair"

Gary Soto, poet, fiction writer, and essayist, is the author of many collections for adults and young readers, including "Black Hair" (1985), *A Summer Life* (1990), *Baseball in April* (1990), and *Buried Onions* (1997). The following selection appears in his book of essays *Living Up the Street* (1985). He is a member of the Royal Chicano Navy, a cultural group in Fresno, California, where he was born and raised.

Black Hair
GARY SOTO

1   There are two kinds of work: One uses the mind and the other uses muscle. As a kid I found out about the latter. I'm thinking of the summer of 1969 when I was a seventeen-year-old runaway who ended up in Glendale, California, working for Valley Tire Factory. To answer an ad in the newspaper I walked miles in the afternoon sun, my stomach slowly knotting on a doughnut that was breakfast, my teeth like bright candles gone yellow.

2   I walked in the door sweating and feeling ugly because my hair was still stiff from a swim at the Santa Monica beach the day before. Jules, the accountant and part owner, looked droopily through his bifocals at my application and then at me. He tipped his cigar in the ashtray, asked my age as if he didn't believe I was seventeen, but finally, after a moment of silence, said, "Come back tomorrow. Eight-thirty."

3   I thanked him, left the office, and went around to the chain-link fence to watch the workers heave tires into a bin; others carted uneven stacks of tires on hand trucks. Their faces were black from tire dust, and when they talked—or cussed—their mouths showed a bright pink.

4   From there I walked up a commercial street, past a cleaners, a motorcycle shop, and a gas station where I washed my face and hands; before leaving I took

a bottle that hung on the side of the Coke machine, filled it with water, and stopped it with a scrap of paper and a rubber band.

5   The next morning I arrived early at work. The assistant foreman, a potbellied Hungarian, showed me a time card and how to punch in. He showed me the Coke machine and the locker room with its slimy shower, and also pointed out the places where I shouldn't go: the ovens where the tires were recapped and the customer service area, which had a slashed couch, a coffee table with greasy magazines, and an ashtray. He introduced me to Tully, a fat man with one ear who worked the buffers that resurfaced the whitewalls. I was handed an apron and a face mask and shown how to use the buffer: Lift the tire and center it, inflate it with a foot pedal, press the buffer against the white band until cleaned, and then deflate and blow off the tire with an air hose.

6   With a paintbrush he stirred a can of industrial preserver. "Then slap this blue stuff on." While he was talking a coworker came up quietly behind him and goosed him with the air hose. Tully jumped as if he had been struck by a bullet and then turned around cussing and cupping his genitals in his hands as the other worker walked away calling out foul names. When Tully turned to me, smiling his gray teeth, I lifted my mouth into a smile because I wanted to get along. He has to be on my side, I thought. He's the one who'll tell the foreman how I'm doing.

7   I worked carefully that day, setting the tires on the machine as if they were babies, because it was easy to catch a finger in the rim that expanded to inflate the tire. At the day's end we swept up the tire dust and emptied the trash into bins.

8   At five the workers scattered for their cars and motorcycles while I crossed the street to wash at a burger stand. My hair was stiff with dust and my mouth showed pink against the backdrop of my dirty face. I ordered a hotdog and walked slowly in the direction of the abandoned house where I had stayed the night before. I lay under the trees and within minutes was asleep. When I woke my shoulders were sore, and my eyes burned when I squeezed the lids together.

9   From the backyard I walked dully through a residential street, and as evening came on, the TV glare in the living rooms and the headlights of passing cars showed against the blue drift of dusk. I saw two children coming up the street with snow cones, their tongues darting at the packed ice. I saw a boy with a peach and wanted to stop him but felt embarrassed by my hunger. I walked for an hour, only to return and discover the house lit brightly. Behind the fence I heard voices and saw a flashlight poking at the garage door. A man on the back steps mumbled something about the refrigerator to the one with the flashlight.

10   I waited for them to leave but had the feeling they wouldn't because there was a commotion of furniture being moved. Tired, even more desperate, I started walking again with a great urge to kick things and tear the day from my life. I felt weak and my mind kept drifting because of hunger. I crossed the street to a gas station where I sipped at the water fountain and searched the Coke machine for change. I started walking again, first up a commercial street, then into a residential area where I lay down on someone's lawn and replayed a scene at home—my mother crying at the kitchen table, my stepfather yelling with food in his mouth. They're cruel, I thought, and warned myself that I should never forgive them. How could they do this to me?

11   When I got up from the lawn it was late. I searched out a place to sleep and found an unlocked car that seemed safe. In the backseat, with my shoes off, I fell asleep but woke up startled about four in the morning when the owner, a nurse on her way to work, opened the door. She got in and was about to start the engine when I raised my head to explain my presence. She screamed so loudly when I said "I'm sorry" that I sprinted from the car with my shoes in hand. Her screams faded, then stopped altogether, as I ran down the block, hid behind a trash bin, and waited for a police siren to sound. Nothing. I crossed the street to a church where I slept stiffly on cardboard in the balcony.

12   I woke up feeling tired and greasy. It was early and a few streetlights were still lit, the east growing pink with dawn. I washed myself from a garden hose and returned to the church to break into what looked like a kitchen. Paper cups, plastic spoons, a coffee pot littered on a table. I found a box of Nabisco crackers and ate until I was full.

13   At work I spent the morning at the buffer, but was then told to help Iggy, an old Mexican who was responsible for choosing tires that could be recapped without the risk of exploding at high speeds. Every morning a truck would deliver used tires, and after I unloaded them Iggy would step among the tires to inspect them for punctures and rips on the sidewalls.

14   With yellow chalk he marked circles and Xs to indicate damage and called out "junk." Tires that could be recapped got a "goody" from Iggy, and I placed them on my hand truck. When I had a stack of eight I kicked the truck at an angle and balanced off to another work area, where Iggy again inspected the tires, scratching Xs and calling out "junk."

15   Iggy worked only until three in the afternoon, at which time he went to the locker room to wash and shave and to dress in a two-piece suit. When he came out he glowed with a bracelet, watch, rings, and a shiny fountain pen in his breast pocket. His shoes sounded against the asphalt. He was the image of a banker stepping into sunlight with millions on his mind. He said a few low words to workers with whom he was friendly and none to people like me.

16   I was seventeen, stupid because I couldn't figure out the difference between an F78 14 and a 750 14 at sight. Iggy shook his head when I brought him the wrong tires, especially since I had expressed interest in being his understudy. "Mexican, how can you be so stupid?" he would yell at me, slapping a tire from my hands. But within weeks I learned a lot about tires, from sizes and makes to how they are molded in iron forms to how Valley stole from other companies. Now and then we received a truckload of tires, most of them new or nearly new, and they were taken to our warehouse in the back, where the serial numbers were ground off with a sander. On those days the foreman handed out Cokes and joked with us as we worked to get the numbers off.

17   Most of the workers were Mexican or black, though a few redneck whites worked there. The base pay was a dollar sixty-five but the average was three dollars. Of the black workers, I knew Sugar Daddy the best. His body carried 250 pounds and armfuls of scars, and he had a long knife that made me jump when he brought it out from his boot without warning. At one time he had been a singer

and had cut a record in 1967 called *Love's Chance,* which broke into the R & B charts. But nothing came of it. No big contract, no club dates, no tours. He made very little from record sales, only enough for an operation to pull a steering wheel from his gut when, drunk and mad at a lady friend, he slammed his Mustang into a row of parked cars.

18   "Touch it," he smiled at me one afternoon as he raised his shirt, his black belly kinked with hair. Scared, I traced the scar that ran from his chest to the left of his belly button, and I was repelled but hid my disgust.

19   Among the Mexicans I had few friends because I was different, a pocho[1] who spoke bad Spanish. At lunch they sat in tires and laughed over burritos, looking up at me to laugh even harder. I also sat in tires while nursing a Coke and felt dirty and sticky because I was still living on the street and had not had a real bath in over a week. Nevertheless, when the border patrol came to round up the nationals, I ran with them as they scrambled for the fence or hid among the tires behind the warehouse. The foreman, who thought I was an undocumented worker, yelled at me to run, to get away. I did just that. At the time it seemed fun because there was no risk, only a good-hearted feeling of hide-and-seek, and besides, it meant an hour away from work on company time. When the police left we came back, and some of the nationals made up stories of how they were almost caught—how they outraced the police. Some of the stories were so convoluted and unconvincing that everyone laughed and shouted "mentiras,"[2] especially when one described how he overpowered a policeman, took his gun away, and sold the patrol car. We laughed and he laughed, happy to be there to make up such a story.

20   If work was difficult, so were the nights. I still had not gathered enough money to rent a room, so I spent the nights sleeping in parked cars or in the church balcony. After a week I found a newspaper ad for a room for rent, phoned, and was given directions. Finished with work, I walked the five miles down Mission Road looking back into the traffic with my thumb out. No rides. After eight hours of handling tires I was frightening to drivers, I suppose, since they seldom looked at me; if they did, it was a quick glance. For the next six weeks I would try to hitchhike, but the only person to stop was a Mexican woman who gave me two dollars to take the bus. I told her it was too much and that no bus ran from Mission Road to where I lived, but she insisted that I keep the money and trotted back to her idling car. It must have hurt her to see me day after day walking in the heat and looking very much the dirty Mexican to the many minds that didn't know what it meant to work at hard labor. That woman knew. Her eyes met mine as she opened the car door, and there was a tenderness that was surprisingly true—one for which you wait for years but when it comes it doesn't help. Nothing changes. You continue on in rags, with the sun still above you.

---

[1]Mexican slang meaning "outsider."
[2]Spanish, meaning "lies."

21   I rented a room from a middle-aged couple whose lives were a mess. She was a schoolteacher and he was a fireman. A perfect setup, I thought. But during my stay there they would argue for hours in their bedroom.

22   When I rang at the front door both Mr. and Mrs. Van Deusen answered and didn't bother to disguise their shock at how awful I looked. But they let me in all the same. Mrs. Van Deusen showed me around the house, from the kitchen and bathroom to the living room with its grand piano. On her fingers she counted out the house rules as she walked me to my room. It was a girl's room with lace curtains, scenic wallpaper of a Victorian couple enjoying a stroll, a canopied bed, and stuffed animals in a corner. Leaving, she turned and asked if she could do laundry for me. Feeling shy and hurt, I told her no; perhaps the next day. She left and I undressed to take a bath, exhausted as I sat on the edge of the bed probing my aches and my bruised places. With a towel around my waist I hurried down the hallway to the bathroom where Mrs. Van Deusen had set out an additional towel with a tube of shampoo. I ran water into the tub and sat on the closed toilet, watching the steam curl toward the ceiling. When I lowered myself into the tub I felt my body sting. I soaped a washcloth and scrubbed my arms until they lightened, even glowed pink, but I still looked unwashed around my neck and face no matter how hard I rubbed. Back in the room I sat in bed reading a magazine, happy and thinking of no better luxury than a girl's sheets, especially after nearly two weeks of sleeping on cardboard at the church.

23   I was too tired to sleep, so I sat at the window watching the neighbors move about in pajamas, and, curious about the room, looked through the bureau drawers to search out personal things—snapshots, a messy diary, and high-school yearbook. I looked up the Van Deusen's daughter, Barbara, and studied her face as if I recognized her from my own school—a face that said "promise," "college," "nice clothes in the closet." She was a skater and a member of the German Club; her greatest ambition was to sing at the Hollywood Bowl.

24   After a while I got into bed, and as I drifted toward sleep I thought about her. In my mind I played a love scene again and again and altered it slightly each time. She comes home from college and at first is indifferent to my presence in her home, but finally I overwhelm her with deep pity when I come home hurt from work, with blood on my shirt. Then there was another version: Home from college she is immediately taken with me, in spite of my work-darkened face, and invites me into the family car for a milkshake across town. Later, back at the house, we sit in the living room talking about school until we're so close I'm holding her hand. The truth of the matter was that Barbara did come home for a week but was bitter toward her parents for taking in boarders (two others besides me). During that time she spoke to me only twice: Once, while searching the refrigerator, she asked if we had any mustard; the other time she asked if I had seen her car keys.

25   But it was a place to stay. Work had become more and more difficult. I worked not only with Iggy but also with the assistant foreman, who was in charge of unloading trucks. After they backed in I hopped on top to pass the tires down, bouncing them on the tailgate to give them an extra spring so they would be less difficult to handle on the other end. Each truck was weighted down with more than

two hundred tires, each averaging twenty pounds, so that by the time the truck was emptied and swept clean I glistened with sweat and my T-shirt stuck to my body. I blew snot threaded with tire dust onto the asphalt, indifferent to the customers who watched from the waiting room.

26   The days were dull. I did what there was to do from morning until the bell sounded at five; I tugged, pulled, and cussed at tires until I was listless and my mind drifted and caught on small things, from cold sodas to shoes to stupid talk about what we would do with a million dollars. I remember unloading a truck with Hamp, a black man.

27   "What's better than a sharp lady?" he asked me as I stood sweaty on a pile of junked tires. "Water. With ice," I said.

28   He laughed with his mouth open wide. With his fingers he pinched the sweat from his chin and flicked at me. "You be too young, boy. A woman can make you a god."

29   As a kid I had chopped cotton and picked grapes, so I knew work. I knew the fatigue and the boredom and the feeling that there was a good possibility that you might have to do such work for years, if not for a lifetime. In fact, as a kid I had imagined a dark fate: to marry Mexican poor, work Mexican hours, and in the end die a Mexican death, broke and in despair.

30   But this job at Valley Tire Company confirmed that there was something worse than fieldwork, and I was doing it. We were all doing it, from the foreman to the newcomers like me, and what I felt heaving tires for eight hours a day was felt by everyone—black, Mexican, redneck. We all despised those hours but didn't know what else to do. The workers were unskilled, some undocumented and fearful of deportation, and all struck with uncertainty at what to do with their lives. Although everyone bitched about work, no one left. Some had worked there for twelve years; some had sons working there. Few quit; no one was ever fired. It amazed me that no one gave up when the border patrol jumped from their vans, batons in hand, because I couldn't imagine any work that could be worse—or any life. What was out there, in the world, that made men run for the fence in fear?

31   Iggy was the only worker who seemed sure of himself. After five hours of "junking," he brushed himself off, cleaned up in the washroom, and came out gleaming with an elegance that humbled the rest of us. Few would look him straight in the eye or talk to him in our usual stupid way because he was so much better. He carried himself as a man should—with Old World "dignity"—while the rest of us muffed our jobs and talked dully about dull things as we worked. From where he worked in his open shed he would now and then watch us with his hands on his hips. He would shake his head and click his tongue in disgust.

32   The rest of us lived dismally. I often wondered what the others' homes were like; I couldn't imagine that they were much better than our workplace. No one indicated that his outside life was interesting or intriguing. We all looked defeated and contemptible in our filth at the day's end. I imagined the average welcome at home: Rafael, a Mexican national who had worked at Valley for five years, returned to a beaten house full of kids dressed in mismatched clothes and playing kick the can. As for Sugar Daddy, he returned home to a stuffy room where he would read and reread

old magazines. He ate potato chips, drank beer, and watched TV. There was no grace in dipping socks into a washbasin where later he would wash his cup and plate.

33   There was no grace at work. It was all ridicule. The assistant foreman drank Cokes in front of the newcomers as they laced tires in the afternoon sun. Knowing that I had a long walk home, Rudy, the college student, passed me waving and yelling "Hello" as I started down Mission Road on the way home to eat out of cans. Even our plump secretary got into the act by wearing short skirts and flaunting her milky legs. If there was love, it was ugly. I'm thinking of Tully and an older man whose name I can no longer recall fondling one another in the washroom. I had come in cradling a smashed finger to find them pressed together in the shower, their pants undone and partly pulled down. When they saw me they smiled with their pink mouths but didn't bother to push away.

34   How we arrived at such a place is a mystery to me. Why anyone would stay for years is an even deeper concern. You showed up, but from where? What broken life? What ugly past? The foreman showed you the Coke machine, the washroom, and the yard where you'd work. When you picked up a tire, you were amazed at the black it could give off.

Analysis: A Moment of Revelation

Much of the power of memoirs, as Gary Soto's "Black Hair" illustrates, is their capacity to bring to life a moment of personal experience. Notice that Soto provides little information about why he was a runaway or how his experience at the Valley Tire Factory ended. Instead, he concentrates the reader's attention on the physical experience of work—the dirt, the noise, the smells, the sweat and bodily exhaustion of a day's labor. Soto seems to want us as readers to feel this remembered moment as intensely as he does. But he also wants the intensity of his recalled experience to unlock its significance—for readers and for himself. As the best memoirs do, Soto's "Black Hair" turns a moment of personal experience into a moment of revelation. Looking back on himself as a seventeen-year-old, Soto uses his account of this moment in the past to explain what he found out about work.

FOR CRITICAL INQUIRY

1. In the opening lines of his memoir, Gary Soto explains that there are "two kinds of work" and that he found out about work that "uses muscle" when he was a seventeen-year-old runaway. When you reach the end of the memoir do you feel he has adequately explained his point? How does Soto's account of his experience develop the point about work with which he begins?

2. The final six paragraphs seem to offer Soto's closing evaluation of his experience. Explain the conclusions he appears to reach at the end. Do they seem justified based on his account of his experience?

3. Soto does not tell us why he was a runaway or how his experience working at the Valley Tire Factory ended. Why do you think he has decided not to provide this information? How does it affect the way you read his memoir?

4. Consider the title of the memoir "Black Hair." What are the various meanings this title might hold?

Annie Dillard, *An American Childhood*

Annie Dillard is a poet, novelist, essayist, and memoirist. She won the Pulitzer Prize in 1974 for *Pilgrim at Tinker Creek,* an account of the year she spent observing nature in the Roanoke Valley of Virginia. The following selection is a chapter from *An American Childhood,* her memoir of growing up in Pittsburgh.

An American Childhood
ANNIE DILLARD

1   Some boys taught me to play football. This was fine sport. You thought up a new strategy for every play and whispered it to the others. You went out for a pass, fooling everyone. Best, you got to throw yourself mightily at someone's running legs. Either you brought him down or you hit the ground flat out on your chin, with your arms empty before you. It was all or nothing. If you hesitated in fear, you would miss and get hurt; you would take a hard fall while the kid got away, or you would get kicked in the face while the kid got away. But if you flung yourself whole-heartedly at the back of his knees—if you gathered and joined body and soul and pointed them diving fearlessly—then you likely wouldn't get hurt, and you'd stop the ball. Your fate, and your team's score, depended on your concentration and courage. Nothing girls did could compare with it.

2   Boys welcomed me at baseball, too, for I had, through enthusiastic practice, what was weirdly known as a boy's arm. In winter, in the snow, there was neither baseball not football, so the boys and I threw snowballs at passing cars. I got in trouble throwing snowballs, and have seldom been happier since.

3   On one weekday morning after Christmas, six inches of new snow had just fallen. We were standing up to our boot tops in snow on a front yard on trafficked Reynolds Street, waiting for cars. The cars traveled Reynolds Street slowly and evenly; they were targets all but wrapped in red ribbons, cream puffs. We couldn't miss.

4   I was seven; the boys were eight, nine, and ten. The oldest two Fahey boys were there—Mikey and Peter—polite blond boys who lived near me on Lloyd Street, and who already had four brothers and sisters. My parents approved of Mikey and Peter Fahey. Chuckie McBride was there, a rough kid, and Billy Paul and Mackie Kean too, from across Reynolds, where the boys grew up dark and furious, grew up skinny, knowing, and skilled. We had all drifted from our houses that morning looking for action, and had found it here on Reynolds Street.

5   It was cloudy but cold. The cars' tires laid behind them on the snowy street a complex trail of beige chunks like crenellated castle walls. I had stepped on some earlier; they squeaked. We could have wished for more traffic. When a car came, we all popped it one. In the intervals between cars we reverted to the natural solitude of children.

6   I started making an iceball—a perfect iceball, from perfectly white snow, perfectly spherical, and squeezed perfectly translucent so no snow remained all the way through. (The Fahey boys and I considered it unfair actually to throw an iceball at somebody, but it had been known to happen.)

7   I had just embarked on the iceball project when we heard tire chains come clanking from afar. A black Buick was moving toward us down the street. We all spread out, banged together some regular snowballs, took aim, and, when the Buick drew nigh, fired.

8   A soft snowball hit the driver's windshield right before the driver's face. It made a smashed star with a hump in the middle.

9   Often, of course, we hit our target, but this time, the only time in all of life, the car pulled over and stopped. Its wide black door opened; a man got out of it, running. He didn't even close the car door.

10   He ran after us, and we ran away from him, up the snowy Reynolds sidewalk. At the corner, I looked back; incredibly, he was still after us. He was in city clothes: a suit and tie, street shoes. Any normal adult would have quit, having sprung us into flight and made his point. This man was gaining on us. He was a thin man, all action. All of a sudden, we were running for our lives.

11   Wordless, we split up. We were on our turf; we could lose ourselves in the neighborhood backyards, everyone for himself. I paused and considered. Everyone had vanished except Mikey Fahey, who was just rounding the corner of a yellow brick house. Poor Mikey, I trailed him. The driver of the Buick sensibly picked the two of us to follow. The man apparently had all day.

12   He chased Mikey and me around the yellow house and up a backyard path we knew by heart: under a low tree, up a bank, through a hedge, down some snowy steps, and across the grocery store's delivery driveway. We smashed through a gap in another hedge, entered a scruffy backyard and ran around its back porch and tight between houses to Edgerton Avenue; we ran across Edgerton to an alley and up our own sliding woodpile to the Hall's front yard; he kept coming. We ran up Lloyd Street and wound through mazy backyards toward the steep hilltop at Willard and Lang.

13   He chased us silently, block after block. He chased us silently over picket fences, through thorny hedges, between houses, around garbage cans, and across streets. Every time I glanced back, choking for breath, I expected he would have quit. He must have been as breathless as we were. His jacket strained over his body. It was an immense discovery, pounding into my hot head with every sliding, joyous step, that this ordinary adult evidently knew what I thought only children who trained at football knew: that you have to fling yourself at what you're doing, you have to point yourself, forget yourself, aim, dive.

14   Mikey and I had nowhere to go, in our own neighborhood or out of it, but away from this man who was chasing us. He impelled us forward; we compelled him to follow our route. The air was cold; every breath tore my throat. We kept running, block after block; we kept improvising, backyard after backyard, running a frantic course and choosing it simultaneously, failing always to find small places or hard places to slow him down, and discovering always, exhilarated, dismayed, that only bare speed could save us—for he would never give up, this man—and we were losing speed.

15   He chased us through the backyard labyrinths of ten blocks before he caught us by our jackets. He caught us and we all stopped.

16   We three stood staggering, half blinded, coughing, in an obscure hilltop backyard: a man in his twenties, a boy, a girl. He had released our jackets, our pursuer, our captor, our hero: he knew we weren't going anywhere. We all played by the rules. Mikey and I unzipped our jackets. I pulled off my sopping mittens. Our tracks multiplied in the backyard's new snow. We had been breaking new snow all morning. We didn't look at each other. I was cherishing my excitement. The man's lower pants legs were wet; his cuffs were full of snow and there was a prow of snow beneath them on his shoes and socks. Some trees bordered the little flat backyard, some messy winter trees. There was no one around: a clearing in a grove, and we the only players.

17   It was a long time before he could speak. I had some difficulty at first recalling why we were there. My lips felt swollen; I couldn't see out of the sides of my eyes; I kept coughing.

18   "You stupid kids," he began perfunctorily.

19   We listened perfunctorily indeed, if we listened at all, for the chewing out was redundant, a mere formality, and beside the point. The point was that he had chased us passionately without giving up, and so he had caught us. Now he came down to earth. I wanted the glory to last forever.

20   But how could the glory have lasted forever? We could have run through every backyard in North America until we got to Panama. But when he trapped us at the lip of the Panama Canal, what precisely could he have done to prolong the drama of the chase and cap its glory? I brooded about this for the next few years. He could only have fried Mikey Fahey and me in boiling oil, say, or dismembered us piecemeal, or staked us to anthills. None of which I really wanted, and none of which any adult was likely to do, even in the spirit of fun. He could only chew us out there in the Panamanian jungle, after months or years of exalting pursuit. He could only begin, "You stupid kids," and continue in his ordinary Pittsburgh accent with his normal righteous anger and the usual common sense.

21   If in that snowy backyard the driver of the black Buick had cut off our heads, Mikey's and mine, I would have died happy, for nothing has required so much of me since as being chased all over Pittsburgh in the middle of winter—running terrified, exhausted—by this sainted, skinny, furious redheaded man who wished to have a word with us. I don't know how he found his way back to his car.

Analysis: Re-creating Experience

At their best, memoirs re-create experience so that readers can actually feel what it was like to be alive at that moment in the writer's life. In this chapter from *An American Childhood,* Annie Dillard isn't just recalling the time she and some friends were out throwing snowballs and this guy stopped and chased them around the neighborhood. Instead she takes us with her as she flees from the man pursuing her. To make the chase come alive, Dillard has re-created the young girl she was at the age of seven. Accordingly, as readers, we experience what takes place from the young girl's perspective and share her sense of excitement and exhilaration. In many respects, this memoir hinges on Dillard's ability to shape the person she once was into a believable character.

FOR CRITICAL INQUIRY

1. In the opening paragraphs, Dillard talks about playing football and baseball. What does this reveal about the character of Dillard as a seven-year-old? How does this information prepare readers for what's to come?

2. Dillard doesn't just tell a story about something that happened. She invests the experience with meaning: "I got in trouble throwing snowballs, and have seldom been happier since." What made her so happy? Point to particular words, sentences, and passages where she develops the meaning of the experience.

3. In the final paragraph, Dillard describes the man who chased her as "this sainted, skinny, furious red-headed man who wanted to have a word with us." How do the adjectives *sainted, skinny, furious,* and *red-headed* go together in her description? Why does she use the word *sainted*?

4. One could argue that throwing snowballs is dangerous and irresponsible behavior. In fact, that is probably what the man who chased Dillard and her friends was thinking. Dillard avoids the issue, however, and puts the emphasis instead on her "immense discovery." What assumptions about readers' reactions does she seem to count on in doing so?

Henry Louis Gates, Jr., "In the Kitchen"

This selection from Henry Louis Gates, Jr.'s memoir, *Colored People,* first appeared as an essay in the *New Yorker.* Gates is a professor of English, and the chairman of Afro-American Studies at Harvard University, as well as one of the leading literary and cultural critics of our time. As you will see, this memoir takes Gates from the 1950s to the present and from the kitchen of his childhood home in Piedmont, West Virginia, to the island of Zanzibar, off the coast of East Africa. Throughout the essay, Gates offers memories and reflections about the cultural meanings of hair-straightening in African-American communities.

In the Kitchen

HENRY LOUIS GATES, JR.

1   We always had a gas stove in the kitchen, in our house in Piedmont, West Virginia, where I grew up. Never electric, though using electric became fashionable in Piedmont in the sixties, like using Crest toothpaste rather than Colgate, or watching Huntley and Brinkley rather than Walter Cronkite. But not us: gas, Colgate, and good ole Walter Cronkite, come what may. We used gas partly out of loyalty to Big Mom, Mama's Mama, because she was mostly blind and still loved to cook, and could feel her way more easily with gas than with electric. But the most important thing about our gas-equipped kitchen was that Mama used to do hair there. The "hot comb" was a fine-toothed iron instrument with a long wooden handle and a pair of iron curlers that opened and closed like scissors. Mama would put it in the gas fire until it glowed. You could smell those prongs heating up.

2   I liked that smell. Not the smell so much, I guess, as what the smell meant for the shape of my day. There was an intimate warmth in the women's tones as they talked with my Mama, doing their hair. I knew what the women had been through to get their hair ready to be "done," because I would watch Mama do it to herself. How that kink could be transformed through grease and fire into that magnificent head of wavy hair was a miracle to me, and still is.

3   Mama would wash her hair over the sink, a towel wrapped around her shoulders, wearing just her slip and her white bra. (We had no shower—just a galvanized tub that we stored in the kitchen—until we moved down Rat Tail Road into Doc Wolverton's house, in 1954.) After she dried it, she would grease her scalp thoroughly with blue Bergamot hair grease, which came in a short, fat jar with a picture of a beautiful colored lady on it. It's important to grease your scalp real good, my Mama would explain, to keep from burning yourself. Of course, her hair would return to its natural kink almost as soon as the hot water and shampoo hit it. To me, it was another miracle how hair so "straight" would so quickly become kinky again the second it even approached some water.

4   My Mama had only a few "clients" whose heads she "did"—did, I think, because she enjoyed it, rather than for the few pennies it brought in. They would sit on one of our red plastic kitchen chairs, the kind with the shiny metal legs, and brace themselves for the process. Mama would stroke that red-hot iron—which by this time had been in the gas fire for half an hour or more—slowly but firmly through their hair, from scalp to strand's end. It made a scorching, crinkly sound, the hot iron did, as it burned its way through kink, leaving in its wake straight strands of hair, standing long and tall but drooping over at the ends, their shape like the top of a heavy willow tree. Slowly, steadily, Mama's hands would transform a round mound of Odetta kink into a darkened swamp of everglades. The Bergamot made the hair shiny; the heat of the hot iron gave it a brownish-red cast. Once all the hair was as straight as God allows kink to get, Mama would take the well-heated curling iron and twirl the straightened strands into more or less loosely

wrapped curls. She claimed that she owed her skill as a hairdresser to the strength in her wrists, and as she worked her little finger would poke out, the way it did when she sipped tea. Mama was a southpaw, and wrote upside down and backward to produce the cleanest, roundest letters you've ever seen.

5   The "kitchen" she would all but remove from sight with a handheld pair of shears, bought just for this purpose. Now, the kitchen was the room in which we were sitting—the room where Mama did hair and washed clothes, and where we all took a bath in that galvanized tub. But the word has another meaning, and the kitchen that I'm speaking of is the very kinky bit of hair at the back of your head, where your neck meets your shirt collar. If there was ever a part of our African past that resisted assimilation, it was the kitchen. No matter how hot the iron, no matter how powerful the chemical, no matter how stringent the mashed-potatoes-and-lye formula of a man's "process," neither God nor woman nor Sammy Davis, Jr., could straighten the kitchen. The kitchen was permanent, irredeemable, irresistible kink. Unassimilably African. No matter what you did, no matter how hard you tried, you couldn't de-kink a person's kitchen. So you trimmed it off as best you could.

6   When hair had begun to "turn," as they'd say—to return to its natural kinky glory—it was the kitchen that turned first (the kitchen around the back, and nappy edges at the temples). When the kitchen started creeping up the back of the neck, it was time to get your hair done again.

7   Sometimes, after dark, a man would come to have his hair done. It was Mr. Charlie Carroll. He was very light-complected and had a ruddy nose—it made me think of Edmund Gwenn, who played Kris Kringle in "Miracle on 34th Street." At first, Mama did him after my brother, Rocky, and I had gone to sleep. It was only later that we found out that he had come to our house so Mama could iron his hair—not with a hot comb or a curling iron but with our very own Proctor-Silex steam iron. For some reason I never understood, Mr. Charlie would conceal his Frederick Douglass-like mane under a big white Stetson hat. I never saw him take it off except when he came to our house, at night, to have his hair pressed. (Later, Daddy would tell us about Mr. Charlie's most prized piece of knowledge, something that the man would only confide after his hair had been pressed, as a token of intimacy. "Not many people know this," he'd say, in a tone of circumspection, "but George Washington was Abraham Lincoln's daddy." Nodding solemnly, he'd add the clincher: "A white man told me." Though he was in dead earnest, this became a humorous refrain around our house—"a white man told me"—which we used to punctuate especially preposterous assertions.)

8   My mother examined my daughter's kitchens whenever we went home to visit, in the early eighties. It became a game between us. I had told her not to do it, because I didn't like the politics it suggested—the notion of "good" and "bad" hair. "Good" hair was "straight," "bad" hair kinky. Even in the late sixties, at the height of Black Power, almost nobody could bring themselves to say "bad" for good and "good" for bad. People still said that hair like white people's hair was "good," even if they encapsulated it in a disclaimer, like "what we used to call 'good.'"

9   Maggie would be seated in her high chair, throwing food this way and that, and Mama would be cooing about how cute it all was, how I used to do just like

Maggie was doing, and wondering whether her flinging her food with her left hand meant that she was going to be left-handed like Mama. When my daughter was just about covered with Chef Boyardee Spaghetti-O's, Mama would seize the opportunity: wiping her clean, she would tilt Maggie's head to one side and reach down the back of her neck. Sometimes Mama would even rub a curl between her fingers, just to make sure that her bifocals had not deceived her. Then she'd sigh with satisfaction and relief: No kink…yet. Mama! I'd shout, pretending to be angry. Every once in a while, if no one was looking, I'd peek, too.

10   I say "yet" because most black babies are born with soft, silken hair. But after a few months it begins to turn, as inevitably as do the seasons or the leaves on a tree. People once thought baby oil would stop it. They were wrong.

11   Everybody I knew as a child wanted to have good hair. You could be as ugly as homemade sin dipped in misery and still be thought attractive if you had good hair. "Jesus moss," the girls at Camp Lee, Virginia, had called Daddy's naturally "good" hair during the war. I know that he played that thick head of hair for all it was worth, too.

12   My own hair was "not a bad grade," as barbers would tell me when they cut it for the first time. It was like a doctor reporting the results of the first full physical he has given you. Like "You're in good shape" or "Blood pressure's kind of high—better cut down on salt."

13   I spent most of my childhood and adolescence messing with my hair. I definitely wanted straight hair. Like Pop's. When I was about three, I tried to stick a wad of Bazooka bubble gum to that straight hair of his. I suppose what fixed that memory for me is the spanking I got for doing so: he turned me upside down, holding me by my feet, the better to paddle my behind. Little nigger, he had shouted, walloping away. I started to laugh about it two days later, when my behind stopped hurting.

14   When black people say "straight," of course, they don't usually mean literally straight—they're not describing hair like, say, Peggy Lipton's (she was the white girl on "The Mod Squad"), or like Mary's of Peter, Paul & Mary fame; black people call that "stringy" hair. No, "straight" just means not kinky, no matter what contours the curl may take. I would have done anything to have straight hair—and I used to try everything, short of getting a process.

15   Of the wide variety of techniques and methods I came to master in the challenging prestidigitation of the follicle, almost all had two things in common: a heavy grease and the application of pressure. It's not an accident that some of the biggest black-owned companies in the fifties and sixties made hair products. And I tried them all, in search of that certain silken touch, the one that would leave neither the hand nor the pillow sullied by grease.

16   I always wondered what Frederick Douglass put on his hair, or what Phillis Wheatley put on hers. Or why Wheatley has that rag on her head in the little engraving in the frontispiece of her book. One thing is for sure: you can bet that when Phillis Wheatley went to England and saw the Countess of Huntingdon she did not stop by the Queen's coiffeur on her way there. So many black people still get their hair straightened that it's a wonder we don't have a national holiday for

Madame C. J. Walker, the woman who invented the process of straightening kinky hair. Call it Jheri-Kurled or call it "relaxed," it's still fried hair.

17   I used all the greases, from sea-blue Bergamot and creamy vanilla Duke (in its clear jar with the orange-white-and-green label) to the godfather of grease, the formidable Murray's. Now, Murray's was some serious grease. Whereas Bergamot was like oily jello, and Duke was viscous and sickly sweet, Murray's was light brown and hard. Hard as lard and twice as greasy, Daddy used to say. Murray's came in an orange can with a press-on top. It was so hard that some people would put a match to the can, just to soften the stuff and make it more manageable. Then, in the late sixties, when Afros came into style, I used Afro Sheen. From Murray's to Duke to Afro Sheen: that was my progression in black consciousness.

18   We used to put hot towels or wash-rags over our Murray-coated heads, in order to melt the wax into the scalp and the follicles. Unfortunately, the wax also had the habit of running down your neck, ears, and forehead. Not to mention your pillowcase. Another problem was that if you put two palmfuls of Murray's on your head your hair turned white. (Duke did the same thing.) The challenge was to get rid of that white color. Because if you got rid of the white stuff you had a magnificent head of wavy hair. That was the beauty of it: Murray's was so hard that it froze your hair into the wavy style you brushed it into. It looked really good if you wore a part. A lot of guys had parts cut into their hair by a barber, either with the clippers or with a straightedged razor. Especially if you had kinky hair—then you'd generally wear a short razorcut, or what we called a Quo Vadis.

19   We tried to be as innovative as possible. Everyone knew about using a stocking cap, because your father or your uncle wore one whenever something really big was about to happen, whether sacred or secular: a funeral or a dance, a wedding or a trip in which you confronted official white people. Any time you were trying to look really sharp, you wore a stocking cap in preparation. And if the event was really a big one, you made a new cap. You asked your mother for a pair of her hose, and cut it with scissors about six inches or so from the open end—the end with the elastic that goes up to the top of the thigh. Then you knotted the cut end, and it became a beehive-shaped hat, with an elastic band that you pulled down low on your forehead and down around your neck in the back. To work well, the cap had to fit tightly and snugly, like a press. And it had to fit that tightly because it was a press: it pressed your hair with the force of the hose's elastic. If you greased your hair down real good, and left the stocking cap on long enough, voilá: you got a head of pressed-against-the-scalp waves. (You also got a ring around your forehead when you woke up, but it went away.) And then you could enjoy your concrete do. Swore we were bad, too, with all that grease and those flat heads. My brother and I would brush it out a bit in the mornings, so that it looked—well, "natural." Grown men still wear stocking caps—especially older men, who generally keep their stocking caps in their top drawers, along with their cufflinks and their see-through silk socks, their "Maverick" ties, their silk handkerchiefs, and whatever else they prize the most.

20   A Murrayed-down stocking cap was the respectable version of the process, which, by contrast, was most definitely not a cool thing to have unless you were an entertainer by trade. Zeke and Keith and Poochie and a few other stars of the

high-school basketball team all used to get a process once or twice a year. It was expensive, and you had to go somewhere like Pittsburgh or D.C. or Uniontown— somewhere where there were enough colored people to support a trade. The guys would disappear, then reappear a day or two later, strutting like peacocks, their hair burned slightly red from the lye base. They'd also wear "rags"—cloths or handkerchiefs—around their heads when they slept or played basketball. Do-rags, they were called. But the result was straight hair, with just a hint of wave. No curl. Do-it-yourselfers took their chances at home with a concoction of mashed potatoes and lye.

21   The most famous process of all, however, outside of the process Malcolm X describes in his "Autobiography," and maybe the process of Sammy Davis, Jr., was Nat King Cole's process. Nat King Cole had patent-leather hair. That man's got the finest process money can buy, or so Daddy said the night we saw Cole's TV show on NBC. It was November 5, 1956. I remember the date because everyone came to our house to watch it and to celebrate one of Daddy's buddies' birthdays. Yeah, Uncle Joe chimed in, they can do shit to his hair that the average Negro can't even think about—secret shit.

22   Nat King Cole was clean. I've had an ongoing argument with a Nigerian friend about Nat King Cole for twenty years now. Not about whether he could sing—any fool knows that he could—but about whether or not he was a handkerchief head for wearing that patent-leather process.

23   Sammy Davis, Jr.'s process was the one I detested. It didn't look good on him. Worse still, he liked to have a fried strand dangling down the middle of his forehead, so he could shake it out from the crown when he sang. But Nat King Cole's hair was a thing unto itself, a beautifully sculpted work of art that he and he alone had the right to wear. The only difference between a process and a stocking cap, really, was taste; but Nat King Cole, unlike, say, Michael Jackson, looked good in his. His head looked like Valentino's head in the twenties, and some say it was Valentino the process was imitating. But Nat King Cole wore a process because it suited his face, his demeanor, his name, his style. He was as clean as he wanted to be.

24   I had forgotten all about that patent-leather look until one day in 1971, when I was sitting in an Arab restaurant on the island of Zanzibar surrounded by men in fezzes and white caftans, trying to learn how to eat curried goat and rice with the fingers of my right hand and feeling two million miles from home. All of a sudden, an old transistor radio sitting on top of a china cupboard stopped blaring out its Swahili music and started playing "Fly Me to the Moon," by Nat King Cole. The restaurant's din was not affected at all, but in my mind's eye I saw it: the King's magnificent sleek black tiara. I managed, barely, to blink back the tears.

Analysis: An Insider's Perspective

Henry Louis Gates, Jr.'s memoir "In the Kitchen" begins as a loving and nostalgic evocation of the hair-straightening he witnessed as a child in his mother's kitchen, and proceeds to an elaborate cataloging of hair-straightening methods. By the end of his essay, however, we realize that Gates is not simply reminiscing or reporting on the intricacies of African-American hairstyles but, rather, is reconstructing a way of life and affirming his loyalty to his memories of growing up and to the people from his past. Particularly striking, perhaps, is how Gates resists representing hair-straightening as an acceptance of white standards of beauty by African-Americans. Though he acknowledges the famous criticism of the "process" in Malcolm X's autobiography, Gates does not seek to position himself as a critic in relation to the people from his past he is writing about. Instead, he reveals, from an insider's perspective, how the ritual of hair straightening, far from simply the product of a desire to look white, reflects a uniquely African-American style and sensibility.

For Critical Inquiry

1. You may have noticed that Henry Louis Gates, Jr., has broken his essay into three sections. Annotate and write a summary of each section. Now consider how the sections connect to each other to form a whole.

2. Memoirs depend in part on re-creating scenes from the past so that readers can share the lived experience of the writer. Mark passages in the essay where you think Gates is especially effective in using specific detail and sensory impressions to re-create the past. What makes these passages work effectively? Many of the details, naturally, relate to hair and hair-straightening techniques and products. List some of these details. How are they crucial to the essay?

3. In the final lines of the essay, as Gates remembers Nat King Cole's "magnificent sleek black tiara," he says, "I managed, barely, to blink back the tears." One of the issues memoirists face is avoiding sentimentality in explaining to readers how they feel looking back on the past. How does Gates handle the problem of potential sentimentality at the close of the essay? Consider the final lines in the context of the entire essay.

4. The essay combines purely personal references with broader cultural references. Give some examples of each. Why is this combination effective?

VISUAL DESIGN: RECORDS OF THE PAST

Individuals and families often put together photo albums and scrapbooks to create their own records of the past. Photo albums, of course, consist of photographs, while scrapbooks are often multimedia compositions that use photos, newspaper clippings, report cards, certificates of achievement, concert tickets, pressed flowers, letters, and other souvenirs and keepsakes. The following examples offer a look at these differences. The first is a page from a high school student's scrapbook, and the second is a page from a young boy's photo album.

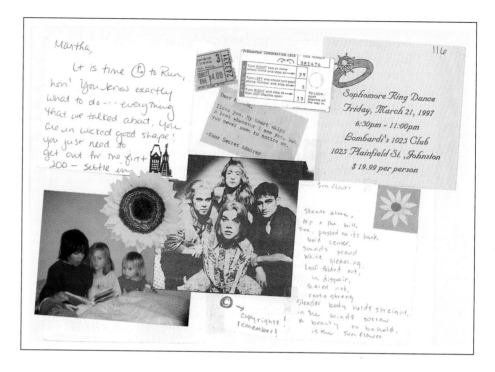

Analysis: The Composition of Visual Memories

Like written memoirs, visual memories have the power, years later, to bring the past back to life, and just as we can analyze how written memoirs are composed, we can do the same with visual memories. Consider, for example, the differences between photo albums and scrapbooks. Notice that the two pages are composed in quite different ways. The young boy's photo album is arranged in rows. Visually, the rows create an orderly sense of sequence in which one thing seems inevitably to lead to the next, telling the story of a life as it unfolds over time. In contrast, the scrapbook page is composed as a collage. It uses the association of visual memories rather than temporal sequence as the principle of composition, linking disparate images and materials together to create a moment in time.

FOR CRITICAL INQUIRY

1. How do the visual elements on the photo album and scrapbook pages interact to tell a story? What difference does the arrangement of the material make?

2. If you keep or have kept a scrapbook, what have you put in it? What determines your selection and the arrangement of materials? How do you feel when you look again at the scrapbook after time has passed?

3. High school and college yearbooks are another genre that creates visual memories. Working together in small groups, gather three or four year-books. If your own high school yearbook is available, you can use it. Otherwise, use yearbooks from your college. You can usually find these in the library; ask a librarian where they are. You could work with college yearbooks from different decades.

   a. Survey the yearbooks' contents. How are they divided? What standard features do they all have? What differences are there?

   b. Now focus on design. How are the yearbooks similar and different in their design? How do the differences in design affect the reader?

   c. Next, consider the yearbooks as repositories of memories. How do they shape people's high school or college experiences? How effective are they as memoirs—what are their strengths and weaknesses in this regard? To what extent do the yearbooks reflect the history of the times?

   d. If friends and teachers have written in your yearbooks, consider what people write in yearbooks. How does this writing seem similar to and different from the actual yearbook text in the picture it creates?

4. Compose a page or two for a scrapbook. Include things that will remind you of what it was like to be you at that moment. You can use many different kinds of materials—such as photos, printed matter, drawings, or pressed flowers. Consider what different arrangements of your material are possible.

When you have completed the assignment, bring your pages to class. Discuss with classmates how the process of composing visual materials differs from producing written texts and how it is similar.

FOR DISCUSSION AND ANALYTICAL WRITING

RHETORICAL ANALYSIS

Consider the writers' ethos in the memoirs you've just read. You can focus on one memoir or compare them. How do the writers construct their characters? Take into account the role each author plays as a character in the memoir and the relationship between the writer's present-day self and as a character in the memoir. How have the writers handled their ethical responsibility to others involved in the memoir? What kind of relationship do they want to establish with their readers?

GENRE CHOICES

Gary Soto's "Black Hair" and the International Ladies Garment Workers Union ad "The Price of Corporate Greed at Leslie Fay" both provide accounts of life in the workplace, though one is a memoir and the other an appeal to support a boycott. Compare them in terms of what each brings to light about the nature of work. What, if anything, do they have in common? How might their differences as genres of writing affect readers?

GOING ONLINE

Visiting Home Pages

Personal home pages might be thought of as another type of visual memory—a cyber-scrapbook that uses multimedia to create a sense of a person at a moment in time. Find three personal home pages that, for one reason or another, interest you. Try to find ones that differ in their use of text, graphics, photos, sound, video, and links to other sites. Then, work in a group with two other students at a computer screen. Take turns showing the three home pages you have chosen. Using the guidelines in Chapter 19, "Visual Design," and any other considerations that seem relevant to you, work as a group to select three home pages from the nine you've visited—one that you think is good or outstanding, one that is fair, and one that is not as good as the other two. Write a short report or make an oral presentation that explains the reasoning that led to these judgments.

WORKING TOGETHER

Creating a Time Capsule

Time capsules contain items that are meant to represent a particular moment or period of history. The term *time capsule* was coined in 1938 for a cylinder the Westinghouse Electrical Company filled with more than one hundred articles used for scientific, industrial, or everyday purposes, along with microfilms and newsreels, It was buried on the grounds of the New York World's Fair of 1939, to be opened in 6939. Sometimes time capsules are buried in the foundations of buildings for future generations (or aliens visiting the planet Earth) to excavate as archaeological evidence about the culture that lived in times past.

Work together in groups of four or five to create a time capsule that can serve to capture the present moment in history. To do this, select twenty-five things that, in your judgment, best represent what it means to be alive in the first decade of the twenty-first century. Write a list of the items with brief explanations of why you have included each one. Make enough copies of the list for the other members of your class or circulate it on a class listserv.

Compile the items on each group's list in a master list. You should have a considerable number. Now work together as a class to narrow the items down to twenty-five that the majority can agree on. Provide a rationale for each item: What does it represent about the present culture that would help future generations (or aliens) understand current ways of life?

WRITING ASSIGNMENT

Recall a person, a place, or an event from your past and write a memoir. You will want to use detail and sensory impression to re-create the moment for your readers. Remember that the point of a memoir, as you have seen, is to reveal the meaning of the past so that readers can understand the significance your memories hold for the present. Since memoirs function to help both writers and their readers understand the past, this assignment can be a good time for you to probe significant times in your life, revisiting them now that you have some distance from them. You can learn more about yourself in the present by looking into events in your past. You might decide to begin with some of the ideas listed below, or you might try some of the exercises in the sections that follow.

1. Focus on a job you have held at some time in the past, as Gary Soto does. How could you reconstruct the experience of work in order to reveal something about its significance to you and others?

2. Pick a photograph that holds memories and emotional associations. You might, for example, focus on a particular detail that recalls a particular moment in the past to explore how your family's history intersects larger

social and historical forces. Look through old photo albums, scrapbooks, and collages if you have them.

3. Recall a particular family ritual, such as visits to grandparents, Sunday dinners, summer vacations, holiday celebrations, weddings, and so on, as a way to focus on an event or a person that is especially significant to you.

4. Consider some aspect of your own cultural ancestry—whether it is the language your ancestors spoke, a kind of food or music, a family tradition, an heirloom that has been passed down from generation to generation—to explain how the past has entered your life and what it reveals about your relationship to the culture of your ancestors.

5. Focus on a childhood incident, as Annie Dillard does, to re-create the event and your own perspective as a younger person.

6. Look through an old diary or journal, if you have kept one. Look for moments when you faced an occasion that challenged your values or where you had a difficult decision to make, experienced a situation that turned out unexpectedly, or were keenly disappointed. Consider using these memories as the starting point for your memoir, in which you can reflect upon the experience and put it in a larger context.

ETHICS OF WRITING

BEARING WITNESS

Part of a memoirist's authority derives from the fact of his or her having been there as an eyewitness to the events recounted. In effect, by offering an eyewitness account, the memoirist is claiming a privileged perspective on what took place. But unlike, say, news reporters, who present themselves as detached observers, memoirists are typically central characters in the events they retell. They are participants as well as observers. For these reasons, memoirists face some important ethical issues concerning their responsibility as witnesses to the past. How does the memoirist represent the other people involved? What are the memoirist's responsibilities to these people? What is the memoirist entitled to divulge about his or her private life? What are the memoirist's loyalties to those he or she writes about? Might such loyalties conflict with obligations to readers? What impact will the memoir have on the writer's relationship with others in the present, and does this potential impact affect the retelling? In cases where the memoirist feels hurt, angry, or offended by what took place, can he or she nonetheless be fair? These are questions that memoirists invariably struggle with, and there are no easy answers, especially when a memoir treats situations that are difficult or painful. The memoir, don't forget, is an act of self-discovery, and yet memoirs are written for the public to read. As witnesses to the past, memoirists can handle their responsibility to others in an ethical way by seeking to understand the motives and character of those involved, including themselves.

Invention

Sketching

Consider what moves you to write. The call to write often begins with the memory of a single detail or an image from everyday life. The seemingly mundane memory of an old bicycle, the refrain from a song, or the smell of your grandparents' kitchen can unlock a series of emotional associations worth exploring. To see what such memories hold for you, do some sketching of scenes or memories from the past.

Just as artists often sketch as preliminary work, you can use sketching as a form of exploratory writing to recall the details, sensory impressions, emotional associations, and social allegiances that moments in the past contain for you. Here's an example of what a sketch might look like:

> It was a green ten-speed Schwinn bike that I remember, a gift for my eleventh birthday. It was sleek and racy-looking, with handbrakes that could stop you on a dime and the exotic-sounding derailleur with its levers to change gears. This was no child's bike, this was an instrument of speed and effortless motion. When I rode this ten-speed, I felt weightless and free, an anonymous blur of cycling energy zooming through my neighborhood and beyond. I could go, and the bike brought me a mobility I had never imagined before. I named my bike "The Green Wind" and rode out of my childhood and into the adventure of adolescence and parts of town my parents would have been horrified to know I visited. The Green Wind took me many places and I learned to be silent about my travels.

Another way to approach sketching is to take a mental walk through the house in which you grew up. Begin by drawing a floor plan of that house, making it as specific as you like. Next, think of a strong memory associated with that house. Once you have chosen a particular memory for further reflection, mark the room on your map in which this memory took place. Sketch out as full a picture as you can of the memory and of the room. Describe the room as you narrate the memory and try to draw connections between the two of them. You can use this information in your memoir.

EXERCISE

1. Using the guidelines below, sketch a scene, memory, event, or incident from the past—something you can recall in reasonable detail that has important associations for you.

2. Exchange your sketch with a classmate. Read your partner's sketch.

3. Take turns interviewing each other. Ask your partner about the sketch you wrote:

   a. What does your partner feel is most interesting about the sketch?

   b. What would your partner like to know more about?

   c. What themes or issues does he or she see in the sketch?

Guidelines for Sketching

1. Visualize the moment in the past. Imagine you are photographing or videotaping. What exactly do you see? List as many specific items and details as you can. Think about the time of day, the season of the year, and what the weather was like. If your memoir is located mostly indoors, try to recall what particular rooms looked like—the furniture, the color of the walls or the design of wallpaper, anything hanging, such as pictures, posters, photographs, and so on. Recall, too, the movement of people. How do they move through the physical space in which your memoir is located? What are they doing?

2. Note other sensory perceptions, such as sounds, smells, tastes, and textures. What do you hear in the physical space you're writing about? What produces the sounds—people's voices, people's work, animals, machines, city traffic, the wind? Are there characteristic smells associated with the place? If there is a meal or food involved in your memoir, what do various dishes taste like? Are there particular textures to objects that you can recall?

3. Describe the people involved in your memoir. What do they look like? How do they move? What are they doing? What are they wearing? Recreate conversation among the people in your memoir. What are they talking about? Can you capture particular ways of speech? Can you use snatches of dialogue to define people and issues?

Exploring Past and Present Perspectives

To clarify the purpose of your memoir and what you want it to mean to readers, consider what your feelings were at the moment things were taking place in the past and what they are now as you look back from the perspective of the present.

In the sketch about the ten-speed bicycle, the writer has re-created the excitement and sense of adventure he felt as an eleven-year-old. However, as the writer reflected on and wrote about the importance of the bike from the perspective of the present, he realized that his travels to the "wrong side" of town not only opened up a whole new world of class and cultural differences but also created a barrier of silence between him and his parents. Some of the work ahead for this writer is to decide how much he wants to emphasize the physical freedom, mobility, and new knowledge he acquired and how much he wants to emphasize what the consequences of his silence have been for his relationship with his parents.

Considering the memory you're writing about from past and present perspectives can help you to clarify the double role of the memoir writer—as a participant and as an observer—and to decide what relative emphasis each of the two perspectives will take on in your memoir.

EXERCISE

1. **Past perspective:** Recall in as much detail as possible what your feelings were at the time. Spend five minutes or so responding to these questions in writing:

   a. What was your initial reaction to the moment in the past you're writing about? What did you think at the time? How did you feel? What did other people seem to think and feel?

   b. Did you share your reaction with anyone at the time? If so, how did they respond?

   c. Did your initial reaction persist or did it change? If it changed, what set of feelings replaced it? What caused the change? Were other people involved in this change?

2. **Present perspective:** Now think about your present perspective. Write for another five minutes or so in response to these questions:

   a. Looking back on the moment in the past, how do the feelings you experienced at the time appear to you today? Do they seem reasonable? Why or why not?

   b. If you were in the same situation today, would you act the same way? Why or why not? If you would act differently, what would you change? How? Why?

   c. What are your present feelings about the event you're describing? Have your feelings changed? Do things look different from the perspective of the present? If so, how would you explain the change?

   d. As you compare your feelings from the past and your feelings in the present, what conclusions can you draw about the significance the memory has for you? Are your feelings resolved, or do they seem unsettled and changing? In either case, what do you think has shaped your current perspective?

3. **Review the two writings:** Use them to write a third statement that defines what you see as the significance of the memory you're writing about and what your purpose is in re-creating it for your readers. What does the memory reveal about the past? How do you want to present yourself in relation to what happened in the past? If there is conflict or crisis, what are your loyalties toward the people and the events?

Exploring Cultural and Historical Perspectives

Just as you have looked into your past and present for new insights, you can also try exploring by considering the cultural and historical backdrop of the event or events you are examining. In other words, you can place your own memories and experience within a broader context, linking your life with social trends and political events happening around you at the time.

You may want (or need) to look in the library and on the Internet for more help in responding to these questions. Check, for example, *The New York Times Index* for that particular year, or the *Facts on File Yearbook.* Weekly periodicals such as *Time, Newsweek,* and *U.S. News & World Report* have an end-of-year issue that can help provide both cultural and historical perspectives. In addition, you can browse the Web to find all kinds of information. As a starting point, take a look at the following sites:

- **The White House Virtual Library:** This links to the White House and government organizations, and provides historical documents online. Address: <www.whitehouse.gov/wh/html/library.html>

- **EINet Galaxy:** This site is a good starting point if you are searching for a specific subject. Address: <www.galaxy.einet.net/galaxy.html>

- **WWW Virtual Library:** Like the site listed above, this one is also a good starting point for specific subjects. Address: <www.w3.org/vl/>

- **Your own institution's resource section:** There may be one linking from the main home page, or there may be a section for writing and learning resources through your campus Writing Center.

EXERCISE

1. Isolate the year that your chosen event happened. If you are examining a ritual that occurred many times, pick one such instance and focus only on that. In answering the following questions, you might need to ask family members or friends for their impressions, insights, and suggestions.

   a. What was the year in question? Was there anything remarkable about that year in the context of national and world events? Is that year "famous" for anything?

   b. Who was president that year? Was the United States involved in any wars or conflicts? What international figures were seen as the "villains"?

   c. How was the economic outlook that year? How has it been characterized in retrospect? How did your event reflect the national economic scene?

   d. Is there a generation associated with that year (World War II veterans, baby boomers, Generation X)? Was any particular ethnic or racial group prominent during this time?

e. What were the major social conflicts that year? Were there important political demonstrations, social movements, or riots in any part of the country? If so, what were they about? Were there any natural disasters that captured national attention that year?

f. What was the "news story" of the year? What was the "success story" of the year? Who were the "heroes" that year?

g. What were the new technological innovations?

h. What kind of music was most popular or notable? Did that music represent anything about society? Was it a reaction to anything?

2. Review your responses. What links, if any, can connect your own experience and the experiences of others at the historical moment you are considering? What cultural and historical contexts might be illuminating in your memoir?

Planning

Arranging Your Material

One thing you have seen from the memoirs gathered in this chapter is that memoir writers often tell a story in chronological order, from beginning to end, as Gary Soto and Annie Dillard do.

Notice the way Gary Soto begins many of the paragraphs in his narration so that readers can easily keep track of the events as they unfold over time:

¶5: "The next morning, I arrived early at work."

¶7: "I worked carefully that day...."

¶8: "At five the workers scattered...."

¶9: "From the backyard I walked dully through a residential street, and as evening came on...."

¶11: "When I got up from the lawn it was late."

¶13: "At work I spent the morning at the buffer...."

¶15: "Iggy worked only until three in the afternoon...."

On the other hand, Henry Louis Gates, Jr., presents a sequence of memories that create one dominant impression. Consider the cues Gates gives readers so that they can locate what is taking place in the separate sketches he puts together in his memoir:

¶1–7: In the kitchen at home (before "we moved ... in 1954").

¶8: Early 1980s ("whenever we went home") and late 1960s (at "the height of Black Power").

¶9–20: "My childhood and adolescence," "black-owned companies in the fifties and sixties," "in the late sixties, when Afros came into style."

¶21–23: "November 5, 1956," the "night we saw" the Nat King Cole TV show.

¶24: In Zanzibar, "one day in 1971."

Here are some questions to help you design a working draft:

1. How will you begin? Do you want to ease into the moment from the past or state it outright? How can you capture your readers' interest? Do you need to establish background information? How will you present yourself—as a participant in the past or as an observer from the perspective of the present?

2. What arrangement best suits your material? If you are telling a single story, how can you keep the narrative crisp and moving? Do you need to interrupt the chronology with commentary, description, interpretation, asides? If you are using selected incidents, what order best conveys the point you want them to make? Do the separate incidents create a dominant impression?

3. How will you set up the moment of revelation that gives your memoir its meaning and significance? Do you want to anticipate this moment by foreshadowing, which gives readers a hint of the revelation that is to come? Or do you want it to appear suddenly?

4. How will you end your memoir? Do you want to surprise readers with an unsuspected meaning? Or do you want to step back from what has taken place to reflect on its significance? Is there a way in which you can echo the opening of the memoir to make your readers feel they have come full circle?

Based on your answers to these questions, make a working outline of your memoir. If you're planning to tell a story from start to finish, indicate the key incidents in the event you're remembering. If you're planning to use a sequence of memories, block out the separate events. Then you can consider the best order to present them.

Working Draft

Review the writing you have done so far. Draw on the sketching you have done, the writing that compares past and present perspectives, and your analysis of cultural and historical contexts. Consider the tentative decisions you've made about how to arrange your material—in chronological order or as a related sequence of events. As you begin composing a working draft of your memoir, you'll need to think about how you can best bring out the significance of your memories.

Beginnings and Endings: Framing Your Memoir

Notice how the writers frame their memoirs to highlight the revelations that make these writings meaningful. For example, in his opening paragraph Gary

Soto introduces the idea that there are "two kinds of work," and then, after telling about his experience at the tire factory, he returns in the last six paragraphs to explore what he found out about work that "uses muscle."

Annie Dillard also uses this strategy to frame her essay. In the opening passage she anticipates the larger significance of the event she is about to re-create: "I got in trouble throwing snowballs, and have seldom been happier since." Then she tells the story of the man who chased her and of her "immense discovery." At the end of the memoir, Dillard extends the meaning of the opening lines: "If in that snowy backyard the driver of the black Buick had cut off our heads, Mikey's and mine, I would have died happy, for nothing has required so much of me since as being chased all over Pittsburgh in the middle of winter—running terrified, exhausted."

Henry Louis Gates, Jr., balances two scenes that have to do with home and straightening hair—his recollection of the kitchen at home in the opening section and the final paragraph, where, "feeling two million miles from home," he hears a Nat King Cole song on the radio that brings back the memories he has just explored.

Selecting Detail

Memoirists often use techniques you can find in fiction: scene-setting, description of people, action, and dialogue. These techniques enable memoirists (like fiction writers) to re-create the past in vivid and convincing detail. Designing a memoir (like fiction writing) involves decisions about the type and amount of detail you need to make your re-creation of the past memorable to readers.

- **Scene-setting:** Use vivid and specific description to set the scene; name particular objects; give details about places and things; use description and detail to establish mood.

- **Description of people:** Use descriptions of people's appearances to highlight their personalities in your memoir; describe the clothes they are wearing; give details about a person's physical presence, gestures, facial features, and hairstyle; notice personal habits; use description and detail to establish character.

- **Dialogue:** Put words in your characters' mouths that reveal their personalities; invent dialogue that is faithful to people's ways of speaking (even if you don't use their exact words); use dialogue to establish relationships between characters.

- **Action:** Put the characters in your memoir in motion; use narrative to tell about something that happened; use narrative to develop characters and reveal the theme of your memoir.

Peer Commentary

Once you've written a working draft, you are ready to get feedback from others. Before exchanging papers, work through the following exercise. Then, you can guide your partner or group members in how to best help you.

> **EXERCISE**
>
> 1. Write an account of your working draft.
>   a. What made you want to write this memoir? Describe in as much detail as you can what you experienced as the call to write.
>   b. What is your purpose in the working draft? What are you trying to reveal about the moment in the past? What significance does this moment hold for you?
>   c. What problems or uncertainties do you see in your working draft? Ask your readers about particular passages in the draft so that you can get specific feedback.
> 2. Your readers can offer you feedback, either oral or written, based on your working draft and the commentary you have written. Here are questions for your readers to take into account.
>   a. Does the writer's purpose come across clearly? Are you able to see and understand the significance of the moment in the writer's past? If the significance of the moment is not revealed clearly enough, what suggestions can you offer?
>   b. Is the memoir organized effectively? Does the moment of revelation appear in the best place? Does the essay begin with sufficient background information and scene setting? Comment on the ending of the memoir. Does the writer pull things together in a way that is satisfying to the reader?
>   c. Is the writing vivid and concrete in re-creating particular scenes and moments from the past? Point to passages that are particularly vivid. Are there passages that are too vague, obscure, or abstract? Do the narrative passages move along crisply or do they seem to drag?

Revising

Use the commentary you have received to plan a revision.

1. Do you re-create the experience you're remembering, as opposed to just telling your readers what happened?
2. Can readers easily follow what you're remembering?
3. Will readers be able to see clearly how you experienced the events in the past and how you think about them now?

4. Are the events and people in the memoir vivid? Do you need more detail?

5. What, if anything, should you cut? What do you need to add?

6. Is there a moment of revelation that gives the memoir significance?

From Telling to Showing

Jennifer Plante revised the opening paragraphs of her memoir (a complete draft of the memoir is included in the Writers' Workshop below) to move from a summary of Sunday afternoons at her grandparents' house to a much fuller scene setting. Jennifer's revision is a good example of the difference between telling and showing. Jenn said she wanted to begin by just telling about these family gatherings. Telling about them helped her to bring her memories to consciousness. At the same time, however, she wasn't satisfied that the first version really captured the feeling of those afternoons. There's more she wanted to show about what those afternoons were really like. Notice how the memories in one paragraph of the early draft generate two paragraphs.

EARLY DRAFT

When I was ten years old, my family used to go to my grandparents' house every Sunday for dinner. It was a kind of ritual. My grandmother would cook a pot roast—I should say she overcooked it—and at the dinner table, my grandfather would carry forth on his political views. He was an intimidating, opinionated man. Nonetheless, this was a special time for me. As a ten-year-old, I didn't really understand the politics but I did know I was a special granddaughter. After dinner, my grandfather and I would watch the New England Patriots if they were on TV that week. He was the kind of hardcore fan who shouted at the Patriots players as if he were the coach, and I imitated him.

REVISED VERSION

The smell of over-cooked pot roast still magically carries me back to Sunday afternoons at my grandparents' house. I was all of ten years old; a tom-boyish, pig-tailed girl who worshiped the ground that her elders walked on. Back then, my grandfather seemed like an enormous man, every bit as intimidating as he was loving. He knew what he wanted, what he believed in, he thought that President Reagan was a demigod, and he thought that his only granddaughter was one of the biggest joys of his life. I remember that every time my family went over to my grandparents' humble home, I would run into my grandfather's warm arms and get swallowed up in a loving hug. Then, he'd sweep me off of my feet and twirl me around in the air until I was giggling so hard that I could no longer breathe.

After we ate the charcoaled roast, I would follow my grandfather into the living room. Light always seemed to radiate from the huge picture window spreading warmth into the living room; it never seemed to rain while I was at my grandparents' house. I would proceed to sit on my grandfather's lap while he stretched out in his La-Z Boy and flipped through the T.V. channels to find the New England Patriots' football game. He would often shout at the players as if he was their coach, and trying to emulate him, I would shout equally as loud not knowing what the hell I was talking about (face-masking means nothing to a ten year old girl). This is how every Sunday afternoon of my childhood was spent; the sequence of events was very ritualistic, the only thing distinguishing one Sunday from another was which meal my grandmother would decide to burn.

WRITERS' WORKSHOP

Jennifer Plante wrote the following two pieces in response to an assignment in her composition class that called on students to write a memoir.

The first piece is Jennifer's commentary on an early working draft of a short memoir based on her recollections of Sunday afternoon visits to her grandparents' house. In this commentary, Jennifer describes the call to write that got her started on the piece in the first place and her own sense of both the potential and the problems of her work in progress. You'll notice that Jennifer wrote her commentary as a kind of interim report—to explain what she was trying to do and to request feedback, constructive criticism, and suggestions from her readers.

The second piece of writing is the working draft itself, before Jennifer went on to revise it. As you read, remember that Jennifer's memoir is work in progress. Try to read it through her commentary, to see what advice or suggestions you would give her concerning revision.

JENNIFER PLANTE'S COMMENTARY

What got me started on this piece of writing is exactly what I begin with—the smell of over-cooked pot roast. For some reason, when I was thinking about a memoir I might write, this smell suddenly seemed to leap out at me and bring me back to the Sunday afternoons we spent at my grandparents. In one way, I wanted to remember these days because I loved them so much. I felt so safe and secure and loved, with not only my parents but my grandparents surrounding me. I tried to find images of warmth, light, and enclosure to re-create this feeling. I wanted the opening to have a Norman Rockwell-like, almost sentimental feel to it—of the "typical" American family living out the American dream of family gatherings. A ritualistic feel.

But I also wanted the paragraphs to serve as a set-up for what was to come, which is really the point of the memoir. It was on a typical Sunday when I was ten that my father and grandfather argued, and my grandfather made these incredibly racist and homophobic comments. I didn't understand at the time exactly what my grandfather meant but I did understand the look on my father's face—and that something had happened that was going to change things.

I think I've done a decent job of setting this scene up, but I don't think it fully conveys what I want it to. So I had to add the final section reflecting back on it and how I now feel betrayed by my grandfather. I think this last part is probably too obvious and maybe even a little bit preachy or self-righteous, though I try to explain how my grandfather is a product of his upbringing. I want readers to understand how my feelings toward my grandfather went from completely adoring to totally mixed and contradictory ones. I don't think this is coming out clearly enough and I would appreciate any suggestions about how to do it or to improve any other parts of the essay.

JENNIFER PLANTE, "SUNDAY AFTERNOONS"

The smell of over-cooked pot roast still magically carries me back to Sunday afternoons at my grandparents' house. I was all of ten years old; a tom-boyish, pig-tailed girl who worshiped the ground that her elders walked on. Back then, my grandfather seemed like an enormous man, every bit as intimidating as he was loving. He knew what he wanted, what he believed in, he thought that President Reagan was a demigod, and he thought that his only granddaughter was one of the biggest joys of his life. I remember that every time my family went over to my grandparents' humble home, I would run into my grandfather's warm arms and get swallowed up in a loving hug. Then, he'd sweep me off of my feet and twirl me around in the air until I was giggling so hard that I could no longer breathe.

After we ate the charcoaled roast, I would follow my grandfather into the living room. Light always seemed to radiate from the huge picture window spreading warmth into the living room; it never seemed to rain while I was at my grandparents' house. I would proceed to sit on my grandfather's lap while he stretched out in his La-Z Boy and flipped through the T.V. channels to find the New England Patriots' football game. He would often shout at the players as if he was their coach, and trying to emulate him, I would shout equally as loud not knowing what the hell I was talking about (face-masking means nothing to a ten year old girl). This is how every Sunday afternoon of my childhood was spent; the sequence of events was very ritualistic, the only thing distinguishing one Sunday from another was which meal my grandmother would decide to burn.

One Sunday afternoon, my grandfather and I had assumed our normal positions on the brown, beat-up chair and found our Patriots losing to some random team. I'm not exactly sure how the subject came up, but my grandfather and my dad began discussing politics and our society. My grandfather and my dad held different opinions about both topics, so as usual, the debate had gotten pretty heated. I began feeling a bit uncomfortable as the discussion wore on; they talked for what seemed like hours and they must have discussed every issue that was of importance to our society. To numb my discomfort, I became focused on the T.V. screen—Steve Grogan had just completed a 30-yard touchdown pass, but the referee had called that "face-masking" thing on the offense, sending Patriot fans into a frenzy. Then, just as quickly as it had started, the debate ended in dead silence. My father sat, open-mouthed, in disbelief at what he'd just heard; my grandfather had finally spoken his mind.

"What is this interracial marriage garbage? Decent white people shouldn't be marrying those blacks. And what is this perverted gay business? All the gays should go back into the closet where they belong!"

I didn't understand what my grandfather had said at the time, but I did notice the look on my father's face. It was as if my grandfather had just slapped him, only I somehow knew that what he'd said had hurt my father much more than any slap ever could have. And I did notice that, for the first time ever, a hard rain began to fall outside.

I look back on that day now and I understand why my father looked so hurt. I also understand now what my grandfather had said, and can't help but feel betrayed that a man that I admired so much had managed to insult over half of the population in one breath. I do feel bitter towards my grandfather, but I can't really blame him for his ignorance; he is a product of his time, and they were taught to hate difference. But ever since that day, I have vowed that, when my grandchildren come to visit me on Sunday afternoons, they will never see a hard rain falling outside of my picture window.

WORKSHOP QUESTIONS

1. Do you agree with Jennifer Plante that she has done a "decent" job of scene-setting in the opening sections of her memoir? Does it effectively re-create the "ritualistic feel" of family gatherings? Does it become too sentimental? Explain your responses to these questions and make any suggestions you might have for strengthening the opening.

2. Plante's memoir relies on a moment of revelation—when her grandfather makes racist and homophobic remarks and the effect these remarks have on her father. Does this moment have the dramatic value and emotional force it needs as the pivotal point in the memoir—the moment that

"changed things"? What suggestions, if any, would you offer to strengthen this crucial point in the memoir?

3. Plante seems dissatisfied with the final section of the memoir, in which she writes from the perspective of the present reflecting back on a moment in the past. She worries about seeming "obvious," "preachy," and "self-righteous" in describing her sense of betrayal. Do you think this is a problem in the draft? What advice would you offer to strengthen this section of the memoir?

REFLECTING ON YOUR WRITING

Write an account that explains how you handled the dual role of the memoir writer as a participant and as an observer. How did you re-create yourself as a character in your memoir? What is the relationship between your self in the past and the perspective of your present self? If memoirs are in part acts of writing that bear witness to and thereby take responsibility for the past, how do the selves you have created and re-created express loyalties and social allegiances?

A CLOSING NOTE

Events and people from the past worth writing about often contain powerful emotional associations for the writer—associations that may not have been put into words before. Part of the work of writing a memoir is to bring such associations forward to explain why they are so powerful and what influence they continue to have on the writer. For this reason, bringing a memoir to closure is likely to involve work creating a mood and portraying the writer's attitude. Memoirists want readers to get a sense of what it felt like to be there, and at the same time they know that readers expect a memoir to have its revelations—to make a point as well as tell a story or describe a moment.

CHAPTER SIX

Public Documents: Codifying Beliefs and Practices

THINKING ABOUT THE GENRE

People in contemporary society rely on public documents to organize and carry out a wide range of social activities. In fact, an individual's life can be charted by following the documents that mark key moments. Notice how the following documents describe the course of a life as it is entered into the public record:

- Birth certificate

- Religious records (baptism, first communion, confirmation, or bar mitzvah)

- School records (report cards, standardized test results, high school and college diplomas, awards and scholarships)

- Driver's license

- Social Security card

- Marriage license

- Employment contracts

- Mortgage

- Tax returns

- Last will and testament

- Death certificate and obituary

People are so surrounded by public documents that they may well take this form of writing for granted. After all, documents just seem to appear out of a file in school, at work, in a bank or a government office as though they were always there. In fact, nowadays many public documents are available online, and people can fill out their tax forms on a home computer. Documents seem to be natural parts of the bureaucratic maze of contemporary life, and so people get used to documents just as you get used to a piece of furniture that's always been in your grandparents' house.

No one seems to have written these documents. You just use them, fill in the blanks and sign, as you'd sit in a familiar chair. But precisely because written documents are an ever-present part of our social reality, it's worthwhile taking a closer look at the purposes documents serve.

Public documents serve to codify the beliefs and practices of a culture, a community, an organization—any group of people who share a mutual concern. Unlike many of the genres of writing in this textbook, public documents derive their authority from collective sources instead of from the individual who wrote them. Public documents speak on behalf of a group of people to articulate the principles and procedures that organize their purposes and guide their way of life.

Some public documents, such as the Ten Commandments or the Declaration of Independence, have taken on a sacred or nearly sacred character because they codify principles of morality and political liberty that are considered fundamental to a whole way of life. Their power resides in the authority people have invested over time in these documents as basic accounts of what they believe and hold most dear.

These documents shape public life. For example, the commandment that the Sabbath be a day of rest is evident in state laws that prohibit the sale of alcohol or regulate hours of business on Sunday. By the same token, the Fourth of July was established as a national holiday to commemorate the Declaration of Independence and the birth of the United States.

Other public documents serve to codify customary behavior and conventional social arrangements. Marriage vows, contracts, wills, and other agreements commit parties to binding relationships that are publicly and legally recognized. Articles of incorporation enable companies to do business, while documentation of not-for-profit status enables civic and arts groups to carry out their purposes. Codes of ethics govern the practice of such professions as medicine, law, scientific research, engineering, social work, and teaching.

Still other documents charter the mission and activities of voluntary associations people have formed to respond to particular needs—organizations such as student clubs, neighborhood associations, trade unions, advocacy groups, and community service projects. Writing a constitution for such a group literally constitutes it as a public entity by giving the group a name and a statement of purpose. Not only does this establish an identity for members of the group, it also enables them to be heard on the public record and to shape public opinion.

The call to write public documents grows out of a culture's need to establish institutions, social order, and predictable patterns of interaction among people. Since written words take on visible shape in documents, they can be stored as a relatively permanent and authoritative account of a culture's beliefs and practices so that people can consult them in order to consider and reconsider their meanings. Public documents create an archive, the collective memory of a culture.

The public documents that form a culture's archive do not themselves change, though their meanings can and often do. The words on the page remain the same, for written documents serve as a kind of external memory to preserve what people or institutions want to commit to writing at a particular time. This is in part what gives documents such as the Ten Commandments or the Declaration of Independence or the Bill of Rights their special authority—their language seems to be fixed once and for all.

At the same time, however, the judgments readers draw from these documents can change over time. Readers will return repeatedly to documents such as the Bill of Rights to invoke its authority to interpret new situations. The language of the First Amendment guaranteeing Americans freedom of speech defines one of the fundamental principles of a democratic society. Nonetheless, even though the language of the First Amendment seems to be fixed and precise, its meaning remains in flux as citizens debate how its principles should be applied to cases of violence in the media, pornography, or hate speech. Likewise, Jews and Christians continually debate what the commandment "You shall not kill" means and whether factors such as self-defense or war modify the meaning of the commandment.

Public documents can tell us a lot about the culture we're living in. The encounters people have with public documents reveal how writing links individuals to social institutions. Just as important, you can write and use documents on your own behalf to accomplish your ends—to establish new voluntary associations and their purposes, to define policies and procedures you're willing to live by, to recruit sympathizers to a cause you believe in, to articulate new social identities, and to define new directions for the future.

EXPLORING YOUR EXPERIENCE

List as many documents from your college or university as you can that involve students. Pick one that in your view reveals something interesting about students' relationship to others. It could be your college's honor code or its policy on sexual harassment, a student loan form, or a job description. Analyze the relationship the document seeks to establish between the individual student and others. Describe what the document covers. What rights and responsibilities does it assign to the individual student? What rights and responsibilities does it assign to others? What beliefs does the document attempt to put into practice?

READINGS

Encounters with Public Documents. Abraham Verghese, from *My Own Country,* and Ellen Cushman, from *The Struggle and the Tools*

The following two reading selections offer accounts of how ordinary people encounter public documents and glimpses of what is at stake in these encounters. The first reading is taken from Abraham Verghese's book *My Own Country,* an account of his experience as a doctor working with HIV-positive and AIDS patients in Johnson City, Tennessee. This selection recounts a medical emergency where Verghese had to determine whether to put a patient on life support machines. As you will see, legal documents concerning both the patient's wishes and who will make the decision play prominent roles in shaping the outcome.

The second reading is from Ellen Cushman's *The Struggle and the Tools,* a study of how African-Americans in an inner city neighborhood negotiate with various public institutions. This selection focuses on how a particular individual, Lucy Cadens, makes sense of the forms to apply for the Home Emergency Assistance Program (HEAP) that provides help to offset high utility costs.

From *My Own Country*

ABRAHAM VERGHESE

1   Bobby Keller called me in the office as I was about to leave for home. He sounded shrill and alarmed.

2   "Doc? Ed is very sick! He is very, very short of breath and running a fever. A hundred and three. Dr. Verghese, he's turning blue on me."

3   "Bobby, call the emergency ambulance service—tell them to bring you to the Johnson City Medical Center."

4   Ed Maupin, the diesel mechanic, had had a CD4 count of 30 the previous week when I had seen him in clinic; Bobby Keller's was 500. At that visit, Ed's oral thrush had cleared up but he was still feeling tired and had been missing work. When I had examined Ed, the lymph nodes in his neck, which had been as big as goose eggs, had suddenly shrunk: I had thought to myself that this was either a good sign or a very bad sign; his immune system had either given up the fight or successfully neutralized the virus. The latter was unlikely.

5   Bobby, at that visit, had looked well and continued to work in the fashion store. I hoped now that Bobby's description of the gravity of the situation was just histrionics.

6   I was at the Miracle Center well ahead of the ambulance. Soon it came roaring in, all its lights flashing. When the back door opened, I peeked in: Ed's eyes

were rolled back in his head, and he was covered with a fine sheen of sweat. Despite the oxygen mask that the ambulance crew had on, his skin was the color of lead. His chest was making vigorous but ineffective excursions.

7   Bobby, who had ridden in the front, was scarcely able to stand up. His face was tremulous; he was on the verge of fainting.

8   "Don't put him on no machines, whatever you do," Bobby begged me. "Please, no machines."

9   "Why?"

10   "Because that's what he told me. He doesn't want it."

11   "When did he tell you? Just now?"

12   "No. A long time ago."

13   "Did he put it in writing? Does he have a living will?"

14   "No…"

15   In the emergency room, I stabilized Ed as best I could without intubating him. I took his oxygen mask off momentarily and looked at his mouth. His mucous membranes were loaded with yeast again—it had blossomed in just a week. But I was examining his mouth to try to decide how difficult it would be to intubate him. His short, receding lower jaw, which the beard concealed well, could make this a tricky intubation. I asked him to say "aaah." He tried to comply; his uvula and tonsils just barely came into view, another sign that he would be a tough intubation.

16   Ideally, an anesthetist would have been the best person to perform intubation. But I didn't want to call an anesthetist who, given the patient, might or might not be willing to do this procedure. Time was running out.

17   Ed was moaning and muttering incomprehensibly; his brain was clearly not getting enough oxygen. His blood pressure was 70 millimeters of mercury systolic over 50 diastolic. This was extremely low for him, because he had baseline hypertension. His cold, clammy extremities told me that the circulation to his arms and legs had shut down in an effort to shunt blood to the brain; even so, what blood got to the brain was not carrying enough oxygen. Ed's chest sounded dull in the bases when I percussed it; on listening with my stethoscope, he was wet and gurgly. The reason he was not oxygenating his blood was clear: his lungs were filled with inflammatory fluid. I ordered a stat chest x-ray and arterial blood gases. I had only a few minutes before I had to either breathe for him, or let him go. I needed more guidance from Bobby as to Ed's wishes.

18   I had an excellent nurse assisting me; she had already started an IV and brought the "crash cart." The respiratory therapist was administering oxygen and had an Ambu bag ready. I asked them to get goggles and masks in addition to their gloves, and to get a gown, mask and gloves ready for me. They were to put theirs on and wait for me. The curtains were pulled and Ed's presence was largely unnoticed in the bustle of the ER. An orthopedist was putting a cast on an individual in the next room, and patients were waiting in the other cubicles.

19   I came out to the waiting room, but Bobby was not there!

20   I hurried outside.

21   Bobby and three other men and one woman were near the ambulance entrance, smoking. The men bore a striking resemblance to Ed Maupin—the same

sharp features, the slightly receding chin. One of them, the oldest, wore a green work uniform. I recognized his face as a familiar one, someone who worked in an auto parts store where I had ordered a replacement bumper for the rusted one that had fallen off my Z. Bobby Keller, still trembling, introduced me to Ed's brothers, all younger than Ed. The woman was the wife of one of the brothers.

22   "Bobby," I asked, "can I tell them what's going on?"

23   "Tell them everything," Bobby said, the tears pouring down uncontrollably, his body shaking with sobs.

24   I addressed the brothers: "Ed is very sick. A few months ago we found out he has AIDS." (There was no point in trying to make the distinction between HIV infection and AIDS. If Ed had not had AIDS when I saw him in the clinic, he most certainly did now.) "Now he has a bad pneumonia from the AIDS. I need to put him on a breathing machine in the next few minutes or he will die. I have a feeling that the pneumonia he has can be treated. If we put him on the breathing machine, it won't be forever. We have a good chance of getting him off. But Bobby tells me that Ed has expressed a desire not to be put on the machine."

25   The assembled family turned to Bobby who nodded vigorously: "He did! Said he never wanted to be on no machines."

26   The family was clear-eyed, trying to stay calm. They pulled hard at their cigarettes. The smoke rose quietly around their weathered faces. They looked like a Norman Rockwell portrait—small-town America's citizens in their work clothes in a hospital parking lot, facing a family crisis. But this situation was one that Norman Rockwell hadn't attempted, one he had never dreamed of. I felt they were fond of their oldest brother, though perhaps disapproving of his relationship with Bobby. Yet judging by how they had all been standing around Bobby when I walked out, I didn't think they had any strong dislike for Bobby—it was almost impossible to dislike him. They had had many years to get used to the idea of Bobby and Ed, the couple, and it was only the idea, I sensed, that they had somehow not accepted.

27   "We need to discuss this," the older brother said.

28   "We have no time, I need to go right back in," I said.

29   They moved a few feet away from Bobby and me. I asked Bobby, "Do you have power-of-attorney or anything like that to make decisions for Ed?" Bobby shook his head.

30   We looked over to where the family was caucusing. The oldest brother was doing all the talking. They came back.

31   "We want for you to do everything you can. Put him on the breathing machine, if you have to."

32   At this a little wail came out of Bobby Keller and then degenerated into sobs. I put my hand on Bobby's shoulder. He shook his head back and forth, back and forth. He wanted to say something but could not find a voice.

33   The oldest brother spoke again. His tone was matter-of-fact and determined:

34   "We are his family. We are legally responsible for him. We want you to do everything for him."

35   We are his family. I watched Bobby's face crumble as he suddenly became a mere observer with no legal right to determine the fate of the man he had loved

since he was seven years old. He was finally, despite the years that had passed and whatever acceptance he and Ed found together, an outsider.

36   I took him aside and said, "Bobby, I have to go on. There is no way for me not to at this point. There's a really good chance that I can rescue Ed from the pneumonia. If I thought it would only make Ed suffer, I wouldn't do it. If this is Pneumocystis, it should respond to treatment."

37   Bobby kept sobbing, shaking his head as I talked, fat tears rolling off his eyes onto the ground, onto his chest. He felt he was betraying Ed. He could not deliver on his promise.

38   I had no time to pacify Bobby or try to convince him. I rushed back in. Ed looked worse. As I went through the ritual of gowning and masking (it was reassuring to have rituals to fall back on, a ritual for every crisis), it struck me that the entire situation had been in my power to dictate. All I had to do was to come out and say that the pneumonia did not look good, that it looked like the end. I mentioned the respirator, I offered it as an option. I could have just kept quiet. I had, when it came down to the final moment, given Ed's brothers the power of family. Not Bobby.

39   But there was no time to look back now.

From *The Struggle and the Tools*
ELLEN CUSHMAN

1   Community members often interpreted the demeaning attitudes of institutional agents by assessing the oral and literate language used in day-to-day proceedings of public service organizations. The first example shows typical forms required to access programmatic services. Whether a DSS, Medicaid, or HUD application, they all came with a list of documents required in order to validate the completed form, an information sheet describing the program, and the actual application. Applicants completed the Home Emergency Assistance Program (HEAP) forms when they needed to offset their high utility costs. In January of 1996, Lucy Cadens picked up a HEAP application when she received a notice of termination of service from her utility company. Although she paid $45 or more a month on her bill, the high costs of gas and electric heat for a poorly insulated three-bedroom apartment continued to add up over the cold months. Her bill for January alone was close to $400, bringing her total owed to just over $960 for the winter of 1996. Lucy had heard about HEAP from a neighbor. Working on a limited budget of state funds, the HEAP office, was opened only through January and mid-February before its funding ran out. Lucy and I looked over the ten pages of the application materials in my car.

2   *"Jesus, these things are long," I flipped through my copies before I started the car. We were headed to our favorite buffet.*

3   *"They try to scare you out of applying. Try to discourage you. And it do for some folks. They see all these forms and all the shit you got to bring with you and they think, 'Hell, it gonna take me four or five hours just to pull this shit together.' And they don't do it. You spend all that time and what do you get in return?" We reached the buffet,*

parked in the slushy snow and buttoned our coats against the wind and flurries. I brought the application with me hoping she would talk more about it. We got our first round of food, chicken and rice soup, salads, and rolls, and we sat in a booth. Lucy took the "documentation requirements" sheet off the top of the stack and shook her head.

4

"Look at the hoops they make us jump through. Like we got nothing better to do than give them 'One or more of the following'" she read from the sheet. "Why would they need more than my Social Security card anyways?" She shook her head, poked at her pasta salad, and checked off the listed items she already had. She decided she needed to make more photocopies of everyone's birth certificates, but resented the assumptions behind the application: "They think we give up easy. Or that if we really need it, then we better be willing to work for it. That's why they need two verifications of my address. They think all poor people be tryin' to get a free ride. Or, we poor so we got to be watched, you know? They be doublechecking us all the time." She sucked on her teeth in disgust and pushed her soup and salad dishes away. Turning to the application, she glanced over the first page. "I can go through this whole thing and tear it up. Every bit of it bullshit."

5

Lucy interprets the class-based prejudices permeating the language of this application. She understands that this public service organization views her as an unethical, shifty person by virtue of her having to complete the application in the first place. While many bureaucracies have long and involved forms to complete, community members attached significance to this length. The number of documents indicates to Lucy that the institution has hidden agendas. With the length of the form alone, the institution daunts the applicants ("They try to scare you out of applying. Try to discourage you."). The application as a whole places high demands on those seeking services. First, the demand is on time and energy and can be seen in the number of hours it takes to complete these forms ("it gonna take me four or five hours just to pull this shit together"). Second, the demands are on literate skills. To make this application successful, individuals selected only information they could convincingly support. Without certain verifications, such as one or more forms of identification, community members' applications would not present a compelling display of need. Residents understood that these demands were shaped from the belief that poor people need to "work" (read: appease gatekeepers) for their public assistance. "Look at the hoops they make us jump through," Lucy says. In order to receive their "awards," residents had to fill numerous institutional requirements.

6

Lucy also perceives the ways the institutions mistrust those they serve. Public service agencies view community members as often trying to manipulate the system of benefits in order to receive more ("they think all poor people be tryin' to get a free ride"). Because poor people are presumably unscrupulous, they will resort to illegal means more quickly, and therefore need to be policed: ("We poor so we got to be watched, you know? They be doublechecking us all the time"). These forms often asked for the same information to be presented in different ways. So verifications must accompany what the applicant lists, and when applicants handed in these forms, they often were asked verbally to recount what appears on the application. The caseworker would ask the applicant to recall specific lines of information (i.e., "so do you receive disability payments?") and doublecheck the verbal answers against the written. While one could argue that caseworkers are merely checking the internal consistency of the application, their verifications and questions indicated to residents that the institution perceives applicants as typically unethical and needing to be kept under surveillance.

7   My point here isn't so much that this literacy artifact represents the insidious values it does, but that Lucy critically reads this artifact, locates these insidious assumptions, and analyzes the politics imbued in this form. As she says, "I can go through this whole thing and tear it up. Every bit of it bullshit." She understands how public service institutions degrade those they seek to serve. She knows how institutional representatives view her using their own classist presumptions. She understands too that despite how much she balks at the institutions present throughout this application, she will still apply because she needs to keep her apartment warm. She did apply for this program, and did receive the aid she sought—four months after she submitted the application.

Analysis: Encountering Public Documents as Literacy Events

We can analyze these two reading selections as describing literacy events, in which pubic documents—or their absence—play a key role in how people interact with each other and make sense of things.

You can find an example of a "living will" or Directive to Physicians on page 192, in the "For Critical Inquiry" section.

In the excerpt from *My Own Country,* the absence of two crucial public documents shapes the outcome of this event. There is no "living will" to express Ed's wishes about medical treatment.

Nor is there a marriage license or power of attorney, entitling Bobby legally to make decisions on Ed's behalf. Instead, as Ed's oldest brother tells Abraham Verghese, "We are his family. We are legally responsible for him." It is precisely because the brothers' relationship to Ed can be documented in the public record that they have the legal right to make decisions. Family ties can be verified, while Bobby and Ed's relationship remains private and unofficial, neither legally recognized nor culturally sanctioned.

The selection from *The Struggle and the Tools* explores a case where a public document—the six-page HEAP application—is a source of mutual suspicion between public assistance workers and poor people seeking help. As Lucy Cadens points out, the sheer length of the application can discourage people from applying. Just as telling, Cadens reads the application as one that expresses mistrust of the applicants—that, in effect, assumes the worst about them.

FOR CRITICAL INQUIRY

1. Describe how the decision to put Ed on the respirator was made. Why is Abraham Verghese conflicted by the decision? Do you think he could or should have acted differently given the circumstances?

2. Here is the main text of a sample "living will," which Ed Maupin did not have on record. What protections does it offer a patient?

LDSS-3421 (Rev. 7/99)
PAGE

SECTION 4: HOUSEHOLD INCOME

CHECK (✓) YES OR NO FOR EVERY QUESTION. REPORT ANY INCOME FOR ALL HOUSEHOLD MEMBERS. ATTACH ADDITIONAL SHEETS IF NECESSARY

INDICATE IF YOU OR ANYONE WHO LIVES WITH YOU GETS MONEY FROM:

TYPE OF INCOME	CHECK ONE (✓)	WHO RECEIVES?	SOURCE OF INCOME	IF YES, GIVE AMOUNT
1. SOCIAL SECURITY/SOCIAL SECURITY DISABILITY including direct deposit	☐ NO ☐ YES			MONTHLY AMT. $
2. SUPPLEMENTAL SECURITY INCOME (SSI)	☐ NO ☐ YES			MONTHLY AMT. $
3. PENSION/RETIREMENT Private and/or government	☐ NO ☐ YES		Source of Pension	MONTHLY AMT. $
4. VETERAN'S BENEFITS	☐ NO ☐ YES			MONTHLY AMT. $
5. DISABILITY private or NYS	☐ NO ☐ YES			WEEKLY AMT. $
6. CONTRIBUTION from someone outside the household	☐ NO ☐ YES		Name of Contributor	MONTHLY AMT. $
7. CHILD SUPPORT (received)	☐ NO ☐ YES			Court ordered weekly amt. $
8. ALIMONY including payments for mortg...				
9. RENTAL INCOME apartment, garage, l...				
10. ROOM/BOARD (received) etc.				
11. WORKER'S COMPENSATION				
12. UNEMPLOYMENT BENEFITS				
13. TAP, PELL, STUDENT LOANS				
14. INTEREST from savings, checking, CD's etc.				
15. DIVIDENDS from stocks, bonds, securit...				

16. Does anyone in the household work?

If yes, submit wage stubs for the past 4 w...

IS THERE ANY OTHER INCOME FROM ANY OTH...

I understand that if I am contacted and sign...
not be required to complete and sign...
awareness of HEAP requirements as e...
agency to verify or confirm information...
requirements for future HEAP years.

If you apply to Bell Atlantic for telephon...
information provided in your application...
Line Telephone Service.

I swear and/or affirm that the informa...
Misrepresentation knowingly made by t...
assistance paid to me or on my behal...
obtaining assistance under this progra...
understand that by signing this Applica...
any other investigation by any Authoriz...

ALL QUESTIONS MUST B...

SIGN HERE: X
NAME OF PERSON, IF Any, WHO ASSISTED YOU...

Application compared to previous in...
☐ No prior application

☐ PENDED   START:

TOTAL INCOME $ CAT...

CERTIFYING AGENCY

WORKER'S SIGNATURE / DATE

SUPERVISOR'S INITIALS / DATE

PAGE 4
LDSS-3421 (Rev. 7/99)

PERSONAL PRIVACY LAW - NOTIFICATION TO CLIENTS

The State's Personal Privacy Protection Law, which took effect September 1, 1984, states that we must tell you what the State will do with the information you give us about yourself and your family. We use the information too find out if you are eligible for the Home Energy Assistance Program and, if so, for how much. The section of the Law gives us the right to collect the information about you is Section 21 of the Social Services Law. To make sure that you are getting all of the assistance you and your family are legally entitled to receive, we check with other sources to find out more about the information you have given us. For example:

- We may check to find out if you were working. We do this by sending your name and Social Security Number to the State Department of Taxation and Finance, and also to known employers, to tell us whether you worked and, if so, how much you made.

- We may ask the State to check with the Unemployment Insurance Division to see if you were getting unemployment benefits.

- We may check with banks to make sure we know about any income you may have received.

Besides using the information you give us in this way, the State also uses the information to prepare statistics about all the people receiving Home Energy assistance. This information...
State to make sure local districts are...
payments to such vendor. Your failure...
assistance and we may then have to...
Support Information Services, 40 North...

Comments, resolutions activities, incom...
expedited regular benefit, vendor conta...

PAGE 2
LDSS-3421 (Rev. 7/99)

IS THERE ANYONE LIVING IN YOUR HOME/APARTMENT, INCLUDING YOURSELF, WHO IS:

BLIND OR DISABLED	☐ NO	☐ YES	IF YES, WHO?
60 YEARS OR OLDER	☐ NO	☐ YES	IF YES, WHO?
UNDER 6 YEARS OLD	☐ NO	☐ YES	IF YES, WHO?

DO YOU OR DOES ANYONE LIVING AT YOUR ADDRESS GET FOOD STAMPS?

☐ NO ☐ YES   IF YES, WHO?   FS CASE NUMBER:

DO YOU OR DOES ANYONE IN YOUR HOUSE/APARTMENT GET PUBLIC ASSISTANCE?

☐ NO ☐ YES   IF YES, WHO?   PA CASE NUMBER:

SECTION 2: HOUSING — CHECK ONE BOX ONLY

☐ HOMEOWNER - Single Family House or Mobile Home

☐ HOMEOWNER - Multi-Family House

☐ CO-OP/CONDO OWNER

☐ RENTER - Public Housing Project or Seni...

☐ RENTER - Private Housing but receive government rent subsidy
Type of Subsidy

☐ RENTER - Private House, Apartment or Mobile Home

☐ RENTER with...

2. MY MONTHLY RENT OR MORTGAGE PAYME...

3. IF APPLICABLE, THE NAME OF THE APARTM...

4. DO YOU OR DOES ANYONE IN YOUR HOUS...

SECTION 3: HEAT AND UTILITY INFO...

**IF YOU PAY FOR YOUR OWN...
SECTION BE...**

My main source of heat is:
☐ Fuel Oil   ☐ Electric Heat
☐ Coal or Wood   ☐ Kerosene

Is the heating bill in your name? ☐ NO...
If "No," the bill is in the name of :

Relationship to you:
Your heating account number (Do no...
(if you have one) is:

Your heating company's name is:

STREET ADDRESS

CITY/TOWN

Do you also pay a utility company di...
cooking or hot water?
☐ NO ☐ YES
Your utility account number (Do...
(if you have one) is:

Your utility company's name is:

Is electric necessary to run the furn...

LDSS-3421 (Rev. 7/99)

HOME ENERGY ASSISTANCE PROGRAM APPLICATION
HEAP
Home Energy Assistance Program

IMPORTANT NOTICE

YOU SHOULD BE AWARE THAT THERE IS LIMITED MONEY AVAILABLE FOR HEAP BENEFIT PAYMENTS. ONCE AVAILABLE MONEY IS USED UP, NO BENEFITS WILL BE ISSUED AND THE PROGRAM WILL CLOSE. THEREFORE, IT IS STRONGLY RECOMMENDED THAT YOU COMPLETE AND RETURN YOUR APPLICATION AS SOON AS POSSIBLE. BE AWARE THAT IN PAST YEARS THE PROGRAM HAS CLOSED DOWN AS EARLY AS MARCH 12.

ANSWER ALL QUESTIONS. DO NOT WRITE IN THE SHADED AREAS. PLEASE PRINT CLEARLY, AND SIGN THE FORM ON PAGE 3.

AGENCY USE ONLY

CONTACT THE AGENCY ABOVE IF YOU NEED HELP

FUEL/UTILITY COMPANY NAME   ACCOUNT NUMBER   DATE RECEIVED   AGE CODE   AGE

OFFICE   APPLICATION DATE   UNIT ID   [WORKER ID.   ]CASE TYPE]CASE NUMBER   REGISTRY NUMBER   VERS.

CASE NAME

SECTION 1: HOUSEHOLD COMPOSITI...

MY NAME, DATE OF BIRTH, SEX, SOCIAL...

FIRST   MI   LAST

MY MAILING ADDRESS (IF DIFFERENT FROM AB...
NO.   STREET

HAVE YOU APPLIED FOR HEAP RECENTLY?...

MY MAIDEN NAME AND/OR OTHER NAMES BY W...
FIRST NAME   MI...

TOTAL NUMBER OF PEOPLE WHO LIVE IN MY HO...

BESIDES MYSELF, THE FOLLOWING PEOPLE LIV...

CD	LN	FIRST NAME	MI	...
1	02			
1	03			
1	04			
1	05			
1	06			
1	07			
1	08			

DSS-3431 (Rev. 6/93) FACE   APPLICANT NAME   DATE

HEAP
Home Energy Assistance Program

HOME ENERGY ASSISTANCE PROGRAM (HEAP)

DOCUMENTATION REQUIREMENTS

☐ WHEN YOU APPLY FOR HEAP ASSISTANCE IN PERSON, YOU MUST PROVIDE PROOF FOR ALL ITEMS LISTED BELOW.

☐ IF YOU HAVE ALREADY APPLIED FOR HEAP ASSISTANCE, YOU MUST PROVIDE PROOF OF THE ITEMS CIRCLED. BRING THESE STATEMENTS NO LATER THAN _____ OR YOUR APPLICATION MAY BE DENIED.

ADDRESS (Where you now live)

You must provide one or more of the following:
- Current rent receipt with name and address
- Copy of lease with address
- Water, sewage, or tax bill
- Mortgage payment books/receipts with address
- Homeowners insurance policy
- Deed

ALL PEOPLE IN YOUR HOUSEHOLD

You must provide one or more of the following for each person in your household:
- Birth certificate
- Baptismal certificate
- School records
- Social Security card
- Driver's license
- Marriage certificate

FUEL/UTILITY BILLS

- If you pay a fuel or utility bill, bring a copy of your most recent fuel/utility bill.
- If you pay for neither heat nor utilities, bring a statement from your landlord that indicates heat and utilities are included in your rent.
- If you have a utility emergency, bring your utility termination notice.

INCOME

You must provide proof of income for all household members who receive any type of income, earned or unearned, including but not limited to:

- Pay stubs for the most recent four weeks
- If self-employed or have rental income, business records for the most recent three months
- Child support or alimony checks
- Bankbook/dividend or interest statement
- Statement from roomer/boarder
- Other _____

COPY OF MOST RECENT CHECK OR AWARD LETTER:
- Social Security/Supplemental Security Income (SSI)
- Veteran's Benefits
- Pensions
- Worker's Compensation/Disability
- Verification of Unemployment Insurance Benefit amount
- Educational Grants/Loans

RESOURCES (For emergency applications only)

- Statement claiming zero resources
- Bank Statement showing current balance for checking, savings, and credit union accounts, IRA's, etc.
- Stocks, bonds, dividends

Depending on your circumstances, additional documentation may be required.

If you have any questions, please call _____

Declaration

If I should have an incurable and irreversible condition that has been diagnosed by two physicians and that will result in my death within a relatively short time without the administration of life-sustaining treatment or has produced an irreversible coma or persistent vegetative state, and I am no longer able to make decisions regarding my medical treatment, I direct my attending physician, pursuant to the Natural Death Act of California, to withhold or withdraw treatment, including artificially administered nutrition and hydration, that only prolongs the process of dying or the irreversible coma or persistent vegetative state and is not necessary for my comfort or to alleviate pain.

If Ed had had a signed living will, do you think Verghese's decision about putting him on a respirator would have been different? Why or why not?

1. Notice how Lucy Cadens identifies assumptions that public assistance agencies make about poor people and how these assumptions are reflected in their application forms. What are these assumptions? What must Cadens assume in order to identify the attitudes expressed in forms such as the HEAP application?

2. What experience, if any, have you had filling out application forms? How does it compare to Cadens' experience? How would you explain differences and similarities?

3. Explain how the two readings could be analyzed as literacy events. In Chapter 1, literacy events are defined as "ways to think about how reading and writing enter people's lives and shape their interactions with others." Apply the definition to the two readings. How does the presence and absence of public documents influence how the literacy event takes place?

Manifestos: *First Things First Manifesto 2000* and "Hacker's Manifesto, or the Conscience of a Hacker"

Manifestos are public declarations of purpose, position, and intention. The American Declaration of Independence, the Rights of Man in the French Revolution, and the Communist Manifesto of 1848 are classic examples of manifestos. These proclamations perform symbolic actions, such as severing the American colonists' ties to England, establishing the basis of free citizenship, or calling for workers of the world to unite. The two manifestos featured here also perform symbolic actions. The first is a manifesto of graphic designers "First Things First Manifesto 2000" that calls for a reorientation of the design profession away from advertising consumer products to more socially useful ends. In contrast, the second manifesto, "Hacker's Manifesto, or The Conscience of a Hacker," was written and signed by an individual rather than a group. The Mentor wrote "The Hacker's Manifesto" to explain and justify the "crime" of hacking shortly after his arrest in 1986.

First Things First Manifesto 2000

We, the undersigned, are graphic designers, art directors, and visual communicators who have been raised in a world in which the techniques and apparatus of advertising have persistently been presented to us as the most lucrative, effective and desirable use of our talents. Many design teachers and mentors promote this belief; the market rewards it; a tide of books and publications reinforces it.

Encouraged in this direction, designers then apply their skill and imagination to sell dog biscuits, designer coffee, diamonds, detergents, hair gel, cigarettes, credit cards, sneakers, butt toners, lite beer and heavy-duty recreational vehicles. Commercial work has always paid the bills, but many graphic designers have now let it become, in large measure, what graphic designers do. This, in turn, is how the world perceives design. The profession's time and energy is used up manufacturing demand for things that are inessential at best.

Many of us have grown increasingly uncomfortable with this view of design. Designers who devote their efforts primarily to advertising, marketing and brand development are supporting, and implicitly endorsing, a mental environment so saturated with commercial messages that it is changing the very way citizen-consumers speak, think, feel, respond and interact. To some extent we are all helping draft a reductive and immeasurably harmful code of public discourse.

There are pursuits more worthy of our problem-solving skills. Unprecedented environmental, social and cultural crises demand our attention. Many cultural interventions, social marketing campaigns, books, magazines, exhibitions, educational tools, television programs, films, charitable causes and other information design projects urgently require our expertise and help.

We propose a reversal of priorities in favor of more useful, lasting and democratic forms of communication—a mind shift away from product marketing and toward the exploration and production of a new kind of meaning. The scope of debate is shrinking; it must expand. Consumerism is running uncontested; it must be challenged by other perspectives, expressed, in part, through the visual languages and resources of design.

In 1964, twenty-two visual communicators signed the original call for our skills to be put to worthwhile use. With the explosive growth of global commercial culture, their message has only grown more urgent. Today, we renew their manifesto in expectation that no more decades will pass before it is taken to heart.

Jonathan Barnbrook
Nick Bell
Andrew Blauvelt
Hans Bockting
Irma Boom
Sheila Levrant de Bretteville
Max Bruinsma
Sian Cook
Linda van Deursen
Chris Dixon
William Drenttel
Gert Dunbar
Simon Esterson
Vince Frost
Ken Garland
Milton Glaser
Jessica Helfand
Steven Heller
Andrew Howard
Tibor Kalman
Jeffrey Keedy
Zuzana Licko
Ellen Lupton
Katherine McCoy
Armand Mevis
J. Abbott Miller
Rick Poynor
Lucienne Roberts
Erik Spiekermann
Jan van Toorn
Teal Triggs
Rudy VanderLans
Bob Wilkinson

Hacker's Manifesto, or the Conscience of a Hacker
THE MENTOR

1   Another one got caught today, it's all over the papers, "Teenager Arrested in Computer Crime Scandal," "Hacker Arrested after Bank Tampering"...

2   Damn kids. They're all alike.

3   But did you, in your three-piece psychology and 1950s technobrain, ever take a look behind the eyes of the hacker? Did you ever wonder what makes him tick, what forces shaped him, what may have molded him?

4   I am a hacker, enter my world...

5   Mine is a world that begins with school...I'm smarter than most of the other kids, this crap they teach us bores me...

6   Damn underachiever. They're all alike.

7   I'm in junior high or high school. I've listened to teachers explain for the fifteenth time how to reduce a fraction. I understand it. "No, Ms. Smith, I didn't show my work. I did it in my head..."

8   Damn kid. Probably copied it. They're all alike.

9   I made a discovery today. I found a computer. Wait a second, this is cool. It does what I want it to. If it makes a mistake, it's because I screwed it up. Not because it doesn't like me...

10   Or feels threatened by me...

11   Or thinks I'm a smart ass...

12   Or doesn't like teaching and shouldn't be here...

13   Damn kid. All he does is play games. They're all alike.

14   And then it happened...a door opened to a world...rushing through the phone line like heroin through an addict's veins, an electronic pulse is sent out, a refuge from the day-to-day incompetencies is sought...a board is found.

15   "This is it...this is where I belong..."

16   I know everyone here...even if I've never met them, never talked to them, may never hear from them again...I know you all...

17   Damn kid. Tying up the phone line again. They're all alike...

18   You bet your ass we're all alike...we've been spoon-fed baby food at school when we hungered for steak...the bits of meat that you did let slip through were pre-chewed and tasteless. We've been dominated by sadists, or ignored by the apathetic. The few that had something to teach found us willing pupils, but those few are like drops of water in the desert.

19   This is our world now...the world of the electron and the switch, the beauty of the baud. We make use of a service already existing without paying for what could be dirt-cheap if it wasn't run by profiteering gluttons, and you call us criminals. We explore...and you call us criminals. We seek after knowledge...and you call us criminals. We exist without skin color, without nationality, without religious bias...and you call us criminals. You build atomic bombs, you wage wars, you mur-

der, cheat, and lie to us and try to make us believe it's for our own good, yet we're the criminals.

20   Yes, I am a criminal. My crime is that of curiosity. My crime is that of judging people by what they say and think, not what they look like. My crime is that of outsmarting you, something that you will never forgive me for.

21   I am a hacker, and this is my manifesto. You may stop this individual, but you can't stop us all...after all, we're all alike.

Analysis: Declaring New Identities

While the two manifestos—"First Things First Manifesto 2000" and "Hacker's Manifesto, or the Conscience of a Hacker"—differ in many respects, they both project a powerful sense of identity. The manifestos begin with a critique of the current state of affairs and then call for or justify alternative actions. In the case of "First Things First," the signers note how they have become "increasingly uncomfortable" with the "mental environment" they have helped to design. Then they propose a "reversal of priorities" away from advertising toward "more useful, lasting, and democratic forms of communication." In the case of "The Hacker's Manifesto," The Mentor first explains what school and the adult world are like for kids like him and how they get labeled ("Damn kids. They're all alike"). Then The Mentor turns the label "criminal" around to justify what hackers do and to assure the authorities that though he has been caught ("You can't stop us all... after all, we're all alike").

Just as the Declaration of Independence contains its list of grievances against the king of England, these two manifestos start with a sense of urgency not just to correct the current state of affairs but to take an entirely different course of action. Both manifestos are, in effect, declarations of independence. By breaking with things as they are, each manifesto declares a new identity—as socially responsible designers or as a hacker—and thereby provides for readers the key point of identification with the aims of the manifesto.

FOR CRITICAL INQUIRY

1. The opening three paragraphs of "First Things First" sketch what is wrong with the profession of graphic design today. What exactly are the signers of the manifesto concerned about? What examples do they provide as evidence? How do these three paragraphs establish the grounds for the following three paragraphs?

2. As noted by the signers, "First Things First Manifesto 2000" renews the original "First Things First Manifesto" of 1964. You can find both manifestos, as well as examples of graphic design work that embodies the spirit of "First Things First" at the Adbusters Web site <www.adbusters.org>. Visit the site. Compare the 2000 manifesto to the 1964 original call.

What do you see as the main differences and similarities? How do the design examples provide an alternative way of thinking about visual communication?

3. One of the key rhetorical moves in "Hacker's Manifesto" is redefining who is a "criminal." Explain how The Mentor makes the redefinition. What is he asking readers to assume about the nature of crime? Do you agree with him? Why or why not?

4. Consider the persona, or ethos, created by each of the manifestos. First, describe the persona in each. How do the manifestos shape a sense of identity? How would you describe the kind of relationship they want to enter into with readers? Second, compare the two manifestos. What do you see as the main differences and similarities in terms of the ethos each seeks to establish?

5. The timing of each manifesto is significant. "First Things First Manifesto 2000" appeared thirty-six years after "First Things First," and the "Hacker's Manifesto" was written a few days after The Mentor was arrested. Explain the call to write in each situation.

Proposition 215. Medical Use of Marijuana: California State Ballot 1996

Proposition 215 is a voter initiative to legalize the use of marijuana for medical purposes that appeared on the 1996 California state ballot. Despite opposition from the American Medical Association and President Bill Clinton, the measure passed decisively, with 55.6 percent of the vote. The following documents include the text of the proposed law, an analysis of Proposition 215, and the arguments in favor of and against Proposition 215 from the 1996 California state ballot. As you read, imagine that you are a voter considering how you will cast your ballot.

Proposition 215: Text of Proposed Law

1   This initiative measure is submitted to the people in accordance with the provisions of Article II, Section 8 of the Constitution.

2   This initiative measure adds a section to the Health and Safety Code; therefore, new provisions proposed to be added are printed in *italic type* to indicate that they are new.

Proposed Law

3   SECTION 1. Section 11362.5 is added to the Health and Safety Code, to read:

4   *11362.5. (a) This section shall be known and may be cited as the Compassionate Use Act of 1996.*

5   *(b)(1) The people of the State of California hereby find and declare that the purposes of the Compassionate Use Act of 1996 are as follows:*

6   *(A) To ensure that seriously ill Californians have the right to obtain and use marijuana for medical purposes where that medical use is deemed appropriate and has been recommended by a physician who has determined that the person's health would benefit from the use of marijuana in the treatment of cancer, anorexia, AIDS, chronic pain, spasticity, glaucoma, arthritis, migraine, or any other illness for which marijuana provides relief.*

7   *(B) To ensure that patients and their primary caregivers who obtain and use marijuana for medical purposes upon the recommendation of a physician are not subject to criminal prosecution or sanction.*

8   *(C) To encourage the federal and state governments to implement a plan to provide for the safe and affordable distribution of marijuana to all patients in medical need of marijuana.*

9   *(2) Nothing in this section shall be construed to supersede legislation prohibiting persons from engaging in conduct that endangers others, nor to condone the diversion of marijuana for nonmedical purposes.*

10   *(c) Notwithstanding any other provision of law, no physician in this state shall be punished, or denied any right or privilege, for having recommended marijuana to a patient for medical purposes.*

11   *(d) Section 11357, relating to the possession of marijuana, and Section 11358, relating to the cultivation of marijuana, shall not apply to a patient, or to a patient's primary caregiver, who possesses or cultivates marijuana for the personal medical purposes of the patient upon the written or oral recommendation or approval of a physician.*

12   (e) For the purposes of this section, "primary caregiver" means the individual designated by the person exempted under this section who has consistently assumed responsibility for the housing, health, or safety of that person.

13   SEC. 2. If any provision of this measure or the application thereof to any person or circumstance is held invalid, that invalidity shall not affect other provisions or applications of the measure that can be given effect without the invalid provision or application, and to this end the provisions of this measure are severable.

Analysis of Proposition 215 by the Legislative Analyst
Background

14   Under current state law, it is a crime to grow or possess marijuana, regardless of whether the marijuana is used to ease pain or other symptoms associated with illness. Criminal penalties vary, depending on the amount of marijuana involved. It is also a crime to transport, import into the state, sell, or give away marijuana.

15   Licensed physicians and certain other health care providers routinely prescribe drugs for medical purposes, including relieving pain and easing symptoms accompanying illness. These drugs are dispensed by pharmacists. Both the physician and pharmacist are required to keep written records of the prescriptions.

Proposal

16   This measure amends state law to allow persons to grow or possess marijuana for medical use when recommended by a physician. The measure provides for the

use of marijuana when a physician has determined that the person's health would benefit from its use in the treatment of cancer, anorexia, AIDS, chronic pain, spasticity, glaucoma, arthritis, migraine, or "any other illness for which marijuana provides relief." The physician's recommendation may be oral or written. No prescriptions or other record-keeping is required by the measure.

17   The measure also allows caregivers to grow and possess marijuana for a person for whom the marijuana is recommended. The measure states that no physician shall be punished for having recommended marijuana for medical purposes. Furthermore, the measure specifies that it is not intended to overrule any law that prohibits the use of marijuana for *nonmedical* purposes.

Fiscal Effect

18   Because the measure specifies that growing and possessing marijuana is restricted to medical uses when recommended by a physician, and does not change other legal prohibitions on marijuana, this measure would probably have no significant state or local fiscal effect.

Argument in Favor of Proposition 215

19   Arguments on this page are the opinions of the authors and have not been checked for accuracy by any official agency.

Proposition 215 Helps Terminally Ill Patients

20   Proposition 215 will allow seriously and terminally ill patients to legally use marijuana, if, and only if, they have the approval of a licensed physician.

21   We are physicians and nurses who have witnessed firsthand the medical benefits of marijuana. *Yet today in California, medical use of marijuana is illegal.* Doctors cannot prescribe marijuana, and terminally ill patients must break the law to use it.

22   Marijuana is not a cure, but it can help cancer patients. Most have severe reactions to the disease and chemotherapy—commonly, severe nausea and vomiting. One in three patients discontinues treatment despite a 50% chance of improvement. When standard anti-nausea drugs fail, marijuana often eases patients' nausea and permits continued treatment. It can be either smoked or baked into foods.

Marijuana Doesn't Just Help Cancer Patients

23   University doctors and researchers have found that marijuana is also effective in: lowering internal eye pressure associated with glaucoma, slowing the onset of blindness; reducing the pain of AIDS patients, and stimulating the appetites of those suffering malnutrition because of AIDS 'wasting syndrome'; and alleviating muscle spasticity and chronic pain due to multiple sclerosis, epilepsy, and spinal cord injuries.

24   When one in five Americans will have cancer, and 20 million may develop glaucoma, shouldn't our government let physicians prescribe any medicine capable of relieving suffering?

25   The federal government stopped supplying marijuana to patients in 1991. Now it tells patients to take Marinol, a synthetic substitute for marijuana that can cost $30,000 a year and is often less reliable and less effective.

26   Marijuana is not magic. But often it is the only way to get relief. A Harvard University survey found that almost one-half of cancer doctors surveyed would prescribe marijuana to some of their patients if it were legal.

If Doctors Can Prescribe Morphine, Why Not Marijuana?

27   Today, physicians are allowed to prescribe powerful drugs like morphine and codeine. It doesn't make sense that they cannot prescribe marijuana, too.

28   Proposition 215 allows physicians to recommend marijuana in writing or verbally, but if the recommendation is verbal, the doctor can be required to verify it under oath. Proposition 215 would also protect patients from criminal penalties for marijuana, but ONLY if they have a doctor's recommendation for its use.

Marijuana Will Still be Illegal for Non-Medical Use

29   Proposition 215 DOES NOT permit non-medical use of marijuana. Recreational use would still be against the law. Proposition 215 does not permit anyone to drive under the influence of marijuana.

30   Proposition 215 allows patients to cultivate their own marijuana simply because federal laws prevent the sale of marijuana, and a state initiative cannot overrule those laws.

31   Proposition 215 is based on legislation passed twice by both houses of the California Legislature with support from Democrats and Republicans. Each time, the legislation was vetoed by Governor Wilson.

32   Polls show that a majority of Californians support Proposition 215. Please join us to relieve suffering and protect your rights. VOTE YES ON PROPOSITION 215.

RICHARD J. COHEN, M.D.
Consulting Medical Oncologist (Cancer Specialist)
California-Pacific Medical Center, San Francisco

IVAN SILVERBERG, M.D.
Medical Oncologist (Cancer Specialist), San Francisco

ANNA T. BOYCE
Registered Nurse, Orange County

Argument Against Proposition 215

33   Arguments on this page are the opinions of the authors and have not been checked for accuracy by any official agency.

Read Proposition 215 Carefully* It Is a Cruel Hoax

34   The proponents of this deceptive and poorly written initiative want to exploit public compassion for the sick in order to legalize and legitimatize the widespread use of marijuana in California.

35   Proposition 215 DOES NOT restrict the use of marijuana to AIDS, cancer, glaucoma and other serious illnesses.

READ THE FINE PRINT. Proposition 215 legalizes marijuana use for *"any other illness for which marijuana provides relief."* This could include stress, headaches, upset stomach, insomnia, a stiff neck...or just about anything.

No Written Prescription Required
Even Children Could Smoke Pot Legally!

36   Proposition 215 does not require a written prescription. Anyone with the "oral recommendation or approval by a physician" can grow, possess, or smoke marijuana. No medical examination is required.

37   *THERE IS NO AGE RESTRICTION.* Even children can be legally permitted to grow, possess and use marijuana...without parental consent.

No FDA Approval* No Consumer Protection

38   Consumers are protected from unsafe and impure drugs by the Food and Drug Administration (FDA). This initiative makes marijuana available to the public without FDA approval or regulation. Quality, purity and strength of the drug would be unregulated. There are no rules restricting the amount a person can smoke or how often they can smoke it.

39   THC, the active ingredient in marijuana, is already available by prescription as the FDA approved drug Marinol.

40   Responsible medical doctors wishing to treat AIDS patients, cancer patients and other sick people can prescribe Marinol right now. They don't need this initiative.

National Institute of Health, Major Medical Groups Say No to
Smoking Marijuana for Medical Purposes

41   The National Institute of Health conducted an extensive study on the medical use of marijuana in 1992 and concluded that smoking marijuana is *not* a safe or more effective treatment than Marinol or other FDA approved drugs for people with AIDS, cancer or glaucoma.

42   The American Medical Association, the American Cancer Society, the National Multiple Sclerosis Society, the American Glaucoma Society and other top medical groups have *not* accepted smoking marijuana for medical purposes.

Law Enforcement and Drug Prevention Leaders
Say No to Proposition 215

The California State Sheriffs Association

The California District Attorneys Association

The California Police Chiefs Association

The California Narcotic Officers Association

The California Peace Officers Association

Attorney General Dan Lungren

43   say that Proposition 215 will provide new legal loopholes for drug dealers to avoid arrest and prosecution...

Californians for Drug-Free Youth

> The California D.A.R.E. Officers Association
>
> Drug Use Is Life Abuse
>
> Community Anti-Drug Coalition of America
>
> Drug Watch International

44   say that Proposition 215 will damage their efforts to convince young people to remain drug free. It sends our children the false message that marijuana is safe and healthy.

Home Grown Pot* Hand Rolled "Joints"
*Does This Sound Like Medicine?

45   This initiative allows unlimited quantities of marijuana to be grown any-where...in backyards or near schoolyards without regulation or restrictions. This is not responsible medicine. It is marijuana legalization.

Vote No On Proposition 215

JAMES P. FOX
President, California District Attorneys Association

MICHAEL J. MEYERS, M.D.
Medical Director, Drug and Alcohol Treatment
Program, Brotman Medical Center, CA

SHARON ROSE
Red Ribbon Coordinator, Californians for Drug-Free Youth, Inc.

Analysis: Expert Testimony and the Voters

The California state ballot uses the standard debate format of presenting arguments for and arguments against the proposition in question—in this case, whether the state of California should legalize the medical use of marijuana. Notice how the arguments differ in the way they approach readers. Supporters of Proposition 215 emphasize potential medical benefits, appeal to voters' desire to alleviate suffering, and provide assurances that the ballot measure limits the use of marijuana to medical cases. On the other hand, opponents of Proposition 215 urge voters to "read the fine print," point out that marijuana for medical use would not be subject to FDA approval, and use the testimony of medical, legal, and drug education groups to raise questions about the wisdom of medical marijuana.

     One striking result of the election is that the lack of support for medical marijuana by such well-established and reputable organizations as the American Medical Association, the National Institute of Health, and the American Cancer Society did not deter voters from passing Proposition 215. In this case, at least, the voters seemed to ignore expert testimony. Why this was so is, of course, a matter of interpretation. Some argue that the public's compassion for suffering patients overwhelmed good sense and the medical evidence, while others hold that mainstream medical and legal organizations are inflexible and out of touch with people's needs. You might come up with other reasons to explain when the public follows the advice of experts and when they don't.

FOR CRITICAL INQUIRY

1. One feature of the California ballot is that the text of all proposed laws is followed by an analysis that provides background information, summarizes the main features of the proposed law, and states its fiscal effect if passed. It is revealing to compare the styles of writing in the proposed law and in the analysis of Proposition 215. First, compare your understanding of the measure when you first read the Text of the Proposed Law to your understanding when you first read the Analysis of Proposition 215. Second, compare the legal writing in the Text of the Proposed Law to the prose in the Analysis. What are the main differences? What makes the Analysis more readable? What, if anything, is left out of the Analysis that appears in the Text?

2. How do the Arguments in Favor of and Against Proposition 215 seek to establish their ethos—their credibility, good will, and good sense?

3. Compare the type of response, or pathos, each Argument attempts to elicit on the part of voters. What emotions does each seek to draw on? What assumptions do the Arguments in Favor of and Against Proposition 215 make about the voters' state of mind and the intensity of their beliefs?

4. Analyze the Argument in Favor of Proposition 215 and the Argument Against. Identify the main claim or claims in each. What evidence is provided to support the claim or claims? What enabling assumptions connect the evidence to the claims?

5. Stage a formal debate in class. Divide the class into two teams—for and against Proposition 215. Each group should prepare a short presentation (5–10 minutes) of its position for or against. In addition, each group should prepare possible rebuttals of the other side's argument. This requires anticipating how the other side is likely to present its position and the reasons and evidence to support it. Then follow this format. Each group presents its position (5–10 minutes). Next, each group presents rebuttals of the other side's arguments (3–5 minutes). Finally, each group makes a closing statement (3–5 minutes). This format enables three members of each group to speak.

Council of Writing Program Administrators, WPA Outcomes Statement for First-Year Composition

The following statement about what students should learn in their first-year writing courses was approved in 2000 by the Executive Committee of the Council of Writing Program Administrators (WPA), the leading professional organization of college writing programs, and published in a number of professional journals. The statement began out of the felt need of writing teachers and program administrators to see whether a common set of goals might be identified that first-year writing programs, given their local differences, could be reasonably expected to follow. As you will see, the Outcomes Statement identified four main areas of knowledge, what writing students should learn in each area, and how faculty in all fields can build on this learning.

Outcomes

Rhetorical Knowledge

By the end of first-year composition, students should

- Focus on a purpose
- Respond to the needs of different audiences
- Respond appropriately to different kinds of rhetorical situations
- Use conventions of format and structure appropriate to the rhetorical situation
- Adopt appropriate voice, tone, and level of formality
- Understand how genres shape reading and writing
- Write in several genres

Faculty in all programs and departments can build on this preparation by helping students learn

- The main features of writing in their fields
- The main uses of writing in their fields
- The expectations of readers in their fields

Critical Thinking, Reading, and Writing

By the end of first-year composition, students should

- Use writing and reading for inquiry; learning, thinking, and communicating

- Understand a writing assignment as a series of tasks, including finding, evaluating, analyzing, and synthesizing appropriate primary and secondary sources
- Integrate their own ideas with those of others
- Understand the relationships among language, knowledge, and power

Faculty in all programs and departments can build on this preparation by helping students learn

- The uses of writing as a critical thinking tool
- The interactions among critical thinking, critical reading, and writing
- The relationships among language, knowledge, and power in their fields

Processes
By the end of first-year composition, students should

- Be aware that it usually takes multiple drafts to create and complete a successful text
- Develop flexible strategies for generating, revising, editing, and proof-reading
- Understand writing as an open process that permits writers to use later invention and re-thinking to revise their work
- Understand the collaborative and social aspects of writing processes
- Learn to critique their own and others' work
- Learn to balance the advantages of relying on others with the responsibility of doing their part
- Use a variety of technologies to address a range of audiences

Faculty in all programs and departments can build on this preparation by helping students learn

- To build final results in stages
- To review work-in-progress in collaborative peer groups for purposes other than editing
- To save extensive editing for later parts of the writing process
- To apply the technologies commonly used to research and communicate within their fields

Knowledge of Conventions
By the end of first-year composition, students should

- Learn common formats for different kinds of texts
- Develop knowledge of genre conventions ranging from structure and paragraphing to tone and mechanics

- Practice appropriate means of documenting their work
- Control such surface features as syntax, grammar, punctuation, and spelling

Faculty in all programs and departments can build on this preparation by helping students learn

- The conventions of usage, specialized vocabulary, format, and documentation in their fields
- Strategies through which better control of conventions can be achieved

Analysis: Establishing Standards of Practice

The WPA Outcomes Statement for First-Year Composition is a good example of the way institutions, government agencies, task forces, panels of experts, and professional associations set standards of practice in a broad range of areas—for doctors, nurses, educators, lawyers, insurance agents, stockbrokers, and engineers. Based on up-to-date knowledge and the best thinking of experts in the field, standards of practice such as the WPA Outcomes Statement provide guidelines for professional work. In this case, the WPA Outcomes Statement is the first in the history of American higher education to define what writing teachers and program administrators think students should learn in first-year composition.

What students should learn, of course, implies what teachers and programs should teach, and one of the delicate balances a document like the WPA Outcomes Statement must find is a clear articulation of common purposes that does not prescribe a rigid uniformity. On the one hand, without a shared sense of expectations, the document can have little meaning or influence. On the other, however, a document that is too prescriptive can unnecessarily infringe on teachers' autonomy, curtail their creativity, and undermine its own appeal. The ideal is not to tell other professionals what to do but to provide them with a set of standards they can use to think about and refine their own courses and programs.

FOR CRITICAL INQUIRY

1. The WPA Outcomes Statement is basically a bulleted list of things students should be able to do by the end of first-year composition. How do the four main areas—rhetorical knowledge; critical thinking, reading, and writing; processes; and knowledge of conventions—help to organize the list? Are there items on the list you find surprising? If so, why?

2. Compare the WPA Outcomes Statement to your expectations when you began your writing course. What goals did you have for yourself as a writer? Have you modified or revised your goals? To what extent do your present goals overlap with those of the WPA Outcomes? Do you have goals not listed by the WPA statement?

3. In each of the four main areas, the WPA Outcomes Statement lists how "faculty in all programs and departments can build on this preparation." Consider the writing you are called to do in your other courses. In what ways does this writing fit with the goals of the WPA statement? Are there other aims not listed by WPA?

4. What does the overall aim of the WPA Outcomes Statement seem to be? If you had to synthesize the outcomes in a sentence or two, how would you state the abilities the outcomes suggest students should have? What would these abilities enable students to do? Are there other things not mentioned in the WPA Outcomes Statement that students should learn about writing or learn to do with writing?

Visual Design: Paula Scher, "Defective Equipment: The Palm Beach County Ballot"

Paula Scher is a graphic designer and partner at Pentagram Design in New York City. Her visual analysis "Defective Equipment: the Palm Beach County Ballot" appeared as op-art in The *New York Times* four days after the 2000 presidential election. As you no doubt recall, the presidential election itself was not decided until a month later when the U.S. Supreme Court refused to allow the recount of contested ballots, thereby making George W. Bush the next president. Al Gore and his camp raised a number of issues about voting irregulari-

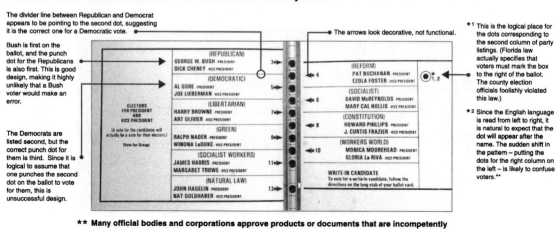

Paula Scher is a partner at Pentagram Design in New York.

ties in Florida. In the case of the now infamous Palm Beach County "butter-fly" ballot, it's hard to forget the frustration of many voters who thought they were voting for Al Gore but, due to the design of the ballot, voted for Pat Buchanan instead.

Analysis: Breaking Visual Design Conventions

The Palm Beach County ballot shows how the design of public documents can have very real consequences. No one knows for sure how many people in Palm Beach County intended to vote for Al Gore but, confused by the design of the ballot, voted for Pat Buchanan instead. Some go so far as to argue that the design of the ballot actually cost Gore the election. This may be, but let's leave that question aside for a moment to look more closely at how the ballot confused voters.

As Paula Scher's analysis points out, the ballot's design violated a number of visual conventions we as readers typically take for granted. We expect, that is, to follow documents from top to bottom and left to right. This is the normal reading path of written English, and any departure from it can cause confusion. Notice that the Palm Beach County ballot does not read consistently from top to bottom. Instead, although the Democratic candidates are listed second, the punch dot for them is third. This confusion, in turn, is caused by the fact that the ballot does not read consistently from left to right (as specified by Florida law). Instead, in the first column of candidates, voters read from the names of candidates on the left to the punch dots on the right, while the second column reverses direction, with the names on the right and the punch dots to the left.

FOR CRITICAL INQUIRY

1. Notice the design of Paula Scher's op-art piece "Defective Equipment: The Palm Beach County Ballot." Scher reproduces the section of the ballot in dispute and then uses arrows and written commentary to point out design flaws. Did you find her analysis easy to follow and understand? Why or why not?

2. Imagine that there was only written text available for the analysis. What would you have to say in writing to make the points that Scher does? What would be lost to the analysis?

3. Scher's analysis develops an argument that is presented in the double asterisked (**) two sentences in bold that appear underneath the ballot. Explain how the analysis leads visually to this point. How do the asterisks link the line of reasoning? Do the two sentences at the bottom seem to follow logically and persuasively from Scher's analysis?

4. The Palm Beach County ballot was designed and approved by Democrats. No one is suggesting that it was intended to rig the election for

George W. Bush, though clearly it helped him. Instead, the ballot appears to be a simple design error. What do you think should have been done immediately following the elections? Do you agree with those who argued that the design flaw literally (though not intentionally) disenfranchised voters—and that new elections should be held with new ballots?

5. Redesign the ballot to eliminate confusion.

FOR DISCUSSION AND ANALYTICAL WRITING

RHETORICAL ANALYSIS

Compare the rhetorical situation of two (or more) public documents presented in this chapter. Examine in particular the relationship between writers and readers that public documents help to establish. Consider on whose behalf (what organizations, institutions, or groups) the writers design the public documents and how readers happen to encounter them.

GENRE CHOICES

Under what circumstances do individuals or groups turn to the manifesto as a public declaration of a position, belief, or plan? What are the advantages and disadvantages of a manifesto as compared to a commentary, proposal, or other genre?

GOING ONLINE

Finding Online Documents at Your College

Colleges and universities are increasingly making important documents available online. Many now have online catalogs and course announcement bulletins. In some cases, students can register for classes online. In addition, many departments and programs have designed Web sites that students can visit to get information about courses, majors, and faculty interests. Work together in groups of three or four to explore what your college, its programs, and departments offer online. Do a search and bring your results to class.

The purpose of this exercise is first to find out what information is available to you and your classmates. Next, once the class has inventoried what is online, consider whether there are other documents or types of information that it would be useful to put online. Finally, if you have suggestions to make, you may want, as a class, to write a letter proposing that something be put or created online and explaining why it would be helpful to students. You will need, of course, to figure out who the proper person is to receive the letter.

WORKING TOGETHER

Writing a Class Charter

For this assignment, you will be working together as a whole class to design and produce a charter for the writing course you are currently taking. One way to do this assignment is to break the class into working groups of four to six, depending on the size of the class, with each group responsible for drafting one section of the charter. Here is one possible way of dividing the charter into sections. Your class, however, may decide to modify this plan.

See the Preamble to the Charter of the United Nations on page 214 for an example.

- **Preamble:** The preamble to a charter explains the purposes and goals of an organization or, in this case, of a writing course.

- **Teacher's rights and responsibilities to the students:** This section explains the role of the teacher in the writing course and what students can legitimately expect from the teacher.

- **Students' rights and responsibilities to the teacher.** This section explains the role of students in their relationship to the teacher in a writing class and what teachers can legitimately expect from them.

- **Students' rights and responsibilities to each other:** This section explains the relationship among students in a writing class and what students can legitimately expect from each other.

- **Bylaws governing classroom life:** While the first four sections will be somewhat general in their explanations of the goals of the course and individuals' roles within it, this section should be more specific, presenting the policies that will govern classroom life. Bylaws often appear in charters as numbered points. Here are some things you will likely want to consider in the bylaws section—such as attendance, timely completion of work, how to ensure that everyone is heard in class discussion, how to handle differences of opinion, and how to make group work productive. There are probably other things, depending on the circumstances, that you will want to cover in this section.

The class as a whole will need to discuss collectively what it wants to see appear in each of the sections. Then the working groups can draft sections, make sufficient copies, and bring them to class for revision. Or the class can work on and respond to the sections electronically through a listserv or Web page.

The "Invention," "Planning," "Drafting," and "Revising" sections in the writing assignment that follow can be helpful no matter which assignment you are doing.

WRITING ASSIGNMENT

The focus on public documents in this chapter can lead to a number of different writing assignments. The following list ranges from writing about public documents to designing your own documents. Your instructor will let you know which possibilities you can consider for this assignment.

(See Chapter 1 for more on analyzing literacy events.)

1. **Encounters with public documents:** Analyze an encounter you have had with a public document. Explain how the document shaped roles, relationships, and outcomes. Consider how encounters with public documents are literacy events.

2. **Rhetorical analysis:** Analyze one (or more) of the documents in this chapter or a public document of your choice. Focus on either the rhetorical situation that surrounds the document (Chapter 2) or the argument (Chapter 3).

3. **Using documents:** You can use documents such as the WPA Outcomes Statement to assess the current situation in light of professional guidelines and standards of practice. You might consider, for example, how your other courses do or do not build on your preparation in composition as suggested in the statement.

4. **Redesigning documents:** You could find a document where the visual design is confusing or hard to follow and redesign it for clarity and readability. Or you could rewrite a public document, such as marriage vows or the Bill of Rights, to redefine relationships, agreements, and courses of action.

5. **Manifesto:** Write a manifesto that explains what calls on you to publicly proclaim a new identity, mission, or purpose. Consider the persona you are inventing in the manifesto and on whose behalf the manifesto is speaking.

6. **Laws, statutes, Constitutional amendments:** You could write a law, statute, or Constitutional amendment. Include an argument for your legislation, using the 1996 Proposition 215 as a model.

Invention

Exploring the Topic

Whether you decide to write about a public document or to design (or redesign) one, a good way to start this assignment is to think about the public documents you have encountered and are likely to encounter in the future. Doing so may help you turn up a personal encounter with a public document you'd like to write about, a public document you'd like to analyze, or the need for a public document you'd like to design.

ETHICS OF WRITING

PLAIN LANGUAGE

Certain public documents—especially legal and financial documents—seem intended to intimidate, baffle, or exclude readers. Application forms for public services, as you can see in the reading selection from *The Struggle and the Tools,* can also have these effects. As a result, a movement to make public documents more accessible has emerged in recent years. The Plain English Campaign, for example, was started in the United Kingdom in 1979 by Chrissie Maher after she witnessed two elderly women die because they couldn't understand an application form for housing benefits. In the United States, in an attempt to make public documents more widely accessible, President Bill Clinton issued a memorandum calling on federal agencies to use plain language in government documents.

The informed participation of citizens in public life depends in part on being able to read and understand a host of documents. Critics have argued that what the Plain English Campaign calls "gobbledygook" and "legalese" amounts to an effort to restrict information to the experts, consolidate their power and prestige, and thereby disenfranchise ordinary people. You can find out more about the Plain English Campaign at <www.plainenglish.co.uk> and about the Plan Language Action Network (PLAN) in the federal government at <204.254.113.225>.

EXERCISE

Work through the following exercise to give yourself plenty of options. At this point, you are just surveying the range of documents and situations. Keep a list of documents that interest you.

1. Think through the stages of your life. What public documents have defined you to others at various times throughout your life? Which ones define you now? Can you imagine changing how these documents have influenced your life?

2. Go through your files of official documents at home. What functions do they serve? Are there any functions that you find position you in undesirable or uncomfortable ways? Is there a power structure implied in these documents that you find troublesome? How might you like to shift the power structure in one of these documents? Now, how would you do it if you were to revise and redesign the document?

3. Of the documents that you interact with in college, have any of them caused you problems or confusion? Which ones, and in what way? Do they need redesign?

4. Talk with parents and friends about public documents that have affected their lives in positive or negative ways. Is a labor union renegotiating a

contract at the factory where a relative works? Is a friend getting married in the near future? Do you have an acquaintance working on a political campaign or with a public interest research group? If so, try to get copies of some of the public documents included in those enterprises. Do they need you to help create one for them?

5. Throughout this chapter you have seen suggestions for public documents that are either missing or are somehow problematic (for example, the lack of legally binding agreements for same-sex couples). Skim back through the chapter, and see if any of those missing pieces provide you with the call to analyze or to write your own public document.

Defining Your Purpose

Once you have generated a list from the exercise above, select three or four situations, relationships, or problems where a public document is central or where one is lacking and seems to be called for. The following questions can help you clarify your purpose.

1. Consider who is involved in the situation. If a document exists, what role does it play in people's interactions? What, if anything, about the document needs clarification or change? If a document does not exist but is needed, how would a new document be used? How would it shape people's interactions?

2. Which of the three or four situations, relationships, or problems do you find most interesting and important? Which one most powerfully calls on you to write about it? What is the most appropriate response on your part to this call to write—to analyze a personal encounter, do a rhetorical analysis, redesign an existing document, or design a new one?

3. Write a one-page statement that describes the situation and explains the type of document you plan to analyze or to write.

4. Exchange the one-page statement with a classmate. Take turns asking your partner what he or she sees as your purpose. Ask your partner if the writing you plan to do seems the best response to the situation. If so, why? If not, why not?

Planning

Public documents often follow a set pattern, making them easily recognizable to readers and easily reproducible by writers to account for new situations. Different types of documents—whether a law, a contract, or an organization's charter—have their own typical design. If you are designing a document, a good way to begin is to find one or more examples of a document like it to identify its typical features. If you are analyzing an existing document, you will also want to pay attention to its design features.

Design of Documents

Consider the following features of the document:

■ **Title and logo:** How is the document titled? Does it use a logo or other identifying graphic feature?

■ **Preamble or background section:** Does the document have a preamble or a background section that explains the occasion that called for it and its general principles? Or does it simply begin by listing points?

See Chapter 19, "Visual Design," for more on white space, page layout, headings, and fonts.

■ **White space:** Does the document use white space to separate sections in the document and to emphasize key points?

■ **Headings and subheadings**: Does the document use headings and subheadings to denote separate sections? How do such divisions make the document easier to read?

■ **Bullets**: Does the document use bullets to emphasize key points?

■ **Fonts:** Does the document use capital letters, italics, boldface, underlinings, or designer fonts to emphasize key words or phrases?

■ **Parallelism:** Does the document use parallel grammatical structures? Here are some of the most commonly used structures:

Infinitives: "to save," "to reaffirm," "to establish," and so on (from the Preamble to the United Nations Charter)

Noun phrases: "Rhetorical Knowledge," "Critical Thinking, Reading, and Writing," "Processes," and "Knowledge of Conventions" (from WPA Outcomes Statement)

Repeated phrases: "By the end of first-year composition, students should…" "Faculty in all programs and departments can build on this preparation by helping students learn…" (from WPA Outcomes Statement)

■ **Signature:** Is the document signed? If so, by whom? What does signing commit people to?

Designing for Readability

The charter or constitution that serves as the founding document for a group, club, organization, or government body typically begins with a preamble that presents the general goals of the organization. It may also explain who is forming the new organization and what gives them the authority to do so. Notice how the Preamble to the United Nations Charter identifies that it is "we the people of the United Nations," through the power invested in their respective governments to represent them, who are founding the organization. By invoking the will of the people of all nations to "combine our efforts," the Preamble takes on a moral authority that goes beyond a simple diplomatic agreement among governments. As you read the Preamble, consider how the design of the document helps you mentally organize the founders' reasons for establishing the UN and the goals it sets forth.

The Preamble to the United Nations Charter

We the People of the United Nations Determined

1   to save succeeding generations from the scourge of war, which twice in our lifetime has brought untold sorrow to mankind, and

2   to reaffirm faith in fundamental human rights, in the dignity and worth of the human person, in the equal rights of men and women and of nations large and small, and

3   to establish conditions under which justice and respect for the obligations arising from treaties and other sources of international law can be maintained, and

4   to promote social progress and better standards of living in larger freedom,

And for These Ends

5   to practice tolerance and live together in peace with one another as good neighbors, and

6   to unite our strength to maintain international peace and security, and

7   to ensure, by the acceptance of principles and the institution of methods, that armed force shall not be used, save in the common interest, and

8   to employ international machinery for the promotion of the economic and social advancement of all peoples,

Have Resolved to Combine Our Efforts to Accomplish These Aims.

9   Accordingly, our respective Governments, through representatives assembled in the city of San Francisco, who have exhibited their full powers found to be in good and due form, have agreed to the present Charter of the United Nations and do hereby establish an international organization to be known as the United Nations.

EXERCISE

1. What effect does the use of the three phrases written in bold letters have on the readability of the document? How do they serve to focus your attention as a reader?

2. Notice that the first two parts of the Preamble comprise a single long sentence, which, if printed in the usual way, might be difficult to follow.

What specific design features does the document use to establish a predictable order that readers can anticipate in reading the sentence?

3. How is white space used in the Preamble? How does it contribute to the document's readability?

Working Draft

Whether you are analyzing a document or designing one of your own, you will want to consider the tone of the writing—the voice readers hear in the written text.

Tone and Rhetorical Distance

A writer's tone of voice is one key way of establishing his or her relationship to readers. Notice how the following examples of informal, standard, and official tone put the writer into quite different relationships to readers:

- Informal: Writing that speaks in the first person singular, addresses readers as "you," uses colloquialisms and contractions, poses rhetorical questions, and generally strives to sound like spoken language creates an informal tone that reduces the distance between the writer and readers. "Hacker's Manifesto," for example, seeks to involve readers and create a sense of intimacy. Whether or not readers agree with The Mentor, it is hard to be neutral or distant from his writing:

    > But did you, in your three-piece psychology and 1950s techno-brain, ever take a look behind the eyes of the hacker?
    >
    > I am a hacker, enter my world…

- Standard: The tone of voice readers hear in many instances of professional communication, journalism, textbooks, and other forms of non-fiction prose can be characterized as "standard" because it relies on a plain, relatively formal (but not elevated or pretentious) style. This tone does not usually call attention to the writer's personality, as is often the case with an informal tone, or address readers intimately as "you." Instead, it seeks to establish a relationship with readers based on shared interests and the mutual respect of reasonable persons exchanging views. Although writers may speak in the first person, the emphasis is on the message. "First Things First Manifesto 2000" is a good example of such a tone:

    > Commercial work has always paid the bills, but many graphic designers have now let it become, in large measure, what graphic designers do. This, in turn, is how the world perceives design.

> We propose a reversal of priorities in favor of more useful, lasting and democratic forms of communication—a mindshift away from product marketing and toward the exploration and production of a new kind of meaning.

- **Official:** An official tone creates the most distance between the written document and readers. The voice that readers hear is not that of an individual writer but of an institution or collective body speaking. The style of writing tends to be more "elevated" than either informal or standard writing, and there is often a certain bureaucratic or legalistic tone at work. Proposition 215 is a typical example. Notice how its official tone differs from the standard tone in the Analysis:

> [Official:] (b)(1) The people of the State of California hereby find and declare that the purposes of the Compassionate Use Act of 1996 are as follows:
> (A) To ensure that seriously ill Californians have the right to obtain and use marijuana for medical purposes where that medical use is deemed appropriate and has been recommended by a physician....
> [Standard:] This measure amends state law to allow persons to grow or possess marijuana for medical use when recommended by a physician.

Peer Commentary

Exchange drafts with a classmate. Depending on whether you have analyzed or designed a public document, use the appropriate guidelines.

For Document Design

1. Is the purpose of your partner's document clear and easy to find? Explain where in the document you became aware of its purpose. Will readers understand what its uses are?

2. What suggestions can you offer to improve or strengthen the format of the document? Consider its layout, organization, use of numbered or bulleted items, and other design features.

3. Is the language of the document precise and easy for readers to understand? Underline words, phrases, or passages that might be written more clearly. Explain why you marked them. Is the tone appropriate for the type of document your partner has designed? Why or why not? Circle words, phrases, or passages where you think the tone does not work well. Explain.

For Analysis of a Document

1. Explain what you see as the writer's purposes—analyzing a personal encounter with a public document, doing a rhetorical analysis, or something else? Is the main point of the analysis clearly stated and easy to find?

2. Describe how the writer develops an analysis. Does the analysis fulfill the writer's purposes or some other purposes? What suggestions can you offer to extend or deepen the analysis?

3. Do you agree with the analysis? If so, explain why. If not, explain why.

Revising

Review the peer commentary you have received and then consider these questions, depending on whether you've designed or analyzed a document:

For Document Design

1. Is the purpose of your document easy for the reader to identify?

2. Have you ordered your points in a way that is easy to follow? Check at this point to make sure similar points are parallel in structure.

3. Is each point clearly separate from other points? Consider the feedback you have received on the tone of the document.

For Analysis of a Document

1. Is the purpose your reader identified what you intended?

2. What suggestions about your analysis does your reader offer? Why do you think your reader made these suggestions?

3. What assumptions about your analysis does your reader seem to be making in agreeing or disagreeing with it? How do these assumptions compare to assumptions you make in the draft?

Locating Common Ground

Public documents such as laws, contracts, and codes are agreements about the way we will conduct ourselves and our relations with others. Because of this, documents rely on consent—through advocacy, voting in elections, and other forms of participation in decision making. When individuals and groups feel their views have not been represented in shaping the policies outlined in public documents, they are less likely to invest authority or abide by these documents.

An interesting case in point occurred at Warehouse State recently. The Ad Hoc Committee on Academic Honesty, consisting of students, faculty, and administrators, issued a draft version of an academic honor code which, if approved, all members of the Warehouse State community would be expected to sign and to follow. (The complete draft appears below.) The following section caused a particular controversy among students:

> As a member of the Warehouse State community, I shall not intentionally or knowingly violate the bonds of academic trust among us, nor shall I tolerate violations of this trust.

A later section in the draft specified students' responsibilities:

Upon witnessing any act of academic dishonesty, a student must:

a. Communicate either verbally or in writing, either directly or anonymously, with the student or students who have committed the act of academic dishonesty, informing this or these students that an act of academic dishonesty has been observed. A student must also:

b. Give prompt notification to the Academic Honor Council that a violation has occurred. The student reporting the violation must identify him or herself and the name(s) of the violator(s).

These provisions in the honor code draft quickly became known as the "rat rule," sparking a heated discussion. Some students argued that they went to Warehouse State to be educated, not to "spy" on other students. Some worried that if they observed cheating during an exam, the responsibility to report violations would interfere with their own academic performance. Others supported the proposed code. Seeking to preserve the spirit of the honor code and, at the same time, to satisfy objections and establish a common ground, the committee revised the two sections. Changes are in italics.

As a member of the Warehouse State community, I shall not intentionally or knowingly violate the bonds of academic trust among us. *I recognize that protecting academic integrity is the collective responsibility of students, faculty, and staff at Warehouse State.*

Upon witnessing any act of academic dishonesty, *a student will be guided by conscience whether to report the act or to take other appropriate action.*

Whether removing the "rat rule" waters down the original intention or provides a common ground all can agree to is an open question.

WRITERS' WORKSHOP

Here is the complete draft, before the revision you've just seen, of the academic honor code for Warehouse State.

The Warehouse State Honor Code

Ad Hoc Committee on Academic Honesty.
Proposal for an Academic Honor Code
February 21, 2001

Preamble

1   At Warehouse State, the bonds of academic trust among all members of the academic community are paramount. Establishing and maintaining these bonds require a unified commitment to the principles of academic integrity and honesty

in all educational interactions. To this end, Warehouse State students, faculty, and administrators affirm the following pledge.

I. Honor pledge

As a member of the Warehouse State community, I shall not intentionally or knowingly violate the bonds of academic trust among us, nor shall I tolerate violations of this trust.

II. Definition of Academic Trust

Academic trust is the assurance that teacher and student will faithfully abide by the rules of intellectual engagement established between them. This trust can exist only when students adhere to the standards of academic honesty and when faculty test and evaluate students in a manner that presumes that students are acting with academic integrity.

III. Definition of Academic Dishonesty

Any willful act that either interferes with the process of evaluation or misrepresents the relation between the work evaluated and the student's actual state of knowledge is an act of academic dishonesty and a violation of academic trust. The following are some examples of dishonesty:

A. *Cheating.* Misrepresentation of the work of another as one's own; use of purchased term papers; copying on exams; submission of homework, programs, projects, and take-home exams with portions done by another; use of unauthorized materials or sources of information, such as "crib sheets" or unauthorized storing of information in calculators; assistance of another person in cases where prohibited.

B. *Fabrication.* Alteration of grades or official records; changing of exam answers after the fact; falsifying or inventing laboratory data.

C. *Facilitating Academic Dishonesty.* Assisting or facilitating any act of academic honesty.

D. *Academic Sabotage.* Sabotage of another student's work or academic record.

E. *Plagiarism.* Representing the work or ideas of another as one's own without giving proper credit.

IV. Responsibilities

A. Student Responsibilities
  1. Know and uphold the Honor Pledge.
  2. Do not commit any acts of academic dishonesty.
  3. Upon witnessing any act of academic dishonesty, a student must:
     a. Communicate either verbally or in writing, either directly or anonymously, with the student or students who have committed the act of academic dishonesty, informing this or these students that an act of academic dishonesty has been observed. A student must also:
     b. Give prompt notification to the Academic Honor Council that a violation has occurred. The student reporting the violation must identify him or herself and the name(s) of the violator(s).

4. When in doubt about classroom or project rules, ask the professor.

11   B. Faculty Responsibilities

1. Know and uphold the Honor Pledge.
2. Foster an educational environment that is consistent with the definition of academic trust.
3. Communicate to students individual policies concerning evaluation procedures and expectations pertaining to academic integrity and trust.
4. Report any act of academic dishonesty to the Academic Honor Council.
5. Recognize that judgments about academic dishonesty are the sole responsibility of the Academic Honor Council. If a student is found not guilty on a charge of academic dishonesty, the instructor will not penalize the student in any way.

12   C. Institutional Responsibilities

1. Disseminate annually the Academic Honor Code to all students, faculty, and staff.
2. Through Faculty and New Student Orientation, promote discussion of the Academic Honor Code and the value Warehouse State places on integrity.
3. Have new students sign the Academic Honor Pledge upon joining the institution.
4. Give administrative support to the Academic Honor Council to ensure ongoing implementation of the Academic Honor Code.
5. Maintain appropriate confidential mechanisms for reporting honor code violations.

V. Acceptance of the Academic Honor Pledge

13   Students sign a pledge they will uphold the principles of academic trust and that they will fulfill their responsibilities concerning the Academic Honor Code as part of their admission to the institution. A student's placing his or her name on an exam, paper, or project shall be understood as a reaffirmation of the student's pledge to abide by the Academic Honor Code. Faculty are expected to conduct classes according to the spirit of academic trust and to follow academic honor code procedures concerning violations.

WORKSHOP QUESTIONS

1. Imagine that the Ad Hoc Committee on Academic Honesty at Warehouse State has asked you to review its draft of the Academic Honor Code. How would you respond? Does the Preamble clearly articulate the purpose of the document? Are the definitions of terms and of student, faculty, and institutional responsibilities clearly stated? Are there things not included that you think the document should contain?

2. Evaluate the revision of the two sections of the honor code that appear in the preceding section. Consider student objections to the "rat rule."

Do you think they are valid? Do you think an academic honor code should require students to report violations?

3. Does your college or university have an honor code? If so, what does it commit students, faculty, and administrators to do? How is it similar to or different from the Warehouse State draft? What revisions, if any, do you think it needs? If your school does not have an honor code, do you think there should be one? What should it cover?

REFLECTING ON YOUR WRITING

Write a short account of your experience analyzing or composing a public document. Take into account the authority you drew on to write the document or the source of authority the document you analyzed drew on. On whose behalf did you write the document or was the document written? What problems or issues did you encounter in your writing? Explain how you dealt with them.

A CLOSING NOTE

Read the draft of the document you have designed or the analysis you wrote. In either case, remember that the purpose of a document is in its uses. Make sure it is clear to readers what use the document is for, what it commits people to, and how it regulates their relationship to others.

CHAPTER SEVEN

Profiles: Creating a Dominant Impression

THINKING ABOUT THE GENRE

Talking about other people—describing them, analyzing their personalities, trying to understand why they do the things they do—is one of the main topics of conversation in most people's lives. Think for a moment about how and why you talk or write about other people in the course of everyday life—whether you're telling your parents what your new roommate is like, discussing with coworkers why your supervisors act the way they do, or writing a letter to a friend trying to explain why someone you both know is leaving school or changing majors. This impulse to describe, to analyze, and to understand what people are all about seems to grow out of a genuine need to come to terms with our social experience and our relationships with others.

It's not surprising, then, that a genre of writing—the profile—is devoted to describing and analyzing particular people or that this genre is extremely popular in magazine and newspaper writing. Profiles are a regular feature in publications such as *Rolling Stone, Sports Illustrated, Ebony, Ms.,* and the *Wall Street Journal,* as well as in local newspapers. Many profiles are of well-known people, and the call to write profiles undoubtedly has a lot to do with readers' fascination with the famous and the powerful. Profiles offer readers a behind-the-scenes look at people they've heard so much about. But the call to write has at least as much to do with our general curiosity about and desire to understand other people and their lives.

One way to understand profiles is to consider how they differ from another genre that focuses on individual people: the biography. While biographies are often long, profiles tend to be relatively brief. Whereas biographies give full chronologies, profiles usually seek to capture their subject at a moment in time (even though they often include information about other times in the subject's life). In fact, the immediate call to write a particular profile often comes because events in that moment in time have brought the person into the public eye. A first-time director makes a movie that becomes the box-office hit of

222

the year. A Wall Street investment banker is under investigation for illegal trading. A sports star unexpectedly retires. In such cases, profile writers seek to fill in the human details behind the headlines.

Note that at times the events are larger than the person profiled. Thus, Dr. Susan M. Love, profiled in Molly O'Neill's "A Surgeon's War on Breast Cancer," although already a prominent physician, became newsworthy to a wider audience because of growing national attention being paid to breast cancer. When an issue moves to the forefront, ordinary people often become the subject of profiles that describe, for example, the lives of undocumented workers or the plight of a corporate executive laid off by downsizing. Such profiles of ordinary people supplement statistical and analytical treatments of issues, illuminating social issues and cultural patterns in a way statistics cannot, making concrete and personal what would otherwise remain abstract and remote. And, working on people's natural curiosity about others, they take readers beyond their preconceptions to explore the remarkable variety of people, backgrounds, lifestyles, and experiences that are frequently reduced to a single category such as "welfare mothers," "the elderly," or "blue-collar workers."

Profiles not only focus on a present moment in time but also in many cases seem to take place in real time. That is, they may tell what the person does over the course of a day or during characteristic activities. As a result, another characteristic of profiles is that they create a sense of immediacy and intimacy, as though the reader were there on the spot, watching and listening to what's going on. Readers of profiles have come to expect that they will be able to visualize the person—What does she look like? What is she wearing? What are her surroundings?—to hear her voice—What does she sound like? How does she talk to the people around her?—and to witness revealing incidents—What is she doing? How and why does she do it? What does this show about her?

To convey this sense of immediacy and intimacy, writers of profiles often rely heavily on interviewing and observation. This doesn't mean, of course, that library research isn't involved. On the contrary, consulting written sources with pertinent background information not only supplements interviewing and observation but also makes them much more effective.

But no matter how immediate profiles seem to be, we are not seeing a person directly but rather through the eyes of the writer. The way a person appears in a profile—and the impact his story has on readers—depends as much on the writer as on the person profiled. Profiles express, explicitly or implicitly, the author's point of view, or dominant impression. No profile will really work for its readers unless it creates this dominant impression—a particular and coherent sense of its subject. Writers of profiles don't just write up the results of their observations and interviews. Instead, they choose the descriptive details, events, daily routines, anecdotes, and quotes and reported speech that will show why and how the profile's subject is unique. A good profile is meaningful as well as vivid.

In some profiles, a dominant impression emerges gradually from the writer's observations. As you'll see, this is what happens in Molly O'Neill's profile of Dr. Susan Love. In other profiles, the writer explicitly states a main point.

An example is Mike Rose's "I Just Wanna Be Average," where profiles of three students illustrate his point that academic tracking affects students intellectually, emotionally, and socially.

Profiles take many forms. O'Neill's is a newspaper article, whereas Rose's profiles appear in a chapter of a book. Jon Garelick's "Kurt Cobain 1967–94" was written shortly after Cobain committed suicide. As you will see, Garelick's profile differs from a newspaper obituary in the same way that profiles in general differ from biography. Garelick doesn't try to give all the biographical details of Cobain's life, but rather tries to bring the meaning of his life into focus and to offer a kind of final judgment.

EXPLORING YOUR EXPERIENCE

People talk about other people all the time. They tell stories about what others do and comment on what they are like. Think about the conversations you have with others—friends, relatives, coworkers, neighbors, acquaintances, or strangers. In these conversations, what kinds of stories and comments about people come up? List four or five occasions when you or someone else told a story or made a comment about another person. What was the purpose?

Compare your list to the lists of your classmates and see whether any patterns emerge. Are there, for example, any differences between men's and women's stories and comments? Can you classify these examples—by purpose or by who is speaking or whom the stories or comments are about?

READINGS

Molly O'Neill, "A Surgeon's War on Breast Cancer."

Molly O'Neill is a staff writer for the *New York Times,* where her profiles, feature stories, and food columns appear regularly. The following profile is of Dr. Susan M. Love, a prominent surgeon, biomedical researcher, and activist. O'Neill effectively uses the techniques of observation and interviewing to build a dominant impression of Dr. Love.

A Surgeon's War on Breast Cancer
MOLLY O'NEILL

1   Three mammography films were clipped to the light box on the wall of a sleek conference room at the U.C.L.A. Breast Center. The different perspectives of a woman's breast looked like black-and-white photographs of the earth taken from a satellite. From each angle, the dark shadow of a tumor hovered like a storm cloud near the center of the gray sphere.

2   A woman born 50 years ago had, on the day of her birth, a 1 in 20 chance of being diagnosed with breast cancer in her lifetime. A woman born today has a 1 in 9 chance, partly due to a longer life expectancy. The U.C.L.A. Breast Center, part of the U.C.L.A. Medical Center, is one of about a dozen clinics in the country that both treat and research the disease. And Dr. Susan M. Love, the director of the U.C.L.A. program, is a leading crusader in the war against breast cancer.

3   A radiologist used a pointer to outline the tumor for a group of radiologists, oncologists, pathologists and surgeons. Dr. Love stood in the back of the conference room, rocking in her bone-colored pumps. Her brown eyes were narrowed behind red-frame glasses.

4   The lab coat she wore was a bulletin board of buttons. "Keep abreast," read one, "Get a second opinion." On another: "T.G.I.F. (Thank God I'm Female)." Under the string of fat white pearls around her neck was a gold chain with an ankh, an ancient symbol of life. Above one of the gold Chanel-style earrings was a tiny labrys, the mythical double-bladed ax used by Amazons.

5   Dr. Love is not without contradictions.

6   She is a traditionally trained surgeon; yet, she believes political action, not surgery, is the only real hope for stemming the increase in breast cancer. She is a feminist, but is skeptical of self-help techniques like breast self-examinations. She was raised Irish Catholic, at one point entered a convent and is now a lesbian mother.

7   With patients, she is funny, warm and accessible. With peers, "Dr. Love constantly challenges dogma," said Dr. Jay Harris, a radiation oncologist and professor at Harvard University, who has known and worked with Dr. Love since her residency at Beth Israel Hospital in Boston nearly 15 years ago. "Surgeons aren't supposed to do that. Susan makes many surgeons uncomfortable."

8   Even the staff of Dr. Love's clinic say that the surgeon's approach is not for every patient. "Some women want to be told what to do," said Sherry Goldman, a nurse practitioner at the U.C.L.A. center. "Options make them nervous."

9   Even before she published "Dr. Susan Love's Breast Book" (Addison Wesley, 1990), a down-to-earth guide that has become the bible of women with breast cancer, she stirred controversy. In Boston, where she practiced before accepting the U.C.L.A. appointment in 1992, Dr. Love questioned the necessity of radical mastectomies and was an early champion of conservative surgeries like lumpectomies and partial mastectomies.

10   She is critical about what she sees as condescending and paternalistic attitudes among traditional breast surgeons. She is indefatigable in raising money—and political consciousness—for breast cancer research and prevention.

11   In 1991, Dr. Love helped found the National Breast Cancer Coalition, a federation of nearly 200 support and advocacy groups that helped raise the national budget for breast cancer research and prevention from $90 million to $420 million. "Thanks to Anita Hill," she likes to say. "After that debacle, congressmen were all looking for a nice, noncontroversial women's issue."

12   Dr. Love, who is 46, is known as a brilliant surgeon. She is also known for her bluntness.

13   She grins puckishly when she describes conventional breast cancer treatment, as "slash, poison and burn." She hopes that hers will be the last generation of surgeons to treat breast cancer with radical and invasive methods. Meanwhile, she performs surgery eight times a week.

14   The woman whose mammogram she was regarding would probably wind up in her operating room.

15   Her tone is kindly, forever big sister. The faint arc of freckles across her nose seems to expand as she smiles. Hers is the sort of open, guileless face that is hard to refuse. But as she rattled off studies, statistics and personal experience to support her recommendations for treating patients, she sounded indomitable.

16   A minute later, as she was entering another examining room, however, her tone was alternately jovial and intimate. "Is it lethal?" asked the 32-year-old patient. The surgeon laughed, pulled up a chair, plunked down and leaned toward the patient, elbows resting on her knees.

17   "Driving in L.A. is lethal," she said. "Your mammogram doesn't say anything about death. We're not talking doom."

18   For the next 40 minutes, using her own left breast to demonstrate each point, Dr. Love discussed the basic purpose of a breast ("it's like a milk factory"), how, under certain circumstances, cells build up on the wall of the duct, "like rust in a pipe," she said, "reversible."

19   The patient was laughing by the time Dr. Love told her: "When those cells break out into the surrounding fatty tissue, that's cancer. It is not reversible. We need to find out where you are on this continuum before we can really talk about options. But there are options. And you have time to think about it."

20   "And you'll take care of me?" the patient asked as they stood.

21   "I will take good care of you," said the surgeon, hugging the patient.

22   In the last 50 years, one-third of women diagnosed with breast cancer died of breast cancer. Dr. Love doesn't claim a better survival rate. She claims to take better care of women, and her patients generally agree.

23   Born in Long Branch, N.J., the oldest of five children, Susan Margaret Love was raised to change the world by doing good work. After two years as a pre-med student at the College of Notre Dame of Maryland in Baltimore, Dr. Love joined a convent but left after four months.

24   "I wanted to save the world," she said, "but they wanted to save their own souls." She enrolled at Fordham University and continued her pre-med studies. In 1970, she applied to medical school.

25   She wasn't fazed by the quota that limited women to 10 percent of the student body in most medical schools. "I wasn't political, I was a nerd," she said. "I've always been mainstream, pretty conservative."

26   After graduating fourth in her class from the State University of New York, Downstate Medical Center, in Brooklyn, she entered the surgical residency program at Beth Israel Hospital in Boston. "The program was modeled after the military," she said. "Most women who survived paid a price. They lost their marriages, or their minds. I did it by being totally out of touch with myself, a good old Irish Catholic."

27   Besides, she loved surgery. "It's so pragmatic, so tactile," she said. "You can fix things."

28   Breast surgery, though, isn't a sure-fire fix. And initially, it didn't interest Dr. Love. "I didn't want to be ghettoized in a women's specialty," she said. But when she established her practice in Boston, doctors referred breast cancer patients to her. "I started to see that this was an area where I could make a difference." Within two years, she had become the breast surgeon for the Dana Farber Cancer Institute in Boston.

29   At the same time, she said, after mounting a "massive find-a-man campaign," she faced her own sexuality. For years, she had avoided another surgeon, Dr. Helen Cooksey, who was gay. "I thought it might be catching," Dr. Love said. "It was."

30   The couple have been together for 13 years. Five years ago, by artificial insemination, Dr. Love had a daughter, Katie Love Cooksey. Dr. Cooksey left surgery to stay home with the child. Last September, the couple won a legal battle that allowed Dr. Cooksey to adopt Katie. "Helen and I have money and privilege, so it's our obligation to pave the way," Dr. Love said.

31   The noblesse oblige theme also rises when she discusses the move from private practice to U.C.L.A.

32   "I was this little person in private practice, and now I have a whole medical school behind me," Dr. Love said. "Of course that means a huge responsibility.

I have to get this clinic up and running and then build an equally serious research effort."

33   At 7 a.m. every weekday, Dr. Love takes her daughter to preschool and goes to the hospital, where she performs any surgeries by 10 a.m. She then dashes down one flight of stairs to the Breast Center to confer, teach and work on grants before patients arrive. One patient was worried. Her aunt had died of breast cancer. "Not close enough to worry," Dr. Love said briskly. She examined the patient, found nothing and said, "Now, what else can I do for you?"

34   "Can you, uh, show me how to do, uh, one of those things?" the patient asked.

35   "Breast self-exam?" Dr. Love responded. "Sure, but it's an overrated activity. The medical establishment would like you to believe that breast cancer starts as a grain of sand, grows to be the size of a pea and on and on until it becomes a grapefruit. Breast cancer doesn't work like that. It grows slow and it's sneaky. You could examine yourself every day and suddenly find a walnut."

36   A 55-year-old patient with a small tumor had been advised by another surgeon to have a complete mastectomy, immediately. "Give me a break," Dr. Love told the patient. "Using a mastectomy to treat a lesion like yours is like using a cannon to shoot a flea."

37   Yet another patient, a 48-year-old woman, had an aggressive cancer but was hesitant to have a mastectomy. Was it possible to save her breast?

38   "Look, breast cancer is like mental health," Dr. Love said. "The early forms are neurotic and can be treated. The later forms are psychotic, and it's more difficult. You have a lot of pre-cancer, a little bit that's crossed the line. I can probably go in and take a wedge out of your breast; it's sort of like taking a dart.

39   "I think I could do it, but I may not get it all. You'll have a 50–50 chance of having to come back for a mastectomy. Go home, sleep on it. The good news is this is not an emergency."

40   The next patient was not so lucky. A 64-year-old who had had a partial mastectomy 10 years previously and had been cancer-free since had found a new lump. Subsequent tests found cancerous lesions in the chest wall, the stomach, the liver, the kidneys and the skull. "It doesn't make any sense," Dr. Love said to the team in the conference room. "Where have these cells been for 10 years?"

41   "Quiescent," said Dr. Dennis Slamon, the chief of oncology.

42   "Why can't we make them all quiescent?" Dr. Love asked. She repeated the question several times as she packed a bulging briefcase, exchanged her lab coat for a smart silk jacket and, after a typical 13-hour workday, walked down the long, cool hall and headed home.

43   The Breast Center is one of a handful of such centers that offer an interdisciplinary approach, using medical specialists and psychologists to care for patients from diagnosis through treatment. The force of Dr. Love's personality is the glue that holds the staff of 30 together. Still, Dr. Love is impatient.

44   "Research is the only way we are going to solve this thing, and I don't mean research into new chemo formulas, I mean research into the cause of breast cancer," she said, as she walked through an empty parking lot to a new Volvo station wagon.

45   "And we're so close," she said. "We know it's genetic. Some people are born with the gene, others develop the gene. We don't know what causes the gene to

change. Pesticides? Pollution? Food additives? They are all possibilities. All we know is that a gene is involved. And we are very close to finding it. Unbelievably close."

46   Sliding behind the steering wheel, she distilled the latest breast cancer research with the same kind of down-to-earth similes that she uses to explain the disease to patients.

47   "You see, the gene is like a robber in the neighborhood," she said. "We have the neighborhood roped off. Now all we have to do is knock on every single door."

Analysis: Open Form to Create Dominant Impression

Molly O'Neill never directly indicates what she wants readers to think of Dr. Susan M. Love. The profile doesn't state and then support a main idea; this isn't the basis of its organization. Nonetheless, the profile effectively conveys a dominant impression of Dr. Love because the information, description, scenes, conversations, and quotes it contains vividly and consistently contribute to this impression.

Moreover, the information, description, and so on are carefully organized into sections. Each section clusters together a particular kind of information or discussion, contributing to the dominant impression in a specific way. If, as in this profile, sections are carefully designed, they can resonate with each other, suggesting connections a reader can make so that the dominant impression created by the whole is that much stronger. If the sections are not carefully designed, readers will likely experience the piece as incoherent and frustrating.

The pattern of organization used in this profile is called *open form*, characterized as having an implicit center of gravity around which parts revolve, rather than an explicit main point that the parts develop.

If you reread the profile, you can see that it divides into the following sections:

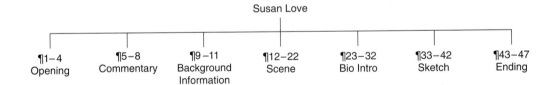

| ¶1–4 | ¶5–8 | ¶9–11 | ¶12–22 | ¶23–32 | ¶33–42 | ¶43–47 |
| Opening | Commentary | Background Information | Scene | Bio Intro | Sketch | Ending |

To see how a section can contribute to a dominant impression, consider the opening scene of the profile (¶s1–4). Effective profiles usually rely on a powerful opening that establishes a perspective for readers. This profile begins in a conference room where a radiologist is showing mammography films to a group of doctors. Readers are immediately immersed in Dr. Love's world. Love herself is initially at the back of the room, and O'Neill takes her time in introducing her.

First O'Neill describes the mammography films, using metaphorical language (they "looked like black-and-white photographs of the earth taken from a satellite" and "the dark shadow of a tumor hovered like a storm cloud") to put what may be unfamiliar to readers into more familiar terms, and then she quickly sketches in statistics on the rising incidence of breast cancer.

It is only after this extended scene that Love appears, "a leading crusader in the war against breast cancer," as though O'Neill were using a camera to zoom in on her subject. Love is seen "rocking in her bone-colored pumps. Her brown eyes were narrowed behind red-frame glasses." The opening concludes with a description of Love. As in most successful profiles, this is by no means a full description. Instead, O'Neill describes only a couple of details—the buttons Love has on her lab coat and the jewelry she wears. Note that these are key details, revealing something important about Dr. Love. Like Dr. Love's posture and gaze, they point to characteristics that are part of the dominant impression the profile goes on to establish.

FOR CRITICAL INQUIRY

1. Reread the profile, paying attention to how your perceptions of Dr. Susan Love develop over the course of the profile. Annotate the profile by indicating what your impression of Love is in the opening scene, at three or four points in the middle, and at the end. Now read back over your annotations to see how your impression of Love has developed. Is your final impression basically similar to your initial one? Are there any changes or shifts along the way? Explain why you think your impressions developed as they did.

2. What dominant impression does the profile seem to create? How do you think O'Neill wants readers to see Love? How does O'Neill establish such a perspective for readers?

3. Point to words (nouns, verbs, adjectives, adverbs), phrases, sentences, and passages that indicate the perspective O'Neill offers to readers.

4. Focus on a particular passage that you feel is especially revealing about the kind of person Love is. What is it about the passage that you find effective in characterizing Dr. Love? Compare the passage you have selected to those chosen by other students in class. Use these comparisons to develop a list of effective strategies for characterizing people in profiles.

Mike Rose, "I Just Wanna Be Average."

Mike Rose is a teacher, poet, scholar, and professor of education at UCLA. The following selection, which in effect contains three profiles, was taken from his award-winning book *Lives on the Boundary*. Rose's book is in part a telling critique of the failures of American schooling to address the needs of all students, and in part an affirmation of the educability of all Americans. And, as this selection shows, it is also partly autobiographical, drawing on Rose's own experience growing up in a working-class neighborhood in Los Angeles. Notice that this selection differs significantly from the previous one both in how the information used was obtained and in how the profiles are organized.

I Just Wanna Be Average
MIKE ROSE

1   Students will float to the mark you set. I and the others in the vocational classes were bobbing in pretty shallow water. Vocational education has aimed at increasing the economic opportunities of students who do not do well in our schools. Some serious programs succeed in doing that, and through exceptional teachers—like Mr. Gross in *Horace's Compromise*—students learn to develop hypotheses and troubleshoot, reason through a problem, and communicate effectively—the true job skills. The vocational track, however, is most often a place for those who are just not making it, a dumping ground for the disaffected. There were a few teachers who worked hard at education; young Brother Slattery, for example, combined a stern voice with weekly quizzes to try to pass along to us a skeletal outline of world history. But mostly the teachers had no idea of how to engage the imaginations of us kids who were scuttling along at the bottom of the pond.

2   And the teachers would have needed some inventiveness, for none of us was groomed for the classroom. It wasn't just that I didn't know things—didn't know how to simplify algebraic fractions, couldn't identify different kinds of clauses, bungled Spanish translations—but that I had developed various faulty and inadequate ways of doing algebra and making sense of Spanish. Worse yet, the years of defensive tuning out in elementary school had given me a way to escape quickly while seeming at least half alert. During my time in Voc. Ed., I developed further into a mediocre student and a somnambulant problem solver, and that affected the subjects I did have the wherewithal to handle: I detested Shakespeare; I got bored with history. My attention flitted here and there. I fooled around in class and read my books indifferently—the intellectual equivalent of playing with your food. I did what I had to do to get by, and I did it with half a mind.

3   But I did learn things about people and eventually came into my own socially. I liked the guys in Voc. Ed. Growing up where I did, I understood and admired physical prowess, and there was an abundance of muscle here. There was Dave Snyder, a sprinter and halfback of true quality. Dave's ability and his quick wit gave him a natural appeal, and he was welcome in any clique, though he always kept a little independent. He enjoyed acting the fool and could care less about studies, but he possessed a certain maturity and never caused the faculty much trouble. It was a testament to his independence that he included me among his friends—I eventually went out for track, but I was no jock. Owing to the Latin alphabet and a dearth of *R*s and *S*s, Snyder sat behind Rose, and we started exchanging one-liners and became friends.

4   There was Ted Richard, a much-touted Little League pitcher. He was chunky and had a baby face and came to Our Lady of Mercy as a seasoned street fighter. Ted was quick to laugh and he had a loud, jolly laugh, but when he got angry he'd smile a little smile, the kind that simply raises the corner of the mouth a quarter of

an inch. For those who knew, it was an eerie signal. Those who didn't found themselves in big trouble, for Ted was very quick. He loved to carry on what we would come to call philosophical discussions: What is courage? Does God exist? He also loved words, enjoyed picking up big ones like *salubrious* and *equivocal* and using them in our conversations—laughing at himself as the word hit a chuckhole rolling off his tongue. Ted didn't do all that well in school—baseball and parties and testing the courage he'd speculated about took up his time. His textbooks were *Argosy* and *Field and Stream*, whatever newspapers he'd find on the bus stop—from the *Daily Worker* to pornography—conversations with uncles or hobos or businessmen he'd meet in a coffee shop, *The Old Man and the Sea*. With hindsight, I can see that Ted was developing into one of those rough-hewn intellectuals whose sources are a mix of the learned and the apocryphal, whose discussions are both assured and sad.

5   And then there was Ken Harvey. Ken was good-looking in a puffy way and had a full and oily ducktail and was a car enthusiast...a hodad. One day in religion class, he said the sentence that turned out to be one of the most memorable of the hundreds of thousands I heard in those Voc. Ed. years. We were talking about the parable of the talents, about achievement, working hard, doing the best you can do, blah-blah-blah, when the teacher called on the restive Ken Harvey for an opinion. Ken thought about it, but just for a second, and said (with studied, minimal affect), "I just wanna be average." That woke me up. Average?! Who wants to be average? Then the athletes chimed in with the clichés that make you want to laryngectomize them, and the exchange became a platitudinous melee. At the time, I thought Ken's assertion was stupid, and I wrote him off. But his sentence has stayed with me all these years, and I think I am finally coming to understand it.

6   Ken Harvey was gasping for air. School can be a tremendously disorienting place. No matter how bad the school, you're going to encounter notions that don't fit with the assumptions and beliefs that you grew up with—maybe you'll hear these dissonant notions from teachers, maybe from the other students, and maybe you'll read them. You'll also be thrown in with all kinds of kids from all kinds of backgrounds, and that can be unsettling—this is especially true in places of rich ethnic and linguistic mix, like the L.A. basin. You'll see a handful of students far excel you in courses that sound exotic and that are only in the curriculum of the elite: French, physics, trigonometry. And all this is happening while you're trying to shape an identity, your body is changing, and your emotions are running wild. If you're a working-class kid in the vocational track, the options you'll have to deal with this will be constrained in certain ways: You're defined by your school as "slow"; you're placed in a curriculum that isn't designed to liberate you but to occupy you, or, if you're lucky, train you, though the training is for work the society does not esteem; other students are picking up the cues from your school and your curriculum and interacting with you in particular ways. If you're a kid like Ted Richard, you turn your back on all this and let your mind roam where it may. But youngsters like Ted are rare. What Ken and so many others do is protect themselves from such suffocating madness by taking on with a vengeance the identity implied in the vocational track. Reject the confusion and frustration by openly defining yourself as the Common Joe. Champion the average. Rely on your own good sense. Fuck this bullshit. Bullshit, of course, is everything you—and the oth-

ers—fear is beyond you: books, essays, tests, academic scrambling, complexity, scientific reasoning, philosophical inquiry.

7 The tragedy is that you have to twist the knife in your own gray matter to make this defense work. You'll have to shut down, have to reject intellectual stimuli or diffuse them with sarcasm, have to cultivate stupidity, have to convert boredom from a malady into a way of confronting the world. Keep your vocabulary simple, act stoned when you're not or act more stoned than you are, flaunt ignorance, materialize your dreams. It is a powerful and effective defense—it neutralizes the insult and the frustration of being a vocational kid and, when perfected, it drives teachers up the wall, a delightful secondary effect. But like all strong magic, it exacts a price.

Analysis: Claim and Evidence

Mike Rose's profiles of three students are part of a larger piece: they are the third through fifth paragraphs in a selection with seven paragraphs, which is itself an excerpt from a book. Notice that the first two paragraphs in the selection establish a main idea, or claim, that the three profiles then support. In the final two paragraphs the author in effect generalizes from the profiles and draws conclusions related to the main point. In contrast to O'Neill's piece, which uses open form, this selection uses an organization familiar from argumentative writing: *claim and evidence.*

Whereas the success of O'Neill's article comes from the way sections establish a dominant impression, the success of a piece with claim and evidence organization comes from the way the evidence supports the claim and serves as a basis for conclusions that say something significant. If these parts and their relationships to one another aren't clear, readers will find the piece hard to follow.

Notice that Rose's piece is just as effective as O'Neill's but in a way that is appropriate to the type of organization he uses. He begins with two memorable sentences that help establish the main idea: "Students will float to the mark you set. I and the others in vocational classes were bobbing in pretty shallow water."

Notice also that the high school students Rose then profiles are much more that just evidence to support this main idea. He sketches Dave Snyder, Ted Richard, and Ken Harvey in vivid detail. Each appears to the reader as a unique individual, with his own characteristics and idiosyncrasies. Yet there is also a sort of shared dominant impression that emerges, an impression that is linked to Rose's main idea. For Rose is showing us, through their experience, a central problem in American schooling: It produces students who, in Ken Harvey's unforgettable words, "just wanna be average." Interpretation on the part of the author, inevitable in any profile, is made explicit in a piece like this one, occurring from the beginning sentences quoted above to the final judgment that the "powerful and effective defense" vocational education students develop "like all strong magic,...exacts a price."

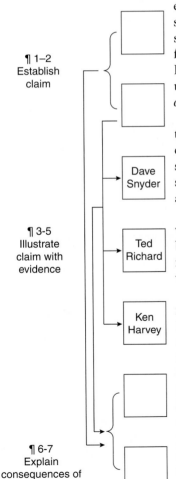

¶ 1–2
Establish
claim

¶ 3-5
Illustrate
claim with
evidence

¶ 6-7
Explain
consequences of
evidence and claim

Dave
Snyder

Ted
Richard

Ken
Harvey

FOR CRITICAL INQUIRY

1. What is the main idea (or claim) that Rose introduces in the two opening paragraphs? How do the profiles of the three students provide evidence for the claim? What enabling assumptions connect this evidence to the claim?

2. Rose wants his profiles of the three students to serve as evidence for his claim, but he also wants to capture the individuality of each student. How does he do this? Point to particular passages, sentences, or words in the text that provide revealing characterization.

3. In the final two paragraphs of this selection, Rose wants to generalize from the experience of the three students he has profiled—to develop further his controlling theme about the effects of schooling by making some final points. What points exactly is Rose making in the final two paragraphs? Do they seem to be justified and to flow naturally from the three profiles? Explain how these points seem to grow logically from the profiles (or why in your view they don't).

Jon Garelick, "Kurt Cobain 1967–1994."

Jon Garelick is a music critic who wrote this tribute to Kurt Cobain for the *Providence Phoenix* shortly after Cobain had committed suicide. Cobain was the lead singer and guitarist in the rock group Nirvana, whose smash hit album *Nevermind*—and its single "Smells Like Teen Spirit"—brought them and the grunge rock scene in Seattle to national prominence in 1988. To many, Nirvana's combination of punk rage, heavy metal guitars, and pop melodies returned rock to its authentic roots in teenage working-class rebellion. To others, the group epitomized all that had gone wrong with young people in America. In any case, Cobain's self-inflicted death presented a moment of cultural reckoning, when people felt compelled to come to terms with Cobain and the meaning of his death.

Kurt Cobain 1967–1994
JON GARELICK

1   Nirvana had just finished a majestic performance of "Smells like Teen Spirit" at the Wallace (MA) Civic Center last November when bassist Krist Novoselic burst into a sudden tantrum aimed at a member of the audience. "I saw you grab that girl! Why don't you come up here, you weenie!"

2   Guitarist/singer/songwriter Kurt Cobain then took a seat to play the ballad "All Apologies," first lecturing the audience about girl groping in the mosh pit. "We've hired goons," he said calmly, "and if we find anyone groping girls' breasts or pinching their asses, they'll throw them out...and then beat the shit out of them."

3   Musically it was a masterful show, perfectly paced, every segue showing off each song to its best advantage, with none of the dead spots that can stall a set at mid

ballad. Through it all, Novoselic was a towering behemoth, hopping and banging out his bass lines. Cobain, by comparison, was a fragile waif. On stage, the band's personal dynamic was as clear as their musical dynamic: with David Grohl's fierce, precise drumming behind them, Novoselic was the kinetic genial giant, Cobain the soft-spoken introvert shuffling across stage in his permanent slouch, emitting howls of vocal and guitar noise mixed with touching, tender melodies. It wasn't hard to imagine that if anyone ever laid a hand on the singer, Novoselic would kill him.

4   If you've followed Nirvana's career at all over the past three years, it was difficult not to feel protective of Cobain. There was reported weirdness with guns, drugs, petulant faxes sent to various publications (including this one)—exploits that made Cobain and wife Courtney Love a notorious rock-and-roll couple.

5   And yet, in interviews and in live performances, Cobain was invariably lucid, modest, intelligent. He denigrated his image as a "pissy, complaining, freaked-out schizophrenic who wants to kill himself." That came from an interview with *Rolling Stone*'s David Fricke after the release of 1993's *In Utero*. Cobain said he looked forward to the development of the band and considered tinkering with extended song forms, allowing that "I don't know if we're capable of it—as musicians." But the set at Wallace Civic Center was not the performance of a band on the verge of breaking up, and there were none of the signs of a frontman who can't, or wouldn't, perform.

6   Even so, when Cobain's shotgun-blasted body was found last week in his Seattle home, the shock wasn't merely at his death. We had been prepared for that (if by none of the other signs) by the "Rome coma" of a month before. And there were hints through his whole career of instability—an incident where he climbed a bank of amplifiers and appeared ready to jump off, his comment to writer Michael Azerrad that if he hadn't "cured" his mysteriously recurring stomach ailment with heroin, he would have blown his brains out.

7   Perhaps we were most shocked by our own sense of shock. At the time, I couldn't imagine another rock star's death that would affect me as profoundly. Bono? Eddie Vedder? Paul Westerberg? Is it simply because I like his songs the most? That I've written the most about him, "studied" him the most in my own rock-crit way? What other comparisons were there? We were more or less prepared for Frank Zappa's death. The jazz gods I worshiped—Mingus, Ellington, Dizzy Gillespie—were likewise in physical decline when they died.

8   But maybe this particular loss is part of the mystery of pop stardom. When it was confirmed that Cobain was dead, I was surprised at my own sense of loss, and of disbelief. The disbelief continued through the Friday-night MTV rebroadcast of the *Unplugged* session, through listening to DJs hopelessly trying to play amateur psychologist to distraught fans. Even the next morning, the shock was still there. There's his face on the front page of the *Times*—he must really be dead.

9   The "unwilling spokesman for a generation" line doesn't exactly fit either. At 41, I'm at least two generations removed from Cobain's. (Gertrude Stein once said that every five years makes a generation, and I didn't grow up in the '70s or the '80s.) The only parallel that fits, and the one that Baby Boom rock crits have been throwing at Gen Xers all week, is that of John Lennon. It's a more unlikely and

awkward parallel than the Boomers will allow, but there it is. Cobain himself told Fricke that Lennon was his favorite Beatle, saying with a laugh, "He was obviously disturbed." Cobain wasn't nearly as famous (it was painful to have to listen to NPR explain who he was to a general audience). Nirvana's influence has been massive but not on a par with the Beatles'. And yet it's that same loss, that same sense of disbelief, and the shock at the violence of his passing.

10   There is, of course, anger as well. Lennon didn't choose his death. The self-destruction of Janis Joplin and Jim Hendrix can nonetheless be seen as accidents. There's compassion for a suicide, but also dismay over the selfishness of the act. A suicide leaves behind guilt for his survivors. And in Cobain's case, a fatherless daughter who'll have to deal with the anger and sense of abandonment for the rest of her life.

11   There is no good answer to the question "Why?" People scoff at the notion that fame alone can do someone in, no matter how sensitive or vulnerable the star. Cobain had access to treatment, he could have "retired," as John Lennon did in order to become a house husband. Cobain's troubled childhood in a broken home, his being shuttled from one guardian to the next, has been well enough documented in band biographies as well as in his own songs. In "Sliver" there's the primal scream of "Grandma take me home!" In "Serve the Servants" there's the ironic self-observation "Oh no, that legendary divorce is such a bore," followed by "I tried to have a father/but instead I had a Dad."

12   None of which excuses Cobain's suicide or makes it completely comprehensible. There's only the understanding that his feelings of shame ran so deep that he finally lost all sense of himself. (In his suicide note, he apparently called himself a "faker.") There were stories that Cobain and Love were in danger of losing custody of their child because of their problems with drugs. There were published reports that in the last couple of weeks of his life he'd fled a rehabilitation center, that Love had called police because of suicide threats. And there was the purchase of the shotgun. It looks as though he went to great effort to isolate himself, so that this time no one could talk him out of it, remind him of the world outside himself, remind him about his daughter.

13   For some, Cobain's suicide validates a portion of his art—the demons in his songs were real after all. But his music was an affirmation. It was about survival. He turned the internalized demons outward and released them as squalling guitar rage and affecting melodies. It was proof that you could emerge from an unbearable isolation and connect, as he did on "Something in the Way," with only two chords and that delicate whisper of a voice. Even at their roughest and most abrasive, he made sense of chaotic feelings.

14   In hindsight, critics talked about the inevitability of Nirvana's success—the surefire mix of metal, punk, and pop that knocked Michael Jackson out of number one on the charts and made Seattle a brand name. But Cobain's art was no formula. His musical style was as personal as his oblique, powerful lyrics. He invented his own language, found his own voice. In the world of pop music—that mass commodity—he was that rare thing: an original.

Analysis: The Meaning of a Life

When important people die, writers often feel called on to account for the meaning of the person's life and its significance to the larger community. Such profiles seek to understand a person's character. Their function is basically an ethical one, to interpret the meaning of an individual's life and to clarify what it tells us about our own communities. For this reason, as you can see in this example, such profiles are centered as much on the judgments and perceptions of the writer as they are on the person profiled.

Notice that there is nothing simple about this profile. Rather, because Kurt Cobain was a complicated and controversial figure, the judgments offered by Garelick are complex and at times ambivalent. What is telling here is that while Garelick praises his subject, he does not dodge Cobain's flaws or evade criticisms. He is looking for the meaning of the person's life, whatever its strengths and weaknesses and contradictions might be, to come to terms with what the person's death represents to the larger community and how we might remember him. And in this sense, the ambitions of this profile are sweeping and powerful because they strive to shape the historical memory of a community.

FOR CRITICAL INQUIRY

1. Jon Garelick opens with an anecdote from a Nirvana concert. How does he use the incident to provide the reader with a perspective on Kurt Cobain? In what light does the anecdote portray Kurt Cobain?

2. What dominant impression of Kurt Cobain emerges? Trace how this impression develops from the opening anecdote to the end of the profile. List some of the words, phrases, and sentences that are central to conveying this dominant impression.

3. Garelick spends part of his profile of Cobain looking for explanations for Cobain's suicide. To what extent is he successful? Do you think Garelick has a plausible explanation? Notice that in the next-to-the-last paragraph Garelick turns to the question of whether Cobain's music is consistent with his death. How does he answer this question? What does his answer say about the plausibility of his explanation?

Visual Design: Profiles in Advertising

In the selection by Mike Rose you saw how profiles can be used to make a larger point. Advertising frequently uses profiles in this way—to promote an organization and its goals.

Following are two examples that combine text and graphics to get their messages across. The first is an advertisement from the pharmaceutical company Pfizer that uses a profile of the former pro basketball player Johnny Moore. The second is from the Service Employees International Union to publicize its campaign for labor law reform.

Johnny never made it to that game back in 1985. Instead, he landed in the hospital with a deadly infection.

His doctors said he might go blind.

Never have kids. Possibly die.

But thanks to excellent care and medicine developed by Pfizer research, Johnny got another shot at life.

And eventually, he even got a daughter to share it with.

"I was thinking, 'If I can just get to the game, I'll be all right.'"

JOHNNY MOORE

SAN ANTONIO, TEXAS

We're part of the cure.

www.pfizer.com
AOL keyword: Pfizer

Analysis: Using Profiles in Advertising Campaigns

Notice that the Pfizer ad is not trying to sell a product. Instead, it's trying to sell the public on the work and reputation of a leading pharmaceutical company. The visual design of the ad combines four main elements: text, the Pfizer logo and slogan ("We're part of the cure"), a quote from Johnny Moore, and a photo. The advertisement paid for by the Service Employees International Union (SEIU) uses the profile of Inmar Hernandez to publicize the plight of janitors and to build support for labor law reform. Notice that, in terms of design, this ad has many

INMAR HERNANDEZ AND THE SHAME IN OUR NATION'S CAPITAL.

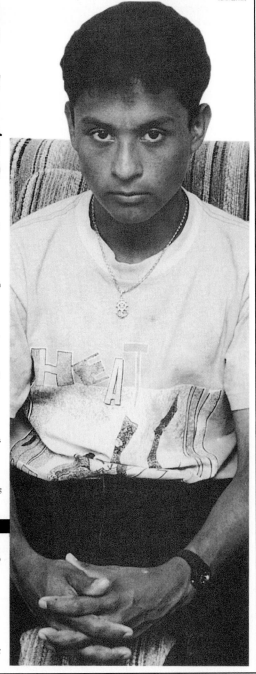

MARTHA TABOR PHOTO

Inmar Hernandez is no ordinary 19-year-old. Since immigrating to this country five years ago, he's been working nights as an office building janitor in downtown Washington, DC to help support his family. During the day, he's been attending Wilson High School and he's graduating this year.

In June, 1992, Inmar and 11 of his co-workers were fired for trying to organize a union in two office buildings where they worked. Inmar worked in an office building owned by wealthy developer Nathan Landow at 1200 G Street. Pritchard Industries, a huge national cleaning contractor, was paying Inmar $4.80 an hour, with no sick days, vacation days, health insurance or holidays.

It took eight months for the National Labor Relations Board (NLRB) to issue a complaint alleging that Pritchard illegally fired Inmar and his co-workers. Rather than go to trial, the company offered back pay and reinstatement. But it took until late May, 1993 for the back wages to be paid. And the 12 still haven't been called back to work.

Inmar couldn't wait, so he took another job working for $5 an hour for Executive Building Maintenance at 1050 Connecticut Avenue. It's a ritzy building owned by a partnership controlled by developers Albert Abramson, Theodore Lerner and their families. Every night, after the rich and powerful of Washington finish dining at Duke Zeibert's Restaurant on the second floor, Inmar goes to work cleaning swank law offices on the fifth floor. On his list are the offices of Arent, Fox, the law firm which represents the Apartment and Office Building Association, an organization of cleaning contractors and downtown building owners which has waged a 5-year anti-union campaign against the janitors.

It's an outrageous shame in our nation's capital. And it's going on in every big city in North America.

Inmar Hernandez is one more reason why we need

LABOR LAW REFORM NOW!

JUSTICE FOR JANITORS DAY IS JUNE 15TH

SERVICE EMPLOYEES INTERNATIONAL UNION, AFL-CIO, CLC

of the same elements as the Pfizer ad: a photo, text, a logo, and a slogan ("Labor Law Reform Now!"). Unlike the Pfizer ad, which balances the text and the quote from Johnny Moore, the SEIU ad uses a prominent headline to organize the page.

FOR CRITICAL INQUIRY

1. How do the brief sketches of Johnny Moore and Inmar Hernandez personalize the message each ad is trying to get across? As readers, how are we asked to understand the meaning of each short profile?

2. Compare the visual design of the ads. How are the various design elements (photos, text, logos, slogans, headlines) combined to create a dominant impression? Do you think the design of one ad is more effective than the other?

3. Look through recent magazines and newspapers for other advertisements and public relations pieces that make use of profiles. Bring two or three examples to class. Work together in a group with several other students. Discuss the dominant impression and the techniques used to create it. Why did the business or organization want to create this dominant impression? How does the person profiled establish a public image for the group or organization? Decide which pieces are most effective—in terms of their use of the profile and their design—and why.

4. Compose your own piece of publicity for a particular group, organization, or cause. Depending on your teacher's directions, work individually or with two or three other students to design a full-page or two-page layout that uses a profile of an individual (or individuals) to convey the desired message and image. When you have finished, bring the design to class and be prepared to explain why you chose the person (or persons) you did and how the profile is meant to express the group's goals.

FOR DISCUSSION AND ANALYTICAL WRITING

RHETORICAL ANALYSIS

Compare the writer's purposes in two of the profiles in this chapter. Take into account the context of issues, the writer's intended audience, and the relationship the writer is trying to establish with readers. How do the writer's purposes influence the presentation of the subject or subjects? How do these purposes influence the amount of description and interpretation in the profile?

GENRE CHOICES

Profiles and biographies are both genres of writing that inform readers about people, but they do so in very different ways. To understand what distinguishes profiles and biographies, read one or two short biographies in a standard reference source, such as an encyclopedia, the *Dictionary of American Biography,* or *Current Biography.* (You can find Susan Love, for example, in the October 1994 issue of *Current Biography* and an entry on Nirvana in *The Rock Who's Who,* 2nd ed., by Brock Helander.) Note the information that is included in— and excluded from—the two writings. Note also the arrangement of information. How do the profile and the biographical entry differ? What do the differences between the two writings tell you about the two genres?

GOING ONLINE

Riotgrrls, Geekgirls, and Other Web Sites for Women and Girls

Visit a number of Web sites designed specifically for women and girls, such as <www.riotgrrl.com>, <www.gurl.com>, <www.oxygen.com>, and (for adolescent girls) <www.purple-moon.com>. Notice how the Web site designers attempt to create a dominant impression, just as profile writers do. Consider the impression of women or girls the site projects to visitors. How does the site represent the identities of, say, riotgrrls or geek girls? How are they pictured visually? What interests, values, and beliefs come across? Who does the intended audience seem to be? What kind of relationship does the Web site seem to establish with this audience? Prepare a brief report—oral, written, or electronic, depending on your teacher's directions—that describes the dominant impression the Web site seeks to create and that lists several features that help project this impression.

WORKING TOGETHER

Analyzing Celebrity Profiles

For this assignment, work together in groups of three or four. Each group should pick a different magazine that regularly features profiles of stars and celebrities (for example, *People, Us, Rolling Stone, Spin, TV Guide,* and *Soap Opera Digest*).

1. Read through five or six issues of the magazine and take notes on the following:
   a. What kinds of people are featured in profiles?
   b. How are they portrayed?
   c. What does the magazine seem to think is interesting and important to readers?
2. How does the magazine represent success, fame, and the good life?
3. Next, use these notes to prepare a written or oral report that analyzes the magazine's profiles.
4. Finally, present oral reports or circulate written reports to all class members. As a class, consider the differences and similarities in how the various magazines treat celebrity profiles. How would you account for the differences? To what extent do they point to differences in their targeted audiences? To what extent do similarities point to wider shared values about what it means to be a celebrity?

WRITING ASSIGNMENT

Choose a person (or a group of people) and write a profile. You should choose someone who is interesting to you and whose social role, distinctive character, unusual job, or prominence in his or her field will interest readers as well. The point of this assignment is to bring that person to life in writing so that you can learn more about your subject while helping your readers to see and understand what makes your subject worth reading about.

The subject you choose for your profile may teach you something about yourself; for instance, you may be able to clarify why this person or group has had a profound influence—positive or negative—on your life and the culture around you. Likewise, you may find that a particular group of readers may have an interest at stake in learning about a subject that interests you; in that case, your call to write a profile can grow from your readers' need to know.

Often profiles are based on observing and interviewing, but as the reading selections indicate, profiles can also be drawn from memory, as in the case of Mike Rose's "I Just Wanna Be Average," or from the public record, as in the case of Jon Garelick's profile of Kurt Cobain. Here are some possibilities to help you think about whom you might profile:

1. Choose someone with an interesting or unusual career or hobby—an AIDS educator, a baseball card collector, an antiques dealer, a forest ranger, a Web site designer.

ETHICS OF WRITING

RESPONSIBILITY TO THE WRITER'S SUBJECT

What is a writer's responsibility to his or her subject? And how does this responsibility interact with the writer's responsibility to readers? What potential conflicts are there between the two responsibilities? These are questions profile writers invariably grapple with.

In many respects, a profile is a collaboration between the writer and the person profiled (unless, of course, the profile is based solely on other sources such as memory and research). Without the subject's cooperation, the profile will be more difficult to write—and perhaps impossible. At the same time, the subject may well have a vested interest in the profile and may, consciously or unconsciously, try to influence the outcome. Or the subject may, inadvertently or not, reveal things that if published would prove embarrassing to the person or others.

Either of these situations can pose a tricky dilemma for the writer. Profiles, after all, are meant to inform readers and offer them the writer's honest perspective—not to serve as publicity or public relations for the person profiled. If profile writers are to have an independent voice, as the ethics of journalism demands, and are to fulfill their responsibilities to readers, they must be able to make their own judgments about what is fit to print. But an important basis for these judgments is a sense of responsibility toward the subject. The writer must resist commercial pressures to sensationalize.

2. Choose someone whose profile will illustrate a larger social issue—a recent immigrant to the United States, a senior citizen, an environmental activist, a consumer advocate, a community organizer, a gang member. Consider submitting this profile to a paper or newsletter interested in addressing such social issues.

3. Choose a local personality—a politician, writer, musician, artist, athlete, or newspaper editor or columnist—or someone prominent on your own campus—a coach, administrator, distinguished teacher, or well-known scholar. Your community or campus newspaper might publish your profile if you write it with your local readership in mind.

4. Follow Mike Rose's example in "I Just Wanna Be Average" and compose a series of personality sketches, from memory or from interviews, that illustrates some larger point or controlling theme.

5. Choose a public figure, living or dead, and write a profile that makes a judgment about the meaning of that person's life.

Invention

Finding a Subject

Take some time to decide on the person (or persons) you want to profile. Don't limit yourself to people you know well, or whose job, hobby, or social role is familiar to you. Writing a profile offers an opportunity to learn about something new, and it will allow you to bring a fresh perspective to that subject. Take some risks in compiling your list: Include people or groups that you would not contact in the course of a typical day. Likewise, take some risks in making your decision—the more you stretch, the more you can learn.

> ### EXERCISE
>
> 1. Make a list: Make a list of people who, for one reason or another, interest you. Try to come up with at least ten people. This will give you some choices. If you have trouble thinking of that many, use memory triggers such as thinking through the different periods of your life or across the different hobbies you have had or the kinds of jobs your relatives hold. What have been the major turning points in your life? What kinds of people had a big impact on you during those times? If all else fails, run through each letter of the alphabet and come up with a name or group to match it.
>
> 2. Talk to others: Meet with two or three other students in your class and share the lists each of you have developed for feedback and advice about who seem to be the most promising as subjects for profiles. Knowing what you know about profiles from the readings in this chapter, which people or groups on each list seem the most promising? Ask the other students to tell you which people are most interesting to them, why, and what they

would like to know about them. Make sure you write down what they say, since their comments will help you decide on interview questions later.

3. Decide tentatively on a subject: Use the feedback you have received to help you make a tentative decision about which subject you will profile. Rank your top three choices at this point, since your first choice might not be available for interviewing, in which case you can try someone else. When you rank your choices, take your partners' reasons for being interested in one person or another into account; remember, they may have different motives and interests from you.

4. Contact your subject: Unless you are writing a profile of a public figure or a personality sketch from memory, you need to interview your subject. For many, this is the hardest part of writing a profile—making the first phone call. Explain that you're a student working on an assignment in a writing course. You'll be amazed—and reassured—by how helpful and gracious most people will be. If they don't have time, they'll tell you so, and then you can go back to your list and try your second choice. Most likely, however, you'll be able to schedule a time to meet and talk with the person. Ask if he or she can suggest anything you might read or research as background information before the interview to help you prepare for it. At this point it may also be helpful for you to sketch out a schedule for yourself. To write this profile, you will need to allow time for the several stages of both research and writing.

Clarifying your Purpose

Write a brief statement of purpose. This can be helpful preparation for an interview or as exploratory writing for a profile from memory or based on research.

EXERCISE

Take fifteen minutes to answer the following questions:

1. Why are you interested in the particular person you're profiling? What is your attitude toward the subject? Why do you want to profile this person?

2. What do you already know about the person and her job, hobby, political or community activity, or social role?

3. What do other people think about the person you're writing about? Do you share these views? What makes your perspective unique?

4. What do you expect to find out by interviewing and observing the person?

5. What is your purpose in profiling this particular person?

Research

Whether you're planning an interview, writing from memory, or profiling a public figure, it will help to do some background research. The nature of this research, of course, will vary depending on whom you're profiling. Your subject may have suggested some things to read before you meet with her. If you're doing a profile of a public personality, there should be material available in your college library or on the Web.

Interviewing your subject can take time, so plan your research schedule accordingly. For example, given the time available to complete this assignment, you will need to decide on the scope of your research—will it be a single observation/interview, an interview and follow-up, or a series of observations and interviews over a period of time?

You will also need to decide whether you plan to tape-record the interview. There are considerable advantages to taping interviews. For one thing, it frees you from the need to write during the interview, so you can devote your attention to the person you're profiling. If you plan to tape, you must, of course, ask the subject's permission, either when you set up the interview or before the interview begins.

Preparing for an Interview

The main point in preparing for an interview is to decide what you want to learn from your subject. One good way to do this is to write out a list of preliminary questions.

Guidelines for Interview Questions

The questions news reporters ask offer useful guidelines in framing these preliminary questions (sometimes known as the 5 Ws):

Who? Ask your subject to tell you something about her background, influences, training, and so on.

What? Ask her to explain the nature of what she does. Try to elicit stories from her.

Where? Ask about the setting in which she does what she does. What is the significance of this setting?

When? Ask your subject to explain the circumstances that call on her to do what she does. When do these circumstances occur?

Why? Ask your subject to explain what motivates her most. What form does this motivation take?

How? Ask your subject to describe the processes of what she does. What particular techniques, procedures, or skills are involved?

During the Interview

It is unusual for interviews to proceed systematically through a series of questions like the ones just listed. More often, interviews turn out to be fluid and free-wheeling conversations. A single question such as "Tell me something about your background and how you came to do what you're doing" may be enough to generate an hour of talk. Nonetheless, preparing such questions in advance helps keep the focus on the person being interviewed by offering invitations to talk. And finally, that's the point of an interview—to get your subject to explain what she knows. In general, interviewers should maintain a low profile and listen. Let the conversation take its own course and be prepared for the emergence of ideas, themes, and issues that you had not anticipated. When and if this happens, go with the line of conversation and follow up on questions that interest you.

After the Interview

After the interview is over, make sure you give yourself time to write some notes. These notes can provide material to add vivid detail to your profile and to build a dominant impression of your subject. Follow the suggestions below to shape your postinterview notes.

Guidelines for Interview Notes

1. Describe in as much detail as possible what your subject looks like, what she was wearing, how she moved around in the particular setting, how she interacted with other people on the scene, and anything else that seems striking.

2. Describe the setting in which the interview occurred, particularly if you met with your subject in her place of work.

3. If you tape-recorded the interview, transcribe the tape. Otherwise, use your notes to reconstruct dialogue. Keep vocal mannerisms intact as much as possible, and make special note of any memorable phrases the interviewee used.

4. What was the most important thing you discovered? Try to write it in a sentence, and then try to explain more about it in a paragraph.

5. What, if anything, seemed contradictory or incongruous in your encounter with your subject? Jot down a quick explanation of why it seemed odd.

6. In what ways did your subject confirm your preconceptions? What surprised you?

7. What larger ideas, themes, or issues were raised in the interview?

Planning

Deciding on the Dominant Impression

As you have seen from the reading selections in this chapter, the purpose of a profile is to capture your subject at a particular moment in time and to take your readers into your subject's world. In these ways, profiles offer readers a dominant impression of the person (or persons) being profiled. In a profile, you need to inform your readers about the person in question, but you also need to provide your readers with a point of view—a way of seeing and understanding the significance of the person being profiled.

Here are some questions to help you determine the dominant impression you want to create:

1. What is the most interesting, unusual, or important thing you have discovered about your subject?

2. What are your own feelings about your subject?

3. What do others say about your subject? Are these responses to your subject consistent, or do people differ?

4. Can you think of two or more dominant impressions you could create to give readers a way of understanding your subject?

5. Use your answers to these questions to refine your sense of purpose. It may help at this point to talk to a friend or classmate. Explain the different ways in which you might portray your subject. Ask how the dominant impressions you are considering affect the way your classmate or friend understands your subject.

Arranging Your Material

1. Inventory the material you have to work with: Look over your notes and notice how many separate items about your subject you have. These are the building blocks of your profile, the raw material that you will put together to construct it. Label each item according to the kind of information it contains—such as physical description, biographical background, observed actions and procedures, revealing incidents or anecdotes, direct quotes, things you have read, and things other people have told you.

2. Decide on a tentative arrangement of your material that suits your purposes. Once you have inventoried the material you have to work with, your task now is to sketch a tentative plan for your profile.
   The arrangement of your material will depend, of course, on your purpose in writing the profile. As you have seen, Molly O'Neill and Mike Rose use quite different arrangement patterns in their profiles. O'Neill uses open form to present clusters of information about Dr. Susan Love, while Rose uses claim and evidence to present a main point and then illustrates it with individual profiles. Reread the two profiles. Do you want to use open form to create a dominant impression of your subject by presenting loosely arranged clusters of information? If so, what order will best enable you to establish a perspective for your readers? Or do you want to use your profile to illustrate a main point? If so, how can you make sure to present the main point clearly and then show how the profile meaningfully illustrates it?

3. Write a working outline: Arrange the items of information you have labeled in a working outline. You are likely to have more material than you can use, so don't worry if you can't fit everything in.

Working Draft

By this time you have organized a lot of material from your research, and you have probably gained some new insight into the person or group you are profiling. Now that you have learned something new, your challenge is to teach your readers what is interesting, unusual, and important about the person or group. Use your working outline to write a working draft.

Beginnings and Endings: Using Figurative Language

As you draft, consider whether *figurative language* can make your profile more vivid and interesting. The use of figurative language, such as *similes* and *metaphors,* implies a comparison by describing one thing in terms of another. The main difference between similes and metaphors is that similes use the linking term *like.* The profile of Dr. Susan Love, for example, has a powerful ending that makes good use of figurative language:

> "You see, the gene is like a robber in the neighborhood," she said. "We have the neighborhood roped off. Now all we have to do is knock on every single door."

Susan Love, of course, is not asking us to believe genes are really robbers. Rather, the simile asks us to think of how genes are like robbers in one sense. Love then extends the comparison by using a metaphor that makes cancer researchers into detectives who have the "neighborhood roped off" and are going to "knock on every single door." This use of figurative language gives the search for breast cancer genes a dramatic character and enables readers to visualize Love's appraisal of current breast cancer research.

Mike Rose uses a metaphor to begin and end the first paragraph of his profile. The paragraph starts with this sentence:

> Students will float to the mark you set. I and the others in the vocational classes were bobbing in pretty shallow water.

And the paragraph ends by returning to the metaphor:

> But mostly the teachers had no idea of how to engage the imaginations of us kids who were scuttling along at the bottom of the pond.

Using figurative language in these ways can help readers understand the points you want to make in your profile.

Comparing and Contrasting

Comparison and contrast is another way to help readers understand your main points. Comparison and contrast enable writers to draw attention to features in their subjects that are similar and dissimilar from others to help illustrate their points. When a clearly recognizable pattern of comparison and contrast is present in a paragraph, readers can use it to follow the writer's thinking.

Jon Garelick, for example, compares and contrasts the death of various rock stars to the death of Kurt Cobain. In the paragraph that follows, Garelick sounds as if he is trying to make sense of his own reaction to the death, and he brings the readers into his mind by sharing the process of his comparison and contrast.

> Perhaps we were most shocked by our sense of shock. At the time, I couldn't imagine another rock star's death that would affect me as profoundly. Bono? Eddie Vedder? Paul Westerberg? Is it simply because I like his songs the most? That I've written the most about him, "studied" him the most in my own rock-crit way? What other comparisons were there? We were more or less prepared for Frank Zappa's death. The jazz gods I worshiped—Mingus, Ellington, Dizzy Gillespie—were likewise in physical decline when they died.

Later, Garelick picks up the comparing and contrasting development pattern again.

> The only parallel that fits, and the one that Baby Boom rock crits have been throwing at Gen Xers all week, is that of John Lennon. It's a more unlikely and awkward parallel than the Boomers will allow, but there it is. Cobain himself told Fricke that Lennon was his favorite Beatle, saying with a laugh, "He was obviously disturbed." Cobain wasn't nearly as famous….Nirvana's influence has been massive but not on a par with the Beatles. And yet it's that same loss, that same sense of disbelief, and the shock at the violence of his passing.
> There is, of course, anger as well. Lennon didn't choose his own death.

EXERCISE

If you think comparing and contrasting might work in your profile but can't think of a way to do it off the top of your head, try the following exercise.

1. Put aside the information you have gathered on the person or people you are profiling.

2. Think about a person who might be in some way similar to your subject. It might be someone who performs a similar social function or who just reminds you of your subject for some other reason. Write down as many similarities as you can think of. At the same time, you may realize more differences between them—so note those too.

3. Think about the person or group who seems to stand for the opposite of your subject. List as many of the differences as you can; in the process you might realize some similarities. Keep track of those as well, especially if they surprise you.

4. Make a list of inanimate objects that you might be able to use to describe your person or group: a kitchen table, a Model-T Ford, a biology textbook. As above, keep track of the features your subject has in common with that object, and where the analogy falls flat.

Peer Commentary

Exchange drafts with a partner. Respond in writing to these questions about your partner's draft:

1. Describe what you see as the writer's purposes. Does the working draft create a dominant impression? Does it imply or state a main point? Explain how and where the draft develops a dominant impression (and main point, if pertinent).

2. Describe the arrangement of the working draft. Divide the draft into sections by grouping related paragraphs together. Explain how each section contributes to the overall impression the profile creates. Do you find the arrangement easy to follow? Does the arrangement seem to suit the writer's purposes? If there are rough spots or abrupt shifts, indicate where they are and how they affected your reading.

3. How effective are the beginning and ending of the draft? What suggestions would you make to strengthen the impact, increase the drama, or otherwise improve these two sections of the draft? Should the writer have used a different strategy?

4. Do you have other suggestions about how the writer could enhance the profile? Are there details, reported speech, descriptions, or incidents that he could emphasize? Are there elements you think he should cut?

Revising

Use the peer commentary to do a critical reading of your draft.

1. Consider first how your reader has analyzed the arrangement of your profile. Notice in particular how the commentary has divided the draft into sections. Do these sections correspond to the way you wanted to arrange the profile? Are there ways to rearrange material to improve its overall effect?

2. If you are presenting a claim and evidence, was this pattern of organization clear to your reader? Are there ways to enhance its presentation?

3. If you are using open form, are the clusters of information clear to your reader? Are there ways to enhance the presentation?

4. Does the draft create the kind of dominant impression you intended?

5. What did your writing partner suggest? Evaluate specific suggestions.

Establishing Perspective from the Beginning

The beginning of your profile is a particularly important place to establish a perspective on the person or group you're writing about. The strategy you use to design an opening will depend both on your material and on the attitude you want your readers to have toward your subject. Notice how Richard Quitadamo revised the opening paragraph of his profile. The early draft reads more like a paragraph from a biography of Edward Sweda, while the revised version takes us into Sweda's world.

EARLY DRAFT OF "A LAWYER'S CRUSADE AGAINST TOBACCO"

Edward Sweda began his career as an anti-smoking activist over twenty years ago, when he became involved as a volunteer in a campaign to provide non-smoking sections in restaurants. He is currently the senior staff attorney for the Tobacco Product Liability Project (TPLP) at Northeastern University. Since 1984, when TPLP was established, Sweda and his associates have battled the powerful tobacco interests.

REVISED VERSION OF "A LAWYER'S CRUSADE AGAINST TOBACCO"

The office of the Tobacco Product Liability Project (TPLP) at Northeastern University in Boston is decorated with anti-smoking propaganda. One poster shows the damage that smoking has done to someone's lungs. The office secretary sat at her desk and typed busily, while Edward Sweda, senior attorney of the TPLP, conversed on the phone with Stanton Glantz, author of the well-known exposé of the tobacco industry *Cigarette Papers.*

Here is a list of techniques for establishing perspective at the beginning of a profile:

1. Set the scene: Describe the place where you encounter your subject; give details about the physical space; describe other people who are there; explain what the people are doing; set the stage for your subject's entrance. (See opening of Molly O'Neill's "A Surgeon's War on Breast Cancer" or the revised version of Richard Quitadamo's profile for examples.)

2. Tell an anecdote: Narrate an incident that involves your subject; describe how your subject acts in a revealing situation. (See opening of Jon Garelick's "Kurt Cobain 1967–1994" for an example.)

3. Use a quotation: Begin with your subject's own words; use a particularly revealing, provocative, or characteristic statement. (Notice use of quotation throughout Garelick's profile of Cobain.)

4. Describe your subject: Use description and detail about your subject's appearance as an opening clue to the person's character. (See openings of both O'Neill's profile of Susan Love and Garelick's profile of Cobain.)

5. Describe a procedure: Follow your subject through a characteristic routine or procedure at work; explain the purpose and technical details; use them to establish your subject's expertise. (See opening of O'Neill's profile of Susan Love.)

6. State your controlling theme: Establish perspective by stating in your own words a key theme that will be developed in the profile. (See opening of Mike Rose's "I Just Wanna Be Average" for an example.)

WRITERS' WORKSHOP

Richard Quitadamo wrote the following profile, "A Lawyer's Crusade against Tobacco," for a course that focused on the politics of public health. Quitadamo plans on becoming a lawyer, and he wanted to find out more about the kind of work lawyers do in the public interest, particularly in the area of product liability. What appears here is Quitadamo's working draft, followed by his questions for a peer commentary. Read the draft, keeping in mind that it is a work in progress. Then consider how you would respond to the questions Quitadamo raises in his note.

A Lawyer's Crusade against Tobacco [Working Draft]
RICHARD QUITADAMO

1   The office of the Tobacco Product Liability Project (TPLP) at Northeastern University in Boston is decorated with anti-smoking propaganda. One poster shows the damage that smoking has done to someone's lungs. The office secretary sat at her desk and typed busily, while Edward Sweda, senior attorney of the TPLP, conversed on the phone with Stanton Glantz, author of the well-known exposé of the tobacco industry *Cigarette Papers*.

2   Sweda seemed fixated on one subject, the recent banning of RJ Reynolds' "Joe Camel" cartoon character from Camel cigarette advertisements. He felt it was a small victory in the ongoing war against smoking. "Look, Stanton, Joe is gone and that's great, but that really doesn't affect the foreign market. It seems the percentage of people outside the US who smoke has risen dramatically. There's got to be something we can do." They talked for a few more moments, and then Sweda hung up the phone.

3   Edward Sweda, a tall, slender man, with graying hair, turned in his office chair. A button on his sweater read "No Smoking." He began to discuss the history of the war on tobacco and the part he has played in it.

4   Sweda began his career in 1979 as a local volunteer against cigarette smoking in Massachusetts. "I hated smoking from day one. It was disgusting, and besides it can kill you." In the late 1970s, the dangers of smoking were a novel concept, and industry leaders were quick to cover up the ill effects of smoking. It was also at this time that medical professionals, political activists, and health care advocates began pushing for stronger regulation of tobacco products.

5   In 1980, Sweda worked in Newton, MA for regulations that would require restaurants to provide at least 15% of its seating to non-smokers. "People have to

breathe, and if other people are smoking in close proximity to you, then they are infringing on your right to breathe fresh air. That's a crime. I as a non-smoker really feel strongly about this issue."

6 Sweda has also worked to stop free samples of cigarettes from being dispersed. "It reminded me of drugs. The first time was free, but after that, you had to pay. I figured I could stop this vicious cycle before it got a chance to start. That's why we eventually formed the TPLP, to use litigation as a tool to make the tobacco industry take responsibility for its actions."

7 TPLP was established in 1984, and since then Sweda and his associates have battled the tobacco industry. "Tobacco industry knew smoking was bad long before TPLP ever showed up. The first report of the Surgeon General on smoking in 1964 proved that cigarette smoking could have harmful effects on human health." But, Sweda continued, the only thing that the anti-smoking campaign got out of the Surgeon General's report was the Fanning Doctrine, which stated that there must be a comparable number of anti-smoking public service announcements (PSAs) to the number of cigarette advertisements. This doctrine, Sweda said, may or may not have led to the drop off of cigarette sales noticeable between 1966 and 1970.

8 However, on January 1, 1971, cigarette advertising was banned from TV, and along with them, the antismoking PSAs. "At first, I was overjoyed," Sweda said, smiling. "What a fool I was. The tobacco industry used other methods to lure potential smokers to their products, the PSAs were gone, and the levels of smoking increased nationwide. It seemed they could sidestep every regulation we imposed."

9 As Sweda spoke, his secretary called attention to the flashing computer screen. Sweda rose from his chair and observed the screen. "You see this? This is something I'm working on right now." Sweda was looking at the next date scheduled for hearings of the Massachusetts State Public Health Council on new proposed legislation to force the tobacco industry to disclose their secret ingredients. "What we want to do at this hearing is to make the industry sweat. They failed to block the hearing and were forced to appear. They didn't even testify on their own behalf, and I just kept talking about the list of secret ingredients and the falsified tests. You should have seen their faces."

10 Yet, Sweda is cautious with his optimism about the future of anti-smoking initiatives. He has seen things go wrong before. The tobacco industry has many influential lobbyists on their side, along with the political backing of tobacco state politicians. They are able to hide information and falsify reports to government officials. This makes the industry virtually untouchable at the federal level. Nonetheless, Sweda said he was more confident this time around. "Things are different in this day and age. People are more educated about the dangers of smoking. With the banning of Joe Camel and the Liggett case of 1996, we seem to be gaining ground on them. The Liggett case is probably the biggest breakthrough in our struggle because it's the first time a tobacco manufacturer cracked and admitted what we've known all along about the health hazards of smoking. And it actually resulted in a settlement."

11 Sweda paused, then sighed. "But there is still the problem of youth. They seem more susceptible to smoking. Maybe it's the age, maybe it's a rebellion thing, or

12 maybe it's the advertisements. The ads seem to target youth. That's why I'm glad Joe Camel is gone."

The TPLP has been working with the Federal Drug Administration on a game plan that focuses specifically on the youth smoking problem. The plan centers on keeping youth from smoking through education and other programs. "I hate to admit it, but it seems our best bet for beating smoking and the industry is to forget adult smokers. They've made their decisions, and it's their choice to continue smoking. Cessation programs and medical help groups exist for those who want to quit. But by focusing on youth, we are taking away the customers of the future. This is important because as the older generation of smokers fades away, the tobacco industry will be looking to recruit new smokers."

13 As Sweda stepped away from the computer, he said, "We'll get them, the industry, that is," and stepped to his desk, picked up the phone, and began to dial a number. This is all in a day's work for Edward Sweda and his TPLP group. They exist to promote public health and stop the growth of the tobacco industry, or as Sweda refers to them, "the merchants of death."

Quitadamo's Note on His Working Draft

I think I do a pretty good job in this draft of setting the scene and showing Sweda at work. The guy was a great interview, and I got a lot of good quotes to use. Do these seem effective? Are they easy to understand? Do you need more information at points? Is it clear, for example, what happened in the Liggett case and why anti-smoking people consider it such a huge victory? Any suggestions in this regard would be greatly appreciated.

Another thing I'm not certain about is whether I should give more information about Sweda himself. I don't provide much background information on him or talk about his personal life. I wanted to focus on him mainly as an anti-smoking activist and felt too much biographical detail would distract from this. What do you think?

My last question involves the notorious "dominant impression" we've been talking about in class so much. Do you feel that this draft gives you a strong perspective on the person? I wasn't sure whether I should provide more commentary on my own. I want readers to see Sweda as an embattled crusader but not a fanatic. Does this come across?

WORKSHOP QUESTIONS

1. Consider Richard Quitadamo's first set of questions concerning the information in the draft. Are there places where you felt you needed more information to understand the issues? If so, indicate the passage or passages in question and explain what's not clear to you.

2. Quitadamo's second question focuses on whether he should give more background on Sweda. What is your opinion? To answer this question, take into account what Quitadamo's purpose seems to be in this profile. Would more biographical detail further his purpose or, as he worries, distract from it? Explain your response.

3. As Quitadamo notes, one mark of a successful profile is that it creates a dominant impression of the subject. Explain in your own words the impression of Sweda this draft created for you. Given what you've read here, what kind of person does he seem to be? How well does the impression you've formed match Quitadamo's goals in portraying Sweda? How could Quitadamo strengthen or enhance his portrayal?

REFLECTING ON YOUR WRITING

Write an account of how you put your profile together. Explain why you selected your subject. Then describe the interview if you did one. Explain whether your final version confirmed or modified your initial preconceptions about your subject. Finally, explain how writing a profile differs from other kinds of writing you have done. What demands and satisfactions are there to writing profiles?

A CLOSING NOTE

Part of the etiquette of writing profiles is to make sure the subject of the profile gets a copy. The purpose is not to get the subject's approval, for the writer will bear the final responsibility for how the writing portrays the person profiled. Still, it is common courtesy to send your subject a copy of the profile so that she can see the final results.

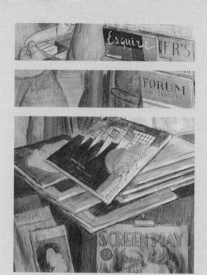

CHAPTER EIGHT

Fact Sheets and FAQs, Brochures, and Web Sites: Informing and Explaining

THINKING ABOUT THE GENRE

The purpose of this chapter is to look at three strategies for selecting, organizing, and delivering information to readers. We feature three common genres of writing. Fact sheets and FAQs (frequently asked questions), brochures, and Web sites are among the most readily available means writers use when they want to inform and explain. On the page or on the screen, these genres enable writers to present ideas and information in forms that are easy for their intended audiences to read and to use.

Writers typically turn to these genres when they believe there exists a need or a desire to know on the reader's part. This recognition leads writers to do everything from informing readers about the dangers of global warming to explaining what to do in cases of domestic abuse to detailing the rise and fall of punk music. Fact sheets and FAQs, brochures, and Web sites range across the spectrum of human activity—from the most serious matters that face us in private life and public affairs to the ways we have fun. But whether writers are describing how to attract songbirds to your backyard, presenting a summary of recent NASCAR rule changes in stock car racing, or explaining the Jubilee 2000 campaign to forgive the debts of Third World countries, the genres described in this chapter give writers a way to design information in convenient packages that meet readers' need to know.

As you will see in the reading selections, informative genres such as fact sheets and FAQs, brochures, and Web sites organize information into manageable chunks that readers can easily identify and use. Fact sheets often use the familiar format of questions and answers, and FAQs always do. (Fact sheets sometimes use a chronological or topical scheme of organization.) Brochures typically divide information into clearly marked sections and sometimes include such visual aids as lists, maps, schedules, and charts. Web sites use linked pages and frequently offer readers a menu or site map to help them navigate. In each of these genres, the design of information is a crucial aspect of informing and explaining.

People talk about the historical era we are living in as the "Age of Information." The sheer amount of information has multiplied dramatically in past decades, and it's hard not to feel overwhelmed at times by the magnitude—some would say glut—of information found in libraries, museums, the mass media, print journalism, bookstores, the Internet, government records, and various data storage systems. Consider, for example, some of the topics in this chapter—affordable housing, Alzheimer's disease, ghost towns in Colorado, Mary Shelley's *Frankenstein*. There are shelves of books and pages of articles on these subjects, and more are being written and published each year.

Fact sheets and FAQs, brochures, and Web sites give writers a strategy to help readers deal with the barrage of information. The genres described in this chapter offer writers the opportunity to sort out the most important information for readers who don't have the time, resources, or inclination to do so on their own. The writer's task is to research, select, and present the best available information on the subject, according to their readers' need to know. To do this, writers need to assess carefully both what is known about the topic at hand and what is most relevant to their readers. Given the amount of information available on so many subjects, writers typically distill the crucial points by determining what use readers are going to make of the information chosen.

To put it another way, these genres are informative, but they are not simply information containers. More important, they also embody their writers' purposes. As you will see, determining your purposes in these genres of informative writing is a key step in deciding what information to include and how to organize it. Is the purpose, say, to alert readers to the warning signs of depression or alcohol abuse; to help them identify landmarks and interesting places on a walking tour or in a national park; or to show them how to do emergency first aid? In some cases, informative writing is linked to the writer's persuasive purposes—for example, to persuade women to have annual pap smears or to convince readers that the Living Wage Movement or organizations such as Habitat for Humanity are worthy of their support.

Whatever the reasons writers turn to the genres in these chapters, it's worth noting that fact sheets and FAQs, brochures, and Web sites offer individuals and organizations a relatively inexpensive and easy way to produce means of organizing and distributing information. Part of the attraction of these genres is that they can be put together rather quickly—and in the case of Web sites updated easily—thereby enabling prompt responses to the situations that call on people to write.

EXPLORING YOUR EXPERIENCE

When you need to know something, where do you turn? What are your main sources of information, both in and out of school, and what are your purposes in using them? (For example, you may have used an encyclopedia to prepare a written report for a class, read a pamphlet about date rape, or checked the Web for sports scores or movie and music reviews.) Compare your list to those of your classmates. Next, pick three or four information sources to analyze them in some detail, choosing sources that differ from each other. Analyze the way each source makes information available. What is the purpose of the information source? How does the source select information to include? How does the source organize the information? What uses do people make of the information?

READINGS

Fact Sheets and Frequently Asked Questions (FAQs): *Habitat for Humanity Fact Sheet; The Living Wage Campaign, Frequently Asked Questions*

The Habitat for Humanity Fact Sheet and the Frequently Asked Questions (FAQs) from the Living Wage Campaign represent one convenient way to introduce readers (or Web site visitors) to a particular topic, issue, organization, or campaign. Both of these selections appear on Web sites, but fact sheets and FAQs can be found in print form as well. The principle of organization you'll find here is simple and intuitive: Use the questions people are likely to have as the scheme to present the information.

Habitat for Humanity Fact Sheet

Other languages: French - German - Hindu - Japanese
Korean - Norwegian - Portuguese - Russian - Spanish

What is Habitat for Humanity International?

1   Habitat for Humanity International is a nonprofit, ecumenical Christian housing ministry. HFHI seeks to eliminate poverty housing and homelessness from the world, and to make decent shelter a matter of conscience and action.

2   Habitat invites people of all backgrounds, races and religions to build houses together in partnership with families in need.

3   Habitat has built more than 100,000 houses around the world, providing more than 500,000 people in more than 2,000 communities with safe, decent, affordable shelter. HFHI was founded in 1976 by Millard Fuller along with his wife, Linda.

How Does it Work?

4   Through volunteer labor and donations of money and materials, Habitat builds and rehabilitates simple, decent houses with the help of the homeowner (partner)

families. Habitat houses are sold to partner families at no profit, financed with affordable, no-interest loans. The homeowners' monthly mortgage payments are used to build still more Habitat houses.

5   Habitat is not a giveaway program. In addition to a down payment and the monthly mortgage payments, homeowners invest hundreds of hours of their own labor—sweat equity—into building their Habitat house and the houses of others.

What does a Habitat house cost?

6   Throughout the world, the cost of houses varies from as little as $800 in some developing countries to an average of $46,600 in the United States.

7   Habitat houses are affordable for low-income families because there is no profit included in the sale price and no interest charged on the mortgage. Mortgage length varies from seven to 30 years.

What are Habitat affiliates?

8   Habitat for Humanity's work is accomplished at the community level by affiliates—independent, locally run, nonprofit organizations. Each affiliate coordinates all aspects of Habitat home building in its local area—fund raising, building site selection, partner family selection and support, house construction and mortgage servicing.

9   Habitat for Humanity International's headquarters, located in Americus, Ga., U.S.A, provides information, training and a variety of other support services to Habitat affiliates worldwide.

10   All Habitat affiliates are asked to "tithe"—to give 10 percent of their contributions to fund house-building work in other nations. Some affiliates in developing countries also receive funding grants from Habitat for Humanity International.

Where does Habitat for Humanity operate?

11   Habitat is a worldwide, grass-roots movement. There are more than 1,900 active affiliates in 79 countries, including all 50 states of the United States, the District of Columbia, Guam and Puerto Rico. Use our affiliate search to find Habitat affiliates in your area.

12   See our Habitat Affiliates Worldwide section for information on each country in which Habitat is at work, including progress reports, project descriptions and affordable housing needs.

How are the partner families selected?

13   Families in need of decent shelter apply to local Habitat affiliates. The affiliate's family selection committee chooses homeowners based on their level of need, their willingness to become partners in the program and their ability to repay the no-interest loan. Every affiliate follows a nondiscriminatory policy of

family selection. Neither race nor religion is a factor in choosing the families who receive Habitat houses.

14   If your family, or a family you know, is in need of decent, affordable housing, contact the Habitat affiliate nearest you. If you're not sure where a local Habitat affiliate might be, use our search engine to find the names and phone numbers of affiliates in your area, or contact the Habitat help line at (800)422-4828, ext. 2551 or 2552. Your local affiliate can give you information on the availability, size, costs and sweat-equity requirements for Habitat houses in your area, as well as information on the application process.

How are donations distributed and used?

15   Donations, whether to a local Habitat affiliate or to HFHI, are used as designated by the donor. Gifts received by HFHI that are designated to a specific affiliate or building project are forwarded to that affiliate or project. Undesignated gifts are used where most needed and for administrative expenses. HFHI's most recent audited financial statement is available online.

Who controls and manages Habitat for Humanity International?

16   An ecumenical, international board of directors determines policy and oversees and guides the mission of Habitat for Humanity International. Board members are dedicated volunteers who are deeply concerned about the problems of poverty housing around the world.

17   The HFHI headquarters office operates with an administrative staff, assisted by a core group of professional and support employees and supplemented by long-term and short-term volunteers. Each Habitat for Humanity affiliate is managed by its own local volunteer board.

How does Habitat work with the government?

18   Habitat for Humanity International is not a government agency, nor does it accept government funds for the construction of houses. However, Habitat considers all levels of government and governmental agencies important partners in its mission to eliminate poverty housing. We encourage governments to do what they can to help alleviate the suffering of all those who have no decent, adequate place to live.

19   Habitat for Humanity welcomes partnerships with governments to help "set the stage" for the construction of houses. Stage-setting funding and gifts might include land, houses for rehabilitation, infrastructure for streets, utilities and administrative expenses.

How does a Habitat for Humanity affiliate get started?

20   Habitat affiliates start when concerned citizens of diverse backgrounds come together to address the problem of poverty housing in their community. These vol-

unteers research the community's affordable housing needs and resources, and evaluate the potential success of Habitat's self-help model in their community. The group then applies to HFHI to become an official Habitat affiliate.

21   If you are interested in eliminating poverty housing in your community, please contact HFHI headquarters for information on establishing a Habitat affiliate. Persons calling from inside the United States can call (800)HABITAT—(800)422-4828. Those calling from outside the United States may contact HFHI headquarters at 01-(229) 924-6935.

How can I become a volunteer?

22   To volunteer where you live, use our affiliate search engine to find contact information for your local affiliate. Other opportunities to support Habitat's work also are available—see our get involved section.

How can I get more information?

23   For additional information, see the other sections of this Web site, see our contact information page, or write or phone our international headquarters:

Habitat for Humanity International
121 Habitat Street
Americus, GA 31709-3498
U.S.A.
(229) 924-6935

The Living Wage Campaign

Frequently Asked Questions

1   *"What do we mean by a 'living wage?'"*

2   It's simple. At an absolute minimum, it means that someone working full-time should never fall below the poverty line. The exact amount varies from state to state or city to city, but we've generally pushed for between $6.50 and $7.50 an hour, with health benefits. Hard-working people should be able to afford the necessities of life for themselves and their families.

3   Some call that radical. We call it a "family value."

4   *"Will living wage requirements cause unemployment?"*

5   A study of the Baltimore's living wage ordinance concluded that it had not produced layoffs. Likewise, a study of the Los Angeles living wage proposal concluded that it would not increase unemployment. These studies are described in more detail below.

6   *"Will employers leave town rather than pay living wages?"*

7   Business always threatens that. But they rarely do. Moreover, some corporations take the subsidies and then leave anyway. And service contractors, such as cleaning or security services, can't move out of the city where they work.

8   *"How much will it cost?"*

9   A study in Baltimore found that the real cost of city contracts had decreased since the city began requiring service contractors to pay their employees a living wage. This decrease was statistically significant. The study also found that administrative costs to taxpayers were "minimal...about 17 cents per taxpayer annually" and that no contractor had reduced their number of employees as a result of the ordinance. Click here to read the executive summary of the study.

10   Another illuminating study looked at the original living wage in Los Angeles. The authors concluded that "the living wage ordinance can be implemented while causing no net increase in the City budget, no employment loss, and no loss of City services." In fact, they concluded that the ordinance would save state and local taxpayers $33.3 million, primarily by reducing the need for food stamps and health entitlements. This study was done by a team led by Prof. Robert Pollin of the University of California-Riverside. Click here to read the executive summary of the study.

11   *"Did Congress just do this?"*

12   After talking for years, the President and Congress finally raised the minimum wage from $4.25 to $5.15. We call that a good start, but little more than that. Even so, the minimum wage is still 26% lower than it was in 1980 (after correcting for inflation). So while the two parties in Washington play election year politics over a tiny increase, NP chapters and our labor and community allies are working hard to achieve a real living wage for working Americans.

13   *"Shouldn't we let the free market decide wage levels?"*

14   This isn't a choice between the free market and government regulation. The government already intervenes in the economy, with billions in subsidies for corporations and often lucrative contracts. By placing conditions on these subsidies, we're trying to make sure that those interventions help the great mass of American working families rather than only a few CEOs.

15   *"Who gets the minimum wage?"*

16   Only one out of fourteen minimum wage workers fits the stereotype of a teenager from a rich family. Instead, almost 40% of minimum wage workers are the sole support of their family.

17   *"Is this just a union thing?"*

18   A lot of unions have supported living wage campaigns in their communities. But so have others, particularly religious and community organizations. Many small business owners also favor living wage ordinances, because they know that

subsidies give an unfair advantage to big companies which show little concern for their communities.

19   The St. Paul living wage initiative, for example, was endorsed by

Minnesota NOW and other women's groups;

Nine religious groups, including the Catholic archdiocese;

Grassroots groups including ACORN (Assn. of Community Organizations for Reform Now) and the Urban Coalition;

Progressive organizations including the New Party and the Minnesota Alliance for Progressive Action;

Several unions, including the Teamsters, the United Transportation Union, the Electrical workers and the UFCW;

and over ten thousand citizens of St. Paul who signed our petitions.

20   Elsewhere on this site you can find links to some of these organizations and statements from various individuals about the living wage.

21   *"Sounds like an interesting concept. But has anyone actually tried it?"*

22   Yes. Santa Clara County, California (which includes San Jose) requires manufacturing firms which get tax abatements from the county to pay $10 an hour to all permanent employees, and to provide them with health insurance. The city of Minneapolis requires large businesses which get over $100,000 in economic development assistance to pay $8.25 an hour. Baltimore requires companies which get service contracts from the city to pay $6.50 an hour. An extensive list of precedents for living wage requirements is included elsewhere on this site.

23   *"You're right: wages are important. But our economy is failing us in a lot of other ways."*

24   The movement for corporate responsibility has also pushed business to provide health care, to maintain good labor relations, to improve workplace safety, to provide health and other benefits to domestic partners, to invest in worker training, and to reform our economy in other ways. Click here for an extensive list.

25   This site is maintained by the New Party.

For more information contact:
Adam Glickman, 227 West 40th St. Suite 1303, NY, NY 10018
1-800-200-1294

Send Web site comments to the webmaster. Last updated July 1997.
www.newparty.org/livwag

Analysis: Information and Persuasion

The idea that information exists independently of the people who gather, organize, distribute, and use it is an old one. There is a profound—and understandable—

wish that if we could only get all the information, we would know what is true and what decisions we should make about private and public affairs. For better or for worse, however, from a rhetorical perspective, such a wish is just that—wishful thinking. Information doesn't come to us innocently. It comes through the intentions of other people, organizations, and institutions. Even in such seemingly neutral and objective forms as news articles or encyclopedia entries, the information we get is not the whole picture but a version, selected according to the best judgment of the writer. We may well have good reason to believe that these sources provide accurate and reliable accounts, but this belief also shows how we have been persuaded to invest credibility and authority in the information the writer presents.

This point is worth mentioning to underscore the fact that information and persuasion are closely linked. The questions and answers you have seen in the two reading selections are meant, certainly, to inform readers about Habitat for Humanity and the Living Wage Campaign. At the same time, the information conveyed is meant to establish the purposes and credibility of those organizations. Notice, for example, how Habitat for Humanity describes itself as "a non-profit, ecumenical Christian housing ministry" and "not a giveaway program." By the same token, the Living Wage Campaign cites two studies (and provides links to them), as well as union, feminist, grassroots, and religious groups that support the living wage initiative.

FOR CRITICAL INQUIRY

1. What do you see as the overall purpose of the Habitat for Humanity Fact Sheet? To what extent is it providing information? To what extent is it trying to persuade readers about the aims of the organization? Are these purposes easy to separate? Explain your answer.

2. How does the Living Wage Campaign FAQs define "a living wage"? Is this meant to be an informative or a persuasive definition? What examples of the definition are offered? What consequences of the living wage do the FAQs highlight?

3. The readings use questions that Habitat for Humanity and the Living Wage Campaign assume are on readers' minds. Consider the choice of questions asked and answered in the two examples. What assumptions are being made about what readers know and need to know?

4. Does the order of questions follow a logical pattern? Does the order provide emphasis? What influence on readers is the order likely to have?

5. The tone of voice differs somewhat in the two readings. Describe each of them and explain why you think they were chosen.

Brochures: Alzheimer's Association, "You Can Make a Difference: 10 Ways to Help an Alzheimer Family." Aspen Historical Society, "Ashcroft: Ghost Town."

Brochures are another common way of conveying information. The two presented on pages 266–267 are good examples of how brochures are especially well suited to explaining how to do things. The brochures are meant not just to inform readers but to be of practical use to them. In these instances, the brochure from the Alzheimer's Association "You Can Make a Difference" tells what individuals can do to help an Alzheimer family, while the brochure on the ghost town Ashcroft provides information for people who are visiting the historic site in the Colorado Rockies, ten miles south of Aspen.

Analysis: Information Design

The two brochures follow a design format you have no doubt seen before. The layout is based on three or four vertical folded panels. Such brochures are easy to distribute and easy to use. You can find them in information racks at health services, bookstores, tourist centers, and other public places.

In the following two examples of informational brochures, the design embodies the purpose. The Alzheimer's Association presents what you can do to help an Alzheimer family. The list on the inside of "10 Easy Ways to Help" provides a range of possibilities, enabling readers to see how they can address the needs of Alzheimer families in a variety of ways. The information offered here, of course, is meant not simply to inform readers but to persuade them that they can make a difference in other people's lives.

The Ashcroft brochure merges information and persuasion in a different way. It wants to give visitors information about the historical background of Ashcroft and to guide their tour of the ghost town. But the information is also intended to persuade visitors to appreciate the historical significance of the site. Accordingly, it contains numerous illustrations to help visitors visualize Ashcroft's past.

FOR CRITICAL INQUIRY

1. Look at the order in which you encounter information in the Alzheimer's Association brochure "You Can Make a Difference." To do this, you have to imagine that you are unfolding the brochure rather than reading it on the page. Consider first what you see on the front cover. Next notice the two panels you see when you open the brochure. Then imagine that the brochure is fully unfolded and that you see the four inside panels. Finally,

ALZHEIMER'S® ASSOCIATION
Someone to Stand by You

919 North Michigan Avenue
Suite 1100
Chicago, Illinois 60611-1676
(800) 272-3900
fax: (312) 335-1110
web site: http://www.alz.org

Alzheimer's Association – RI Chapter
245 Waterman Street, Suite 306
Providence, RI 02906
HELPLINE: (401) 421-0008 / (800) 244-1428
www.alz-ri.org

YOU CAN MAKE A DIFFERENCE

10 WAYS

TO HELP AN

ALZHEIMER

FAMILY

ALZHEIMER'S® ASSOCIATION
Someone to Stand by You

WHAT IS ALZHEIMER'S DISEASE?

Alzheimer's disease attacks the parts of the brain that control memory, thinking and judgment. A person with Alzheimer's may be physically healthy but require 24-hour-a-day assistance with basic daily activities. At some point, he'll forget the names and faces of family and friends. He may become withdrawn, and his behavior may change. Later, he'll decline physically as well.

ALZHEIMER'S AFFECTS THE ENTIRE FAMILY

Alzheimer's causes significant changes in family life. Spouses and children – often including school age youngsters – become caregivers. Caregiving can make recreation, chores and even employment difficult or impossible to maintain. The uninsured cost of care can wipe out savings, too. It's no wonder that 80 percent of Alzheimer caregivers report high levels of stress and stress-related illness.

FRIEND TO FRIEND *messages from caregivers*

"We like to go out, but my husband's too much to handle alone. I could use some help."

"Call me. If I can't talk, I'll let you know."

"It's difficult when friends stay away."

FAMILIES NEED FRIENDS

One in ten American families has a loved one with Alzheimer's disease; and one in three adults knows someone with the disease. Chances are, you do, too. You may want to offer your help, but worry that you'll say or do the wrong thing. You should know that:

Alzheimer caregivers

* *feel alone and disconnected from friends*
* *need assistance, but are reluctant to ask*
* *are often unable to do errands or complete household tasks*
* *experience stress, sometimes severe*
* *need a break from caregiving, but may not have anyone to relieve them or refuse assistance when it's offered*
* *are looking for someone to listen*

And those with Alzheimer's

* *face an uncertain future*
* *must adjust to new schedules and changing roles and responsibilities*
* *worry about overwhelming family caregivers*
* *strive to maintain an active and independent lifestyle*
* *may look the same, but act differently*

---

10 EASY WAYS TO HELP AN ALZHEIMER FAMILY

A friend is an important source of support for the Alzheimer family. Even if they live far away, there's still plenty you can do. Here are ten easy ways to help:

1 Keep in touch
Maintain contact with family members. A card, a call, or visit all mean a great deal. Family members, including the person with Alzheimer's, will benefit from your visits or calls. Continue to send cards, even if you don't get a response. It's a simple, yet important way to show you care.

2 Do little things – they mean a lot
When cooking, make extra portions and drop off a meal (in a freezable and disposable container). If you're on your way out to do an errand, check with a family member to see if there's anything they need. Surprise the caregiver with a special treat, such as a rented movie, an audiotape of last week's church service or a gift certificate for a massage or dinner out.

3 Give them a break
Everyone needs a little time for themselves. Offer to stay with the Alzheimer person so family members can run errands, attend a support group meeting or take a short trip. Even if the caregiver does not leave the house, this will provide some personal time. Chances are, the person with Alzheimer's will also enjoy a break.

4 Be specific when offering assistance
Most friends are good about saying they're available to "do anything," but many caregivers find it hard to ask for something specific. Have the family prepare a "to do" list of hard-to-get-to projects (e.g., laundry, dusting, yard work, medical bills). Figure out what you can do, then dedicate some time – on a weekly or monthly basis – to helping the family tackle some of these tasks.

5 Be alert
Learn about Alzheimer's and how it impacts the family. Most people with Alzheimer's "wander" at some point, and could become lost in their own neighborhoods. Know how to recognize a problem and respond. Take time to learn about other common behaviors and helpful care techniques.

6 Provide a change of scenery
Plan an activity that gets the whole family out of the house. Make a reservation at a restaurant and ask for a table with some privacy. Be sure to include the person with Alzheimer's, if the caregiver feels it's appropriate. If not, make arrangements for someone to stay at home while you're out. Or, invite the family to your house or to a nearby park for a picnic.

7 Learn to listen
Sometimes, those affected by Alzheimer's just need to talk with someone. Ask family members how they're doing and encourage them to share. Be available when the caregiver is free to talk without interruptions. You don't need to provide all the answers – just be a compassionate listener. Try not to question or judge, but rather, support and accept.

8 Care for the caregiver
Encourage caregivers to take care of themselves. Pass along useful information and offer to attend a support group meeting with them. Local chapters of the Alzheimer's Association have information available and sponsor telephone "Helplines" and support groups in your area.

9 Remember *all* family members
The person with Alzheimer's will appreciate your visits, even if unable to show it. Talk with the person the way you'd want to be talked to. Spouses, adult children and even young grandchildren are all affected in different ways by a relative's Alzheimer's disease. Be attentive to their needs, too.

10 Get involved
Unless a prevention is found, 14 million Americans will have Alzheimer's disease in coming years. There are many things you can do to help families today, and prevent further devastation tomorrow. Make a contribution to the Alzheimer's Association or volunteer at your local chapter. Join in the Association's annual Memory Walk to raise awareness and funds for chapter programs and services. Ask your legislator to support funding of research and programs to help Alzheimer families. You can make a difference!

**The Alzheimer's Association:
Someone to Stand by You**

The Alzheimer's Association is the only national voluntary organization dedicated to conquering Alzheimer's disease through research and to providing information and support to people with Alzheimer's disease, their families, and caregivers.

Founded in 1980 by family caregivers, the Alzheimer's Association has more than 200 chapters nationwide providing programs and services to assist Alzheimer families in their communities. The Association is the leading funding source for Alzheimer research after the federal government.

Information on Alzheimer's disease, current research, patient care and assistance for caregivers is available from the Alzheimer's Association. For more information or the location of the chapter nearest you, call:

(800) 272-3900

or e-mail: info@alz.org

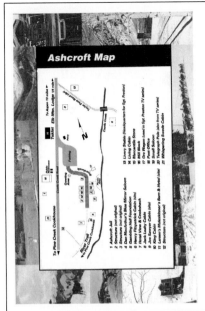

look at the back cover. How is information organized in these four locations on the brochure? Why do you think the designers chose the order in which the information appears?

2. The Ashcroft brochure consists of three oversized panels instead of the four-panel format of the Alzheimer's Association brochure. In fact, the pan-

els are big enough to use columns of text on the inside and still have room for illustrations. Look carefully at the illustrations that appear on the front and inside. How do they work together with the text to produce an impression of the place? Do you think the illustrations were well chosen? Why or why not?

3. Notice where brochures appear around campus. For a day or two, pick up a brochure whenever you see one, noting where you found it. Bring the brochures to class. Work with two or three other students. Make a list of all the places brochures can be found. What range of purposes do you see in the brochures? How are they meant to be used?

4. From the brochures you and your classmates have brought to class, pick out two or three that you think are especially well-designed and two or three that you think are not so well-designed. Explain your judgment. What criteria are you using in your evaluation?

Web Sites: "Evolution of Daytime TV Talk" and "My Hideous Progeny: Mary Shelley's *Frankenstein.*"

The two Web sites included here give an idea of the kind of informative writing you can find online. "Evolution of Daytime TV Talk" is a series that appears as part of a talk show Web site. As you will see, the six-part series appeared in weekly install-

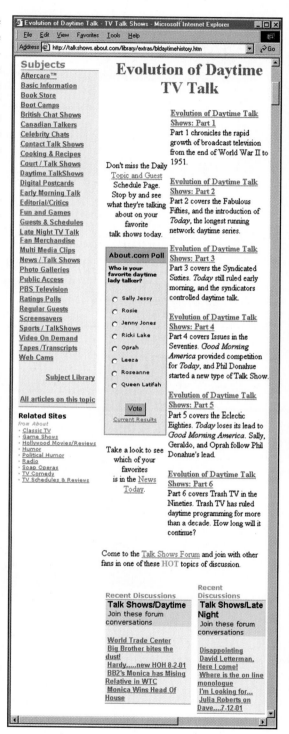

ments. Here we present the first of two pages from Parts 1, 2, and 3 and both pages from Parts 4, 5, and 6. You can find the entire series at <talkshows.about.com/tvradio/talkshows/library/extras/bldaytimehistory.htm>. "My Hideous Progeny: Mary Shelley's *Frankenstein*" was developed by Cynthia Hamberg as part of her master's thesis on literary Web sites. We include the home page, each of the sections listed on the menu, and pages from three of the six sections. You can find the Web site at <home1.worldonline.nl/~hamberg>.

Evolution of Daytime Talk Shows

Part 1: Post War—1951

1   With the end of World War II came a sudden flurry of activity centered around this wonderful new world of television. The post-war economy was booming. More and more young families were buying their first homes (with the aid of VA loans), and Americans were eager to have this new form of family entertainment in their own living rooms. The early television stations began to "steal away" the actors and writers from  older, established radio stations. The writers brought their scripts with them, and suddenly, many of the shows which had been favorite radio programs for years were being adapted for television.

2   The first, and longest running TV Talk Show of all time is, of course, NBC's classic Meet the Press. This panel discussion program, created by Lawrence Spivak and Martha Rountree, began as a radio show in 1945 and moved to television on November 6, 1947. Martha Rountree was the first moderator of Meet the Press, and remains the only female moderator in the show's history. There have only been nine moderators in over half a century of weekly broadcasts. NBC has preserved some of history's greatest moments for us, and you can view them on their official MSNBC Web site. You can view video clips from these very memorable TV appearances of Joseph McCarthy (1950), Eleanor Roosevelt (1957), Fidel Castro (1959), Martin Luther King, Jr. (1960), and others.

3   New York City was the center of TV activity in the late forties, but Chicago was about to change that. After some test broadcasts of World Series baseball games and election returns in late 1948, NBC's own WNBQ station in Chicago began a regular commercial television broadcast schedule on January 7, 1949.

4   The Chicago School of Television
Come back next week for Part 2 on the Evolution of Daytime Talk Shows, but in the meantime, stop by our Talk Shows Chat Room and share your early memories with other fans. Check the Talk Show Events Calendar for scheduled chat times,

and drop by the Talk Shows Discussion Forum to share your memories or discuss the current daytime Talk Shows. Here are the current HOT topics of discussion in our forums today.

Part 2: Fabulous Fifties

5   Just as NBC's *Tonight* show dominated late-night programming in the early years of television, the *Today* show has been the standard in early-morning programs. For almost 50 years, American viewers all over the country have been drinking one last cup of coffee while watching the *Today* show, then rushing off to start the workday. *Today* is network television's longest running daytime series, as well as one of the most profitable shows in the history of television. NBC has preserved a little bit of this early television history on the MSNBC Web site. You can even watch a video clip of the opening segment of that first January 14, 1952 *Today* show broadcast. The first host of *Today* was Dave Garroway, from the Chicago School of Television, with Jack Lescoulie (former UCLA football star) and Jim Fleming rounding out the first early-morning news team. Though off to a shaky start with what was considered at that time very "high tech" electronic gadgetry, Garroway and crew quickly moved to a more relaxed, personal atmosphere, and started to pick up new commercial sponsors and station affiliates.

6   An unusual part of that early *Today* show was the appearance of the first non-human cast member, J. Fred Muggs in 1953. Though popular with the viewers, Muggs was never popular with the show's staff. Animal actors can be difficult to work with, and this chimpanzee was more than a handful for the *Today* crew. He was eventually replaced with another chimp, Komomo, Jr., who proved to be a talented addition to the cast. While Kokomo Jr. (pictured above) appeared only briefly on *Today*, he and Nick Carrado went on to appear on many daytime and late-night Talk Shows.

7   But 1953 marked another first for the *Today* show. They began to feature a different young woman each day, and the "*Today* Girl" soon became a permanent part of the early-morning program. The first "*Today* Girls" were little more than window-dressing. They were attractive young women who were featured for one day only, and had very few responsibilities on the show. The role and responsibilities of the "*Today* Girl" expanded slowly over the years, and it was not until much later (1974) that the "*Today* Girl" evolved into a full-fledged "co-host" on the *Today* show. The following up-and-coming personalities took a turn as a "*Today* Girl" during the fifties: Estelle Parsons, Lee Meriwether, Helen O'Connell, Betsy Palmer, and Florence Henderson.

Part 3: Syndicated Sixties

8   The sixties marked a decade of change for television viewers. The first communications satellite, "Echo 1 A" was launched by the U.S. The Sony corporation

developed the first television set assembled with transistors instead of electron tubes. The first transatlantic television transmission, via the Telestar Satellite, made worldwide television and cable networks a reality in 1962. And color television made its debut in U.S. homes in 1964. But the change that more Americans noticed was the departure of Dave Garroway from the *Today* show. After more than nine years as the face of early morning TV, Dave was replaced by John Chancellor in 1961. But John was a serious newsman, not an entertainer, and his assignment as host of *Today* didn't last long. Hugh Downs took over in 1962 and stayed with the show for the remainder of the decade. Joe Garagiola (ex St. Louis Cardinals catcher) brought a new lively personality to *Today* in the late sixties. Garagiola's quick wit was a nice diversion when Downs lapsed into longwindedness.

9   The female face was becoming a more common sight on *Today*. Pat Fontaine and Maureen O'sullivan started off this decade of "*Today* Girls." Although hired as a writer, Barbara Walters was pressed into on-camera service in November of 1963 because of the assassination of President John F. Kennedy. After her successful coverage of the JFK funeral, Barbara made regular appearances on the *Today* show, and succeeded Maureen O'Sullivan as the next "*Today* Girl."

10   CBS made another attempt at a morning show in the sixties. From 1963–1966, the *CBS Morning News* was broadcast as a half hour hard news program with veteran newsman Mike Wallace. In 1966, Joseph Benti took over the show, and the show was expanded to a full hour in 1969. But this show was a very dry, straight news broadcast, with none of the morning conversation, celebrity interviews, and friendly banter that was popular with *Today* show viewers.

11   The *Today* show continued to be the early-morning programming standard, but a few fresh faces that would remain with us throughout the next two decades made their debut on daytime TV in the sixties. The next page continues with a look at this new group of Talk Show hosts.

Page 2: Changing Times, Changing Faces

12   Join me next week for another article in this series, as we confront U.S. Talk Shows in the Seventies. Until then, you can look here for more information on your favorite Talk Show or host, current or classic.

Part 4: Issues in the Seventies

13   The *Today* show marched into its third decade without competition, but it seemed as if there was a revolving door at NBC during the seventies. Hugh Downs left *Today* in 1971, and was replaced by Frank McGee. Frank McGee proved to be difficult to work with, unpopular with most of the staff. After Frank died of bone cancer in 1974, another Oklahoman newsman, Jim Hartz was brought in as host. Both McGee and Hartz were serious newsmen, and ratings had begun a downhill slide. Barbara Walters (then an official co-host) decided to switch from NBC to ABC in 1976, and NBC chose this time to drop Jim Hartz from the lineup.

14   ABC launched its first real early morning competitor in November of 1975. *Good Morning America* was similar to *Today* in that it used a blend of news, interviews, and

feature articles; but the set of *GMA* was a living room, instead of a newsroom. That seemed to give *GMA* a far more personal feeling, like inviting friends over for coffee and conversation. David Hartman was the first host of *GMA*, with Nancy Dussault as his co-host. Nancy didn't stay long, and was replaced by Sandy Hill in 1977. *GMA* started off slowly in the ratings, but climbed steadily throughout the last half of the seventies.

15   Tom Brokaw was brought in to take over the helm of the *Today* show on August 29, 1976, and a major search was launched to find a replacement for the co-host position left vacant by Barbara Walters. Six women (including Linda Ellerbee and Betty Furness) were seriously considered for the spot, but Jane Pauley was finally selected to round out the *Today* team. It was this team of Tom Brokaw, Jane Pauley, and Gene Shalit that stopped the ratings slide, and brought *Today* back to life at the close of the seventies.

16   There were two choices for early morning programming in the seventies, and Phil Donahue brought a new attitude to daytime programming. The next page continues with a look at Phil Donahue's new type of Talk Show.

Page 2: Phil Donahue Arrives

17   Join me next week for another article in this series, as we move into the controversial eighties with Part 5 of the Evolution of Daytime Talk Shows. Until then, you can look here for more information on your favorite Talk Show or host, current or classic.

Part 5: The Eclectic Eighties

18   We had a strange mixture of old and new in the eighties, and constant change seemed to be the "order of the day" for early morning shows. Tom Brokaw left *Today* at the end of 1981, and former sportscaster Bryant Gumbel, along with news correspondent Chris Wallace (son of Mike Wallace) arrived on the scene in 1982. Chris Wallace left after less than a year, and was replaced by John Palmer. Jane Pauley was on maternity leave at the end of 1983, but returned in early 1984. Linda Ellerbee, who did popular weekly "T.G.I.F." spots, defected to ABC in late 1986. During all these changes, *Today* was running second to *Good Morning America*, and even went to third place (after the *CBS Morning News*) once in 1983. Ratings began to recover in the late eighties, up until Bryant Gumbel wrote a memo (very critical of Willard Scott and Gene Shalit) to his superiors. This internal memo was somehow leaked to the press, and created quite a backlash. Then NBC decided to bring in Deborah Norville (at first only to read the news), but somehow managed to squeeze Jane Pauley out completely. Ratings started to slide again, and *Today* was again running a consistent second to *GMA*.

19   Sandy Hill left *GMA* in the summer of 1980, and was replaced by Joan Lunden. The David Hartman/Joan Lunden team remained in place until David Hartman decided to leave in February of 1987. Charlie Gibson succeeded Hartman in 1987, and the new Charlie Gibson/Joan Lunden team proved to be an extremely suc-

20   cessful partnership for ABC. Except for minor fluctuations, *GMA* stayed at the top of the early morning ratings throughout most of the eighties.

The CBS early morning program during the seventies had been strictly a news show, but in the fall of 1980, *Morning* made its debut as a ninety-minute daily program with Charles Kuralt and Diane Sawyer as co-hosts. In early 1982, the program expanded to two hours, the same as its competitors, *GMA* and *Today*. Shortly after *Morning* expanded to two hours, Kuralt left the program and was replaced by Bill Kurtis. Diane Sawyer decided to leave in late 1984, and Diane's replacement turned out to be a disaster. Phyllis George, a former Miss America, was teamed up with Bill Kurtis. Kurtis expressed extreme disappointment in CBS's choice, and left in September 1985. Bob Schieffer hosted temporarily, until Forrest Sawyer took over. Phyllis George was replaced by Maria Shriver. The Forrest/Shriver team lasted less than a year, and was replaced by the team of Bruce Morton and Faith Daniels.

21   After so many unsuccessful attempts with *Morning*, CBS decided to start with a fresh format in 1987. On January 12, 1987 CBS launched *The Morning Program*, a ninety-minute show hosted by Mariette Hartley and Rolland Smith. The team included weather by Mark McEwen, comedy bits by Bob Saget, and a studio audience was thrown in for good measure. But this show failed to attract viewers and was cancelled after only 10 months. A new show called *CBS This Morning* debuted in November, 1987. This time, CBS tried out Kathleen Sullivan and Harry Smith as co-hosts, and Greg Gumbel (brother of Bryant Gumbel) as sports anchor.

22   The balance of power in early morning programming shifted frequently in the eighties, but Phil Donahue continued to lead the way in afternoon programming. The next page continues with the changing styles of Talk Shows in the eighties.

Page 2: Controversy Sells
23   Join me next week for the last article in this series. We will take a look back at the nineties, and the current status of Talk Shows in the U.S. Until then, you can look here for more information on your favorite Talk Shows, past or present.

Part 6: Trash TV in the Nineties
24   Despite the efforts of CBS, the competition for early morning ratings remained mainly a race between NBC's *Today* and ABC's *Good Morning America* throughout the nineties. Katie Couric replaced *Today*'s Deborah Norville in 1991, and Matt Lauer took over Gumbel's co-host position in 1996. The Matt Lauer/Katie Couric team, along with Ann Curry as the news anchor, Al Roker reporting the day's weather, and Gene Shalit with entertainment reviews and interviews, has proved to be quite successful for NBC, with improved ratings for the last half of the decade. Willard Scott, who has been with the *Today* show since 1980, functions as roving reporter and all-around funny man.

25   NBC has attempted to build on *Today*'s popularity by launching a new morning show called *Later Today* in the fall of 1999. With a mixture of news, entertainment

and issue-related segments, *Later Today* attempts to build on the momentum created by the last hour of *Today*. Three lovely ladies, Jodi Applegate, Asha Black, and Florence Henderson discuss everything from current fashion and home decorating trends to personal health and fitness issues.

26   For the first half of the nineties, *GMA* stayed in first place for early morning shows. The Charlie Gibson/Joan Lunden team was hard to beat. But *GMA*'s ratings stumbled when Joan Lunden was replaced by Lisa McRee in 1997. And they tumbled further when Kevin Newman stepped into the chair left vacant by Charlie Gibson in 1998. ABC attempted to boost ratings by bringing Charlie back, and teaming him with Diane Sawyer. This was supposed to be only a temporary arrangement, but ABC doesn't seem to be in any hurry to replace what has turned out to be a successful pairing for them.

27   In spite of two early morning shows on weekdays, The *CBS Morning News* and *CBS This Morning*, plus two weekend shows, the *CBS New Saturday Morning* and *CBS New Sunday Morning*, they weren't a serious early morning contender during the first half of the decade. But CBS began to gain in ratings during the second half when both NBC and ABC were going through major changes. And they fired a major volley in the "Early Morning Talk Show War" with their new *Early Show*, which launched in November of 1999 with Bryant Gumbel and Jane Clayson. Only time will tell if Gumbel and the Early Show, will be an early morning contender again.

28   While early morning Talk Shows continued to focus on news and information (with a splash of entertainment thrown in), the other daytime Talk Shows shifted into a progressively trashy trend in the first half of the nineties.

Page 2: Trashy Trends

29   If you enjoyed this article, but came into this series at the end, you might want to go back and start at the beginning with Part 1 of the Evolution of Daytime Talk Shows. Do you have a personal favorite daytime or late-night program? You can find more information on your favorite Talk Shows, past or present, right here on the About.com Talk Shows site.

My Hideous Progeny

Home
Mary Shelley
Frankenstein
Gothic
Literature
Links
Feedback
About This Site

Mary Shelley's *Frankenstein*

On this site, you will find everything you have ever wanted to know about Mary Shelley. There are pages dealing with Mary's life, her family, her friends and her novels.

A large section of this Web site is specifically devoted to her most famous novel *Frankenstein*, offering a summary, a title explanation, character descriptions and information about the genre of Gothic literature. The text of *Frankenstein* is available in a fully annotated HTML format.

Mary Shelley

3 In this section you can find:

- A biography of Mary Wollstonecraft Shelley
- short biographies of Mary's relatives
- A bibliography of Mary Shelley's work as well as work relating to Mary Shelley or her novel *Frankenstein*

Biography
Mary Wollstonecraft Shelley (1797–1851)

4 Mary is born in Somers Town, Great Britain, in 1797 to well-known parents: author and feminist Mary Wollstonecraft and philosopher William Godwin. Unfortunately, Wollstonecraft dies as the result of Mary's birth. Mary is therefore raised by her father and a much resented stepmother.

5 When Mary is sixteen she meets the young poet Percy Bysshe Shelley, a devotee of her father's teachings. Together with Mary's stepsister, they run off to continental Europe several times, not hindered by the fact that Shelley was already married.

6 In 1816, they go abroad again, this time spending time with Byron and his friend Polidori in Geneva. There Byron suggests that they should all write a ghost story. Mary writes *Frankenstein*, the only story of the four that was ever to be published as a novel. Later that same year, Percy's wife drowns herself: Percy and Mary marry in December 1816.

7 The last years of married life are filled with disaster for Mary. Her half sister dies as do two of her children. Mary becomes depressed, a tendency she probably inherited from her mother. She is only partly relieved by the birth of Percy, their only surviving child.

8 Mary and Percy eventually move to Italy where Percy drowns during a sailing trip in 1822. Mary is determined to keep the memory of her late husband alive. She publishes several editions of Percy's writings and adds notes and prefaces to them.

9 She also continues writing her own novels, the most famous one being *The Last Man* (1826). This book deals with human isolation just as her earlier novel *Frankenstein* did. She writes numerous short stories and contributes biographical and critical studies to the *Cabinet Cyclopædia*.

10 Mary spends the last years of her life in the loving company of her son and two good friends. She tries very hard to free herself from the strains put on her by being the daughter and wife of such well-known people. She maintains her liberal opinions but at the same time tries to fit into a more conservative society. She even writes an *apologia* in her journal, which reveals "the stresses of a life spent trying to measure up to the example, yet to escape the obloquy, of her parents and husband."[1]

[1]"Mary Wollstonecraft Shelley," *The Norton Anthology of English Literature*, ed. M.H. Abrams, 6th ed., vol. 2 (New York: Norton, 1993). 844–862.

11   Mary Wollstonecraft Shelley dies in 1851 at the age of fifty-three.

SOURCES:

Abrams, M.H., ed. *The Norton Anthology of English Literature*. 6th ed. Vol. 2. New York: Norton, 1993.

Spark, Muriel. *Mary Shelley*. New York: Meridian, 1988.

Relatives

12   Here you can find short biographies of people who played an important role in Mary Shelley's life:

- her mother Mary Wollstonecraft
- her father William Godwin
- her husband Percy Bysshe Shelley

13   **Mary Wollstonecraft (1759–1797)**

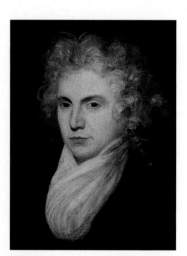

14   Mary Wollstonecraft does not grow up in a very harmonious household. Her father is a heavy drinker and tyrannizes her mother. As she witnesses and sometimes even tries to stop the abuse, it was perhaps inevitable that Mary would turn out to be one of the first feminists.

15   At the age of 27, she writes her first article "Thoughts on the Education of Daughters" in 1786. It does not take long for people to recognize her for her remarkable writing skills. Besides writing original works, she also writes reviews and does translations.

16   In earlier works, Mary Wollstonecraft writes about "the disabilities and sufferings of the English lower classes."[1] But in her most famous works, Mary focuses more on the oppression of women. This is the central theme of her most famous work *A Vindication of the Rights of Woman*. Never before were the sufferings and indignities of women so passionately described. In writing this work, Mary "had found the cause she was to pursue for the rest of her life."[2]

17   In her personal life, she also has to deal with indignities. She falls in love with a man, who leaves her just after she gives birth to their daughter. Wollstonecraft is so depressed that she tries to commit suicide twice.

18   In 1793, she renews a friendship with the well-known philosopher William Godwin. They fall in love and marry in 1797. However, this new-found happiness

---

[1]"Mary Wollstonecraft Shelley," *The Norton Anthology of English Literature*, ed. M.H. Abrams, 6th ed., vol. 2 (New York: Norton, 1993) 844–847.

[2]"Mary Wollstonecraft Shelley," *The Norton Anthology of English Literature*, ed. M.H. Abrams, 6th ed., vol. 2 (New York: Norton, 1993) 844–847.

does not last for a long time. Six months after their marriage, Mary gives birth to her second daughter Mary Wollstonecraft Godwin. Unfortunately, Mary is diagnosed with blood poisoning and dies ten days later.

19   Her husband publishes *Memoirs of the Author of "A Vindication of the Rights of Women"* in the year following her death. In this publication, he tells all about Mary's affairs, suicide attempts and her liberal ideas about religion and sexual relations. The unfortunate result is that Mary is saddled with a scandalous reputation. It was only in the 20th century that Mary Wollstonecraft's writings become recognized as classic works, not only dealing with women's issues but also critiquing the prevailing social circumstances.

William Godwin (1756–1836)

20   Godwin is born on March 3, 1756. Before he becomes a novelist and philosopher, he serves as a minister. In 1785 however, he changes his views and becomes a convinced atheist. He has very strong beliefs which often conflict with the ruling public opinion. He strongly believes in man's individual perfectness and its ability to reason. A person should not be restricted by another person (he was therefore opposed to marriage) or any form of government. He is also in favor of the redistribution of property. He believes that each person should have enough property to fit his needs, because each man deserves a state of well-being.

21   At that time he was considered a courageous and original thinker, although he was probably too left-wing for the larger part of the population. In 1793, Godwin writes his best-known work: *The Enquiry Concerning Political Justice, and Its Influence on General Virtue and Happiness.*

22   Four years later, Godwin marries feminist author Mary Wollstonecraft. A clear indication of his love for her, as Godwin disapproves of marriage. Later he states that "nothing but a regard for the happiness of the individual, which I [Godwin] have no right to injure, would have induced me to submit to an institution which I [Godwin] wish to see abolished."[1] The marriage does not last long as Mary dies six months later of complications from the birth of their daughter. In 1801, Godwin marries again, this time to Jane Clairmont. Besides writing for adults, he also writes books for children. The rest of his time he is devoted to publishing the work of others. William Godwin dies in London in 1836.

Percy Bysshe Shelley (1792–1822)

23   In 1792, Percy Bysshe Shelley is born into a conservative, aristocratic family. It was obvious from a very early age that Shelley would not follow the same

[1]Muriel Spark, *Mary Shelley* (New York: Meridian, 1988) 10.

conservative path in life. While studying at Oxford University, he decides to dedicate his life to fighting injustice and oppression. In 1810, after being expelled from Oxford, Shelley goes to London where he marries the sixteen-year-old Harriet Westbrook. He quickly becomes a disciple of William Godwin, a radical social reformer.

24   In 1813, Shelley prints his first important work, "Queen Mab," which describes "religion and codified religion as the roots of social evil."[1] The following year, Shelley falls in love and runs off with Godwin's daughter, Mary. His family and friends who already thought of him as a revolutionary and an atheist, now also regard him immoral.

25   After the suicide of Shelley's wife Harriet Westbrook, Percy and Mary marry in 1816. A short time later, they move to Italy. However, Percy still feels like an "outcast, scorned and rejected by the human race to whose welfare he [Percy] had dedicated his powers and his life."[2]

26   In times of the greatest despair (the death of their two children), Shelley writes his greatest works, including "Prometheus Unbound" (1819), and the tragedy "The Cenci."

27   Just before his death in 1822, Shelley regains some joy in life. This was mostly thanks to a small group of friends that gathers around him. Percy Shelley dies unexpectedly. When he and a friend are on a sailing trip, they are caught by a heavy rainstorm. The ship sinks and Shelley drowns on July 8, 1822.

28   Shelley's work is now regarded as one of the greatest of all English poets, although some find his poems too pretty and over-sentimental.

SOURCES:

Abrams, M.H., ed. *The Norton Anthology of English Literature*. 6th ed. Vol. 2. New York: Norton, 1993.

Spark, Muriel. *Mary Shelley*. New York: Meridian, 1988.

Encarta '95. CD-ROM. United States of America: Microsoft Corporation, 1994.

[1]"Percy Bysshe Shelley", *The Norton Anthology of English Literature*, ed. M.H. Abrams, 6th ed., vol. 2 (New York: Norton, 1993) 643–647.

[2]"Percy Bysshe Shelley", *The Norton Anthology of English Literature*, ed. M.H. Abrams, 6th ed., vol. 2 (New York: Norton, 1993) 643–647.

Bibliography

29   Here you can find a bibliography of all the writings of Mary Shelley (fiction and non-fiction) as well as a selected bibliography of reference works.

Mary Shelley
Fiction

- *Frankenstein, or The Modern Prometheus* (1818)
  A young student's discovery of animating lifeless matter leads to disaster when he creates a monster. You can read more about this novel in the Frankenstein section of this web site.

- *Valperga, or The Life and Adventures of Castruccio, Prince of Lucca* (1823)
  A romance set in medieval Italy, dealing with inquisition, superstition and ancestral warfare.

- *The Last Man* (1826)
  An apocalyptic tale in which protagonist Lionel Verney is followed through a distant future world which has been depopulated by a plague.

- *The Fortunes of Perkin Warbeck* (1830)
  A historical romance set in the 15th century, dealing with the rise and fall of Perkin Warbeck, the alleged Duke of York, son of Edward IV.

- *Lodore* (1835)
  This novel deals with two young lovers who are forced to keep their relationship a secret while continually fleeing their creditors.

  It can be said to be autobiographical, as the relationship between Ethel Lodore and Edward Villiers strongly resembles the initial stages of Mary and Percy Shelley's relationship.

- *Falkner* (1837)
  A novel focussing on the relationship between a young orphan and her protector.

- *Mathilda* (1959)
  The novel deals with a father's passionate (incestuous) love for his daughter. This novel represents Mary's emotional state at the time: she had lost three children and the relationship with her father and her husband were strained. The novel is a melodramatic representation of this period of her life.

Although this short novel was written in the summer of 1819, it was not published until 1959, over a hundred years after Mary's death. It was Mary's wish not to publish the novel, as she probably realized that it was too personal to be published.

■ *Collected Tales and Stories* (1976)

Mary wrote short stories throughout her life but they were only collected and published in 1976.

Non-Fiction[1]

■ *History of a Six Weeks' Tour* (1817)
This was co-written by her husband Percy Bysshe Shelley.

■ *Lives of the Most Eminent Literary and Scientific Men of Italy, Spain, and Portugal* (1835–37)
First published in the Cabinet Cyclopædia. *Lives of the Most Eminent Literary and Scientific Men of France* First published in the Cabinet Cyclopædia.

■ Preface and Notes to *The Poetical Works of Percy Bysshe Shelley* (from 1839 onwards)

■ *The Letters of Mary Wollstonecraft Shelley* ed. Betty T. Bennett. (3 volumes, 1980, 1983, 1988)

■ *The Journals of Mary Shelley* ed. Paula R. Feldman and Diana Scott-Kilvert. (2 volumes, 1987)

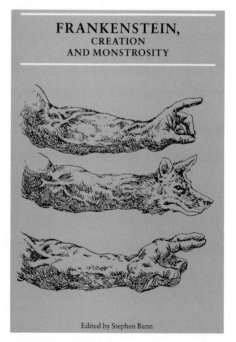

Works of Reference

■ Bann, Stephen, ed. *Frankenstein, Creation and Monstrosity*. London: Reaktion Books, 1994.

■ Botting, Fred. *Making Monstrous: Frankenstein, Criticism, Theory*. Manchester: Manchester University Press, 1991.

■ Kilgour. *The Rise of the Gothic Novel*. London: Routledge, 1995.

■ Spark, Muriel. *Mary Shelley*. New York: Meridian, 1988.

---

[1]Muriel Spark, *Mary Shelley* (New York: Meridian, 1988) 237.

SOURCE:

■ Spark, Muriel. *Mary Shelley*. New York: Meridian, 1988.

Frankenstein, or The Modern Prometheus

30 On this page, you can find information about Shelley's famous novel *Frankenstein, or The Modern Prometheus*.

31 At this point, the following information is available:

■ a very short and a more detailed summary of the novel

■ a description of the novel's main characters

■ the full text of *Frankenstein* in an annotated HTML format

■ an explanation of the novel's subtitle *The Modern Prometheus*

■ a not yet completed list of literary works to which the text of *Frankenstein* refers

■ an equally uncompleted list of film as well as theatrical adaptations of *Frankenstein*

Summary

A really short synopsis of *Frankenstein, or The Modern Prometheus* would be:

32 A young Swiss student discovers the secret of animating lifeless matter and, by assembling body parts, creates a monster who vows revenge on his creator after being rejected from society.

A more detailed summary would go like this:

33 An English explorer, Robert Walton, is on an expedition to the North Pole. In letters to his sister Margaret Saville, he keeps his family informed of his situation and tells about the difficult conditions on the ship. One day when the ship is completely surrounded by ice, a man in bad condition is taken aboard: Victor Frankenstein. As soon as his health allows it, he tells Walton the story of his life.

34 He grew up in Geneva, Switzerland as the eldest son of a higher class family. He was brought up with an orphan, Elizabeth and also had two younger brothers. He did not have many friends, Henry Clerval being the only exception. At the age of nineteen, Frankenstein became interested in natural philosophy, electricity, chemistry and mathematics. After the death of his mother, who succumbed to scarlet fever, Frankenstein left for Ingolstadt, Germany, to attend university. There, his interest in natural philosophy quickly became an obsession. He was particularly fascinated with the human frame and the principle of life. After four years of fanatic studying, not keeping in contact with his family, he was able to "bestow animation upon lifeless matter" and created a monster of gigantic proportion from assembled body parts taken from graveyards, slaughterhouses and dissecting rooms. As soon as the creature opened his eyes, however, the beauty of Frankenstein's

dream vanished: it became a horrible creature. He realized he made a mistake in creating this monster and fled from his laboratory. On his return the next day, the monster had disappeared. Victor was consequently bedridden with a nervous fever for the next months, being nursed back to health by his friend Clerval. On the eve of the return to his parental home, he received a letter that his youngest brother had been found murdered. On his way home, Frankenstein saw the daemon he has created and immediately realized that it is he who is responsible for his brother's death. Frankenstein decided not to tell his family about the daemon because they would simply dismiss it as insane. As he arrived home, he was informed that the murderer of his brother had been found. The accused was Justine, a good friend of the family. When Justine has been found guilty and has been hanged, Frankenstein's heart was tortured. He could not stay in the house and started wandering in the Alpine valleys. There, Frankenstein was confronted with his creation who tells him his life story.

After leaving Frankenstein's laboratory, he went to the village where he was insulted and attacked by the frightened villagers. He eventually went to the country and found refuge in a hovel next to a small house inhabited by a old, blind man and his two children. By observing the family and by reading their books, the monster learnt how to speak and read. He felt compassion for the family who have to struggle to get by, and anonymously did chores for them. Longing for some kindness and protection, he decided to meet his hosts. He got into a pleasant conversation with the blind man but his children return unexpectedly. Horrified by his appearance, they beat him and he fled the house. Completely disillusioned, the monster was filled with rage and decided to find his creator. By chance he met Frankenstein's younger brother in the forest. As soon as he discovered that the boy "belongs to the enemy" he choked him. He also placed a portrait in the lap of a sleeping young girl, Justine, thereby incriminating her with his crime.

The daemon's only request from Frankenstein was that he should create another being: a female to accompany him. If Frankenstein complies, he and his bride will stay away from other people and keep to themselves in the wild. Frankenstein saw some justice in the monster's arguments and also felt that he has a duty towards his fellow-man, so he agreed to the daemon's request. Victor left for England to finish his work accompanied by his friend Clerval, promising to marry Elizabeth on his return. When the work on his second creation was advanced, he started to question his promise. He was afraid that they might hate each other, or that they might produce a whole race of these creatures. When the monster visits to check on the progress, Frankenstein destroyed his work. The monster swore revenge and promised to be with him on his wedding night. The following day a body was found and Frankenstein was accused of murder. He was taken to the body which he identified as Henry Clerval. He was eventually cleared of all charges and returned to Geneva in a very bad condition. Frankenstein married Elizabeth after promising her to tell her his horrifying secret the following day. Remembering the monster's threat, Frankenstein was convinced that he would be killed that night. The monster, however, kills Elizabeth instead. Frankenstein lost another family member as his father died after hearing the news about Elizabeth's death. Frankenstein had now lost every sensation except for revenge. He followed the monster everywhere which eventually led him to the Arctic region, where he was taken aboard Walton's ship.

35   After telling Walton his story, Victor asks him to kill the monster if he dies before he can do it himself. The ship has in the meantime been freed from the ice and pressured by his crew, Walton has decided to abandon his trip and return home. Victor's health eventually deteriorates and he dies. Just after his death, Walton finds the monster hanging over Victor's body. The daemon speaks of his sufferings. Because of all the murders he has committed, he now hates himself. Since his creator is dead, he decides it is time that he too will rest in death. After stating that he will build a funeral pile for himself, he leaves the ship and disappears on his ice-raft in the darkness.

Gothic Literature

36   On this page, you can find information about:

■ the genre of literature which best describes *Frankenstein*

■ important gothic novelists other than Mary Shelley

Genre

37   Frankenstein. or The Modern Prometheus contains elements of two major genres of literature: the gothic and science fiction.

38   Gothicism is part of the Romantic Movement that started in the late eighteenth century and lasted to roughly three decades into the nineteenth century. The Romantic Movement is characterized by innovation (instead of traditionalism), spontaneity (according to Wordsworth good poetry is a "spontaneous overflow of powerful feelings,"[1]) freedom of thought and expression (especially the thoughts and feelings of the poet himself), an idealization of nature (Romantic poets were also referred to as "nature poets") and the belief of living in an age of "new beginnings and high possibilities."[2]

39   The first novel that was later identified as Gothic was Horace Walpole's *Castle of Otranto: A Gothic Story* in 1764. The *Castle of Otranto*, like many other Gothic novels, is set in a medieval society, has a lot of mysterious disappearances as well as other supernatural occurrences. The main protagonist is usually a solitary character who has an egocentrical nature. Even though the genre is a phase in the Romantic movement, it is regarded as the forerunner of the modern mystery or science fiction novel.

40   Many of the above mentioned elements appear in Frankenstein. For example, nature is used frequently to create atmosphere. The bleak, glacial fields of the Alps and the mists of the Arctic serve to indicate the isolation of the two protagonists.

[1]"Neoclassic and Romantic", *A Glossary of Literary Terms*, ed. M.H. Abrams, 5th ed., (United States of America: Holt, Rinehart and Winston, 1988) 113–117.
[2]"Neoclassic and Romantic", *A Glossary of Literary Terms*. ed. M.H. Abrams, 5th ed. (United States of America: Holt, Rinehart and Winston, 1988) 113–117.

The solitary character in Frankenstein can apply to both Victor as his creation as they both live their lives in social isolation.

41   Although Gothic novels were written mainly to evoke terror in their readers, they also served to show the dark side of human nature. They describe the "nightmarish terrors that lie beneath the controlled and ordered surface of the conscious mind."[1] Surprisingly, there were a vast number of female Gothic authors. It is not unlikely that this kind of fiction provided a release for the "submerged desires of that...disadvantaged class."[2]

42   The Gothic genre also extends to poetry. Poems by Coleridge and Keats ("Christabel" and "Eve of St. Agnes" respectively) deal with "the fantastic and the exploration of the unconscious mind."[3]

43   Science fiction explores "the marvels of discovery and achievement that may result from future developments in science and technology."[4] Mary Shelley used some of the most recent technological findings of her time to create Frankenstein. She has replaced the heavenly fire of the Prometheus myth with the spark of newly discovered electricity. The concepts of electricity and warmth led to the discovery of the galvanization process, which was said to be the key to the animation of life. Indeed, it is this process which animates Frankenstein's monster.

SOURCES:

- Abrams, M.H., ed. *A Glossary of Literary Terms*. 5th ed. United States of America: Holt, Rinehart and Winston, 1988.

- Abrams, M.H., ed. *The Norton Anthology of English Literature*. 6th ed. Vol. 2. New York: Norton, 1993.

- *Encarta '95*. CD-ROM. United States of America: Microsoft Corporation, 1994.

- *Encarta '99 Encyclopedie Winkler Prins Editie*. CD-ROM. United States of America: Microsoft Corporation/Elsevier, 1993–1998.

Links

44   On this page, you can find links to Web sites dealing with:

- Mary Shelley and/or her novel Frankenstein
- Romantic or Gothic literature in general

[1]"The Romantic Period," *The Norton Anthology of English Literature*, ed. M.H. Abrams, 6th ed., vol. 2 (New York: Norton, 1993) 1–17.
[2]"The Romantic Period," *The Norton Anthology of English Literature*, ed. M.H. Abrams, 6th ed., vol. 2 (New York: Norton, 1993) 1–17.
[3]"The Romantic Period," *The Norton Anthology of English Literature*, ed. M.H. Abrams, 6th ed., vol. 2 (New York: Norton, 1993) 1–17.
[4]"Utopias and Dystopias," *A Glossary of Literary Terms*, ed. M.H. Abrams, 5th ed. (United States of America: Holt, Rinehart and Winston, 1988) 195–196.

■ Mary Shelley's relatives

■ the (authors of) literary works that are referred to in *Frankenstein*

All these links will open a new window in your browser.

Mary Shelley and/or her novel *Frankenstein*

■ Mary Shelley and *Frankenstein*
A very extensive and informative site about Mary Shelley.

Romantic or Gothic Literature

■ The Gothic: Materials for Study
A very informative Web site with articles about the Gothic style of writing, such as the intriguing "The Female Gothic."

■ The Gothic Literature Page: The English Gothic Novel from 1764 to 1820
A Web site which provides you with the basic characteristics about Gothicism as well as a lot of links to other sites dealing with the Gothic.

■ A Celebration of Women Writers
This site is not about Romantic authors specifically, but is completely devoted to women writers of all genres and countries.

■ Voice of the Shuttle: English Literature: Romantics
There is not one definitive site on Romanticism, so instead this Voice of the Shuttle page provides enough links for you to find what you are looking for.

■ The Readers Vine: A Booklovers' Paradise

A very extensive and informative Web site for all booklovers with information about authors, books and genres. Users can discuss the various aspects of literature on bulletin boards; links to other literary sites are also provided.

Mary Shelley's Relatives

■ Mary Wollstonecraft
One of the few sites completely dedicated to Mary Shelley's mother: Mary Wollstonecraft. It provides a biography, a bibliography with electronic texts as well as several reviews.

■ Godwin Archive
A small Web site with Godwin's biography, bibliography, commentary and even some graphics.

■ The Poetry Archives: Percy Bysshe Shelley
A Web site with electronic versions of nineteen of his poems.

Literary Works in *Frankenstein*

- The Poetry Archives: George Gordon, Lord Byron
  A selection of his poetry can be found on this Web site.

- Homer's Iliad and Odyssey
  This excellent page provides ample information about these two famous classical works, including electronic texts.

- The Internet Classics Archive: The Iliad by Homer
  The complete Iliad in electronic form, divided in its twenty-four books.

- Albertus Magnus - Doctor Universalis
  A newly created Web site completely devoted to Albertus Magnus

- The Milton-L Home Page
  Self-described, this Web site is devoted to "the life, literature and times of John Milton." It is actually the home of a John Milton discussion group. It provides archives of the group, as well as electronic texts, images and audio excerpts.

- The Complete Works of William Shakespeare
  The Web's first edition of the Complete Works of William Shakespeare. Besides offering the electronic texts for all of Shakespeare's plays and some of his poetry, this site also has a discussion area.

- The Ever Reader: The Online Magazine of the Shakespeare Oxford Society
  For a more scientific approach, this site by this Shakespeare Society is ideal. It provides articles, analyses and interviews with Shakespeare scholars.

- TCG's Wordsworth Page
  A page with information about the life and works of William Wordsworth.

- The Complete Poetical Works of William Wordsworth
  The definitive page if you are looking for electronic versions of Wordsworth's poems.

Feedback

46   I really enjoy feedback from the visitors of my Web site! About what you like or don't like, but especially about what things you miss on this Web site.

47   Personally, I'm thinking of adding a section dealing with films based on *Frankenstein*. But for that I need your contributions! So if you'd like to write a (short) essay on a *Frankenstein* film that you saw (i.e. did it do justice to the novel, why (not)? etc. etc.) let me know through e-mail!

48   Contributions on any other topic (relating to Mary Shelley or *Frankenstein*) are always welcome too!

49   You can leave a message in my guestbook (clicking on this link will open a new window in your browser).

50   It is also possible to view the guestbook (this link will also open a new browser window).

51 For questions and discussions you can use the My Hideous Progeny WWW Board (again, this link will open a new window).

52 Of course, there is also the possibility to e-mail me personally.

53 I also own a mailing list which you are most welcome to join called "Mind The Gap." The list is especially for Anglophiles (like me) who want to discuss all things British: from tea to scones, from music to television, from film to literature (Mary Shelley for example!).

54 If you'd like to join, just enter your e-mail address in the box below and click the join button.

About This Site

55 This Web site was created as part of my MA thesis on the functionality of literary Web sites (opens a new window). In my essay, I discussed the importance and relevance of Web sites dealing with authors, literary works and genres. To gain some insight into the already existing literary Web sites, I compared two Web sites on the basis of criteria dealing with browser compatibility, navigation and content. The outcome was that the average literary Web site leaves a lot to be desired.

56 In order to explain what to me would be an ideal Web site, I have determined some key elements that literary Web sites must have. To make it more practical, I created this Mary Shelley Web site. Due to time restrictions, however, I was unable to realize the entire Web site. For the time being, this site will consist of several pages that can be seen as representative of the entire Web site. I will continue to update this Web site; I am striving to 'complete' (if such a thing is indeed possible) it eventually.

57 Of course, I would be very interested in your opinion of this Web site, so please feel free to e-mail me with questions, comments or constructive criticism.

Analysis: Web Site Design

The two Web sites are typical in many respects of how this genre organizes information—in bite-sized, or you might say "screen-sized," chunks. The Web is a great source of information, but nothing looks quite so intimidating on a small-screen monitor as a Web page that contains a long text (which is why people print such pages and read them from hard copy). For this reason, Web site designers think in terms of breaking information into chunks that fit on a single screen or require minimal scrolling down.

As you can see from visiting the two Web sites, the information in both examples is designed for the screen. The text at each site generally appears in short and to-the-point clusters, so visitors aren't being asked to read too much at once. For example, "Evolution of Daytime TV Talk" divides each of its six segments into two pages and uses graphics to break up the stretches of text. The Mary Shelley Web site, similarly, uses relatively short paragraphs, graphics, and lots of white space to enhance readability. (On the other hand, notice how the ads, links, and activities surrounding "Evolution of Daytime TV Talk" create a busy and distracting look—a design problem with many commercial sites.)

Finally, notice that each of the Web sites makes its organizational scheme immediately apparent to visitors, with clear cues on the home page about where we can find which items of information. These principles of organization do differ. "Evolution of Daytime TV Talk" uses a chronological approach, with each of the six segments devoted to a decade, while the Mary Shelley Web sites use topical organization. In both cases, however, the organization seems logical and intuitive because the sites use familiar principles.

FOR CRITICAL INQUIRY

1. What does the purpose of "Evolution of Daytime TV Talk" seem to be? Who do you imagine the intended audience to be? The series, as you have seen, is located at the Web site. What clues to answer the two questions can you find by examining the rest of the Web site?

2. Describe the writer's tone of voice in "Evolution of Daytime TV Talk." What kind of relationship does she seem to want to establish with her readers? What kinds of things does she invite her readers to do?

3. What do you see as the purpose of "My Hideous Progeny: Mary Shelley's Frankenstein"? Consider the relationship between this purpose and the design of the Web site. Do they match well?

4. Go online and browse the Mary Shelley Web site in any order you see fit. Follow whatever links interest you. Notice as you browse how your choices participate in your experience of the Web site. Compare the path you took to those of your classmates. Did they differ? If so, how? If not, why? What inferences can you draw from these differences and similarities about how people use Web sites?

5. Read "Feedback" and "About This Site." How would you respond to Cynthia Hamberg? What suggestions would you make about updates, additional information, new topics?

Visual Design: "A Jazzography: From Storyville to Lincoln Center."

A *chronology* is another kind of fact sheet writers use to select and display information. Instead of questions and answers, chronologies use key dates over a span of time as the principle of organization. "A Jazzography: From Storyville to Lincoln Center" appeared in a special section of the *New York Times Magazine* devoted to the resurgence of interest in jazz.

Analysis: The Story in the Chronology

Chronologies such as "A Jazzography" are not simply lists of dates and explanations of what happened. They provide the highlights and thereby tell a particular story of what happened that depends on the chronicler's selection of events and judgment about what's most significant. Notice how this chronology

A JAZZOGRAPHY
FROM STORYVILLE TO LINCOLN CENTER . . .

The singer as jazz soloist: Billie Holiday in 1948.

c. 1840 Adolphe Sax, a Belgian, invents the saxophone.

1902 The 12-year-old Jelly Roll Morton "invents" jazz, or so he later claims. A habitué of Storyville, the red-light district of New Orleans, Morton combines ragtime, French quadrilles, and the hot blues played by Buddy Bolden, the notoriously hard-living cornetist.

1917 The Dixieland Jazz Band, a white group, makes the first jazz recording, "Livery Stable Blues." It sells a million copies, launching jazz as popular music. Freddie Keppard, a black band leader, had rejected the chance to make the first jazz record — he was afraid other musicians would copy his style.

1925–1928 Take it away, Satchmo: With his Hot Fives and Hot Sevens recordings, Louis Armstrong revolutionizes the jazz form, encouraging solo improvisation over ensemble playing.

1929–1945 The swing era rises and falls. Duke Ellington, Jimmie Lunceford and Count Basie lead influential groups. Most of the big hits, though, are recorded by white band leaders like Glenn Miller, Benny Goodman and Tommy Dorsey.

c. 1935–1955 The jam session as art form: West 52nd Street in Manhattan, packed with clubs, becomes the playground for Charlie Parker, Dizzy Gillespie, Miles Davis, Thelonious Monk and all their friends.

1936 Well before the rest of the country, jazz becomes integrated. At the Congress Hotel in Chicago, Lionel Hampton and Teddy Wilson sit in with Benny Goodman's ensemble. Two years later, Billie Holiday joins Artie Shaw's big band.

1939 While playing "Cherokee" during a Harlem jam session, Charlie Parker happens upon a harmonic discovery that leads to be-bop, a far more intricate style of jazz, both harmonically and rhythmically.

1943 Jazz ascends to the concert hall: The first of Duke Ellington's annual Carnegie Hall programs and the premier of "Black, Brown and Beige," his influential long-form work about the history of American blacks.

1951 On the heels of Miles Davis's "Birth of the Cool," musicians like Chet Baker and Gerry Mulligan form the so-called cool school, turning down the volume and intensity. It happens, of course, in California.

1951 Sidney Bechet relocates to Paris, the first of many American jazz expatriates including Kenny Clarke, Arthur Taylor and Bud Powell. Racial tension was less pronounced, and European audiences were more appreciative.

A jazz progenitor: Buddy Bolden. c. 1900

(continued)

(continued)

1954 Jazz goes outdoors: George Wein, a pianist and singer, rewrites his jazz résumé by inviting musicians to Newport, R.I., for the first of many Jazz Festivals.

1956 A crossover dream: Ella Fitzgerald makes the first of several "Songbook" recordings for Verve, the impresario Norman Granz's new label. The Songbooks make Fitzgerald an international star.

1959 A pivotal year, with several records that expand the very possibilities of improvisation: Miles Davis's "Kind of Blue," John Coltrane's "Giant Steps," Ornette Coleman's "Shape of Jazz to Come."

1964 The avant-garde gains mainstream recognition as Thelonious Monk makes the cover of *Time* magazine, which christens him the high priest of be-bop.

1969 Miles Davis's "Bitches Brew," a primordial jazz-rock fusion record, sells 500,000 copies, turning many rock fans on to jazz but leaving some hard-core Miles followers groaning.

1972–1977 New York's "loft jazz" scene blooms, with experimental, post-bop players performing in lofts like Ali's Alley. Among the players on the scene are Joe Lovano and David Murray.

1979 On Jan. 5, the famously cosmic Charles Mingus dies in Cuernavaca, Mexico, at the age of 56. That same day, 56 whales beach themselves on the Mexican coast.

1984 The new generation gets a leader who looks backward: Wynton Marsalis, at 22, wins a Grammy for his "neo-bop" record "Think of One." The same night, he takes a classical grammy for his recording of trumpet concertos.

1989–1991 Frontmen and backlash: Trying to duplicate Marsalis's commercial success, record labels snap up straight-

Miles Davis, keeper of the cool, at the Columbia Records studio in 1955.

ahead players like Roy Hargrove, Antonio Hart and Christopher Hollyday. Much grumbling ensues from those who consider these so-called Young Lions too imitative or too green.

1991 Jazz as institution: Marsalis is appointed artistic director of the new Jazz at Lincoln Center program. Big audiences but big detractors, too, who claim that Marsalis is anti-modernist and anti-white.

1992 A new fusion trip: The British "acid jazz" group Us3, which blends hip-hop and electronic samples of jazz cuts, gets permission to raid the Blue Note archives. Meanwhile, in Brooklyn, the hip-hop group Digable Planets records "Rebirth of Slick (Cool like Dat)," using the horn lines of James Williams's "Stretchin'." Suddenly, a new degree of jazz cool.

1993 Jazzmen can be pop stars, too: Joshua Redman, the Harvard summa cum laude saxophonist, chooses jazz over Yale Law and releases two records within a year. Critics love the records and fans love Redman; in concert, young women shriek and young men pump their fists in the air.

June 1995 The Impulse record label, one of the most important in jazz history, is revived after a 21-year dormancy. It is the seventh major jazz label to be launched or relaunched in the past 10 years.

Duke Ellington at the Paramount Theatre, 1947.

creates emphasis in the stream of jazz history: In 1902 Jelly Roll Morton "invents" (or claims to invent) jazz; in 1925–1928, Louis Armstrong "revolutionizes the jazz form"; 1959 was a "pivotal year." In this sense, chronologies are both "factual," recounting actual events, and "interpretive," providing readers with a way of seeing what matters most (at least according to the chronicler's account).

FOR CRITICAL INQUIRY

1. There are twenty-four entries in this chronology, starting in c. 1840 with the invention of the saxophone and ending in June 1995 with the revival of the Impulse record label. How does the chronicler get from the first entry to the last? What story is he telling? Is there a plot to it? How would you describe the plot? How does the plot guide the chronicler's selection of events to include?

2. Why do you think the chronicler included the detail in the entry for 1979 that on the day Charles Mingus died at the age of 56, fifty-six whales beached themselves in Mexico? What does this detail contribute to the chronology?

3. Consider the relationship of the photos to the text. What do they add?

4. Under the entry "1951," the chronicler writes that the cool jazz of Gerry Mulligan and Chet Baker "happens, of course, in California." Why "of course"? What assumptions does the chronicler make here about his readers?

FOR DISCUSSION AND ANALYTICAL WRITING

RHETORICAL ANALYSIS

Pick one (or more) of the examples of informative writing in this chapter. Write a rhetorical analysis that explains what called the writers and designers to produce it. Take into account how the example defines its readers' need to know and what it wants them to do. How would you describe the relationship the informative writing seeks to establish with its readers?

GENRE CHOICES

Pick a reading in one of the other chapters on a topic you find particularly interesting. Consider how you could present the information in that reading in the form of a fact sheet or brochure. What would your purposes be for doing so? Who would your intended readers be? What would you imagine them doing with the information? When would it make sense to choose a genre of informative writing, as presented in this chapter, and a genre in another chapter?

GOING ONLINE

The Triangle Shirtwaist Factory Fire

The Triangle Shirtwaist Factory Fire occurred on March 25, 1911, killing 147 factory workers. This tragedy led to heightened union organizing activities by the International Ladies Garment Workers Union (now UNITE) and the establishment of the Factory Investigation Commission by the state of New York, which prompted important sweatshop reforms. What follows is a brief report on the fire, taken from the *Dictionary of American History.* Read this short account. Then visit the Web site <ilr.cornell.edu/trianglefire/> designed by the Kheel Center for Labor-Management Documentation and Archives at Cornell University. Compare how the dictionary entry and the Web site present information about the fire. What do you see as the main differences? In what circumstances would the information in the dictionary entry be sufficient for your purposes? When would you want the more extended treatment in the Web site?

The Web site is divided into essays, images, audio, and archival material with accompanying links. In what order did you follow the links? Compare the way you navigated the Web site to the way other students in your class navigated it. How does taking different paths through the Web site (and on to related Web sites) affect your experience as a reader?

"Triangle Fire," Alvin F. Harlow

The Triangle Shirtwaist Company, occupying the three top floors of a ten-story loft building in New York City, suffered a disastrous fire on Mar. 25, 1911, in which an estimated 147 lives, mostly women and girls working there, were lost. More than fifty persons jumped from the windows to the street; the others were burned or trampled to death. The cause of the fire was unknown; perhaps a lighted cigarette or match was dropped into flammable waste. It was found that little provision had been made for fighting fire; that there was only one narrow fire escape; that some of the doors through which the women might have fled were habitually kept locked; and that stairway entrances were cluttered with boxes and rubbish. The elevator men did their best, but could not work rapidly enough. The proprietors of the business were indicted and tried, but acquitted. Public opinion had been aroused, however, and the disaster led to sweeping reforms in building and factory laws, especially as to precautions against fire.

WORKING TOGETHER

Constructing a Chronology

Use the "Jazzography" as a model to construct your own chronology of a subject that interests you: the history of photography, psychology, television situation comedies, the American automobile industry, the films of Woody Allen, major league football, social welfare policy, relations between the U.S. government and American Indian tribes, twentieth-century women painters, or molecular biology. Anything that has been around and developing for fifty years or more will work for this assignment. Assume that you are preparing the chronology for general readers who will be interested in your topic but who are not specialists.

Work together in groups of three or four. Decide on a topic you are all interested in researching. Make sure there is enough information available on the topic. Decide on a division of labor so that each group member will be responsible for a particular period or aspect in the history of the topic. When you are researching, watch for key moments, whether or not they fit into the part you are responsible for.

Once you have completed the research, construct a tentative chronology with fifteen or twenty dated entries on highlights or trends. It may be helpful to involve a peer reader at this point to give you feedback on what is clear in the chronology and what needs more explanation. Make revisions based on this input and, depending on your teacher's directions, design graphics to accompany the text.

WRITING ASSIGNMENT

For this assignment, choose one of the genres in this chapter to present information on a subject that interests you and that you think your intended readers have a need to know about. Your work here will involve determining the purpose of your informative writing and deciding what information is relevant to your readers. Here are some preliminary ideas about how to approach this assignment.

1. Design a fact sheet or FAQs. Fact sheets and FAQs are particularly suitable if you want to introduce readers to a subject or issue they may not know much about. You could, for example, design a fact sheet or FAQs on a current issue to give readers a quick understanding of what is at stake concerning, say, the use of medical marijuana, U.S. military support of the Colombian government, gay and lesbian civil unions, or mad cow disease. Or you could use the genre to publicize a particular campus, community, political, or cultural organization you belong to—to explain, as Habitat for Humanity does, what the organization's goals and activities are and how people can become involved. Fact sheets can be organized in a chronological or topical arrangement. FAQs, on the other hand, always use questions and answers.

2. Design a brochure. Brochures give you a different kind of space to work with than fact sheets and FAQs do. Like fact sheets and FAQs, they are certainly suitable for introducing readers to a subject, and you might want to design a brochure that uses the panels to present clusters of

information about, say, the dangers of lead paint in older houses, how you can detect it, what you should do about it, and how you can get more information. Because brochures enable you to integrate text and graphics, they are a good choice for illustrating how things work, how to do something, or where things are located. You could, for example, explain what to do if someone falls through the ice on a local pond or how to recognize and treat sunstroke. Or you could use maps to design a walking tour or point out special attractions on campus or in a neighborhood, section of the city, museum, or park.

3. Design a Web site. Web sites enable you to do the same things fact sheets and FAQs and brochures do in terms of organizing information into easily managed and readable clusters. One of the main differences, of course, is how visitors navigate Web sites and how designers link pages inside a site and provide links to external Web sites. Because of the web's multimedia capacities, Web sites also give you a broad range of design options—not only text and graphics but also animation, live action, and sound.

Invention

One of the first things you need to do is identify situations that call for the kind of informative writing featured in this chapter. Consider your hobbies, community groups, campus interests, social organizations, and family activities. Make a list of subjects and activities that interest you. Think about information people could use and issues that involve you and others.

ETHICS OF WRITING

RESPONSIBLE INFORMATION

Because informative genres respond to people's need to know, it is crucial that writers select and emphasize the most reliable information available. As just mentioned, this means that writers need to evaluate carefully their sources of information. But it also means that they must avoid sensationalism in their presentation of information. Writers may be tempted to use sensational details for dramatic effect to make their fact sheet or brochure stand out. Take, for example, a pamphlet on eating disorders. In the section on what causes eating disorders, a pull-quote jumps off the page, exclaiming that "a growing body of evidence suggests a link between sexual abuse and eating disorders." The text of the pamphlet, however, explains that "data are mixed" and that "a trauma is not necessary to trigger an eating disorder." Nonetheless, the impression readers will get from the page is that there is a connection. The problem is not only that the claim rests on sketchy evidence. The link to sexual abuse also stigmatizes eating disorders and may discourage people from acknowledging their condition and seeking help.

Subjects and Activities	Needed Information	Issues
Bicycling	Good bike rides	When is the city going to develop more bike paths?
Resident assistants	—	Should RAs be required to turn in students for drinking?
Volunteering literacy center	How to teach adults	—
International students	Available services	—

As you can see, the chart helps visualize needed information and issues. If you are a weekend bicyclist, for example, you could design a brochure of easy, moderate, and difficult bike rides. On the other hand, you might find the situation calls on you to write a fact sheet that explains the current status of public bike paths in your city or town and how and why they should be extended. Or you might develop a Web site on the debate about requiring RAs to report underage students for drinking, a brochure on how to teach adults to read and write, or a fact sheet on services available to international students.

Clarifying Your Purpose and Your Readers' Need to Know

Once you have some tentative ideas about information people could use and issues facing you and others, you can begin to ask what gives these topics an urgency or importance that would make them worth writing about. You need to consider why readers need or want information about the subject and how this information will help them learn or do something new, important, or otherwise worthwhile. At the same time, you need to ask what is at stake for you as a writer and a person in informing your readers—to make sure your purposes match what your readers need.

EXERCISE

Pick one (or more) of the subjects of interest on your chart. Then write on each subject for five minutes or so:

1. What interests you about this subject? Why is it important to you?

2. Who are your intended readers? Why do they need information about your subject? What are they likely to know already about it? What information do you think they need? What should they be able to do with this information?

3. Read over what you have just written. What do you now see as the purpose of informing your readers about the subject? Do you want to help them understand something, show them how to do something, persuade them about an issue, identify something of interest, or do you have some other purpose? Assess whether this purpose is consistent with what you see as your readers' need to know. What genre appears most suitable? Why?

Researching Your Subject

Once you have determined your purpose and what your readers need to know, the next step is to assess your current state of knowledge—to determine whether the information you already have available is adequate to your purposes or whether you need to do more research.

EXERCISE

1. Write a list of questions that cover what you think your readers need to know. Here, for example, is a list concerning the status of public bike paths that you can use as a model:

   a. What is the current status of the bike path system?

   b. What actions or land acquisitions are pending?

   c. How do such acquisitions generally take place?

   d. What local action is needed to support additional acquisitions?

   e. How have other communities responded?

   f. What has been done in this community in the past?

   g. What are the greatest obstacles to getting more land for this project?

2. Use your list of questions to quickly survey the information you have. Can you answer the questions with the information at hand? Is your information up-to-date, reliable, and authoritative? Is it relevant to your readers' needs? If you need more information, where can you get it?

3. Take into account the information you have at hand, the information you need to get, and the amount of time you have to complete this assignment. Will you be able to find what you need in the time available? If not, consider whether the scope of your project is too broad. How can you set priorities based on your sense of purpose and of what your readers need to know?

Planning

Planning fact sheets and FAQs, brochures, and Web sites involves designing information so that readers can see at first glance what your purpose is and how the information is organized. Unlike genres such as memoirs or commentary, where readers discover the writer's purpose in a continuous flow of words and paragraphs, informative genres typically divide information into parts and use headings and other visual design features to make the organization readily visible.

Here are some general guidelines for organizing informative writing:

1. Make sure the purpose of the information is immediately apparent.
2. Break the information into a series of parts (think here of bite-sized chunks).
3. Organize the information in a consistent and easily recognizable order, such as questions and answers, enumeration, chronology, and steps in a process.

Let's look now at the way each of the genres described in this chapter organizes information and what is involved in planning.

Fact Sheets and FAQs

Fact sheets often use a question-and-answer format, but they can also use a topical or chronological arrangement (as in the case of "A Jazzography"). If you decide to write a fact sheet, the organizational plan should follow from your purposes.

On the other hand, FAQs, by definition, consist of questions and answers. The way the questions and answers are presented, however, can vary, particularly in the case of online FAQs. In some instances, as is the case with the Living Wage Campaign's FAQs, questions and answers appear together as a dialogue or call and response. In other instances, however, as in the case of "Death Penalty Frequently Asked Questions," the questions appear on one page as links you click on to go to the answer on another page.

There are advantages and disadvantages to either type. When questions and answers are on one page, people are more likely to read through the entire sequence; the arrangement thereby enables you to lead your reader from point to point. And you can easily print hard copies as handouts if needed. On the other hand, if answers are separate pages, they can be much longer than a back-and-forth, question-and-answer format allows. Readers typically browse through the FAQs to find those that best correspond to their needs and interests—and then click on the links.

FAQs have become a common feature in online communication—at listservs, newsgroups, and chat rooms as well as at Web sites. (New visitors are smart to read any available FAQs before they join in the conversation; otherwise they risk getting flamed.) Sometimes, however, the FAQs just accumulate, as a running record of questions people send in. The list gets longer, and it becomes more difficult for readers to see a logical order or find the questions they are looking for. Online FAQs may well need reorganizing and pruning from time to time.

Death Penalty Frequently Asked Questions

- WHICH STATES retain the death penalty?
- How many EXECUTIONS have there been in the US since 1976?
- WHICH COUNTRIES retain or have abolished the death penalty?
- Have any states with the DP imposed a MORATORIUM?
- What states have LIFE WITHOUT PAROLE?
- Which countries RETAIN the Death Penalty?
- How can I WRITE to a PENPAL on Death Row?"

- Are people ever WRONGFULLY CONVICTED or EXECUTED?
  - In Illinois, 13 as of January, 2000
  - Innocence and the Death Penalty (DPIC)
  - A partial list of Wrongful Executions (M. Radelet)

- WHO was executed in...?
  - WHO was executed in 2000?
  - WHO was executed in 1999?
  - WHO was executed in 1998?
  - WHO was executed in 1997?
  - WHO was executed in 1996?

- WHAT METHODS do states use to execut
  - A list of State's Execution

- LETHAL INJECTION
  - What drugs are used in a l
  - Is LETHAL INJECTION Pa

- Does RACE matter in determining who is
  - Yes. Race & DP Studies fro

- WHO were the VICTIMS of Executed Inn

- WHO WAS THE FIRST - LAST....?
  - Who was the FIRST WOM
  - Who was the FIRST PRE-
  - When was the last executi

- JUVENILES and the Death Penalty
  - Are Juveniles Executed?

- Are there any general statistics on the DI

- What makes a crime CAPITAL ELIGIBLE

- Are People Ever Wrongfully Convicted or
  - Examples of Wrongful Cor
  - Wrongful Convictions in I

- Is it cheaper to execute somebody than k
  - Some figures
  - Is the Death Penalty Chea

- Does the Death Penalty Deter?
  - DPIC & Deterrence
  - Mike Radelet's paper on D

- Should even BRUTAL KILLERS BE SPAR

- Are some names more likely to be "execu

- WOMEN AND CAPITAL PUNISHMENT
  - Where can I find info abou
  - How many WOMEN are o
  - Women on Death Row Sp

- Can "mentally retarded" offenders be exe

Executions in the US since 1976

Date: Fri, 3 Mar 2000 01:23:38 – 0600
From: Rick Halperin
Reply-To: deathpenalty@lists.washlaw.edu
Subject: EXECUTION STATS BY YR. & STATE

Execution Statistics Summary —
State and Year (as of 3/3/00)

State		
Texas	209	
Virginia	75	
Florida	46	
Missouri	41	
Louisiana	25	
South Carolina		24
Georgia	23	
Oklahoma	22	
Alabama	21	
Arkansas	21	
Arizona	20	
North Carolina		15
Illinois	12	
Delaware	10	
Nevada	8	
California	7	
Indiana	7	
Utah	6	
Mississippi		4
Maryland	3	
Nebraska	3	
Pennsylvania		3
Washington		3
Kentucky	2	
Montana	2	
Oregon	2	
Colorado	1	
Idaho	1	
Ohio	1	
Wyoming	1	

Total executions since 1976 618
Executions by Year

Year	#	Year	#
1976	0	1988	11
1977	1	1989	16
1978	0	1990	23
1979	2	1991	14
1980	0	1992	31
1981	1	1993	38
1982	2	1994	31
1983	5	1995	56
1984	21	1996	45
1985	18	1997	74
1986	18	1998	68
1987	25	1999	98

EXERCISE

1. List as many questions and answers as you can without worrying at first about their order or even if they are repetitive.

2. Read what you have written. Combine questions and answers that are repetitive or closely related.

3. Decide on a tentative order in which to present them. Early questions typically offer definitions and statements of purpose, giving readers enough background to understand the questions and answers that follow.

4. Evaluate and, if necessary, revise the order. Is needed information missing? Is some information irrelevant or repetitive?

Brochures

Planning brochures requires visualizing how readers will encounter the panels as they unfold. Notice, for example, in the Alzheimer's Association brochure "You Can Make a Difference," how information appears:

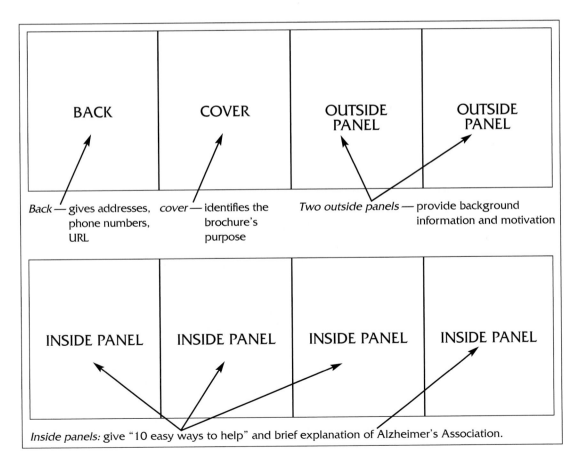

BACK   COVER   OUTSIDE PANEL   OUTSIDE PANEL

Back — gives addresses, phone numbers, URL

cover — identifies the brochure's purpose

Two outside panels — provide background information and motivation

INSIDE PANEL   INSIDE PANEL   INSIDE PANEL   INSIDE PANEL

Inside panels: give "10 easy ways to help" and brief explanation of Alzheimer's Association.

EXERCISE

Use the sketch of "You Can Make a Difference" to visualize the panels of your brochure.

1. List as many separate items of information as you can. Use this list to select information, according to what your readers need to know. Tentatively decide what information will go on each panel or combination of panels.

2. On a sheet of paper, sketch the outside panels on one side and the inside panels on the other.

3. Fold the sheet. Test your design by evaluating how the information appears as you unfold it.

Web Sites

Designing a Web site involves a number of considerations—how the information is organized, how much information appears on each page, how visitors will navigate the site.

Notice how the two Web sites "Evolution of Daytime TV Talk" and "My Hideous Progeny: Mary Shelley's Frankenstein" answer these questions by charting the organization of information and the links for visitors to move from page to page.

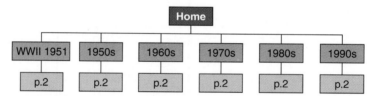

Organization of "Evolution of Daytime TV Talk"

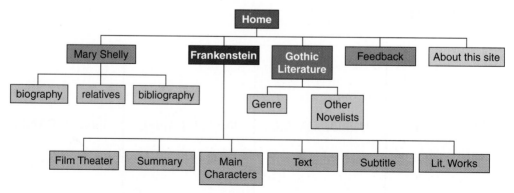

Organization of "My Hideous Progeny: Mary Shelley's *Frankenstein*"

As you can see, "Evolution of Daytime TV Talk" has a relatively simple structure. From the homepage, you can choose one of six parts, where you will find two pages. There are many links to external sites on each page but the six parts are not fully linked. You can go, for example, from Part 1 to Part 2 but not to the other parts.

The structure of the Mary Shelley Web site is more varied and linked. Three of the pages on the homepage menu—Mary Shelley, Frankenstein, and Gothic Literature—offer further choices (and in some cases provide internal links so that you can go, say, from the Frankenstein summary to links on the main characters). The other three pages—Links, Feedback, and About This Site—don't lead to other pages but do provide external links.

EXERCISE

Use the sketches of the two Web sites' designs to make a preliminary sketch of your Web site.

1. List as many topics as you can, taking into account what you have determined visitors want or need to know.

2. Select the topics you want to include, and write each topic on a separate note card. Each note card will represent a Web site page. Make sure to designate one note card as the homepage.

3. Decide what visitors need to know when they visit the homepage. The title, menu, and any introductory text should make the site's purposes clear and enable visitors to see how to navigate the site.

4. Now organize the note cards to try out designs for your Web site. Put the homepage at the top, as the entry point. Experiment with various arrangements of your information, imagining how visitors might move from page to page.

Drafting

Writing headings is a good way to break the information you're presenting into manageable chunks, whether you're drafting a fact sheet, FAQs, brochure, or Web site. Headings can help readers see the organization of the document and know where to find particular items of information.

Setting up headings amounts to devising a logical and consistent system. They should be brief and informative. Avoid witty or clever headings. They do not always convey information clearly to readers. Be consistent, and use parallel phrases as much as possible.

The most common styles of headings are questions, *-ing* phrases, noun phrases, and imperative sentences.

Questions

Questions, of course, provide the organizing structure of FAQs and many fact sheets. They elicit reader interest and involvement as well as mark the content of sections. Take for example the following headings from a brochure on sexually transmitted diseases (STDs):

What Is an STD?

How Are STDs Transmitted?

Can STDs Be Treated?

How Can You Prevent Contracting STDs?

-ing Phrases

Because phrases that begin with -ing verb forms imply action, they are a good choice for writing that explains how to do something or that concentrates on solving problems. Here is an example from a Web site on global warming.

Defining Global Warming

Understanding the Causes

Calculating the Effects

Designing a Response

Planning for the Future

Noun Phrases

Noun phrases can be quite useful in documents that cover a variety of topics. Here are the section headings that might appear on a fact sheet about a corporation's current productivity program:

Characteristics of the Corporation

Productivity Planning of the Corporation

Obstacles to Productivity Planning

A Plan for Future Productivity Growth

Imperative Sentences

Imperative sentences are best suited for giving advice or directions about how to do something. The headings from the inside of Alzheimer's Association's "You Can Make a Difference" use imperative sentences:

Keep in touch.

Do little things.

Give them a break.

Be specific when offering assistance.

Be alert.

Provide a change of scenery.

Learn to listen.

Care for the caregiver.

Remember all family members.

Get involved.

Peer Commentary

Exchange your working draft with a classmate and then answer these questions in writing:

1. Explain to the writer what you knew about the subject before you read the working draft, what you learned from reading it, and what (if anything) surprised you.

2. Explain to the writer whether you found the working draft easy to understand. Point to sections that are especially clear or interesting. Also point to any parts you found confusing.

3. What questions, if any, does the draft raise in your mind that you feel are not adequately answered? Are there points in the draft where you wanted more information from the writer? If so, explain.

4. Comment on the design. Is the purpose clear at the outset? Does the draft break the information into manageable chunks? Is the order of information easy to follow?

5. What suggestions do you have for revision?

Revising

Use the peer commentary to do a careful critical reading of your working draft.

1. Did your reader find the purpose to be clear?

2. Are the amount and type of information adequate? Is the information easy to understand?

3. Is it presented in the best possible order?

4. Does the design enable your reader to move easily from point to point?

Getting the Right Order

In many cases, revising the order of information can be the key to taking your draft to the next level. Thinking about the order you present information can help you see whether one item leads to the next, what you have left out, and what you can combine.

Here are the questions on a student's working draft of a fact sheet about the herpes simplex virus:

- Is there a cure for herpes?
- How contagious is the virus?
- Besides the unappealing sores, does the virus pose any other health risk?
- What can be done to prevent it?
- How does herpes really spread?
- What about the possibility of herpes being spread by a toilet seat?
- How often do the symptoms recur?
- How is herpes treated?
- What can I do to prevent herpes?

After getting a peer commentary, the student revised the order by combining information, adding further information, and developing a new set of questions:

- What is herpes?
- What are the symptoms?
- How does it spread?
- What are the health risks?
- How is herpes treated?
- How can I prevent herpes?

WRITER'S WORKSHOP

The brochure on eating disorders that appears here is a draft Kevin Candiloro did for a course on public health. Before you look at the draft, read Kevin's commentary on the feedback he wants from peer commentaries:

> This is a draft, so I think there are still changes I can make. In terms of the content, I'm not sure I've got the best order. Should I explain what eating disorders are before I explain why some people have them? I'm also not sure what should come first, talking about how to help someone with an eating disorder or helping yourself if you've got one. I don't have to keep the questions I'm using at this point, so if you have any suggestions about them, please tell me. It seems that I've got a lot of text. Can you suggest how to break it up into smaller parts? I don't like the bit of text on the back cover, above the section about where to find help, that continues from the inside. Do you have any ideas about how to fix this?

WORKSHOP QUESTIONS

1. How would you respond to Kevin's concerns about his draft? First, consider whether the purpose of the brochure comes across clearly. Were you able to see right away what reader needs the brochure was designed to meet?

2. Consider the order of questions. Is it the most effective? What changes, if any, would you suggest?

3. Is the information adequate, given Kevin's purposes? What, if anything, should be added or deleted?

4. Look at the design. Can you think of ways to break up the information into smaller chunks? Should Kevin use more headings? Imagine you are opening the brochure. You see the panel from the outside ("How can I help myself to combat my eating disorder?") next to the first panel from the inside ("Why do some people have eating disorders?" and "What is an eating disorder?"). Is this a problem? If you think so, what should Kevin do?

 **How** can I help myself to combat my eating disorder?

You have completed the first part already. Admitting that you need to change your lifestyle to adopt healthier habits is the first step toward change.

If you fast or go on highly restrictive diets one thing you can start with is to learn about proper nutrition and why it is necessary to eat right. It is possible to eat so that you remain at a healthy weight. Maintaining a healthy weight will result in higher energy and your body will be better able to maintain itself and fight illness. Learn what your ideal healthy weight is and how many calories you need to eat to maintain it. Make a meal and snack plan and try to keep with it even if you don't feel hungry or interested in eating.

Binging and dieting can be controlled by making an effort to reduce the amount of calories in your binges and increasing the amount of calories in your diets. It is also a good idea to learn about proper nutrition techniques and why they are important.

Overeating can be helped by taking a few steps to limit yourself. Do not shop when you are hungry and buy only what you need. You should learn how to eat nutritionally balanced meals at specific times of the day and stick to a regular eating schedule. Eat slowly and do not continue eating if you feel full.

No matter what type of eating disorder a person might have, one can always benefit from seeking support from a councilor, nutritionist or other people who have had similar problems with food. Sometimes a therapist can be helpful in helping people to face their illness. Changing habits is a very hard thing to do and it often takes time to be successful.

Poor eating habits make people sick and unhappy. Setting short term goals for oneself can help to show progress in controlling an eating disorder. Anyone should feel proud that they are able to accomplish such a difficult task and one should always remember that eating disorders are treatable.

Where to find help

Eating Disorder Referral and Information Center
2923 Sandy Pointe, Suite 6
Del Mar, CA 92014-2052
(858) 481-1515

National Association of Anorexia Nervosa and Associated Disorders (ANAD)
Box 7
Highland Park, IL 60035
(847) 831-3438

American Anorexia/ Bulimia Association, Inc. (AABA)
165 West 46th Street, Suite 1108
New York, NY 10036
(212) 575-6200

Overeaters Anonymous
World Service Office
P.O. Box 44020
Rio Rancho, NM 87174-4020
(505) 891-2664

Massachusetts Eating Disorders Association, Inc. (MEDA)
92 Pearl Street
Newton, MA 02158
(617) 558-1881

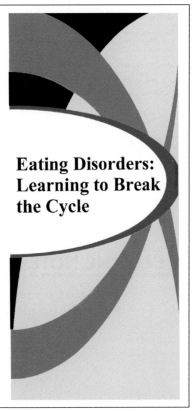

Eating Disorders: Learning to Break the Cycle

(continued)

(continued)

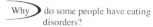 do some people have eating disorders?

Society and the media place an enormous importance upon being thin. Because of this many people seek to control their lives through their body. It is when food and eating begin to control a person's life that eating disorder sets in. Eating disorders imprison a person in beliefs that how they eat determines their worth as a person. Additionally many athletes who compete in weight emphasizing sports (wrestling, body building, etc.) can also develop eating disorders.

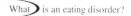 is an eating disorder?

The most common forms of eating disorders diagnosed in the United States are anorexia nervosa and bulimia nervosa. Many also consider compulsive overeating to be an eating disorder.

Anorexia is characterized by severe episodes of restrictive dieting or starvation. Anorexics are afraid to gain weight in any capacity and often drop to weights well below healthy tolerances. Symptoms caused by this severe type of weight loss include: pale or gray skin, cold hands and feet, fatigue, digestive problems, irregular sleeping patterns, amenorrhea in women (loss of menstrual periods), growth of fine body hair, unusual eating habits, dizziness, headaches, mood swings and depression. Symptoms of severe, long term anorexia might include susceptibility to infection, bone fractures, general chemical imbalances and atrophy of the heart muscles which can be life threatening.

Bulimia is defined by periods of rapid weight loss and gain. This is caused by the cycle of binging an purging in which the bulimic participates. Most often the shame of their condition forces bulimics to binge and purge in secret. Purging is done by forced vomiting, taking diuretic drugs or laxatives, fasting or over-exercising. Both phases of this illness take their toll on the body.

Throat and mouth wounds, tooth decay, bruising of the eyes and cheeks, digestive disorders, dehydration, muscle fatigue, ulcers and heart irregularities are all symptoms of bulimia.

Compulsive overeating leads to being overweight and eventually leads to obesity. The health problems associated with being overweight have been studied intently in the recent past. The fear of these health issues even motivates some anorexics and bulimics to their illnesses. Symptoms that result from compulsive overeating include: joint pain, fatigue, high blood pressure, and in later stages: osteoarthritis, heart disease and gall bladder disease.

 is at risk?

People who become trapped in the cycle of an eating disorder usually show similar external signs. Often, people with eating disorders become anxious at meals, are obsessed with their body image or repeatedly count their daily calorie intake. In many cases a person with one of these illnesses will show remorse for eating a meal in the form of self-degrading or self-punishing statements. They often complain of "feeling fat" even when they are thin or even unhealthily so. They judge themselves and their character by the food that they eat and keep to themselves when acting upon their disorder.

Most diagnosed cases of anorexia and bulimia occur in adolescent girls. The ages of 14 and 18 are the peaks for the occurrence of these illnesses. When young girls are struggling to become young women the pressures of society are often too much to handle and a person will lapse into eating disorder as a way to try to gain control over their life. Unfortunately, this is a mistake that often leads to years of illness.

 can I help someone who may have an eating disorder?

The most important thing to remember if you suspect that your friend or a family member may have an eating disorder is that the person is likely to be very protective of their illness and may not immediately acknowledge its existence at all. You should try to learn about eating disorders for yourself so that you can get a better sense of the problem and how it affects people.

Be persistent, but not overbearing. Try to bring up the topic by stating that you are worried about how their behavior is impacting your relationship. Do not bring up any concerns about their weight or appearance. If the person is not receptive, tell them you will talk about it again later.

If your friend or family member becomes angry or upset when you try to talk to them about their problem, do not force the issue. Do not try to take the roll of a counselor or eating monitor. You cannot help anyone before they have admitted to having a problem.

You may often be rejected by the person that you are trying to help. This is common. Do not take the rejection personally. People with eating disorders often have trouble admitting that they have a problem controlling themselves, since a sense of control is what drives their illness.

REFLECTING ON YOUR WRITING

Think about how you wrote and revised the informative writing you did as this chapter's work. What did you discover along the way about informative writing that you didn't know before?

A CLOSING NOTE

Once you have revised and redesigned your work, consider how it could be distributed to people who need or could use the information.

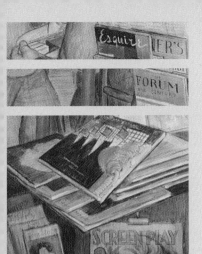

CHAPTER NINE

Commentary: Identifying Patterns of Meaning

THINKING ABOUT THE GENRE

Commentary is a genre of writing that uses analysis and interpretation to find patterns of meaning in events, trends, and ideas. The purpose of commentary is not simply to report on things but to give readers a way to make sense of them.

This purpose should be clear if you think about the commentaries you've heard on radio and television and read in newspapers and magazines. For example, when television news commentators such as Sam Donaldson or Cokie Roberts present their nightly remarks, you don't see news footage on the television screen—just the commentator speaking directly to you. Thus, the focus has shifted away from the news itself to the commentator's analysis and interpretation of the news. Even without this visual cue, people generally don't mistake radio commentary by, say, Rush Limbaugh or Andrei Codrescu for news reports or the commentaries of newspaper columnists such as Mollie Ivens or George Will.

Whether commentaries are on TV or radio or in print, we expect them to give us something to react to, to think about, and to use to make sense of contemporary experience. We have this expectation because of the feature that most clearly distinguishes the commentary from news reports and articles: Commentary doesn't use the objective tone and neutral stance of reporting but instead is written from a particular perspective. Commentary takes a position and presents an interpretation that the writer hopes readers will find convincing.

The call to write commentary grows in part out of people's desire to have satisfying accounts of their experience, to identify patterns of meaning that make the world cohere for them in their daily pursuits. Commentary offers explanations of events in the news that can help readers, viewers, and listeners organize their worlds and imagine the future.

In contemporary society, in which new ideas emerge and trends and events occur at a dizzying pace, commentators perform several crucial functions. For one thing, they perform a *labeling* function, identifying current trends and giving readers labels for these trends (for example, "Generation X," "downsizing and corporate restructuring," "the information age," "the New World Order"). For another, by seeking to find patterns of meaning in events, trends, and ideas, commentators call on readers to think about the causes and consequences of what is happening in the world today (for example, "NAFTA has led to the loss of jobs," "The drop in reading scores results from the neglect of phonics instruction"). Finally, in the process of explaining, commentators often apportion praise and blame and take a moral stance on events—whether of solidarity, indignant reaction, or ironic distance (for example, "Vermont has taken the right stand by approving civil unions for gay couples," "Allen Iverson should grow up and stop pretending to be a gangsta rapper," or "It's amusing to watch the baby boomers of the psychedelic sixties tell their children not to use drugs").

Because of the functions they perform, commentators help shape our sense of issues and the differences that divide people. For example, students, trade unionists, human rights activists, and environmentalists have recently staged demonstrations, protests, and campaigns against what they see as the negative effects of globalization, focusing in particular on the World Trade Organization, the International Monetary Fund, and sweatshop working conditions. Some commentators have identified themselves with the protestors' views, arguing that "free trade" is largely a strategy to open new markets to American corporations and that the results have been the loss of jobs at home and labor, human rights, and environmental abuses abroad. Other commentators offer an alternative view. They argue that globalization has been instrumental in the "new prosperity" in the United States and that "free trade," for whatever its short-term difficulties may be, represents the best means to modernize Third World countries. Thus, while both sets of commentators agree that globalization and free trade are undeniable economic trends, they differ dramatically in their evaluations and the positions they take. In writing their respective commentaries, they all want to make readers see the merits of their perspectives. For commentary seeks not only to disclose patterns of meaning but also to persuade and shape public opinion.

These functions largely determine the relationship between the writers of commentaries and their readers (or listeners). In analyzing and interpreting events and trends, commentators approach readers as cothinkers, asking readers to look at the world from their perspective, whether readers ultimately agree with them or not. One of the pleasures (and aggravations) of reading commentary is to follow the commentator's line of reasoning—to see how his or her mind works to make sense of the world. For this reason, commentators tend to acquire regular readers who become familiar with the writer's views and look forward to reading what he or she will say about new issues.

Commentary is by no means limited to print and broadcast journalism, even though those may be the most familiar forms. It is also an important genre in academic and professional writing, where books and articles seek to provide persuasive explanations of issues in a particular field—whether it is the meaning of Hamlet's melancholia, the causes of slavery in the New World, the nature of human-computer interactions, the role of trade in Paleolithic economies, or the results of new AIDS therapies. In academic commentaries, the issues are often more technical and specialized than the issues commentators treat in the popular media. But in many respects, it is the same desire to go beyond the given facts—to find patterns of meaning, identify underlying causes, explain consequences—that drives academic inquiry.

Whatever the context may be, the call to write commentary grows in part out of this desire to analyze and explain what happens around us—to have satisfying accounts of our experience and to find patterns of meaning that can make the world cohere. In conversation, we routinely offer commentary on events, trends, and other people. We want to get a handle on the local scene at work, in school, in our neighborhood, and so we talk about what is going on, analyzing the motives for actions and the reasons for events. A good deal of everyday talk in fact serves as a kind of social analysis that shapes how we negotiate our relationships with others.

EXPLORING YOUR EXPERIENCE

Think of a place where you routinely talk with others. It could be your workplace, the family dinner table, your dormitory, or any place you hang out. What topics come up in conversations—events, trends, ideas, people? What makes these topics of interest to the people involved? Characterize the kinds of comments people make. What role does such talk play in the particular setting? Use your findings to see if you can form any tentative generalizations about how people use conversation to find patterns of meaning and manage their lives.

READINGS

Eric Liu, "Remember When Public Spaces Didn't Carry Brand Names?"

Eric Liu is a regular commentator on MSNBC. A second-generation Chinese-American, Liu has written a memoir, *The Accidental Asian: Notes on a Native Speaker* (1998) that raises questions about assimilation, ethnicity, and race. His commentary on "branding" appeared in *USA Today*.

Remember When Public Spaces Didn't Carry Brand Names?
ERIC LIU

---

1   In a few weeks, when the world champion New York Yankees open their home season, will they take the field at Trump Stadium? Time Warner Park? Maybe AT&T Arena?

2   Chances are the park will still be called Yankee Stadium. But it won't be that way for long. Quietly, and with strikingly little protest, the Yankees have

announced that they are planning to sell the "naming rights" to their Bronx homestead. By the time the 2000 season arrives, some lucky corporation may well have bought the sign outside the House that Ruth Built. And frankly, that turns my stomach.

3   It's not just that Yankee Stadium is a national treasure. It's not just that allowing the highest bidder to rename this 76-year-old icon feels like an insult—to New Yorkers, to tradition and to the memory of Yankees past, such as Joe DiMaggio. It's also that what is about to happen to Yankee Stadium is part of a deeper, accelerating trend in our society, the relentless branding of public spaces.

4   The sports world gives us piles of examples. San Francisco's fabled Candlestick Park is now 3Com Park. The selling of bowl names has reached sublimely ridiculous levels. (Remember the Poulan/Weed Eater Independence Bowl?) And the trend is hardly confined to sports. Branding—the conspicuous marking of places and things with corporate names and logos—is now everywhere in the civic square.

5   Consider the public schools, some of which are flooded with advertising for merchandise and fast food. Districts around the country are raising money by making exclusive deals with Pepsi or Coke or with credit card companies or banks. In one Texas district, Dr. Pepper recently paid $3.45 million in part to plaster its logo on a high school roof to attract the attention of passengers flying in and out of Dallas.

6   Other efforts to turn public spaces into commercial vessels are no less corrosive. Rollerblade now hawks its wares in Central Park under the banner "The Official Skate of New York City Parks." Buses in Boston and other cities don't just carry ad placards anymore; some of them have been turned into rolling billboards.

7   How far can this go? Over in England, the legendary white cliffs of Dover now serve as the backdrop for a laser-projected Adidas ad. Here in America, we haven't draped Mount Rushmore with a Nike "swoosh." But things are heading in that general direction.

8   You might say at this point, "What's the big deal? America is commercialized—get over it!" And I admit my views may sound a bit old-fashioned. But this isn't a matter of priggishness or personal nostalgia.

9   Public spaces matter. They matter because they are emblems, the physical embodiments, of a community's spirit and soul. A public space belongs to all who share in the life of a community. And it belongs to them in common, regardless of their differences in social station or political clout. Indeed, its very purpose is to preserve a realm where a person's worth or dignity doesn't depend on market valuations.

10   So when a shared public space, such as a park or a schoolhouse, becomes just another marketing opportunity for just another sponsor, something precious is undermined: the idea that we are equal as citizens even though we may be unequal as consumers.

11   What the commercialization of public spaces also does, gradually and subtly, is convert all forms of identity into brand identity.

12   We come to believe that without our brands, or without the right brands, we are literally and figuratively no-names. We question whether we belong in public, whether we are truly members.

13   We forget that there are other means, besides badges of corporate affiliation, to communicate with one another.

14   It could, of course, be said, with a place like Times Square in mind, that brands, logos, and slogans are now our most widely understood public language. It could be said that in this age of cultural fragmentation, the closest thing we have in common is commerce.

15   But is this the best vision of American life we can muster?

16   In the military, they worry about "mission creep." In civilian life, the problem is "market creep." And the question now is how to stem this creeping sickness. We know that there is some limit to what people will accept: A 1996 April Fools announcement that the Liberty Bell had been purchased and rechristened the "Taco Liberty Bell" provoked a storm of angry calls. Drawing the line there, though, isn't protecting an awful lot.

17   Maybe the renaming of Yankee Stadium will shame some legislators or zoning czars into action. Maybe the "corporatization" of our classrooms will spark some popular protest. Maybe the licensing away of Central Park will awaken us to the disappearance of public space—and to the erosion of the public idea.

18   Then again, maybe not. In which case, we'd better keep a close eye on Mount Rushmore.

Analysis: Conversing with Readers

Eric Liu's commentary is typical in many respects of the kind of commentary you'll find in newspapers and on television. The tone is informal and the paragraphs are short; though the topic is serious, Liu treats it with a good deal of humor. As readers, we feel Liu is a person of goodwill who wants to engage us in a conversation about something he's noticed lately (not unlike the way we talk about things with friends).

Liu's breezy presentation, however, does not just make his commentary inviting to readers and easy to read. Notice at two key points how he incorporates what readers might be thinking. In the eighth paragraph, after he has substantiated the reality of the "branding" by giving a series of examples, Liu addresses readers directly and says, "You might say at this point, 'What's the big deal?'" Next, after acknowledging that he "may sound old-fashioned," Liu pinpoints the main issue of his commentary, namely that public spaces belong to everyone and that branding threatens to "convert all forms of identity into brand identity." Then, in the fourteenth paragraph, Liu anticipates his readers again, this time by imagining that people might say that brands "are now our most widely understood public language" and the "closest thing we have in common in commerce." By conversing with his readers at two pivotal points in his commentary, Liu establishes the groundwork for readers to join him in asking the question, "Is this the best vision of American life we can muster?"

FOR CRITICAL INQUIRY

1. Almost half the commentary—the first seven paragraphs—is devoted to establishing the reality of the branding phenomenon. As you read, when did you become aware of Liu's perspective on this trend? What cued you to Liu's point of view?

2. What exactly is Liu's argument against branding? Is there a sentence or sentences anywhere that express his main claim? What evidence does Liu offer to support his claim? What enabling assumptions connect the evidence to the claim? Are these assumptions stated explicitly or implied?

3. As noted, Liu anticipates what readers might be thinking at two key points in the commentary—at the beginnings of paragraphs 8 and 14. How does Liu handle these possible differing views? How successful do you think he is in countering or negotiating such differences?

4. Branding may be spreading faster than even Liu imagined at the time he published this commentary in 1999. Here is an agreement between the city of Halfway, Oregon (population of 345), and Halfway.com, Inc., an Internet company based in Conshohocken, Pennsylvania, to rename the town Half.com, Oregon. Read the agreement. Take into account this small and poor town's efforts to raise money and promote development. It should be obvious what Liu would say. What is your evaluation of the agreement?

1   From an agreement reached in January between Halfway, Oregon, a city of 345, and Half.com, Inc., an Internet company based in Conshohocken, Pennsylvania.

2   WHEREAS, the Company Half.com markets and promotes its innovative person-to-person electronic commerce site on the World Wide Web; and

3   WHEREAS, the City desires to promote its quality of life and economic stability, and is willing to do so by renaming the City to incorporate the Company's name;

4   NOW, THEREFORE, the City and Company agree as follows: the City will change its name to "Half.com, Oregon" and make reasonable efforts to change the names of any City-owned buildings, place Company marks on uniforms of City employees, and place signs at the entrance of the City and elsewhere throughout the City.

5   The Company will donate twenty-two computers to the City, contribute $5,000 to the Pine Valley Fair Association, and commit $75,000 to carry out the intent and purpose of the Agreement.

6   Each sign created or modified, whether it is placed on a road near the City or used in advertising, will include no less than the following language: "Welcome to the First dot Com City in America, Half.com, Oregon (a.k.a. Halfway, Oregon)."

7   The font size of "Half.com, Oregon" on any sign or in any advertisement shall be twice the size of "Halfway, Oregon." The Company will have final approval on each sign and advertisement, including the font, size, and style.

8   The Company will make reasonable attempts to promote the City using the Company's site and take measures to ensure that the City is portrayed in a respectable light.

Commentary on Shannon Faulkner's Resignation from The Citadel: "Sadness and Shame at the Citadel"; Susan Faludi, "Shannon Faulkner's Strength in Numbers"; Captain Erin Dowd, "Ex-Cadet's Actions Didn't Match Her Words"

After having fought for more than two years to be admitted to The Citadel, a military academy which then had a males-only policy, Shannon Faulkner resigned on August 18, 1995, at the end of her first week. As shown by the dates above, commentary on her resignation appeared on the heels of the event. This is typical of commentary that is focused on events: Writers move swiftly to have their say while the news is still current. They can assume familiarity with the event and show readers a particular way of making sense of it—of its meaning, its causes, and its larger implications. While the three pieces here represent somewhat different forms—an editorial, an op-ed piece, and a letter to the editor—all clearly belong to the genre of commentary. In reading the pieces, notice how each looks at the event from a different perspective—that is, finds a different way of making sense of it.

Sadness and Shame at The Citadel

1   When Shannon Faulkner took on the task of becoming the first female student at The Citadel, South Carolina's all-male military college, she also took on a broader responsibility. Like it or not, she was acting not only for herself but for all other Americans who believe that a school financed by taxpayers' money has no right to discriminate on the basis of gender.

2   When Ms. Faulkner, emotionally exhausted and physically depleted, dropped the banner she herself had raised, many of those rooting for her were doubtless disappointed. But she is right to hope that "next year a whole group of women will be going in" and will succeed where she failed. There are already many American women serving in the United States armed forces and performing with distinction in its service academies. West Point's top graduate this year, in fact, was Second Lieut. Rebecca E. Marier.

3   As many of these women warriors will attest, Shannon Faulkner waged a more lonely battle than they did. Her "enemy," apart from tradition and sexism, was an unremittingly hostile corps of cadets whose maturity was evidenced in their behavior the day she quit. They ripped off their shirts and chanted "C-I-T-A-D-E-L," banged pipes on windowsills and shouted their joy at the school's remaining a male preserve. Whether it will stay that way is a question the Supreme Court has been asked to decide.

4   Ms. Faulkner surely feels sad about leaving The Citadel, but she has no reason to feel shame. More than 30 male cadets dropped out as well. In fighting as hard and long as she did, she may have opened the door for other women. It is

those yahoos, those future first citizens of South Carolina and its neighbors, who shook their fists and yelled their catcalls who should feel shame. So should their commanding officers who did little to dilute their pleasure in driving a lone intruder from their turf.

Shannon Faulkner's Strength in Numbers
SUSAN FALUDI

1   Out of all the nearly 2,000 cadets who enrolled in an all-male military academy called The Citadel this year, the only one whose name we know was the one the school didn't want: Shannon Faulkner.

2   This distinction seems, on its face, too obvious to mention. Of course she's famous—that she was admitted to the academy at all was a cause célèbre. But the distinction is important, because it goes to the heart of the issue. One reason the other Citadel cadets loathed Shannon Faulkner (aside from her sex) was her individuality, which affronted The Citadel's ethic. The academy purports to educate young men by making them conform. Conformity is enforced through anonymity. From the day the cadets arrive, when they are issued identical uniforms and haircuts, they become so homogeneous that, as an upperclassman explained to me, "mothers can't even tell their sons apart."

3   Through communal living and endless drills and rigid codes of conduct, the cadet's individuality is subordinated to the identity of the group, his strength founded in numbers and teamwork, in esprit de corps and long tradition. Going it alone, as a maverick, isn't done. "Individuals do not make it here," the commandant of cadets warned this year's freshmen on their first day. "If you want to stay an individual, every day will be a tough day."

4   This is what is called a military education, and it was exactly what Shannon Faulkner wanted and could not find elsewhere in her home state of South Carolina. From the start her quest seemed hopeless: by seeking military anonymity in an all-male corps, she had to stand out. But her downfall was hastened by forces beyond The Citadel.

5   The largest obstacle she faced was the popular illusion that history is driven not by the actions and changing beliefs of large numbers of ordinary people, but by a few heroic giants who materialize out of nowhere to transform the landscape.

6   The media inflate this fairy tale by anointing a hero in every story and letting the surrounding political issues slide off their camera lenses. Paula Coughlin wasn't the only woman who said she was assaulted at Tailhook, just as Shannon Faulkner wasn't the only woman who was denied admission to The Citadel. But they were the first to raise their voices and so they were the ones the press put in the spotlight, all too often failing to illuminate the problem: male behavior that created the problem in the first place.

7   For the heroine of the moment, caught in the temporary spotlight of celebrity culture, it can be terribly flattering to be elevated above the masses by the mass media. But it's also dangerous to be isolated and stranded, with so far to fall in public. Especially since, according to common consent, the entire women's movement must fall along with her.

8   This is the paradox that Shannon Faulkner was trying, in her way, to counter: women are only allowed the solidarity and esprit de corps of the women's movement when they are defeated. A constant refrain of Ms. Faulkner's opponents—and those of Ms. Coughlin—was that she was a stalking horse for feminism. Each of these women was accused of being a pawn of some grand and malevolent conspiracy. They weren't. They fought alone. But let them fall or prove to be only human, and the women's movement must take the hit. In an inverse of The Citadel ethic, women are condemned to fight alone and condemned to fall communally.

9   Solidarity is fostered in men—whole state-supported academies teach it to them—but it is suspect in women. Lately, that message has been reinforced by so-called feminist pundits, from Camille Paglia to Christina Hoff Sommers, who tell women over and over: "You can do it on your own. You don't need any help from the organized women's movement."

10   But once Shannon the individual stumbled, her humiliation instantly became all women's. It was a reversal Shannon Faulkner seemed achingly aware of. Standing beside her father in a pelting rain, she said in a shaky voice, "It's hard for me to leave, because...I don't know what's going to happen with the case." A USA Today headline put the last nail in the coffin: "Even Some Feminists Fear She Hurt Cause."

11   Shannon Faulkner had sensed the dangers of this early on. Any journalist who followed her around—or tried to—in the last two and a half years can tell you she was not a willing heroine. With an agility and savvy remarkable in anyone, much less someone barely out of high school, she kept reporters at arm's length and thwarted their efforts to plunder her personality, to forage through her private life for tidbits they could use to ornament their creation: Shannon Faulkner the media star.

12   But at the same time, she accepted the bargain: she agreed to fight alone. She was not a feminist, she said. She was "an individualist." And when a Federal judge finally ordered The Citadel to admit her to its corps of cadets, she told The New York Times that she didn't consider the ruling a victory "just for women"—only a confirmation of her belief that if you want something, you have to "go for it." She avoided the feminist label for all the usual reasons, living in the Deep South being only the most obvious. And she got lots of press points for playing the role of the lone and apolitical female ranger, with no need for a meddlesome women's movement.

13   But as Shannon Faulkner stood before the press last week, she shared with us her feminist epiphany, one that generally doesn't dawn on most women until much later in life: making a lone woman a star is not the same as advancing women's equality. In fact, it's counterproductive. She said, "I really hope that next year a whole group of women will be going in, because maybe it would have been different if there had been other women with me."

14   As I heard that remark, it occurred to me that she had received a Citadel education after all. She had grasped the only aspect of the Citadel teachings that really matters: there is strength in numbers; solidarity counts.

15   It's a lesson that gleeful pundits, disappointed feminists and conservative detractors of Shannon Faulkner can learn as well. "It would have been different if there had been other women with me." That's not an excuse. That's a valedictory.

Ex-Cadet's Actions Didn't Match Her Words

To the Editor:

1   I am writing in response to Shannon Faulkner's failed attempt to join the cadet ranks at The Citadel (front page, Aug. 19). I applaud her effort in gaining recognition from the women's equality movement. Ms. Faulkner's drive and persistence in challenging the outdated "men only" policy at a public, federally funded institution are respectable.

2   I am concerned, however, that her half-hearted attempt will perpetuate the perception that women cannot achieve or exceed military standards. I am also concerned that The Citadel will be perceived as different from other academies and too difficult for the average woman.

3   I am a United States Army officer, and I am greatly disappointed by Ms. Faulkner's lack of preparation for the challenges of a military career. Her actions did not match her verbal public stand, so strong and unyielding.

4   Ms. Faulkner is visibly unfit and apparently mentally uncommitted. She does not walk her talk.

5   Women can and do succeed in the military and at military institutions. The success at West Point of First Lieut. Kristen Baker and Second Lieut. Rebecca Marier are prime examples.

6   I have successfully worked side by side with men while carrying a load equal to more than half my body weight. I experienced combat from the front lines in Iraq and have endured the hardships common to other military veterans. I enjoy a network of female friends who jump out of planes, rappel from helicopters and meet social and physical military demands daily.

7   The military is designed to stress an individual both physically and mentally. It is not a game. Like many other professions, the military sets goals and standards for its officer candidates in preparation for potential experiences. Success in the military is achieved very easily: one must possess basic perseverance.

8   Respect is not a prerequisite; it is earned by living up to individual statements and meeting organizational standards.

9   Ms. Faulkner's failure is a lesson for those who attempt to achieve equality without preparing to meet the standards. Women's liberation is a necessary and productive movement. We can be physically, mentally and technically prepared to meet professional demands.

10   It is unfortunate that Ms. Faulkner's young shoulders bear the controversial weight of one failed attempt for women's liberation and equality. It is more unfortunate that she so quickly deprived herself of achieving a goal that could have strengthened her self-confidence and physical stamina. May women continue to challenge the admission policies at The Citadel and display the stamina and commitment to endure more than one hot day of work.

(Capt.) Erin Dowd
Nashville, Aug. 20, 1995

Analysis: Interpreting an Event from Different Perspectives

The three readings are typical in many respects of commentaries that interpret current events. Notice, for one thing, that none of the three writers spends much time describing the event. Instead, they use phrases, like "Shannon Faulkner's failed attempt" in the first line of Dowd's letter, that assume that the event is common knowledge. The writers are able to dispense with background explanation and move quickly to presenting their main points.

Although the commentaries respond to the same event, each offers a different interpretation of Faulkner's resignation from The Citadel. Taken together, they present an interesting case study of how different writers construct the call to write in different ways. In fact, the three commentaries seem to agree fully on only one point: Each comes out against The Citadel's males-only admission policy. Aside from that point of agreement, they seem to have quite different interests in the event.

These different interests in what is at stake in the Faulkner resignation can be explained in part by the writers' backgrounds. The *New York Times,* as a national "establishment" newspaper, seeks in its editorials to speak on behalf of the general public interest. Susan Faludi, a feminist and author of *Backlash: The Undeclared War Against American Women,* is most interested in what the implications are for the woman's movement, while Captain Erin Dowd, herself an officer in the U.S. Army, seems most concerned with how the Faulkner resignation will affect other women's situations in the military.

FOR CRITICAL INQUIRY

1. What does each commentator see as the cause(s) of Shannon Faulkner's resignation from The Citadel?

2. What does each commentator see as the main lesson to be learned?

3. In one or two sentences, state what you think is the main point of each commentary. Consider how the three commentaries differ in their interpretations. How might you account for these differences?

4. How do the three commentaries seek to shape public understanding of the event? What values or attitudes does each seek to tap? How does each commentary align itself with people, ideas, or movements? Who does each commentary distance itself from?

Michael Rock, "Since When Did *USA Today* Become the National Design Ideal?"

Michael Rock is both a graphic design professional and an academic. He is a partner in the Michael Rock/Susan Sellers firm in New York City and a member of the faculty at the Yale School of Art. He is also a contributing editor to *I.D.* magazine, one of the leading graphic design publications, where this commentary on the design of the national newspaper *USA Today* appeared in 1992.

Since When Did *USA Today* Become the National Design Ideal?
MICHAEL ROCK

1   In a recent *New York Times* Sunday magazine article on school textbooks, writer Robert Reinhold described California's new history series as "...filled with colorful charts, graphs, time lines, maps, photographs in a format suggestive of the newspaper *USA Today*." There it is again. Since when did *USA Today* become the national design ideal? Everywhere you look you find *USA Today* used as an analogy to describe a noteworthy design format. Making ideas "accessible" is the operative term for the information age. But too often information is drained of its significance in the name of accessibility.

2   Some things are designed for reading: scholarly journals, literary reviews, financial pages, and their ilk are fairly impenetrable to the casual page flipper. Other objects like *USA Today*, annual reports, fashion magazines, and so on are for looking. (Haven't you heard in the course of a design project someone say, only half in jest, "No one actually reads the copy, just make it look good.") Then there are the gray areas. These include newsmagazines and textbooks, which imply reading but are increasingly about looking. If you compare *Time* or *Newsweek* or a fifth grade schoolbook of twenty years ago to their present incarnations, the change is remarkable. The headlines are bigger, the captions are bigger, the photographs, charts, and call-outs are all bigger. Something had to go, someone must have decided, and what went was the text.

3   The trend in typography is clearly towards a destruction of narrative text, with images increasingly responsible for carrying the content. Running copy is being replaced with exaggerated hierarchies, charts, graphs, sidebars, bars, boxes, captions, and call-outs that reduce the "story" to a collection of visualized pseudo-facts. It is the design equivalent of the video sound-bite, with complex ideas boiled down (in the words of Nigel Holmes, *Time's* design direction) to "manageable chunks."

How to Compete Against TV

4   The resulting designs often have the look of information, but without real content. Beyond its stylistic implications, this new typographic sensibility represents a change in the consumer's relationship to information, the author's authority, and the significance of the form. There is a fragmentation of communication, with the model of contemporary typography no longer being the linear argument but the simultaneous slogan. For instance, a *Newsweek* story may now open with an image that takes up as much as ninety percent of the spread, with only a small introductory paragraph of text as accompaniment. We are rapidly approaching the critical point where the graphics overtake the meaning.

5   The rationale behind the accessibility movement is that information is easier to absorb in small pieces. Prodded along by marketing data, publishers and designers feel the need to compete with television and video for consumer attention. We have all heard that newspaper readership is down and that television has surpassed reading as the information source-of-choice for the majority of Americans. In response, publishers seem inclined to apply the TV info-tainment format to newspapers and magazines. The logic is something along the lines of "TV is fast, vapid, and unbelievably successful. Publications should employ the same techniques as TV."

6   This perhaps makes sense in mass market magazines like *Entertainment Weekly* or *Spy* or even in corporate annual reports, where the message is not necessarily crucial; those products are not intended to challenge your intellect. When the same stylistic formats are applied to newsmagazines, newspapers, and school books, the implication may be more troubling. The distinction between what is news, opinion, entertainment, and propaganda is blurry enough. The turn toward graphic oversimplification may make the boundaries even more obscure. U.S. Education Secretary T. H. Bell referred to this phenomenon as part of the "dumbing down" of American textbooks that removes all complex information in an attempt to capture the reader's attention. But if students are unable to read and to grasp complex subjects, is the problem in the book? Is simplifying the content to fit into "exciting" *USA Today* formats going to solve the problem?

Designing Fictional Facts

7   Publications made for looking rather than for reading can suggest entire themes with carefully composed photographs or coded design forms that avoid the kind of supporting evidence demanded in expository writing. (Consider the photograph from *People* of November 1991 showing Clarence and Virginia Thomas curled up on their couch reading the Bible. How can you respond to that image? How can you reason against it?) These formats emphasize the incredible power of the art-directed image, buttressed by the decontextualized quotation, the boldface caption, the "scientific" diagram, and the brightly colored map. Charts and diagrams are certainly useful for offering general, relational explications of an issue but they necessarily shave away the ambiguous, nuanced, or obscure aspects of any idea. The information has been preprocessed, prechewed; it can only lead to

one conclusion. And so the design of these pages controls the reading, siphoning off all complexity and presenting a slyly fictional "fact."

8   At the most fundamental level, the spread of the *USA Today* style represents a destruction of traditional narrative ideals. Narrative implies an author as well as a reader. The reader negotiates the process of the rational argument, checking any specific point against the entire premise. The credibility of the content is measured against the author's authority. The argument set forth is understood to be limited by the perspective inherently implied in the narrative voice. But images and charts seem to not imply an inherent point-of-view. They radiate a kind of false objectivity because the concept of the image-as-opinion is difficult for most people to grasp.

9   Cultural critics may see this shift toward the fragmented layout as an example of the continuing decline of textual authority, with the author's intention giving way to the reader's interpretation. They may praise this impulse. "Design becomes a provocation to the audience to construct meaning, consider new ideas, and reconsider preconceptions," says Cranbook's Katherine McCoy. The philosophy of deconstruction may indeed serve as a tool to describe the original move toward fragmentation. But when the concept becomes codified and adopted as mainstream style, when the devices of mass culture adopt "deconstructed" typographic mannerisms, you can be sure it is not done to put greater interpretive power into the hands of the audience.

10   Fighting to grab one second from the harried, over-informed consumer, the makers of the mass media have concluded that messages must be instantaneous, offering about the same content level as a fifteen-second television commercial. (As Nigel Holmes puts it, "... the dentist may well get through his first appointment sooner than you thought.") If a chart with a picture of Uncle Sam and a Russian bear on a seesaw balanced over an oil barrel can replace several paragraphs of text, all the better. No one has time to think about a rational argument; it takes too long, it's too boring. A sharp image and a few well chosen words can produce the same idea without the nuances but with a kind of prefabricated logic.

Low-Cal Reading

11   Setting aside the more sinister interpretations of this trend, one could argue that it actually relates to basic shifts in the way typography and design are produced. The Macintosh opened up to designers a vast array of new graphic possibilities, giving them access to what is the equivalent of sophisticated typesetting terminals. Intricate settings, overlapping or run-around type, complex charts and graphs that were once too costly and time consuming to design are now within the scope of even the smallest studio. Similarly, book and magazine publishers have greater digital composition possibilities and more four-color printing forms.

12   Or maybe the best explanation for the spread of *USA Today* look-alikes is that it is an inevitable extension of the LITE phenomenon. If beer or mayonnaise or individually wrapped slices of American cheese make you fat, then: a) stop eating and drinking so much; b) remanufacture the products with fewer calories. We are more comfortable with the idea of changing our products than with changing our habits.

Maybe publication design is under the same pressure. Maybe we want the "experience" of reading without all that heavy, annoying thinking. Maybe its LITE design; it tastes great and it's less filling.

Analysis: Explaining Causes and Effects

In "Remember When Public Spaces Didn't Carry Brand Names?" Eric Liu argues against the branding of public spaces, but he doesn't really explain why this trend came about in the first place. Justifiably, he assumes that readers will already know. Michael Rock's commentary is similar to Liu's in the way it raises questions about another current trend, in this case the subordination of text to images in the design of newspapers, magazines, and textbooks. The difference is that Rock is interested in the causes of the trend as well as in its effects.

Rock offers a series of reasons to explain why this trend has occurred. He notes how television (with its video sound bites), the "accessibility movement," pressures on the "harried, over-informed consumer," and new computer technologies have contributed to what he calls "graphic oversimplification." In the final reason he gives, Rock joins cause and effect together metaphorically as "an inevitable extension of the LITE phenomenon....it tastes great and it's less filling."

FOR CRITICAL INQUIRY

1. Michael Rock draws a key distinction between "reading" and "looking." What does he mean? How does he use this distinction throughout the commentary?

2. There is a clear sense that Rock feels something is lost in the new "design ideal." What is he defending? What does he think is at stake?

3. Evaluate Rock's position in this commentary. As a graphic designer, Rock is not opposed to visual information. The question is where he draws the line between useful images and pseudo-facts.

4. Bring a copy of *USA Today, Time,* or *Newsweek* to class. Analyze the presentation of visual information. To what extent does your analysis confirm Rock's perspective? What differences, if any, does it bring to light?

Lundy Braun, "How To Fight the New Epidemics."

Lundy Braun does research on cervical cancer and the history of disease. She also teaches pathology to medical students and courses on the biological and social origins of disease to undergraduates at Brown University. "How To Fight the New Epidemics" appeared in the *Providence Journal-Bulletin* on May 29, 1995. Braun wrote this commentary in response to public fascination with media accounts of "killer viruses" and other epidemic diseases. But, as you will see, the issues she addresses go far beyond the often sensationalistic media coverage of infectious diseases.

How to Fight the New Epidemics
LUNDY BRAUN

1   One of the hottest topics in the news these days seems to be "killer" viruses. With the outbreak of Ebola virus in Zaire and the popular accounts of epidemics of virus infection in feature films, made-for-television movies and best-selling non-fiction, the public has been captivated by the apparent power of microorganisms to sweep through towns and villages unfettered.

2   But hidden behind our fascination with these real and fictional epidemics is a profound feeling of betrayal, stemming from the widely held view that science had won the war against microbial infections.

3   The recent outbreaks have taken us by surprise, threatening our carefully nurtured sense of health and well-being. We diet, consume vitamins and exercise vigorously to ward off heart disease and cancer. But infectious diseases strike in a seemingly unpredictable pattern, leaving us feeling unprotected and vulnerable. With the re-emergence of tuberculosis as a significant public health problem in the United States, cholera in Latin America, the plague epidemic in India last year and the Ebola virus infection in Zaire, HIV infection, formerly considered an isolated occurrence confined to marginalized populations, now seems a harbinger of ever more terrifying microbial agents.

4   Yet, the reasons for the re-emergence of infectious diseases are not particularly mysterious. In reality, infectious diseases never were conquered, and the recent epidemics are quite predictable. For centuries, infectious diseases have been the major cause of death in the developing world. Moreover, even in the developed world, successful management relies on active disease surveillance and public health policies.

5   In 1966, the eminent Australian immunologist Sir MacFarlane Burnet declared, "In many ways one can think of the middle of the 20th Century as the end of one of the most important social revolutions in history, the virtual elimination of infectious disease as a significant factor in social life." Shared by most of the scientific community, this view is rooted in the rise of the germ theory in the late 19th and early 20th centuries that associated specific microbial agents with particular diseases.

6   The germ theory took hold not only because of the spectacular technical achievements represented by the isolation of the microorganisms, but also because infectious disease, once seen as divine retribution for past sins, now appeared potentially controllable. The discovery of antibiotics and the development of vaccines lent further support to this notion of control. Thus, the germ theory effectively replaced disease prevention policies based on sanitary reforms, including improvement in sewage systems and better housing conditions, which were primarily responsible for the dramatic decline in the death rates from infectious disease.

7   The possibility of control over these great afflictions of humankind became even more appealing in the post-World War II period when a sense of endless optimism about the future was fueled by economic expansion in industrialized countries. Unfortunately, during this period, we also began to rely exclusively on science

to solve the problems of disease. Throughout this century the role of the natural and social environment in the development of disease has been largely ignored by the scientific and medical communities and policy-makers.

8   Yet, the obstacles to management of many infectious diseases are social as well as scientific, and disease prevention policies based exclusively on science leave us ill-prepared to respond effectively to the current epidemics.

9   In the case of tuberculosis, we know how the bacterium is transmitted, how it causes disease and until recently, we had drugs that were relatively effective in reducing transmission and the development of disease. Despite this wealth of medical knowledge, tuberculosis continues to thrive, primarily in marginalized groups with minimal or no access to medical care. Without a concerted effort to improve access to the health care system, tuberculosis will remain a formidable challenge irrespective of the development of new drug treatments or more effective vaccines.

10   In the case of AIDS, basic scientific research coupled with education, public health measures and the political will to address difficult social issues are essential to managing this epidemic.

11   There are many other examples of microbial diseases where the failure to integrate scientific knowledge with social programs has hampered the development of sound disease prevention policies. Cervical cancer, for example, is the second most common cause of cancer-related mortality in women worldwide. Over a decade ago, sexually transmitted human papillomaviruses were linked to this cancer. Yet years later, we still know relatively little about the mechanisms by which human papillomaviruses contribute to the development of cervical cancer. To reduce the morbidity and mortality associated with this infection we need to develop more precise ways of identifying women at increased risk of progression to cancer.

12   An investment in basic microbiological research will be required to answer these questions. Meantime, however, we have more than sufficient scientific information to begin to educate the population most at risk of contracting the disease, namely adolescents. Again, the failure to implement such programs is fundamentally a political issue, reflecting our reluctance as a society to deal with adolescent sexuality.

13   Effective management of infectious diseases is achievable. Many of the agents associated with recent outbreaks are not new microbes but rather newly recognized ones that have appeared in human populations as a consequence of social disorganization and ecological disruption. To be successful, disease-prevention policies must be based on more than technical solutions. They must be firmly rooted in an ecological perspective of disease that does not separate scientific knowledge from an understanding of the influence of the natural environment on disease and a commitment to social justice.

14   There are no magic bullets. We will have little impact on infectious diseases without addressing the living conditions of large segments of our society and rebuilding our public health infrastructure. In the absence of such a policy, however, future outbreaks will continue to be viewed with the mixture of fascination, fear, helplessness and misdirected social policy that has characterized our response to the recent epidemics.

Analysis: Identifying the Right Occasion

"How To Fight the New Epidemics" is an interesting example of a specialist turning to commentary to address a wider audience. Braun's writing for the most part grows out of her research on cervical cancer—such as grant proposals and reports in specialized journals. However, when new and mysterious "killer diseases" became hot topics in the news, Braun felt called on to explain the "fascination" with these epidemics and the "profound feeling of betrayal" among the public that science had not won the war against infectious diseases.

For Braun, the purpose of characterizing this public mood goes beyond simply labeling a trend in the popular mind. As her commentary unfolds, readers quickly become aware that this public mood is only an occasion for her to make a larger argument about the limits of the germ theory of disease and the failure of scientific and medical policy-making to take social conditions into account in preventing and controlling disease.

"How To Fight the New Epidemics" is a good example of how successful writers find occasions that link their own particular knowledge to what is on the public's mind. The appearance of "killer viruses" in the media gives Braun's argument about the germ theory a sense of urgency. By connecting her research into the history of disease to the present moment, Braun's commentary takes on timeliness and relevance.

FOR CRITICAL INQUIRY

1. How does Braun use the hot news topic of "killer viruses" to frame her commentary?

2. What is the central problem Braun identifies in her commentary? What does she see as its causes? What does she see as its consequences? What are her policy recommendations for dealing with the problem?

3. Describe the writer's strategy by grouping paragraphs into sections and labeling their function. What does each section contribute to the commentary as a whole?

Visual Design: Parody

Visual commentary often uses humor to get its point across—to poke fun at the rich and famous, to expose hypocrisy in public life, and to underscore the foibles of contemporary society. Editorial cartoons in newspapers and magazines, comic strips such as Gary Trudeau's *Doonesbury* and Scott Adams' *Dilbert,* and skits on *Saturday Night Live* typically rely on humorous exaggerations that are funny and often painfully true. The following two examples of visual commentary provide satirical looks at bioengineered food and the image of masculinity in Calvin Klein ads. The first appeared on the op-art page of the *New York Times,* the second in *Adbusters* magazine.

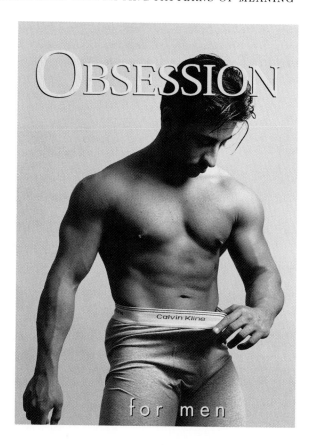

Analysis: Reworking Visual Design

Both of these visual commentaries are parodies (or satirical imitations) of familiar forms of visual communication—ads for supermarket specials and for Calvin Klein's line of men's fashions and accessories. The two parodies rely on readers' recognition of the visual design of the original ads. The humor—and the insight—of the parodies plays off this knowledge by imitating the originals in order to reveal unsuspected meanings. Reworking visual designs that have become so familiar causes us to stop for a moment and to see the original ads in a new light. The persuasive power of the two parodies does not rest on a reasoned interpretation, as is the case in written commentary, but rather on a change of perception. In this sense, parody can expose hidden logics in genetically altered foods and in the image of high fashion and hard bodies in Calvin Klein ads.

FOR CRITICAL INQUIRY

1. What design features make it immediately recognizable that the two parodies are imitations of an original? How do the parodies rework these originals to elicit new responses?

2. Put together a group of editorial cartoons that offer commentary on a recent event or issue in the news. (*Newsweek,* the Sunday edition of the *New York Times,* and the Saturday edition of the *Washington Post* all feature cartoons from the past week.) How do the cartoons combine images and text to fashion their commentary? Which cartoons do you find particularly effective?

3. Choose an image to rework—an ad, a cereal box or any other packaged product, a magazine or book cover, a poster, or a sign. Rework the image in a way that clearly imitates the original and at the same time brings to the surface a new perception of the original.

FOR DISCUSSION AND ANALYTICAL WRITING

RHETORICAL ANALYSIS

Pick one of the commentaries (or compare two) to analyze the rhetorical situation. Pay particular attention to how the writer identifies the key issue and how this perspective on the topic shapes the commentary. See guidelines and sample rhetorical analysis in Chapter 2.

GENRE CHOICES

Michael Rock and the signers of the *First Things First Manifesto 2000* (see Chapter 6) are all graphic designers concerned with the current direction of the design profession. Yet they have chosen to address the issue in quite different ways. Consider why they chose the particular genre they did—a commentary and a manifesto. What does each genre enable the writers to do? What kind of relationship to their readers do the genres make possible?

GOING ONLINE

Following a Thread About Matthew Shepard

Matthew Shepard, a 21-year-old student at the University of Wyoming who happened to be gay, was kidnapped, robbed, and beaten on October 6, 1998. After being left tied to a fence, Matthew Shepard died on October 12. Shepard's death prompted not only the prosecution of his murderers but also a tremendous amount of commentary on message boards. To see how people have tried to make sense of this hate-based crime, check out the following Web sites—Memorial to Matthew Shepard <www.truthtree.com/matthew.stml>, Welcome to Matthew's Place <www.matthewsplace.com>, and Matthew Shepard Online Resources Bulletin Board <ww.wiredstrategies.com/wwwboard>. Consider what people are talking about and how they respond to each other. How is this kind of online commentary different from or similar to the commentaries you've read in this chapter?

WORKING TOGETHER

Assembling a Casebook

A casebook brings together writings on a topic. You may have used casebooks in other courses—on the causes of World War I, say, or on interpretations of *The Scarlet Letter.* A casebook typically organizes a range of perspectives on the topic so that readers can reconstruct for themselves the context of issues surrounding the topic.

Work together in groups of two or three. Pick a current issue that has generated debate. It could be affirmative action, bilingual education, immigration, eligibility standards for college athletes, or any other issue that has provoked a good deal of commentary.

Assemble a casebook on the issue for high school students.

First you'll need to do some library research—to search newspapers and magazines for commentaries written from different positions. (Don't assume that there are just two sides—most controversies have many sides.) Select five or six commentaries that are representative of the various positions you find.

After rereading the commentaries you've selected, design your casebook in the following way:

1. Write a brief introduction that gives readers an overview of the issue—what it is, how it began, why it is controversial—and mentions the articles you have selected.

2. Include the readings. Before each reading give a headnote that tells who the writer is and briefly introduces the reading. After each reading provide discussion questions to promote thinking about it. (You can use the headnotes and discussion questions in this book as models.)

3. At the end of the casebook include several questions that pull together the various readings to make sure the other students have understood the overall issue.

WRITING ASSIGNMENT

For this assignment, write a commentary that addresses a topic of interest to you. As you have noticed throughout the readings in this chapter, writing a commentary involves making an argument about an issue circulating in your culture. Commentary can also provide you with a chance to understand a curious cultural phenomenon a bit better. You may be called to write a commentary to help yourself make sense of an issue, or to bring the implications of an issue to your readers' attention. There may be issues you want to address that arise from reading you are doing in one of your other classes. To help you get ideas for this assignment, consider what has called on the writers represented in this chapter's reading selections to write commentary.

- **Current events:** Stories that break in the news, such as Shannon Faulkner's battle with The Citadel, seem to call for a swift response to coalesce readers' feelings and influence public reaction. Here is writing at the point of opinion making, shaping the public mood and sense of issues. You might draw on a recent event to serve as the springboard for your commentary, something current that your readers are likely to know about but where the meaning is still up for grabs.

- **Historical events:** You could also write about a historical event—the Civil War, the Great Depression, the dropping of the atomic bomb, the beginning of rock and roll, the Clinton-Lewinsky scandal. Commentators often analyze past events and point out implications that would otherwise go unnoticed. You could write a commentary about the significance of a historic event, an invention, a social movement, or an everyday occurrence.

- **Trends:** Labeling trends is a strategy commentators use to give readers a handle on what is taking place around them. Trends are not objective phenomena waiting to be discovered, like some new species of animal. Rather they rely on the interpretive powers of commentators to name what's happening, thereby giving a series of events a distinct identity and making it available as a topic for public discussion. The idea of "branding" in Eric Liu's commentary or the takeover of *USA Today* style design in Michael Rock's are good examples of how identifying and labeling trends can bring an issue into focus. There are plenty of other trends as well: Body-piercing, tattooing, cybercafes, nostalgia for the 1970s, the rising use of Ecstasy, the growth of microbreweries, the declining crime rate, and corporate downsizing are just a few. You might write about the significance of a particular trend that is already well-known, or you can invent a new label to characterize a trend that has not been noticed before.

- **Policy issues:** Commentators often address issues of public policy. For example, Lundy Braun's commentary, "How to Fight the New Epidemics," analyzes the causes of infectious disease and the adequacy of the "germ theory" to control disease. You might write a commentary that focuses on the causes of an issue that interests you and the implications for public policy. Accounting for why things happen is often the first step in explaining what should be done—to endorse, alter, or control the situation.

- **Satire and humor:** As you have seen, visual commentaries often use satire to bring out the unstated logic of an event or situation. Satire and humor can be used effectively to question conventional ideas. You might write a satirical commentary that uses humor to rework existing ways of thinking. Or, if your instructor is agreeable, you might design and produce a poster, a cartoon, or a comic strip to comment on a current event, issue, or idea. Or write and perform a comic skit either as a monologue or with others.

- **Responses to readings:** Another strategy for finding issues for your commentary is to respond to one of the reading selections in this book or to something you have read recently in another course. You can frame your commentary by agreeing or disagreeing with another writer, or you can use that writer's presentation of an issue as a jumping-off point to develop your own perspective and position.

ETHICS OF WRITING

IN WHOSE INTEREST?

Commentators often seek to persuade readers (or listeners or viewers) that their commentaries represent the best interests of the public and the common good. By speaking on behalf of the public, commentary plays a vital role in a democracy, holding accountable those in positions of power and explaining what the public's stake is in events, trends, and ideas.

Speaking in the name of the public, however, is rarely a simple matter, and it brings with it ethical responsibilities that writers need to take into account. Since commentary offers explanations, it presumes, for example, to represent other people's motives. Commentators therefore need to avoid falling into stereotyped representations of groups of people ("Single

mothers on welfare have more children to get more benefits," "Gay men are promiscuous," "Young people today don't have a social conscience"). Such stereotypes not only characterize groups unfairly, they also turn these groups into "them" who are different from "us," and often present the interests of these groups as incompatible with the public interest.

In other words, writers need to be aware that speaking in the name of the public may in fact amount to speaking on behalf of some people or groups and distancing themselves from others. Writers need to examine their own assumptions about who is included in the public and try to understand how the people they write about perceive themselves and their experience.

Invention

As you have seen, the reading selections in this chapter offer perspectives after the fact—after events have taken place; personalities have emerged in the media; or ideas, styles, fads, and moods have started floating around in the public consciousness. The point of commentary is to name a topic, identify an important issue, and explain its significance. Commentators, in effect, are asking their readers to consider one possible way of making sense of what has happened in the past and what is going on in the present.

Naming the Topic

Corporate branding, Shannon Faulkner's struggle to enter The Citadel, *USA Today*'s design style, or the new epidemics are topics because they refer to things your readers are likely to have read about in the news or observed in their personal experience—events, situations, trends, ideas, conflicts, or debates that people are talking about.

Topics are forms of knowledge, the facts and information that have acquired public recognition and that you can assume your readers will recognize and be familiar with. Topics have names—whether those of individuals (Shannon Faulkner, O. J. Simpson), historical and political events (slavery, the Persian Gulf War, the Bush presidency), social and cultural trends (increase in two-career families, video games, animal rights advocacy), or concepts (natural selection, Einstein's theory of relativity, the germ theory of disease). You can look up a topic and find information on it in the library. Your topic is the source of your commentary, the information whose significance you want to explore.

> **EXERCISE**

Here are some suggestions for naming your topic:

1. To locate **current events** that might be fruitful for your commentary, find at least four different news sources (for example, a big-city newspaper, a campus newspaper, a newsmagazine, or a TV broadcast). Within those sources, see which stories recur in all the formats—these are probably the most popular stories right now. Make a list of the issues that show up in at least three of the sources, and mark those that seem most compelling or disturbing to you. If any remind you of another issue that you have felt strongly about, consider making connections between them in your commentary.

2. For **historical events,** you might look in several places for ideas. To start, you might look through a history book and look for pictures or boxed anecdotes that capture your attention. If they don't offer you any ideas, trace through the significant social movements in your life from the time you were born, and think of specific events that were a part

of those larger social movements. You might also watch movies about events that take place in historical times and note the real events that weave into the plots; if one interests you, learn more about it for your commentary. Finally, if you are learning about an interesting historical event in another class, take the opportunity to write about it in this class as well.

3. Although you should feel free to use any of the **trends** already mentioned in this chapter, there are many other possible topics. To identify a trend or fad that compels you to write, take an inventory of the aspects of your life. This means breaking down the aspects of your life into decision-making moments and then examining them to see if they fit into a larger trend. For example, when you wake up in the morning, what kinds of clothes do you put on? Are they related to any trend (like Birkenstock clogs or a specific kind of jeans)? When you eat breakfast, what do you choose (something loaded with sugar, something with whole-wheat bran, or nothing at all)? What form of transportation do you take? Could that be part of a trend? Notice, too, the choices that people around you seem to make. By the end of the day, you should have a lengthy list of topics.

4. One way to find **policy issues** of interest to you is to identify the issues that might influence you directly—either right now or in the future. Think through your life systematically and make a list of the communities that have an impact on your daily existence. For example, label the various parts of your identity: college student, parent of a toddler, copy shop employee, volunteer emergency medical technician, amateur photographer, weekend auto mechanic, member of a religious youth organization. Next, for each label you wrote down, think of at least three policy issues that matter to that community. As a student, for instance, you might have been affected by need-blind admissions or particular financial aid policies and procedures. As a parent, you might have a stake in arguing for more and better child care options for your college or work community. As a copy shop employee, you might be interested in recent copyright legislation that makes it more difficult for copy shops to create course packs for classes. By the time you have gone through your list of community identities, you should have a sizable list of policy issues that are important to you and ripe for commentary.

5. Reconstruct conversations you've had with friends and family, either recently or in the past, and find the **sources of humor** in those conversations. Those moments can form the basis of your commentary; after selecting a defining moment growing out of humor, you can write more seriously about its implications.

Exploring the Topic

State your topic in the form of a noun phrase (the Protestant Reformation, conversation patterns between men and women, global warming). To explore the topic, respond to the following questions in writing:

1. What do you know about the topic? How do you know what you know about it? What is the source of your knowledge? List as many sources as you can. Which, if any, of these sources are available to you? Which might it be helpful to locate and reread?

2. What do you think other people know about the topic? Is it widely known, or is it likely to be of interest to a more limited readership? How are other people likely to have learned about the topic—through newspapers, television news, or personal experience?

3. Are there conflicting views or a range of opinion on the topic? If so, how would you describe the conflict or difference of opinion? Are there readily distinguishable sides involved? If so, do you tend to have allegiances to one side rather than the other? Explain how you align yourself to the topic and to what others have said about it.

Identifying the Issue

An issue refers to how the writer focuses attention on what he or she thinks is important about the topic. This is where the function of commentary comes in. Commentators establish issues to explain some meaningful aspect of the topic according to their own perspective.

Notice how, in the following chart, the same topic can generate a number of different issues.

Topic:	The Shannon Faulkner case		
Source:	The media		
	The *New York Times*	Susan Faludi	Capt. Erin Dowd
Issues:	gender equity	gender equity	gender equity
	immaturity of cadet behavior	popular illusions about heroes and celebrities	Faulkner's lack of preparation

Notice that there is some overlap in the three selections. Each writer announces early on where he or she stands on the central controversy in Shannon Faulkner's two-and-a-half-year struggle to gain admission to The Citadel—the issue of gender equity in the military. All three make it clear that they support an end to discrimination at men-only military academies and a woman's right to attend The Citadel. As you can see, however, while the writers all share a similar position on the issue of gender equity, they go on to introduce and explore very different issues concerning the Shannon Faulkner case.

After you have identified the issue that most interests you within the topic, you can begin to explain the particular urgency of your issue. Why should your readers be concerned and interested? Why is the issue being raised in the first place? (Or, if you're writing about an issue that has not received attention, why has the issue been ignored and why do you want to raise it?)

EXERCISE

1. Locate three readings (from newspapers, magazines, journals, or books) on the topic you are planning to write about. Use the chart above as a model to name the topic, indicate the source, and identify the issues others have written about.

2. List as many other issues as you can. You don't have to agree with the sense of the issue or be interested in writing about it just yet. The point at this stage is to get as wide a picture as possible of available issues. For now, just brainstorm for all the issues you can; you will pare the list down to the most interesting ones later.

3. Circle the three or four issues that interest you most. Consider what, if anything, they have in common with one another. Do they overlap in any way? How do they differ? Does one bring to light something that the others don't? If you notice a connection between the issues you've circled, that connection may well be worth writing about in your commentary.

4. Decide tentatively on one issue to write about. What would you say about the issue in a commentary? What do you imagine as your main point? How does this perspective align you with some people and positions? What common ground do you share?

5. Consider the position of people who differ with you. What are the key points of difference? What objections might people have to your commentary? Are any valid? Are there any points of agreement or common values? How can you use these in your commentary? What differences do you feel need to be addressed in your statement?

6. Think about the implications of your commentary. If people were persuaded by your position, what would happen? How would this be an improvement over the present condition of things? If your readers take your commentary seriously, what would you hope to achieve? Is there something you would like them to do?

Planning

Framing the Issue

Like the frame of a painting, the frame of a commentary goes on the outside to give it boundaries and a focus of attention. Commentaries typically open by framing an issue—defining it, explaining its relevance to readers, and using it to set up the writer's position. Framing, then, has two main purposes.

First, it focuses readers' attention on a particular aspect of the topic. It establishes a perspective for readers to see significant features of a topic they already know something about. Framing the issue often begins with the familiar and then seeks to add a new or different angle or way of analyzing and explaining what is known.

Second, framing the issue sets up the writer to present the main point of his or her commentary. Depending on how the writer frames the issue, he or she will enter into one or another relationship to the topic and to what other people have said about it.

Planning the Introduction

Commentary writers use various techniques in their introductions to name the topic and frame the issues. Here are a few:

1. Describe an event or an existing situation. The point is to establish what is known in order to set yourself up to explain what new perspective you are going to bring to the issue. The amount of detail will depend on how familiar you think your readers will be with your topic.

2. Describe the sides of a controversy, conflict, or debate. On issues where people differ or find themselves on opposing sides, commentary writers often briefly sketch the different views in order to explain what they believe is at stake. By analyzing and evaluating the sides that already exist, you can set yourself up to present your own perspective and to show how it allies you with some people and positions but not with others.

3. Explain the causes or origins of an issue. Giving readers accounts of how something got started raises underlying issues of cause and effect: Why does something occur in the first place? What causes things to happen over a period of time? What are the results? Who is affected? Who is responsible? By explaining the causes or origins of an issue, you can set yourself up to show readers how something came to have the shape and importance it does.

4. Explain how you became aware of the issue. Writers draw on what through reading, observation, or experience brought a particular issue to their attention—how something hit home for them. This technique can

help set up writers to explain an event, a situation, a conflict, or a debate by showing why and on what terms the writer is invested in the issue.

5. Explain points and principles you have in common with readers. Writers often join with others on certain shared points or principles. Affirming common values and attitudes gains you consideration for your views, which can help set you up to introduce ideas that may not fit in readily with the thinking of others.

6. Use examples or personal anecdotes. Begin with an example or anecdote that illustrates the issue you are writing about. More important, draw explicit connections between the example or anecdote and the larger issue. Is the example or anecdote representative of the situation your position addresses, or is it an exception? Make this clear in your framing of the commentary.

Planning the Ending

Endings apply the final frame to the writer's position. They give the writer the chance to have the last word, to leave readers with a closing sense of the issue and the writer's stand. Here are some ways writers design endings:

1. Point out the consequences of your position. What would happen if your position were taken up? How would that improve the current situation?

2. Reaffirm shared values and beliefs. What common values and beliefs does your commentary draw on? How does your position express these values and beliefs?

3. Make recommendations. What would your commentary look like if it were carried through in practice? What concrete proposals does it lead to?

4. Call on readers to take action. What steps can readers take, assuming they agree with you? What changes in thinking, personal habits, or public policy follow from your commentary?

The Working Draft

Write a page or two as quickly as you can. Write as if you were warming up to write the "real" first draft. Begin by identifying the topic and the issue you're writing about. Explain your perspective on the issue, and quickly sketch an ending. Now you can use this writing as a discovery draft to clarify your own perspective on the issue you are writing about, to explore your own sympathies, and to understand on whose behalf you want to speak and with whom you differ. Use this draft to produce a working draft of your commentary.

Emphasizing the Main Point: Distinguishing Your Perspective from That of Others

Readers of commentary expect a writer to give them something to think about. They assume that the point of reading a commentary is not just—or even primarily—to be informed about an issue but to consider what the writer has to say about it. For this reason, it is important that the writer's main point is easy to find.

One way to make sure readers can readily see your perspective is to distinguish it from another perspective. This is a widely used technique in commentary, as we can see in the opening paragraph of Michael Rock's "Since When Did *USA Today* Become the National Design Ideal?":

> Everywhere you look you find *USA Today* used as an analogy to describe a noteworthy design format. Making ideas "accessible" is the operative term for the information age. But too often information is drained of its significance in the name of accessibility.

It's easy enough to see in this passage where Rock is coming from, in part because he shows how his perspective differs from what others think. He's leading us as readers from a common view ("Everywhere you look") to his own take, set up with the words "But too often." Along similar lines, Lundy Braun's "How To Fight the New Epidemics" first explains how the germ theory has influenced public health practices and then offers an alternative perspective.

Peer Commentary

Exchange working drafts and respond in writing to these questions about your partner's draft:

1. Identify the topic of the draft. How does the writer frame the main issue? Point to a phrase or sentence. Where did you become aware of what the writer has to say about the issue? Point to a phrase or sentence where you first got the writer's point. If you can't point to particular phrases or sentences, what answers does the writer seem to imply to these questions?

2. Who is likely to agree with the writer's commentary? What beliefs and values does the commentary appeal to? Does the commentary seem to choose sides? If so, who else is on the writer's side? Who is excluded?

3. Do you share the writer's perspective on the issue? If so, does the writer make the most effective case in presenting that perspective? Can you offer suggestions about ways to improve it? If you don't share the writer's perspective, explain why. Describe your own perspective.

Revising

Read the peer remarks on your working draft. Use them to take the following questions into account:

1. Does the introduction frame the issues and forecast the main point and the direction of your commentary?

2. Is the main point located at an effective place in the commentary? How much background or context is necessary for your main point to take

on significance? When it does appear, is the main point stated as clearly as possible?

3. Are details, facts, and other information about the topic clearly related to your main point? If you use examples, is it clear what point or points they are intended to illustrate?

4. Do your explanations develop the main point of the commentary, or do they raise other issues? If they do, is this intended on your part, or are you starting to jump from issue to issue? Can you point out the connection between issues so that readers will be able to follow your line of thought?

5. Does the ending offer a satisfying sense of closure? Will readers find it easy to see how you arrived at your final point? Does the ending help to emphasize the main point or lesson of the commentary?

Maintaining a Reasonable Tone

One of the appeals of writing commentary is that the genre offers writers the opportunity to stake out a position on issues they are passionate about. Commentators often want to make sense of things because they are invested and believe there is really something that matters. For this reason, commentators typically pay attention to the tone of their writing so that their readers, whether they share the writer's perspective or not, will at least take the commentary seriously as a reasonable effort to explain and analyze.

The two following passages show how Rachel Smith modulated the tone of her commentary, "Sociably Acceptable Discrimination" which appears in full in the next section.

EARLY DRAFT

I am so sick of the way born-again Christians are portrayed in the media. What's wrong with people? Do they think all born-agains are narrow-minded, Bible-waving bigots?

Is the desire for sensationalism so strong that the media has to make every born-again a Bible-waving fanatic who chains herself to abortion-clinic doors and supports the madmen who shoot the doctors that perform abortions? It is so unfair to focus on the extremist fringe and ignore all the normal people who are born-again Christians.

In this draft, as the peer commentary suggested to Rachel, her anger, though arguably justified, was getting in the way of her analysis of how born-again Christians are portrayed in the media. The peer reviewer thought Rachel was calling too much attention to her own feelings ("I am so sick" and "It is so unfair") and blaming others ("What's wrong with these people?") when she should have been explaining the issue and its significance. The peer reviewer also mentioned that the rhetorical questions at the end of the opening paragraph and beginning of the second made her feel that Rachel was trying to strong-arm her readers instead of persuading them. Notice in the revised version how Rachel turns the sequence of questions into analytical statements that explore the issue at hand instead of assuming agreement on the reader's part. Rachel also enhances the reasonable tone of the commentary by making the rhetorical question in the second paragraph into a concession on her part that it's true some born-agains are extremists.

> This movie is only one example of the way that born-again Christians are portrayed in the media. America's most popular image of a born-again Christian is a narrow-minded, Bible-waving, bigot who doesn't know how to have fun.
>
> Now, don't get me wrong; I'm not saying that we don't sometimes wave our Bibles around. There are people who call themselves born-again Christians who find it absolutely imperative that they shove their beliefs down everyone's throat, "waving their Bible" all the while. They chain themselves to abortion-clinic doors and support the madmen who shoot the doctors that perform abortions.

WRITERS' WORKSHOP

Rachel Smith, "Socially Acceptable Discrimination"

Rachel Smith wrote the following commentary, "Socially Acceptable Discrimination" as an assignment in her first-year writing course. It is followed by an interview with the writer.

SOCIALLY ACCEPTABLE DISCRIMINATION?

Rachel Smith

I looked up at the billboard as we drove home from church one Sunday and saw the advertisement for the newest Steve Martin movie *Leap of Faith*. Martin stood in the center of the board, arms raised above him, his suitcoat gaudy and sparkling. His face was tilted upwards. A slight smile on his lips, his eyes were squinted. His stance suggested religious worship. Lights shone down from behind him, and the words *Leap of Faith* were pasted on the board over his head. At first glance, the picture looked sincere; here was a man worshipping God. However, when I noticed the overdone clothes and the pious look on his face, I knew that this was not a picture of a man praising his God. This was an advertisement for a movie whose sole purpose was to make a "hilarious" comedy out of the life of a television evangelist. Later, when I saw the preview trailers for *Leap of Faith* on television, I saw Steve Martin pushing fat, sweating women to the floor in a cheap imitation of what sometimes happens at real evangelical tent meetings. He had this look of intense pleasure on his face, his body language wide and over-the-top, almost as if he was getting a sexual kick out of what he was doing. The character was described as being "a born-again, Spirit-filled, holy-rollin' Christian," and often spouted "Well, Peraaaise God!" This movie is only one example of the way that born-again Christians are portrayed in the media. America's most popular image of a born-again Christian is a narrow-minded, Bible-waving, bigot who doesn't know how to have fun.

Now, don't get me wrong; I'm not saying that we don't sometimes wave our Bibles around. There are people who call themselves born-again Christians who find it absolutely imperative that they shove their beliefs down everyone's throat, "waving their Bible" all the while. They chain themselves to abortion-clinic doors and support the madmen who shoot the doctors that perform abortions. There are people in every group, whether it is feminists, African-Americans, those of Middle Eastern descent, or teenagers, who are the "black sheep," so to speak, of the group. They are the radicals and therefore are sensational. They get the publicity and portray their group as being as radical and unbalanced as they are. Not all African-Americans harbour deep, hateful grudges against whites. Actually, a large majority of them don't. Often, in movies, they are portrayed in the stereotype that they all hate whites, as in Malcolm X. This portrayal is the most sensational, and therefore the most newsworthy. Why hasn't anyone made a major, widely-released movie about the life of Martin Luther King, Jr.? Because he didn't have a checkered past, his life wasn't filled with violence and anger (on his part, at least), and he preached a message of forgiveness. Those things aren't sensational. They aren't as newsworthy as the radical, insane things that the media prefers to focus on.

Because of the media's attraction to the sensational, often groups are represented erroneously. What's sensational about the rest of the born-again Christians? They don't attack doctors and plant explosives in office buildings. They don't all go around condemning everyone they meet to hell. They live just like everyone else. Granted, they don't frequent too many bars and brothels, they tend to spend more time in church than most Americans, and they live, very strictly, by the Bible. Because of this last point, many believe that Christians don't have any fun. That is one of the main reasons movies like *Leap of Faith* were made. The media says that underneath that "good" image, Christians are probably really warped human beings, following some long-dead cult that says the world will come to an end pretty soon, so all the rest of us had better join up or we'll be in lots of trouble. *Leap of Faith* just gives people a laugh and helps relieve them of the little suspicion that those crazy, born-again Christians just might have something. When a prominent televangelist is exposed, the media jumps into the fray and triumphantly holds up the tattered pieces, flaunting the fall of someone supposed to be "good." This concentration on the negative side of Christianity lends itself to making the public see born-again Christians as completely unbalanced, non-rational, bigoted people. We are portrayed in only the worst ways.

My intent in writing on this subject is not to whine about injustice and the liberal media, but to bring out the other side of the issue. To put it plainly, every special interest group in America has gained a lot of publicity for fighting discrimination, except for the born-again Christians. Politically correct speech is the newest fad; everyone is careful about what they say. More movies are being released that center on the lives of homosexuals, there is a rise in the frequency of African-American sit-coms, Greenpeace gets news coverage every time they try to sue a lumber company, and whenever there is a story on abortion, a majority of the personal interviews come from the Pro-choice side. In all this "political correctness," born-again Christians are invariably left out by the media because the beliefs that we hold do not embrace all the personal preferences that people have. We live by a definite standard of right and wrong, and because people do not want to be told that something they are doing is wrong, they invent their own morality: situation ethics. Born-again Christians do not fit into that jelly-mold of American society. When a movie like *Leap of Faith* came out, the only protests against such discrimination were in Christian magazines and books. We fight the currents, and yes, we do make people uncomfortable sometimes, but why is discrimination against us more culturally acceptable?

Interview with Rachel Smith

Q: *What prompted you to write "Socially Acceptable Discrimination"?*

A: I have felt for a long time that people unfairly judge born-again Christians like myself. If you go by the newspapers, born-agains are narrow-minded bigots, madmen who kill abortion doctors, or hypocrites like Jim Bakker. I know this isn't the real story, but it seemed that these stereotypes of born-agains are just something I had to live with—that I couldn't really do anything about it. Then I saw the Steve Martin movie, *Leap of Faith,* and I began to think that this might give me an occasion to try to correct perceptions.

Q: *How did you decide to focus on the particular issues you explore in "Socially Acceptable Discrimination"?*

A: I knew I wanted to change the way people perceive born-again Christians but I also knew I couldn't just say, "Hey, you've got it all wrong. That's not the way we really are." I'd be asking people to accept my personal experience, and I was pretty sure this wasn't going to work. So I thought that if I focused on how the media portrayed born-again Christians, and tied this to the idea that the media loves to sensationalize things, I might get a different response from readers. I figured most people think the media is sensationalistic and that by using this as a kind of common ground with readers, I could introduce my own point of view in a way that might get a hearing.

Q: *What conflicts, if any, did you experience writing this commentary?*

A: It's hard because movies like *Leap of Faith* and all the media coverage of crazed evangelicals really gets me angry. I know it's a false picture and totally unfair to me and other born-agains, who are just normal people who happen to believe in God and want to follow the Bible. I wanted to make this point, but I also knew that if I let my anger come out too strongly, I was going to lose readers—or maybe even confirm their impression that we're all nuts. So I definitely experienced this conflict of wanting to be loyal to other believers and to get their real story out and, at the same time, knowing that I had to write in a reasonable tone. That's where the Steve Martin movie and the idea of media sensationalism were so helpful to me. By analyzing them (instead of screaming at people, which is what I felt like doing), I think I got some critical distance and could still be true to what I wanted to say.

WORKSHOP QUESTIONS

1. As Rachel Smith notes in the interview, her main purpose is to "correct perceptions" of born-again Christians. What was your attitude toward born-again Christians before you read "Socially Acceptable Discrimination"? Did reading her commentary confirm, modify, change, or otherwise affect the attitude you began with? Given your experience reading the essay, what suggestions would you offer Smith to help achieve her purpose?

2. Smith says that she realized she couldn't persuade people solely on the basis of her personal experience as a born-again Christian. Instead, she focuses on how the media portrays born-agains. Evaluate this strategy. To what extent does it offer the common ground with readers that she hopes to find? Are there ways she could strengthen this appeal?

3. Smith notes a conflict between her loyalty to other believers and her desire to reach out to her readers. One way this conflict manifests itself is in the tension between the anger she feels about being portrayed unfairly and the need she acknowledges to maintain a reasonable tone in her writing. How well do you think she handles this tension? What suggestion would you offer about how to manage this conflict?

REFLECTING ON YOUR WRITING

Use the following questions from the interview with Rachel Smith to interview someone who has recently written a commentary. It could be a classmate; but also consider interviewing columnists of your student or local newspaper.

1. What prompted you to write the commentary?
2. How did you decide to establish the focus of the piece?
3. What conflicts, if any, did you experience when you wrote it?

Compare the writer's experience writing the commentary with your own.

A CLOSING NOTE

As you have seen throughout this chapter, commentary involves speaking on behalf of others. Reread the commentary you've written to see how the perspective you offer in your commentary allies you with some people and divides you from others. Use the information you get to make sure you are comfortable with the way your commentary establishes your relationship to others and to assess whether there are passages you want to revise.

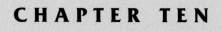

CHAPTER TEN

Proposals: Formulating and Solving Problems

THINKING ABOUT THE GENRE

Proposals put forth plans of action and seek to persuade readers that those plans should be implemented. Like commentary, proposals involve analyzing issues, taking a position, and making an argument. However, proposals go beyond commentaries by recommending a course of action, often a solution to a problem that has been identified as needing attention. Like commentaries, proposals use arguments to influence readers' beliefs, but they do so with the aim of advancing a new program or policy.

This difference between commentaries and proposals is not an absolute one but a matter of emphasis. After all, the positions writers take in commentaries have consequences. Whether writers make it explicit or not, their positions imply certain policies, courses of action, and ways of living. But proposals emphasize this dimension of making policy, devising courses of action, and negotiating the demands of everyday life. The focus of attention shifts from the statement and explanation of the writer's position to what we ought to do about it. Thus, in proposals, a writer's position has a practical or applied dimension in that it involves identifying problems and offering solutions.

Making proposals, of course, is a familiar, everyday activity that people perform routinely, often without being conscious that they are engaging in a fairly predictable pattern—defining a problem, surveying alternatives, and choosing a course of action. Let's say you're making a plan for Saturday night—whether with your family or with your friends—and you have a limited budget. The problem here is to propose something that others will enjoy but that still fits within your finances.

You survey the possibilities, immediately ruling out a first-run movie or dinner in an expensive restaurant. You realize you could go out for pizza and still have enough money left for a second-run movie or a movie playing on campus; or eat at a Chinese or Mexican restaurant, then rent a movie for your family to

344

watch at home; or go with your friends to the campus coffeehouse, which is featuring a local band with no door charge.

To persuade your family or your friends to go along with your proposal, you first need to make sure that it really solves the problem (that's why you ruled out the expensive dinner and first-run movie). In addition, you'll want to make sure that you've considered all possible alternatives (maybe there's a free concert at your church, or you can get into a basketball game on campus with your student ID) and that you've anticipated possible objections (what if one of your children doesn't like Chinese food or one of your friends had it just last night?). As you can see, this real-life example illustrates several features proposals must have in order to be effective. You need to persuade others that the solution proposed is possible—that budgetary and other constraints have been taken into account—and that it is a good one—that it considers alternatives and anticipates objections.

People in many walks of life do this kind of problem solving when they write proposals. One common type of proposal is the grant proposal, in which a writer requests funding to support a project. For example, scientists define research problems in their field and write a proposal to the National Science Foundation or some other potential sponsor in which they explain why the line of investigation they intend to pursue promises to yield significant findings. Bids for contracts by, say, engineering firms are proposals explaining how the firms would solve a manufacturing company's problem of solid waste disposal or improve the efficiency of assembly-line production.

Many proposals involve problems and solutions in matters of public policy. For example, private foundations and government agencies commission bodies of experts to study problems in their fields—education, the environment, civil rights, international trade, labor relations—and to issue reports with proposals for change. By the same token, citizens' organizations and advocacy groups of all sorts—from neighborhood and church associations to local preservationist and environmental groups to national organizations such as Greenpeace, the National Organization for Women (NOW), and the National Rifle Association (NRA)—also study problems, consider alternatives, and make recommendations to appropriate government bodies. Their proposals seek to gain public support and influence government policy.

In order to explore the main features shared by these different kinds of proposals, let's look at a situation that might call for a written proposal. A local community group thinks that a vacant lot the city owns could be converted into a neighborhood park. The group knows that there's strong support for local parks and recreation among city residents and municipal officials. But it also knows that the city's resources are limited, so any proposal involving spending would need ample justification—to show that the proposed park would solve a problem of some urgency and consequence. For example, the group might show that, compared to other areas of the city, the neighborhood lacks recreational facilities. Or, if the lot has given rise to other problems—if, for example, it is becoming a site for drug dealing or vandalism—the group might argue that a park could simultaneously solve those problems. For the proposal to be persuasive, it would require a clear and convincing statement of the problem and of the general goals and specific objectives being proposed.

In its proposal, the group would need to show that the proposed solution will have the intended effects. If the group claims that drug dealing is part of the problem, then its proposal needs to explain exactly how turning the lot into a park can, in fact, get rid of the dealers. But this isn't enough. The group would also need to show that the solution deals with the problem in the best, most appropriate way, given the alternatives available and the needs and values of the people affected (perhaps drug dealing could be dealt with more cheaply and effectively through increased police surveillance; perhaps the lot is too small to serve all age groups, and the neighborhood and city would be better off expanding a park in an adjoining neighborhood). A proposal that is both capable of solving the problem and suitable for doing so is said to be *feasible.* To have a chance of being implemented, a proposal needs to establish that it passes the *feasibility test*—that its solution will have the intended effects and that it fits the situation.

Proposals often require research. The community group proposing the park could strengthen its case considerably, for example, by showing that the proposed park fits the needs of the neighborhood, given the age and interests of its residents. This information could be obtained by surveying households, as could specifics about the kinds of recreational facilities to include in the park. And by comparing the parks in their neighborhood to those elsewhere in the city, the group could argue that their neighborhood needs to be brought up to the city standard.

Depending on the situation, proposal writers may be called on to present certain information in a certain order. Funding agencies often have particular guidelines that writers need to follow, and companies often have standard forms for preparing proposals. More generally, proposals tend to have a structure that reflects their two basic elements: statement of a problem and proposal of a solution.

Proposals need to convince readers—to fund a project, to implement a solution, to change a policy. Proposals are a form of persuasive writing, and clear statements of problems and solutions, demonstrations of feasibility, documentation through research, and careful organization can all help make a proposal persuasive to readers.

EXPLORING YOUR EXPERIENCE

In our daily lives, as just noted, we are constantly making proposals. Analyze one such proposal by describing an instance in which you encountered a situation, defined it as a problem, and proposed a solution. Explain the steps you followed to define the problem, consider alternatives, anticipate objections, and formulate a feasible solution—even though you probably did not experience the problem solving you engaged in as a series of steps. Looking back on this experience, what made your solution successful or unsuccessful? Were there any unforeseen consequences?

READINGS

Leon Botstein, "Let Teenagers Try Adulthood"

Leon Botstein is the president of Bard College and author of *Jefferson's Children: Education and the Promise of American Culture.* The following proposal appeared on the op-ed page of the *New York Times* in May 1999, shortly after the school shootings in Littleton, Colorado.

Let Teenagers Try Adulthood
LEON BOTSTEIN

1   The national outpouring after the Littleton shootings has forced us to confront something we have suspected for a long time: the American high school is obsolete and should be abolished. In the last month, high school students present and past have come forward with stories about cliques and the artificial intensity of a world defined by insiders and outsiders, in which the insiders hold sway because of superficial definitions of good looks and attractiveness, popularity, and sports prowess.

2   The team sports of high school dominate more than student culture. A community's loyalty to the high school system is often based on the extent to which varsity teams succeed. High school administrators and faculty members are often former coaches, and the coaches themselves are placed in a separate, untouchable category. The result is that the culture of the inside elite is not contested by the adults in the school. Individuality and dissent are discouraged.

3   But the rules of high school turn out not to be the rules of life. Often the high school outsider becomes the more successful and admired adult. The definitions of masculinity and femininity go through sufficient transformation to make the game of popularity in high school an embarrassment. No other group of adults young or old is confined to an age-segregated environment, much like a gang in which individuals of the same age group define each other's world. In no workplace, not even in colleges or universities, is there such a narrow segmentation by chronology.

4   Given the poor quality of recruitment and training for high school teachers, it is no wonder that the curriculum and the enterprise of learning hold so little sway over young people. When puberty meets education and learning in modern America, the victory of puberty masquerading as popular culture and the tyranny of peer groups based on ludicrous values meet little resistance.

5   By the time those who graduate from high school go on to college and realize what really is at stake in becoming an adult, too many opportunities have been

lost and too much time has been wasted. Most thoughtful young people suffer the high school environment in silence and in their junior and senior years mark time waiting for college to begin. The Littleton killers, above and beyond the psychological demons that drove them to violence, felt trapped in the artificiality of the high school world and believed it to be real. They engineered their moment of undivided attention and importance in the absence of any confidence that life after high school could have a different meaning.

6   Adults should face the fact that they don't like adolescents and that they have used high school to isolate the pubescent and hormonally active adolescent away from both the picture-book idealized innocence of childhood and the more accountable world of adulthood. But the primary reason high school doesn't work anymore, if it ever did, is that young people mature substantially earlier in the late 20th century than they did when the high school was invented. For example, the age of first menstruation has dropped at least two years since the beginning of this century, and not surprisingly, the onset of sexual activity has dropped in proportion. An institution intended for children in transition now holds young adults back well beyond the developmental point for which high school was originally designed.

7   Furthermore, whatever constraints to the presumption of adulthood among young people may have existed decades ago have now fallen away. Information and images, as well as the real and virtual freedom of movement we associate with adulthood, are now accessible to every fifteen- and sixteen-year-old.

8   Secondary education must be rethought. Elementary school should begin at age four or five and end with the sixth grade. We should entirely abandon the concept of the middle school and junior high school. Beginning with the seventh grade, there should be four years of secondary education that we may call high school. Young people should graduate at sixteen rather than eighteen.

9   They could then enter the real world, the world of work or national service, in which they would take a place of responsibility alongside older adults in mixed company. They could stay at home and attend junior college, or they could go away to college. For all the faults of college, at least the adults who dominate the world of colleges, the faculty, were selected precisely because they were exceptional and different, not because they were popular. Despite the often cavalier attitude toward teaching in college, at least physicists know their physics, mathematicians know and love their mathematics, and music is taught by musicians, not by graduates of education schools, where the disciplines are subordinated to the study of classroom management.

10   For those sixteen-year-olds who do not want to do any of the above, we might construct new kinds of institutions, each dedicated to one activity, from science to dance, to which adolescents could devote their energies while working together with professionals in those fields.

11   At sixteen, young Americans are prepared to be taken seriously and to develop the motivations and interests that will serve them well in adult life. They need to enter a world where they are not in a lunchroom with only their peers, estranged from other age groups and cut off from the game of life as it is really played. There is nothing utopian about this idea; it is immensely practical and efficient, and its

implementation is long overdue. We need to face biological and cultural facts and not prolong the life of a flawed institution that is out of date.

Analysis: Facing the Facts

Leon Botstein's proposal to abolish high school as we currently know it is likely to come as a surprise to many readers. After all, high school is one of those institutions we take for granted, and we think of it, whether fondly or not, as a stage of life that everyone goes through. Botstein wants to change all that. In his view, high school has such serious problems that we should rethink the whole schooling system instead of trying to reform it.

Notice that Botstein is assuming that his intended readers will recognize the problems of high schools that he details in the opening paragraphs (cliques, the dominance of athletics, recruitment and training of teachers). To get his readers to take seriously his proposal to abolish high schools, however, Botstein needs to take them further—to "face the fact" that American high schools are obsolete because they've been used to isolate young people who are biologically and culturally mature from the world of adulthood. Whether readers will agree that Botstein's proposal is a feasible one, of course, remains to be seen. Nonetheless, by defining the problem of high school as that of an obsolete system of age segregation, Botstein is able to show how his proposal "faces the fact" that teenagers are ready to be taken seriously and to join the adult world.

FOR CRITICAL INQUIRY

1. What are the reasons Botstein gives to support his view that "high school doesn't work anymore"? Notice that he reserves the "primary reason" for the sixth paragraph. Consider the effect on readers of the way he has arranged his reasons.

2. What assumptions about high schools and American teenagers is Botstein counting on his intended readers to share with him? How do these shared assumptions help to establish the grounds for Botstein's proposal?

3. What are the "facts" Botstein thinks we need to "face"? How does Botstein's call to "face the facts" appeal to his readers?

4. How feasible is Botstein's proposal? What differing views would have to be addressed to establish the proposal's feasibility?

Barbara Ehrenreich, "Stop Ironing the Diapers"

Barbara Ehrenreich is a contributing editor of *Harper's*, a regular contributor to the *Nation*, and the author of a dozen books, including *Fear of Falling: The Inner Life of the Middle Class* (1989) and *Nickel and Dimed: On (Not) Getting By in America* (2000). The following essay, which originally appeared in *Ms.* magazine, is typical of her witty and pointed writing on gender and class.

Stop Ironing the Diapers

BARBARA EHRENREICH

1   I was saddened to read, a few weeks ago, that a group of young women is planning a conference on that ancient question: is it possible to raise children and have a career at the same time? A group of young *men*—now that would be interesting. But I had thought that among women the issue had been put to rest long ago with a simple retort, Is it possible to raise children *without* having some dependable source of income with which to buy them food, clothing, and Nintendo?

2   Of course, what the young women are worried about is whether it's possible to raise children *well* while at the same time maintaining one's membership in the labor force. They have heard of "quality time." They are anxious about "missing a stage." They are afraid they won't have the time to nudge their offsprings' tiny intellects in the direction of the inevitable SATs.

3   This is not only silly but dangerous. Except under the most adverse circumstances—such as homelessness, unsafe living conditions, or lack of spouse and child care—child-raising was not *meant* to be a full-time activity. No culture on earth outside of mid-century suburban America has ever deployed one woman per child without simultaneously assigning her such major productive activities as weaving, farming, gathering, temple maintenance, and tent building. The reason is that full-time, one-on-one child-raising is not good for women *or* children. And it is on the strength of that anthropological generalization, as well as my own two decades of motherhood, that I offer you my collected tips on *how to raise your children at home in your spare time.*

4   1. *Forget the "stages."* The women who are afraid to leave home because they might "miss a stage" do not realize that all "stages" last more than ten minutes. Sadly, some of them last fifteen years or more. Even the most cursory parent, who drops in only to change clothes and get the messages off the answering machine, is unlikely to miss a "stage." Once a "stage" is over—and let us assume it is a particularly charming one, involving high-pitched squeals of glee and a rich flow of spittle down the chin—the best thing you can do is *forget it* at once. The reason for this is that no self-respecting six-year-old wants to be reminded that she was once a fat little fool in a high chair; just as no thirteen-year-old wants to be reminded that she was ever, even for a moment, a six-year-old.

5   I cannot emphasize this point strongly enough: the parent who insists on remembering the "stages"—and worse still, bringing them up—risks turning that drool-faced little darling into a *lifelong enemy*. I mean, try to see it from the child's point of view: suppose you were condemned to being two and a half feet tall, unemployed, and incontinent for an indefinite period of time. Would you want people reminding you of this unfortunate phase for the rest of your life?

6   2. *Forget "quality time."* I tried it once on May 15, 1978. I know because it is still penciled into my 1978 appointment book. "Kids," I announced, "I have forty-five minutes. Let's have some quality time!" They looked at me dully in the man-

ner of rural retirees confronting a visitor from the Census Bureau. Finally, one of them said, in a soothing tone, "Sure, Mom, but could it be after *Gilligan's Island?*"

7   The same thing applies to "talks," as in "Let's sit down and have a little talk." In response to that—or the equally lame "How's school?"—any self-respecting child will assume the demeanor of a prisoner of war facing interrogation. The only thing that works is *low-quality* time: time in which you—and they—are ostensibly doing something else, like housework. Even a two-year-old can dust or tidy and thereby gain an exaggerated sense of self-importance. In fact, this is the only sensible function of housework, the other being to create the erroneous impression that you do not live with children at all.

8   Also, do not underestimate the telephone as a means of parent-child communication. Teenagers especially recognize it as an instrument demanding full disclosure, in infinite detail, of their thoughts, ambitions, and philosophical outlook. If you want to know what's on their minds, call them from work. When you get home, they'll be calling someone else.

9   3. *Do not overload their intellects.* Many parents, mindful of approaching nursery-school entrance exams, PSATs, GREs, and so forth, stay up late into the night reading back issues of *Scientific American* and the *Cliff's Notes* for the *Encyclopedia Britannica*. This is in case the child should ask a question, such as "Why do horses walk on their hands?" The *overprepared* parent answers with a twenty-minute disquisition on evolution, animal husbandry, and DNA, during which the child slinks away in despair, determined never to ask a question again, except possibly the indispensable "Are we there yet?"

10   The part-time parent knows better, and responds only in vague and elusive ways, letting her voice trail off and her eyes wander to some mythical landscape, as in: "Well, they don't when they fight....No, then they rear up....Or when they fly...like Pegasus...mmmm." This system invariably elicits a stream of eager questions, which can then be referred to a more reliable source.

11   4. *Do not attempt to mold them.* First, because it takes too much time. Second, because a child is not a salmon mousse. A child is a temporarily disabled and stunted version of a larger person, whom you will someday know. Your job is to help them overcome the disabilities associated with their size and inexperience so that they get on with being that larger person, and in a form that you might *like* to know.

12   Hence, the part-time parent encourages self-reliance in all things. For example, from the moment my children mastered Pidgin English, they were taught one simple rule: Never wake a sleeping adult. I was mysterious about the consequences, but they became adept, at age two, at getting their own cereal and hanging out until a responsible hour. Also, contrary to widespread American myth, no self-respecting toddler enjoys having wet and clammy buns. Nor is the potty concept alien to the one-year-old mind. So do not make the common mistake of withholding the toilet facilities until the crisis of nursery-school matriculation forces the issue.

13   5. *Do not be afraid they will turn on you, someday, for being a lousy parent.* They *will* turn on you. They will also turn on the full-time parents, the cookie-making parents, the Little League parents, and the all-sacrificing parents. If you are at work every day when they get home from school, they will turn on you, eventually, for being a selfish,

neglectful careerist. If you are at home every day, eagerly awaiting their return, they will turn on you for being a useless, unproductive layabout. This is all part of the normal process of "individuation," in which one adult ego must be trampled into the dust in order for one fully formed teenage ego to emerge. Accept it.

14   Besides, a part-time parent is unlikely to ever harbor that most poisonous of all parental thoughts: "What I gave up for you...!" No child should have to take the rap for wrecking a grown woman's brilliant career. The good part-time parent convinces her children that they are positive assets, without whose wit and insights she would never have gotten the last two promotions.

15   6. *Whether you work outside the home or not, never tell them that being a mommy is your "job."* Being a mommy is a relationship, not a profession. Nothing could be worse for a child's self-esteem than to think that you think that being with her is *work*. She may come to think that you are involved in some obscure manufacturing process in which she is only the raw material. She may even come to think that her real mom was switched at birth, and that you are the baby-sitter. Which leads to my final tip:

16   7. Even if you are not a part-time parent, even if you haven't the slightest intention of entering the wide world of wage earning, *pretend that you are one.*

Analysis: Finding a Solution by Redefining the Problem

Barbara Ehrenreich opens her apparently light-hearted proposal to "raise your children at home in your spare time" by establishing a serious context of issues, namely the conflicts women feel about having a career and raising children. Notice that she is assuming her intended readers will acknowledge this conflict as a real and pressing problem. The solution Ehrenreich proposes speaks directly to the feelings of guilt young women have about being good mothers when they are pursuing careers. But instead of giving advice on how to balance the two, Ehrenreich says the problem itself needs to be redefined—that it is "silly and dangerous" to think that child-rearing was meant to be a full-time occupation.

The seven numbered proposals that follow—Ehrenreich's "collected tips"—use the standard format of advice giving you find in women's magazines and elsewhere to explain exactly how you can "raise children in your spare time." As you can see, the proposals contain a good deal of common sense, and yet, at the same time, they also call into question some of the dominant expectations about parenting young women (and men) are likely to have. And in this way, Ehrenreich uses the genre of proposals not only to give sound advice but to redefine a problem and thereby to show how her solutions logically follow.

FOR CRITICAL INQUIRY

1. How does Ehrenreich establish a problem and then redefine it?

2. Ehrenreich's proposal to "raise children in your spare time" is based on the claim that "full-time, one-on-one child-raising is not good for women

or children." What evidence does she use to support this view? Where does it appear?

3. The tone of Ehrenreich's proposal is light-hearted and serious at the same time. How does this combination shape Ehrenreich's ethos? Why do you think she has chosen this strategy?

4. Bring to class a women's magazine such as *Mademoiselle, Glamour,* or *Cosmopolitan* that features an advice-giving article. These are typically titled "Twelve Signs Your Love Life Is Going Wrong" or "Who Needs Plastic Surgery?" Consider how the advice-giving article and Ehrenreich's proposal use a similar format. What do you see as the main differences? What does Ehrenreich do that the article does not do?

Shonda Anderson, "Female Boxing: A Fieldwork Proposal for Soc. 215 Participant Observation"

The following proposal was written for a sociology course on participant observation. The course required students to design and carry out a fieldwork project by both observing and participating in a setting of their choice. Shonda Anderson decided to investigate the world of female boxing by regularly visiting a gym where she could watch other women in training as well as do some training herself. The fieldwork proposal she wrote is fairly typical of the writing researchers of all sorts do to explain the problem they want to investigate and the steps they propose to carry out the research.

Female Boxing: A Fieldwork Proposal

SHONDA ANDERSON

Shonda Anderson
Soc. 215
January 25, 2001

Introduction

1   Over the past several years, female boxing has emerged on the professional sports scene. The daughters of Muhammed Ali, Joe Frazier, and George Foreman have been heavily promoted as undercards at major prize fights. The film *Girl Fight* received critical acclaim and increased media attention to female boxing. It remains to be seen, though, whether professional female boxing has a future or whether the heightened publicity is short-lived and dependent on nostalgic narratives of legendary heavyweight champions at a time when highly talented and charismatic male heavyweights are hard to find.

2   In any case, the boxing matches seen on TV and pay-per-view are not representative of the sport overall but encompass a mere 5% of boxers. My hypothesis

is that there are many levels at which men and women box—professional, amateur, and recreational. To understand the sport and the attraction it has for women, I want to look at the many reasons and different ways women participate in the sport and not just at the media spectacle that represents female boxing as a gimmick and a sideshow. I want to understand why ordinary women take up boxing and what role it plays in their lives.

Research Question

3   Boxing has traditionally been coded as a male sport, the so-called "manly arts." Recently, however, gender barriers have been dropping in the world of sports, and women have become involved in sports once reserved for men, from pole vaulting in track and field to the new professional women's football league. My main research question asks how women boxers negotiate their gender roles and create a sense of self in the formerly all-male world of the gym and the ring. What obstacles do they encounter and how do they cope with them? How do women learn to fight—to take on behaviors traditionally identified with males and proscribed in females?

Research Plan

4   The site of my participant observation is Gleason's Gym, a longtime boxing gym in Brooklyn, New York. Some 800 boxers—professional, amateur, and recreational—train with over 68 trainers at Gleason's. Gleason's is known in the world of boxing as one of the liveliest, happening, and serious gyms in New York. Gleason's also trains a fair number of female boxers. These women come from all classes of society and all walks of life. They include whites, African Americans, and Latinas, gay and straight women.

5   My plan is to visit Gleason's Gym once a week for four hours each time over a twelve week period. My research strategy is based on observation, interviews, and participation.

6   *Observation.* I plan to observe both men and women training and sparring. I am particularly interested in what trainers say to men and women, what advice they give, and whether they hype up their boxers by appealing to gender identities. I am interested too in what spectators say when male and female boxers enter the ring to spar. I also plan to observe the physical setting to identify gendered signs, such as the mannequin I saw on my preliminary visit that had "ex-husband" written on it.

7   *Interviewing.* I plan to talk to female and male boxers, trainers, and managers—to gain a broad perspective on why men and women box and what people in the boxing world think about female boxers. I will ask both men and women boxers why they go to the gym, what appeals to them about boxing, and how training makes them feel. I will ask trainers how they devise training plans for men and women and how they decide someone has enough training to enter the ring and spar. Finally, I will ask female boxers what they think of other female boxers and what their feelings are about violence.

8   *Participation.* One of the best ways for me to understand the world of female boxing is to work with a trainer. I plan to devote part of my time at the gym each week to my own training as a boxer. At this point, I do not know whether I want to enter the ring and spar with a partner. Entering the ring is a heavily symbolic moment for boxers, a rite of passage from training with weights, bags, jump ropes, and so on to actually boxing with another person. Whatever I decide to do, encountering the choice will help me understand the mentality of boxers.

Significance of Research

9   My research should shed some light on how women devise strategies and identities to deal with the obstacles they confront as participants in largely male sports. It may also help develop an understanding of women's relationship to violence, as they turn from the conventional image of females as the victims of violence to become originators of violence.

Analysis: Research Proposals

Research proposals are similar in many respects to other types of proposals, whether to change a policy or improve a service. The same task of defining a problem and then proposing a satisfactory solution is common to all. What distinguishes a research proposal is that the problem is one of understanding something—the structure of DNA, the effects of mass media, or the phenomenon of female boxing—and the solution is to design a workable research plan to investigate the subject and produce new insights. Most research proposals seek to persuade the reader about the merit of the research and the researcher's ability to carry it out. In the case of Shonda Anderson's "Female Boxing: A Fieldwork Proposal," the goal is that her instructor will approve the proposal.

The research question or questions in a proposal are crucial. As you can see in "Female Boxing: A Fieldwork Proposal," Shonda Anderson's research plan follows from the questions she wants to answer. Explaining the central research questions accomplishes two things in the proposal. First, it tells readers why the research is meaningful. Second, it enables them to judge whether the proposed plan of action is in fact well-suited to make sense of Shonda's questions.

FOR CRITICAL INQUIRY

1. Consider the relationship between the two paragraphs in the introduction. How does the first paragraph establish a context for the hypothesis presented in the second paragraph? What is the function of this hypothesis in terms of defining the research problem?

2. Evaluate the match between the research question and the research plan. Does the research plan seem capable of providing answers to the questions Shonda raises? Why or why not?

3. What do you see as the strengths and weaknesses of the research proposal? Would you approve it? What suggestions would you offer to modify or refine the proposed research?

Henry Jenkins, "Lessons from Littleton: What Congress Doesn't Want to Hear About Youth and the Media"

Henry Jenkins directs the Comparative Media Studies program at MIT and is the author of a study of *Star Trek* fans, *Textual Poachers: Television Fans and Participatory Culture,* and of video games, *From Mortal Kombat to Barbie.* In the wake of the shootings at Columbine High, Jenkins testified at the Senate Commerce Committee's hearings on the marketing of violent entertainment to youth.

Lessons from Littleton:
What Congress Doesn't Want to Hear About Youth and the Media
HENRY JENKINS

Part I: Profile of Moral Panic

1   In Risk and Blame, Anthropologist Mary Douglas describes the cultural basis for witch hunts in traditional societies. "Whether the witch is able to do harm or not, the attribution of a hidden power to hurt is a weapon of attack against them....A successful accusation is one that has enough credibility for a public outcry to remove the opportunity of repeating the damage." A moral panic starts with an unspeakable tragedy which sparks an attempt to ascribe blame and responsibility. Initially, accusations flow freely but focus on those targets who are already the subject of anxiety. Douglas notes, "Though anyone can accuse, not all accusations will be accepted. To be successful an accusation must be directed against victims hated by the populace. The cause of harm must be vague, unspecific, difficult to prove or disprove." Once one accusation sticks, it becomes easier to pile on charges. Our rush to judgement overwhelms our ability to rationally assess the evidence. Our need to take action supersedes our ability to anticipate consequences. Moral panic shuts down self-examination at the very moment when real problems demand careful consideration.

2   Several weeks after the shootings at Columbine High School in Littleton, Colorado, the United States Senate Commerce Committee launched a series of hearings, chaired by Sen. Sam Brownback (R-Ark.), on the "marketing of violent entertainment to children." Introducing the investigation, Brownback explained, "We are not here to point fingers but to identify the causes of cultural pollution and seek solutions." The phrase, "cultural pollution," of course, already presumed a consensus that popular culture was a worthless irritant which was to blame for various social harms. Brownback was prepared to sweep aside constitutional protections: "We are having endless debates about First and Second Amendment rights while our children are being killed and traumatized." Brownback focused

his ire on forms of popular culture that met youth rather than adult tastes: "I am willing to bet that there aren't many adults who are huge fans of teen slasher movies or the music of Cannibal Corpse and Marilyn Manson." Sen. Orin Hatch (R-Utah) declared Manson's music "tremendously offensive to everyone in America who thinks," a category that seemingly does not include a significant number of high school and college students. William Bennett, former Secretary of Education and self-proclaimed guardian of American virtue, called on Congress to make "meaningful distinctions" between works that used violence to tell "a larger story" such as Braveheart, Saving Private Ryan, or Clear and Present Danger, and works that "gratuitously" exploited violence, such as The Basketball Diaries, Cruel Intentions, or Scream. His "commonsense" distinction was at heart an ideological one, separating works that offered adult perspectives from those which expressed youth concerns.

3   Though they understood the hearings as a "ritual humiliation" of the entertainment industries, the senators were feeding a "cultural war" which was more and more focused on teenagers. As a GOP operative Mike Murphy explained in that week's Time, "we need Goth control, not gun control." Hatch engaged in homophobic banter about whether Manson was "a he or a she" while Brownback accused members of the Goth subculture of giving themselves over to "the dark side." Such comments reinforced bigotry and fear. Adult fears about popular culture were being transferred towards those people who consumed it. The Goths were a relatively small subculture whose members drew inspiration from Romantic literature and constructed their personal identity by borrowing from the iconography of the horror film and S/M pornography. The group could claim a twenty year history without much public attention because they had previously not been associated with violent crime. However, the Columbine shooters had been mistakenly identified in some early news reports as Goths and as a result, this group had been singled out in the post-Littleton backlash.

4   From the outset, Congress was unlikely to set federal policies to regulate media content, which would not have sustained constitutional scrutiny. They counted on public pressure to intimidate the entertainment industry into voluntarily withdrawing controversial works from circulation. Manson canceled some concerts. MGM stopped selling The Basketball Diaries. The Warner Brothers Network withheld the airing of the season finale of Buffy the Vampire Slayer until midsummer.

5   The biggest impact of the moral panic, however, would be felt in the schools—both public and private—as teachers and administrators increasingly saw their students as "threats" to public safety and suspected popular culture of turning good kids into brutal "monsters." Online journalist Jon Katz's remarkable series, "Voices from the Hellmouth," circulated hundreds of first-person accounts of how American schools were reacting to the shootings. As Katz reported, "Many of these kids saw themselves as targets of a new hunt for oddballs—suspects in a bizarre, systematic search for the strange and the alienated. Suddenly, in this tyranny of the normal, to be different wasn't just to feel unhappy, it was to be dangerous."

6   Many schools took away web and net access. Many kids were placed into therapy based on their subcultural identifications or interests in computer games or

certain kinds of music. Students were punished for taking controversial positions in class discussions or on essay assignments. In one case, a student was suspended for wearing a Star of David to school because his teacher thought it was a gang insignia. Another was sent home for wearing a black coat that was officially part of his ROTC uniform. One school district banned heavy coats. Knowing little or nothing about the popular culture consumed by teens, teachers, principals, and parents were striking out blindly.

7

Other educators took risks, challenging the crackdowns on "Goths" in their schools and bringing the materials that Katz had gathered back into their classrooms for dialogue with their students. Local journalists investigated Katz's reports and found them accurate. Civil rights organizations were confronting a record number of complaints from students who felt their constitutional rights were being infringed. Then-Presidential candidate Dan Quayle added fuel to the fires with a speech attacking the concept of "students rights" as an unjustified interference with classroom discipline, insisting that "Our children cannot learn in an environment of chaos...If we're going to make an error, err on the side of school safety."

Part II: What's Missing from This Picture?

8

Speaking before the Senate Commerce Committee, Lt. Col. David Grossman, the author of On Killing, asserted, "the real media critic isn't Siskel and Ebert. It's the American Medical Association and it's time to place them in charge of the FCC and other such organizations." Grossman argued that current scientific and medical understandings of "media effects" supported his demands that government actively regulate media content. Grossman proposes expanding the current category of pornography to include violent entertainment. His language consistently pathologizes culture, depicting media products as "toxic substances" analogous to cigarettes in their damaging impact on children's mental and physical health.

9

With these hearings, the decades-old "culture war" rhetoric entered a third phase. In the first phase (during the Reagan years), the religious right refashioned itself as the "moral majority" in a belated backlash against the 1960s counterculture. This phase was largely ineffective, since Democrats directly challenged its overt effort to legally mandate religious doctrines and values. The phrase, "culture war," was associated with political extremism. The second phase (the Bush years) was characterized by attacks on "political correctness" within higher education and had much more impact on public opinion, helping to decredentialize those in the Humanities and Social Sciences who sought to better understand the complex nature of American culture. In the third phase, the rhetoric of morality is displaced by the language of medicine and science; doctors are assumed to speak an objective truth about media effects. The shift towards a language of scientific objectivity has made it possible for a significant number of liberal democrats, such as Sen. Joseph Lieberman (D-Conn.) or Sen. Max Cleland (D-Georgia), to align themselves with conservative Republicans in calling for the regulation of media content.

The Pseudo-science of Media Effects

10   However, there are many problems with this "scientific" approach to culture. For starters, the American Medical Association has no specific cultural expertise. We can trace a long history of misdirected attacks by medical authorities against popular culture, dating at least as far back as the efforts in Shakespeare's England to close the theaters in the name of public hygiene. In most cases, the medical establishment promotes a fairly conservative agenda, suspicious of those cultural forms associated with the working class or ethnic and racial minorities, making recommendations that ratify their own tastes and quarantine works they dislike.

11   Despite Grossman's claims, cultural works are not carcinogens: cultural works are complex and contradictory, open to many different interpretations, subject to various unanticipated uses. Popular culture's complex relationship with its consumers cannot be reduced to simple variables or tested through lab experiments. Even if such rigor were possible, media activists exaggerate the body of scientific evidence supporting their claims. To date, relatively few studies have examined the impact of video and computer games upon teens and nobody knows how relevant research on television is to our consumption of interactive media.

12   The best media effects researchers qualify their findings and few argue for a direct link between consuming media images and performing real world violence. If video game violence was an immediate catalyst, we would have difficulty explaining why none of the shootings involving teens have occurred in movie theaters or video arcades where the direct stimulus of game playing would be most acute. Instead, these murders have tended to occur in schools and we need to look at real world factors to discover what triggers such violence. A more careful analysis would read video games as one cultural influence among many, as having different degrees of impact on different children, and as not sufficient in and of themselves to provoke an otherwise healthy and well-adjusted child to engage in acts of violence. Some children, especially those who are antisocial and emotionally unbalanced, should be protected from exposure to the most extreme forms of media violence, but most children are not at risk from the media they consume. Parents, not governments, are in the best position to know what kinds of culture their children should consume. Media activists strip aside those careful qualifications, claiming that the computer games are "murder simulators" teaching our children to kill.

13   Our current legal definitions of obscenity insist that the work must be "taken as a whole," read according to prevailing community standards, and judged to be "utterly without redeeming…value." Media effects research, on the other hand, places little or no interest on the work as a whole or to the work's meanings or values. It adopts a crude stimulus-response model of media consumption and focuses on localized "media images" not on their function within larger stories. In many cases, research subjects are forced to watch a rapid succession of violent images removed from any narrative context. Much of this research makes little or no distinction between different kinds of stories our culture might tell about violence.

14   Much media effects research removes media consumption from real world contexts and situates it in a laboratory. But media never functions in a vacuum. Playing a game in an arcade is a very different experience than playing it in one's own home or as part of a military training exercise. Media consumption gains its meaning through association with a range of other activities that constitute our everyday life.

15   Media effects research shows limited interest in what those stories mean to the people who consume them. The focus has been on measurable biological responses—neural stimulation, pulse, heart beat, pupil dilation. Such research essentially measures the adrenaline rush that occurs when we play an exciting video game. Yet, neural stimulation is only part of the story. As current cognitive research into emotion suggests, the human body experiences remarkably similar degrees of neural stimulation riding a car off a bridge and riding a roller coaster, but one is experienced as terrifying and the other pleasurable. The difference has to do with our interpretations of those initial neural stimulations.

16   Much media effects research assumes a casual connection between the physiological reactions or attitudinal shifts measured in the laboratory and subsequent real world behavior. In a 1994 study, on the other hand, Ann Hagell and Tim Newburn noted that prisoners serving time for violent crimes had, on average, consumed far less media than the general population.

17   Media effects research systematically deskills children, often assuming that they cannot separate fantasy from reality. Activists compound this problem by ignoring considerable developmental differences between small children and teens. Children at a relatively early age, around four or five, began to make basic distinctions between realistic and fantastic representations of violence, with documentary images (news reports of local crime, historical footage of war, nature footage of predators and prey) far more emotionally disturbing than cartoons or video games. Primatologists note that many mammals make basic distinctions between play violence and actual violence. The same two animals might jostle playfully in one context or fight to the death in another, depending on the presence or absence of "play faces" or reassuring noises. Surely, our children can make the same distinctions.

Part III: A More Humanistic Perspective

18   Media effects research enjoys its current government support not because it is the best methodology for understanding the relationship between media consumption and real world behavior but because its stimulus-response model offers simple solutions to complex problems. To really understand the place of violent entertainment in contemporary youth culture, we must broaden the conversation to include researchers of many different methodologies—anthropologists, criminologists, social and cultural historians, media scholars, experts on children's play and literature, and so forth. Rather than starting from the assumption that we are investigating what media content is doing to our children, we should ask what our children are doing with the media they consume. We are living through a period of profound media transition: the availability of new entertainment and informa-

tion technologies impact all aspects of our social, cultural, political, economic, and educational experience. Children are often the first to embrace these new technologies and have discovered complex new ways to employ them in their social interactions with their friends, their recreational activities, their creative expression, their homework, and their political lives. We trivialize these changes when we reduce the important conversations we should be having about future directions for technological development into a moralistic debate about violent video games. My field, Comparative Media Studies, adopts humanistic and qualitative social science methodologies to better understand those changes and explain them to the general public. Humanistic research paints a very different picture of media consumption than found in the media effects literature.

19 First, media consumption is assumed to be active (something we do) not passive (something that happens to us). Media technologies are tools and we can use them in a variety of different ways—some constructive, some destructive.

20 Second, media consumption is assumed to be a process; we work on media content over a long period of time; our immediate emotional reactions are only part of what one needs to understand if you want to predict real world consequences of media consumption.

21 Third, different consumers react to the same media content in fundamentally different ways as it is fit into their larger understanding of the world and so universalizing claims are fundamentally inadequate for accounting for media's social and cultural impact.

22 Fourth, consumer response to media is more often creative than imitative. All of us construct our own personal mythologies from the contents made available to us through the mass media and we are drawn towards images and stories that are personally meaningful to us because they match the way we see the world. We use them as vehicles to explore who we are, what we want, what we value, and how we relate to other people. Harris and Kleibold were drawn towards darker and more violent images and invested those images with their most anti-social impulses. Another child might use those same images to emphasize the need for community and friendship in a world marked by violence and competition.

23 Finally, real life trumps media images every time. Media images are read against our perception of the world which is built up through countless direct experiences. Real life has the power to exert material consequences. Harris and Kleibold were legally required to go to school; they were subjected to real ridicule and abuse from their classmates and this real world brutality helped to motivate their actions. Popular entertainment does not exert this same kind of coercive control over us. Media content is more likely to reinforce—rather than fundamentally alter—our existing prejudices and predispositions.

The Meaningfulness of Violent Entertainment

24 Media effects research has had little to say about why children are drawn towards violent entertainment, except to ascribe a universalized blood lust. Humanistic research, on the other hand, offers useful tools for understanding why children find media violence attractive and meaningful. The materials of popular

culture are read as modern myths that reflect the values and desires of the people who produce and consume them. Although we need to spend much more time talking with teens about their relationship to popular culture before we can offer a full account, one can point to a number of possible explanations for the appeal of violent entertainment.

25　　First, violent entertainment offers teens a fantasy of empowerment. The "Quake girls," for example, are a subculture of young women who understand playing violent video games in explicitly feminist terms—as an opportunity to compete aggressively with boys without regard to biological differences and by doing so, to rehearse for later professional competitions. But, many boys come home from being bullied at school and also experience an enormous release in playing violent games. Blood and thunder imagery runs through the history of boyhood play and fantasy. Game images echo the pictures another generation of boys drew with crayons on their notebooks or had in their heads as they hurled pinecones on the playground. The new technologies make these images more vivid and more open to adult scrutiny, but they do not fundamentally alter the contents of boys' imaginations.

26　　Second, violent entertainment offers teens a fantasy of transgression, a chance to test the limits of their parent's culture. Slasher films, for example, often depict a world where parents' attempts to protect teens from harsh realities place kids at risk and where adults dismiss youth efforts to explain monstrous events they have observed. Such films are often the only works that take seriously the experience of nonconformist teens who do not get the positive reinforcement received by football heroes and homecoming queens. After a decade of attacks on political correctness, is it any surprise that many students prefer to be politically incorrect, to embrace forms of culture that seek to shock adults or that express fundamentally antisocial fantasies (whether in the form of South Park or Red Neck Rampage)?

27　　Third, violent entertainment offers teens an acknowledgment that the world is not all sweetness and light. The child psychologist Bruno Bettelheim argues that the violence and darkness of fairy tales is important for children to confront as a means of acknowledging the darker sides of their own nature. Without such a depiction, children might take their own transgressive impulses as evidence that they are a "monster," rather than learning how to recognize and control those aspects of themselves. One Goth teen told me that he had been treated like a monster all of his life, by parents, teachers, and classmates, and so he had adopted a Goth persona because for the first time, it allowed him to decide what kind of monster he wanted to be and helped him to identify other teens who also felt stigmatized. Many teens come from broken homes, encounter domestic violence, confront poverty, and worry about crime in their own neighborhoods. Not surprisingly, they are drawn towards representations of the world which are dark and pessimistic and which acknowledge these troubling experiences.

28　　Fourth, violent entertainment offers teens an intensification of emotional experience. Adolescence is a time of powerful, often overwhelming feelings. If teens are going to escape the intense feelings of rejection or damaged self-esteem they often experience, they require forms of popular culture that are loud and raucous, have pumped up style, promise speed and spectacle, offer abrupt shifts between the comic and the violent. Their fascination with violent video games is as much a response to their aesthetic qualities as to their explicit content.

29   In short, teens aren't drawn to Quake or Scream because they are blood thirsty or because they think violence is the best real world response to their problems. These works offer them the best available vehicle for their fantasies of empowerment, take seriously what young people feel and think about the adult world, acknowledge the darker sides of the teenagers' everyday experiences, and offer an intense release from real world tensions. If, for moral, political, or aesthetic, reasons we find such violent entertainment reprehensible, then we are going to have to offer new genres that satisfy those basic urges at least as well.

Part IV: Proposals for the Future

30   All of the above suggests a fairly simple conclusion: we should not let moral panic push us to abandon our commitment to free expression and to embrace increased government regulation of cultural content. We should take seriously our children's relationship to popular culture and create contexts where we can better understand what roles media plays in their lives. The knee-jerk reactions to the Littleton shooting caused tremendous damage as adult authorities struck out blindly against nonconformist students, insuring that we further alienated those already feeling alien and closed the door to meaningful adult-youth communication. As the one-year anniversary of the Littleton shootings approaches, we need to reassess how we engage with controversies over popular culture. Educators should adopt a basic ethical principle—above all, do no harm. The following are some aspects of a more constructive response to these issues:

I. Supportive digital communities for youth

31   Harris and Kleibold weren't alienated because they went online. The online world offers many teens a new opportunity for social connections, for finding friends outside the often closed community of their own high schools. For example, online interventions are a powerful weapon for slowing the rate of gay and lesbian teen suicide at a time when many other institutions have failed to respond to the homophobia in their daily lives or offer basic information about their emerging sexuality. For kids who are social pariahs, the online world offers a chance to find someone out there, anywhere on the planet, who doesn't think you are a hopeless geek. Some concerned adults responded to Littleton by constructing welcoming communities for teens who feel alienated from their classmates and school authorities. Projects, such as hsunderground.com, channel antisocial impulses into more constructive directions, offering a degree of free speech not found in even the most progressive private school, connecting angry kids to a larger social community.

2. The demand for K–12 media education

32   Media education has historically been an occasional treat but not a central aspect of the educational process. As media change influences all of our core institutions and practices, we need to acknowledge that media literacy is a basic skill,

part of what it means to be a good researcher and writer, an intelligent citizen or a shrewd consumer. Children already have a greater degree of media literacy than we imagine but our refusal to mobilize those skills in the classroom, to value what teens have taught themselves about media, helps to build a wall between school teaching and real world experience. Media education can take many forms, ranging from whole courses dealing with media and modern culture to more localized lessons on the ways communication technologies influenced the development of American democracy or on how to assess the reliability of different information sources.

3. Adult knowledge and respect for popular culture

33 The "moral panic" embodied adult anxieties and ignorance about youth culture. Media education too often functions as an excuse for adults to impose their judgements, rather than as a means for mutual learning. Adults need to take the time to listen to what their children have to say about popular culture, just as we make time to listen to what children tell us about their little league games or band practices. We need to listen and learn because these forms of cultural consumption are an important part of children's lives. Schools can create opportunities for open dialogue about popular culture, but only if they lower the emotional temperature. Youths can't speak openly or honestly about their culture if the immediate adult response is to ban whatever comes to light. Adults need to enter into those conversations with an open mind, ready to rethink their prejudices, but they also must be prepared to justify their own aesthetic choices and moral values.

4. A more tolerant school environment

34 Talk to most high school students and they offer a similar explanation for the shootings: Harris and Kleibold were cut off from their classmates because they were different; their isolation turned rancid inside them until they struck out blindly against their classmates. Many teens recognize those feelings within themselves, even if most of them have the self control not to act on them. Kids, whose cultural tastes are outside their school's mainstream, feel at risk, ridiculed by their classmates and held suspect by their teachers. Our schools need to invest at least as much efforts into understanding and responding to the cultural differences introduced by contemporary youth cultures as we spend examining the historical differences between various races and ethnic groups. Every kid has the right to feel safe and welcome in their own school.

5. Parental discussion groups about media content

35 If we are going to place the responsibility of policing culture onto parents, then we have to provide the resources they need to respond intelligently to a complex and changing cultural environment. A one-size-fits-all solution doesn't work because our children aren't the same size and don't mature at the same rate and our families come from many different backgrounds and don't have the same values. The web enables parents to compare notes with other parents before purchasing a birthday or holiday gift. Such exchanges between parents about specific media content are much more valuable than ratings systems, because these ongoing interactions allow us to determine the values behind these assessments.

6. Creative responses from media producers

36   Much popular culture isn't so much dangerous as it is banal and mind-numbing. Game designers and developers depend too heavily upon formulas as a safe way of anticipating market demand. In doing so, they fall back on violent content as much out of laziness as from any desire to exploit bloodlust. For those reasons, we need to encourage the games industry to enter a phase of self-examination, to try to better understand what draws children to the existing games. The challenge is to broaden the range of available options, so that every consumer finds forms of culture that reflect their values and give expression to their fantasies. We probably can't tell stories without some element of conflict, but those conflicts can take various forms. We must explore other ways of representing and resolving conflict that supplement, even if they do not altogether replace, those currently on the market.

Analysis: From Critique to Constructive Proposals

As everyone knows, there is a long-standing debate in the United States about the effects of media violence on young people. This debate resurfaced again in the wake of the shootings at Columbine High in 1999, as commentators searched for whom or what to blame and education officials devised new policies to make their schools safe. Henry Jenkins locates his critique of current research on media effects and proposals for the future in this context of issues.

Because Jenkins is, in many respects, arguing against conventional views of media violence, he needs to do three things in order for readers to take his proposals for a very different kind of media policy seriously. First, he characterizes the current context of issues as a "moral panic" that has led to unconstitutional and oppressive school policies, as well as the threat of government regulation of cultural content. Second, he explains what's wrong with the "media effects" research that has drawn causal connections between media and actual violence. Third, he introduces an alternative type of research—what he calls a "more humanistic perspective"—that leads to very different conclusions about how young people use the media.

Notice how these three moves provide the groundwork for the six proposals at the end ("All of the above suggests....").

FOR CRITICAL INQUIRY

1. How does Jenkins give the notion of "moral panic" a sense of urgency that calls on him to write this critique and proposal?

2. In Jenkins' view, what are the shortcomings of "media effects" research?

3. What arguments does he give to explain why a "more humanistic perspective" represents a better approach to understanding the media and young people?

4. Do the six proposals he offers follow logically? What assumptions would readers have to share with Jenkins to think of these proposals as a feasible response?

Visual Design:
Advocacy Group Appeals

Advocacy group appeals often make proposals for changes in public policy. The two appeals that follow both define problems and propose solutions. The first is an open letter to President Clinton from the National Urban League calling on the Justice Department to take a series of steps to stop police killings of black unarmed civilians. The second, from U.S. English, proposes making English the official language of government in the United States.

NATIONAL URBAN LEAGUE

President Bill Clinton
The White House
Washington, DC

Dear President Clinton:

The African-American community is enraged by the recent exoneration of police officers in the fatal shootings of unarmed black civilians in several cities across the country. And we are profoundly disturbed by the unfolding scandals in the Los Angeles Police Department and in other local law enforcement agencies.

When state courts winked at lynching earlier this century and when governors defied the U.S. Constitution by maintaining segregated schools, we turned to the federal government to protect our lives and enforce our civil rights. We call upon you to exert comparable leadership today to stem police brutality and abuse and to rebuild the trust between the police and minorities that is so essential to reducing crime.

I implore you to invoke all of the statutory, regulatory and financial leverage at the federal government's disposal to compel local police departments to reform their policies and practices regarding the recruitment, training and supervision of police officers and the permissible use of firearms.

Washington actually bears some responsibility for the brutality and abuse suffered by minorities at the hands of the police. When the federal government declared war on crime, it underwrote the rapid expansion of local police departments to combat crime. But Washington did not condition the receipt of federal aid on the implementation of sound recruitment, training and supervision policies.

Thus, over the years, the federal government has subsidized the addition of thousands of ill-suited, inadequately trained and unsupervised officers who, once on the streets, have become a law unto themselves. Many of these officers have been trained in paramilitary techniques that are woefully out of synch with today's emphasis on community policing. In effect, the elite anti-crime units that were created declared unofficial martial law in the inner city and unilaterally suspended the civil liberties of minority citizens. Therefore, the National Urban League calls upon the U.S. Justice Department to:

- Promulgate a series of best practices based on the real world experience of police departments that have successfully reduced crime with minimal citizen complaints and fatalities involving unarmed civilians;
- Challenge concerned governors, mayors and police chiefs to jumpstart the reform effort by voluntarily embracing these best practices;

- Require local police departments that receive federal assistance to institute these recommended practices as a condition of continued receipt of federal aid;

- Terminate federal aid to police departments that refuse to implement best practices or that fail to resolve chronic problems of police brutality, abuse and avoidable use of deadly force; and

- Press Congress to pass the newly introduced Law Enforcement Trust and Integrity Act.

Most police officers serve our community with compassion and distinction. We welcome the sharp reduction in urban crime. Yet the repeated killings of unarmed civilians and the routine trampling of our civil rights have undermined our faith in the ability of state courts to bring the accused officers to justice and in the capacity of local police departments to police themselves. With Washington's help, police departments across the country are getting a grip on crime. It's the Justice Department's job now to make certain the police get a grip on themselves.

Sincerely,

Hugh B. Price
President,
National Urban League
120 Wall Street, NYC, 10005
www.nul.org

Analysis: Borrowing Genres to Make Proposals

The two advocacy group appeals differ in important respects from the other examples of proposals in this chapter. The earlier examples follow roughly the same pattern of organization: They define a problem, present a solution, and explain the consequences. In this sense, they are easy to recognize as proposals. The two advocacy group appeals, on the other hand, borrow from other genres to make their proposals. The National Urban League uses the genre of the open letter to define a problem ("fatal shootings of unarmed black civilians") and, in a bulleted list, to propose a series of steps to solve the problem. U.S. English uses the techniques of advertising (what is often called "social marketing") to define a problem (immigrants are being told they don't have to learn English to "assimilate") and propose a solution (make English the official language). The two appeals are noteworthy because they show that genres are not air-tight forms with a single purpose but in fact can be—and often are—combined to get messages across.

FOR CRITICAL INQUIRY

1. The National Urban League could have issued a conventional proposal to make the changes it is calling for. Why do you think the organization chose an open letter? How does the open letter establish a relationship to its intended readers (President Clinton and readers of the *Progressive*, where it appeared on May 2000)?

2. How does the U.S. English appeal use advertising techniques to fashion its message? Note in particular the photo that depicts immigrants of an earlier era. How does this photo work together with the text to convey a message?

They knew they had to learn English to survive.

How come today's immigrants are being misled?

They learned without bilingual education. And without government documents in a multitude of languages. They knew they had to learn English before anything else.

But today, a whole new generation of Americans are being fed a lie by bureaucrats, educators and self-appointed leaders for immigrant groups. The lie says "you don't have to learn English because you can make it here without assimilating." The truth is this: without learning our shared language, an immigrant's dream of a better life will fade.

With nearly 700,000 members, we're the largest organization fighting to make English the official language of government at all levels. *Join us. Support us. Fight with us.* Because now more than ever, immigrants need to be told the truth.

Speak up for America. Call 1-800-U.S.ENGLISH

U.S.ENGLISH

1747 Pennsylvania Avenue, NW, Suite 1100
Washington, DC 20006

3. Bring to class an appeal—an advertisement, flyer, poster, or letter—from a public interest group that makes a proposal. What problem does it define, what solution does it propose, and what, if anything, does it call on readers to do? How effective is the visual design? Why do you think the group decided on this particular form of appeal?

FOR DISCUSSION AND ANALYTICAL WRITING

RHETORICAL ANALYSIS

Analyze the argument in one (or more) of the proposals in this chapter. Pay particular attention to the enabling assumptions that connect the claim (the writer's proposal) and the evidence. What backing of these assumptions is offered explicitly or assumed implicitly? Consider how the shape of the writer's argument is likely to influence readers' evaluations of whether the proposal is feasible or not.

GENRE CHOICES

Think of a current problem—on campus, local, national, or international. Imagine a feasible solution to the problem. You could write a formal proposal to solve the problem, as the students who proposed a campus coffee house did. (See the proposal in "Writer's Workshop" later in this chapter.) Let's assume you're really serious about getting your proposal implemented. What other genres of writing might you use to publicize your proposal? What do you see as the purpose of those genres?

GOING ONLINE

Proposal Writing Guides

You can find a number of guides to proposal writing online. Check out one or more of the following: The Art of Proposal Writing from the Social Science Research Council <www.ssrc.org/artprop.htm>, EPA Grant-Writing Tutorial from the Environmental Protection Agency <www.epa.gov/grtlakes/seahome/grants.html>, Proposal Writing Short Course from the Foundation Center <fdncenter.org/learn/shortcourse/prop1.html>, and Hints for Writing Successful NIH Grants by Ellen Barrett at the University of Miami School of Medicine <chroma.med.miami.edu/research/Ellens_how_to.html>.

Consider the advice the Web sites offer. What seems to be crucial in writing successful proposals?

WORKING TOGETHER

Advocacy Group Proposals

Advocacy groups do a wide range of writing to publicize their proposals—including advertisements in newspapers and magazines and on radio and television, flyers, letters of appeal, posters, bumper stickers, articles in the opinion pages of newspapers, petitions, and proposals.

Work together in a group of three or four to write two pieces of different types. Follow these steps:

1. Choose an issue that could interest an advocacy group. What is a key problem connected with the issue? What might be a feasible solution to the problem? As a group, come to a consensus about a problem and feasible solution.

2. Once you have defined the problem you want to address, think about the types of writing listed above that might be most relevant for presenting your solution, and choose two. What will the specific purpose of each piece be? Who is the likely audience for each piece and how can you most effectively address this audience?

3. When you are finished, write an introduction to the project, explaining the problem you defined and the solution you proposed, why you chose the types of writing you chose, how audience and purpose were reflected in what you wrote, and what you did to make the visual design of the pieces effective.

WRITING ASSIGNMENT

For this assignment, write a proposal that formulates a problem and offers a solution. You will need to think of an existing situation that calls for attention, whether it is on campus or at the local, national, or international level. Something may be wrong that needs to be changed or corrected. Something may be lacking that needs to be added. Something worthwhile may not be working properly and therefore needs to be improved. Or it may be that a situation needs to be redefined in order to find new approaches and solutions.

Here are some specific possibilities:

■ **Proposals for new or improved services:** Proposals call on government agencies, professional associations, educational institutions, and private foundations to provide new or improved services—for example in health care, education, and recreation. The student "Proposal for a Campus Coffee House" is a good example of such a proposal for a college campus. You might write a proposal based on a situation you see on campus—to improve residential life, food service, social climate, advising, or academic programs. Or you may want to write a proposal for new or improved services in your local community or at the state or federal level.

■ **Public policy proposals:** These range from editorials in newspapers and journals of opinion to actual legislation that proposes to do things such as change immigration laws, recognize gay and lesbian relationships, require a balanced budget, or devise a national health care plan. Leon Botstein's proposal to abolish American high schools, as well as the National Urban League's proposal to improve the recruitment, training, and supervision of police officers or FAIR's call for a moratorium on immigration, offer examples of short public policy proposals that seek to influence public opinion and create a favorable political climate for the writer's plan.

■ **Proposals that redefine a well-known problem in order to present a new solution:** Proposal writers may find that the real issue begins with the way a well-known problem has been formulated. There are times when the current understanding of an issue can actually inhibit new and creative thinking to find solutions. For example, in "Lessons from Littleton: What Congress Doesn't Want to Hear About Youth and Media," Henry Jenkins identifies a problem with how media experts and politicians have understood the media's effects on young people. To set up his six "proposals for the future," Jenkins first needs to redefine the problem by showing what's wrong or missing from the current understanding of the media's effects and establish an alternative perspective. You might write a proposal that examines the conventional wisdom about an issue, redefines the problem, and presents a solution that follows.

■ **Proposals on customs, habits, and everyday life:** Barbara Ehrenreich's "Stop Ironing the Diapers" is a good example of how writers offer proposals about the way we conduct daily life. Ehrenreich, of course, uses the personal advice approach found in men's and women's magazines and in the columns of Ann Landers and Dear Abby. Proposals about manners and morals are frequent topics of journalists, and essayists offer "tips" on dealing with the complexities of daily living. Consider writing a proposal about contemporary relations between the sexes, family matters, life at work, or balancing careers and children.

■ **Research proposals:** Shonda Anderson's "Female Boxing: A Fieldwork Proposal" offers a representative example of the kind of research proposal undergraduates may well be called on to write. You might draw on one of the classes you're taking right now to write a research proposal. What is an interesting and important problem or issue that has emerged in readings, lectures, and discussions? How would you go about researching it?

ETHICS OF WRITING

PROBLEMS AND CONFLICTS

Turning the situations that confront us in everyday life and in public affairs into problems is a powerful way of making reality more manageable. Once you have something defined as a problem, after all, it then becomes possible to think in terms of a solution. From this, however, it follows that problems don't just exist, waiting for solutions, but rather take shape according to the way people define them. Consider the controversy over abortion. Some define the problem in terms of the fetus's right to life, while others define it in terms of the woman's right to control her own body. Depending on how the problem is defined, particular solutions seem more—or less—logical than others. And, of course, a proposal aims to do precisely that: define a problem in a way that makes a particular solution appear logical.

Yet, as the abortion controversy makes quite clear, underlying many definitions of problems are real conflicts about values and beliefs. That is, genuine differences in beliefs lead to very different statements of the problem and thus to different proposed solutions.

Formulating a problem invariably means taking a position in relation to what others think and believe—aligning yourself with particular values and beliefs and distancing yourself from others. If you assume that you can simply define a problem objectively, you might well wind up ignoring the underlying conflicts in the situation and interpretations and in the needs of others. Such ethical issues arise with other genres, but they become especially important with proposals because proposals are focused on action and in many cases influence decisions about the use of limited resources.

Invention

To think more systematically about proposals you might be called to write, try working through the following exercises. Your proposal may well grow out of a situation you are currently in, or it may stem from an experience you have had in the recent past.

1. Start by taking an inventory of the issues around you that might call for a solution. As you could tell from the readings, there is a wide range of possibilities open to you. Begin by thinking small and local. Make a list of those positions in which you have the most power to enact change. Are you an officer of any groups, clubs, or organizations? Are you in any classes where the teacher allows the students to carry a lot of responsibility? Are you a leader or captain on a team? If so, write down each example where you find yourself speaking from a position of authority. Then think through the issues that confront those groups, and keep track of them as possibilities.

2. Next, identify those positions where you would be listened to as a fellow member rather than as a leader. What other groups are you a part of? What are the issues that circulate in each of those groups? Do any of

these issues call you to propose a solution (even if you haven't thought of one yet)? If so, write them down as good possibilities.

3. Now that you have thought about the options that might be closer to home, you can broaden your thinking to national and international issues. Which do you identify as real problems? Which do you care enough about to spend time thinking of and proposing a solution to? What kind of a power position are you in when you talk about these types of issues? Who might listen to you? What is the best forum for getting people to hear your proposal?

4. Once you have created your list of possibilities, narrow it down to the three most promising options, beginning with the ones you care most about or have the potential to make your life (or that of someone you know) markedly better. Then try the exercises in the sections on formulating a problem, assessing alternatives, and matching problems and solutions. After you have thought about your potential proposals from all those directions, you should be able to tell which one will make the best proposal.

5. Decide tentatively on the audience. Who can realistically make changes happen? To whom do you have realistic access? With whom do you have credibility? Is there a specific person or governing body who is in a position to enact the changes you will present? Create a list of at least three possible audiences and consider the implications each audience holds for the successful implementation of your proposal. Notice how your definition of the problem may change depending on your audience. Do these shifts in definition hold any consequences for you or for those you are trying to help?

Formulating the Problem

As you have seen, problems don't just come in prepackaged form, calling on us to solve them. They first have to be defined. By formulating problems, writers take situations that already exist and point out what aspects call for urgent attention and action. In this sense, problem formulation is always in part an interpretation—a way of establishing the relevance of a problem to readers. This is a powerful move, since, as a writer, you are taking a group of people and defining them (and their problems) in a particular way. As a proposal writer, you establish criteria for deciding what is good and normal and what is bad and in need of some sort of repair. There are, of course, many ways to define problems, so part of your job is to do so responsibly and ethically.

Illegal drugs are a good example of how problems can be defined in a number of ways. If you ask most Americans about the problems that currently beset American society, many of them will quite likely name "drugs." But what exactly is the problem with drugs? There is little question that millions of

Americans use illegal drugs and that there is a flourishing criminal drug trade. To say as much, however, only describes an existing situation in the broadest sense: What, if anything, should we do about illegal drugs? To propose solutions to the issue, you will have to define more precisely what you see as the problem raised by drugs.

Depending on the writer's perspective, the problem can vary considerably and lead to very different proposals. For example, some would say that the problem with drugs is that illegal drug trade results in police corruption and powerful underworld drug cartels. Others would argue that drugs are causing social decay and destroying the moral fiber of a generation of American young people. Still others would hold that Americans and drug laws haven't distinguished adequately between recreational drugs like marijuana and addictive drugs like heroin and cocaine. In the following chart notice how different problem formulation leads to different proposals. Notice, too, how each solution growing from the problem formulation will impact a different community.

Issue:	Illegal drug use		
Problem:	Underworld drug trade	Social decay	Need for redefinition
Proposed Solution:	Step up war against major drug dealers	Education, jobs programs	Decriminalize marijuana
	Cut off drugs at point of distribution	Eliminate conditions of drug use, such as poverty and hopelessness	Make legal distinctions that recognize differences between kinds of drugs (recreational versus addictive)

Use the chart as a guide to analyze an existing situation by breaking it down into a number of problems. You will probably not be able to address in one proposal all the aspects of the situation that you identify as problems. In fact, you may find that the proposed solutions suggested by the various problems are contradictory or mutually exclusive. The idea at this point is to see how many different problems you can formulate so that you will be able to decide which seems to be most pressing or important.

1. Begin by considering the current situation. In a short phrase (such as "illegal drug use") describe the main topic as you see it.
2. Now consider what problems this topic raises. What's wrong? What's lacking? What, if anything, could be redefined? In short phrases, state a number of problems that you see in the current situation.

3. Next, consider what proposed solutions emerge from the problems as you have defined them. What are people currently doing? How effective are current solutions? What have people proposed to add to, change, or redefine the situation?

4. Finally, go back to the first two steps and reconsider the way you are defining the problem itself. Why did you choose this particular tack? What are some other possibilities? How does your definition of the problem position the people it most concerns? How else might they be positioned if you used a different definition? Whom are you hoping to represent? Once you have answered these questions, you may want to revise your responses to the first three parts of this exercise.

Assessing Alternatives

Once you have identified a number of possible solutions to the problems you've defined, you can then assess the relative strengths and weaknesses of proposals. One way to do this is to test the feasibility of proposed solutions—their capability and suitability to solve problems. Again this can be done by using a chart:

Problem:	What policy on international drug trade should the government follow?	
Proposed Solution:	Legalize drug trade under state control.	Step up the war against international drug trade.
Capability:	Unknown. Costs and benefits uncertain. Would require considerable administration. What about possible black market?	Could reduce amount of illegal drugs to enter the U.S. However, very costly to have widespread effect. What about domestic trade?
Suitability:	Politically unpopular. Voters would interpret as a state endorsement of drug use.	Foreign policy implications need to be carefully considered.

Construct your own chart to assess the feasibility of solutions.

1. State the problem in the form of a question.

2. List two or more potential solutions to the problem. Even if you do not support or endorse one or more of the solutions, by thinking through the feasibility of each one you can develop the benefits of your solution and explain why it is preferable to other approaches.

3. Spend some time figuring out what the criteria might be for a good solution. That means making a list of the qualities a good solution might

have. What are the requirements for a good solution? What other characteristics are desirable? And what qualities would be like icing on the cake, nice but not absolutely necessary? Test your tentative solutions against your list of criteria.

4. Consider whether each proposed solution is in fact capable of solving the problem as it has been stated. Evaluating the capability of a proposed solution, as is the case on the chart above, may not lead to a yes or no answer. Rather, it may lead to further questions that need to be addressed, in this case about the expense and possible consequences of the proposal.

5. Consider the suitability of the proposed solutions. Here you are likely to uncover conflicts of values and interests. In the case of the two proposals listed above, one (legalizing the drug trade) conflicts with many Americans' values, while the other (stepping up the war against the international drug trade) raises potential conflicts of interest with American foreign policy objectives, particularly in regard to countries that export illegal drugs. Uncovering such conflicts can help you clarify what readers you can most effectively appeal to for support and what values and attitudes you might emphasize as a basis of support.

Planning

Relative Emphasis on the Problem and the Solution

As the readings in this chapter show, the amount of space devoted to formulating the problem and to explaining the solution may vary considerably, depending on the writer's situation and purposes. Look, for example, at the relative emphasis on the problem and on the solution in Barbara Ehrenreich's "Stop Ironing the Diapers" and Henry Jenkins' "Lessons from Littleton."

"Stop Ironing the Diapers"
¶¶1–4: Defines the problem.
¶¶5–6: Solution 1—Forget the stages.
¶¶7–9: Solution 2—Forget quality time.
¶¶10–11: Solution 3—Do not overload their intellects.
¶¶12–13: Solution 4—Do not attempt to mold them.
¶¶14–15: Solution 5—Do not be afraid they will turn on you.
¶16: Solution 6—Never say being a mommy is your job.
¶17: Solution 7—Pretend you are a part-time parent.

Notice in this case, that approximately 25 percent of the proposal (¶¶1–4) is concerned with formulating the problem, while the bulk of the proposal consists of explaining the solution. On the other hand, Henry Jenkins devotes 29 paragraphs to formulating the problem (almost 80 percent) and only 7 to presenting solutions.

"Lessons from Littleton"

¶¶1–7: Part I—Defines moral panic.

¶¶8–17: Part II—Critiques current understanding.

¶¶18–29: Part III—Proposes an alternative perspective.

¶¶30–36: Part IV—Proposes six solutions to the problem.

Ehrenreich clearly feels that her readers will understand quite quickly what the problem is and how she redefines it. In contrast, Jenkins assumes that his readers need a much longer, in-depth analysis of how the problem of media effects on young people has been formulated in the past in order to propose a new way of thinking about the issue. As you begin to sketch a working outline of your proposal, take into account your readers' needs. Is a quick sketch of the problem adequate, or should you go into greater detail? Your answer will depend in large part on the situation you're facing and what your purposes are.

Developing a Working Outline

Review the writing and thinking you've done so far. Use the following guidelines to sketch a working outline of your proposal. The guidelines indicate the main issues that writers typically address to design persuasive proposals. As you have just seen, the relative proportion of space devoted to the problem statement and to your explanation of the solution is something you must determine.

Guidelines for a Working Outline

1. **Statement of the problem:** Decide how readily readers will recognize the problem and how much agreement already exists about how to solve it. Your first task is to establish the relevance of the problem to your intended audience. Who does the problem affect? What makes it urgent? What will happen if the problem is not addressed?

2. **Description of the solution:** Since effective proposals present both general goals that appeal to shared values and attitudes and the specific solution to be accomplished, you need to state the goals you have identified and then state clearly how and why your proposed solution will work. Describe the solution and the steps needed to implement it. Decide on the level of detail required to give readers the necessary information to evaluate your proposal.

3. **Explanation of reasons:** Identify the best reasons in support of your proposal. Consider the available alternatives and to what length you need to address them. Finally, think about what counterarguments are likely to arise and to what length you need to deal with them.

4. **Ending:** Some proposals have short endings that reinforce the main point. Others, such as the advertisements commonly found in magazines and newspapers, end by calling on readers to do something.

Working Draft

Use the working outline you have developed to write a draft of your proposal.

Matching Problems and Solutions

Perhaps the most important feature of a persuasive proposal is the match between the problem as the writer defines it and the solution as the writer describes and explains it. Unless the two fit together in a logical and compelling way, readers are unlikely to have confidence in the proposal.

Proposal writers often link solutions to problems in two ways—in terms of long-term, overall goals and in terms of objectives that specify the outcome of the proposal. In the case of Barbara Ehrenreich's "Stop Ironing the Diapers," for example, the overall goal is to identify how women can balance careers and child rearing, while the specific objective is to get women to recognize that parenting is not meant to be a full-time activity—that, in fact, the idea of parenting "at home in your spare time" makes a lot of sense.

Objectives normally tell who is going to do what, when they are going to do it, what the projected results will be, and (in some instances) how the results will be measured. Notice how the seven suggestions in Ehrenreich's proposal offer concrete steps to accomplish both the overall goal and the specific objective.

As you design your proposal, consider how you can effectively present your goals and objectives. Your goals will give readers a sense of your values and offer common ground as the basis for readers' support, while your objectives will help convince readers you have a concrete plan of action that can succeed.

Peer Commentary

Once you have written a draft proposal, exchange drafts with a classmate. If you are working in a group, exchange drafts between groups. Write a commentary to the draft, using the following guidelines.

1. How does the proposal establish the need for something to be done—by defining a problem, describing a situation, using an example, providing facts and background information? Is the need for action convincing? Who is likely to recognize and want to address the main issue of the proposal? Who might feel excluded? Is there any way to include more potential supporters?

2. Where does the proposal first appear? Is it clear and easy to find? Put the proposal in your own words. If you cannot readily paraphrase it, explain why. What is the objective of the proposal? Is it clear who is going to do what, when, how much and (if appropriate) how the results will be evaluated? Do you think the proposal will have the results intended? Why or why not? What other results might occur?

3. What reasons are offered on behalf of the proposal? Do you find these reasons persuasive? Why or why not? Are these the best reasons available? What other reasons might the writer use?

4. Does the solution appear to be feasible? Why or why not? Does the writer need to include more information to make the proposal seem more feasible? What would it take to convince you that this proposal would work?

5. Is the proposal addressed to an appropriate audience? Can the audience do anything to support the actions suggested in the proposal? If not, can you suggest a more appropriate audience? If so, does the way the proposal is written seem suitable for that audience? Point to specific places in the text that need revision. What kinds of changes would make the proposal work better for the audience?

Revising

Now that you have received feedback on your proposal, you can revise those points you feel are necessary—to make sure that the solution you propose follows logically and persuasively from the problem as you have defined it. To help you assess the relationship between your problem formulation and the solution you propose, consider this early draft of the problem and solution sections of the "Proposal for a Campus Coffee House."

Notice two things. First, this proposal devotes approximately equal space to the problem and to the solution. Second, the early draft does not clearly separate the problem statement from the solution statement. In fact, as you can see, the problem is initially defined as the lack of a solution—a logical confusion that will make readers feel the reasoning is circular (the reason we need X is because we don't have it), which is not likely to be very persuasive. To see how the writer straightened out the relationship between problems and solutions, compare this early draft to the revised version that appears in the next section.

EARLY DRAFT

THE PROBLEM: DRINKING ON CAMPUS

The absence of an alcohol-free social life has become a major problem at Warehouse State. Because there are no alternatives, campus social life is dominated by the fraternities, whose parties make alcohol easily available to minors. Off campus, local bars that feature live bands are popular with students, and underage students have little difficulty obtaining and using fake IDs.

The Student Counseling Center currently counsels students with drinking problems and has recently instituted a peer counselor program to educate students about the risks of drinking. Such programs, however, will be limited and largely reactive unless there are alcohol-free alternatives to social life on campus.

THE SOLUTION: CAMPUS COFFEE HOUSE

The Student Management Club proposes to operate a campus coffee house with live entertainment on Friday and Saturday nights in order to provide an alcohol-free social environment on campus for 200 students (capacity of auxiliary dining room in Morgan Commons when set up cabaret-style).

Such a campus coffee house would have a number of benefits. It would help stop the high levels of drinking on campus by both legal and underage students (Martinez & Johnson, 1998), as well as the "binge drinking" that has increased the number of students admitted to the student infirmary for excessive drinking by almost 50% in the last four years. It would serve as a public endorsement of alcohol-free social life, enhance student culture by providing low-cost alcohol-free entertainment on campus, and support current ongoing alcohol abuse treatment and prevention programs.

WRITERS' WORKSHOP

A group of three students wrote the following "Proposal for a Campus Coffee House" in response to an assignment in a business writing class that called on students to produce a collaboratively written proposal to deal with a campus problem. Their commentary on the decisions they made formulating problems and solutions and designing the format appears after the proposal.

PROPOSAL FOR A CAMPUS COFFEE HOUSE

To meet the problem of excessive drinking on campus, we propose that a coffee house, open on Friday and Saturday nights with live entertainment, be established in the auxiliary dining room in Morgan Commons and operated by the Student Management Club to provide an alcohol-free alternative to undergraduate social life.

THE PROBLEM: DRINKING ON CAMPUS.

A recent study by the Student Health Center indicates high levels of drinking by undergraduates on campus (Martinez & Johnson, 1998). Both legal and underage students drink frequently (Fig. 1). They also increasingly engage in unhealthy "binge drinking" to the point of unconsciousness. The number of students admitted to the student infirmary for excessive drinking has increased almost 50% in the past four years (Fig.2). These patterns of drinking conform to those observed in a recent national study (Dollenmayer, 1998). Like many other colleges and universities, Warehouse State is faced with a serious student drinking problem (Weiss, 1997).

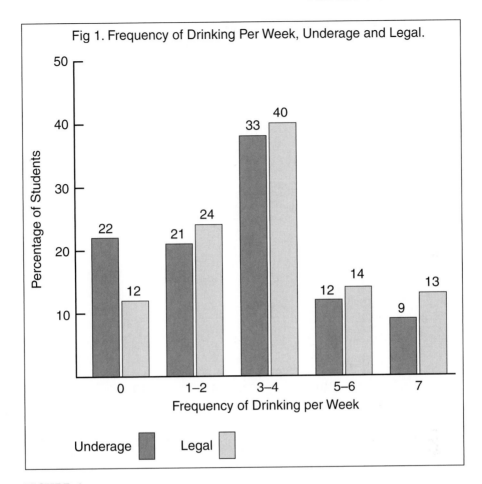

Fig 1. Frequency of Drinking Per Week, Underage and Legal.

FIGURE 1

Currently there are few alternatives for students seeking an alcohol-free social life. Campus social life is dominated by the fraternities, whose parties make alcohol easily available to minors. Off campus, local bars that feature live bands are popular with students, and underage students have little difficulty obtaining and using fake IDs.

THE SOLUTION: CAMPUS COFFEE HOUSE.

The Student Management Club proposes to operate a campus coffee house with live entertainment on Friday and Saturday nights in order to provide an alcohol-free social environment on campus for 200 students (capacity of auxiliary dining room in Morgan Commons when set up cabaret-style).

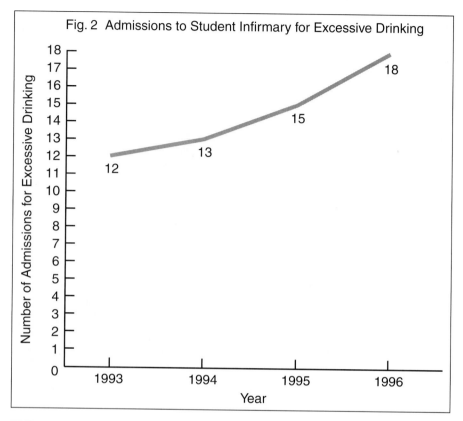

FIGURE 2

Such a campus coffee house would have a number of benefits. It would serve as a public endorsement of alcohol-free social life, enhance student culture by providing low-cost alcohol-free entertainment on campus, and support current ongoing alcohol abuse treatment and prevention programs. The Student Counseling Center currently counsels students with drinking problems and has recently instituted a promising peer counselor program to educate students about the risks of drinking. Such programs, however, will be limited and largely reactive unless there are alcohol-free alternatives to social life on campus.

ORGANIZATIONAL CAPABILITY

The Student Management Club has the experience and expertise needed to run the proposed coffee house. Since 1991, it has successfully run a coffee counter in Adams Union, open five days a week from 8 to 3:30. Management majors are interested in expanding their work into the areas of arts programming and publicity.

TABLE 1 *Initial Expenditures*

Supplies (mugs, plates, spoons, forks, paper products, etc.)	$ 750
Coffee, tea, milk, pastries	250
Publicity	250
Total	$1,250

TABLE 2 *Projected Budget*

Per evening of operation			
Income		Expenses	
(estimated)	$400	Entertainment (band or singer)	$100.00
		Staff (2 persons, 5 hrs each @ $5.35)	53.50
		Supplies	75.00
		Food	100.00
		Publicity	25.00
		Total	$353.50

BUDGET

The proposed campus coffee house will require initial funding of $1250 to begin operations. See cost breakdown in Table 1, Initial Expenditure. We believe, however, that such expenditures are one-time only and that the campus coffee house should become self-supporting. See projected budget in Table 2.

REFERENCES

Dollenmayer, L.C. (1998). Patterns of alcohol use among American college students. *Journal of the American Medical Association, 275* (16), 223–29.

Martinez, M., & Johnson, R. (1998). Alcohol use and campus social life. Livingston, NM: Student Health Center, Warehouse State University.

Weiss, I. (1997, December 2). Drinking deaths prompt concern on campus. *New York Times,* pp. 1, 7.

Writers' Commentary

Following are excerpts from a group meeting, which the participants taped. Here are some passages from the transcript where the three group members, Kathy, Andrea, and Bruce, talk about why they got involved in the coffee house project and how they went about writing the proposal.

KATHY: One of the things that has been interesting about working in this group is that the members come to it from different perspectives. Andrea and I see the coffee house more as a crusade against drinking, which we've watched do a lot of damage to some people we know. So that's a pretty big motivation to get involved, to provide alternatives. Bruce, I think, is into it more out of his interest in folk music and running coffee houses.

BRUCE: Yeah, I mean I do support the idea of having alcohol-free alternative places for students to go. That makes sense to me. But, I agree, definitely. My main thing is arts programming and administration, that whole business. If I can, that's what I want to do when I graduate.

BRUCE: Some of that came up when we were trying to think of reasons for the coffee house, and I was into how it would help promote the arts on campus. We ended up not using that stuff.

ANDREA: Right, but I think Kathy and I became more aware of how we had to make sure the proposal didn't sound moralistic. Remember at first we defined the problem as "drinking on campus" and only later changed it to "excessive drinking." We wanted the proposal to sound positive— that a coffee house would enhance student life.

BRUCE: Exactly. We didn't want it to sound like punishment. And you're right, the proposal doesn't really come out against drinking as the problem but against excessive drinking, binge drinking. I mean alcohol is legal for people over twenty-one. Besides it's unrealistic to think a campus coffee house or anything else for that matter is going to end drinking on campus.

ANDREA: Another thing I felt we tried to do in the proposal was link the coffee house concept to other campus anti-drinking programs. I thought we did a pretty good job of listing benefits in the solution section.

WORKSHOP QUESTIONS

1. Consider how well the proposed solution matches the problem defined in this proposal. Is the problem well-defined and substantiated by adequate evidence? Does the proposed solution seem to offer a feasible approach to excessive drinking on campus? Are there other important factors the writers have not taken into account?

2. The writers, as you may have noticed, are reasonably concerned that their proposal doesn't sound moralistic, even though Kathy and Andrea were initially interested in the idea because of their strong feelings about drinking. Do you think they have been successful in presenting their proposal as a "positive" step to "enhance student life"? If so, what is it about the proposal that creates this impression? If not, why?

3. Imagine that you are on a campus committee that reviews proposals and decides which ones to support. There are more worthy proposals than there are funds available, so you will have to make some hard decisions. The proposal for a campus coffee house is one of the finalists, and the committee plans to meet each group of proposers before making its decision. Draw up a list of questions you would ask Kathy, Andrea, and Bruce to help you make a decision.

REFLECTING ON YOUR WRITING

If you did a group proposal, when you have finished, hold a meeting to look back and evaluate the experience of working together.

1. Explore the reasons each member was drawn to the problem the proposal addresses. To what extent do these reasons overlap? How are they distinct from each other? How did they combine in the group? What influence did this have on writing the proposal?
2. Describe how the group went about writing the proposal. What parts went smoothly? What problems, if any, did the group have? How did individual members and the group deal with problems in the writing?

If you wrote an individual proposal, ask similar questions: What called you to the problem you address? What made it important or urgent? How did you go about writing the proposal? What was easy about it? What problems, if any, did you have? How did you deal with these problems?

A CLOSING NOTE

The real test of a proposal, of course, is whether it works on its intended audience—whether readers will support the goals and objectives of the proposal and do what they can to implement it. For this reason, if you want to find out how effective your proposal is, you need to send it out. Your instructor and classmates can offer useful advice in the context of a writing classroom, but you are likely to get a very different and potentially interesting response by sending your proposal to the group, agency, or institution that can actually implement it.

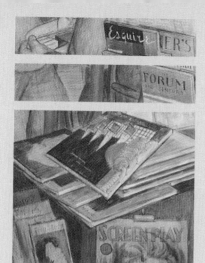

CHAPTER ELEVEN

Reviews: Evaluating Works and Performances

THINKING ABOUT THE GENRE

Reviews are a genre of writing people turn to when they are called on to make evaluations. Of course, reviewers normally describe and analyze whatever they are reviewing—whether it is a movie, a CD, an employee's performance, or a government program. Still, as readers are aware, reviewers provide this background information and analysis as evidence for the evaluation they are making. In some cases, reviewers also offer recommendations ("Avoid this slasher unless you like to be entertained with pointless blood and gore" or "Develop quality control measures to monitor the new manufacturing process"). But what is invariably present is the evaluation itself. As Roger Ebert's movie reviews demonstrate quite literally, reviewers are in the business of saying "thumbs up" or "thumbs down."

Reviews take place informally all the time in everyday life. Part of daily conversation is talking about what people need, what they have seen and done, and what kinds of judgments they make about their experience. It's not unusual to ask, What kind of lawnmower should I buy? Is the psychology course you're taking any good? Is the latest Spike Lee movie worth seeing? Do you like your new car? Where's a good place to get a cheap meal?

At times the informal judgments that result from such questions can spark extended debate. Sports fans, for example, can argue endlessly about everything from who was the best quarterback of the 1990s to which team is going to win the game on Saturday. In these debates, individuals not only make claims— "Babe Ruth was the greatest baseball player of all time"—but must also be able to state the criteria these claims are based on—"No one else has been able to hit the way Babe Ruth did." And, if necessary, they have to justify these criteria. After all, someone might respond that Willie Mays was the greatest because he was the best all-round player. Then the first person would have to justify using hitting as the main criterion. Making evaluations based on justified criteria is at the heart of these informal reviews—and of their formal, written counterparts as well.

Perhaps the most familiar written reviews are newspaper and magazine reviews of the arts—reviews of books, music, film, art, architecture, television, and dance. But newspapers and magazines also feature other kinds of reviews. For example, *Consumer Reports* reviews a broad range of products, and specialized magazines like *Runner's World* or *Wired* routinely assess the particular products that interest their readers. Most newspapers review local restaurants, and most have a travel section that reviews tourist attractions and vacation spots, often with tips on what to see and do and where to stay. As these examples suggest, readers use reviews in a variety of ways—to get information, to get advice from experts, and to compare their judgments to the reviewer's.

The workplace also uses reviews. Annual reviews that evaluate employee performance and productivity are standard features in both the private and public sectors, often determining salaries and promotions. And it's not just individuals who are assessed. Organizations periodically bring in consultants to review programs and procedures and to make recommendations about how they should operate.

At the center of all these reviews are the criteria used to make evaluations. The criteria on which a movie might be evaluated, for example, include the performance of the actors, the plot and its pacing, and the effectiveness of the direction and camera work. The criteria on which *Consumer Reports* bases its evaluation of a car include the car's features, fuel efficiency, and repair record.

The criteria reviewers use may be explicit or implicit. *Consumer Reports,* for example, uses explicit criteria based on quantitative data. Readers can find them listed and explained on the page. Often, however, the criteria are far less explicit. In movie reviews readers must frequently figure out the criteria from the critic's discussion and analysis of the film.

The way readers respond to a review and whether they find its evaluation persuasive will depend to a large extent on whether they believe the criteria used are justifiable. Car reviews in *Consumer Reports,* for example, are likely to persuade readers who accept repair records and gas mileage as the most important considerations in buying a car. Readers who are more interested in style, luxury, and comfort may not find these criteria to be the most compelling.

Readers, of course, may agree with the criteria used and yet not agree with the assessments. This sometimes happens when readers disagree with how the criteria are applied. For example, a film critic and readers might share the belief that the leading actress' performance is crucial to the success of a film but disagree nonetheless about the performance of a particular actress in a particular movie.

In other cases of evaluation, however, people disagree not because they apply shared criteria in different ways but because their criteria of evaluation differ altogether. This is why professional reviewers and critics get into such heated debates about the quality of a book, a movie, a musical performance, or a television show. Take the ongoing debate over daytime talk shows, for example. Some critics see Rikki Lake, Sally Jesse Raphael, Jennie Jones, and Geraldo as offering little more than sensationalism. Others hold that these talk shows raise important issues and give ordinary people a chance to be heard in a medium dominated by celebrities and experts. Clearly these critics are using different criteria to evaluate these talk shows and are making different assumptions about the role of television and the mass media in contemporary culture. In a heterogeneous society such as our own, it is virtually inevitable that people's evaluations—whether in politics, the arts, or other areas—and the criteria and assumptions that underlie them will differ considerably. The reading selections in this chapter offer examples of how reviewers establish justifiable criteria as the basis for their evaluations and of how reviewers' judgments can differ.

EXPLORING YOUR EXPERIENCE

How do you and the people you know find out about movies, CDs, television shows, live music, books and magazines, restaurants, plays, dance performances, concerts, and Web sites? Do you read reviews that appear in newspapers, magazines, or online? How often do you hear and make use of informal, word-of-mouth reviews from family, friends, or coworkers? Think of a discussion you had in which people's evaluations differed. What was being reviewed? What did people say? Why did their evaluations differ? Did they seem to be using the same criteria but applying them differently, or were they using different criteria? How did the discussion end? Did anyone modify their views?

READINGS

Rob Marriott, "Fathers and Sons: Jay-Z Makes His Fifth Album a Family Affair"

Rob Marriott's review of Jay-Z's fifth album *The Dynasty Roc La Familia* (2000–   ) appeared in the December 7, 2000 issue of *Rolling Stone*. Typical of music magazines, in its review section, *Rolling Stone* uses a rating system that ranges from 5 stars for a "classic" to one star for "poor." Thus, for reviewers like Rob Marriott, the writing task involves both assigning stars to the recording under consideration and then explaining the evaluation. As you can see at the top of the review, Marriott gives Jay-Z's album 4 stars for "excellent." In turn, readers will understandably expect Marriott to explain his evaluation.

Fathers and Sons: Jay-Z Makes His Fifth Album a Family Affair
ROB MARRIOTT

1   ★ ★ ★ ★ In the pantheon of street-cultural gods, the hustler is the bejeweled strategist, a ghetto politician who moves with the money and mommies—the cat who can hang out with the thugs, high rollers, Los Angeles Bloods and Brooklyn

gods with equal grace. And Jay-Z is his pop personification. Outside of Iceberg Slim, no one has offered a more detailed portrait of the hustler as a young man.

2   Over the last four albums of his reign, Jay-Z has offered crime-born insights edged with a razor awareness of not only the dangers and angles of the streets but also the consequences of his actions—on himself, his family and his community. For every glamorous "Big Pimpin," there is a document of his fear and loathing like "Streets Is Watching." In return for his crimes, he gave us a window into the process of his evolution from hustler to pop phenom—all the while keeping count of his progress in diamonds, cars and bottles of Cristal.

3   In his latest offering, the strangely titled *The Dynasty Roc La Familia* (2000-   ), Jay settles into a more natural role: that of the hustler-teacher. Sensing correctly that bling fatigue has set in, Jay steps away from the flash and floss of *Volume 1, 2,* and *3* and focuses on more weighty subject matter. *La Familia* is not without its pimping and posturing ("Get Your Mind Right Mami," "Parking Lot Pimpin'"), but it is much more about family. On track after track, Jay confronts the new, unfamiliar demands of being a father figure with the same determined egoism and intelligence that he used while hustling in the streets of Brooklyn. "Soon You'll Understand" finds Jay having to confront a young girl's tears instead of rival drug dealers and FBI surveillance. There are unanswered questions and unresolved emotions. And throughout, Jay returns to a core theme. In an offhand moment, Jay calls to the father he hardly knew: "But I ain't mad at you, Dad/Holla at your lad."

4   The production is as reflective as his lyrics: pulled back, less frenetic and more full-bodied than on his previous album, *Volume 3...Life and Times of S. Carter*. *La Familia* is closer, in many ways, to his seminal 1996 debut album, *Reasonable Doubt*, and his pre-Timbaland days. *Dynasty* is Jay-Z working back toward his roots musically, all the while creating a solid foundation for the next generation.

5   Jay-Z sought out new talent like Rich Rock and the Neptunes to give the entire work a just-left-of-pop feel. The meat of the album—"Stick 2 the Script," "The R.O.C." and "Holla"—are slightly abstract and cinematic cuts that are rubbed up against such straight-out pop fare as "Parking Lot Pimpin'." Where *Volume 3* was scatter-dash, *Dynasty* rocks smoothly between the club bump of the Neptunes' "I Just Wanna Love U (Give It 2 Me)" and the more introspective material of the album's best track, "This Can't Be Life."

6   Often, Jay stays in the background, spitting a scant verse or two and giving more of the spotlight to his proteges Amil, Memphis Bleek and Beanie Sigel. Beanie and Memphis, for their parts, continue to find their voices and play their roles: Memphis as thug celebrant, Beanie as street-wary preacher reminiscent of a young KRS-One. The two become representatives of Jay's own dual nature: half floss-king still thugging it, half street teacher offering warnings and experience to those who have ears to hear.

7   Jay's tendency to associate with Southern and West Coast cats reveals not only his market savvy but also his recognition of where the current heat in hip-hop resides. Interestingly, it's Houston's Scarface who has the most poignant moment on the album: On "This Can't Be Life," he emotionally devotes his verse to mourning

with a friend for a dead child: "I could have talked about my hard times on this song/But heaven knows I would have been wrong/It wouldn't be right/This can't be us/This can't be life." And that's something, considering the powerful final track, "Where Have You Been," on which Jay and Beans recount in full technicolor the pain and rage they have about their absentee fathers.

8   As he continues to develop, Jay's turn to family-building adds another dimension to an already intriguing figure. The hustler now seeks to become the father he never had. He articulates new struggles with love, and defines his next levels of success in familial rather than financial terms. Perhaps this change in emphasis by hip-hop's most credible voice suggests a new reorientation in the culture's priorities as well. We can only hope.

Analysis: Establishing the Reviewer's Credibility

Record reviews that appear in music magazines such as *Rolling Stone* need, of course, to make a judgment about the quality of the album under consideration. After all, that's what reviews are all about. Music reviews, however, are not just a matter of saying whether you liked a record or not. To persuade readers that a review is worth taking seriously, reviewers need to establish their credibility as a knowledgeable and reliable source. Notice how Rob Marriott does this in the opening two paragraphs by giving readers a perspective on Jay-Z and his previous recordings. Marriott's familiarity with Jay-Z's work in turn enables him, in the third paragraph, to point out what is new and different about *The Dynasty Roc La Familia (2000–   )*. Marriott, readers are likely to believe, knows what he is talking about. This impression, moreover, is reinforced in the rest of the review, as Marriott shows he knows not only about Jay-Z but about the hip-hop scene in general, when, for example, he says Jay-Z's protégé Beanie is "reminiscent of a young KRS-One" and talks about "Southern and West Coast" styles "where the current heat in hip-hop resides."

FOR CRITICAL INQUIRY

1. Consider your own experience reading this review. No doubt you noticed right away the 4 stars (for "excellent") at the top of the review. But, aside from this rating, where in the body of the review did you become aware of Rob Marriott's evaluation of Jay-Z's album? Is there a particular passage you can point to?

2. What reasons does Marriott give to support his evaluation? Where do these reasons appear in the review?

3. What do you see as the criteria Marriott uses to make his evaluation of Jay-Z's album? Are the criteria stated explicitly or implicitly?

4. In the opening paragraph, Marriott says "no one has offered a more detailed portrait of the hustler as a young man" than Jay-Z. Then, in the

final paragraph, he says that the "hustler now seeks to become the father he never had." Explain how Marriott gets from paragraph one to paragraph eight. How does this movement establish grounds for Marriott's evaluation of the album?

Karen Durbin, "Razor Thin, But Larger than Life"

Ally McBeal first appeared on Fox during the 1997–1998 television season and quickly became the source of heated discussion about the show's portrayal of young career women and whether those representations amounted to a betrayal of feminist ideals. Durbin is the film critic for *Mirabella* magazine. The following review appeared in the Arts and Leisure section of the Sunday *New York Times* in December 1998, halfway through the second season of *Ally McBeal*—when the debate over the show was at its height. Durbin identifies herself unapologetically as a "confirmed *Ally McBeal* fan," though she admits her "passion" for the show and its main character "is not boundless."

Razor Thin, But Larger than Life
KAREN DURBIN

1   The CBS sitcom *Everybody Loves Raymond* now regularly beats Fox's *Ally McBeal* in the Monday night Nielsens. Recently, an executive producer of *Raymond*, Philip Rosenthal, expressed his delight to *Entertainment Weekly* with a notable shortage of grace, semantic and otherwise. Asked how he accounted for the superior ratings, Mr. Rosenthal said, "Everyone on our show has no problem eating." Sore winners are bad enough; boorish ones should guffaw to themselves in private.

2   Mr. Rosenthal wasn't even being original; he's just the latest to jump on the Ally-bashing bandwagon, a vehicle that rolls with some regularity over the slender bones of the show's lawyer heroine and Calista Flockhart, the gifted young actress who plays her. The hysteria over Ms. Flockhart's putative anorexia reached such a pitch of meanness a couple of months ago that the actress took to eating large meals in public as self-defense.

3   Ms. Flockhart is hardly the only young woman on television these days who looks like a line drawing. In the print ads for HBO's *Sex and the City*, Sarah Jessica Parker's hips are no wider than the laptop she's typing on. According to my laptop, that's 11.5 inches, and she's sitting down. But nobody's rushing to stitch an "A" for anorexia on the skimpy little dresses Ms. Parker wears in the show. Nor, for that matter, has she been attacked for wearing them. *Sex and the City*, like the autobiographical sketches by Candace Bushnell that the show is based on, is a not-quite-tongue-in-cheek portrait of the educated young urban woman as a man-hungry gold digger. Nevertheless, when the editors of *Time* magazine felt moved last summer to ask the question "Is Feminism Dead?" they didn't make

Ms. Parker or Ms. Bushnell the punch line of what must surely be the silliest cover of the year. Instead, their hilarious array of disembodied female heads floating in a funereal black sea proceeded from Susan B. Anthony through Betty Friedan and Gloria Steinem to—who else?—Ally McBeal.

4   The death of feminism tends to be greatly exaggerated, but journalists have been writing its obituary since 1974, when *Harper's* magazine did its own cover article. "Requiem for the Women's Movement," just in time to ride the antifeminist backlash while criticizing the movement for not being radical enough. *Time* does something similar, only the movement's problem now is that it's not serious enough. Ally is the antithesis of true feminism because (1) she gets upset when the supermarket doesn't have enough of her favorite snack, (2) her skirts are too short, and (3) she's a ditz who (4) thinks too much about her lousy love life.

5   I'm a confirmed *Ally McBeal* fan who first took to the streets with knees knocking and feminist fist upraised not quite 30 years ago, when my dress size was considerably smaller than it is now, and what dresses I owned seldom extended more than 12 inches down from the waist. I've never thought that her skirt length or eating habits were a threat to my political health. On the contrary, I identify. As for points (3) and (4), I come from a family of opinionated motormouths, but when I feel rattled or shy, heredity deserts me and my brain shifts into park. So when Ally gets that slightly wild deer-in-the-headlights look her eye (it generally has to do with sex) and blurts something embarrassing, I identify with that too. It's a comfort to know that there's another woman out there, even an imaginary one, for whom the dance of desire begins with a foot in the mouth.

6   None of that would matter if Ally were just an airhead, but she isn't. She wins her cases with ingenious, sometimes inspired arguments that have less to do with the law than with an attempt to discern some rules to live by in the blur of a rapidly changing world.

7   At its uneven best, *Ally McBeal* is neither yuppie sitcom nor courtroom drama but an absurdist morality play that gives off sparks of screwball comedy. Its heroine is basically smart and thoughtful, with a prissy streak that's the downside of her penchant for worrying about what's right. If she's also confused and conflicted, that's because she exists in a state of uncomfortable dissent from the world around her. With her somewhat nutty integrity, Ally McBeal has always struck me as the weird little sister of Mary Richards, although she's not nearly so nice. Alone among her newsroom colleagues on *The Mary Tyler Moore Show*, Mary submissively called her boss Mr. Grant. When a judge tells Ally he will bar her from his courtroom unless she wears longer skirts, she calls him a pig. This is David E. Kelley, the show's creator, talking back to his critics, but it works within the terms of the character. It's not one of Ally's better moves, but to her own self she's certainly being true (note that she seems to have a choice).

8   And like most eccentrics, she harbors a fugitive longing to be normal. How else to explain her attachment to her terminally bland ex-boyfriend? Handsome Billy and his pretty wife, Georgia, are the show's only true yupsters, a totally conven-

tional couple who resent and make a perfect foil for Ally's stubborn singularity. They gripe at her for making waves, for getting out of line, for being larger than life, for, in other words, not knowing her place. She's that quintessential feminist emblem, the inconvenient woman.

9   The *Time* magazine article lumped *Ally McBeal* together with *Bridget Jones' Diary*. But the heroine of Helen Fielding's comic British novel is consumed with the search for Mr. Right, while Ally spends much of her time turning eligible men away. (A little too much time, it seems to me; will she ever get to have sex again or was that cute nude model it?) *Bridget Jones* reads like something from a 50's time capsule. Candace Bushnell's money-grubbing hard-bodies are more believable (so that's how Donald Trump keeps getting dates), but they don't represent much besides themselves.

10   What rings both timely and true is Ally's mix of doubt, assertiveness and self-mocking humor, the last best expressed in her dissing contests with her roommate, Renee. If Ally is kin to Mary Richards, then Renee descends from Murphy Brown. Pugnacious and competitive, Renee copes with her vulnerability by putting on a tough front. Ally does it by putting on no front at all. Maybe that's why she creates such a disturbance both on and off the show. Her short skirts are a metaphor; she's all but walking naked through the world.

11   My passion for *Ally McBeal* is not boundless. Most of the new episodes lack the emotional heft that gives the show its real payoff. Without that, the absurdism seems unfocused (the whole subplot involving a colleague's pet frog) or worse, unfunny. I've always thought the pristine unisex bathroom was one of the show's more resonant absurdities, another metaphor for that rude and ridiculous place where men and women eventually meet and things happen that nobody can control. But the missing frog pops out of the toilet where Ally is sitting so that she can go eek? Somebody leaves the toilet seat up so that she can fall in? If this is what Ally gets instead of a lover or even a fling, maybe Mr. Kelley should take his subconscious in for a tuneup, before he becomes the worst Ally-basher of all.

Analysis: Establishing the Context of Issues

As Karen Durbin notes, *Time* magazine (June 29, 1998) featured a picture of Calista Flockhart (the actress who plays Ally McBeal), along with Susan B. Anthony, Betty Friedan, and Gloria Steinem, to ask the question, "Is Feminism Dead?" Since then, feminists, media critics, and cultural commentators have all weighed in with their views of *Ally McBeal* and what the show says about popular culture and the future of the women's movement. For many, the "razor thin" and possibly anorexic Ally McBeal represents, as Durbin puts it, the "antithesis of true feminism."

Notice how Durbin sets her review within this context of issues, giving her evaluation of *Ally McBeal* a significance that goes beyond the strengths and weaknesses of the show (though she goes on to discuss both in the course of the review). As Durbin establishes the context, she enables readers to see that there is something at stake in *Ally McBeal*'s representation of young career women and in what the critics are saying about the show. Accordingly, Durbin devotes the opening four paragraphs to describing how *Ally McBeal* has been linked to an antifeminist backlash. As you can see, it is only after she has identified and dealt with four reasons Ally is seen by some as a sign of the death of feminism that Durbin makes her own evaluation clear in the fifth paragraph— "I'm a confirmed *Ally McBeal* fan"—and then devotes the remaining five paragraphs to explaining why.

FOR CRITICAL INQUIRY

1. How does Durbin deal with the four reasons *Ally McBeal* is seen by some as the "antithesis of true feminism"? Do you find her response persuasive? Why or why not?

2. Durbin characterizes the show as "neither yuppie sitcom nor courtroom drama but an absurdist morality play that gives off sparks of screwball comedy." Notice in this characterization how Durbin uses four distinct genres ("yuppie sitcom," "courtroom drama," "absurdist morality play," and "screwball comedy") as descriptive labels and terms of comparison and contrast. What does this comparison and contrast accomplish in the review?

3. Durbin says she is a "confirmed *Ally McBeal* fan." What criteria does she use to make this positive evaluation? Are the criteria stated explicitly anywhere in the review, or are they implied?

4. In the final paragraph, Durbin notes that her "passion for *Ally McBeal* is not boundless." What is the function of this paragraph in the review as a whole? Why do you think Durbin waited until the end to express reservations about the show?

Stephen Holden, "After 20 Years, It Still Comes Out Swinging"

Stephen Holden is a film and music critic for the *New York Times*. His review of *Raging Bull* appeared in August 2000, when a new 35-millimeter print was released to mark the twentieth anniversary of the film. Starring Robert DeNiro in an Academy Award-winning performance as the boxer Jake La Motta and directed by Martin Scorsese, *Raging Bull* was a critical success when it first came out in 1980. As you read, notice that Holden's review amounts to a critical reassessment of *Raging Bull* to put the film in perspective and to see how it holds up to viewing twenty years later.

After 20 Years, It Still Comes Out Swinging

STEPHEN HOLDEN

1 "Raging Bull" is not simply the greatest boxing movie ever made; Martin Scorsese's 1980 masterpiece is arguably the finest American film released in a decade when Hollywood retreated from the tragic realist vision of American life enshrined in Francis Ford Coppola's first two "Godfather" films.

2 It may also have been the last movie to embody an ascendant cinematic vision that stretched neo-realist aesthetics to fit epic Hollywood ambitions. If "Raging Bull" is much closer in look and spirit to Rossellini than Mr. Coppola's films are, it is also an extremely self-conscious masterwork that forces us to feel the metaphorical weight of every bead of sweat, hallway shadow and camera angle.

3 On one level, the black-and-white film (augmented with a short-grainy color home movie sequence), which Film Forum is showing to celebrate the picture's 20th anniversary, is a grim, realistic biography of the boxing legend Jake La Motta. But the 1940's middleweight champion who is its real-life antihero is also emblematic of larger forces. He is the ultimate screen embodiment of raw Italian-American machismo at a certain moment in the ever-shifting melting pot of New York City. Blindly fighting his way to the top, then falling and stumbling into a shabby middle age, undone by the same forces by which he rose, he is a potent tribal symbol who ultimately embarrasses his tribe.

4 The wonder of Mr. Scorsese's vision and of Robert De Niro's Academy Award-winning portrayal of Jake is that we feel any compassion for this flailing, instinctual beast who abuses his wife and, in a fit of paranoia, beats up his brother. Yet by the end of the movie, when Jake is a bloated, chest-puffing stand-up comic pathetically mouthing off in a dive for a few extra dollars, the character has achieved a certain embattled nobility. Encased in rolls of flesh (Mr. De Niro put on 50 pounds to play the older Jake) and flashing an ugly, porcine grin, he is still lunging and punching at life as aggressively (and as blindly) as ever.

5 "Raging Bull," like no movie before, personalizes the "Godfather" films' Darwinian vision of an immigrant urban culture muscling its way up the lower rungs of the social ladder. But where Mr. Coppola celebrated a shadow aristocracy with its own grand, quasi-royal pecking order, rituals and traditions, Mr. Scorsese imagined a world unencumbered by majesty. Even the Copacabana, the legendary Manhattan nightclub, is remembered as a boisterous roughneck dive peopled with fight promoters and Mafiosi dolled up in their Saturday night best. Few movies have so indelibly captured the gritty squall of New York's mean streets in the 1940's and 50's, a world of streetwise men in sweat-stained undershirts in un-air-conditioned tenements.

6 The boxing sequences, with their gorgeous images of sweat and blood flying from smashed heads and the thuds of body blows (made by squashing melons and

tomatoes) echoing in a concentrated silence, are among the most visceral fight scenes ever filmed. They are matched in intensity by an unforgettable scene in which Jake, finally forced into a corner, turns on himself as he would on an opponent. Dragged into a prison cell after being convicted of selling alcohol to minors in his nightclub, he violently butts his head against the wall and howls and screams in pain and frustration.

7   "Raging Bull" brought Joe Pesci to the screen in what remains his greatest role as Jake's devoted, protective brother, who nurtures the fighter until Jake turns on him. As Jake's teenage wife, Vickie, who stoically endures his pathologically jealous tirades and brutal manhandling until the lid blows off, Cathy Moriarty is the essence of sullen, smoldering sexuality. Think of Lana Turner in "The Postman Always Rings Twice," stripped of genteel Hollywood airs and with a tough New York accent.

8   "Raging Bull" is showing in a glistening new 35-millimeter print. It should be seen in a theater. It's one American classic without a misstep.

Analysis: Creating a Classic

The main point of Stephen Holden's review of *Raging Bull* comes out clearly enough in the title "After 20 Years, It Still Comes Out Swinging." Notice how the words in the title alert readers to two key aspects of the review. First, they tell us we are revisiting a highly acclaimed film 20 years after it initially secured its critical reputation, and second, the title lets us know the reviewer thinks the film holds up to scrutiny. If anything, the passage of time, Holden suggests, has clarified the achievement of the film. In retrospect, he claims in the opening paragraph, we can see that *Raging Bull* is not only the "greatest boxing movie ever made" but also "arguably the finest American film" released in the 1980s.

From the first paragraph, where Holden describes *Raging Bull* as "Martin Scorsese's 1980 masterpiece," to the final paragraph, where he calls the film "one American classic without a misstep," he is lavish in his praise. In many respects, Holden seems to assume that his readers already know the film and will readily accept his characterization of it as a "masterwork." The real issue in the review concerns why the film is a classic—the reasons and evidence Holden presents to support and explain his evaluation. Notice in particular how Holden discusses *Raging Bull* in relation to the first two *Godfather* films as a way of explaining what is distinctive about it. In a larger sense, the review raises the question about what we mean when we call a film (or a song, TV show, live performance, play, or novel) a "classic." What exactly is invested in the term *classic* that gives a work such a special standing?

FOR CRITICAL INQUIRY

1. Notice that Holden's purposes in this review go beyond simply offering an evaluation of a film. He is also ranking the film in a larger sense, as an "American classic" and "arguably the finest American film" of the 1980s.

What does it mean to call something a "classic"? How does the term distinguish a work?

2. How does Holden go about justifying his claim that *Raging Bull* is a "classic"? What do his criteria of evaluation seem to be? What reasons does he offer to support his evaluation?

3. In paragraphs 1 and 2 and again in paragraph 5, Holden compares *Raging Bull* to the first two *Godfather* films. What does this comparison and contrast accomplish in the review? What does it enable Holden to highlight that might not be so clear otherwise?

4. In the third paragraph, Holden looks at the film on two levels—as a "grim, realistic biography" and as "emblematic of larger forces." What are these "larger forces"? How are they connected to the realistic details of biography in the film? What do these two levels enable readers to see about the film?

Alan A. Stone, from "Report and Recommendations Concerning The Handling of Incidents such as the Branch Davidian Standoff in Waco, Texas"

Alan A. Stone, a professor of law and psychiatry at Harvard University, was one of ten experts selected by the Deputy Attorney General to review the FBI's handling of the siege on the Branch Davidian compound in Waco, Texas, on April 1993, which resulted in the deaths of approximately 80 Branch Davidians, including more than 20 children. The Branch Davidians were a religious cult, led by David Koresh, who believed the end of the world as prophesied in the Bible was close at hand. In February 1993, agents of the Bureau of Alcohol, Tobacco, and Firearms (BATF) raided the Branch Davidian compound, where members of the cult had gathered in anticipation of the apocalypse, to investigate possible firearm violations as well as allegations that child abuse was taking place. In this "dynamic entry," six Branch Davidians and four BATF agents were killed. At that point, the FBI took over jurisdiction, and on April 1993, following 51 days of attempted negotiation, the FBI attacked the compound with tear gas and tanks.

Stone's review was to be published in a Justice Department report consisting of three parts: a "factual investigation" carried out by the Justice Department; an evaluation of the FBI's handling of the incident by Edward Dennis, a former assistant attorney general; and the reviews by the outside experts. In his section of the report, Dennis concluded that the FBI "exhibited extraordinary restraint and handled this crisis with great professionalism." (This was also the finding of John Danworth, special counsel appointed by Attorney General Janet Reno, in the review issued on July 2000, which exonerated federal agents.) As you will see, Stone disagrees with this conclusion. His review of events argues that things could have been handled differently. However, the government's report was released without Stone's review, excepts from which appear in the following reading selection

From "Reports and Recommendations Concerning the Handling of Incidents such as the Branch Davidian Standoff in Waco, Texas"

ALAN A. STONE

1   In creating its report, the Justice Department sifted through a mountain of information. This evidence overwhelmingly proves that David Koresh and the Branch Davidians set the fire and killed themselves in the conflagration at Waco, which fulfilled their apocalyptic prophecy. My report does not question that conclusion; instead, my concern is whether the FBI strategy pursued at Waco in some way contributed to the tragedy that resulted in the death of twenty-five innocent children along with many adults. The department's factual investigation and the [Edward] Dennis evaluation seem to agree with the FBI commander on the ground, who is convinced that nothing the FBI could have done would have changed the outcome. That is not my impression.

2   On the evening of February 28 and the morning of March 1, the FBI replaced the Bureau of Alcohol, Tobacco, and Firearms [ATF] at the Branch Davidian compound. There had been casualties on both sides during the ATF's attempted "dynamic entry." David Koresh, the leader of the Branch Davidians, had been shot through the hip, and the situation was in flux.

3   During the first phase of the FBI's engagement at Waco, a period of a few days, the agents on the ground at the compound proceeded with a strategy of conciliatory negotiation, which had the approval and understanding of the entire chain of command. In the view of the negotiating team, considerable progress was made— for example, some adults and children came out of the compound—but David Koresh and the Branch Davidians made many promises to the negotiators that they then did not keep. Pushed by the tactical leader, the FBI's commander on the ground began to allow tactical pressures to be placed on the compound in addition to negotiation, e.g., turning off the electricity, so that those in the compound would be as cold as the agents outside during the twenty-degree night. This tactical pressure was applied over the objections of the FBI's own experts in negotiation and behavioral science, who specifically advised against it. These experts warned the FBI command about the potentially fatal consequences of using such measures.

4   By March 21, the FBI was concentrating on tactical pressure alone: first, by using all-out psycho-physiological warfare intended to stress and intimidate the Branch Davidians; and second, by "tightening the noose" with a circle of armored vehicles. The FBI considered these efforts a success because no shots were fired at them by the Branch Davidians.

5   This changing negotiation strategy at the compound from (1) conciliatory negotiating to (2) negotiation and tactical pressure and then to (3) tactical pressure alone evolved over the objections of the FBI's own experts. When the fourth and ultimate strategy, the insertion of C.S. gas [tear gas] into the compound, was presented to Attorney General Janet Reno, the FBI had abandoned any serious effort to reach a negotiated solution and was well along in its strategy of all-out tactical pressure, thereby leaving little choice as to how to end the Waco standoff. By the time the attorney general made her decision, the noose was closed and, as one agent told me, the FBI believed they had "three options—gas, gas, and gas."

6   There is, to my mind, unequivocal evidence that the Branch Davidians set the compound on fire themselves and ended their lives on David Koresh's order. However, I am now convinced that the FBI's noose-tightening tactics may well have precipitated Koresh's decision to commit himself and his followers to this course of mass suicide.

7   There is a wealth of criminology, behavioral-science, and psychiatric literature on the subject of murder followed by suicide that indicates that these behaviors and the mental states that motivate them have very important and complicated links. Even more important is what has been called the "gamble with death." For example, inner-city youths often provoke a shoot-out, "gambling" with death by provoking police into killing them. In the case of the Branch Davidians, there was direct empirical evidence supporting the assumption that those at the compound, because of their own unconventional beliefs, were in the "gamble with death" mode. The evidence for this was their response to the ATF's misguided assault. The ATF claims gunfire came from forty different locations. If true, this means that at least forty Branch Davidians were willing to shoot at federal agents and kill or be killed as martyr-suicide victims defending their "faith." The FBI's behavioral-science unit realized that Koresh and his followers were in a desperate kill-or-be-killed mode. They were also well aware of the significance and meaning of the Branch Davidians' apocalyptic faith. They understood that David Koresh interpreted law-enforcement attacks as related to the prophesied apocalyptic ending. The idea that people with those beliefs, expecting the apocalypse, would submit to tactical pressure is a conclusion that flies in the face of their behavior during the ATF raid.

8   In deciding to move to a show-of-force tactical strategy, the FBI made the critical assumption that David Koresh and the Branch Davidians, like ordinary persons, would respond to pressure in the form of a closing circle of armed vehicles by concluding that survival was in their self-interest and surrendering. This ill-fated assumption runs contrary to all of the relevant behavioral-science and psychiatric literature as well as the understanding that it offered of David Koresh and the Branch Davidians.

9   The ATF investigation report [issued in September] states that the so-called dynamic entry turned into what is described as being "ambushed." As I tried to get a sense of the state of mind and behavior of the people in the compound, the idea that the Branch Davidians' actions were considered an "ambush" troubled me. If

they were militants determined to ambush and kill as many ATF agents as possible, it seemed to me that given their firepower, the devastation would have been even worse. They apparently did not maximize the number of ATF agents killed. This comports with all of the state-of-mind evidence and suggests that the Branch Davidians were neither depressed, suicidal people nor determined, cold-blooded killers; rather, they were desperate religious fanatics expecting an apocalyptic ending, in which they were destined to die defending their sacred ground and destined to achieve salvation.

10   The psychology of such behavior—together with its religious significance for the Branch Davidians—was mistakenly evaluated, if not simply ignored, by those responsible for the FBI strategy of "tightening the noose." The overwhelming show of force was not working in the way the tacticians suppose. It did not provoke the Branch Davidians to surrender, but it may have provoked David Koresh to order the mass suicide.

11   Throughout the [Justice Department's] official factual investigation, there are references to the failure of communication between the tactical and negotiation arms of the FBI. The commander on the ground has said that the official investigation and evaluation exaggerate the extent and significance of that failure. I disagree. Consider the memo of March 5, from Special Agents Peter Smerick and Mark Young, on the subject "Negotiation Strategy and Considerations." Agents Smerick and Young were not Monday-morning quarterbacks, as we panelists are; they were members of the FBI team on the field of play. The agents emphasized that the strategy of negotiations coupled with ever-increasing tactical pressure was inapplicable. They wrote, "This strategy, if carried to excess, could eventually be counterproductive and could result in loss of life." The agents were also fully aware that Koresh's followers believed in his teachings and would "die for his cause."

12   What went wrong at Waco was not that the FBI lacked expertise in behavioral science or in the understanding of unconventional religious groups. Rather, the commander on the ground and others committed to tactical-aggressive, traditional law-enforcement practices disregarded those experts and tried to assert control and demonstrate to Koresh that they were in charge. There is nothing surprising or esoteric in this explanation, nor does it arise only from the clear wisdom of hindsight. The FBI's own experts recognized and predicted in memoranda that there was the risk that the active, aggressive law-enforcement mentality of the FBI—the so-called action imperative—would prevail in the face of frustration and delay. They warned that, in these circumstances, there might be tragic consequences from the FBI's "action imperative." They were correct.

Analysis: Supporting an Evaluation with Analysis

Alan A. Stone's review of the FBI's handling of the crisis at Waco is interesting for several reasons. First, it's a good example of a common type of review in which an outside evaluator assesses the performance of an organization's policies and personnel. Second, in this case, the review concerned an incident that had captured the nation's attention and ended in a tragedy that stirred some people's anger at the government—in other words, it was a controversial, highly charged incident. Third, reviewers' evaluations conflicted. Specifically, Stone's evaluation conflicted with official evaluations, and his review was suppressed.

Stone does not dispute the basic facts established by the Justice Department's investigation. He notes that the investigation had "sifted through a mountain of information" that overwhelmingly proved that David Koresh and his followers "set the fire and killed themselves in the conflagration at Waco." Rather, he disagrees with the evaluation that the FBI did not contribute to the tragedy. His own evaluation is that the FBI's handling of the crisis, far from not being a factor, actually made the final outcome inevitable. Stone backs up this evaluation with background information and analysis: He describes the events, going back to the period when the BATF was still involved and tracing the evolution of strategy once the FBI took over jurisdiction. He also draws on both a "wealth of criminology, behavioral-science, and psychiatric literature" and memos written by FBI agents at the time of the incident.

FOR CRITICAL INQUIRY

1. Stone's review is divided into three sections, each of which has a somewhat different function in the review as a whole. Look back at each section, summarize its content, and identify its function in the review as a whole.

2. Three major elements of the background information and analysis leading to Stone's evaluation are the chronology of events at Waco, relevant literature from a range of fields, and FBI internal communications. Explain how Stone uses these three elements together to arrive at and support his evaluation. Why is each of these elements needed?

3. In his analysis Stone gives a particularly prominent role to the "gamble with death" concept. Why is this concept so important to his overall evaluation?

4. What are some of the criteria that Stone evidently uses to assess the FBI's performance at Waco? Do you agree with these criteria? Why or why not?

5. Recommendations often follow from evaluations of performance. What recommendations for FBI conduct in future situations does Stone's evaluation suggest?

6. The section written by former Assistant Attorney General Edward Dennis concluded that the FBI "exhibited extraordinary restraint and handled this crisis with great professionalism." This assessment is dramatically different from Stone's. Having read Stone's review, what kind of analysis do you think Dennis's very different evaluation could have been based on?

Visual Design: Minisystems Ratings and Superbowl Matchup—Thomas George, "Why the Giants Will Win" and Mike Freeman, "Why the Ravens Will Win"

The following selections offer two common types of visual design—the use of rating systems and of paired reviews. You've already seen how the review of Eminem's *The Marshall Mathers LP* uses letter grades as a rating system. The

---

Minisystems

Ratings

ALL SIZES AND SHAPES (From left to right) The *Yamaha GX-505*; the *JVC MX-J500*, A CR Best Buy; the *Panasonic SC-AK78*, with surround sound; and the compact *Yamaha MCR-E100*.

Shop Smart

What to spend. Most minisystems sell for $100 to $300, although you'll find some selling for a few hundred dollars more. Generally speaking, don't expect top sound quality much below $250.

What to look for. Before buying a minisystem, listen to a few familiar CD recordings in the store, if possible. Adjust the tone controls to see if you like the sound. Ask about the return or exchange policy in case you don't like the system when you get it home.

Where to shop. You'll find the best selection in electronics stores like Best Buy and Circuit City and department stores such as Sears. Prices may be lower in discount chains such as Kmart, Target, and Wal-Mart.

When to buy. New models show up in the spring, so you may get discounts on older models in the winter.

The tests behind the Ratings

Overall score is based largely on the quality of sound. **Sound quality** is the accuracy of the two main speakers with the tone controls optimized for the best sound performance. **Taping quality** combines frequency response, dynamic range, and freedom from flutter of the tape deck(s). **FM tuning** includes sensitivity (picking up weak signals) and selectivity (avoiding crossover of adjacent stations). **CD handling** is how well the player handled defective discs and how long it took the player to go from one track to another on the same disc. **Ease of use** rates each model on ergonomics and the controls on the main unit and remote. **Price** is the national average (provided by Active Research Inc., www.activebuyersguide.com). An asterisk (*) indicates approximate retail. Features and AM tuner are also factored into the overall score, but are not shown on the Ratings chart.

Overall Ratings In performance order

Excellent ● Very good ◕ Good ◑ Fair ◔ Poor ○

KEY NO.	BRAND AND MODEL	PRICE	OVERALL SCORE (P F G VG E)	SOUND QUALITY	TAPING QUALITY	FM TUNING	CD HANDLING	EASE OF USE	COMMENTS
▷	**Yamaha** GX-505	$400*		◕	◕	●	●	◑	Very good overall. Useful features on CD and tape players. Displays time remaining on disc and track. Detachable speaker wires. But only one tape deck.
▷	**JVC** MX-J500 A CR Best Buy	280		◕	◕	◕	◕	○	Very good overall. Useful features on CD and tape players. But some function buttons shared by both tape decks.
▷	**Panasonic** SC-AK78	400		◕	◕	◕	●	◑	Very good overall, top-rated surround-sound system. Useful features on tape player. Heavy bass. But controls shared by both tape decks. Complicated wiring for speakers.
▷	**JVC** MX-J900	450		◕	○	◕	●	◑	Good overall. Useful features on CD player. Heavy bass. But controls shared by both tape decks. Complicated wiring for speakers.
▷	**Sony** MHC-NX1	600		○	●	◕	◕	◑	Good overall. Useful features on CD and tape players. Displays time remaining on disc and track. Detachable speaker wires. Microphone input. But one tape deck lacks some functions. Relatively expensive.
▷	**Sony** MHC-BX7	350		◕	◑	◕	◕	○	Good overall. Useful features on CD and tape players. Displays time remaining on disc and track. But controls shared by both tape decks. Larger than most.
▷	**Panasonic** SC-AK29	250		○	○	◑	●	○	Good overall. Heavy bass. But CD player lacks some useful features. Controls shared by both tape decks. Complicated wiring for speakers.
▷	**Aiwa** NSX-AJ20	145		◕	◕	◕	○	○	Good overall. Useful features on CD player. Displays time remaining on disc. But tape player lacks some useful features. Controls shared by both tape decks.
▷	**Aiwa** NSX-AJ70	235		○	◕	◕	○	○	Good overall. Useful features on CD and tape players. Displays time remaining on disc. Microphone input. But controls shared by both tape decks.
▷	**Philips** FW-P78	300*		◕	◕	◑	◕	○	Good overall, a budget surround-sound system. Useful features on tape player. Heavy bass. But controls shared by both tape decks.
▷	**Aiwa** NSX-HMA56	280		◕	○	◕	○	○	Good overall, a budget surround-sound system. Useful features on CD player. Displays time remaining on disc. Microphone input. But tape player lacks some useful features. Warranty covers surround speakers for only 90 days. Complicated wiring for speakers.
▷	**RCA** RS2520	150*		◕	◑	◔	●	◔	Good overall. But tape player lacks some useful features, including auto-stop for FF/Rewind. One tape deck lacks some functions. Complicated wiring for speakers. Ease of use only fair.
▷	**Aiwa** XR-M200	190		○	○	◕	○	◔	Fair overall. Useful features on CD and tape players. Smaller than most. But holds only one CD and has only one tape deck. Complicated wiring for speakers. Ease of use only fair.
▷	**Sharp** CD-BA200	200*		◕	◔	◑	◕	◔	Fair overall. There are better choices. Amp/speaker accuracy was the worst among the tested models. Complicated wiring for speakers.

This model is rated separately because it lacks a tape player.

| ▷ | **Yamaha** MCR-E100 | 500* | | ◕ | – | ◕ | ● | ◕ | Very good overall. Useful features on CD player. Displays time remaining on disc and track. Detachable speaker wires. Smaller than most. But no tape player. |

▶ **Can't find a model?** Contact the manufacturer. See page 61.   45

Minisystems Ratings in this section illustrate the much more complex schemes of product evaluation *Consumer Reports* has become famous for, providing shoppers with an extensive visual display of information. The second selection uses a different visual design by pairing two contrasting evaluations—in this case predictions made in *The New York Times* on Friday, January 26, 2001, two days before Superbowl XXXV. Of course, we now know that the Baltimore Ravens beat the New York Giants 34–7. Nonetheless, the predictions by Thomas George and Mike Freeman offer a good example of how experienced and knowledgeable sportswriters establish criteria and make evaluations.

Super Bowl Matchup

Why the Giants Will Win

By THOMAS GEORGE

15.4

Points allowed per game

It is difficult to ignore the Ravens' defense in any way. This defense, as the Giants have smartly acknowledged all week, has earned everything it has accomplished. It has produced an effort in style and in numbers that is unmatched in pro football history. It all starts with middle linebacker Ray Lewis, but the other components are more varied and more layered. Combine the coaching, the scheme and the personnel of this defense, and the Giants, like all other teams this season, will find the search for yards and points brutally tough. But the Giants are the pick here because as good as the Ravens' defense is, the Giants' defense is more than capable, especially against the Ravens' offense. The Giants' defense against the Ravens' offense is the game's biggest mismatch. Expect the Giants' offense to do just enough and the Giants' defense, in a surreal twist, to dominate.

Key players to watch for the Ravens are quarterback Trent Dilfer and linebacker Peter Boulware. Dilfer is expected to play the same kind of game that got the Ravens here: methodical, careful and with plenty of handoffs to running back Jamal Lewis. But if the Ravens are forced to play catch-up, will Dilfer make mistakes? The Giants think so. In that case, they will pressure him in the pocket relentlessly. Boulware is a speed rusher on passing downs and will be a force.

Key players to watch for the Giants are receivers Ike Hilliard and Ron Dixon and tight end Pete Mitchell. Hilliard, in the Giants' regular offensive sets, will shake free in the Baltimore secondary. Mitchell will make plays against the Baltimore linebackers. And Dixon is a major X factor. When the Giants use a spread offense — and they will be forced to use it, especially in the second quarter and beyond — it will be Dixon who has the best chance to break loose against the Baltimore nickel and dime packages. Dixon has the speed that will keep that group on its toes and heels.

The Giants' third Super Bowl title will be as sweet as the first two, and as special, especially considering the arduous and stunning road traveled.

GIANTS, 16-10

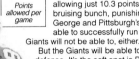

Giants wide receiver Ron Dixon

Why the Ravens Will Win

By MIKE FREEMAN

10.3

Points allowed per game

Have I mentioned that in September I picked the Baltimore Ravens to make it to the Super Bowl?

Just thought I'd remind everyone. I'm no Raven-come-lately. But I am conflicted.

Baltimore's defense is one of the speediest, most aggressive the National Football League has ever seen, allowing just 10.3 points a game, and more important, it is a bruising bunch, punishing the likes of Tennessee's Eddie George and Pittsburgh's Jerome Bettis. No team has been able to successfully run the ball on Baltimore, and the Giants will not be able to, either.

But the Giants will be able to throw on the vaunted Ravens defense. It's the soft spot in Baltimore's tough armor. Quarterback Kerry Collins has enough accuracy to throw pinpoint passes in the intermediate routes. Many in the news media have pointed to what the Jets did to Baltimore — Vinny Testaverde and crew racked up more than 500 yards of offense — as the formula to attack the Ravens. But that is not really the case.

"In that game we did two things wrong," the defensive coordinator Marvin Lewis said. "We missed tackles and we kept peeking in the backfield trying to stop the run, and then the Jets threw the ball over the top. That won't happen again."

The Jets used the no-huddle offense and trick plays. That is not the way to beat Baltimore.

Among the game tapes the Giants have scoured are two: Baltimore's first game against Jacksonville, in which the Jaguars garnered 421 total yards of offense mainly by throwing the football deep, and the Washington game, in which Stephen Davis rushed for 91 yards, including a 33-yard touchdown scamper. It is the latter game the Giants can use to see what blocking schemes the Redskins used to free up Davis.

So the Giants will score some points.

Field goals. But points nonetheless.

Something else that will help the Giants: the Ravens have been extremely distracted this week, from Coach Brian Billick's tirade against the media, to tight end Shannon Sharpe defending Ray Lewis, to some Baltimore defensive backs hinting they can shut out the Giants, to several Ravens players guaranteeing a victory. Meanwhile, the Giants have been quiet and professional. That does not bode well for Baltimore.

Still, despite all those factors, it is defense that wins games, and the Ravens have the best defense and the best defensive player in football in Lewis. Baltimore's D wins it.

RAVENS, 12-9

Analysis: Rating Systems and Paired Reviews

The ratings of audio minisystems from *Consumer Reports* offers a good example of how visual design can make a great deal of information readily accessible to readers. As you can see, the layout contains three separate sections, "Shop Smart," "The tests behind the Ratings," and "Overall Ratings." "Shop Smart" uses bold type and short paragraphs to present a general strategy ("What to spend," "What to look for," "Where to shop," and "Where to buy"). In contrast, "The tests behind the Ratings" uses a dense block of text broken up only by keywords in bold, giving readers the sense that this section contains more technical information and takes more work to read. The main feature, of course, is the "Overall Ratings" with its use of scores and symbols, where visual elements rather than words convey the message.

In contrast, *Superbowl Matchup* relies largely on the written texts, where the two sportswriters explain their predictions. Nonetheless, the visual design of the *Superbowl Matchup* plays a key role in helping readers compare the two predictions. Notice, for example, the parallelism in the two titles ("Why the Giants Will Win" and "Why the Ravens Will Win"), the boxes with team logos and points allowed per game, and the easy-to-find predicted scores at the end of each preview. The written texts themselves have been designed to occupy approximately the same amount of page space. Everything is equal and balanced, with the single figure of Giants wide receiver Ron Dixon providing a focal point in the middle of the design.

FOR CRITICAL INQUIRY

1. The minisystems ratings from *Consumer Reports* uses two sets of criteria—one concerned with shopping strategy and the other with rating the minisystems themselves. In each case, do the criteria seem reasonable? Can you think of anything you would add to these criteria?

2. Consider the design of the "Overall Ratings" that *Consumer Reports* uses. Notice that the overall scores are represented by a bar chart. What is the effect of this design decision? How would this section of the table differ if the overall scores were represented, say, by numbers on a 100 point scale or words ("poor," "fair," "good," "very good," "excellent"). Notice too the symbols used to rate performance and convenience. These are standard features in *Consumer Reports* ratings, and no doubt readers learn the system. But if you aren't familiar with it, did you find you had to consult the box that explains the symbols' values—excellent, very good, good, fair, and poor? How did this affect your reading?

3. What elements of the minisystems ratings make the page easy to read and use? What elements, if any, do you think could be redesigned for greater clarity?

4. How do paired reviews, such as the predictions in *Superbowl Matchup,* compare to the single-author reviews of *The Marshall Mathers LP* or *Ally McBeal* in this chapter? What, if anything, is gained by including conflicting evaluations in one place? What visual design features enable readers to grasp easily the two writers' predictions?

5. To what extent do Thomas George and Mike Freeman apply similar criteria to make their predictions? To what extent do their criteria differ? In the case of shared criteria, how do they use the same criteria to reach different judgments?

FOR DISCUSSION AND ANALYTICAL WRITING

RHETORICAL ANALYSIS

Pick one or two of the reviews in this chapter. Identify the main criteria of evaluation. Notice that in each review's argument, the criteria of evaluation play the role of enabling assumptions. Explain how the criteria enable the reviewer to connect the evidence provided to the review's central claim. Consider how widely shared the criteria of evaluation are likely to be on the readers' part. What does the reviewer's assumption seem to be? Does the reviewer appear to assume that the criteria can be taken for granted as something most readers already believe, or do the criteria seem to require explanation and justification?

GENRE CHOICES

On January 4, 2001, VH-1 released its list of the 100 best albums in rock-and-roll history, based on a poll of 500 music critics. Nirvana's *Nevermind* (1991) was ranked number 2, behind the number 1 album, the Beatles' *Revolver.* A month earlier, *Rolling Stone*'s December 7, 2000, issue presented the 100 greatest pop songs, dating from the Beatles' arrival in the United States in 1963 to the present. On the *Rolling Stone* list, "Smells Like Teen Spirit" from Nirvana's *Nevermind* album was ranked number 3, behind the Beatles' "Yesterday" at number 1 and the Rolling Stones' "(I Can't Get No) Satisfaction" at number 2. Read the review of "Smells Like Teen Spirit" that appears in the December 7, 2000, issue of *Rolling Stone* (and draw on VH–1 if you happened to see the segment on *Nirvana*). The *Rolling Stone* review, understandably, focuses for the most part on Kurt Cobain, who wrote and sang "Smells Like Teen Spirit." Compare the treatment of Cobain in the review to the profile of him in Chapter 7. How does the purpose of the genre in question—review or profile—shape the approaches of the two writers?

GOING ONLINE

Rapstation

Rapstation <www.rapstation.com> is an open-source Web site that includes news, interviews, and reviews of rap recordings and hip-hop culture, as well as songs and software that visitors can download for free. The Web site was founded by Chuck D of Public Enemy, perhaps the most important rap group of the 1980s. Chuck D lists his top ten tunes each week. Visit the Web site. What do Chuck D's criteria of judgment for his weekly lists seem to be? How can you tell?

WORKING TOGETHER

Course Review

Work together as a class to review your writing course. The review will require planning questions and methods, conducting research, compiling and analyzing the information obtained, and finally, evaluating the course based on that information. Here is a basic procedure, which you may want to modify, depending on the size of your class and the scope of your review:

1. Working together in groups of five or six, think about criteria for evaluating the course. What is important in a writing course: interesting readings, lively discussions, group activities, engaging and varied writing assignments, the teacher's presentations and instructions, classroom atmosphere? What about the results: improvement in writing, preparation for writing in other classes or at work, changed attitudes toward writing and a greater understanding of its usefulness? These are, of course, only some criteria you might use.

2. Make a list of specific questions that would give you information related to the criteria you're using. Once you have a list, decide which questions seem the most important and useful. Compile a final list of questions, and make enough copies of the list for everyone in class.

3. Meet together as a whole class. Have each group present its questions. As a class, synthesize the questions into a master list that everyone can agree on. If there are questions on a lot of different areas, you might have to eliminate some areas and focus on others.

4. With your questions in mind, decide how you will get answers—what forms of research you want to use. You could, for example, use any combination of the following: surveys, written evaluations, interviews, discussion groups, video or audio recordings of a class, or outside observers. Decide which methods would be practical as well as most useful for getting the information you need.

5. At this point, separate again into groups, with each group responsible for a particular research method and/or a particular area of inquiry.

Make sure that everyone has a role in the research process. Each group should make final decisions about the specifics of how it will conduct its research.

6. In groups, conduct the research and compile the results. How you compile results will, of course, depend on the method of gathering information you used. For example, survey responses can be tallied, whereas videos would have to be analyzed.

7. The two final steps are to analyze and interpret the results of your research and to prepare a final evaluation based on this analysis. You can begin by having the groups that conducted the research report to the class. These reports should include tentative conclusions and judgments drawn from the data. The class can discuss each report, agreeing or disagreeing with its conclusions and judgments. The reports and discussion can then be the basis of a written course review. A group can be given the responsibility of writing the review, or different groups can write sections, but the entire class should read and approve the final course review.

WRITING ASSIGNMENT

For this assignment, write a review. Pick something to review that you know well or that you find interesting and would like to learn more about. You will write this review for a particular group of readers, so you might target a particular publication, such as a student or local newspaper or one of the national magazines you are familiar with. This will help you anticipate what your readers already know, what they value, and what criteria they accept as a basis of evaluation.

The subject of your review can be drawn from many spheres of life. Here are some common types of reviews:

- **Live performances:** Attend a musical concert, a play, or a club with live music and write a review of the performance.

- **Media:** Television programs, radio shows, movies, and musical recordings are all possible subjects for reviews.

- **The Web.** As the Internet grows more crowded, people can use help finding which sites are worth visiting and which are not. Gather an assortment of related Web sites and write a comparative review of them. Or just focus on one site and review it in depth.

- **Exhibitions:** Local museums, on- and off-campus, may be featuring special art, historical, or scientific exhibitions that you could review.

- **Books:** You could review a best-seller, a recent book in an academic field that interests you, a controversial book such as *The Bell Curve,* a book that is particularly popular with college students, or an older book that invites a revisit.

- **Sports:** Write a preview of an upcoming season of a college or professional sport, or make a prediction about an important game.

- **Leisure and entertainment:** Write a restaurant review, a guide to entertainment on campus, or an evaluation of backpacking routes you have taken. Visit historical places, local parks, or parts of a city, and write an evaluation of what they have to offer.

- **Education:** Write a review of a course you have taken, a textbook, or a program you have been involved in (such as an orientation for first-year students or a summer program).

- **Letters of recommendation:** You may be in a position to write a letter of recommendation for somebody you know. Such letters, in fact, are reviews of the person you are recommending (they are, by nature, generally positive). If you have a friend applying to college or for a position such as orientation leader, peer counselor, or resident assistant that requires recommendations, you can consider the writing you do for that person for this assignment. Likewise, if you have worked with somebody who is searching for a job, consider writing that person a recommendation that he or she can take to interviews.

- **Politics and the public sphere:** Write a review of the 2000 presidential campaign, a particular elected official, a candidate for office, a proposed law, an ongoing program, or a controversial event, such as the FBI's intervention in Waco.

- **Rating systems:** Design a rating system for reviewing consumer products, musical recordings, movies, restaurants, or a host of other things.

- **Greatest or best lists:** You could list the top 10 (or 25 or 100) rap songs, punk bands, teenage movies, game shows, female actresses, hockey players, or presidents and explain your criteria of evaluation. Some lists focus on the best of the year, while others identify the all-time greatest.

- **Paired Reviews:** Work with a partner to write paired reviews that offer differing judgments about a CD, movie, upcoming sports event, or who is going to win an Academy Award.

Invention

Exploring Your Topic

To get started thinking about your topic and how you might approach it in a review, assess what you already know and what further information you need.

ETHICS OF WRITING

REVIEWING AS A PARTISAN ACTIVITY

Reviewers are by no means neutral observers. On the contrary, they are in the business of being partisan. Whatever field of human activity their reviews concern, they support some performances and find fault with others. Reviewers are not only incapable of being neutral but also incapable of being objective. After all, even the more quantitative and objective reviews, such as the product ratings in *Consumer Reports,* require that criteria for evaluation be chosen and weighted.

Reviewers have a clear responsibility to their readers. For example, the purpose of *Consumer Reports* is to provide reliable information to consumers, who are often overwhelmed by manufacturers' claims. The magazine therefore has the responsibility to use the best information and criteria available so that readers can make informed decisions. While reviewers' personal tastes play more of a role in subjective reviews such as movie and book reviews, the responsibility to present information accurately to readers remains.

Reviewers have a responsibility to their readers because something of consequence is at stake: A consumer wants to spend money on the best available product; an employer wants to know which workers to promote; a business or government agency needs to know what changes in the system are needed.

For precisely this reason, reviewers have a responsibility to those whose products and performances are being reviewed. Even if unfair, negative reviews can kill a play or cost an employee his or her job.

As you begin considering what kind of review you might write, these issues of partisanship and responsibility will inevitably arise. On whose behalf will you be writing? What are the potential consequences of the evaluations you will make? What responsibilities does this bring to you as a reviewer?

EXERCISE

Write about your topic using the following points of departure. Write what you know and don't worry if your response is incomplete or you have little or no information. The following questions can help you determine whether you need to do further research.

1. **Describe your subject:** Tell as much as you know about it. If it's a book or movie, identify the genre (for example, coming-of-age novel, action-adventure movie, biography, or political analysis), and write a brief summary. If you're reviewing a musical performance or recording, identify the style (for example, classical, modern jazz, urban blues, heavy metal, or country and western), the musicians and instruments, and the tunes or scores they play.

2. **State your current feelings and opinions:** Do you like or dislike what you are reviewing? Everything or just aspects? Do you think it is a good, average, mediocre, or poor example of its kind? Have you always had the same feelings and opinions, or have your views changed? Are there

similar works you prefer? If so, why? Are there similar works you think are inferior to your subject? If so, why?

3. **Give background information:** What do you know about the author of the book, the director of the film, the composer or musical leader? What other works do you know besides the one you are reviewing? How is this work like or different from other works by the author, director, or composer? What do you know about the history of the genre or style of the work? What other examples can you think of?

4. **List what others have written:** Do you know of reviews or articles on your subject? Are there books on it? What have other people said? Do the critics and reviewers seem to agree, or are there debates, differences, or controversies? If so, what's at stake?

5. **Describe your readers:** Who is likely to be interested in your subject? Why? What values and attitudes are they likely to hold? How knowledgeable are your readers likely to be about your subject and other subjects of similar type? What kinds of judgments have they made in the past? What are they likely to think about your opinion? Do you think they will agree or disagree, be surprised, shocked, amused, or angry? At this point, you might want to look carefully at the readers who tend to read the publication to which you are hoping to submit your review. What kinds of reviews have appeared there before? What kinds of values do the readers of that publication seem to have?

Establishing Criteria of Evaluation

Criteria are the standards critics and reviewers use to justify their evaluations. They will vary, depending on what you are reviewing and who your audience is. For example, the criteria you would use to judge suitable movies for eight-year-olds will quite likely differ in at least some important respects from the criteria you would use for college students or other adults. You might recommend the Disney version of *Pocahontas* or *The Secret Garden* for an eight-year-old but rule out *Pulp Fiction,* even though it won an Academy Award and received generally enthusiastic reviews.

To put it another way, one of your criteria in this example would be age-appropriateness. Applying this criterion of evaluation might lead to assertions such as these:

> I think children (not to mention most adults) will enjoy *Pocahontas* because it has great animation, wonderful music, and most of all a memorable heroine who is intelligent and independent.

or

> Quentin Tarantino may indeed put sex and violence to good cinematic use in *Pulp Fiction,* but it's not a movie for children or the squeamish.

Notice in this case that the assertions are based on the same criterion, namely age-appropriateness. Readers who accept this criterion are likely to agree with your assertions, or at least give them a sympathetic reading.

As a review writer, then, part of your job is to identify the criteria that make for the most appropriate and compelling review. Depending on your purpose and audience, you may not be concerned about age-appropriateness; in this case, that criterion is irrelevant. You, as the writer, need to decide which criteria will matter; you also need to identify the criteria to your readers so that they know whether or not to accept your evaluation. In the case of satirical syndicated movie critic Joe Bob Briggs, he has decided to give movies high marks for violence, swearing, partial nudity, and massive explosions. In his reviews, he makes sure his readers understand that these are the qualities he prizes.

EXERCISE

To identify criteria that may help you in your evaluation, respond to the following questions.

1. What qualities do you look for in a good example of the type of item you are reviewing? List at least seven qualities. Rank them from most to least important.

2. What qualities seem to be acceptable to most people? What qualities seem to be the most attractive? Again, list as many qualities as you can, and rank them in order of importance.

3. What makes a particularly bad example? When you write this list, don't simply write the opposite of the "good" qualities listed above. Instead, think of several specific bad examples, and try to identify what made them really stand out as inferior. List these and rank them.

4. Ask others about their most and least desirable criteria. You may want to do an informal survey of the types of people who read the publication you are writing for.

5. By the time you have completed these questions, you should have a full list of possible criteria. Now you can select those that you feel are most appropriate to your project and those that mean the most to you and your readers. Keep that list handy, as you will need to explain it in your review when you write your working draft.

Simply sharing criteria, however, does not ensure that people will come to the same conclusion; people may draw different conclusions from the same criteria. Or they might not share the same criteria at all. Both possibilities are evident in the two previews of Superbowl XXXV. Notice how George and Freeman apply the same criteria to different ends or use criteria not shared by the other reviewer.

Criteria	George	Freeman
Quality of defense		
Overall	Ravens "unmatched"	Ravens one of the "speediest, most aggressive" ever
	Giants "more than capable," will dominate Ravens' offense	——
Pass rush	Peter Boulware will be a "force"	——
Pass defense	——	Ravens' "soft spot"
Run defense	——	Can't run against Ravens
Quarterbacks	Trent Dilfer may make mistakes under pressure	Kerry Collins "accurate enough" to exploit Ravens' secondary
Receivers	Giants' Ron Dixon has speed to "break loose"	——
Intangibles	——	Pregame distractions for Ravens

At this point you can make some decisions about the criteria you have selected for your own assignment. Remember, you will need to justify your criteria to your readers, so make sure you have fully evaluated their appropriateness.

EXERCISE

1. Write down a series of assertions you want to make about what you are reviewing. Use this form of sentence: "I really liked X because Y" or "What made X a great movie is Y."

2. Analyze the assertions. What criteria are you applying in each instance? Do you think readers are likely to accept these criteria as reasonable ones? Why or why not?

3. How might people apply the same criteria but come up with a different evaluation? Are there criteria of evaluation people might use that differ from those you use? How would these criteria influence a reviewer's evaluation?

Criteria of evaluation in a review can also be described as the enabling assumptions by which reviewers link their claim (the movie was good, bad, disappointing, sensationalistic, and so on) to the available evidence (the movie itself). To justify their criteria, reviewers offer backing.

Planning

Considering the Relation Between Description and Evaluation

One issue reviewers face is how much they need to describe what they are reviewing. How much detail should you give? Should you summarize the plot of the movie or book? If so, where and in what detail? How can you best combine such description with your evaluation?

Answers to these questions will depend in part on what the reviewer assumes readers are likely to know about the topic. Their level of familiarity will shape how much the reviewer feels called on to provide background information and description.

These are very real considerations. At the same time, however, it is important to see description and evaluation not as separate writing strategies that require separate space in a review but as strategies that are related to each other.

Stephen Holden's review of *Raging Bull* offers a good example of how writers integrate description and evaluation. In the third paragraph, Holden describes *Raging Bull* as a "grim, realistic biography of the boxing legend Jake La Motta." But then instead of giving an extended summary of the plot, Holden uses the plot to analyze the film and explain his evaluation.

Notice, for example, in the following sentence, how Holden begins with a description of *Raging Bull*'s plot,

> Blindly fighting his way to the top, then falling and stumbling into a shabby middle age,

but then shifts in the main clause to analysis and evaluation,

> undone by the same forces by which he rose, he [Jake La Motta] is a potent tribal symbol who ultimately embarrasses his tribe.

Similarly, notice how Holden combines description and evaluation, using the final scenes of the film to illustrate his assessment of Robert De Niro's performance. The "wonder" of De Niro's portrayal of Jake La Motta, Holden says, "is that we feel any compassion for this flailing, instinctual beast." In the next two sentences, Holden takes readers to the end of the film,

> Yet by the end of the movie, when Jake is a bloated, chest-puffing stand-up comic pathetically mouthing off in a dive for a few extra dollars,

to see the culmination of De Niro's performance,

> the character has achieved a certain embattled nobility.

And then Holden consolidates his point with a description of De Niro's physical appearance and the sheer energy and physical force of his acting style,

> Encased in rolls of flesh (Mr. De Niro put on 50 pounds to play the older Jake) and flashing an ugly, porcine grin, he is still lunging and punching at life as aggressively (and as blindly) as ever...

Using Comparison and Contrast

Comparison and contrast are good strategies to put what you are reviewing in perspective by seeing how it stacks up to something similar. For example, comparing a record album, movie, book, or live performance to others of its kind can help readers get a handle on what you are reviewing.

Stephen Holden, for example, uses comparison and contrast to explain what *Raging Bull* and the *Godfather* films have in common and how they differ. First, Holden identifies their common ground,

> *Raging Bull,* like no movie before, personalizes the *Godfather* films' Darwinian vision of an immigrant urban culture muscling its way up the lower rungs of the social ladder.

And then he points out the main difference,

> But where Mr. Coppola celebrated a shadow aristocracy with its own grand, quasi-royal pecking order, rituals and traditions, Mr. Scorsese imagined a world unencumbered by majesty.

Working Draft

Use the writing you have already done to get started. Consider how your opening can characterize what you're reviewing and make your evaluation clear to readers. Reviewers do not necessarily point out the criteria of judgment they are using. Nonetheless, to engage your readers, you need to make sure the criteria are easy to identify, even if they are only implied. Consider, too, how you can weave description and other background information into your review. Are there comparisons and contrasts worth making?

Engaging Others

Reviews do not take place in a vacuum. In many cases, reviewers not only tell readers their evaluation of a work or performance but also locate that evaluation in relation to evaluations others have made. Doing so enables them to distinguish their views from what others have said or written and thereby clarify exactly where they are coming from and what criteria they are using.

Take, for example, the opening paragraphs in Karen Durbin's review of *Ally McBeal.* Notice how she presents four reasons for why *Time* magazine thinks Ally McBeal is the "antithesis of true feminism" and then goes on to explain her own perspective.

In some cases, such as in Alan A. Stone's "How the FBI Fueled the Waco Fire," major differences over analysis and evaluation shape the reviewer's stance and purpose. Notice in the opening paragraph how Stone locates his views in relation to the Justice Department's factual investigation and the evaluation by Edward Dennis. First, he acknowledges that the evidence assembled in the Justice Department review "overwhelmingly proves" the Branch Davidians set the Waco compound on fire and killed themselves. But then, when Stone turns to the issue of the FBI's role, he notes that both reviews argue "that nothing the FBI could have done would have changed the outcome." Here is the crux of the matter for Stone, who says bluntly, "That is not my impression." In the rest of the review, Stone explains what he thinks the FBI could have done differently.

Peer Commentary

Exchange the working draft of your review with a classmate. Respond to the following questions in writing:

1. Is the subject defined clearly? Does the review give the reader enough details and background information to understand the reviewer's evaluation? Are there things you wanted to know that the writer left out? Are there things the writer mentions but that you would like to know more about?

2. Does the reviewer's evaluation come across clearly? As you read the draft, where did you become aware of the reviewer's evaluation? Point to the sentence or passage. Do you understand what the reviewer's criteria are? Do they need to be stated more clearly? Are they reasonable criteria? Are there other criteria you think the writer should take into account?

3. Does the review seem balanced? How does the reviewer combine description and evaluation? Does the reviewer talk about good and bad points, positive and negative aspects? Is the tone appropriate?

4. Does the reviewer use comparisons? If so, where and for what purposes?

5. What suggestions would you make to strengthen the review?

Revising

Use the peer responses to reread your working draft. Consider these issues:

1. Do you bring the work or performance into focus for your readers by using strategies such as describing it, characterizing what type or genre it is, explaining how it is similar to or differs from others of its kind, and providing adequate background information?

2. Is your evaluation clear and easy to understand, or are you hedging in one way or another?

3. Does it make sense in your review to engage what others have already written or said about the work or performance? If so, how can you distinguish your own perspective from others'?

4. Do you attend to both good and bad points, positive and negative features? Remember being balanced does not mean being objective or neutral. To make an evaluation you have to commit yourself and explain how, given the good and the bad, you have made a judgment based on criteria.

Options for Meaningful Endings

The ending of your review should do more than just summarize what you have already said. Look at the ending as an opportunity to leave your readers with something further to think about regarding the significance of the work or performance you've reviewed.

Notice, for example, the strategy for ending that Denise Sega uses in her working draft "More Than Just Burnouts," a review of Donna Gaines' book *Teenage Wasteland* that appears in full below. In this case, Denise ends her review by indicating who would be interested in the book and why.

> ### WORKING DRAFT
>
> In conclusion, I believe this is an important book that should be read by anyone interested in finding out more about the "gritty underside of white teen life in the suburbs" (cover notes). Compared to the sensationalistic stories in the press that blame teenage suicide on drugs or heavy metal, Donna Gaines has taken the time to listen—and to hear what the kids have to say.

The strategy Sega has chosen, of course, is not the only possible way to end her review meaningfully. Here are two other strategies reviewers commonly draw on.

1. Anticipate a possible objection. Some readers may feel that Donna Gaines identifies too much with the "burnouts"—and that her research is thereby "contaminated" by her personal allegiances. Gaines' partisanship, however, gives the book its unique authority. By gaining the trust of Bergenfield's heavy metal kids, Gaines is able to give their side of things and to show how they make sense of their world. After reading *Teenage Wasteland*, it's hard not to think these kids need an advocate who can speak on their behalf.

2. Connect to a larger context of issues. Youth-bashing has become a popular spectator sport in recent years, and events such as the school shootings in Littleton, Colorado and elsewhere have fueled adult fears and anxieties about teenagers. Perhaps the most important achievement of Teenage Wasteland is that it cuts through the moral panic and the sensationalistic stories in the press and on TV about young people. Instead, Gaines gives us an understanding of how alienated teenagers experience their lives.

WRITERS' WORKSHOP

Written for a sociology course on youth culture, the following is a working draft of a review of Donna Gaines's book *Teenage Wasteland*. The assignment was to draft a four-page review that evaluated the book, to exchange it with a classmate for peer commentary, and to revise. The writer, Denise Sega, had a number of concerns she wanted her partner to address in the peer commentary. Here's the note she wrote:

> I'm worried that I spend too much time summarizing the book and not enough explaining my evaluation of it. What do you think? Do I say too much about the author and the book's contents? Is my evaluation clear to you? Do you think I give enough explanation of why I liked the book so much? Any other suggestions are also appreciated. Thanks.

As you read, keep in mind what Denise asked her partner. When you finish reading the working draft, consider how you would respond.

MORE THAN JUST BURNOUTS (WORKING DRAFT)

Denise Sega

DONNA GAINES, TEENAGE WASTELAND: SUBURBIA'S DEAD END KIDS. NEW YORK: HARPER PERENNIAL, 1991.

Youth culture. Teenagers have devised many different ways of growing up. From jocks and preps to neo-Beatnicks and hip-hop kids, most high schools contain a range of distinctive social groupings. In *Teenage Wasteland,* Donna Gaines looks at a group of "burnouts" and heavy metal teens in suburban New Jersey, the "dead end" working-class kids who are alienated from school and community. The opening paragraphs explain the situation that led Gaines to write this book:

> When I heard about the suicide pact it grabbed me in the solar plexus. I looked at the pictures of the kids and their friends. I read what reporters said. I was sitting in my garden apartment looking out on Long Island's Jericho Turnpike thinking maybe this is how the world ends, with the last generation bowing out first.
> In Bergenfield, New Jersey, on the morning of March 11, 1987, the bodies of four teenagers were discovered inside a 1977 Chevrolet Camaro. The car, which belonged to Thomas Olton, was parked in an unused garage in the Foster Village garden apartment complex, behind the Foster Village Shopping Center. Two sisters, Lisa and Cheryl Burress, and their friends, Thomas Rizzo and Thomas Olton, had died of carbon monoxide poisoning. (3)

The remainder of the introduction reveals the rationale and research plan for Gaines' investigation of the suicides. What began as an assignment for the *Village Voice,* for which Gaines writes regularly, her investigation eventually became her doctoral work as well as the book in review.

Besides providing more details about the instigating event, the Bergenfield suicide pact, the introductory pages also provide autobiographical details about the author which are essential to understanding

Gaines' devotion to her task, as well as her informed frame of reference. Gaines, too, in many ways, was a "burnout." She describes her growing up years and habits. She explains that "like many of [her] peers, [she] spent a lot of [her] adulthood recovering from a personal history of substance abuse, family trauma, school failure, and arrests" (4). To put this life behind her, Gaines turned to social work, first as a "big sister" with junior high students in Brooklyn and then as a helper on a suicide prevention hotline. After becoming a New York State certified social worker, Gaines worked in the special adoptions and youth services divisions and as a street worker providing services for troubled teens. Eventually she moved into research and program evaluation and finally returned to school to complete her doctorate in sociology.

In the introduction, Gaines also explains the need for the book. Initially, she was reluctant to write about suicidal teens because she felt that "if I couldn't help them, I didn't want to bother them" (6). She did not like the idea of turning vulnerable people like the Bergenfield teens into "research subjects" by getting them to trust her with their secrets. Despite these qualms, however, she did decide to go to Bergenfield and ultimately spent two years hanging out with the "burnouts" and "dropouts" of suburban New Jersey, talking to them about heavy metal music, Satanism, work, school, the future, and many other things. Gaines was angry because these teens had been classified by adults as "losers" and never allowed to tell their side of the story. The press had explained the suicides as the result of the individual problems of troubled teens and failed to see, as Gaines does so clearly in her book, how the suicides "symbolized a tragic defeat for young people" (6) and a wider pattern of alienation.

Teenage Wasteland reveals the sense of sadness among the teens in Bergenfield. "By nineteen," Gaines writes, "you've hit the brick wall and you really need something. Because there is nothing to do here and there is nowhere to go" (78). Young people hanging out seems to annoy and even frighten adults. Nevertheless, for these teens, there does not seem to be anything else to do. According to Gaines, they have been neglected by society for so long, experienced so much lack of care in so many ways, that they see no alternatives. They see no hope for anything better.

The only "ticket out" these teens see is to be like Jon Bon Jovi or Keith Richards. The chances of becoming a rock star, of course, is one in a million. The dream breaks down, the kids realize their limitations, and they feel they have run out of choices for the future. There seem to be no alternatives to their bleak situations:

> At the bottom are kids with poor basic skills, short attention spans, limited emotional investment in the future. Also poor housing, poor nutrition, bad schooling, bad lives. And in their bad jobs they will face careers of unsatisfying part-time work, low pay, no benefits, and no opportunity for advancement.

There are the few possibilities offered by a relative—a coveted place in a union, a chance to join a small family business in a service trade, a spot in a small shop. In my neighborhood, kids dream of making a good score on the cop tests, working up from hostess to waitress. Most hang out in limbo hoping to get called for a job in the sheriff's department, or the parks, or sanitation. They're on all the lists, although they know the odds for getting called are slim. The lists are frozen, the screening process is endless. (155)

According to Gaines, these are "America's invisible classes," the "unseen and unheard...legions of young people who now serve the baby boom and others, in fancy eateries, video stores, and supermarkets" (157). Given this situation, it is no surprise that Bergenfield's teens turn to Satanism and heavy metal to give them a sense of power and a refuge in a world over which they feel they have no control. There are no good jobs, and the social programs for these teens only label them as "troubled" or "deviant" or "burnouts" and do not work.

One truly fascinating part of the book involves Gaines' etymology of the term "burnout." Besides providing at least twenty-five synonyms for the term, she also explains its evolution. Furthermore, she differentiates between "burnouts" and "dirtbags"—a subtle yet significant distinction. Her discussion of how these terms reflect teens feeling "powerless, useless, and ineffectual" is, in itself, powerful, useful, and effectual in helping readers understand the deep sense of alienation afflicting the "teenage wasteland."

In conclusion, I believe this is an important book that should be read by anyone interested in finding out more about the "gritty underside of white teen life in the suburbs" (cover notes). Compared to the sensationalistic stories in the press that blame teenage suicide on drugs or heavy metal, Donna Gaines has taken the time to listen—and to hear what the kids have to say.

WORKSHOP QUESTIONS

1. In her note to her partner, Denise Sega raises a number of issues about her working draft. One of these concerns the amount of description and evaluation that appear in the draft. She seems worried that she spends too much time summarizing the book and talking about the author and not enough on evaluation. How would you respond to this concern? What suggestions would you offer?

2. It is obvious that Sega admires *Teenage Wasteland,* but she raises the question of whether the criteria of evaluation she uses come across clearly enough. Reread the draft and mark those passages that make an evaluation or imply one. What seem to be the criteria Sega uses in each case? If the criteria are not stated explicitly, express in your own words

what they seem to be. What advice would you give Sega about present-ing her criteria of evaluation more explicitly?

3. In the third paragraph, Sega compares the treatment of the Bergenfield suicide pact by the press to Gaines's treatment in *Teenage Wasteland*. What is the point of this comparison? Do you think Sega could do more with it? If so, how could the comparison be extended and strengthened? Do other comparisons appear in the draft? If so, are they effective, or could they use more work? Are there other comparisons you can think of that Sega might use?

REFLECTING ON YOUR WRITING

The assignments throughout the chapter have put you in the role of a reviewer and shown how you might evaluate a performance, a program, or a policy. For your portfolio, shift focus to discuss how you have been reviewed by others—by teachers in school, supervisors at work, judges at performances, and peer commentators in your writing course.

First, give a little background on your experiences of being evaluated in and out of school. What were the circumstances of the evaluations? Why were you being evaluated? What criteria were used? What was your response to the eval-uations? Were these experiences helpful to you? Explain why or why not.

Second, use this background to reconstruct your attitude toward evaluation when you entered your writing course. Has your attitude changed? Why or why not? What has been the effect on you as a writer, a student, and a person of receiving reviews from both your teacher and your peers? What differences, if any, do you see between teachers' and peers' evaluations? What suggestions would you offer for improving the process of evaluation in your writing course?

A CLOSING NOTE

Reviews, of course, are made to be read by the public, by the readers, viewers, listeners, concertgoers, diners, tourists, and fans who care about arts and enter-tainment. By the same token, reviews of educational programs and government actions and policies are meant to be read by the people in charge. Consider pub-lishing your review or sending it to the appropriate officials. Student newspa-pers often publish reviews as well as predictions about sporting events. Electronic mail discussion groups are another possible outlet.

PART THREE

Writers at Work

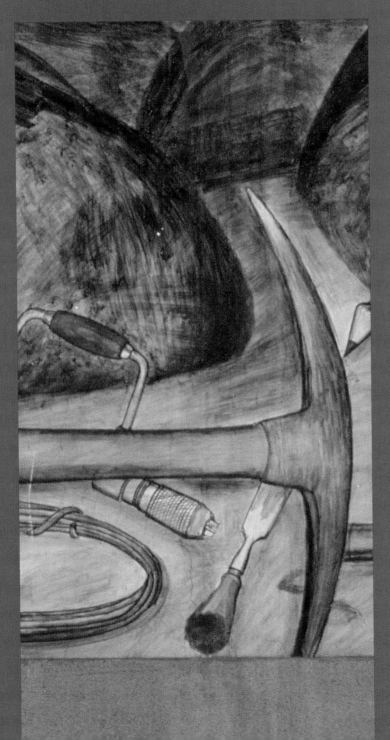

INTRODUCTION:
MANAGING YOUR WRITING PROJECTS

Different writing tasks demand different ways of working. Let's look at writers at work in three different situations to see how they respond to the call to write:

1. A first-year college student receives an e-mail message from a friend at another college and, without stopping to plan, immediately responds with a long e-mail message in return. First she talks about how funny her political science teacher was today in class, and sends along a joke he told. Then, after pausing briefly, she launches into a discussion of two mutual high school friends she saw over the weekend. This makes her think about Christmas vacation coming up, and she asks when her friend is coming home and whether they can plan a get-together of all four friends. Then she stops, rereads what she has written, deletes something she said about one of the friends as too gossipy, adds a short note saying she just saw a really scary movie, and sends the e-message. Two days later her friend replies with details about getting together over Christmas vacation.

2. A local newspaper is planning a special supplement to mark the beginning of the baseball season, and the sports editor asks a freelance writer (and baseball fan) to contribute a thousand-word essay. They talk in a general way about the focus of the essay—to evoke nostalgia for the traditions of America's national pastime. Based on this discussion, the writer goes to work. He sketches a series of notes on a pad and then drafts by hand a personal account of going to Wrigley Field with his dad to see the Chicago Cubs play in the days before the ballpark had lights. He enters the draft on his computer, making a number of changes along the way. When he discusses the draft with a close friend, however, it becomes clear that the piece of writing is really a memoir about the writer's relationship with his father and is not appropriate for the baseball supplement. Nonetheless one section that discusses changes in baseball gives him an idea—to compare the old-fashioned joys of going to the ballpark to see the hometown team with the new era of free-agency, million-dollar salaries, sports complexes, and luxury boxes.

    He writes another draft, focusing this time on how greedy owners, high ticket prices, and players with no team loyalties are ruining the game. When the writer's friend reads this draft, he notices that the tone is wrong—too angry, too much of a scathing criticism of the game. But both he and the writer also notice that the strongest passages are those where the writer describes ballparks from a fan's point of view (something he has carried over from the first version). So the writer decides to write a commentary on how baseball stadiums have changed over the years—from old-fashioned parks such as Wrigley Field to suburban multipurpose sports complexes such as the Oakland Coliseum and back to baseball-only stadiums such as Baltimore's Camden Yards, which embody a nostalgia for tradition. This focus seems to give him the critical distance he needs to adjust his tone and emphasis to the occasion. He writes a new draft in a day, only to realize that he needs some information on the Houston Astrodome. After looking up the facts and incorporating the new material, he spends two days tinkering with sentences and passages, revising on hard copy by hand. He enters the final changes, prints and proofreads the essay, and sends it to the editor.

3. The marketing manager of a regional drugstore chain is asked to prepare a report on the results of the company's decision to add a small grocery and dairy section to its stores. From experience, she has a fairly clear idea of the information and the form of writing her readers expect. Her first step is to create a document on her computer by outlining the main sections of her report. Then she assembles relevant information—the original plan for the grocery and dairy section, sales figures, financial statements, and advertising reports—and spends an hour with the head of marketing research discussing the results of a recent customer survey. As she reads these materials, she marks information and written passages to incorporate into her report. She spends the better part of a day filling in her outline, moving figures, tables, graphs, and passages from other documents into sections of her report. She makes sure adequate summaries, transitions, and explanations hold the parts together. Finally, she returns to the introduction, which had been left as a sketchy few sentences, and drafts a full version. The next day, she reads the report carefully, changes the order of two sentences, rewrites a few others, and corrects some typos. Then she proofreads, checks the figures and tables, adds a title page, and submits the document.

As these examples show, writers manage their writing tasks in very different ways. Sometimes they spend lots of time planning, as the marketing manager does. In other cases the writing comes out spontaneously, as it does for the e-mail writer. Sometimes the purpose and focus of the writing emerge gradually, as you can see in the example of the freelance writer who spends a great deal of time revising. In other cases less revision is needed.

These differences in managing the writing task can be traced in part to the different genres the three writers are using. For the first writer, the openness and informality of the personal letter or e-mail allow her to link observations and anecdotes together loosely, without worrying about transitions or logical connections. For the marketing manager, the predictable form of the business report provides her with a scaffolding to organize her material. For the freelance writer, however, genre poses a problem he needs to solve in order to complete the writing task, and one of his key decisions is to shift from memoir to commentary.

You can see, too, from these examples that writers use feedback and discussion with others in different ways. The e-mail writer, for example, is responding to a friend's message, and in turn her friend sends a reply. Their personal correspondence is likely to continue this way as long as they are friends. The freelance writer and the marketing manager, however, consult with others, which does more than maintain personal relationships. The freelance writer's friend provides careful readings and important feedback that shape the writer's revisions. The marketing manager's discussion with a colleague contributes useful information for her report.

Finally, these examples show how writers use the tools of writing in different ways. Some draft at the keyboard, while others prefer to write with pen in hand. Some revise directly on the screen, while others like to work on hard copy. And as the case of the marketing manager shows, new writing technologies enable writers to move material easily from one document to another.

The chapters in this part explore how writers work. First, we present a case study of a college writing assignment. Next, we look at how writers collaborate on group writing projects. Then we consider the tools writers use, especially the new writing technologies. Finally, we examine how the forms of writing embody writers' purposes.

Before we turn to these matters, however, let's take a closer look at how people manage writing tasks and the habits they develop as writers.

ELEMENTS OF WRITING TASKS

No two writers compose in the same way, and an individual may work in different ways on different writing tasks. Nonetheless, there are predictable elements in a writing project that can be listed. As you can see, these elements appear in the writing assignments in Part Two:

- **Invention:** Developing an approach to the topic and to readers, assessing purpose, doing research, choosing the appropriate genre.

- **Planning:** Designing the arrangement of material, finding an appropriate pattern of organization.

- **Drafting:** Creating a working draft, getting ideas down on paper.

- **Peer commentary:** Getting feedback from others, seeing the working draft through the reader's eyes.

- **Revising:** Rereading the working draft, clarifying purpose and organization, connecting the parts.

- **Manuscript preparation:** Document design, editing, proofreading.

Because of the way the elements of writing have been listed, you may think that they constitute a series of steps you can follow. If you look at writers at work, however, you'll see that they may well manage these elements in quite different ways. Some writers like to start drafting before they develop a clear plan, while others would not think of drafting without a carefully developed outline.

Nor are the elements necessarily separate from each other. Some people revise as they draft, working carefully over each section before going on to the next, while others write quickly and then think about needed revisions. Nor do writers spend the same amount of time on each of the elements. Depending on the writing task and their own writing habits, writers learn how to manage the elements in ways that work for them.

Writing can be exhilarating, but it can be aggravating too. You can probably think of times when writing seemed to pour out, leading you to previously unsuspected ideas and precisely the right way of saying things. On the other hand, you may have had moments when you couldn't begin a writing task or got stuck in the middle. The way to get to the source of such difficulties is to think about how you are managing the elements of your writing task. Are you spending your time doing what needs to be done to get the writing task completed? Should you be revising and editing passages that you may eventually discard? Is this keeping you from figuring out how (or whether) the passage connects to other points? If you see your draft diverge from your outline, should you follow it or go back and revise your plan? When you're stuck in the middle of a draft, do you need to turn to invention—to read more or talk to others?

Answers to these questions will vary, of course, depending on the writing task and your own habits as a writer. The point is that experienced writers learn to ask such questions in order to get their bearings, especially when the writing is not going well, to see where they stand in putting a piece of writing together and what they need to do next.

Reflecting On Your Writing:
How You Managed A Writing Task

Think of a writing task you completed recently, in school or out of school. Analyze how you managed the task. To do this, consider the following questions:

1. What called on you to write? Describe how you defined the writing task. How did you establish your purpose? What did your exploration of the topic involve? How did you imagine your readers and the relationship you wanted to establish with them? What genre did you choose? Did you talk to others about your ideas?

2. Explain how you planned the writing. How much planning did you do? When, and what form did it take?

3. Describe how you drafted. When did you begin? How much invention and planning did you do before you started drafting?

4. Describe what feedback, if any, you received on your draft. What was the effect of this feedback?

5. What kinds of revisions did you make? When did you revise—during drafting, after you had a complete working draft, at various points?

6. What final form did the writing take? Were any considerations of document design involved? Did you edit and proofread the final version?

Now look back over your answers to these questions. What conclusions can you draw about how you managed the elements of the writing process in this instance? What, if anything, would you do differently if you had to do the task again?

WRITING HABITS

We've all got our idiosyncrasies, and writers are no exception, especially when it comes to writing. Most experienced writers have well-developed habits concerning their writing. In fact, often these habits are so developed that they take on the character of a ritual, in much the same way athletes have pregame rituals and superstitions.

It's not surprising that writers develop their own habits. Writing can be hard work, and writers' habits are a way of handling the difficulties and emotional stress of writing. To be productive, they need to be in the right frame of mind, and their writing habits can help them prepare mentally to face their writing task and to pace themselves over its duration. In this sense, individual writing habits are part of the way writers manage the writing process.

- **Time and place:** Some writers like to get up early in the morning to write, while others prefer late-night writing sessions. Some writers need total quiet and solitude, while others prefer public places or music in the background.

- **Technology:** Some writers have special pens they use and particular kinds of lined paper, while others always compose on an old typewriter and still others on a computer equipped with the latest word-processing program.

- **Prewriting habits:** Some writers find that they are most productive if they write after they have run or swum or worked out in the gym. Some writers need to straighten up their desk or work environment as preparation to write. Some play computer games or read for a while before they write. Others even need to put on certain clothes—to dress in a particular way to take on the role of the writer.

■ **Pacing the task:** Some writers like to write for as long as they can, until they're exhausted or have reached an impasse. Others write for a pre-determined amount of time and then stop no matter where they are. Still others stop only at a point where they know exactly what they want to say next so that getting started again will be easy. And some writers play with fire: They wait until the last minute, with a deadline bearing down on them, to start writing.

■ **Breaks:** A break is an opportunity for writers to relax and unwind or to gain some distance and mull over a problem in the writing. Some writers like to take long walks, whether in the city or the country. Others go to the movies or watch television. Still others do household chores or gardening. In any case, it's important to see breaks as part of the writing process, not as a retreat from it.

Reflecting On Your Writing: Describing Your Writing Habits

Describe your writing habits. At what time of day do you like to write? Where do you like to write? What tools of writing best suit you? What prewriting habits, if any, do you follow? How do you pace yourself? When do you take breaks and what do you do on them? Which of your habits are most useful to you? Which, if any, would you consider changing?

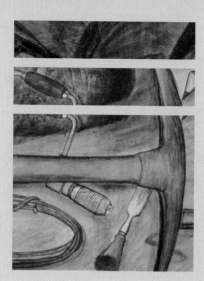

CHAPTER TWELVE

Case Study of a Writing Assignment

If you ask people to describe a writer at work, it is likely that they will describe a lonely figure at a desk, surrounded by books and manuscripts, facing the terrors of the blank page or computer screen, sustained by endless cups of coffee. The image of the writer as an individual struggling in isolation to produce works of writing is deeply engrained in the popular consciousness.

Now it's true that writers often spend a good deal of time working independently. But that does not necessarily mean that they are working in isolation. In fact, writing often involves considerable social interaction. Consider, for example, these two scenarios:

- A group of poets known as the Olney Street Collective have been meeting monthly for over twenty years in Providence, Rhode Island. Members of the group come from many walks of life—teaching, law, public relations, journalism, and business. None of them is a famous poet, but all have been published in small literary magazines. They write in their spare time, when they have the chance, and sometimes they go through long stretches without writing at all. The group's membership has changed over the years as people moved away or lost interest. But the group itself has kept going because it seems to fill a need for people who write poetry to get together and read their poems. The meetings are informal. There's lots of talk about poetry, movies, life, jobs, people's children or lovers or spouses, but little criticism or discussion of the poems the members read. Members come to read their poems and listen to others read.

- A history professor is preparing an article based on her research on the role of women in the anti-Vietnam War movement and its connection to the emergence of contemporary feminism. She has already interviewed many women who played key roles in both the antiwar and women's liberation movements, and she has discussed these issues at length with students in a history seminar. She presented some of her research at a conference of American historians and received responses, questions, and counterinterpretations from her copanelists and from members of the audience. She has also spent a good deal of time talking about her research with a trusted colleague in the history department.

These two scenarios only begin to suggest the range of social interactions that surround and sustain acts of writing. For the poets, the monthly meetings of their poetry group serve as a support system and an occasion to get together with like-minded people to share their writing. Similarly, the history professor's work has benefited from the women she interviewed, the presentation at the conference, and informal discussion with her colleague. In each case, individuals draw on common interests and professional connections with others to foster their writing. At the same time, while they depend in crucial respects on these interactions, the poets and the history professor are working as individual authors to produce their own writing, taking full responsibility for it and receiving the credit.

As you will see in the next chapter, there are other writing situations in which people work together to produce collaboratively written projects. In this chapter, you'll see how writers and readers work together on individual writing projects.

COLLABORATING ON YOUR WRITING PROJECTS

Analyzing writing assignments with classmates, talking with others about ideas for a paper, reading and responding to working drafts, offering suggestions for editing—these are some of the ways that writers and readers can work together on individual writing projects. The writing assignments in Part Two include suggestions for collaborating at various steps in the writing task and directions for peer commentary. Teachers in other classes may also ask you to comment on another student's work-in-progress. For these reasons, it's worth taking a moment to look at some of the benefits of working together on individual writing assignments.

The main premise behind working together on individual writing assignments is the old idea that two (or more) heads are better than one. By interacting with others, you can draw on a wider range of experience, knowledge, and problem-solving strategies. Feedback from readers brings new perspectives to an issue or problem so that you can consider alternatives that might not otherwise have occurred to you and develop ways to negotiate your differences with others.

Besides, working together can be fun and rewarding in its own right. There's something about people working together that seems to create energy and increase everyone's involvement in the work.

Giving and getting feedback and suggestions from other students on individual writing projects can help you in your role as a writer and as a reader who is learning to read carefully and make helpful comments.

- For you as a writer, getting feedback from others helps overcome the sense of isolation writers often experience in working alone by exploring how your work-in-progress communicates to readers. In this way, collaboration with others can help you discover your purpose, clarify your focus, and understand your readers' need for precise language and coherent organization.

- For you as a reader, providing feedback at various stages in the writing process enables you to see how other writers shape their ideas and manage their work-in-progress. In this way, collaboration involves readers in the messy and creative work of planning and drafting, helps them learn to read carefully and critically, and promotes a sense of tactful response to the work of others.

EXPLORING YOUR EXPERIENCE

Have you been involved in writing workshops where you worked with other students on individual writing assignments? What types of interactions took place? Did you discuss ideas for papers with classmates? Did you exchange drafts and respond to other students' writing? Describe your experiences. What has it been like for you to get response to your writing from other students? What has it been like for you to respond to other students' work? What do you see as the difference between a teacher's and a fellow student's response to your writing?

CASE STUDY OF A WRITING ASSIGNMENT

To see how writers and readers can work together effectively, in the rest of this chapter we'll follow a student, Krista Guglielmetti, preparing a paper for a mass communication course. This case study will help you understand how writers and readers can collaborate at various stages of an individual work in progress, what use writers can make of responses from readers, and when the writer needs to work independently. As you will see, collaboration begins with discussion of ideas and approaches before any drafting takes place. At later stages, once the writer has produced a working draft, readers may provide written commentary.

Invention

You don't need to wait until you have a working draft to collaborate with others on your writing. Experienced writers often find that they want—and need—to talk to others before they begin writing to help them think more concretely about their audience and purpose and to brainstorm ideas about their topic.

Assessing Your Purpose

It can be difficult to get started on a writing project if you are uncertain about the call to write and the kind of writing task it presents. You may not be clear, for example, about what an assignment in one of your courses is calling on you to do. If you feel shaky about the purpose of a writing assignment, other students in the class probably do too. Of course, you could talk to the teacher, but you may also want to collaborate with classmates to clarify the purpose of the assignment and develop an approach to it.

Here is the writing assignment Krista Guglielmetti was given in Introduction to Mass Communication. Read the assignment. Then work together with classmates to determine what it seems to call on Krista and her classmates to do.

WRITING ASSIGNMENT

Introduction to Mass Communication

Much as visual representations from the past idealized families huddled around the fireplace for warmth and comfort, we now have idealized pictures of families gathered together in front of the television set. (See the accompanying illustration.) Media critics have raised questions about what

such viewing time actually means for the contemporary family. Does it represent an important moment of family togetherness, a means of avoiding really encountering each other, or something else? Draw on your family's viewing habits to write a short (2-page, 500-word) essay that explains the role television plays in the contemporary family. You will need to describe how your family uses television viewing, but your essay should also analyze what such viewing practices tell us about the role of television in the contemporary family.

EXERCISE

Work together with two or three classmates to analyze this writing assignment and to determine what it is calling on students in the Introduction to Mass Communication class to do. The following guidelines can be used for virtually any writing assignment. Of course, since you are not actually a student in the mass communication class, you won't have all the information available to Krista and her classmates. Nonetheless, you can make some informed guesses by picking up important cues from the assignment.

Guidelines for Analyzing Writing Assignments

1. Look for key words in the assignment—such as *describe, summarize, explain, analyze,* or *evaluate critically.* Discuss what these terms might mean in relation to the material you're being asked to write about and the goals and focus of the course.

2. Consider what information you need to do the assignment successfully. Where can you get this information? Does the assignment call for additional research, or is it based on class readings and discussion? Are there things you know or have learned in other classes that might prove useful?

3. Look for any special directions the assignment provides about the form of writing. Does it call for a specific genre (such as a report, a proposal, or a review)? Does it call for documentation? Consider the assigned length. What is it possible to do well within these limits?

After your group has answered these questions, compare your response to those of other groups. At this point, what advice would you give Krista as she begins the assignment?

Understanding Readers

Another difficulty in getting started on a writing task may be the writers' uncertainty about what will interest their readers. Sometimes writers feel that if they have thought of something, everyone else must have too. Underestimating the importance of their own ideas, they feel reluctant to express them. One way to test your ideas is to discuss them with other people. That way you can not only reassure yourself that your ideas are valid but also begin to formulate a plan for approaching your readers.

Talking out the ideas you have for a paper is one of the best ways to understand your readers. Here are some guidelines for doing this, followed by a transcript of Krista's discussion with her roommate Tamika.

Guidelines for Understanding Your Readers

1. Find a willing listener, describe your writing task, and then tell your listener what you are thinking of writing about and what you are thinking of saying about it.

2. Ask your listener what she already knows about your subject, what she would like to know about it, and whether she has ideas or information you could use in your writing.

TRANSCRIPT OF KRISTA'S DISCUSSION WITH TAMIKA

KRISTA: I've got to write this paper for my mass comm course on families and television viewing. We're supposed to use our own family to explain what television means in terms of family life.

TAMIKA: Sounds cool. In my lit class all we write about is John Milton and Alexander Pope. At least you've met these people. So what are you going to say?

KRISTA: Well, that's the problem. As you know, my family is a disaster. But I don't want to lay on all this dysfunctional stuff. I thought I could maybe say something about how families use television to avoid really relating to each other. That's sure what happens in my family. But I'm worried this is too obvious. What do you think? Does that sound interesting?

TAMIKA: Oh yeah. People these days are definitely using TV as a means of avoidance. You're supposed to be all happy together, only nobody talks to each other because some TV show is going on.

KRISTA: Why is that?

TAMIKA: In my opinion, people care more about what happens to those idiots on *Just Shoot Me* than their own selves.

KRISTA: You really think so? I mean, do you think I can do something here? My teacher has to like it, you know.

TAMIKA: That goes without saying. Just think up some reasons why people like TV more than they like real life. That's the point. You go, girl. You got your main idea.

KRISTA: I hope so. Thanks, Tamika. I better get to work.

TAMIKA: Yeah, but how about cleaning your side of the room first?

Exploring the Topic

At a certain point, writers need to get some ideas down on paper, even if the writing is of a preliminary sort. One way to start is to do exploratory writing, in which you're tentatively working out the focus and direction of your paper. If you want someone to look at your exploratory writing, you can use the guidelines below. Make sure that the person who reads your writing understands that it is an initial attempt to discover what you want to say.

Guidelines for Responding to Exploratory Writing

1. Ask your reader to circle or underline key phrases and interesting ideas, whether or not they seem to be the main point of the writing.

2. Ask your reader to tell you if there seem to be, implied or lurking just off the page, ideas that you could develop.

After thinking about her conversation with Tamika, Krista decided to do some exploratory writing. Below is her writing and the response from her friend Eric.

KRISTA'S EXPLORATORY WRITING

When I was a kid, I dreaded Monday nights. I would be up in my room happily reading a book when I would be summoned by my father to come down and watch TV with the rest of the family. There was no escape. This was supposed to be "quality time"—one of the few moments in the week the family got together. Only we weren't really together. How can you be, sitting silently in front of a TV set? It was pitiful, watching some family in a sit com on TV instead of being a family. All we succeeded in doing was to substitute a fictional family for the real one—us.

ERIC'S RESPONSE

To me, the most interesting point here is the one about how people substitute fictional TV families for real ones. I think you could use this as the basis for your essay. I sense a lot of anger at your family, and I think you need to be careful with this. As I understand it, your assignment is an analytical one, not just a personal essay about your family. Maybe you could look more into why people want to watch TV families. What are the reasons? If you could develop some ideas about why TV families are preferable to real ones, you could explain why and how your family used TV families to create this sense of false togetherness.

Planning

Using discussions with others about their ideas for a writing project, writers need to develop a plan for their writing. The key issue at this point is how to arrange their material so that they highlight the main point and provide supporting evidence.

After Krista talked to Tamika and got response to her exploratory writing from Eric, she mulled over the results. She knew it was time to use this information to plan her essay. Tamika and Eric helped her see that she needed to write an analytical essay that made a central claim and backed it up with evidence. A personal essay that focused on her feelings about her family was not the kind of writing called for by the assignment.

At this point, she worked by herself, developing her main idea and arranging reasons to support it. She sketched the following brief outline so that she could begin drafting.

Krista's Brief Outline

Introduction
    Begin with an anecdote about my family
        Getting called down on Monday night to watch TV with the family
    Generalize this experience
        Claim: the only quality family time left is spent in front of TV
Body
    Give reasons why this is so
        It's easy
        Actors are doing the work of being a family for us
        For TV's fictional families, everything works out
Ending
    How to deal with the problem?
        Turn off the TV and talk to your family

Drafting

Any plan a writer develops needs to be tested by writing a working draft. Outlines, sketches, or other kinds of preliminary planning can tell you only so much. To see where your ideas are going, you must commit them to paper.

After she sketched a brief outline, the next step for Krista was to write a working draft. As you can see, she used ideas and suggestions from Tamika and Eric. But, as is the case in individual writing projects, she worked independently to write the draft. Here is what she came up with.

KRISTA'S WORKING DRAFT

It's 8:00 on a Monday night, and I am sitting at home in my bedroom peacefully reading a novel. Suddenly, the dreaded call comes, "Kris, you been in that room for two hours. Come on out here and be with the family for awhile. *Cosby* is going to start in five minutes. Don't you want to watch it with us?" Well, actually no. I was content with my book. But Dad and the family saw these hours in front of the television as quality, and I was expected to participate. What I constantly wondered every Monday was why? When did sitting in front of the tube become family time?

Unfortunately, my family is not the exception but the rule. People are able to remember it is Monday and at 5:00 they can watch the heartwarming merger of blended families on *Full House*. Yet, without a calendar, they have a difficult time remembering that this particular Monday is their stepmother's or stepfather's birthday and they should get a card or gift on the way home from work or school. They can tell you that the hot couple is headed for divorce on *Melrose Place* more easily than they can see the status of their own marriage. People may not have noticed, but the only quality family time left is that shared on the TV. The family has left the living room and has gone to live in the TV set in the form of fictional families living fictional lives that the real people would be living if they weren't watching TV.

So what happened? When did fiction become stronger than reality? And is there a way out? I propose the theory that it happened because it was easy. It takes no effort to sit and stare at the TV. It takes work to relate to your family. Now, that is what we pay actors for: to do that work for us, to relate to their families in the ways that we no longer can. On TV, blended families always work out, drug addicts are always treated, and no one is ever hurt permanently. It's easy. Just follow the script and everything will be fine. After all, if you're watching TV, you won't fight (except over who has the remote). If you don't fight, no one can get hurt and everyone will be happy. Let the TV characters fight. They always make up on the half hour. What could be simpler?

The solution? That's simpler and more obvious than the problem. If the TV is taking over your life, unplug it. Instead of watching TV dads, watch your own. Ask him questions, find out how his day went. Read those books when you want to escape the family. This way, when you come back, your family won't be under the illusion you were with them, and you may have learned something from your reading you can share with them. One night per week, just unplug the box and have real quality time. That's all it will take. Soon, it will become like a popular series. How did mom's big promotion interview at work go? Tune in next week for the answer. And soon will come the realization that you don't have to wait. You can ask her tomorrow. And more easily than you watched TV your whole life, you have become a family again.

Peer Commentary

Once writers have a working draft down on paper, they need to figure out what kinds of revisions are called for. Clearly, feedback from readers can be useful at this point. To get the most useful kind of feedback to your own working drafts, make sure your readers know they're looking at a work-in-progress and not a final draft.

There are different kinds of commentary you can get from readers at this point. Your readers can:

- *Describe* the writer's strategy.

- *Analyze* the organization of the essay.

- *Evaluate* the argument.

Each kind of commentary provides different information to help you plan revisions. Sometimes you'll want just one kind of commentary; at other times you'll want more than one.

The following sections describe the different kinds of feedback, explain their purposes, and provide guidelines. After each, you'll find an example of the type of peer commentary in response to Krista's working draft.

Describe the Writer's Strategy

A good first step in getting feedback on a working draft is to ask your reader to suspend judgment for a moment and instead to analyze the function of each paragraph in your working draft —how the paragraphs support the main point and how they are connected to each other. In this way, a reader can give you a blueprint of what you have written. This can help you see how (or whether) the parts fit together. You can use this information to decide how well your paragraphs play the roles you intended for them (or whether they perform some other function). This can also be a good basis for the following two types of commentary, in which readers analyze the organization and evaluate the ideas of a working draft.

Guidelines for Describing the Writer's Strategy

1. What is the writer's main point? Identify the sentence or sentences that express the main point. If you don't find such a sentence, write your own version of what you think the main point is.

2. Write a statement about each paragraph that explains the function it performs and how it fits into the organization of the working draft. Use words that describe function, such as *describes, explains, gives reasons, proposes,* or *compares.*

SAMPLE DESCRIPTION OF KRISTA'S DRAFT

Main point: The "only family quality time left is that shared on the TV." Families have substituted fictional for real life.

¶1: Tells a story about her family that introduces the main problem. Asks a series of questions.

¶2: Generalizes from her family's experience to point out that they aren't exceptions. Gives two further examples of the problem. Explains how families have substituted fiction for real life.

¶3: Raises a question about why the problem has developed. Offers a theory to explain the problem.

¶4: Proposes a solution and describes the outcome.

Analyze the Organization

Sometimes, in the struggle to get them down on paper, you may lose perspective on how effectively you've organized your ideas. For this reason, it can be helpful to ask someone else to analyze the organization and presentation of your main idea and examine the supporting evidence.

Again, ask readers to put aside their personal responses to your ideas. Explain that you want them to focus instead on the organization of what you have written. If they have already described the function of paragraphs in the draft, they can use that description as the basis of their analysis. Tell them, in any case, to consider the following questions.

Guidelines for Analyzing the Organization

1. What is the main point of the draft? Is it clear and easy to find? Does the introduction help readers anticipate where the draft will be going?

2. Do the following paragraphs develop the main point, or do they seem to develop some other point? Is it easy to tell how the paragraphs relate to the main point, or do they need to be connected more explicitly to it?

3. Is each of the paragraphs well-focused, or do some of them seem to have several ideas contending for the reader's attention? If a paragraph needs more focus, how could this be achieved?

4. Within the supporting paragraphs, do some points seem to need more development? Are there points that don't belong at all?

5. Is the ending or conclusion effective? Does it provide a sense of closure?

SAMPLE ANALYSIS OF THE ORGANIZATION OF KRISTA'S DRAFT

I like the opening story because I can see what you are getting at. But I wasn't totally clear on the main point for awhile. At first, it seemed like it was just about your family. Then in ¶ 2 you broadened things to include American families in general. I think you could use a clinching statement at the end of the first ¶ that says what your main point is. The questions left me up in the air.

In ¶2, you give two examples that illustrate the problem. I think you could put these in the introduction to show what the problem looks like beyond your family. Then you could expand the final part of ¶2 that explains how we're substituting fictional for real families. That's a great point because it analyzes the problem instead of just describing it. The last sentence is long and hard to follow.

¶3 explains why people have substituted fictional for real families. I like the theory you propose, but I think you should emphasize the point that on TV everything works out and the characters in the shows do the work for us. This seems like the main idea in the ¶ more than TV took over because it was easy.

Finally, your solution in ¶4 makes sense. I wonder whether escaping the family by reading takes away from your main point.

Evaluate the Argument

While the first two kinds of commentary ask readers to set aside their evaluation of your ideas, sometimes you'll really want to know what they think. This is especially likely if you're making an argument or dealing with a controversial topic. For this kind of peer commentary in particular, you'll find it helpful to have more than one reader and to discuss with each reader the comments he or she makes. In this way, you'll have the opportunity to see how your ideas relate to other points of view and to understand the enabling assumptions you and others bring to the issue. This can help you make decisions about how to clarify your own position and handle differing views as you revise.

If your readers have described the function of paragraphs and analyzed the organization of your working draft, they can use these as a basis to evaluate the argument. In any case, your readers should begin by analyzing the parts of your argument before they evaluate it.

Guidelines for Evaluating the Argument

1. Analyze the parts of the argument. What is the claim or main point of the working draft? What supporting evidence is provided? What enabling assumptions connect the evidence to the claim?

2. Do you agree with the essay's main point? Do you accept the essay's assumptions? Explain why.

3. *If you disagree* with the essay's main point or do not accept one or more of its assumptions, what position would you take on the issue yourself? How would you support your position? What assumptions would you make? How would you refute the main point of the essay? What alternative perspectives does the draft need to take into account?

4. *If you agree* with the essay's position, explain why. Do you think the essay makes the best possible argument supporting it? How would you strengthen it? What would you change, add, or omit? Why?

Discuss the responses with your readers. If you disagree, the idea is not to argue about who is right but to keep talking to understand why your positions differ and what assumptions might have led you to take differing positions.

SAMPLE EVALUATIONS OF THE ARGUMENT IN KRISTA'S DRAFT

COMMENTARY 1

Krista, your main claim seems to be at the end of the second paragraph where you say that the only quality family time is watching TV, and you support this idea by talking about how families have substituted fictional families for real families. The reason you give is that it's easier that way—the actors do the work for us and everything works out fine. The assumption that connects this reason to your main claim seems to be that families can't deal with reality any more and so they need a fictional substitute.

I can see what you mean, in that TV shows always have happy endings and wrap up everything in an hour or half hour. But I think there can also be times TV contributes to family life. For example, in my family, watching football together is a big deal, and I have lots of good memories of sitting with my father, grandfather, and brothers watching the 49ers. Maybe this was just a male-bonding ritual but everybody talked and shared. I'm not sure but I feel you're a little too negative.

COMMENTARY 2

[Analysis of the parts of the argument is similar to Response 1.]

I agree totally with your analysis of so-called quality time in front of the tube. What you say is exactly true of my family, and I'm sick of it. My suggestion here is that the evidence you give to back up your main point doesn't seem developed enough. It's all jammed in paragraph 3. To me, the point is not that watching TV is easy but that TV does the work for us in these packaged hour segments. I think that idea would come out more clearly if you developed it more.

The only other thing is the final paragraph. For this kind of assignment, I'm not sure your teacher wants personal advice at the end. Maybe there's some way you could make the ending more analytical by pointing out larger problems or consequences.

Revising

Writing isn't a precise science with right and wrong answers, and neither is talking about written work in progress. When others comment on your writing, each person will have his or her own responses, insights, and suggestions. At times you'll get differing suggestions about what to do with your working draft, as is the case with the two commentaries on Krista's working draft. This doesn't necessarily mean that one reader has seen the true problem in your writing and the other has missed it altogether. By telling you the effect your writing has on each of them, both readers are giving you information to work with.

ETHICS OF COLLABORATION

RESPONSIBILITIES OF WRITERS AND READERS

Productive collaboration depends in large part on the quality of the relationship established between writers and readers. Each have responsibilities toward the others to make sure that open and meaningful communication can take place.

Writers, for example, need to provide their readers with legible working drafts, preferably typed and double-spaced, with any handwritten additions or deletions easy to follow. For readers to respond appropriately, writers should let them know how far along the working draft is—whether it's an early attempt to get ideas down on paper or a full draft based on a working plan. Most important, writers need to keep an open mind and avoid defensiveness when they read peer commentaries or discuss their work with readers. The main responsibility of writers is to understand what their readers are saying and what in their working draft has prompted the readers' responses.

By the same token, the main responsibility of readers is to offer the writer an honest account of their experiences of reading the writer's work. To do this, readers need to understand that they are not playing the role of a teacher (with the authority to instruct, correct, and evaluate that goes along with it) but rather are acting as peers and colleagues. Readers may worry that their comments will hurt the writer's feelings or that they are not qualified to provide useful feedback. These feelings are understandable, but it's just as important to understand that empty praise ("Great ideas, your paper really flowed") and vague comments ("Maybe give more examples") don't really help the writer or convey much information about the writer's work. To be a responsible reader, you don't have to be an expert.

Instead, you need to give a clear and accurate explanation of how and why you responded to the writer's work ("I see how you set up the main point in the opening paragraph, but it wasn't really clear to me how the ideas in the second paragraph are connected to it").

Finally, writers and readers need to understand their responsibilities when they disagree. Disagreements can take various forms. For example, writers and readers may disagree about the organization of a paper. The writer, say, may believe that the introduction or one of the key reasons is particularly effective, but the reader may fail to see the point, feel confused, or just plain disagree. Clearly, their responsibility is to negotiate their differences. They need to keep talking, not so much to decide who is right and who is wrong but rather to understand why they disagree and how the working draft might produce such different readings.

The same is true when writers and readers disagree about ideas and arguments. Such disagreements can at times feel dangerous because people's beliefs about important and controversial cultural, social, and political issues can be deeply held—and genuine conflict may be unavoidable. In such instances, it is the reader's responsibility to explain why he or she disagrees with the writer's views without turning points of difference into an attack on the writer. In turn, it is the writer's responsibility to hear what the reader has to say and to engage in negotiation. Their joint goal is to make their differences—the conflict of ideas and beliefs—into a productive encounter. The point is not to win the argument or convince the other person (though that may occur) but rather to identify the assumptions that divide them and to consider whether there is any common ground that might connect them.

It's important to understand why readers have responded to your writing as they did. Try to imagine their point of view and what in your writing might have prompted their response. Peer commentary doesn't provide writers with a set of directions they can carry out mechanically. Rather, they must analyze and interpret their readers' responses.

Here are some guidelines for revising, followed by Krista's commentary about how she made use of the peer commentary she received on her working draft.

Guidelines for Revising

1. What do your readers see as the main point of your draft? Is that the main idea you intended? If your readers have identified your main point, do they offer suggestions to make it come across more clearly? If you feel they missed your main point, consider why this is so. Do you need to revise the sentence or sentences that express your central point?

2. Do your readers see how the evidence you supply supports your main point? If so, do they offer suggestions about strengthening the evidence you're using to back up your main claim? If not, does this mean you need to revise your main point or revise the supporting evidence?

3. What do your readers think you assume to connect your evidence to your main claim? Is this what you had in mind? If not, how can you change the relationship between your claim and the evidence you provide?

4. If your readers agree with your essay's position, why is this so? Do they think you make the best possible case? If they disagree, consider their positions and the assumptions they are making. Do they offer alternative perspectives you could use?

5. Do you provide a meaningful ending that points out an important consequence or implication of your argument?

KRISTA'S THOUGHTS ON HER PEER COMMENTARIES

After I read the peer commentaries, at first I thought the paper was a mess and I needed to start all over again. So I put them aside for a time. When I reread them, I started to see that the paper could be revised. I realized it was a mistake to use questions at the end of paragraph 1. In fact, I had overused rhetorical questions throughout the essay. My real main point didn't come across until the end of paragraph 2, and I could see that my supporting material was too scattered in paragraphs 2 and 3.

Notice in Krista's revisions of her working draft how she uses ideas from the two commentaries to plan a revision. First, we present two paragraphs from the working draft with Krista's annotated plans for revision. This is followed by the final draft.

It's 8:00 on a Monday night, and I am sitting at home in my bedroom peacefully reading a novel. Suddenly, the dreaded call comes, "Kris, you been in that room for two hours. Come on out here and be with the family for awhile. Cosby is going to start in five minues. Don't you want to watch it with us?" Well, actually no. I was content with my book. But Dad and the family saw these hours in front of the television as quality, and I was expected to participate. What I constantly wondered every Monday was why? When did sitting in front of the tube become family time?

cut

Combine ¶1 & 2

Unfortunately, my family is not the exception but the rule. People are able to remember it is Monday and at 5:00 they can watch the heartwarming merger of blended famlies on <u>Full House</u>. Yet, without a calendar, they have a difficult time remembering that this particular Monday is their stepmother's or stepfather's birthday and they should get a card or gift on the way home from work or school. They can tell you that the hot couple is headed for divorce on <u>Melrose Place</u> more easily than they can see the status of their own marriage. People may not have noticed, but the only quality time that is left is that shared on the TV. ~~The family has left~~ *In families like mine,* ~~the living room and has gone to live in the~~ TV *television viewing too often means evading each other* ~~set in the form of~~ *by replacing real families with fictional ones.* ~~fictional families living fictional lives that the real people would be living if they weren't watching TV.~~

Use in ¶2 as examples

Add concession that TV can be quality time

--Turn next ¶ into 2 ¶s : 1) how TV families do the work for us, 2) how TV families always solve their problems
--Change ending : explain results instead of giving advice

FAMILY LIFE AND TELEVISION

Krista Guglielmetti
Introduction to Mass Communication
October 2, 1998

It's 8:00 on a Monday night, and I am sitting at home in my bedroom peacefully reading a novel. Suddenly, the dreaded call comes, "Kris, you been in that room for two hours. Come on out here and be with the family for awhile. Cosby is going to start in five minutes. Don't you want to watch it with us?" This predictable Monday night call from my Dad reveals one of the ways families use television viewing. It is supposed to be "quality" time, where real families gather together to watch fictional families in sit coms like Cosby. Now it may be true that in some families people actually interact while they are watching television, discussing the meaning of recent news or sharing in the victory or defeat of their favorite team. But in families like mine, television viewing too often means evading each other by replacing real families with fictional ones.

When my family watches television together, what we share is not the experience of actual family members but episodes in the fictional lives of television families. One of the effects of watching these television families is that we use the actors and actresses to do our work for us. The fictional families offer television viewers vicarious experiences that can substitute for real experience. People, for example, remember it is Thursday and at 5:00 they can watch the heartwarming merger of the blended family *Full House.* Yet, without a calendar, they have a difficult time remembering that this particular Monday is their stepmother's or stepfather's birthday and they should get a card or gift on the way home from work or school. Television viewers can tell you that the hot couple on *Melrose Place* is headed for divorce more easily than they can see the status of their own marriage. People may not have noticed, but fiction has become stronger than reality.

Perhaps the greatest attraction to fictional television families is that, unlike real families, they can solve their problems in hour or half hour segments. On TV, blended families always work out, drug addicts are always treated, and no one is ever hurt permanently. It's easy. Just follow the script and everything will be fine. After all, if you're watching TV, you won't fight (except over who has the remote). If you don't fight, no one can get hurt and everyone will be happy. So we let the TV characters do our fighting for us because they always make up on the half hour.

In my family, watching television families work things out doesn't bring us closer together. Instead of being shared quality time, our experience as television viewers brings about a sense of failure and demoralization. Even though no one says so, we all know we'll never measure up to the television families. Our lives are messier, and our problems seem to persist no matter how much we watch *Cosby*.

Final Touches

Writers collaborate with others throughout the writing process, and that includes working on the final touches. Copy editors routinely edit the manuscripts of even the most famous writers, making suggestions about words, phrases, sentences, or passages that might be unclear, awkward, or grammatically incorrect. Then proofreaders carefully review the final draft for any misspellings, missing words, typos, or other flaws.

In school writing, teachers sometimes consider such collaborative work of editing and proofreading as unwarranted assistance from other students. If your teacher permits it, collaboration can be quite useful in applying the final touches to your work.

Directions for Editing

Ask the person editing your manuscript to look for any words, phrases, sentences, or passages that need to be changed. The person can do this in one of two ways: He can simply underline or circle problems, write a brief note of explanation in the margin when necessary, and let you make the changes; or he can go ahead and make tentative changes for you to consider. Your teacher will let you know which method to follow.

SAMPLE EDITING

[Sentence in Krista's Revised Draft:]

Unlike real families, the greatest attraction of fictional television families is that they can solve their problems in hour or half hour segments.

[Final Version:]

Perhaps the greatest attraction to fictional television families is that, unlike real families, they can solve their problems in hour or half hour segments.

Directions for Proofreading

The person proofreading your final copy can underline or circle grammatical errors, usage problems, typos, and misspellings and let you make the final corrections. Or she can supply the corrections. Again, it's up to your teacher which method to follow.

TALKING TO TEACHERS

Much of what has been said here about how writers and readers can collaborate also applies to talking about your writing with teachers. There may be times, for example, when you have trouble figuring out a writing assignment. You may be confused about the suggestions you've received in peer commentaries, or you may not fully understand the teacher's comments. In such situations, you might request a conference with your teacher.

Talking about writing with teachers will be most productive if you prepare ahead of time. If you want to discuss a writing assignment, reread the directions carefully and prepare questions on what isn't clear to you about the assignment. If you want to talk about the feedback you've gotten from peers, reread their commentaries and bring them with you to the conference. If you want to talk about a paper that has already been graded, make sure you read it over carefully, paying particular attention to the teacher's comments.

In any case, have realistic expectations about what can happen at the conference. Don't expect your teacher to change your grade or give you a formula for completing the assignment. The point of the conference is for you to understand what your teacher is looking for in a piece of writing.

GOING TO THE WRITING CENTER

One of the best places to talk about writing is a writing center, where you can meet and discuss your writing with people who are interested in the writing process and in how students develop as writers. Find out if your college has a writing center. It will be listed in the campus directory, and your writing teacher will know about its hours and procedures.

Sometimes students think the writing center is only for those with serious writing problems, but that is not the case. Students of all abilities can benefit from talking to writing tutors. Whether the people who staff the writing center at your college are undergraduates, graduate students, or professional tutors, they are experienced writers who like to talk about writing.

If your campus has a writing center, make an appointment to interview one of the tutors. Ask what kinds of services the center provides and what insights into college writing the tutor can offer. Even better, take a writing assignment you're working on or a paper that's already been graded to serve as the basis for a conversation with the tutor.

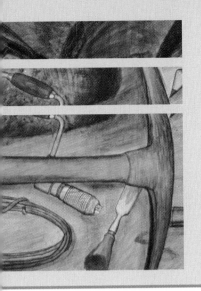

CHAPTER THIRTEEN

Working Together: Collaborative Writing Projects

Working on collaborative writing projects differs in important respects from working with others on individual writing projects. In the case of individual writing projects, the final result belongs to you; you are accountable for it and you get the bulk of the credit, even though the writing reflects the input of others. Collaborative writing, on the other hand, aims for a collective outcome produced jointly by a team of people with shared responsibility for the results.

Here are examples of how people in various settings work together in collaborative writing projects.

- A group of 19 automotive engineers is designing a prototype for a new car model. The engineers are divided into a number of working groups—engine design, emissions control, aerodynamics and body design, suspension, electrical system, interior design and safety features—with a project manager to coordinate the various groups. They meet regularly to discuss ongoing design plans and to ensure that each group's work fits with that of the other groups. At these meetings, the leader of each working group reports orally and submits written progress reports to the project manager. As the work nears its completion, each group drafts a section of what will be the final report to take to the company's executives for approval to build an actual prototype. The project manager edits the various sections and writes an introduction and an executive summary so that the end result is a single, coherent document.

- Home owners meet to form a citizens group opposing a plan to build a gambling casino near their neighborhood. Theirs is a quiet residential area, and they want to keep it that way. The streets are safe, there is little traffic, and their children can play outside. They know that they're in for a tough fight, especially since the real estate firms and developers

447

who are pushing the plan have political clout. They decide to write a petition to take door to door to show widespread opposition to the casino. The group works together to compose the petition, with many people suggesting the appeal and wording they should use. When everyone is satisfied with the petition, one group member volunteers to format it on her computer and make copies for all to circulate.

■ A group of three students is working together on a research project in an environmental studies course. Their task is to create a map of the sidewalk shade trees the city has planted and maintained in the downtown area over the years and to make recommendations about where new trees should be planted. After they have surveyed the downtown area, sketched a preliminary map, and made tentative decisions about where new trees should go, they decide that one group member should write a working draft of their findings. Once the draft is finished, the group meets to consider what revisions are needed to produce a final report. The writer of the working draft makes these changes while the other two members create the map.

As you can see, when individuals are working together on collaborative writing projects, they will manage the writing task in various ways, depending on the nature of the task and the decisions the group makes. Sometimes, as in the case of the automotive engineers, individuals will each write separate sections, which are then compiled into a single document and edited for uniformity of style. Or, as in the case of the neighborhood citizens group, they may work together so closely in planning, drafting, and revising a document that it becomes impossible to distinguish one person's work from another's. In still other cases, such as that of the student group in the environmental studies course, the group will work together planning and doing research, one individual will do the drafting, and then the group will work together again to plan revisions.

There is no single best way to work on collaborative writing projects. Experienced writers learn when it makes sense to produce a collaboratively written document and which writing strategy the situation seems to call for.

Collaborative writing is often called for when tasks are complex, with many separate parts (such as the design work of the automotive engineers), or when extensive time and effort are required (such as the group research project in the environmental studies course). But in other cases, collaboration is appropriate when the writing that results is meant to speak for a group of people rather than an individual (as in the case of the neighborhood citizens group).

While these examples of collaborative writing projects differ in many respects, each of them reveals one of the most important benefits of working together—namely that the final written product is based on the collective judgment of a group of people. When a group works well together, the resulting energy and involvement can lead to writing that goes beyond what anyone in the group could have produced alone.

Successful collaborative writing depends on organization, meetings, and constant communication. This chapter looks at how groups can produce effective collaborative writing. The first section offers some general guidelines about working in groups. The second section considers how groups can manage a collaborative writing project from start to finish. The final section presents further writing suggestions for groups.

EXPLORING YOUR EXPERIENCE

Form a group with three or four other students. Have each student describe an experience in which he or she worked together with other people. The experience can be positive or negative, and it need not involve writing. After everyone has described an experience, try to reach a consensus, even if you agree to disagree, about what makes group work successful or unsuccessful.

GUIDELINES FOR COLLABORATING IN GROUPS

Any group of people working together on a project will face certain issues, and a group collaborating on a writing project is no exception. The following guidelines are meant to keep a group running smoothly and to forestall some common problems.

Recognize that Group Members Need to Get Acquainted and that Groups Take Time to Form

People entering new groups sometimes make snap judgments without getting to know the other people or giving the group time to form and develop. Initial impressions are rarely reliable indicators of how a group will be. Like individuals, groups have life histories, and one of the most awkward and difficult moments is getting started. Group members may be nervous, defensive, or overly assertive. It takes some time for people to get to know one another and to develop a sense of connectedness to the group.

Clarify Group Purposes and Individual Roles

Much of the initial discomfort and anxiety has to do with uncertainty about what the purpose of the group is and what people's roles in the group will be. Group members need to define their collective task and develop a plan to carry it out. That way, members will understand what to expect and how the group will operate.

Recognize that Members Bring Different Styles to the Group

As you have seen in the Introduction to Part Three, individual styles of composing can vary considerably. The same is true of individuals' styles of working in groups. For example, individuals differ in the way they approach problems. Some like to spend a lot of time formulating problems, exploring the complexities, contradictions, and nuances of a situation. Others want to define problems quickly and then spend their time figuring out how to solve them. By the same token, people have different styles of interacting in groups. Some like to develop their ideas by talking, while others prefer to decide what they think before speaking. So successful groups learn to incorporate the strengths of all these styles, making sure that even the most reticent members participate.

Recognize that You May Not Play the Same Role in Every Group

In some instances you may be the group leader, but in other instances you'll need to play the role of mediator, helping members negotiate their differences; or critic, questioning the others' ideas; or timekeeper, prompting the group to stick to deadlines. You may play different roles in the same group from meeting to meeting or even within a meeting. For a group to be successful, members must be willing and able to respond flexibly to the work at hand.

Monitor Group Progress and Reassess Goals and Procedures

It's helpful to step back periodically to take stock of what has been accomplished and what remains to be done. Groups also need to look at their own internal workings to see if the procedures they have set up are effective and if everyone is participating.

Quickly Address Problems in Group Dynamics

Problems will arise in group work. Some members may dominate and talk too much. Others may withdraw and not contribute. Still others may fail to carry out assigned tasks. If a group avoids confronting these problems, the problems will only get worse. Remember, the point of raising a problem is not to blame individuals but to promote an understanding about what's expected of each person and what the group can do to encourage everyone's participation.

Encourage Differences of Opinion

One of the things that makes groups productive is the different perspectives individual members bring to group work. In fact, groups of like-minded people who share basic assumptions are often not as creative as groups where there are differences among members. At the same time, group members may feel that they can't bring up ideas or feelings because to do so would threaten group harmony. That feeling is understandable. Sometimes it's difficult to take a position that diverges from what other members of the group think and believe. But groups are not forms of social organization to enforce conformity; they are working bodies that need to consider all the available options and points of view. For this reason, groups need to encourage the discussion of differences and to look at conflicting viewpoints.

HOW TO WORK TOGETHER ON COLLABORATIVE WRITING PROJECTS

Because collaborative writing differs from individual writing, it is worth looking at each step involved in working on a joint project.

Organizing the Group

One of the keys to collaborative writing is to get off to a good start. You'll need to decide on the size of the group, its composition, and what to do at your first meeting.

Group Size

For many collaborative writing projects in college classes, a group of three or four is often the best size. A smaller size—only two students—doesn't offer the group as many resources, and anything larger than four can create problems in managing the work with so many involved.

Of course, there can be exceptions. For example, your teacher may decide to do a collaborative project involving the entire class—developing a Web home page for the class or a Web site devoted to a particular topic with everyone's participation.

Group Composition

Some teachers like to put groups together themselves. Others like to give students input into the group they will be in. If the teacher puts the groups together, it's a good idea to ask each student if there is someone in class he or she particularly wants to work with or particularly wants to avoid working with. It can help, too, to take schedules into account and match students who have free time in common when they can meet.

The First Meeting

The first meeting should focus on the basics:

1. Exchange phone numbers, e-mail addresses, campus box numbers, and the best times to reach group members.
2. If possible, establish a listserv of group members on the campus network.
3. Identify the best times for meetings.
4. Agree on some basic procedures for running meetings. For example, do you want a group coordinator to lead meetings? If so, will one person serve throughout the project, or will you rotate that position? How do you plan to keep records of meetings? Will you have a recorder for the project, or rotate? How long will each meeting last? Who is responsible for developing the agenda?

Division of Labor, or Integrated Team?

Some groups approach collaborative projects by developing a division of labor that assigns particular tasks to group members who complete them individually and then bring the results back to the group. This has been the traditional model for collaborative work in business, industry, and government. It is an efficient method of work, especially when groups are composed of highly skilled members. Its limitations are that weak group members can affect the quality of the overall work and that some group members may lose sight of the overall project because they are so caught up in their own specialized work.

More recently, groups have begun to explore an integrated approach in which the members all work together through each stage of the project. An integrated-team approach involves members more fully in the work and helps them maintain an overall view of the project's goals and progress. But it also takes more time—that must be devoted to meetings and, often, to developing good working relationships among members.

These two models of group work are not mutually exclusive. In fact many groups function along integrated-team lines when they are planning and reviewing work, but also farm out particular tasks to individuals or subgroups. So you need to discuss and develop some basic guidelines on group functioning.

Organizing the Project: The Proposal

The first task is to decide what the project is and what its goals are. One of the best ways to do this is to write a proposal. Your teacher is the logical audience for your proposal. If you are doing a project with an on- or off-campus group, members of that group should also receive your proposal.

Proposals should include:

■ **A statement of purpose:** Define the topic or issue you are working on. Explain why it is important or significant. What have others said about it? State what you plan to do and explain why.

■ **A description of methods:** Explain how you plan to go about the project. What research will you need to do? How will you do it?

■ **A plan for managing the work:** Explain what roles group members will play and what skills they will bring to the task.

■ **A task breakdown chart:** A task breakdown (or Gantt) chart shows the tasks involved and their scheduling. Such a chart is especially useful for planning collaborative projects because it shows how tasks relate to each other.

Once the group is up and running, it will need to figure out how to stay on track—how to keep the work moving ahead and how to deal effectively with problems as they arise.

Incorporating a calendar into your task breakdown chart is one way to stay oriented. Two other ways are to run productive meetings and to write interim progress reports.

Productive Meetings

Group meetings are productive when they get work done, address issues and conflicts, and keep group members accountable. Although failing to meet can cause group members to feel disconnected, meeting for no reason can be just as demoralizing. For meetings to be productive, there must be a real agenda and work that needs to be done. One way to set an agenda is to agree at the end of each meeting what will be accomplished before the next meeting, and by whom. That way the agenda grows out of the progress of the project and group members are kept accountable. If problems in group functioning come up, they need to be addressed immediately at the next meeting.

Progress Reports

Progress reports are another way to enhance group members' accountability—both to one another and to their teacher. They serve to chart the development of a project at regular intervals. On your task breakdown chart you will want to include one or two progress reports that follow the completion of major parts of the project. Include in your reports the following:

■ **Tasks completed:** Describe with details what you have done.

■ **Tasks in progress:** Be specific about what you are doing and give completion dates.

■ **Tasks scheduled:** Describe briefly tasks you haven't yet started, including any not originally entered on the task breakdown chart.

■ **Issues, problems, obstacles:** Explain how these emerged and how your group is dealing with them.

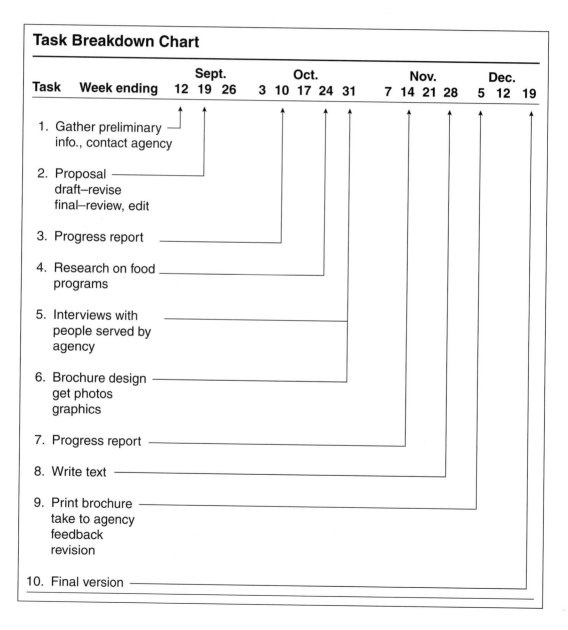

Task Breakdown Chart

Task Week ending	Sept. 12 19 26	Oct. 3 10 17 24 31	Nov. 7 14 21 28	Dec. 5 12 19

1. Gather preliminary info., contact agency

2. Proposal draft–revise final–review, edit

3. Progress report

4. Research on food programs

5. Interviews with people served by agency

6. Brochure design get photos graphics

7. Progress report

8. Write text

9. Print brochure take to agency feedback revision

10. Final version

In some cases, teachers may ask groups for oral as well as written progress reports. This is a good way for everyone in class to see what the other groups are doing.

Confidential Self-Evaluation

In addition to requiring group progress reports, some teachers also like to ask individual students to assess how their group has been functioning and what their role in it has been. These self-evaluations are confidential and directed only to the teacher. They can be useful in helping the teacher anticipate when groups are having difficulties or personality problems. They are also useful to individual students because they offer an occasion to reflect on the experience of group work and what it means to them as writers, learners, and persons.

Drafting, Revising, and Editing

One thing that often surprises students working in groups for the first time is finding out that they have already started to draft their document from the moment they began to put their proposal together.

For many writing tasks, the final document will draw and expand on what is in the proposal—explaining why the issue or problem is important, what others have said about it, what the group has learned about it, and what recommendations the group has to make.

But whatever the writing task happens to be, groups need to make decisions about how to handle drafting, revising, and editing collaboratively written documents. Here are some possible approaches. Your group will need to decide which one best suits your purposes.

- Members draft individual sections. The group compiles the sections and revises together.

- One person writes a draft. The group revises together.

- Members draft individual sections. One person compiles the sections and revises the document.

With any of these approaches, a final editing needs to be done by an individual or by the group.

However you decide to organize drafting, revising, and editing, make sure everyone contributes to the final document. The draft does not become final until everyone has signed off on it.

Collaborative drafting and revising can raise sensitive issues about individual writing styles and abilities. Some people can be protective of their writing and defensive when it is criticized or revised. Be aware of this. If you think other group members either are trying to impose their own style or are feeling discouraged, bring these matters to everyone's attention and try to sort them out before you continue on the writing task.

Giving Credit

Some teachers ask collaborative writing groups to preface their final document with an acknowledgments page that explains who should get credit for what in the overall project. You should also acknowledge anyone outside your group who helped you on the project.

Final Presentation

The final presentation of a collaborative project takes place when the document reaches its intended destination—whether it's the teacher, the Web, a politician or government official office, or a community organization. You may want to schedule an oral presentation to go along with the delivery of the document.

Online Collaboration

The new electronic communication technologies have created new ways for groups to work together, even when their members are far apart. It's no longer necessary to meet face to face to have the kind of exchange that gives a joint project energy and creativity. With the nearly instantaneous transmission of documents, commentary, and conversation, collaborators can now stay in touch, confer, argue, and refine their ideas with an immediacy that was unimaginable in the past.

ETHICS OF WRITING

GIVING CREDIT AND TAKING RESPONSIBILITY

One of a writer's ethical obligations is to acknowledge collaborators. How this is done varies. In the case of single-authored works, writers will often acknowledge their debt to people who helped with ideas and discussion and who read and commented on drafts. If you look at the preface or acknowledgments of nonfiction books, you'll see that writers typically thank friends, colleagues, editors, and family for their input and support. They will then also take responsibility, noting that they alone are responsible for the views expressed and for any errors.

In collaborative writing, all coauthors should get credit and take responsibility. This is not always as simple as it sounds. People participate to different extents, and sometimes it can be difficult to determine just who should be included among the coauthors. Ethical controversies on this issue have arisen, especially in the area of science research. For example, many have argued that Rosalind Franklin's contributions entitled her to be a coauthor with James Watson and Francis Crick on their Nobel Prize-winning work on the structure of DNA but that she was excluded because she was a woman.

Of course, group members don't need to be halfway around the world from each other to take advantage of the new technologies. Here are some good ways of how to use these technologies in collaborative writing projects:

1. **Stay in touch with group members:** Ongoing communication among group members is one of the keys to successful group work. Setting up a listserv on e-mail can help members to stay in touch in and out of class.

2. **Consult with people everywhere:** Through e-mail, newsgroups, and Web sites your group can contact a wide range of people who are knowledgeable about your topic—to ask questions, get information, and try out ideas. Online communication can be much quicker and simpler than letters or phone calls.

3. **Share working drafts:** To put together a successful collaboratively written document, coauthors need easy access to one another's working drafts. Drafts can be shared in ways that range from downloading files on e-mail to state-of-the-art hypertext authoring systems.

4. **Confer on drafts:** Online conferences make it easy for all group members to have input on drafts. New methods include "real-time" synchronous conferences facilitated by networking software.

IDENTIFYING THE CALL TO WRITE: TYPES OF PROJECTS

When is the call to write best answered by collaborative writing? As already indicated, collaborative writing is most appropriate for complex projects—for example, projects that require developing an initial proposal, doing research of various kinds, analyzing the results of this research, designing a document, and producing text and graphics. The amount and variety of work needed for such projects is better handled by a group than by one person working alone. Partly for this reason, collaborative writing is also especially appropriate to projects that involve significant community issues and require working closely with one or more community groups.

Below you'll find listings of possible topics for collaborative writing projects. The topics are organized by genre, or writing type (see Part Two for discussions of genres). These projects are meant to be more than simply multiauthor versions of conventional research papers. They are intended to be the sorts of projects collaborative writing is most conducive to—projects in which the call to write grows out of the needs of people in our society and out of issues that touch people's lives.

How these topics are used is up to you and your teacher. You may want to use one of them, or similar topics that you think of, as the basis for an actual project that you undertake this term. Or you might just read them to get a better sense of how to identify a call to write that can be answered collaboratively. For in collaborative writing, as in any writing, the first step is to identify a call to write.

Reports and Recommendations

To do this type of project, a group identifies an issue that is controversial or that needs to be raised, researches the issue (for example, at the library and through surveys and interviews), prepares a report, and makes recommendations.

Local Issues

- Should the city or town impose a curfew on those under 18?

- Should a state permit gambling casinos?

- What kind of property tax reform is called for?

- How adequate are local services, such as shelters for the homeless and for battered women, food and nutrition programs, and adult literacy and English as a Second Language classes?

You might want to look at just one of these categories.

School Issues

- What kind of bilingual program, if any, should the local school system have?

- Should the schools have a dress code?

- What kind of sex education is appropriate at each grade level?

- Should the schools dismantle tracking and replace it with multiability classrooms?

Campus Issues

- How can the campus food service be improved?

- What steps should be taken to deal with underage and excessive drinking?

- Should fraternities and sororities be abolished?

- How can students' first-year experience be improved?

Proposals for Grant Funding

Working with a community, student, or other organization, the group identifies a need of the organization, locates and contacts possible funding sources, develops a budget, and writes and submits a grant proposal on behalf of the organization.

Community Organizations

- Proposal to fund a photography class for adolescents at a community center
- Proposal to fund a midnight basketball league
- Proposal to fund a community garden using vacant lots owned by the city
- Proposal to fund job preparation workshops for recent immigrants

Student Organizations

- Proposal to fund a speakers series
- Proposal to fund a film series
- Proposal to fund AIDS awareness workshops and counseling
- Proposal to fund community service projects

Informative Writing

Working with a community organization, social service agency, health care facility, or other organization, the group researches a topic and designs and produces one or more pieces of informative writing.

Community Organizations

- Brochure on domestic violence and what battered women can do
- Leaflet on how to compost
- Series of bilingual flyers on furniture and clothing banks, and on adult literacy, English as a Second Language, and GED classes
- Poster advertising the services of a local community center

Social Service Agencies

- Brochure on how recent immigrants can qualify for green cards, permanent resident, and citizenship status
- Brochure on the availability of food programs

- Bilingual flyers on emergency heat and rent programs
- Poster on child care options

Health Care Facilities
- Posters advertising immunization programs
- Brochure on sexually transmitted diseases
- Flyers advertising programs on alcohol abuse
- Brochures on risks of and ways of dealing with radon, asbestos, lead, and/or other substances that may occur in the home

Other Possibilities

The possibilities are broad—both for the content of the writing and for its form. Here are several more suggestions:

1. Prepare a briefing on a current issue (such as NAFTA, corporate downsizing, tax reform proposals, U.S.-Cuban policy) for a politician, government official, or legislative body.
2. Develop a multimedia educational exhibit on a current topic (for example, gene therapy, the aftermath of the breakup of the Soviet Union, new directions in telecommunications) for a junior high school class.
3. Design a museum exhibit with captions together with a leaflet.
4. Design a guide to your campus and local community for first-year students.
5. Design a Web site on a topic or issue you are interested in.
6. Develop a MUD or MOO environment with opportunities for role-playing.

REFLECTING ON YOUR WRITING: ANALYZING COLLABORATIVE WRITING

Consider a collaborative writing task you have completed. Explain why the particular situation seemed to call for a collaboratively written document instead of an individually written one. How did your group go about organizing and managing the writing task? What role or roles did you play in the group? What problems or issues did you confront and how did you handle them? What was the result of the group's work? From your own perspective, what do you see as the main differences between collaborative and individual writing? What do you see as the benefits and limits of each?

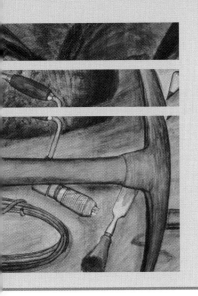

CHAPTER FOURTEEN

The Form of Nonfiction Prose

I n this chapter we look at the *craft* of writing—at the way in which writers shape their thoughts, feelings, and experiences into written forms. Now, of course, this entire book is devoted to deepening your understanding of the craft of writing. The role of this chapter is to help you understand how the form of nonfiction prose embodies a writer's purposes and provides the groundwork for readers to engage a writer's ideas. Such an understanding of the formal aspects of writing can help you gain greater control over your own writing projects. We will look in particular at how writers organize their work, write introductions and endings, connect the parts, and design paragraphs.

THINKING ABOUT FORM

Understanding how form works in nonfiction prose is a matter of understanding how the parts of a piece of writing are related to one another and how that arrangement guides and enables readers to follow the writer's thoughts and purposes.

In some genres of writing, writers and readers alike rely heavily on formal conventions. You can tell, for example, that a piece of writing is a letter simply by looking at it. The same is true for certain kinds of academic writing, such as lab reports and scientific articles, with their fixed sections—introduction, materials and methods, results, discussion. Public documents such as wills, contracts, laws, and resolutions also have highly predictable features that make them immediately recognizable. In fact, writing some public documents is largely a case of filling in a predetermined form.

However, other genres in writing, such as memoirs, commentary, proposals, and reviews, may well vary more in terms of form. In these genres, writers cannot always use a preexisting form to shape their material. Instead they often need to devise a form that is adequate for their purposes and appropriate to the materials at hand.

Whether the form of a piece of writing is standardized or improvised for the occasion, form has two key dimensions—the visual and the psychological.

- **The visual dimension** of form refers to the way written texts are laid out on a page. Writing materializes people's thoughts and purposes in visible form, and written texts take on a particular "look" as they occupy the space of a page. Paragraph breaks, headings and subheadings, the use of bullets and illustrations, the size and style of fonts, the layout of the page—these aspects of writing provide readers with visual cues to follow a piece of writing.

- **The psychological dimension** of form places readers in a particular frame of mind by creating a set of expectations about the writer's purposes and where a piece of writing is going. The form of written texts arouses the reader's anticipation and then goes on to fulfill it in one way or another, whether the resolution is temporary or permanent, expected or surprising.

Looking at how the visual and psychological dimensions of form work together can help you see that organizing a piece of writing is not simply providing a series of containers to pour your thoughts into—at the rate, say, of one main point per essay and one idea per paragraph. This rather mechanical view of form is often the result of learning the five-paragraph theme (and its thesis, three paragraphs of support, and conclusion) without taking into account how the form of writing serves, both visually and psychologically, to manage the interaction between the writer and readers. Whether the form of writing is fixed in advance or needs to be invented for the occasion, its key function, as you will see, is to produce common expectations and shared understanding between writers and readers.

THREE PATTERNS OF ORGANIZATION

Let's look first at the overall organization of nonfiction prose. To see how form works to bring writers and readers together, we will look at three common patterns:

1. **Top-Down Order:** This pattern of organization is perhaps the most familiar. It can be found in newspaper and magazine articles and in many kinds of academic and professional writing. Writers tell readers at the outset what their main point is and then go on to develop and support it. This pattern of organization enables readers to hold in mind the writer's central idea and to evaluate its merits based on the evidence that follows. The success of top-down order depends in large part on how well writers deliver on what they have led their readers to anticipate.

2. **Culminating Order**: This form reserves or delays the presentation of the writer's central idea until late in the piece of writing. Instead of announcing a claim early on and then using the rest of the writing to support it, here the writing is organized so that it culminates with the payoff for readers. With this pattern of organization, the success of a piece of writing will often depend on how effectively the writer establishes a central issue or set of issues and then organizes the rest of the essay so that when the culminating point arrives it seems inevitable and logical.

3. **Open-Form**: An open-form pattern of organization gives readers much less guidance than either top-down or culminating order. Instead of explicitly pointing out the connections among the parts, open form often leaves it to the readers to provide these links. If top-down and culminating order operate logically, open form operates associatively, and the parts of the writing take on meaning implicitly by how they are juxtaposed to each other. In this case, the success of a piece of writing largely depends on how skillfully the writer combines apparently disparate materials to create a dominant impression that may never be named outright but that is available to the reader nonetheless.

EXERCISE

Read the following three selections. Pay special attention to their patterns of organization. Use the terms we've just introduced—top-down order, culminating order, and open form—to identify how the writing is organized. Note when you became aware of the writer's main point and how she developed it. Be prepared to discuss your reading experience.

I Shop, Ergo I Am: The Mall as Society's Mirror
SARA BOXER

1   In certain academic circles, "shop till you drop" is considered a civic act. If you follow cultural studies—the academic scrutiny of ordinary activities like eating fast food, buying a house in the suburbs, watching television and taking vacations at Disneyland—you will know that shopping is not just a matter of going to a store and paying for your purchase.

2   How you shop is who you are. Shopping is a statement about your place in society and your part in world cultural history. There is a close relationship, even an equation, between citizenship and consumption. The store is the modern city-state, the place where people act as free citizens, making choices, rendering opinions and socializing with others.

3 If this sounds like a stretch, you're way behind the times. The field of cultural studies, which took off in England in the 1970's, has been popular in this country for more than a decade.

4 The intellectual fascination with stores goes back even further. When the philosopher Walter Benjamin died in 1940, he was working on a long study of the Paris arcades, the covered retail passageways, then almost extinct; which he called the "original temples of commodity capitalism." Six decades later, the study of shopping is well trampled. Some academics have moved on from early classical work on the birth of the department store and the shopping arcade to the shopping malls of the 1950's and even the new wide aisles of today's factory outlets and superstores—places like Best Buy, Toys "R" Us and Ikea.

5 Historically, the age of shopping and browsing begins at the very end of the 18th century. In a paper titled "Counter Publics: Shopping and Women's Sociability," delivered at the Modern Language Association's annual meeting, Deidre Lynch, an associate professor of English at the State University of New York in Buffalo, said the word "shopping" started to appear frequently in print around 1780. That was when stores in London started turning into public attractions.

6 By 1800, Ms. Lynch said, "a policy of obligation-free browsing seems to have been introduced into London emporia." At that point, "the usual morning employment of English ladies," the 18th-century writer Robert Southey said, was to "go-a-shopping." Stores became places to socialize, to see and be seen. Browsing was born.

7 The pastime of browsing has been fully documented. Benjamin wrote that the Paris arcades, which went up in the early 1800's, created a new kind of person, a professional loiterer, or *flâneur*, who could easily turn into a dangerous political gadfly. The philosopher Jürgen Habermas, some of his interpreters say, has equated consumer capitalism with the feminization of culture. And now some feminists, putting a new spin on this idea, are claiming the store as the place where women first became "public women."

8 By imagining that they owned the wares, women were "transported into new identities," Ms. Lynch said. By meeting with their friends, they created what feminist critics like Nancy Fraser and Miriam Hansen called "counter publics," groups of disenfranchised people.

Putting Merchants in Their Place

9 Some feminists point out that as shoppers, women had the power to alter other people's lives. Women who spent "a summer's day cheapening a pair of gloves" without buying anything, as Southey put it, were "fortifying the boundaries of social class," Ms. Lynch said. They were "teaching haberdashers and milliners their place," taunting them with the prospect of a purchase and never delivering. It may not have been nice, but it was a sort of political power.

10 Women could also use their power for good. In 1815, Ms. Lynch points out, Mary Lamb wrote an essay called "On Needle-work," urging upper-class ladies who liked to do needlework as a hobby to give compensatory pay to women who

did it to make a living. Lamb's biographer recently noted that this was how "bourgeois women busily distributed the fruits of their husbands' capitalist gains in the name of female solidarity."

11 The idea that shopping is a form of civil action naturally has its critics. In one of the essays in a book titled "Buy This Book," Don Slater, a sociologist at the University of London, criticized the tendency of many academics to celebrate "the productivity, creativity, autonomy, rebelliousness and even…the 'authority' of the consumer." The trouble with this kind of post-modern populism is that it mirrors "the logic of the consumer society it seeks to analyze," he said. Such theories, without distinguishing between real needs and false ones, he suggested, assume that shoppers are rational and autonomous creatures who acquire what they want and want what they acquire.

12 Another critic, Meaghan Morris, author of an essay called "Banality in Cultural Studies," has faulted academics for idealizing the pleasure and power of shopping and underestimating the "anger, frustration, sorrow, irritation, hatred, boredom and fatigue" that go with it.

13 The field of shopping studies, whatever you think of it, is now at a pivotal point. In the 19th century, emporiums in London and arcades in Paris turned shopping into social occasions; in the 20th century, academics turned shopping into civic action; and in the 21st century, it seems that megastores will bring us into a new, darker era.

14 Shoppers' freedoms are changing. According to Robert Bocock, writing in "Consumption," the mall walkers of today do not have the rights that the *flâneurs* of the 19th century had. "In the United States, 'policing' of who is allowed entry to the malls has become stricter in the last two or three decades of the 20th century."

15 In superstores, the role of shoppers has changed even more radically. Superstores are warehouses that stock an astounding number of goods picked out at a national corporate level, said Marianne Conroy, a scholar of comparative literature at the University of Maryland. Shoppers educate themselves about the goods and serve themselves. Thus, the superstore effectively "strips shopping of its aura of sociality," Ms. Conroy said. There is no meaningful interaction between the salespeople and the shoppers or among the shoppers. The shoppers' relationship is not with other people but with boxes and shelves.

16 Does the concept of the shopper as citizen still hold? The real test is to see how the citizen-shopper fares at the superstore. In a paper she delivered to the Modern Language Association, titled "You've Gotta Fight for Your Right to Shop: Superstores, Citizenship and the Restructuring of Consumption," Ms. Conroy analyzed one event in the history of a superstore that tested the equation between shopping and citizenship.

17 In 1996 Ronald Kahlow, a software engineer, decided to do some comparison shopping at a Best Buy outlet store in Reston, VA., by punching the prices and model numbers of some televisions into his laptop computer. When store employees asked him to stop, he refused and was arrested for trespassing. The next day, Mr. Kahlow returned with a pen and paper. Again, he was charged with trespassing and handcuffed.

18   When he stood trial in Fairfax County Court, he was found not guilty. And, as Ms. Conroy observed, the presiding judge in the case, Donald McDonough, grandly equated Mr. Kahlow's comparison shopping to civil disobedience in the 1960's. Mr. Kahlow then recited Robert F. Kennedy's poem "A Ripple of Hope," and the judge said, "Never has the cause of comparison shopping been so eloquently advanced."

Like Canaries in the Mines

19   At first, Ms. Conroy suggested they both might have gone overboard in reading "public meaning into private acts," but then she reconsidered. Maybe, she said, it's just time to refine the model.

20   Ms. Conroy suggested that consumerism should be seen no longer as the way citizens exercise their rights and freedoms but rather as "an activity that makes the impact of economic institutions on everyday life critically intelligible." In other words, shoppers in superstores are like canaries in the mines. Their experience inside tells us something about the dangers lurking in society at large.

21   What does one man's shopping experience at Best Buy tell us about the dangers of modern life in America? The fact that Mr. Kahlow was arrested when he tried to comparison shop shows that even the minimal rights of citizen-shoppers are endangered, said Ms. Conroy. Not only have they lost a venue for socializing, but they are also beginning to lose their right to move about freely and make reasoned choices.

22   Without the trappings of sociability, it's easier to see what's what. Stores used to be places that made people want to come out and buy things they didn't know they wanted. And they were so seductive that by the end of the 20th century they became one of the few sites left for public life. But in the superstores, the *flâneurs* and the consumer-citizens are fish out of water. They have nowhere pleasant to wander, no glittering distractions, no socializing to look forward to and no escape from the watchful eyes of the security guards. If this is citizenship, maybe it's time to move to another country.

Minneapolis Pornography Ordinance
ELLEN GOODMAN

1   Just a couple of months before the pool-table gang rape in New Bedford, Mass., *Hustler* magazine printed a photo feature that reads like a blueprint for the actual crime. There were just two differences between *Hustler* and real life. In *Hustler*, the woman enjoyed it. In real life, the woman charged rape.

2   There is no evidence that the four men charged with this crime had actually read the magazine. Nor is there evidence that the spectators who yelled encouragement for two hours had held previous ringside seats at pornographic events.

But there is a growing sense that the violent pornography being peddled in this country helps to create an atmosphere in which such events occur.

3   As recently as last month, a study done by two University of Wisconsin researchers suggested that even "normal" men, prescreened college students, were changed by their exposure to violent pornography. After just ten hours of viewing, reported researcher Edward Donnerstein, "the men were less likely to convict in a rape trial, less likely to see injury to a victim, more likely to see the victim as responsible." Pornography may not cause rape directly, he said, "but it maintains a lot of very callous attitudes. It justifies aggression. It even says you are doing a favor to the victim."

4   If we can prove that pornography is harmful, then shouldn't the victims have legal rights? This, in any case, is the theory behind a city ordinance that recently passed the Minneapolis City Council. Vetoed by the mayor last week, it is likely to be back before the Council for an overriding vote, likely to appear in other cities, other towns. What is unique about the Minneapolis approach is that for the first time it attacks pornography, not because of nudity or sexual explicitness, but because it degrades and harms women. It opposes pornography on the basis of sex discrimination.

5   University of Minnesota Law Professor Catherine MacKinnon, who co-authored the ordinance with feminist writer Andrea Dworkin, says that they chose this tactic because they believe that pornography is central to "creating and maintaining the inequality of the sexes....Just being a woman means you are injured by pornography.

6   They defined pornography carefully as, "the sexually explicit subordination of women, graphically depicted, whether in pictures or in words." To fit their legal definition it must also include one of nine conditions that show this subordination, like presenting women who "experience sexual pleasure in being raped or...mutilated...." Under this law, it would be possible for a pool-table rape victim to sue *Hustler*. It would be possible for a woman to sue if she were forced to act in a pornographic movie. Indeed, since the law describes pornography as oppressive to all women, it would be possible for any woman to sue those who traffic in the stuff for violating her civil rights.

7   In many ways, the Minneapolis ordinance is an appealing attack on an appalling problem. The authors have tried to resolve a long and bubbling conflict among those who have both a deep aversion to pornography and a deep loyalty to the value of free speech. "To date," says Professor MacKinnon, "people have identified the pornographer's freedom with everybody's freedom. But we're saying that the freedom of the pornographer is the subordination of women. It means one has to take a side."

8   But the sides are not quite as clear as Professor MacKinnon describes them. Nor is the ordinance. Even if we accept the argument that pornography is harmful to women—and I do—then we must also recognize that anti-Semitic literature is harmful to Jews and racist literature is harmful to blacks. For that matter, Marxist

literature may be harmful to government policy. It isn't just women versus pornographers. If women win the right to sue publishers and producers, then so could Jews, blacks, and a long list of people who may be able to prove they have been harmed by books, movies, speeches or even records. The Manson murders, you may recall, were reportedly inspired by the Beatles.

9   We might prefer a library or book store or lecture hall without *Mein Kampf* or the Grand Whoever of the Ku Klux Klan. But a growing list of harmful expressions would inevitably strangle freedom of speech.

10   This ordinance was carefully written to avoid problems of banning and prior restraint, but the right of any woman to claim damages from pornography is just too broad. It seems destined to lead to censorship.

12   What the Minneapolis City Council has before it is a very attractive theory. What MacKinnon and Dworkin have written is a very persuasive and useful definition of pornography. But they haven't yet resolved the conflict between the harm of pornography and the value of free speech. In its present form, this is still a shaky piece of law.

Los Angeles Notebook
JOAN DIDION

1   There is something uneasy in the Los Angeles air this afternoon, some unnatural stillness, some tension. What it means is that tonight a Santa Ana will begin to blow, a hot wind from the northeast whining down through the Cajon and San Gorgonio Passes, blowing up sandstorms out along Route 66, drying the hills and the nerves to the flash point. For a few days now we will see smoke back in the canyons, and hear sirens in the night. I have neither heard nor read that a Santa Ana is due, but I know it, and almost everyone I have seen today knows it too. We know it because we feel it. The baby frets. The maid sulks. I rekindle a waning argument with the telephone company, then cut my losses and lie down, given over to whatever it is in the air. To live with the Santa Ana is to accept, consciously or unconsciously, a deeply mechanistic view of human behavior.

2   I recall being told, when I first moved to Los Angeles and was living on an isolated beach, that the Indians would throw themselves into the sea when the bad wind blew. I could see why. The Pacific turned ominously glossy during a Santa Ana period, and one woke in the night troubled not only by the peacocks screaming in the olive trees but by the eerie absence of surf. The heat was surreal. The sky had a yellow cast, the kind of light sometimes called "earthquake weather." My only neighbor would not come out of her house for days, and there were no lights at night, and her husband roamed the place with a machete. One day he would tell me that he had heard a trespasser, the next a rattlesnake.

3   "On nights like that," Raymond Chandler once wrote about the Santa Ana, "every booze party ends in a fight. Meek little wives feel the edge of the carving

knife and study their husbands' necks. Anything can happen." That was the kind of wind it was. I did not know then that there was any basis for the effect it had on all of us, but it turns out to be another of those cases in which science bears out folk wisdom. The Santa Ana, which is named for one of the canyons it rushes through, is a *foehn* wind, like the *foehn* of Austria and Switzerland and the *hamsin* of Israel. There are a number of persistent malevolent winds, perhaps the best known of which are the mistral of France and the Mediterranean sirocco, but a *foehn* wind has distinct characteristics: it occurs on the leeward slope of a mountain range and, although the air begins as a cold mass, it is warmed as it comes down the mountain and appears finally as a hot dry wind. Whenever and wherever a *foehn* blows, doctors hear about headaches and nausea and allergies, about "nervousness," about "depression." In Los Angeles some teachers do not attempt to conduct formal classes during a Santa Ana, because the children become unmanageable. In Switzerland the suicide rate goes up during the *foehn*, and in the courts of some Swiss cantons the wind is considered a mitigating circumstance for crime. Surgeons are said to watch the wind, because blood does not clot normally during a *foehn*. A few years ago an Israeli physicist discovered that not only during such winds, but for the ten or twelve hours which precede them, the air carries an unusually high ratio of positive to negative ions. No one seems to know exactly why that should be; some talk about friction and others suggest solar disturbances. In any case the positive ions are there, and what an excess of positive ions does, in the simplest terms, is make people unhappy. One cannot get much more mechanistic than that.

4   Easterners commonly complain that there is no "weather" at all in Southern California, that the days and the seasons slip by relentlessly, numbingly bland. That is quite misleading. In fact the climate is characterized by infrequent but violent extremes: two periods of torrential subtropical rains which continue for weeks and wash out the hills and send subdivisions sliding toward the sea; about twenty scattered days a year of the Santa Ana, which, with its incendiary dryness, invariably means fire. At the first prediction of a Santa Ana, the Forest Service flies men and equipment from northern California into the southern forests, and the Los Angeles Fire Department cancels its ordinary non-firefighting routines. The Santa Ana caused Malibu to burn the way it did in 1956, and Bel Air in 1961, and Santa Barbara in 1964. In the winter of 1966–67 eleven men were killed fighting a Santa Ana fire that spread through the San Gabriel Mountains.

5   Just to watch the front-page news out of Los Angeles during a Santa Ana is to get very close to what it is about the place. The longest single Santa Ana period in recent years was in 1957, and it lasted not the usual three or four days but fourteen days, from November 21 until December 4. On the first day 25,000 acres of the San Gabriel Mountains were burning, with gusts reaching 100 miles an hour. In town, the wind reached Force 12, or hurricane force, on the Beaufort Scale; oil derricks were toppled and people ordered off the downtown streets to avoid injury from flying objects. On November 22 the fire in the San Gabriels was out of control. On November 24 six people were killed in automobile accidents, and by the

end of the week the Los Angeles Times was keeping a box score of traffic deaths. On November 26 a prominent Pasadena attorney, depressed about money, shot and killed his wife, their two sons, and himself. On November 27 a South Gate divorcee, twenty-two, was murdered and thrown from a moving car. On November 30 the San Gabriel fire was still out of control, and the wind in town was blowing eighty miles an hour. On the first day of December four people died violently, and on the third the wind began to break.

6   It is hard for people who have not lived in Los Angeles to realize how radically the Santa Ana figures in the local imagination. The city burning is Los Angeles's deepest image of itself: Nathanael West perceived that, in The Day of the Locust; and at the time of the 1965 Watts riots what struck the imagination most indelibly were the fires. For days one could drive the Harbor Freeway and see the city on fire, just as we had always known it would be in the end. Los Angeles weather is the weather of catastrophe, of apocalypse, and, just as the reliably long and bitter winters of New England determine the way life is lived there, so the violence and the unpredictability of the Santa Ana affect the entire quality of life in Los Angeles, accentuate its impermanence, its unreliability. The wind shows us how close to the edge we are.

2

7   "Here's why I'm on the beeper, Ron," said the telephone voice on the all-night radio show. "I just want to say that this Sex for the Secretary creature—whatever her name is—certainly isn't contributing anything to the morals in this country. It's pathetic. Statistics show."

8   "It's Sex and the Office, honey," the disc jockey said. "That's the title. By Helen Gurley Brown. Statistics show what?"

9   "I haven't got them right here at my fingertips, naturally. But they show."

10   "I'd be interested in hearing them. Be constructive, you Night Owls."

11   "All right, let's take one statistic," the voice said, truculent now. "Maybe I haven't read the book, but what's this business she recommends about going out with married men for lunch?"

12   So it went, from midnight until 5 a.m., interrupted by records and by occasional calls debating whether or not a rattlesnake can swim. Misinformation about rattlesnakes is a leitmotiv of the insomniac imagination in Los Angeles. Toward 2 a.m. a man from "out Tarzana way" called to protest. "The Night Owls who called earlier must have been thinking about, uh, The Man in the Gray Flannel Suit or some other book," he said, "because Helen's one of the few authors trying to tell us what's really going on. Hefner's another, and he's also controversial, working in, uh, another area."

13   An old man, after testifying that he "personally" had seen a swimming rattlesnake, in the Delta-Mendota Canal, urged "moderation" on the Helen Gurley Brown question. "We shouldn't get on the beeper to call things pornographic before

we've read them," he complained, pronouncing it porn-ee-oh-graphic. "I say, get the book. Give it a chance." The original provocateur called back to agree that she would get the book. "And then I'll burn it," she added.

14   "Book burner, eh?" laughed the disc jockey good-naturedly.

15   "I wish they still burned witches," she hissed.

3

16   It is three o'clock on a Sunday afternoon and 105° and the air so thick with smog that the dusty palm trees loom up with a sudden and rather attractive mystery. I have been playing in the sprinklers with the baby and I get in the car and go to Ralph's Market on the corner of Sunset and Fuller wearing an old bikini bathing suit. That is not a very good thing to wear to the market but neither is it, at Ralph's on the corner of Sunset and Fuller, an unusual costume. Nonetheless a large woman in a cotton muumuu jams her cart into mine at the butcher counter. "What a thing to wear to the market," she says in a loud but strangled voice. Everyone looks the other way and I study a plastic package of rib lamb chops and she repeats it. She follows me all over the store, to the Junior Foods, to the Dairy Products, to the Mexican Delicacies, jamming my cart whenever she can. Her husband plucks at her sleeve. As I leave the check-out counter she raises her voice one last time: "What a thing to wear to the Ralph's," she says.

4

17   A party at someone's house in Beverly Hills: a pink tent, two orchestras, a couple of French Communist directors in Cardin evening jackets, chili and hamburgers from Chasen's. The wife of an English actor sits at a table alone; she visits California rarely although her husband works here a good deal. An American who knows her slightly comes over to the table.

18   "Marvelous to see you here," he says.

19   "Is it," she says.

20   "How long have you been here?"

21   "Too long."

22   She takes a fresh drink from a passing waiter and smiles at her husband, who is dancing.

23   The American tries again. He mentions her husband.

24   "I hear he's marvelous in this picture."

25   She looks at the American for the first time. When she finally speaks she enunciates every word very clearly. "He...is...also...a...fag," she says pleasantly.

5

26   The oral history of Los Angeles is written in piano bars. "Moon River," the piano player always plays, and "Mountain Greenery." "There's a Small Hotel" and "This

is Not the First Time." People talk to each other, tell each other about their first wives and last husbands. "Stay funny," they tell each other, and "This is to die over." A construction man talks to an unemployed screenwriter who is celebrating, alone, his tenth wedding anniversary. The construction man is on a job in Montecito: "Up in Montecito," he says, "they got one square mile with 135 millionaires."

27   "Putrescence," the writer says.

28   "That's all you got to say about it?"

29   "Don't read me wrong, I think Santa Barbara's one of the most—Christ, the most—beautiful places in the world, but it's a beautiful place that contains a...putrescence. They just live on their putrescent millions."

30   "So give me putrescent."

31   "No, no," the writer says. "I just happen to think millionaires have some sort of lacking in their...in their elasticity."

32   A drunk requests "The Sweetheart of Sigma Chi." The piano player says he doesn't know it. "Where'd you learn to play the piano?" the drunk asks. "I got two degrees," the piano player says. "One in musical education." I go to a coin telephone and call a friend in New York. "Where are you?" he says. "In a piano bar in Encino," I say. "Why?" he says. "Why not," I say.

1965–67

FOR CRITICAL INQUIRY

1. As you read the opening sections of each selection, what did they lead you to anticipate would follow? Were your predictions realized?

2. Explain when you became aware of the writer's main point in each selection. Is it stated explicitly? If so, how did that statement guide your reading? If it was not stated explicitly, how did you identify the writer's purposes?

3. Compare your reading experience in each selection. How did you organize mentally the presentation of material? What patterns of organization in the written text did you rely on? Were there other cues for readers in the text that you used? What do you see as the main differences and similarities in how you read each selection?

SEEING PATTERNS OF ORGANIZATION: HOW FORM EMBODIES PURPOSE

As you can see, the pattern of organization each writer chose embodies a particular purpose and establishes a different relationship with readers. In the first selection "I Shop, Ergo I Am," Sarah Boxer wants to inform *New York Times* readers about a new development in the academic world. For this reason, she makes clear early on how the idea that shopping "is a statement about your place in society" has been taken up by cultural studies scholars. We can diagram the top-down pattern of organization in her article:

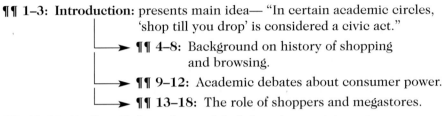

¶¶ 1–3: **Introduction:** presents main idea— "In certain academic circles, 'shop till you drop' is considered a civic act."

➤ ¶¶ 4–8: Background on history of shopping and browsing.

➤ ¶¶ 9–12: Academic debates about consumer power.

➤ ¶¶ 13–18: The role of shoppers and megastores.

¶¶ 19–22: **Ending:** Refines the model of shopping as civic action.

Boxer moves from a general statement about shopping and citizenship in the introduction to particular evidence in the middle section back to a general level in the ending.

In contrast, Ellen Goodman's "Minneapolis Pornography Ordinance" more nearly resembles the rising action of a short story, with an opening exposition of the issues, a mounting conflict, a crisis where two principles seem irreconcilable, and a resolution in the form of Goodman's main claim. By delaying the presentation of her own position, Goodman leads the readers of her syndicated column through an explanation of what the Minneapolis ordinance is trying to accomplish and the logic it is based on. A good half of her writing, the first six paragraphs, gives a generous and informative description of the ordinance before Goodman starts to raise questions about its relationship to the values of free speech.

Notice how she slowly raises doubts about the merits of the ordinance, gradually building a case about how it clashes with the values of free speech, up to the final paragraph when she culminates the column by unequivocally stating her position.

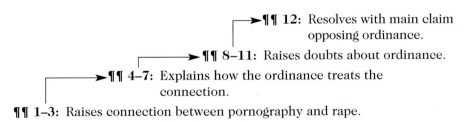

➤ ¶¶ 12: Resolves with main claim opposing ordinance.

➤ ¶¶ 8–11: Raises doubts about ordinance.

➤ ¶¶ 4–7: Explains how the ordinance treats the connection.

¶¶ 1–3: Raises connection between pornography and rape.

In turn, Joan Didion's "Los Angeles Notebook" consists of five sections that at first glance have a kind of free-standing character, as if each were meant to be read by itself. Didion is audacious here in using an open form that operates as a mosaic or collage does by juxtaposing disparate parts to form a whole. The five sections are separate units of attention; yet the fact that they appear under one title sets us to work as readers to see how they resonate with each other and what the unstated connections might be between and among them.

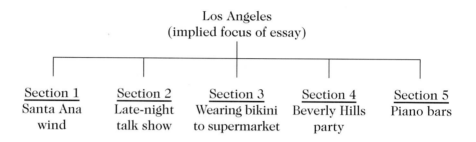

Los Angeles
(implied focus of essay)

Section 1	Section 2	Section 3	Section 4	Section 5
Santa Ana wind	Late-night talk show	Wearing bikini to supermarket	Beverly Hills party	Piano bars

EXERCISES

1. Locate a piece of writing that uses a top-down pattern of organization. This could be your own writing or one of the reading selections. Now diagram the pattern of organization in the writing you have chosen by following these steps:

   a. Divide the writing into sections by grouping paragraphs together.

   b. Lay out the sections so that supporting sections are indented in relation to the main point.

   c. Draw arrows to show how the sections are connected.

   d. Write a commentary on your diagram that explains how the sections elicit readers' expectations and then goes on to resolve or fulfill these expectations.

2. Rewrite the opening of Ellen Goodman's "Minneapolis Pornography Ordinance" so that it follows a top-down pattern of organization. What, if anything, do you gain by doing so? What do you lose?

3. Use Joan Didion's "Los Angeles Notebook" as a model to experiment with open form. Write a sequence of sketches that are somehow thematically or attitudinally related. Exchange your writing with a partner in class. Write an analysis of your partner's essay, explaining what you see as the implied focus and what seems to pull the parts together.

A Note on Mixed Form

The three examples presented here—top-down order, culminating order, and open form—offer relatively pure cases of each pattern of organization. That does not mean, however, that all writing will necessarily fall strictly into one of the patterns. In fact, a good deal of writing combines aspects of the three patterns and therefore might best be described as examples of *mixed form.*

PUTTING THE PARTS TOGETHER

We have looked at the overall form of some short essays. Now we need to look a little more closely at how writers combine the parts of an essay to form a whole. In the following sections, we look first at how writers organize introductions and endings and then at how they connect the parts.

Introductions

The purpose of an introduction is obvious. The opening section needs to let the reader know what the writing is about and how the writer is going to approach the topic.

Sometimes, depending on the situation and the genre, writers just outright tell readers: "This report summarizes the results of the pilot project and makes recommendations for the second stage of implementation" or "This proposal requests funding for a day-care center to serve students, faculty, and staff." In other cases, however, introductions need to do more work in establishing a central issue and explaining what is at stake.

Introductions work when they produce a certain meeting of the minds between the writer and reader. This is not to say that they necessarily agree about anything, only that they are mutually engaged in thinking about an issue, problem, or experience. Effective introductions are able to produce this kind of engagement because they identify something that the reader recognizes as interesting, important, controversial, amusing, urgent, whatever—a shareable concern whose relevance is evident.

In other words, writers need to frame their issues in a way that connects to what readers know and care about. Such a framework, then, can become the base from which the writer ventures his or her own views on the matter. The following are some common strategies writers use to establish a common framework and to explain how their own perspective connects to it.

- Describe an existing situation.

- Tell an anecdote.

- Raise a question to answer or problem to solve.

- Use a striking fact, statistic, or other background information.

- Define terms.

- Provide historical background.

- Describe a place, person, or object.

- State a common view and replace it with an alternative perspective.

- Forecast what your writing is designed to do.

EXERCISE

Bring to class three pieces of writing (or draw on readings in this book) that use different strategies in their introductions. Work in a group with three or four other students. Take turns explaining the strategies you have found. Consider the differences and similarities among the examples you have found. What generalizations can you draw about how introductions work?

Endings

In terms of the psychological dimensions of form, endings are key moments in writing. Writers know that endings need to provide readers with a sense of closure by resolving their expectations. Without a satisfying sense of an ending, readers are likely to feel let down. Writing that ends abruptly or fails to deliver at the end is going to leave readers up in the air, frustrated, and perhaps annoyed at the writer. In this section, we look at some ways writers typically end short pieces of writing so that they offer readers a satisfying sense of resolution.

Perhaps the most important thing writers can learn about endings is that they perform a function no other part of an essay can perform: They address a question that it doesn't make sense to raise until the writer has developed his or her line of inquiry. This question can be phrased rather bluntly as "so what?"

So what if it is the case, as Sarah Boxer points out, that cultural studies scholars are looking at shopping as civic action? Readers may well have been interested in what Boxer reports about shopping studies. At the same time, it is quite likely that the question "so what?" is lingering at the back of their minds. What's the big picture here, readers will want to know, the consequences and wider implications?

The function of endings is precisely to answer the question "so what?"—to give readers a way to connect the information in Boxer's article with broader issues. Notice how Boxer has effectively resolved in her ending section the expectations raised in readers' minds when she draws out the connection between shopping and the "dangers of modern life." What might have seemed an esoteric academic topic takes on a wider meaning as Boxer explains how the rise of megastores are changing the character of shopping—and the nature of socializing in contemporary America.

Notice, too, that Boxer is not trying to wrap up everything once and for all in a neat package. Closure doesn't necessarily mean having the final word. In fact, Boxer's ending gives readers something further to think about—to consider what is at stake for them in the whole matter of shopping.

Here are some techniques writers commonly use to write endings that provide a satisfying sense of resolution and closure.

- Point out consequences or the wider significance of the main point.

- Refine the main point in light of the material presented in the piece of writing.

- Offer a recommendation or a solution.

- Consider alternatives.

- Create an echo effect by looping back to something you presented in the introduction.

- Offer a final judgment

EXERCISE

Compare the endings in three pieces of writing. (Jon Garelick's "Kurt Cobain 1967– 1994," page 234, Eric Liu's "Remember When Public Space Didn't Carry Brand Names," page 309, and Henry Jenkins' "Lessons from Littleton: What Congress Doesn't Want to Hear About Youth and the Media," page 356, make a good combination.) First identify where the ending begins in each piece. What cues does the writer give? Next, explain the strategy it uses. How does this strategy embody the writer's purposes?

Connecting the Parts: Keeping Your Purposes Visible

If introductions help readers anticipate what is to come and endings explore the consequences or wider implications of the writer's ideas, the middle section (or main body) is where writers unfold their thinking and develop their ideas. The success of the middle section partly depends on readers being able to see how the reasons, evidence, and other supporting materials connect to the main idea presented in the introduction. Writing that is easy to follow, even if the ideas are complex, will use various devices to keep the writer's purposes visible so that readers can stay oriented, identify the relevance of the writer's discussion, and connect it to expectations set up in the introduction.

Here are three standard techniques for connecting the parts.

Use Reasons to Explain

A common way of connecting the parts is to use reasons to explain how the discussion in the middle section develops the main point. In the following sequence of paragraphs, notice how Laurie Ouellette uses reasons to explain why "young women have shunned feminism."

> [W]hat can explain why so many young women have shunned feminism? In her survey of young women, *Feminist Fatale: Voices from the Twentysomething Generation Explore the Future of the Women's Movement,* Paula Kamen found that media-fueled stereotypes of feminists as "man-bashers" and "radical extremists" were behind the fact that many young women don't identify with the women's movement.
>
> But these are not the only reasons. Kamen also points to the lack of young feminist role models as an important factor. The failure of a major feminist organization such as NOW to reach out to a wider spectrum of women, including young women, must be acknowledged as a part of this problem. While individual chapters do have young feminist committees and sometimes officers, they and the national office are led and staffed primarily by older women, and consequently often fail to reflect the interests and needs of a complex generation of young women.
>
> Yet another reason young women have turned away from feminism may lie within its history. If the young women who have gained the most from feminism—that is, white, middle-class women who took advantage of increased accessibility to higher education and professional employment—have been reluctant to associate themselves with feminism, it is hardly surprising that most economically disadvantaged women and women of color, who have seen fewer of those gains, have not been eager to embrace feminism either. The women's movement of the seventies has been called an upper-middle-class white women's movement, and to a large degree I believe that is true. More than a few young feminists—many influenced by feminists of color such as Flo Kennedy, Audre Lorde, and bell hooks—have realized that feminism must also acknowledge issues of race and class to reach out to those women whose concerns have been overlooked by the women's movement of the past. Indeed, numerous statistics, including a poll by the *New York Times,* have noted that young African-American women are more likely than white women to acknowledge many of the concerns conducive to a feminist agenda, including a need for job training and equal earning power outside the professional sector. But for them, feminism has not provided the only answer. Only by making issues of class and race a priority can feminism hope to influence the lives of the millions of women for whom the daily struggle to survive, not feminist activism, is a priority. Will ours be the first generation of feminists to give priority to fighting cuts in Aid to Families with Dependent Children, establishing the right to national health care, day care, and parental leave, and bringing to the forefront other issues pertinent to the daily struggle of many women's lives? If there is to be a third wave of feminism, they must.
>
> *Laurie Ouellette*

We can diagram the pattern of development in the three paragraphs to make visible how it embodies Ouellette's purposes. Notice how the form creates a hierarchy of levels—the main point, the reasons and the supporting evidence.

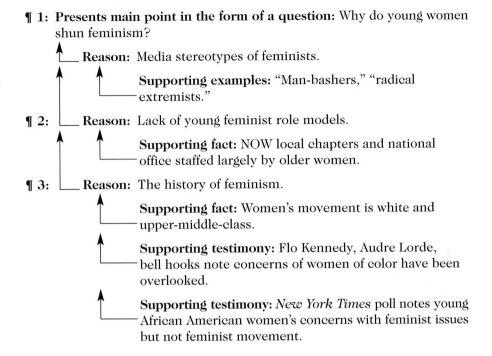

¶ **1: Presents main point in the form of a question:** Why do young women shun feminism?

Reason: Media stereotypes of feminists.

Supporting examples: "Man-bashers," "radical extremists."

¶ **2: Reason:** Lack of young feminist role models.

Supporting fact: NOW local chapters and national office staffed largely by older women.

¶ **3: Reason:** The history of feminism.

Supporting fact: Women's movement is white and upper-middle-class.

Supporting testimony: Flo Kennedy, Audre Lorde, bell hooks note concerns of women of color have been overlooked.

Supporting testimony: *New York Times* poll notes young African American women's concerns with feminist issues but not feminist movement.

Create Topic Chains

Topic chains help readers establish links between the parts of a piece of writing and allow them to feel that they know where the writer is going. Writers create topic chains by repeating key words, using pronouns and synonyms, and restating main points. Notice the topic chain Sarah Boxer develops by regularly emphasizing the notion of shopping at the beginning of many paragraphs.

¶¶**1–3:** In certain academic circles, 'shop till you drop' is considered a civic act.

¶**4:** The intellectual fascination with stores...

¶**5:** Historically, the age of shopping and browsing begins...

¶**7:** The pastime of browsing...

¶**9:** Some feminists point out that as shoppers...

¶**11:** The idea that shopping is a form of civic action...

¶**13:** The field of shopping studies...

¶**14:** Shoppers' freedoms...

¶**15:** In superstores, the role of shoppers...

¶**16:** Does the concept of the shopper as citizen...?

¶20: Ms. Conroy suggested that consumerism...

¶21: What does one man's shopping experience...?

Use Transitions

Writers use transitional words, phrases, and sentences to show readers how one statement, paragraph, or section in a piece of writing relates to the next.

Temporal transitions indicate the sequence of events that takes place and the passage of time. In "Black Hair" (page 147), Gary Soto begins a number of paragraphs with temporal transitions to help readers see the order in his narrative account of work:

¶5: *The next morning,* I arrived early at work.

¶7: I worked carefully *that day*....

¶8: *At five,* the workers scattered....

¶9: From the backyard I walked dully through a residential street, and *as evening came on*...

¶11: When I got up from the lawn *it was late.*

¶13: At work I spent the *morning* at the buffer....

¶15: Iggy worked only *until three in the afternoon*....

Spatial transitions help locate the position of things, people, and events. In her profile of Dr. Susan Love (page 224), Molly O'Neill uses spatial transitions so that readers can visualize the scene she is describing.

A radiologist used a pointer to outline the tumor for a group of radiologists, pathologists, and surgeons. Dr. Love stood in the back of the conference room, rocking in her bone-colored pumps. Her brown eyes were narrowed *behind* red-frame glasses.

The lab coat she wore was a bulletin board of buttons. "Keep abreast," read one, "Get a second opinion." On another: "T.G.I.F. (Thank God I'm Female)." *Under* the string of fat white pearls *around* her neck was a gold chain with an ankh, an ancient symbol of life. *Above* one of the Chanel-style earrings was a tiny labyrs, the mythical double-bladed ax used by Amazons.

Logical transitions help readers understand how ideas are related to one another. Transitional words and phrases link ideas as the writers move from one paragraph to the next—building on what they have just said as the basis for the paragraph that follows.

Notice how Henry Jenkins, in "Lessons from Littleton" (page 356), lists a sequence of four points using parallel phrases and then summarizes the consequences:

First, violent entertainment offers teens a fantasy of empowerment....

Second, violent entertainment offers teens a fantasy of transgression....

Third, violent entertainment offers teens an acknowledgement that the world is not all sweetness and light....

Fourth, violent entertainment offers teens an intensification of emotional experience....

In short, teens aren't drawn to *Quake* or *Scream* because they are bloodthirsty....

Leon Botstein, in "Let Teenagers Try Adulthood" (page 347), signals an addition to his argument:

An institution intended for children in transition now holds young adults back well beyond the developmental point for which high school was originally designed.

Furthermore, whatever constraints to the presumption of adulthood among young people may have existed decades ago have now fallen away.

In "Why the Ravens Will Win" (page 403), Mike Freeman draws a consequence.

Among the game tapes the Giants have scoured are two: Baltimore's first game against Jacksonville, in which the Jaguars garnered 421 total yards of offense mainly by throwing the football deep, and the Washington game, in which Stephen Davis rushed for 91 yards, including a 33-yard touchdown scamper. It's the latter game the Giants can use to see what blocking schemes the Redskins used to free up Davis.

So the Giants will score some points.

Jon Garelick, in "Kurt Cobain 1967–1994" (page 234), expresses contrast between one point and the next.

There was reported weirdness and with guns, drugs, petulant faxes sent to various publications (including this one)—exploits that made Cobain and wife Courtney Love a notorious rock-and-roll couple.

And yet, in interviews and live performances, Cobain was invariably lucid, modest, intelligent.

And in "How To Fight the New Epidemics" (page 321), Lundy Braun compares ("not only") and contrasts ("but also") ideas:

This view is rooted in the rise of the germ theory in the late 19th and early 20th centuries that associated specific microbial agents with particular diseases.

The germ theory took hold *not only because* of the spectacular technical achievements represented by the isolation of microorganisms, *but also because* infectious diseases, once seen as divine retribution for past sins, now appeared potentially conquerable.

DESIGNING PARAGRAPHS

Paragraphs are the building blocks writers use to assemble larger pieces of writing. That does not mean, of course, that paragraphs come ready-made in standard, prefabricated forms. They need to be designed to perform particular

COMMON TYPES OF TRANSITIONS

To mark sequence and passage of time:	next, later, after, before, earlier, meanwhile, immediately, soon, shortly, often, frequently, again, during, finally, at last
To locate spatially:	near, next to, alongside, facing, adjacent, far beyond, away, off in the distance, between, through, up, down, across, above, below, inside, outside
To give examples:	for example, for instance, namely, specifically, that is
To add further points:	and, in addition, also, furthermore, moreover
To show consequences:	thus, therefore, so, consequently, hence, as a result, for this reason
To compare:	similarly, likewise, also
To contrast:	however, in contrast, but, yet, nevertheless, nonetheless
To compare and contrast:	not only/but also, on the one hand/on the other
To make a concession:	although, even though, granted that

functions depending on the kind of writing and where the paragraph takes place in the larger piece of writing.

Seeing Paragraphs: The Visual Dimension

As mentioned earlier, the form of nonfiction prose has both a visual and a psychological dimension, and this is true as well of paragraphs. Visually, paragraphs are graphic units that mark units of attention for readers by indenting. Paragraph breaks help readers see where a related sequence of ideas begins and ends. In turn, paragraphs provide writers with a means to establish the reader's focus of attention for a period of time.

Experienced writers have learned that the beginning and ending of paragraphs are the points at which readers are most attentive. When a paragraph begins, readers look for cues to tell them what the paragraph is going to be about so that they can concentrate on that particular point and how the writer develops it. When the paragraph ends, readers often pause briefly, to catch their breath and consolidate their sense of what they have just read, before going on to the next paragraph.

In newspaper writing, for example, in part because of the narrow columns in the page layout, paragraphs tend to be short. One of their functions is to make the experience of reading as easy as possible so that readers can get the gist of an article by scanning it quickly. The same thing applies to many kinds of writing in the workplace and the public sphere, where writers and readers alike put a premium on making the information in memos, reports, proposals, news briefings, and brochures concise and easy to process.

In other genres of writing, however, paragraphs have a very different look on the page. Academic writing, essays, and magazine articles often use longer paragraphs, and readers expect that writers will develop their points in greater depth and detail.

The length of a paragraph, in other words, depends on the kind of writing in which it appears and the function it serves.

EXERCISE

Following is a passage from Susan Faludi's "Shannon Faulkner's Strength in Numbers" without paragraph indentation. You will probably notice right away how dense and forbidding the passage seems. It looks like a lot of extra work to get through it. Your task here is to provide paragraphing to make the passage easier for readers. Follow these steps:

1. On your own, read through the passage and insert paragraph breaks where you think they are most useful.

2. Now work with two or three classmates and compare how each of you has divided the passage into paragraphs. To what extent are the paragraphs alike? To what extent do they differ? In the case of differences, does the effect on readers differ? If so, how? Working together, see if you can come up with one version that everyone in the group can live with. If you can't agree, explain what your differences are and what seems to be at stake.

3. Finally, compare what your group has come up with to the way paragraph breaks appear in the printed version on page 314. To what extent are the paragraphs alike or different? In the case of differences, how does the effect on readers differ?

Out of all the nearly 2,000 cadets who enrolled in an all-male military academy called The Citadel this year, the only one whose name we know was the one the school didn't want: Shannon Faulkner. This distinction seems, on its face, too obvious to mention. Of course she's famous—that she was admitted to the academy at all was a cause célèbre. But the distinction is important, because it goes to the heart of the issue. One reason the other Citadel cadets loathed Shannon Faulkner (aside from her sex) was her individuality, which affronted The Citadel's ethic. The academy purports to educate young men by making them conform. Conformity is enforced through anonymity. From the day the cadets arrive, when they are issued identical uniforms and haircuts, they become so homogeneous that, as an upperclassman explained to me, "mothers can't even tell their sons apart." Through communal living and endless drills and rigid codes of conduct, the cadet's individuality is subordinated to the identity of the group, his strength founded in numbers and teamwork, in esprit de corps and long tradition. Going it alone, as a maverick, isn't done. "Individuals do not make it here," the commandant of cadets warned this year's freshmen on their first day. "If you want to stay an individual, every day will be a tough day." This is what is called a military education, and it was exactly what Shannon Faulkner wanted and could not find elsewhere in her home state of South Carolina. From the start her quest seemed hopeless: by seeking military anonymity in an all-male corps, she had to stand out. But her downfall was hastened by forces beyond The Citadel. The largest obstacle she faced was the popular illusion that history is driven not by the actions and changing beliefs of large numbers of ordinary people, but by a few heroic giants who materialize out of nowhere to transform the landscape.

Unity and Coherence: The Psychological Dimension

Unity and coherence are workshop terms referring to the psychological dimension of writing and to how writing arouses the reader's expectations and then goes on to fulfill them. *Unity* means that a piece of writing has some central point, focus, or center of gravity that readers can readily identify. They don't wonder what the writer is getting at or try to figure out the main point on their own. *Coherence* means that the ideas in the writing seem to come in the right order, leading logically from one point to the next. Readers don't feel that the writing rambles or jumps around from point to point but instead moves along purposefully.

Often, readers are not even aware that well-crafted writing is unified and coherent. They simply experience the writing as easy to read: The writer's ideas seem to be where they belong, and readers can easily follow the writer's thoughts from point to point. The writing just seems to flow, and readers don't feel confused about its direction. Moreover, when this happens, readers feel they are in good hands—and, as a result, are likely to invest a certain amount of confidence and credibility in what the writer is saying. Whether they agree with the ideas or not, they at least feel that the writer knows what he or she is doing and is therefore worth considering. In short, unity and coherence are devices for making a meeting of minds possible.

You can see how unity and coherence work at the level of a whole piece of writing by looking back at the writing samples in this chapter. Take, for example, Sarah Boxer's "I Shop, Ergo I Am." Here the unity comes from the opening paragraphs, where Boxer explains how the connection between shopping and civic action has been taken up as a topic by cultural studies scholars. Readers at this point will justifiably expect the article to tell them more about such shopping studies. And that is exactly what Boxer does. She develops the idea in a coherent order, starting with studies of eighteenth-century shopping and then moving to contemporary instances. In other words, she enables readers to see how the article's parts are relevant to the main idea.

To see how paragraphs use unity and coherence to enhance readability, look at the following paragraph:

> Public toilets...have become the real frontline of the city's war on the homeless. Los Angeles, as a matter of deliberate policy, has fewer public toilets than any other major North American city. On the advice of the Los Angeles police, who now sit on the "design board of at least one major Downtown project, the redevelopment agency bulldozed the few remaining public toilets on Skid Row. Agency planners then considered whether to include a "free-standing public toilet" in their design for the upscale South Park residential development; agency chairman Jim Wood later admitted that the decision not to build the toilet was a "policy decision and not a design decision." The agency preferred the alternative of "quasi-public restrooms"—toilets in restaurants, art galleries, and office buildings—which can be made available selectively to tourists and white-collar workers while being denied to vagrants and other unsuitables. The same logic has inspired the city's transportation planners to exclude toilets from their designs for Los Angeles's new subway system.
>
> *Mike Davis, from* City of Quartz

Topic Sentences and Unity

Notice how Davis begins with a topic sentence ("Public toilets...have become the real frontline on the city's war on the homeless"). Topic sentences typically focus on a single idea or on a sequence of related ideas that will be developed in the paragraph. At this point, readers can reasonably expect Davis to devote the rest of the paragraph to explaining how public toilets figure into Los Angeles's "war on the homeless."

Discussion and Unity and Coherence

As you can see, the rest of the paragraph, or the discussion, is indeed devoted to explaining how planners eliminated the availability of public toilets; it thereby contributes to the unity of the paragraph and to fulfilling readers' expectations. Notice, furthermore, how the order of sentences seems coherent. Each sentence not only follows from the topic sentence but also picks up on the sentence that precedes it. The way one sentence leads to the next can be analyzed by imagining that each sentence answers a question in the reader's mind raised by the preceding sentence or sentences:

> *Topic Sentence*
> Public toilets...have become the real frontline in the city's war on the homeless.
> *(Question: What is this "war"?)*

> *Discussion*
> Los Angeles, as a matter of deliberate policy, has fewer public toilets than any other major North American city.
> *(Answers question and raises another about how "policy" was made)*

On the advice of the Los Angeles police, who now sit on the design board of at least one major Downtown project, the redevelopment agency bulldozed the few remaining public toilets on Skid Row.

(Answers question about how "policy" was made)

Agency planners then considered whether to include a "free-standing public toilet" in their design for the upscale South Park residential development; agency chairman Jim Wood later admitted that the decision not to build the toilet was a "policy decision and not a design decision."

(Amplifies answer about how "policy" was made by giving another example)

The agency preferred the alternative of "quasi-public restrooms"—toilets in restaurants, art galleries, and office buildings—which can be made available selectively to tourists and white-collar workers while being denied to vagrants and other unsuitables.

(Answers question about how "policy" amounts to "war on the homeless")

The same logic has inspired the city's transportation planners to exclude toilets from their designs for Los Angeles's new subway system.

(Gives a final example of how "policy" makes "war on the homeless")

EXERCISE

Work together in a group of four or five. Read the following passage aloud. Then answer the questions.

I have always wanted to be a high school American history teacher. Many teachers are now feeling the pressure to teach the test rather than educate their students in historical understanding. There are certainly skills and knowledge that high school students should acquire in their American history classes. Historical understanding gives students a way to see how the past shapes the present. In American history courses, students have too often memorized facts and dates rather than learning to understand why historical events took place and how they affect the present. I realize that many students are not interested in the past, but my desire is to help students think about American history and the unresolved questions it raises about the legacy of slavery, the American belief in individualism and free enterprise, and the Vietnam War. The current trend to make high schools more accountable emphasizes testing at the expense of genuine learning. Historical understanding is crucial if we want to have an informed citizenry who can make decisions about the complex issues that face us as a nation.

1. What question does the first sentence raise?

2. How is this question answered?

3. Are there other questions that the paragraph seems to raise?

4. How are these questions answered?

5. How would you revise this paragraph for unity and coherence?

A Note on the Placement of Topic Sentences

Topic sentences typically appear at the beginning (or near the beginning) of a paragraph to focus the readers' attention and enable them to forecast what is to come. In some instances, however, writers will vary the position of topic sentences, delaying it until late in the paragraph. Let's take two examples from "Letters" in Chapter 4 to see how these different (underlined) placements of topic sentences work. In the first instance, notice how Mark Patinkin puts the topic sentence first in this paragraph from "Commit a Crime, Suffer the Consequences" (page 117):

> *All this is just part of the new American game of always saying, "It's not my fault."* No one, when caught, seems ready to admit having done wrong anymore. They just whine and appeal. As in: "Your honor, the stabbing was not my client's fault. He had a bad childhood. And was caught up in a riot at the time. In fact, he's not a criminal at all, he's one of society's victims."

On the other hand, writers may choose to position the topic sentence at the end of the paragraph—to use the paragraph to lead up to it, as James Baldwin does here in the second paragraph of "My Dungeon Shook: Letter to My Nephew" (page 124):

> I have known both of you all your lives, have carried your Daddy in my arms and on my shoulders, kissed and spanked him and watched him learn to walk. I don't know if you've known anybody from that far back; if you've loved anybody that long, first as an infant, then as a child, then as a man, you gain a strange perspective on time and human pain and effort. Other people cannot see what I see whenever I look into your father's face, for behind your father's face as it is today are all those other faces which were his. Let him laugh and I see a cellar your father does not remember and a house he does not remember and I hear in his present laughter his laughter as a child. Let him curse and I remember him falling down the cellar steps, and howling, and I remember, with pain, his tears, which my hand or your grandmother's so easily wiped away. But no one's hand can wipe away those tears he sheds invisibly today, which one hears in his laughter and in his speech and in his songs. I know what the world has done to my brother and how narrowly he has survived it. And I know, which is much worse, and this is the crime of which I accuse my country and my countrymen, and for which neither I nor time nor history will ever forgive them, that they have destroyed and are destroying hundreds of thousands of lives and do not know it and do not want to know it. One can be, indeed one must strive to become, tough and philosophical concerning destruction and death, for this is what most of mankind has been best at since we have heard of man. (But remember: most of mankind is not all of mankind.) But it is not permissible that the authors of devastation should also be innocent. *It is the innocence which constitutes the crime.*

HOW PARAGRAPHS MAKE PATTERNS OF ORGANIZATION EASY TO RECOGNIZE

Readers recognize paragraphs first by their visual features, as indentation marks the transition from one paragraph to another. Readers' expectation, of course, is that the paragraph they are embarking on will relate both to the one before and to the overall meaning in the piece of writing. As you have seen, topic sentences are key to making this transition easy for readers to follow. But you also need to keep readers with you throughout the paragraph.

Readers will be looking, largely unconsciously, for a pattern of development in the paragraph—some ordering system that weaves the sentences into a pattern of meaning. When a clearly recognizable pattern is present, readers will be able to concentrate on the content of the paragraph—to think about what you are saying. What follow are some common techniques for making the pattern of development in a paragraph easy for readers to recognize.

Narration

Narration tells a story, relates an anecdote, or recreates an event or a sequence of events. Memoirs often use narration as their pattern of organization, as you can see in Gary Soto's "Black Hair" (page 147) and the excerpt from Annie Dillard's *An American Childhood* (page 154). In other cases, writers will weave narration into their writing. Consider, for example, how the two following excerpts (pages 516 and 398) use narration to develop key points:

> My flesh-and-blood family long ago grew accustomed to the way I sit in my office early in the morning and late at night, chuckling and cursing, sometimes crying, about words I read on the computer screen. It might have looked to my daughter as if I were alone at my desk the night she caught me chortling online, but from my point of view I was in living contact with old and new friends, strangers and colleagues.
>
> *(Howard Rheingold, from* The Virtual Community*)*

> During the first phase of the FBI's engagement at Waco, a period of a few days, the agents on the ground at the compound proceeded with a strategy of conciliatory negotiation, which had the approval and understanding of the entire chain of command. In the view of the negotiating team, considerable progress was made—for example, some adults and children came out of the compound— but David Koresh and the Branch Davidians made many promises to the negotiators that they then did not keep. Pushed by the tactical leader, the FBI's commander on the ground began to allow tactical pressures to be placed on the compound in addition to negotiation, e.g., turning off the electricity, so that those in the compound would be as cold as the agents outside during the twenty-degree night. This tactical pressure was applied over the objections of

the FBI's own experts in negotiation and behavioral science, who specifically advised against it. These experts warned the FBI command about the potentially fatal consequences of using such measures.

(Alan Stone, from "Report and Recommendations Concerning the Handling of Incidents Such as the Branch Davidian Standoff in Waco, Texas")

Description

Description enables readers to see what you are writing about. Writers use description to create word-pictures of a scene or a person. Notice how the following passage locates readers in an America Online chatroom (page 511):

"Yo yo yo, what's up what's up?" The lines scroll up my screen. Different fonts, different colors, the words whiz by, everyone's screen name sounding vaguely pornographic. I'm on America Online, in a chat room for young adults. There are hundreds of such chat rooms on AOL, and it has taken a lot of Net navigating simply to find one that has room enough to let me in.

(Camille Sweeney, "In a Chat Room, You Can Be NE1: Constructing a Teenage Self On Line")

But description can also be used to explain a concept or a state of mind, as Mike Rose does in the following paragraph, where he analyzes the defenses vocational education students erect (pages 232–233):

The tragedy is that you have to twist the knife in your own gray matter to make this defense work. You'll have to shut down, have to reject intellectual stimuli or defuse them with sarcasm, have to cultivate stupidity, have to convert boredom from a malady into a way of confronting the world. Keep your vocabulary simple, act stoned when you're not or act more stoned than you are, flaunt ignorance, materialize your dreams. It is a powerful and effective defense—it neutralizes the insult and the frustration of being a vocational kid and, when perfected, it drives teachers up the wall, a delightful secondary effect. But like all strong magic, it exacts a price.

(Mike Rose, from Lives on the Boundary)

Definition

Definitions provide the meaning of a term or a concept. In some instances, a simple and clear definition of terms is needed to explain basic concepts in a public document, as is the case here (page 219):

II. Definition of Academic Trust
Academic trust is the assurance that teacher and student will faithfully abide by the rules of intellectual engagement established between them. This trust can exist only when students adhere to the standards of academic honesty and

when faculty test and evaluate students in a manner that presumes that students are acting with academic integrity.

> *(Ad Hoc Committee on Academic Honesty,*
> *Proposal for an Academic Honor Code)*

In other instances, however, writers use extended definitions to develop
their thinking about a subject, as Michael Rock does in the final paragraph of
his analysis of *USA Today* design style, where he defines what he calls the "LITE
phenomenon" (pages 320–321):

> Or maybe the best explanation for the spread of *USA Today* look-alikes is that
> it is an inevitable extension of the LITE phenomenon. If beer or mayonnaise or
> individually wrapped slices of American cheese make you fat, then: a) stop eat-
> ing and drinking so much; or b) remanufacture the product with fewer calories.
> We are more comfortable with the idea of changing our products than with
> changing our habits. Maybe publication design is under the same pressure.
> Maybe we want the "experience" of reading without all that heavy, annoying
> thinking. Maybe it's LITE design; it tastes great and is less filling.
>
> *(Michael Rock, "Since When Did USA Today*
> *Become the National Design Ideal?")*

Classification

Classification is a way of sorting things and people into groups by creating categories. *The Call to Write,* for example, divides the various forms of writing into
genres, enabling us then to classify the pieces of writing we encounter into one
or another of these categories. By the same token, in her review of *Ally McBeal,*
Karen Durbin classifies the show by first explaining what categories it doesn't
fit into (page 392):

> At its uneven best, *Ally McBeal* is neither yuppie sitcom nor courtroom drama

and then she tells us which ones the show is like,

> but an absurdist morality play that gives off sparks of screwball comedy.
>
> *(Karen Durbin, "Razor Thin, But Larger Than Life")*

In other instances, classification can provide an overall pattern of organization for a document or piece of writing. For example, the "WPA Outcomes
Statement for First-Year Composition" (page 203) uses a classification
scheme—"Rhetorical Knowledge," "Critical Thinking, Reading, and Writing,"
"Processes," and "Knowledge of Conventions"—to set up four criteria for assessing what takes place in writing classes.

Comparison and Contrast

Comparison and contrast refer to the way in which writers note differences and similarities. Either can appear by itself, but writers frequently use the two strategies together to show how things, people, and ideas are like or unlike others of their type. You can find discussions of how writers use comparison and contrast in Chapter 7 "Profiles" and Chapter 11 "Reviews."

EXERCISE

Locate one or more examples of narration, description, definition, classification, or comparison and contrast in the piece of writing where it appears. As you put the example back into its original context, note how you became aware of what the writer was doing at that point. What cues alert you to the fact that you're reading a narration, description, definition, classification, or comparison and contrast? What function does the particular strategy perform?

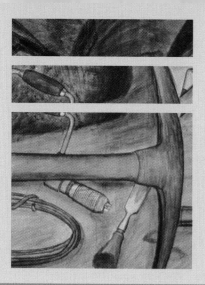

CHAPTER FIFTEEN

Communicating Online: Writing in the Age of Digital Literacy

We are living in a transitional time. The personal computer, word processing, scanners, graphics programs, and desktop publishing have changed the way writers produce printed texts. Increased access to the Internet and the Web—the so-called "information superhighway"—though distributed mainly among privileged groups in the wealthy nations, has made the term *cyberspace* a household word, and in some cases appears to be on the verge of replacing printed texts with digital ones—e-mail, listservs, attached files, message boards, palm pilots, Web sites, MUDs, and MOOs.

For many writers, these are changes that need to be reckoned with. If writers once composed their manuscripts in longhand, only gradually replacing quill and ink first with fountain pens and then with ballpoint pens, writers have now abandoned their typewriters as composing has become a matter of word processing. For some writers, computers simply offer a better way to do the same old work. For others, however, the new technologies have changed the way they imagine writing.

Researchers, for example, no longer go to the card catalog in the library but now search a library's holdings online and browse the Web. For many people, the rapid transmission of an e-mail or fax message seems vastly preferable to the slower "snail-mail." Both corporate executives and environmentalists talk enthusiastically about the benefits of the "paperless" office. Desktop publishing enables writers to do the kind of work that was once the business of graphic designers in print shops. The Internet and Web provide interactive public forums that make possible a kind of participation and feedback that is difficult to achieve with printed texts. And hypertext and multimedia present new ways of designing documents that organize data, create links to other sources, and incorporate sound, graphics, and video.

For these reasons, it is fair to assume that writing will increasingly involve familiarity with word processing and the new forms of electronic communication. Of course, individuals have different reactions to the new writing technologies.

Some are intimidated, while others are enthusiastic users. You may have considerable knowledge and experience, or you may have little or none.

Whatever the case may be, a point to keep in mind is that the new writing technologies are tools for you to use, just as skilled craftspeople use the tools of their trade. The more you know about them, the more effectively you'll be able to use them. And the more you learn about these new technologies, the more you'll understand their impact on contemporary life.

The writing classroom can be an ideal setting in which to investigate the world of cyberspace. Throughout this book are opportunities to go online and explore the Internet and the Web. But even if the new technologies are not a focus of your course, you might want to learn more by going to your campus computer center and by talking to staff and students who have knowledge and experience.

In this chapter, we look at some of the ways writers use the new digital literacies, how they communicate online, and the virtual communities in which they participate.

EXPLORING YOUR EXPERIENCE

Spend fifteen minutes or so responding to these questions in writing:

1. Do you normally use a word processor? Do you know how to scan images or use graphics programs? Do you know document design programs?

2. What experience, if any, have you had using e-mail or instant messages? Do you know how to send attachments? Do you participate in chat rooms, listservs, newsgroups, or other electronic forums? Do you use the Web or take part in MUDs or MOOs? If you have used these technologies, what purposes do they serve for you?

3. How would you describe your attitude toward the new writing technologies and the new forms of electronic communication?

4. What would you like to learn about the new writing technologies? If you are just beginning, what skills would you like to acquire? If you already have some experience, how would you like to enhance your skills? What are some realistic goals you might set for yourself? If you do have some knowledge of these writing tools, would you be willing to share it with other students? What do you know that you could teach others?

WORKING TOGETHER

Once you have completed the individual responses, meet with a group of three or four other students. Take turns explaining what you have written. If you know a lot about computers, the Internet, and the Web, tell what you know and what purposes the new writing tools have served for you. If you are inexperienced, don't feel defensive or intimidated by the other students' knowledge. The point of this discussion is to find out what knowledge and experience are available within your class, what goals individual students have for themselves, and how students might draw on one another's expertise to meet their goals.

After you have discussed your responses, decide on one person to report to the whole class. The report should give a brief summary of what people already know, what their goals are, and who might be willing to help other students. Without attributing attitudes to specific students, characterize the range of attitudes that were expressed in the group.

WORD PROCESSING

There can be little question that word processing has some very real benefits for writers. Time permitting, writers can now revise extensively without having to retype an entire document. They can add, delete, and move material with ease. In addition, most word-processing programs make available spell-checkers, which compare each word in a text to an online dictionary; various kinds of style-checkers, which can locate passive constructions, wordy phrases, and clichés and can indicate the number of words in a text, average sentence length, and readability level; and an online thesaurus, which lists alternative word choices.

Steven Johnson. "How the Computer Changed My Writing"

In the following passage from Steven Johnson's book *Interface Culture: How New Technology Transforms the Way We Create and Communicate,* Johnson looks at how the computer changed his writing. As you will see, the change he describes involves not only the added convenience and resources that computers make available but also the way word processing altered what he wrote— and how he thought.

> ### How the Computer Changed My Writing
> #### STEVEN JOHNSON

1   The truly interesting thing here is that using a word processor changes how we write—not just because we're relying on new tools to get the job done, but also because the computer fundamentally transforms the way we conjure up our sentences, the thought process that runs alongside the writing process. You can see this transformation at work on a number of levels. The most basic is one of sheer volume: the speed of digital composition—not to mention the undo commands and the spell checker—makes it a great deal easier to churn out ten pages where we might once have scratched out five using pen and paper (or a Smith-Corona). The perishability of certain digital formats—e-mail being the most obvious example—

has also created a more casual, almost conversational writing style, a fusion of written letter and telephone speak.

2   But for me, the most intriguing side effect of the word processor lies in the changed relationship between a sentence in its conceptual form and its physical translation onto the page or the screen. In the years when I still wrote using pen and paper or a typewriter, I almost invariably worked out each sentence in my head before I began transcribing it on the page. There was a clear before and after to the process: I would work out the subject and verb, modifiers, subsidiary clauses in advance; I would tinker with the arrangement for a minute or two; and when the mix seemed right, I'd turn back to the yellow legal pad. The method made sense, given the tools I was using—changing the sequence of words after you'd scrawled them out quickly made a mess of your document. (You could swap phrases in and out with arrows and cross-outs, of course, but it made reading over the text extremely unpleasant.) All this changed after the siren song of the Mac's interface lured me into writing directly at the computer. I began with my familiar start-and-stop routine, dutifully thinking up the sentence before typing it out, but it soon became clear that the word processor eliminated the penalty that revisions normally exacted. If the phrasing wasn't quite right, you could rearrange words with a few quick mouse gestures, and the magical "delete" key was always a split second away. After a few months, I noticed a qualitative shift in the way I worked with sentences: the thinking and the typing processes began to overlap. A phrase would come into my head—a sentence fragment, an opening clause, a parenthetical remark—and before I had time to mull it over, the words would be up on the screen. Only then would I start fishing around for a verb, or a prepositional phrase to close out the sentence. Most sentences would unfold through a kind of staggered trial and error—darting back and forth between several different iterations until I arrived at something that seemed to work.

3   It was a subtle change, but a profound one nonetheless. The fundamental units of my writing had mutated under the spell of the word processor: I had begun by working with blocks of complete sentences, but by the end I was thinking in smaller blocks, in units of discrete phrases. This, of course, had an enormous effect on the types of sentences I ended up writing. The older procedure imposed a kind of upward ceiling on the sentence's complexity: you had to be able to hold the entire sequence of words in your head, which meant that the mind naturally gravitated to simpler, more direct syntax. Too many subsidiary clauses and you lost track. But the word processor allowed me to zoom in on smaller clusters of words and build out from there—I could always add another aside, some more descriptive frippery, because the overall shape of the sentence was never in question. If I lost track of the subject-verb agreement, I could always go back and adjust it. And so my sentences swelled out enormously, like a small village besieged by new immigrants. They were ringed by countless peripheral thoughts and show-off allusions, paved by endless qualifications and false starts. It didn't help matters that I happened to be under the sway of French semiotic theory at the time, but I know those sentences would have been almost impossible to execute had I been scribbling

them out on my old legal pads. The computer had not only made it easier for me to write; it had also changed the very substance of what I was writing, and in that sense, I suspect, it had an enormous effect on my thinking as well.

EXERCISE

Comparing Writing Technologies

Use Johnson's reflections on how word processing changed his writing to perform an experiment. Write a paragraph on your favorite rock musician, movie star, TV show, sports team, politician, fast-food chain, style of clothing, or whatever (the topic isn't that important in this experiment) by hand, using pen or pencil and paper. Then write another paragraph, changing the topic, using a word processor. Consider the differences, in terms of both the physical act of writing and the effect of the technologies, on your writing and thinking. What conclusions can you draw? Do they support Johnson's findings?

Suggestions for Word Processing

1. **Label and organize your computer files and folders.** Develop your own system of labeling and organizing your files. Make sure the names you give to individual files will call to mind what you have in them. Organize individual files in folders. You might, for example, set up separate folders for each of your courses or use one folder for all the files you've produced for a research project.

2. **Save your work frequently.** A power failure, technical glitch, or wrong command can cause your writing to disappear, so don't wait until the end of a work session to save. Saving every fifteen minutes or so is a sensible practice. Some word-processing programs have a function you can set to come on the screen at regular intervals and ask whether you want to save; others will save your work automatically at preset intervals.

3. **Back up your work.** Computers basically have three options for saving files: You can store them on the hard drive, on a disk, or over a network to a file server. The best practice is to store files in two different places. This gives you an added measure of protection should something malfunction on your computer, your disk get damaged, or the network or file server go down.

4. **Make a hard copy of work you want to protect.** As a final protective measure, make hard copies of your work. If you are concerned about wasting paper, there are some ways to minimize the amount of paper you use when you make hard copies. You might, for example, print backup copies single-spaced instead of double, print on both sides, or obtain paper that has already been used, and print on the other side.

5. **Develop your own work habits.** Writers differ in the way they incorporate word processing into their writing process. Some writers do all their work on the screen—planning, drafting, revising, and editing. Others find that the size of the computer screen doesn't allow them to view enough text, so they like to work on hard copy, where they can more easily shuffle pages back and forth.

6. **Develop revision strategies.** To make sure they don't lose working drafts, many writers create a sequence of drafts on the computer. When you begin a revision session, simply create a new file to work in. You can do this in a number of ways, depending on your word-processing program. If you have a "Save As" function, use it to create a new file. Or you can mark your original file and use the "Copy" function to transfer it into a new file. Either method allows you to keep the original in one file and have a new one to work on.

7. **Learn and use your tools.** Use the spell-checker (but remember that it can't decide whether the word you want is *their* or *there, its* or *it's,* or *affect or effect*). If your program has a style-checker, see what information it can provide you about sentence length, readability level, and so on. Use your online thesaurus as you would a print version to consider word choices.

INTERACTIVITY: COMMUNICATING ONLINE

Perhaps the most revolutionary feature of online communication is its interactivity. Unlike earlier forms of communication—whether printed material such as books and magazines, the radio, or television—computer-mediated communication enables immediate feedback. While the older means of communication are organized hierarchically, with top-down distribution from centralized sources such as publishing houses or radio and television broadcasting stations, the Internet uses a distributed, or shared, delivery system that has no central point. Messages can originate from anywhere someone has access to a connection. Anyone can start or participate in discussions that intersect other discussions and branch out in many directions, as users shape and reshape a spreading web of meanings.

As you can see from the following exchange, the Internet seems to incite people to write in the new public forums created in cyberspace. Notice how the following discussion "thread" develops, in this case prompted by the first writer's comments that the shootings at Columbine High School in Littleton, Colorado, on April 1999 were "an awesome plan." This thread comes from the message board linked to the Columbine Shrine Web site, maintained by TSW: The Semicool World, a commercial entertainment Web site.

TSW Message Boards, The Columbine Shrine Thread

Comment
ExuBiu, Unregistered User (1/4/00 12:23:29 am)

1   I think it was an AWESOME PLAN!

2   I think what they did needed to be done. I think the way the media handled it was over-rated. I think the way the media turns every negative things into something like a circus needs to stop. I think people need to stop feeling sorry for themselves and what happens. I think people need to @#%$ live their lives and forget about everyone else's business. I also think that, if the media didn't concentrate so heavily on the negatives things, that there would be a lot more positive influence in the world, and then…no matter what music the kids listened to…or what games they played, they would have a positive outlook. It's the media's fault this @#%$ happens, and I think it's pathetic how weak we all are to feel sorry for the ones weak enough to break under the strain of @#%$ up societal views.

From: Will, webmaster
Re: I think it was an AWESOME PLAN!

3   Maybe the media over-did-it a little, but in no way are we to FORGET these people. We are remembering. And maybe you should learn to have a little sympathy and compassion. That's what this world needs…everyone talks of hate breeding hate…well that's what you're doing now. Show some caring….I hope this doesn't have to happen again or at your school or to your best friend for you to realize just what you are saying is compassionless. I just pray to God that nothing like this EVER happens again. Step back and read what you wrote again from a 180 degree turn.

bearden13, Unregistered User (1/5/00 10:10:58 am)
They were not right!!!

4   What these two boys did was not an awesome plan! No matter what is done to you, you don't have a right to kill innocent people. How could you even think that? Just because you're not part of the in-crowd doesn't mean you should go around killing people. Be yourself and don't worry about what people think about you. It's what you think that matters most.

From: angel, Unregistered User (1/6/00 10:29:51 pm)
Grow Up

5   I think what you are thinking is underrated, so many of you sickos just like eric and dylan are in this world and since you guys are getting so tough and taking a stand, I think WE should get tough and take a stand. No more just sitting on the couch thinking how sad. I can do something about this and I will. I don't know what your problem is but you think you can just go around shooting whoever you don't like because you're too immature to handle it. Grow up.

From: Mac1080, Unregistered User (1/13/00 4:25:59 pm)
They were merely pawns
6   Eric and Dylan were merely pawns in the sick lifestyle that the world calls high school. Can anyone remember what it felt like to be teased at school? Well try to live with that everyday before you condone what the boys did. They merely lashed out in the only way that they felt would be recognized. To me they were like modern day Robin Hoods who stole from the world future bigots and idiots and returned to us something to really consider. So before you judge and condone them, look at yourself and see if you know what they felt like. If you can honestly say that you can't then you would have been one of the tormentors. If you wish to give an intelligent reply to this then do so but I will not respond to the "holier-than-though" people who I know will write me.

Exercise

Analyzing a Thread

You probably noticed right away that the discussion of the Columbine shootings contains some "shocking" views that would never appear in mainstream public forums such as the press or TV. Chat rooms, message boards, and newsgroups sometimes include such "forbidden" discourses. To see how computer-mediated communication works in this instance, first examine the online discussion.

1. What do you notice about how each person presents his or her views?
2. How do the writers interact? How would you describe the style of writing that appears?
3. Compare the online discussion to more conventional writing you find in newspapers and magazines. What do you see as the main differences and similarities in the way writers make arguments and exchange views?

Going Online: Finding Newsgroups and Listservs

Newsgroups and listservs are two forums for interaction on the Internet.

Newsgroups

Newsgroups are Internet sites where news, articles, personal postings, and other types of information and argument are made available to users. Thousands of newsgroups exist, devoted to virtually any topic you can think of—such as politics, the environment, health, sports, and popular culture. Some groups are moderated—that is, a moderator decides what postings will appear—but most are unmoderated and open to anyone. Newsgroups range from "serious" discussions by informed participants to "chat" and the exchange of personal opinions.

You can find newsgroups by going to <www.liszt.com/news/> or <tile.net/news> on the Web. Your college probably subscribes to Usenet, an extensive network of public newsgroups. Newsgroups are organized into categories you can identify by prefixes. Here are some of the most common:

Prefix	Category	Example
alt:	alternative topics	alt.fan.u2
clari:	newsfeeds from wire services	clari.news.immigration
comp:	computer topics	comp.binarie.ms-windows
misc:	miscellaneous topics	misc.immigration.canada
rec:	recreational topics	rec.sport.biking
soc:	social topics	soc.culture.Irish
talk:	discussion	talk.politics.gun

A Note on the Reliability of Newsgroup Information

Keep in mind that you need to read what appears on newsgroups with special care. Newspapers, national magazines, scholarly journals, and books from commercial and university presses use a number of filtering procedures—professional training, peer review, editing, fact checking—that enhance the legitimacy and reliability of these print sources. Information and opinion on newsgroups, on the other hand, can come from anywhere. Newsgroups are wide open, and the tone of discussion can get quite heated. Part of the excitement of the Internet is that it is not regulated, but that means you need to evaluate carefully what you read. It can be particularly helpful to compare newsgroup comments with conventional sources and to consider users' personal investments in the issues, especially when their remarks are heated, passionate, questionable, or extreme.

Listservs

Listservs usually consist of people who are interested in a particular topic and want to share information and participate in ongoing discussions with others. Individuals generally subscribe to listservs because they are serious about the topic and have chosen for personal or professional reasons to keep up on current issues.

You can find thousands of listservs on a wide range of topics by going to <www.liszt.com/> or <tile.net/lists> on the Web. You can also find a list of academic discussion groups, the Directory of Scholarly Electronic Conferences, at <www.mid.net/KOVACS/>.

Although the style of writing on listservs can vary dramatically, the tone of listserv discussion is typically thoughtful and reasonable, even when users disagree. Listserv members generally expect informed, up-to-date contributions to the ongoing discussion, requests for information, and well-considered questions for list members to think about. Listservs for academic and professional purposes have a kind of legitimacy and reliability that is not always the case with newsgroups.

Further Links

Many colleges and universities now restrict access to Usenet newsgroups, sometimes because of space/bandwidth limitations but sometimes because of the controversial nature of some newsgroups. To read about a famous case of restricting access, go to *The English Server* at Carnegie-Mellon University <english-server.hss.cmu.edu/>.

INTERACTIVITY IN WRITING PROJECTS

You can integrate the interactive capabilities of online communication into your own writing projects in a number of ways. Here are four suggestions about how you can use online tools.

Use Collaborative Writing Software

Software programs now enable writers to communicate online and work collaboratively on a document. In the workplace, it has become common for several writers in different locations to work simultaneously on a writing project by using software that includes such features as chat windows for discussion, split screens that provide space for marginal comments, and color coding or individually identified cursors that show what changes a particular writer has made on the document. If your college has such software available, you can use it to get peer reviews of your work in progress or to work together on group writing projects.

Use E-Mail

E-mail is particularly useful in planning group projects. When it's hard to find convenient meeting times, e-mail enables group members to communicate online.

Notice how the following exchange incorporates the reader's response into the text of the writer's original message. The first writer begins with her ideas for a group project, and the reader/second writer offers commentary and suggestions.

>I've been thinking about our group project on
>document design and maybe we should do a poster or
>brochure on AIDS.

I'd rather do a brochure because we can use my Pagemaker program and scan in illustrations if we need to. I'm not so sure about how to make a high quality poster.

>We could pitch it to high school kids and explain risky
>behaviors and prevention methods like using condoms.

OK, good idea. One thing we'll need to decide is whether the brochure is pitched to girls, boys, or both. The approach would probably differ some, depending.

>And we could make a prototype and get some feedback
>from high school kids before we do the final version.

Right! I can ask my sister to get some kids from her school together. I'm sure they'd help us with a pilot version.

Use Listservs

For discussion among a larger group, listservs are especially appropriate. Teachers often set up a class listserv so that everyone will be on the same mailing list for announcements and discussion.

Notice in the following exchange, taken from a listserv set up in an introduction to literature course, how the first writer identifies her purpose and how the second posting responds in a thoughtful yet probing manner:

> **To: listserv_intro.lit@wpi.edu**
> **From: melanie@wpi.edu**
> We've been trying to decide whether Willie Loman [in Arthur Miller's play *Death of a Salesman*] is really a tragic hero—and I'm more confused than ever. Can someone help me out? Willie doesn't exactly fit Aristotle's definition that tragedy needs a noble protagonist (Willie is a "low man"), a moment of recognition (I'm not sure this happens in the play), and a reversal (which definitely does) that evokes pity and fear in the audience. I do pity Willie, but sometimes I think he's more pathetic than tragic. At the same time, I do feel some fear anybody could end up like Willie.

> **To: listserv_intro.lit@wpi.edu**
> **From: armando@wpi.edu**
> I have the same problem with *Death of a Salesman* that Melanie talks about. My thinking right now is that Arthur Miller is trying to update Aristotle's definition of tragedy by writing what he calls a tragedy of the common man— common person :-) and raise questions about the tragic consequences of staking everything on being "well liked." In Modern Tragedy, Raymond Williams talks about tragedy of ordinary people and that seems right for Miller.

Use Online Writing Centers

Many colleges now have Online Writing Labs (OWLs) where students can communicate online with writing tutors about work in progress. If your college has an OWL, consider using it. The writing center may have a Web site where you can get information about online tutoring.

Further Links

Even if your college does not have an OWL, you can visit the Virtual Writing Center at Salt Lake Community College <www.slcc.englab.wc.edu>. This is a

MOO where you can move around in the various rooms at the site and read the conversations that are taking place. You can log onto the site as a guest and participate in the discussions. Consider how the online communication in a virtual writing center differs from the face-to-face communication in an actual writing center. What do you see as the advantages and disadvantages in each case?

ETHICS OF WRITING IN CYBERSPACE

NETIQUETTE

Cyberspace is a new world with its own culture and rules of behavior. Netiquette (*net* + *etiquette*) refers to an evolving code of practices on the Internet. Here are some of the basics.

1. Most newsgroups and listservs expect newcomers (or "newbies") to "lurk" for awhile, consult FAQs, read current postings, and learn the issues and concerns of participants.

2. When you do post a message, identify your purpose—to comment on a thread of discussion, ask a question, propose an answer or solution. In general, be brief—and make sure your posting is relevant. *Spam* is the cyber-term for worthless or irrelevant posts that waste people's time. If you are replying to e-mail by way of the reply command, make sure you delete any addresses of people for whom your reply is not intended.

3. Don't flame—or attack—another person online. Remember that you are sending messages to other humans, not to your computer monitor. Think twice before you hit the send key.

4. Assume that nothing is secure in cyberspace and that any message you write and send could end up being read by people you never intended it for. The safest rule is not to write anything you're not willing to let the whole world see.

5. The style of writing used online is often quite informal compared to printed texts. It is often acceptable—and considered good form—to use emoticons and abbreviations, but remember what your purpose is and who your reader will be. For example, if you are asking your instructor to clarify a writing assignment or interviewing an expert on a research project, be businesslike and use standard English.

Common e-mail emoticons and abbreviations:

:-)	smile	IMHO	in my humble opinion
:-(	frown	VBG	very big grin
;-)	wink	LOL	laughing out loud
;-P	tongue sticking out	TTL	talk to you later
8 -)	googly eyes	BRB	be right back

6. Consider personalizing your e-mail messages with a signature line.

Personalized signature line:

Dolores Fuentes Phone: (602) 555-0000
Box 143
Arizona State University
Tempe, AZ 85287
"When other races have given up their tongue we've kept ours."
—Gloria Anzaldua

Further Links

To learn more about netiquette, check out *The Net: User Guidelines and Netiquette* <www.fau.edu/~rinaldi/net/index/htm> or *I'm Not Miss Manners of the Internet* <www.fau.edu/rinaldi/netiquette.html>.

TROUBLE IN CYBERSPACE

One of the attractions of the Internet is the lack of regulation. As mentioned earlier, anyone with a connection can post messages or create a Web site. From one angle, this openness has enabled new public forums where people can share opinions, information, and ideas. At the same time, there is growing concern about the pornography, hate groups, and offensive messages you can find online—and a growing call on the part of some for filtering devices which would allow parents, libraries, and universities to block certain Web sites and for closer monitoring of what appears on message boards and electronic discussion groups.

The following article "By the Water Cooler in Cyberspace, the Talk Turns Ugly" by *New York Times* reporter Reed Abelson provides a look at the disturbing messages that are turning up on message boards for company employees.

By the Water Cooler in Cyberspace, the Talk Turns Ugly
REED ABELSON

1   The talk was about a woman, a former senior manager in the Minneapolis office of PricewaterhouseCoopers who had won a $1.625 million sex discrimination case.

2   "A man who complains about things being unfair gets nothing," someone said. "A woman or minority who complains about things being unfair gets what—a well-deserved $1 million and free ride to partner?" He named one female partner as "a prime candidate."

3   "You guys are a bunch of idiots," came one angry reply.

4   "Anyone have any example of the stellar work she has done that earned her the position?" another asked sarcastically, referring to the female partner. "She wouldn't know how to fill out a corporate or partnership tax return if her life depended on it."

5   This conversation was not conducted sotto voce around the water cooler or over a lunch far from the office. It happened recently in a far more public place: an Internet message board, a kind of e-mail bulletin board.

6   Thousands of message boards for individual companies have emerged over the last few years, creating a window on what some employees feel but never say publicly. Often the view through this window is rather ugly.

7   On message boards for particular companies on third-party Web sites like Yahoo and Vault, some employees are anonymously expressing thoughts they

would not dare say out loud. They are freely showing their prejudices or denouncing other employees by name, sometimes accusing them of incompetence or misconduct or recounting salacious rumors about their sex lives.

8   "This is a problem that has exploded recently, in the last six months," said Parry Aftab, a lawyer at Darby & Darby in New York who specializes in Internet-related issues.

9   All this makes for enormous challenges in the new electronic communities. It can be useful for managers to find out what their employees really think of them, but also devastating when hurtful and hateful gossip is laid out for all to see.

10   While message boards are popular for companies, they are also common for schools, professional groups and other interest groups. All raise troubling questions about how to permit free and often useful exchanges that tend to be intertwined with vicious gossip and hateful comments. And for companies, some of which are not even aware that the discussions are taking place, these electronic dialogues represent a whole new challenge and area of potential liability.

11   Yahoo relies on the users of its boards to complain about messages. Others monitor what is said and will delete offensive material.

12   In the case of the PricewaterhouseCoopers partner, Vault, which bills itself as an electronic water cooler, has deleted some of the messages about the partner, according to users of the board. Vault says it does monitor its boards but may not catch every offensive message.

13   Asked about the rest of the offending messages, PricewaterhouseCoopers said it would contact the Web site about removing them.

14   Sometimes employees or managers at a company are attacked in vicious detail. In recent months, for example, a Yahoo message board on Startec Global Communications in Potomac, Md., has been the site of a pointed discussion by people who claim to be employees or former employees. The company, which went public in 1997, has struggled over the last year as its stock has plummeted from $15 to under 50 cents.

15   The message board has had numerous references to the ethnicity of some of the managers. "The Indians I encountered at STGC were racist, jingoistic and narrow-minded," reads one message, referring to the company by its stock symbol.

16   Other messages on the Startec board seem like personal attacks. Offering a list of people who should resign, one individual describes an employee as the girlfriend of an executive, whose first name is given. "How does it feel knowing that the only reason why you are still around is because you are sleeping" with the executive, the individual wrote in one posting.

17   Another message describes another executive, by name, as "a bankrupt alcoholic with no business sense."

18   In a written response, Startec said its "management does not focus on posts." The company, which described many of the messages as "less than professional," said it discouraged its staff from participating in the discussions.

19   Disgruntled employees and former employees are increasingly using the Internet to harass colleagues, executives or the company itself, according to Ms. Aftab,

who is also the executive director of CyberAngels.org, a not-for-profit group that helps individuals attacked this way.

20   In one recent example, she said, a company executive was being harassed through e-mail messages sent to his family, employees and investors that said he molested his children. In another, an employee set up a Web site claiming to be another employee and offering to have sex.

21   In some cases the messages appear to come from white men who think they are being discriminated against by companies favoring women or minorities. On one site devoted to United Parcel Service, called the Brown Cafe, employees have complained about what they say is unfair treatment. United Parcel's "policy to promote from within seems to have become promote only those of minority status," reads one message.

22   United Parcel declined to comment.

23   Diversity training can also be fodder for outbursts. When Lucent Technologies tried to make its employees more sensitive to gay colleagues, there was an outpouring. "Always the Bulletin Board at HQ in Murray Hill, N.J., secretly 'promotes' this deviant activity," one message said.

24   Lucent, which says it seeks to balance the right of its employees to express themselves with its other responsibilities, says it prohibits the sending of threatening or harassing messages.

25   Employees and former employees are also using the Internet to make claims of sexual harassment. On a message board for American Express, for example, someone complained last August about a manager at American Express Incentive Services who "keeps hitting on me and/or saying totally inappropriate things about women's breast size, etc." The person says that she "went to our H.R. person," whom she identifies by first name, but that the woman dismissed her concerns.

26   "We take all allegations very, very seriously," said a spokeswoman for American Express Incentive Services, who declined to comment on the specific claims.

27   Some messages encourage people to come forward with similar tales. In a posting about Home Depot, for example, one individual who identifies himself by name claims to be a district manager who is "having sex with the employees."

28   "I love this, and they can't do a thing about it."

29   In the ensuing debate over whether he was lying, one person identified two other managers as examples of this behavior. "It's a free-for-all orgy behind the scenes in some of these stores," the person said. Home Depot said it investigated any claims brought to its attention.

30   In addition to several lawsuits in which offensive e-mail was used as an example of a work environment hostile to blacks or women, there has already been one lawsuit that claimed electronic dialogue alone constitute harassment. A Continental Airlines pilot, Tammy Blakey, sued Continental because of messages sent by other pilots in what was known as the Crew Members Forum, a computer bulletin board. She claimed to have forwarded the offending messages to the company.

31   The messages, written in 1995, railed against the pilot's earlier harassment lawsuit and criticized what some described as the "feminazis among us."

BACKGROUND CHATTER, INTERNET-STYLE

Thousands of Internet message boards for individual companies have emerged on Web sites like Yahoo and Vault, and some people use them to anonymously express thoughts they would not dare say out loud. Here are some examples, with names, some identifying descriptions and some vulgar language deleted.

From a message board on PricewaterhouseCoopers:

> Again someone please tell me or give me an example of any partner in the 100+ year history of both Legacy firms of any male that has worked for them on a part-time or "flex-time" basis and made partner? It just so happens that a woman by the name of ▮▮▮▮▮▮▮▮
>
> ▮▮▮▮▮▮▮▮▮▮▮▮▮▮▮▮
>
> ▮▮▮▮▮▮▮▮▮▮ Anyone have any example of the stellar work she has done that earned her the position? Furthermore, was it even a good choice by the firm? They gave her the clients...she has never (to this day) brought ANY new business into PwC. ▮▮▮▮▮▮▮▮
>
> ▮▮▮▮▮▮▮▮▮▮▮▮▮▮▮▮
>
> What also adds to the confusion is that she wouldn't know how to fill out a corporate or partnership tax return if her life depended on it. Hey▮▮...ever use FastTax, Prosystems, Ultra Tax, etc...or any kind of tax software?

From a message board on Lucent Technologies, referring to an executive:

> Ignor this User | Report Abuse
>
> **Re: QUEER DAY at Lucent..**▮▮▮▮▮▮▮ 04/08/01 07:11 pm EDT
> by:▮▮▮▮▮▮ Msg. 222261 of 228860
>
> I HEARD THAT HE WAS A BIT TIME QUEER? ALL MAJOR COMPANIES NOW PROMOTE GAY ▮▮ BUT NOT AS LARGE AS LUCENT, HMMMM?

From a message board on EGL Inc. referring to an employee's discrimination suit:

> From what I've read of the ▮▮▮▮▮ case ▮▮▮▮▮ he played the race card after he was terminated. If that's the case, shame on him for wasting taxpayers time and money and shame on him for throwing fuel onto the Eagle fire.
>
> It's time the courts started awarding money to companies who have been wrongly accused of discrimination or harassment. As it stands, the employee has nothing to lose and the company has everything to lose. Maybe a few more companies need to defend these suits instead of settling up to make them go away.

32   She "doesn't really belong here anyway, at least to my mind," wrote one, "and I personally don't care what she has to say about anything. I believe her lawsuit is bogus, the charges patently false, and that she is out to get a quick buck."

33   While the case was resolved confidentially last year, the New Jersey Supreme Court had already ruled that Continental could be liable for the messages sent by these pilots.

34   In a written statement, Continental said, "While Tammy Blakey's individual matter has been amicably resolved, Continental continues to feel strongly that our society should not attempt to hold employers responsible for individual statements made in Internet chat rooms over which employers have no control."

35   While individuals may think they can remain anonymous when they write these messages, companies can typically use technology to identify the writers, according to Internet experts and lawyers.

36   Some companies have taken action. Richard M. Scrushy, chief executive of the HealthSouth Corporation, brought a lawsuit against someone who posted messages claiming an affair with Mr. Scrushy's wife.

37   Mr. Scrushy hired a lawyer who worked with an investigator to uncover the identity of the writer, who turned out to be a former employee who did not know either individual. The lawsuit was settled, and the Scrushys dropped their criminal charges after the former employee apologized for the postings and agreed to perform community service and make donations to charity.

FOR CRITICAL INQUIRY

1. Reed Abelson says that message boards where employees can post anonymous messages "raise troubling questions about how to permit free and often useful exchanges that tend to be intertwined with vicious gossip and hateful comments." Abelson does not explain exactly what these "troubling questions" are, but rather seems to assume readers will know. What do you see as the "troubling questions" raised by the kinds of messages that accompany the article?

2. To what extent do you think the anonymity of the messages accounts for their particular character? Should companies require employees to sign their messages? What would be gained? What lost?

3. When hateful and offensive messages start to appear, what should companies do? What policy for online communication would you recommend?

Going Online: Napster and Intellectual Property

One of the most interesting developments in how people use the Web is the emergence of Napster, a file-sharing Web site that enables members to find and download music on their own personal computers' hard drive and then record the music on CDs or transfer it to portable MP3 players.

Hate Groups

can enter your

HOME

without even

Knocking.

The same Internet that has revolutionized how we communicate has also given hate groups just what they need. They can now easily coordinate with other extremists who share their views. They can recruit. They can harass victims through e-mail. And they can all too easily spread the poison of prejudice to our children.

Yet in spite of these frightening developments, the rest of us can use the Internet to fight back. The Anti-Defamation League has developed effective strategies for dealing with Internet extremism, including HateFilter,® a computer program which blocks hate sites.

For more information on how ADL fights anti-Semitism, bigotry and hatred wherever it occurs, visit www.adl.org or call 1-866-STOP-HATE.

Anti-Defamation League
823 United Nations Plaza, New York, NY 10017
Glen A. Tobias, National Chairman
Abraham H. Foxman, National Director

Visit the Anti-Defamation League's Web site <www.adl.org> to see how the organization defines hate groups. Do you think there are circumstances when the use of filtering devices are justified? If so, what are they? If not, why not?

According to some record companies, music agents, and musicians, Napster amounts to illegal pirating that violates copyright and an artist's fair share of royalties. The heavy metal group Metallica and the rapster Dr. Dre sued Napster, and a number of colleges prohibit access to Napster through their computer services. On the other hand, Napster claims it is not selling the music but simply making it possible for individuals to share (much as many people make audiocassettes for each other), and some musicians such as Chuck D of Public Enemy and the veteran rocker Neil Young have defended Napster as a means to evade the corporate stranglehold on what music gets circulated and thereby keep the music scene fresh and alive to new trends.

Recent court decisions have ruled that Napster has indeed violated copyright protection and the rights of intellectual property. Nonetheless, the issue of intellectual property on the Internet is not likely to go away soon. To form your own views of whether Napster (and the newer, more difficult to trace file-sharing systems such as Gnutella and Freenet) represents a danger to recognized principles of intellectual property, an important precedent in ensuring freedom of communication, or something else, visit the Napster Web site <www.napster.com> and the Napster message board <forum.napster.com>. You can find the debate between Chuck D and Metallica's Lars Ulrich that was televised on PBS's *Charlie Rose Show* on May 12, 2000, on the Rapstation Web site <www.rapstation.com/promot/lars_vs_chuckd/htm/>. Rapstation includes audio and video excerpts of the debate. Evaluate the arguments on each side. Do you find Chuck D or Lars Ulrich more persuasive? Why?

Further Links

For some, one of the key notions that distinguishes online communication from earlier print literacy is the idea that information wants to be free. The open source movement has argued for the sharing of information and software. To get a sense of the issues involved in the idea of open sources—and how it differs from older notions of intellectual property—visit the Open Source Initiative <www.opensource.org>. In particular visit the History page to see how the idea of open sources has emerged.

LIFE IN VIRTUAL COMMUNITIES

Cyberspace, says cyberpunk author William Gibson who coined the term, is a "consensual hallucination," the virtual reality created where the circuits of our brains meet and are mediated by the electronic circuitry of computer networks, video games, artificial intelligence, and simulation technologies. This matrix— "the point," as Gibson puts it, "at which the media flow together and surround us"—may be "the ultimate exclusion of daily life," but it is certainly a place where people are spending a lot of time these days.

People shape their online selves in various ways. In role-playing environments such as MUDs and MOOs, participants can invent their own personae by becoming older or younger and switching genders or races if they wish. In chat rooms and discussion groups, individuals often use screen names that provide anonymity and a certain freedom to experiment. But even in those cases where people use their own names and speak in what they assume to be their own voices, the question comes up about the relationship between their online and offline selves. Are these identities identical? Or, as some cybertheorists have suggested, are we all really a multiplicity of selves, constantly shifting in our relationships with others, moving back and forth between the virtual and the real? For some, such as Howard Rheingold, cyberspace offers the possibility of constructing virtual communities where people "live in each other's brains as voices, images, words on screens. We are multiple personalities and we include each other."

We present two reading selections here that explore what is taking place in cyberspace. In her *New York Times Magazine* article, "In a Chat Room, You Can Be NE1: Constructing a Teenage Self On Line," the journalist Camille Sweeney investigates identity formation in cyberspace. The second reading selection is taken from the introduction to Rheingold's book *The Virtual Community: Homesteading on the Electronic Frontier.*

In a Chat Room, You Can Be NE1: Constructing a Teenage Self On Line
CAMILLE SWEENEY

1   "Yo yo yo, what's up what's up?" The lines scroll up my screen. Different fonts, different colors, the words whiz by, everyone's screen name sounding vaguely pornographic. I'm on America Online, in a chat room for young adults. There are hundreds of such chat rooms on AOL, and it has taken a lot of Net navigating simply to find one that has room enough to let me in.

2   For all the crowds and clamoring, there's not much being said in this chat room, or rather, not much that's being paid attention to. A 16-year-old girl is talking about her baby due in two months. A grumpy 15-year-old guy reluctantly wishes her well. Another girl, 17, asks, "Are your parents cool with it?" The lines continue to scroll, a word here, a phrase there, live text that reads much like a flow of conversation you might overhear in a crowded high-school hallway or parking lot between classes in old-fashioned meat space (that is, anyplace not in the cyberworld).

3   I've been on line, off and on, for months trying to determine if there is such a thing as a cyberself and, if so, what goes into the making of this most modern of personality constructs. Teen-agers especially are fitting specimens for this experiment because they are the first generation saturated in this new medium. In any given week, according to Teenage Research Unlimited, nearly 70 percent of all 12- to 19-year-olds go on line. The Internet has shaped them—just as television

shaped their parents, and radio their grandparents. Once a generation saw itself grow up on TV; now a generation is watching itself grow up on line. It would follow then that the 31 million teen-agers of Gen Y or Generation Why or Echo Boomers or Millennials, as this group is variously called, would have completely new ways of perceiving one another and themselves. I went undercover as a cyber-teen to find out.

4   Teen-age years—at least in my memory—are reserved largely for trying out different personas. As the psychoanalyst Erik Erikson contended, adolescence is a period "during which the individual through free role experimentation may find a niche in some section of his society, a niche which is firmly defined and yet seems to be uniquely made for him."

5   Herein lies the thrill of the on-line self: its malleability, its plasticity, the fact that it can be made up entirely of your own imagination. You can take your old self, or don a fresh one, and hang out in a group of jocks for a postgame chat, argue the banality of Britney Spears with an international posse of pop connoisseurs, post a note to a cool-sounding guy from Detroit—all without ever having to leave your bedroom. Maybe this is the Internet's greatest asset to teendom: access, and the confidence to slip in and out of personalities, the ability to try on identities, the adolescent equivalent of playing dress-up in the attic, standing before the mirror in heels and lipstick long before you own your own.

August 1999

6   The measure of a successful site, an Internet entrepreneur tells me, is its "stickiness." This is the number of hits a site receives, people checking it out, multiplied by the amount of time they spend on it. Bolt.com is a sticky, a cyber-friend says, definitely a place where a lot of teenagers go to hang and mostly talk about stuff teenagers talk about—romance being No. 1. I log on to the friendly blue-and-orange home page, with features and bulletins, a quote of the day and a daily poll: "Would you date someone of different ethnicity?" "Would you date someone your parents don't approve of?" "Where would you say you get your style from?" Unlike so many dismally designed sites for teenagers, Bolt seems like a breezy, busy, cool community. I choose "camarules" as my screen name, ditching my letter-digit combo. Dan Pelson, cofounder of the site, is right—if being on AOL is like driving your father's Oldsmobile on the Interstate, being on Bolt.com is like riding a Day-Glo mountain bike with a beefy shock absorber and no particular place to go.

7   Though there are plenty of other places for teenagers to hang out on line, I spend most of my time on Bolt's bulletin boards. There are many to choose from, with topics ranging from Activism and Jobs and Money to Style and Sex and Dating. This is where you can post a message that either attracts a response or goes completely unheeded. The success of a message depends on a lot of factors: the catchiness of the subject line, the popularity of the board and, most important, the general level of boredom of those on line. If people are bored, they'll check out just about anything.

8   And judging from my time on line, people are bored. "I'm so bored," writes a 16-year-old guy who refers to himself as Baron Vampire. Unlike a lot of Bolsters, but like a lot of teenagers, Baron Vampire doesn't really follow the topic being discussed on the board; instead, he turns the conversation back to himself. And he seems to attract attention—maybe because he's a bored vampire, maybe because the icon he uses with his screen name is a tiny bat, hanging upside down, blinking. I feel a maternal tug to respond, but I hold back, letting some of the girls on the board jump in to console him—it would be like getting in the way of a tribal dance.

9   Before long a group of female Bolsters have virtually surrounded the wounded vampire. "Why are you bored V?" they ask, firing him note after note. Doubtless some are even using a private note system that only he can see. He responds with an emoticon -:*(- that evokes both childhood pathos and "Rebel Without a Cause." "Crying on the net strange," one girl writes without punctuation. After several messages of concern, the vampire seems to perk up. "So how is everyone else?" he writes. "I don't want to hear if you're bored." I skate away.

10   A girl who calls herself Cool_P2 is giving a party in an area marked Miscellaneous. It's got the feel of a younger girls' party—too much soda, no boys. I look up the personal profile Cool_P2 filled out for Bolt: it includes things like date of birth, favorite movies, music. She has written that she's 11. Unlike many adult boards on the Net where everyone claims to be a teenager (even when no one is), the registered members of Bolt, now approaching 1.5 million worldwide, are mostly actual teenagers. Even if Cool_P2 is lying about her (or his) age, I think a party's a great idea. Imagine letting your kids go to a party and not having to worry what time they come home. Cool_P2 kicks off using the asterisks code, which means that anything written between asterisks is considered action as opposed to dialogue. It's like a scene from a screenplay or a little theater piece, written, starring and directed by teenagers, each line added onto by someone else.

11   9:05:51   *puts on music and shakes her thang*
12   9:07:02   Oh, so we're going to try this party thing again? Good luck!
13   9:07:03   Oh god...*shakes her head and walks away*
14   9:07:14   *busts a move*
15   9:07:52   Yumphf humphf! You people are weiiiiiiird!

16   It gets later. I go to the Sex Questions board. A 15-year-old girl wants to know if cybering with a guy she met on line is cheating on her boyfriend. There's a frenzy of response. One guy writes, "You're so stupid!!" I consider writing something about lust in the heart, but decide to let them work it out on their own and scroll to the next posting. A real problem is being discussed. A 14-year-old girl writes: "My bf doesn't like taking off his hat when we make out. I like to rub my fingers threw [sic] his hair but I can't with his hat!!?? How do I get it off??? Help." A 15-year-old girl from Australia replies, "I bet he has some nasty, nasty hat hair." A guy of the same age writes that she should start playing the national anthem so he'll be forced to take it off. "I know that wasn't funny," he writes. "I'm bored." A younger girl writes that she should just tell him that "it's hard for u 2 make out

when he's got his hat on." A 16-year-old girl calling herself Lollypop writes, "Let him kiss your ears if he lets you fondle his hair." That seems fair.

17   A few days later, I meet Stifbizkit. His screen name's a rip-off of Limp Bizkit, a popular hip-hop rock band out of Florida. Stif says he is 16 and posts a message on the Girl Trouble board; "popping the question" is his subject. He wants to know the sweetest way to do it: should he play a song, give her a letter or play a song and give her a letter. He writes that he is open to suggestions. I write asking him exactly what question he wants to pop. He jets me a note saying he wants to ask her to go out with him. We have several back-and-forths over the next couple of days. I'm happy to give him "girl" advice, and he is happy to report that in the interim he has spent a non-cyber evening with her and another couple. The girl from the other couple has told him that the girl he's after likes him. "She thinks I'm really hot," he writes, but also reports that despite a long night spent on top of a mountain, in his parent's hot tub and on a beach, all they did was talk. I tell him that sounds like cool progress and to keep it up.

18   No sooner have we finished than the board becomes transfixed with the plight of Fourtraxman, a 14-year-old whose girlfriend, he says, broke up with him two hours ago and has already got back together with her ex. He says "she's one of those girls that's hard to get over." In the short time since the breakup, Fourtraxman has solicited a lot of advice. I watch as guys and girls from all over the world weigh in with remedies, consolation and just pure commiseration.

19   The on-line immediacy is astounding. This is not something that has to wait until first period Monday morning. Gold_Angel, an 18-year-old girl, writes that what that girl's done to him is just plain mean. "To ditch your current man for an ex is just wrong!" she writes, adding, "write me if you need to talk more!"

20   Where was this when I was their age? Where was this when Wade turned me down for the junior prom? In my teenage world, to get that rapid-fire attention would have taken several phone calls and lots of jockeying for phone time with my sisters, and maybe because of it my predicament would have gone undiscussed, at least through an entire evening. It's difficult to know just what has changed for teenagers today. Much of it is a general overexposure to the adult world, but the new teenage cyberself is demanding to be acknowledged and won't go away. The new teen-ager says: Here's what I'm thinking about. Here's what's happening to me right now. What am I going to do?

21   Maybe this isn't all that new. After all, speaking from my own increasingly distant experience, teenagers have never been free from self-absorption. What is different is that, like everything in this cyberworld, kids are moving through their teenage years at a lightning pace. The songs of teenage life remain the same, but they're being remixed, played at a faster speed and at a much higher volume.

22   Once online, you can get the definitive word on the date you left an hour ago, a review of a concert that just ended, advice on the right sling-pack to carry, a report on the latest come-on line. But you also get something else, something no other generation has ever had: the ability to leave your teenage body behind and take advantage of the almost limitless freedom to explore your personal identity.

Today's teenagers can discover themselves (or the many parts of themselves) by roaming the boards and the chat rooms, connecting, disconnecting, shooting questions out into the universe—and maybe, just maybe, receiving answers.

Introduction to *The Virtual Community*
HOWARD RHEINGOLD

1   "Daddy is saying 'Holy moly!' to his computer again!"

2   Those words have become a family code for the way my virtual community has infiltrated our real world. My seven-year-old daughter knows that her father congregates with a family of invisible friends who seem to gather in his computer. Sometimes he talks to them, even if nobody else can see them. And she knows that these invisible friends sometimes show up in the flesh, materializing from the next block or the other side of the planet.

3   Since the summer of 1985, for an average of two hours a day, seven days a week, I've been plugging my personal computer into my telephone and making contact with the WELL (Whole Earth 'Lectronic Link)—a computer conferencing system that enables people around the world to carry on public conversations and exchange private electronic mail (e-mail). The idea of a community accessible only via my computer screen sounded cold to me at first, but I learned quickly that people can feel passionately about e-mail and computer conferences. I've become one of them. I care about these people I met through my computer, and I care deeply about the future of the medium that enables us to assemble.

4   I'm not alone in this emotional attachment to an apparently bloodless technological ritual. Millions of people on every continent also participate in the computer-mediated social groups know as virtual communities, and this population is growing fast. Finding the WELL was like discovering a cozy little world that had been flourishing without me, hidden within the walls of my house; an entire cast of characters welcomed me to the troupe with great merriment as soon as I found the secret door. Like others who fell into the WELL, I soon discovered that I was audience, performer, and scriptwriter, along with my companions, in an ongoing improvisation. A full-scale subculture was growing on the other side of my telephone jack, and they invited me to help create something new.

5   The virtual village of a few hundred people I stumbled upon in 1985 grew to eight thousand by 1993. It became clear to me during the first months of that history that I was participating in the self-design of a new kind of culture. I watched the community's social contracts stretch and change as the people who discovered and started building the WELL in its first year or two were joined by so many others. Norms were established, challenged, changed, reestablished, rechallenged, in a kind of speeded-up social evolution.

6   The WELL felt like an authentic community to me from the start because it was grounded in my everyday physical world. WELLites who don't live within driving

distance of the San Francisco Bay Area are constrained in their ability to participate in the local networks of face-to-face acquaintances. By now, I've attended real-life WELL marriages, WELL births, and even a WELL funeral. (The phrase "in real life" pops up so often in virtual communities that regulars abbreviate it to IRL.) I can't count the parties and outings where the invisible personae who first acted out their parts in the debates and melodramas on my computer screen later manifested in front of me in the physical world in the form of real people, with faces, bodies, and voices.

7   I remember the first time I walked into a room full of people IRL who knew many intimate details of my history and whose own stories I knew very well. Three months after I joined, I went to my first WELL party at the home of one of the WELL's online moderators. I looked around at the room full of strangers when I walked in. It was one of the oddest sensations of my life. I had contended with these people, shot the invisible breeze around the electronic watercooler, shared alliances and formed bonds, fallen off my chair laughing with them, become livid with anger at some of them. But there wasn't a recognizable face in the house. I had never seen them before.

8   My flesh-and-blood family long ago grew accustomed to the way I sit in my home office early in the morning and late at night, chuckling and cursing, sometimes crying, about words I read on the computer screen. It might have looked to my daughter as if I were alone at my desk the night she caught me chortling online, but from my point of view, I was in living contact with old and new friends, strangers and colleagues.

9   I was in the Parenting conference on the WELL, participating in an informational and emotional support group for a friend who had just learned that his son had been diagnosed with leukemia.

10   I was in MicroMUSE, a role-playing fantasy game of the twenty-fourth century (and science education medium in disguise), interacting with students and professors who know me only as "Pollenator."

11   I was in TWICS, a bicultural community in Tokyo; CIX, a community in London; CalvaCom, a community in Paris; and Usenet, a collection of hundreds of different discussions that travel around the world via electronic mail to millions of participants in dozens of countries.

12   I was browsing through Supreme Court decisions, in search of information that could help me debunk an opponent's claims in a political debate elsewhere on the Net, or I was retrieving this morning's satellite images of weather over the Pacific.

13   I was following an eyewitness report from Moscow during the coup attempt, or China during the Tiananmen Square incident, or Israel and Kuwait during the Gulf War, passed directly from citizen to citizen through an ad hoc network patched together from cheap computers and ordinary telephone lines, cutting across normal geographic and political boundaries by piggybacking on the global communications infrastructure.

14   I was monitoring a rambling real-time dialogue among people whose bodies were scattered across three continents, a global bull session that seems to blend wit and sophomore locker-room talk via Internet relay chat (IRC), a medium that

combines the features of conversation and writing. IRC has accumulated an obsession subculture of its own among undergraduates by the thousands from Adelaide to Arabia.

15   People in virtual communities use words on screens to exchange pleasantries and argue, engage in intellectual discourse, conduct commerce, exchange knowledge, share emotional support, make plans, brainstorm, gossip, feud, fall in love, find friends and lose them, play games, flirt, create a little high art and a lot of idle talk. People in virtual communities do just about everything people do in real life, but we leave our bodies behind. You can't kiss anybody and nobody can punch you in the nose, but a lot can happen within those boundaries. To the millions who have been drawn into it, the richness and vitality of computer-linked cultures is attractive, even addictive.

16   There is no such thing as a single, monolithic, online subculture; it's more like an ecosystem of subcultures, some frivolous, others serious. The cutting edge of scientific discourse is migrating to virtual communities, where you can read the electronic pre-printed reports of molecular biologists and cognitive scientists. At the same time, activists and educational reformers are using the same medium as a political tool. You can use virtual communities to find a date, sell a lawnmower, publish a novel, conduct a meeting.

17   Some people use virtual communities as a form of psychotherapy. Others, such as the most addicted players of Minitel in France or multiuser dungeons (MUDs) on the international networks, spend eighty hours a week or more pretending they are someone else, living a life that does not exist outside a computer. Because MUDs are not only susceptible to pathologically obsessive use by some people but also create a strain on computer and communication resources, MUDding has been banned at universities such as Amherst and on the entire continent of Australia.

18   Scientists, students, librarians, artists, organizers, and escapists aren't the only people who have taken to the new medium. The U.S. senator who campaigned for years for the construction of a national Research and Education Network that could host the virtual communities of the future is now vice president of the United States. As of June 1993, the White House and Congress have e-mail addresses.

19   Most people who get their news from conventional media have been unaware of the wildly varied assortment of new cultures that have evolved in the world's computer networks over the past ten years. Most people who have not yet used these new media remain unaware of how profoundly the social, political, and scientific experiments under way today via computer networks could change all our lives in the near future.

FOR CRITICAL INQUIRY

1. According to Camille Sweeney, what is the appeal of having an online identity—or what she calls a "cyberself"? What does she see as the benefits of online identities? How do these online identities differ from offline ones?

2. Interview several teenagers about the time they spend in chat rooms and elsewhere in cyberspace. Ask about how their relationships with others online and offline are different and similar. Try to find out what their sense of themselves is online and offline. Identify patterns in the responses. What do these patterns suggest about identity formation and cyberspace?

3. What does Howard Rheingold see as the attractions of life online? In his view, what is the relationship between experience online and in real life (IRL)? Do you find his view that life online actually creates virtual communities? What kind of communities are they? What would you have to assume to call them "communities"?

4. Notice that Rheingold says he spends an average of two hours a day, seven days a week online. How much time do you spend online? Follow Rheingold's example when he lists where he went online and what he did. Keep a daily journal of where you went and what you did for a week. (If you're not currently online, use this exercise as an occasion to start.) Figure on spending at least an hour a day online for this exercise. Pay particular attention to the virtual communities you visit, what goes on there, and the relationship to real life. Turn your notes into a report (written or oral, depending on your teacher's direction) that explains where you have been and the effect of the virtual communities on your real life.

Further Links

You can find an interesting study of gender swapping on the Internet by Amy S. Bruckman, one of the pioneer researchers on identity and cyberspace. Go to <ftp.media.mit.edu/pub/asb/papers/gender-swapping.txt>. You can find Howard Rheingold's book *The Virtual Community* online at <www.well.com/user/hlr/vcbook/>.

PART FOUR

Guide to Research

INTRODUCTION: DOING RESEARCH

People do research in one form or another all the time, perhaps without even being aware of it. You may associate research with the kinds of formal research projects assigned in school, but research takes place in virtually every sphere of life:

- If you need to buy a birthday present for your mother, you may well ask other family members for suggestions. Many students do considerable research to decide which colleges to apply to. People who want to buy a new car often consult *Consumer Reports* and talk to friends to find the best deal. If you are planning a vacation, you might look at travel guides in your local bookstore or library.

- Many types of research take place in the workplace—for example marketing research, product development, or productivity studies. People in business need to research current trends in the market, state and federal regulations, and tax codes. The professions, such as law and medicine, are defined in many respects by the kind of research practitioners in those fields do to deal with clients' legal situations or to diagnose patients' conditions and recommend treatment.

- Public opinion polling has become a common feature of politics and journalism, a way to keep track of the public mood and people's attitudes about the issues of the day. Public advocacy groups often conduct their own research on questions that matter to them—whether it's the impact of mining on national lands, the effect of NAFTA on American jobs, drunk driving, or impending changes in the welfare law.

- Research, of course, is a familiar part of academic life for students and faculty alike. You may recall some of the research assignments you encountered in elementary school and high school—term papers, book reports, science fair projects, history posters, oral presentations—and you will almost certainly do research in your college courses. Faculty do research when they prepare for their classes or plan new ones. The saying "publish or perish" reveals the importance of research in the professional careers of faculty. Their work is defined in part by the research of their academic disciplines and the expectation that they will participate in the creation of new knowledge in their fields.

As you can see, not all research enters into the written record. Sometimes research is just a matter of getting information to make a decision or take an action. In other cases, such as a teacher's lecture notes or a memo to coworkers, research leads to writing but not to formal publication. But in many instances, research is intended for a wider readership—a journalist's investigative reporting on child labor in American-owned factories abroad, a study of global warming by a panel of scientists, an article in a history journal presenting a new interpretation of American attitudes toward immigration, or a recent book by a team of sociologists on the causes and consequences of homelessness in San Francisco.

Research Techniques

These various examples reveal that research not only takes many different forms but also involves different research techniques. Some research deals largely with **written records**—previous work published on a subject, historical archives, old newspapers and magazines, government documents, unpublished manuscripts, letters, and personal journals or diaries. Much of this material can be found in college libraries, but some researchers travel around the world to visit special collections, local historical societies, or families and individuals who hold important documents.

In other cases, research projects require **field research.** Marketing researchers, for example, use focus groups, telephone interviews, and surveys to accumulate data. A journalist working on child labor may well visit plants around the world and talk to company executives and experts on labor relations. A wildlife biologist is likely to spend considerable time in the field observing the behavior of birds or animals.

In still other cases, researchers conduct **experiments in laboratories.** Molecular biologists, for example, use highly sophisticated techniques and equipment to study the function of genes. Psychologists routinely use laboratory conditions to study how people solve particular kinds of tasks or respond to sex and violence in the media.

Scale of Research

The scale of the research will also vary, often depending on the amount of time and the resources a researcher has available. A team of sociologists studying homelessness, for example, decided to concentrate their research on one city, San Francisco, instead of trying to investigate homelessness everywhere in the United States or in the world. This is no doubt a wise decision, for whatever the researchers may lose in the scope of their research they are likely to make up for in the amount of detail and the depth of analysis they can achieve by focusing on a single location.

The historian investigating American attitudes toward immigration faces a similar situation. To offer a persuasive interpretation of American attitudes from the colonial period to the present is a massive undertaking that would undoubtedly take years to complete, and the results would require a book-length (or even multivolume) treatment. For these reasons, the historian decides to focus his research on a particular time frame, 1880 to 1920, which is widely recognized as an important period in immigration history, as millions of immigrants came to the United States from southern and eastern Europe. As a necessary background, he will want to understand American attitudes in earlier periods, as well as attitudes toward the "new" immigration from Southeast Asia, India and Pakistan, Korea, the Caribbean, and Central and Latin America of recent years. But by concentrating on the period from 1880 to 1920, the historian has set a manageable research task that can realistically lead to an article offering a new interpretation of the issue.

Need to Know

As you have seen, the forms, techniques, and scale of research may vary widely. Nonetheless, there is one thing all the examples of research have in common. They are all motivated by the need to know. In each case, something is calling on a person or a group of people to do research—to get the information needed, to investigate a problem, to provide a new way of seeing things. To put it another way, research begins when people have questions they need answers to: What kind of computer should I buy? How are consumers likely to respond to a new product or service? What does the public think about George W. Bush's first term in office? What causes breast cancer? Why did Lyndon Johnson escalate the war in Vietnam?

Researchers in different fields of study, of course, have different ways of asking questions and different ways of answering them. Take the AIDS epidemic, for example. Scientific researchers have been asking questions about the nature and behavior of the human immunodeficiency virus (HIV) and about the kinds of treatment that can alter the course of infection. Psychologists and sociologists, in contrast, have studied the effect of AIDS on the identities of HIV-negative gay men and the benefits and drawbacks of needle-exchange programs. Economists have calculated the financial impact of AIDS on medical institutions, health insurance companies, government programs, and employers.

Researchers, as you can see, do not just think of a topic and start to investigate it. They turn the general topic of AIDS into specific questions that concern people in their field of study. This gives them an angle on the problem and a way of starting their research. In many cases, you can discover what led a researcher to ask a particular question or set of questions by looking at the preface or introduction to book-length research studies.

The following excerpts from the introduction to Donna Gaines's *Teenage Wasteland* offer a personal account of why she decided to do research on the suicide pact of four working-class teenagers in Bergenfield, New Jersey. Gaines's research is interesting because it began as an assignment from her editor at the *Village Voice,* then turned into the basis of her doctoral thesis in sociology at the State University of New York at Stony Brook, and was finally published as a book directed to a general readership, not just an academic audience.

As you read, notice how Gaines explains her motivation for doing research, the questions she is asking, and how these questions shape the kind of research she did.

Introduction from *Teenage Wasteland*
DONNA GAINES

1   When I heard about the suicide pact it grabbed me in the solar plexus. I looked at the pictures of the kids and their friends. I read what the reporters said. I was sitting in my garden apartment looking out on Long Island's Jericho Turnpike thinking maybe this is how the world ends, with the last generation bowing out first.

2   In Bergenfield, New Jersey, on the morning of March 11, 1987, the bodies of four teenagers were discovered inside a 1977 rust-colored Chevrolet Camaro. The car, which belonged to Thomas Olton, was parked in an unused garage in the Foster Village garden apartment complex, behind the Foster Village Shopping Center. Two sisters, Lisa and Cheryl Burress, and their friends, Thomas Rizzo and Thomas Olton, had died of carbon monoxide poisoning.

3   Lisa was sixteen, Cheryl was seventeen, and the boys were nineteen—they were suburban teens, turnpike kids like the ones in the town I live in. And thinking about them made me remember how it felt being a teenager too. I was horrified that it had come to this. I believed I understood why they did it, although it wasn't a feeling I could have put into words.

4   You could tell from the newspapers that they were rock and roll kids. The police had found a cassette tape cover of AC/DC's *If You Want Blood, You've Got It* near the bodies. Their friends were described as kids who listened to thrash metal, had shaggy haircuts, wore lots of black and leather. "Dropouts," "druggies," the papers called them. Teenage suburban rockers whose lives revolved around their favorite bands and their friends. Youths who barely got by in school and at home and who did not impress authority figures in any remarkable way....

5   A week or two after the suicide pact, *The Village Voice* assigned me to go to Bergenfield. Now this was not a story I would've volunteered for. Usually I write about things I enjoy: computers, guns, pornography, tattoos, rock and roll, cars. I don't like the idea of "research subjects" or getting vulnerable people to trust me with their secrets so I can go back and tell about them. Generally, I prefer leaving people alone.

6   But one day my editor at the *Voice* called to ask if I wanted to go to Bergenfield. She knew my background—that I knew suburbia, that I could talk to kids. By now I fully embraced the sociologist's ethical commitment to the "rights of the researched," and the social worker's vow of client confidentiality. As far as suicidal teenagers were concerned, I felt that if I couldn't help them, I didn't want to bother them.

7   But I was really pissed off at what I kept reading. How people in Bergenfield openly referred to the four kids as "troubled losers." Even after they were dead, nobody cut them any slack. "Burnouts," "druggies," "dropouts." Something was wrong. So I took the opportunity.

8   From the beginning, I believed that the Bergenfield suicides symbolized a tragic defeat for young people. Something was happening in the larger society that was not yet comprehended. Scholars spoke ominously of "the postmodern condition," "societal upheaval," "decay," "anomie." Meanwhile, American kids kept losing ground, showing all the symptoms of societal neglect. Many were left to fend for themselves, often with little success. The news got worse. Teenage suicides continued, and still nobody seemed to be getting the point.

9   Now, in trying to understand this event, I might have continued working within the established discourse on teenage suicide. I might have carried on the tradition of obscuring the bigger picture, psychologizing the Bergenfield suicide pact, interviewing the parents of the four youths, hounding their friends for the gory details. I might have spent my time probing school records, tracking down their teachers and shrinks for insights, focusing on their personal histories and intimate relationships. I might have searched out the individual motivations behind the words left in the note written and signed by each youth on the brown paper bag found with their bodies on March 11. But I did not.

10   Because the suicide pact was a *collective act*, it warrants a social explanation— a portrait of the "burnouts" in Bergenfield as actors within a particular social landscape.

11   For a long time now, the discourse of teenage suicide has been dominated by atomizing psychological and medical models. And so the larger picture of American youth as members of a distinctive generation with a unique collective biography, emerging at a particular moment in history, has been lost.

12   The starting-off point for this book, then, is a teenage suicide pact in an "upper-poor" white ethnic suburb in northern New Jersey. But, of course, the story did not begin and will not end in Bergenfield.

13   Yes, there were specific sociocultural patterns operating in Bergenfield through which a teenage suicide pact became objectively possible. Yes, there were particular conditions which influenced how the town reacted to the event. Yes, there were reasons—that unique constellation of circumstances congealed in the lives of the four youths in the years, weeks, and days prior to March 11—that made suicide seem like their best alternative.

14   Given the four youths' personal histories, their losses, their failures, their shattered dreams, the motivation to die in this way seems transparent. Yet, after the suicide pact, in towns across the country, on television and in the press, people asked, "Why did they do it?" But I went to Bergenfield with other questions.

15   This was a suicide pact that involved close friends who were by no accounts obsessed, star-crossed lovers. What would make four people want to die together? Why would they ask, in their collective suicide note, to be waked and buried together? Were they part of a suicide cult?

16   If not, what was the nature of the social bond that tied them so closely? What could be so intimately binding that in the early morning hours of March 11 not one of them could stop, step back from the pact they had made to say, "Wait, I can't do this"? Who were these kids that everybody called "burnouts"?

17   "Greasers," "hoods," "beats," "freaks," "hippies," "punks." From the 1950s onward, these groups have signified young people's refusal to cooperate. In the social order of the American high school, teens are expected to do what they are told—make the grade, win the prize, play the game. Kids who refuse have always found something else to do. Sometimes it kills them; sometimes it sets them free.

18   In the eighties, as before, high school kids at the top were the "preps," "jocks," or "brains," depending on the region. In white suburban high schools in towns like Bergenfield, the "burnouts" are often the kids near the bottom—academically, economically, and socially.

19   To outsiders, they look tough, scruffy, poor, wild. Uninvolved in and unimpressed by convention, they create an alternative world, a retreat, a refuge. Some burnouts are proud; they "wave their freak flags high." They call themselves burnouts to flaunt their break with the existing order, as a form of resistance, a statement of refusal.

20   But the meaning changes when "burnout" is hurled by an outsider. Then it hurts. It's an insult. Everyone knows you don't call somebody a burnout to their face unless you are looking for a fight. At that point, the word becomes synonymous with "troubled loser," "druggie"—all the things the press and some residents of the town called the four kids who died together in Tommy Olton's Camaro.

21   How did kids in Bergenfield *become* "burnouts," I wondered. At what point were they identified as outcasts? Was this a labeling process or one of self-selection? What kinds of lives did they have? What resources were available for them? What choices did they have? What ties did these kids have to the world outside Bergenfield? Where did their particular subculture come from? Why in the 1980s, the Reagan years, in white, suburban America?

22   What were their hopes and fears? What did heavy metal, Satan, suicide, and long hair mean to them? Who were their heroes, their gods? What saved them and what betrayed them in the long, cold night?

23   And what was this "something evil in the air" that people spoke about? Were the kids in Bergenfield "possessed"? Was the suicide pact an act of cowardice by four "losers," or the final refuge of kids helplessly and hopelessly trapped? How different was Bergenfield from other towns?

24   Could kids be labeled to death? How much power did these labels have? I wanted to meet other kids in Bergenfield who were identified as "burnouts" to find out what it felt like to carry these labels. I wanted to understand the existential situation they operated in—not simply as hapless losers, helpless victims, or tragic martyrs, but also as *historical actors* determined in their choices, resistant, defiant.

25   Because the suicide pact in Bergenfield seemed to be a symptom of something larger, a metaphor for something more universal. I moved on from there to other towns. For almost two years I spent my time reading thrash magazines, seeing

shows, and hanging out with "burnouts" and "dirtbags" as well as kids who slip through such labels....

26   From the beginning, I decided I didn't want to dwell too much on the negatives. I wanted to understand how alienated kids survived, as well as how they were defeated. How did they maintain their humanity against what I now felt were impossible odds? I wondered. What keeps young people together when the world they are told to trust no longer seems to work? What motivates them to be decent human beings when nobody seems to respect them or take them seriously?

FOR CRITICAL INQUIRY

1. Explain Gaines's decision to cover the teen suicide pact for the *Village Voice.* What was her initial reluctance? What considerations overcame this reluctance?

2. What questions and approaches to researching the suicide pact does Gaines reject? Why does she reject them?

3. What questions does Gaines think are more important? Why?

4. How do Gaines's questions shape how she carried out her research?

In the following chapters, you will learn more about how to carry out research. As you will see, the focus of these chapters is on academic research, the kind of assignments you are likely to get in college courses. Nonetheless, the information is just as pertinent to research in other spheres. Chapter 16 explains how to organize a research project and use print and electronic sources. Chapter 17 discusses field research. (We do not include research that involves experimental work in laboratories, a specialized topic better handled in a science or social science course devoted to research design.)

CHAPTER SIXTEEN

Research Projects: Using Print and Electronic Sources

The way people do research is changing. For most college research projects, the library is still likely to be your main source of information, so you can count on spending a large part of your research time reading and evaluating what you find in books and articles from newspapers, magazines, and academic journals (although your topic and research questions may also lead you to conduct field research—which is treated in the next chapter).

What has changed is that a good deal of the information you'll need for a research project is now available online or on CD-ROMs—everything from the library's catalog and subject headings to indexes, bibliographies, and other electronic databases. In addition, there is a world of information that you can access over the Internet—material that ranges from serious scholarly discussion to wildly opinionated debates of questionable value. Now that anyone can start a discussion group or put up a Web site, you can find useful electronic sources of information created and maintained by individuals, museums, advocacy groups, and government agencies—and some that are just plain crackpot. For these reasons, doing research today is a matter of knowing your way around both print and electronic sources and understanding the difference between sources that are credible and those that are not.

This chapter covers a number of helpful sources that you can find in your library and on the Internet. Before you plunge into the library or cyberspace, however, it's worth looking first at how to organize your research project so that you can make the best use of the sources you turn up. We begin with an overview of the research process. Then we follow the research process step by step to show how you can find, read, and evaluate print and electronic sources.

OVERVIEW OF THE RESEARCH PROCESS

As you saw in the Introduction, research typically begins when people need to know something and have important questions to answer. Now it is only fair to say that in college the call to do research most often comes from teachers in the form of a research assignment. Most faculty believe that an important part of a college education is learning how to pose a meaningful problem to investigate, to research and evaluate what others have said about it, and to form your own judgment. The following overview of the research process identifies the main steps in responding to this call to write, and lists the tasks involved at each point:

- **Getting started:** Analyze the research assignment. Do preliminary research to get an overview of your topic. Start to focus your reading to develop a research question. Evaluate your research question and revise or modify it, if necessary. Write a proposal to clarify the purpose of your research.

- **Finding sources:** Use your library's card catalog, indexes, bibliographies, and other databases to identify print and electronic sources. Browse sites on the Internet. Keep a working bibliography.

- **Reading and evaluating sources:** Take notes. Photocopy sources. Assess the relevance and credibility of the sources. Look for assumptions and biases. Keep an open mind. Be prepared to revise or modify your own thinking in light of what you've read.

- **Planning and drafting:** Reread your notes and photocopies. Develop a working outline of your paper. Start drafting. Reread sources and find additional information as needed. Revise or modify your outline if necessary.

This chapter looks in more detail at each of these steps in the research process.

GETTING STARTED

Research depends in part on knowing what you are looking for. This will depend, of course, on the research assignment. In some cases, the assignment will provide specific directions, but in others, it will be open-ended. If you have questions about what the assignment is calling on you to do, make sure you consult with your instructor.

Let's say you are taking a course on American popular music and your teacher assigns an open-ended research paper. The topic is yours to determine, and you decide you want to write something about rock 'n' roll as a cultural phenomenon. Good start. The problem, however, is that such a broad topic is not likely to give you much direction in your research. The first step in organizing a research project, then, is to develop a focused question to guide your investigation.

Preliminary Research

Sometimes you may know right away what you want to research—what, for example, was the public reaction to Elvis Presley in the mid-1950s, how did folksingers influence the development of rock in the 1960s, or what does the emergence of punk in the late 1970s tell us about American culture at that time? In other cases, especially when the topic you're researching is new to you, you'll need to do some preliminary research to develop a research question. The following sources offer good places to start:

- **The Web:** Web sites can offer helpful starting places for research projects. See "Finding a Research Path" for an example of how a student used the Web to do preliminary research and develop a research question.

- **Encyclopedias:** You can find an overview of many topics in general encyclopedias. It can also be helpful to consult specialized encyclopedias that cover a particular field of study and often include bibliographies for each entry. See the list of general and specialized encyclopedias.

- **Recent books:** Skim a recent book on your topic, looking in particular at its introduction to see how the writer describes the issues the book addresses. Notice, too, what the book seems to cover by reading the table of contents. And don't forget to see whether it has a bibliography.

- **Recent articles:** Find a recent article in a scholarly journal or a popular magazine on your topic. Read the article, noticing what question or questions the writer poses and (in the case of academic articles) what sources are listed in the references.

- **Classmates, librarians, teaching assistants, faculty members:** Talk to other people who know something about your topic and the current questions people are asking about it. They can help you understand what the issues are and what sources you might look for.

Your preliminary research should give you some ideas about the way others have approached the topic you're interested in, the kinds of questions they raise, and the differences of opinion and interpretation that divide them. This research should also help you identify other books and articles on the subject that you may want to consult.

General Encyclopedias

Collier's Encyclopedia, 24 vols.

Encyclopedia Americana, 30 vols. plus yearbooks

Grolier Multimedia Encyclopedia (CD-ROM)

Microsoft Encarta (CD-ROM, includes 24 vol. Funk and Wagnalls *New Encyclopedia*)

The New Encyclopedia Britannica, 32 vols.

World Book Encyclopedia, 22 vols. plus yearbooks

Specialized Encyclopedias

Art, Film, Television

Encyclopedia of World Architecture
Encyclopedia of World Art
International Encyclopedia of Film
International Encyclopedia of Television
International Television Almanac

Economics and Business

Encyclopedia of Advertising
Encyclopedia of American Economic History
Encyclopedia of Banking and Finance
Encyclopedia of Management
Handbook of Modern Marketing
McGraw-Hill Dictionary of Modern Economics

Education

Encyclopedia of Education

Foreign Relations

Encyclopedia of American Foreign Policy
Encyclopedia of the Third World

History

An Encyclopedia of World History
Cambridge Ancient History
Cambridge History of China
Dictionary of American History
Encyclopedia of Latin-American History
Harvard Guide to American History
New Cambridge Modern History

Literature

Cambridge Guide to English Literature
Encyclopedia of World Literature in the 20th Century
Funk and Wagnall's Standard Dictionary of Folklore, Mythology, and Legend
McGraw-Hill Encyclopedia of World Drama
Oxford Companion to American Literature

Music

Dance Encyclopedia
Encyclopedia of Pop, Rock, and Soul
New Grove Dictionary of American Music
New Grove Dictionary of Music and Musicians

Religion and Philosophy

Dictionary of the History of Ideas
Encyclopedia of Philosophy
Encyclopedia of Religion
Encyclopedia of Bioethics
New Standard Jewish Encyclopedia
Oxford Dictionary of the Christian Church

Science and Technology

Encyclopedia of Biological Sciences
Encyclopedia of Chemistry
Encyclopedia of Computer Science and Technology
Encyclopedia of Oceanography
Encyclopaedic Dictionary of Physics
Introduction to the History of Science
McGraw-Hill Dictionary of Earth Sciences
McGraw-Hill Encyclopedia of Science and Technology
The Software Toolworks Multimedia Encyclopedia
Van Nostrand's Scientific Encyclopedia

Social Sciences

Dictionary of Anthropology
Encyclopedia of American Political History
Encyclopedia of Crime and Justice
Encyclopedia of Educational Research
Encyclopedia of Psychology
International Encyclopedia of the Social Sciences
Literature of Geography
Literature of Political Science
New Dictionary of the Social Sciences

Women's Studies

Women's Studies Encyclopedia

FINDING A RESEARCH PATH

THE WORLD WIDE WEB

Here is Amira Patel's account of how she got started on a research project in her American immigration history course using the Web:

I was assigned a ten-page research paper on any aspect of immigration. I wasn't sure what I wanted to write about—maybe something on attitudes toward immigrants—so I decided to check out the Web and see if I could get some ideas for the paper. First, I selected Infoseek as a search engine and entered the keyword "immigration." I got 56,518 pages so I felt a little overwhelmed. I decided to try "anti-immigration" and got a more manageable number, 218. Unfortunately, Infoseek couldn't process my request because the system was flooded with other requests.

Therefore, I decided to switch to Yahoo! Yahoo! can be good because it lets you match a keyword like "immigration" to categories. I first chose "Arts: Humanities: History: U.S. History: Immigration" and got four hits. I browsed each quickly. "Immigration in the Gilded Age and Progressive Era" brought up the issue of nativism and anti-immigration sentiment in the early 20th century, but I wasn't really sure I wanted to research that historical period.

I decided to switch to another Yahoo! search for more recent information. I chose "Full Coverage: U.S. News" and typed in "immigration" as the keyword (see Fig. 16.1). This gives both news stories and related Web sites. I clicked on the National Immigration Forum's Web site because Yahoo! noted that it "fights immigrant prejudice." I checked out the page "Immigration Facts" (see Fig. 16.2) and then clicked on another link "Issue Brief: Cycles of Nativism in U.S. History" (see Fig. 16.3).

(continued)

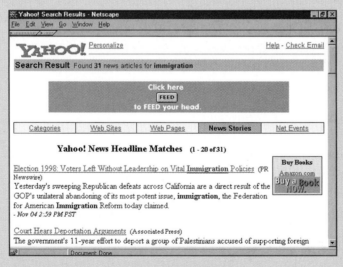

FIGURE 16.1   Results of a Yahoo! search

Full Coverage: US News: Immigration Web site. Reproduced with permission of YAHOO! Inc. Copyright ©2000 by YAHOO! Inc. YAHOO! and the YAHOO! logo are trademarks of YAHOO! Inc.

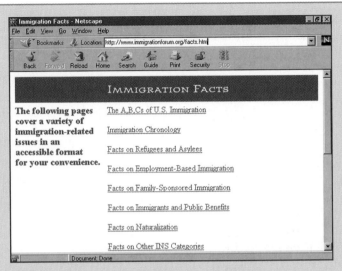

FIGURE 16.2   **A page from the National Immigration Forum's Web site**

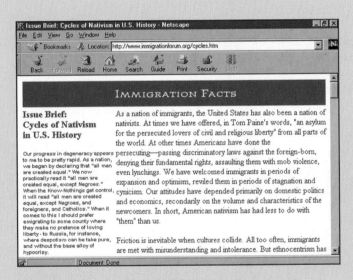

FIGURE 16.3   **Historical information available at the National Immigration Forum's Web site**

(continued)

I read through it and became interested in the "English Only" movement. I got curious about why so many people think English should be the official language and why they feel that way right now, when there are so many new immigrants from Asia and Latin America coming into the United States.

Now that I had narrowed my search down to "English Only," I stayed with Yahoo! and typed in "English Only." The first site I got, "Language Policy Research Center," is about languages in Israel and was not helpful to my search. I tried a second site, James Crawford's "Language Policy Web Site and Emporium" (Fig. 16.4), and found a ton of information on the history of the English Only movement and English Only legislation. It also gives links to other Web sites so that I could read what supporters of English Only, such as the advocacy group U.S. English, had to say about the issue.

By this point, I felt confident I had found a good topic in "English Only" and enough bibliographical sources to get started in the library. I decided I wanted to do research to explain why the English Only movement has emerged in recent years.

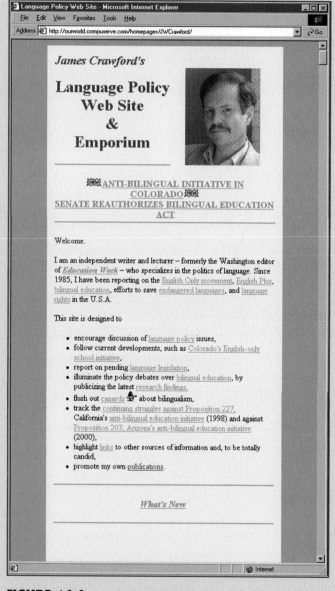

FIGURE 16.4
Language Policy Web site and Emporium

Diagram of a Research Path

Here is a visualization of Amira's research path. Notice that, typical of most Web searches, it is a wandering one, with some dead ends as well as important leads.

Infoseek

   "immigration"—56, 518 pages

   "anti-immigration"—218 pages

      system couldn't process request....

   Yahoo!

      "Immigration in the Gilded Age and Progressive Era"

         not sure....

      "National Immigration Forum"

         "Immigration Facts"

            "Issue Brief: Cycles of Nativism"

               English Only

                  "Language Policy Research Center"

                     not relevant....

               "Language Policy Web Site & Emporium"

                  "English Only movement"

                     FOCUS!

Using Search Engines to Explore the Web

The search engines that are readily available through Web browsers such as Netscape may search different sites, so if you don't find what you are looking for with one, try another.

The key to using search engines is finding the right keyword or combination of keywords for your purposes. For example, when Amira used *immigration* as a keyword on Infoseek, she got over 50,000 hits, clearly an unmanageable number. But when she shifted to *anti-immigration,* she got 218. And as you can see in the account of her search, switching from the broad topic "immigration" to the more limited one "English Only" helped make her search more focused and more productive.

Using Boolean Operators

Another way to focus a search is to combine keywords with Boolean operators—AND, OR, NOT, and quotation marks. For example, if you type the two words *death penalty* you will be inundated with sources because your search will find documents that contain either of the words entered. (One search engine found 15,819, most of which had nothing to do with the death penalty.) However, if you put quotation marks around the words—"death penalty"—you turn it into one phrase and set up a more focused search. Furthermore, if you combine the phrase *death penalty* with another keyword, such as *abolish* or the phrase *supreme court,* you can focus your search considerably. By using

"death penalty" AND abolish

a search turned up 21 hits, most or all of which are likely to be relevant.

Choosing a Search Engine

Search engines vary in how they are organized, and different search engines may well produce different results. For this reason, the best way to do research with search engines is to use more than one, as Amira does in her preliminary research. Virtually all search engines enable keyword searching, and some offer subject trees that enable you to search within categories as well as by keywords. Many search engines support Boolean operators, but some do not, including such popular ones as Yahoo! and Infoseek.

Here is a list of some of the most popular search engines available at the time this chapter was written:

Google <www.google.com>	AltaVista <altavista.digital.com>
Excite <www.excite.com>	Galaxy <galaxy.einet.net/galaxy.html>
Infoseek <www.infoseek.com>	Lycos <www.lycos.com>
Yahoo! <www.yahoo.com>	Hotbot <www.hotbot.com>
Webcrawler <www.webcrawler.com>	ProFusion <profusion.ittc.ukans.edu>

Developing a Research Question

Once you've done some preliminary research, answer the following questions to refine your own sense of the research question you want to investigate:

1. What questions, issues, and problems appear repeatedly? Why do people think they are important?

2. Are there arguments, debates, or controversies that appear in what you've read? What positions have others taken? What seems to be at stake in these arguments? Do you find yourself siding with some people and disagreeing with others?

3. Is there some aspect of your topic that people don't seem to pay much attention to? Why do you think this is so? Are they neglecting questions or issues that could provide a good focus for research?

4. Given what you've read so far, what questions, issues, arguments, and controversies do you find most interesting? What, in your view, makes them important?

Evaluating a Research Question

Let's say that your preliminary research for a course on the history of postwar America has led you from the general topic of Race in America to the more specific topic of Asian Americans to the research question, "Do media portrayals of Asian Americans perpetuate social stereotypes?" That sounds like a good starting point, but it's worth pausing for a moment to make sure. Here are some questions that can help you evaluate your research question:

1. Are you genuinely interested in the question? (Research is work and takes time, so you want to be sure you are committed enough to sustain your efforts.)

2. Is the question an important one that will have significance for others? Does the question pose a significant problem, investigate a controversy, or participate in an ongoing debate? (You'll be making the results of your research public, so you need to make sure others will find it meaningful. It doesn't make sense, for example, to research the question, "Was Captain Cook the first European to travel to Australia?" because the answer is already accepted as established fact.)

3. Is your research question limited enough to handle in the amount of time you have available and in the length of the paper you've been assigned? (Plenty of good research questions may be too big to treat effectively given constraints of time and space.)

4. Are there enough sources available to find the information you need to answer your research question? (If not, you need to revise, modify, or abandon your research question.)

Writing a Proposal

Some teachers ask students to write a proposal that defines the purpose of their research, explains its significance, and indicates their research plan. Even if your teacher does not require a proposal, writing one can be a useful exercise to help you clarify your purpose. To say that you want to investigate a particular question is only the beginning. You will also need to decide how you plan to handle the information you turn up in your research. Your purpose and the stance you take toward your readers and the material can vary considerably. Here are some typical purposes of research:

■ **To provide an overview of the current thinking of experts:** In this case, your purpose is largely an informative one—to report on what experts in the field think about an important issue. You might, for example, explain the current views of experts on the extinction of dinosaurs or report on the latest results of drug treatment of HIV-positive people.

- **To review the arguments in a controversy:** Again, your purpose is largely informative—to explain to readers the positions people have taken in a current debate. You might, for example, explain current debates in literary studies between those who believe that there is an established canon of masterpieces all students should read and those who believe the traditional canon excludes women, minority, working-class, and Third World writers. Or you could report on the current legal controversy prompted by the prosecution of pregnant women for doing harm to their fetuses by drinking or taking drugs.

- **To answer an important question or solve a problem:** In this case, your purpose is not simply to report on what is known but to put forward your own analysis and interpretation. You might, for example, explain why there has been a resurgence of tuberculosis or the consequences of deregulation in the telecommunications industry.

- **To position your own interpretation in relation to what others have said:** In this case, your purpose is similar to that of answering an important question. The key difference is that instead of simply using what others have written as evidence for your interpretation, you also explain how your analysis or interpretation relates to the views of others—how and why it differs, how and why it shares common ground. You might, for example, position your own interpretation of Madonna as a cultural symbol in relation to other interpretations of her. Or you might explain how your analysis of Martin Luther King's "I Have a Dream" speech differs from and is similar to the analyses of others.

- **To take a stand on a controversy:** Here your purpose is not simply to report and analyze but also to persuade. In this case, you have an argument to make. You might claim, for example, that there should (or should not) be mandatory testing for the HIV virus. Or you could argue that the United States should (or should not) adopt more stringent limits on commercial fishing in the North Atlantic.

Here is an example of what a research proposal might look like. Notice that it does three things:

1. Explains the purpose of the research.
2. Indicates its significance.
3. Sketches briefly the research plan.

SAMPLE RESEARCH PROPOSAL

My plan is to research the question "Do media portrayals of Asian Americans perpetuate social stereotypes?" Given what I've read so far, my basic purpose will be to show that this is an important question and to provide some answers. I haven't found any major differences of opinion or interpretation, so I don't foresee any major controversies I'll need to talk about. I will need to explain how the media portrays Asian Americans and define what a social stereotype is and the effects it has. From what I've read, it seems the media pictures Asian Americans as good at math and science, hardworking, serious, and eager to assimilate. As I see it, the problem here is that this picture lumps all Asian Americans together and overlooks significant differences between Chinese, Japanese, Koreans, and Southeast Asians. The "all work, no play" stereotype also ignores the poverty and gang life in certain Asian American communities. I plan to do more reading. I've got plenty of sources that look good. And I'll probably watch some recent movies, such as *Joy Luck Club* and *Wedding Banquet*.

FINDING SOURCES

Once you have established a direction for your research project, the next step is to do in-depth research. By this point, you have probably turned up a number of promising sources through your preliminary research. This section provides information on setting up a working bibliography and finding further sources online and in print.

Keeping a Working Bibliography

A working bibliography is just what it says: a list of the sources you plan to work with on your research project. A working bibliography can save you a lot of time and aggravation by serving two important purposes: (1) It enables you to keep track of the sources you want to consult; (2) when you're finishing your paper, it makes preparing your Works Cited or References page easier, since you don't have to make last-minute trips to the library to get bibliographical information.

Include in your working bibliography more sources than you expect to use in the final paper. Some of the sources may be unavailable at your library, and others may not be useful to your purposes. If you've done a good job of research, you won't use all the sources you've found.

Researchers have different styles of keeping working bibliographies. You can use three- by five-inch cards, with a new note card for each entry. This enables you to order your entries by topic when you're doing research and alphabetically when you're preparing your paper. Or you might prefer to use a computer. Many word-processing, spreadsheet, and database programs allow you to sort entries and print out lists, which can be added to as you go along and turned into the final Works Cited or Reference page when you've finished.

The working bibliography should contain the information that you need to find the source as well as the information you'll need for your Works Cited or Reference page.

Books

Call number

Author(s), editor(s), translator(s)

Title and subtitle

City of publication, name of publisher, and date of publication

Articles

Author(s)

Title and subtitle of article

Periodical name

Volume and issue number (if periodical uses them)

Date

Page numbers

Electronic Information

Name of source

Date you accessed information

Name of sender, if e-mail

Electronic address

The Library Catalog

Your college library is likely to be your main source for books and periodicals. A library catalog lists the library's holdings by author, title, periodical, and subject. Libraries traditionally used card catalogs, and researchers shuttled from drawer to drawer to find the information they were looking for. Today, most libraries have replaced the unwieldy card catalog with catalogs online.

As you can see from the screen introducing users to the online catalog at the University of South Florida (Fig. 16.5), you can search by author, title, periodical, subject, or keyword. Your library's catalog may differ from the one shown here, so check with your reference librarian for information on how to use it.

To do a subject heading search, you can save time by first consulting the Library of Congress Subject Headings (LCSH), a reference source that lists the standard subject headings used in catalogs and indexes. As you can see from the entry for the book *Nativism Reborn?: The Official English Only Movement and the American States* (Fig. 16.6), online catalogs provide a good deal of information about the library's holdings. In addition, some online catalogs allow users to browse the shelf where the book is located to see other related titles.

UNIV OF SOUTH FLORIDA

University of South Florida Catalog

(Copyright 1985, State University System of Florida)

Type command WITH search term:	To search by:	Examples:	
A=	Authors=twain mark		
T=	All titles	t=	tom sawyer
TJ=	Journal/magazine/newspaper titles	tj=	newsweek
S=	General subject headings	s=	ecology
SM=	Medical subject headings	sm=	myocardia
CL=	Library of Congress call numbers	cl=	qh546.3
K=	Keywords	k=	solar energy

or WITHOUT search term:

    K to get Keyword input screen

    EXS to enter a complex keyword search

Search statements are made up of a letter representing the type of search desired, followed by = (equals sign) and the search term(s).

Example: A=SHAKESPEARE   Find all authors with the last name SHAKESPEARE

FIGURE 16.5   **An online catalog**

Indiana University Libraries

INDYCAT

Subject Search Request: Language policy—United States.

Search Results: 17 results

TITLE LIST

   Select item and click on location code for call number and available copies.

| Browse Line | New Subject Search | Search Menu |

English Language Empowerment Act of 1996 : report together with m	1996
Held by: [I-IUPUI UL]	
English-only question : an official language for Americans? /	1990
Held by: [I-IUPUI UL]	
English—our official language? /	1994
Held by: [I-IUPUI UL] [Columbus]	
Ethnicity and language /	1987
Held by: [I-IUPUI UL]	

FIGURE 16.6   **Search results in an online catalog**   *(continued)*

Hearing on English as a common language : hearing before the Subc Held by [I-IUPUI UL]	1996
Hearing on English as the common language : hearing before the Su Held by [I-IUPUI UL]	1996
Hold your tongue : bilingualism and the politics of English only Held by: [I-IUPUI UL]	1992
Language loyalties : a source book on the official English contro Held by: [I-IUPUI UL]	1992
Languages in America : a pluralist view /	1996
Latino language and education : communication and the dream defer Held by: [I-IUPUI UL]	1995
Nativism reborn? : the official English language movement and the Held by: [I-IUPUI UL]	1995
Official English, English only : more than meets the eye / Held by: [I-IUPUI UL]	1998
Only English? : law and language policy in the United States / Held by: [I-IUPUI UL]	1990
Perspectives on official English : the campaign for English as th Held by: [I-IUPUI UL]	1990
S. 356—Language of Government Act of 1995 : hearings before the Held by: [I-IUPUI UL]	1996
Voting Rights Act Language Assistance Amendments of 1992 : hearin	1993
Voting Rights Act Language Assistance Amendments of 1992 report t	1992

FIGURE 16.6   *(continued)*

Indiana University Libraries
INDYCAT

Subject Search Request: Nativism reborn? : the official English language movement and the

LONG VIEW

| Help | New Subject Search | Return to Title List | Search Menu |

Author   Tatalovich, Raymond.

FIGURE 16.7   **A book entry in an online catalog**   *(continued)*

Title	Nativism reborn? : the official English language movement and the American states / Raymond Tatalovich.
Published	Lexington, Ky. : University Press of Kentucky, 1995.
Description	xiii, 319 p. ; 23 cm. ←*Number of pages, whether illustrated, size*
Notes	Includes bibliographical references and index. ←*Information on content*
Subjects	Language policy—United States. ←*Related Library of Congress*
	English language—Political aspects—United States ←*subject headings*
	English-only movement
ISBN	0813119189 (acid-free) ←*Book number useful for locating or purchasing*
Location	IUPUI UNIV LIB
Call Number	P119.32.U6 T38 1995
Status	Checked in

| Help | <u>New Subject Search</u> | <u>Return to Title List</u> | <u>Search Menu</u> |

FIGURE 16.7   *(continued)*

FINDING A RESEARCH PATH

THE LIBRARY CATALOG

Let's return to Amira Patel's research on the English Only movement. Here is her account of how she used the library catalog.

I already had the titles of some books from browsing the Web, but I wanted to do a systematic search of the university library.

First, I tried "English-only movement" as a subject heading and got the titles of two books. When I looked up one of the book titles on the online catalog, I noticed that the entry listed a number of other subjects: "Language policy—United States," "English language—Political aspects—United States," and "English language—social aspects—United States."

So next, I tried each of the three subject headings. The best one by far was "Language policy—United States" (Fig. 16.7). It turned up seventeen references.

Finally, I decided to take a little different approach and do a keyword search using "immigration and language." This gave me a list of eleven other books. Not all of these are relevant, but a number look like they might give me a useful perspective on language policy issues like English Only.

I printed out all the searches and started to look for individual books. Then I headed for the stacks.

WEB RESOURCES

VIRTUAL LIBRARIES AND WEB DIRECTORIES

The sheer amount of information that is organized and made available on the Web has increased dramatically in recent years, changing what it means to do research and to find sources. You can now visit virtual libraries that make databases, documents, and image collections available online. You can also find web directories organized by academic fields that will point you to resources that include Web sites of professional associations, online discussion groups, and electronic texts and journals.

The best way to learn about the various resources you can find on the Web is to visit a number of sites that pertain to your research topic. For example, if you are doing research on the artist Vincent Van Gogh, you will probably start exploring the Web by using a search engine and Van Gogh's name as the keyword. You may, however, be able to find additional information and Web sites by visiting art history directories, such as the Art History Research Centre and Art History Resources on the Web.

Here is a list of virtual libraries and web directories for a number of academic and professional fields:

Virtual Libraries
Infosurf
<www.library.ucsb.edu/subj/resource.html>

Internet Public Library
<www.ipl.org/re/RR/>

New York Public Library Resource Guides
<www.nypl.org/admin/genweb/guides.html>

Online Reference Tools
<www.library.cmu.edu/bySubject/CS+ECE/lib/reftools.html>

Purdue's Virtual Library
<www.thorplus.lib.purdue.edu/vlibrary/index.html>

University of California-Berkeley, LibWeb
<sunsite.berkeley.edu/cgi-bin/welcome.p1>

Yale University Subject Guides
<www.library.edu/Internet/yalesir.html>

Web Directories
Humanities and Arts
General Directories
Humanities Hub
<www.gu.edu.au/gwis/hub/hub.home.html>

Humbul Gateway
<users.ox.ac.uk/~humbul>

Voice of the Shuttle
<humanitas.ucsb.edu>

African-American Studies
University of Texas Center for African and African American Studies
<www.utexas.edu/depts/canas>

University of Georgia Institute for African American Studies
<www.uga.edu/~iaas>

Art and Film
Art History Research Centre
<www.fofa.concordia.sbc.edu/ARTHLinks.html>

Art History Resources on the Web
<witcombe.sbc.edu/ARHTLinks.html>

Internet Movie Database

Museums in the USA
<www.museumca.org/usa/ >

The Parthenet
<Home.mtholyoke.edu/'klconner/parthenet.html/>

(continued)

Classics
Ancient World Web
<www.julen.net/aw/>

Classics Resources on the Internet
<www.usask.ca/classics/resourcesurls.html>

History
Indexes of Resources for History
<history.cc.ukans.edu/history/>

Library of Congress American Memory Project
<lcweb2.loc.gov/amhome.html>

Literature and Drama
The English Server

Literary Resources on the Net
<dept.english.upenn.edu/~jlynch/Lit>

(continued)

If you are looking for a sociology department in the U.S., look <u>here</u>!

Reference

- <u>Open Directory Project</u>: <u>Science: Social Sciences: Sociology</u>
- <u>WWW Virtual Library: Sociology</u>
- <u>Academic Info Sociology</u>
- <u>Agora Sociologique</u> (French)
- <u>Ally & Bacon Sociology Links</u>
- <u>Argus Clearinghouse: Sociology</u>
- <u>FAQ-Soziologie</u> (German)
- <u>Galilei – Global directory of universities: Sociology</u>
- <u>Gattungswesen: Página de Sociología</u> (Spanish)
- <u>GESIS SocioGuide</u> (German)
- <u>H-Net, Humanities and Social Sciences OnLine</u>
- <u>Hipersociología</u> (Spanish)
- <u>International Encyclopedia of the Social and Behavioral Sciences</u>
- <u>Links2Go: Sociology</u>
- <u>Página de Sociología de Artemio Baigorri</u> (Spanish)
- <u>Research Resources for the Social Sciences</u>
- <u>Scout Report for the Social Sciences</u>
- <u>Social Science Information Gateway</u>

Homepage of Princeton Sociology links

Theatre Links Page
<www.theatre-link.com>

Music
Music Education Links
<www.geocities.com/Athens/2405/resources
.html>

MusicLink: Music on the Internet
<toltec.lib.utk.edu/~music/www.html>

Philosophy and Religion
American Philosophical Association
<www.udel.edu/apa/index.html>

Comparative Religion
<www.academicinfo.net/religindex.html>

Handilinks to Philosophy
<ahandyguide.com/cat1/p/p95.htm>

Rhetoric
Rhetoric and Argumentation Sites
<www.drc.utexas.edu/stures/index.cfm>

Rhetoric Resources at Georgia Tech
<www.lcc.gatech.edu/gallery/rhetoric/>

Rhetoric Server, University of California,
Berkeley

Women's Studies
Women's Resource Project
<sunsite.unc.edu/cheryb/women>

WSSLINKS: Women and Gender Studies
Web Sites
<www.yale.edu/wss/>

Social Siences
General Directories
Social Science Information Gateway

Social Sciences Virtual Library
<www.clas.ufl.edu/users/gthursby/
socsci/>

Anthropology
Anthropology Resources on the Internet
<www.nitehawk.com/alleycat/anth-faq.html>

UCSB Anthropology Web
<www.anth.ucsb.edu/netinfo.html>

Economics and Business
Commercenet

Hoover's Online

WebEc
<netec.wustl.edu/WebEc/>

Education
AskEric

Online Education WWW Server

Law and Political Science
Internet Legal Resources Guide
<www.ilrg.com>

Law Resources on the Internet
<www.lawyernet.com/legal.htm>

Political Science Resources on the Web
<www.lib.umich.edu/libhome/Documents.
center/polisci.html>

Psychology
PsychNET
<www.apa.org/psychnet/>

Psychology Virtual Library
<www.clas.ufl.edu/users/gthursby/psi/>

Social Psychology Network
<www.wesleyan.edu/spn/>

Sociology
Princeton Sociology Links
<www.princeton.edu/~sociolog/links.html>

SocioWeb
<www.socioweb.com/~markbl/socioweb/>

(continued)

Science, Medicine, and Engineering
General
National Academy of Science
<www.nas.edu>

Network Science
<www.netsci.org>

Science Hypermedia
<www.scimedia.com/index.htm>

Astronomy
Astroweb
<www.stsci.edu/astroweb/astronomy.html>

Handilinks to Astronomy
<www.ahandyguide.com/cat1/a/a166.htm>

Biology
Cell and Molecular Biology
<,www.cellbio.com/>

Marine Biology
<life.bio.sunysb.edu/marinebio/mbweb.html>

Chemistry
American Chemical Society
<www.acs.org/>

The Learning Matters of Chemistry
<www.knowledgebydesign.com/time/tlmc.html>

Computer Science
Computer Science Research Resources
<www.cs.umd.edu/documents/Csresources.html>

Virtual Computer Library
<www.utexas.edu/computer>

Engineering
Cornell's Engineering Library
<www.englib.cornell.edu/>

Engineering Information Village
<hood2.ei.org/eivill/plsql/village.serve_page?p=1280>

National Academy of Engineering
<www.nae.edu/nae/nae.nsf/>

Environmental Studies
Envirolink
<envirolink.org>

International Institute for Sustainable Development
<iisd1.iisd.ca/>

Geography and Geology
American Geological Institute
<www.agiweb.org/>

Geological Society of America
<www.geosociety.org/index.htm>

WWW Virtual Library: Geography
<www.icomos.org/WWW_VL_Geography.html>

Mathematics
E-Math
<e-math.ams.org>

Math Archives
<archives.math.utk.edu>

Medical and Health Sciences
Doctor's Guide to the Internet
<www.plsgroup.com/docguide.htm>

Martindale's Health Science Guide
<www.sci.lib.uci.edu/HSG/HSGuide.html>

Medline Plus, National Library of Medicine
<www.nlm.nih.gov/>

Medscape
<www.medscape.com>

Physics
PhysLink
<www.physlink.com/>

Physics Resources, Case Western University
<Erebus.phys.cwru.edu/phys/resource/resources.html>

Bibliographies and Indexes

One place to look for bibliographies is in the books and articles you're using in your research. You may notice that some books and articles appear frequently in bibliographies, Works Cited, or References in what you are reading. If so, the book or article listed is probably an important one and therefore worth looking at.

There are also reference bibliographies and indexes that can enable you to deepen your search for sources. You'll find them in the reference section of your library, and they may appear in print, online, or on a CD-ROM. Consult with your librarian about the bibliographies and indexes available at your library. Many college libraries offer workshops on how to use these and other research sources. Check with your library to see what programs it offers students.

Bibliographies

Bibliographies list books and articles published on particular subjects and fields of study. Some bibliographies are annotated, including brief descriptions of the entries and sometimes evaluations. Make sure you consult an up-to-date bibliography. The *Bibliographic Index* is published every year, providing a master list of bibliographies from that year. Check back over several years to see which ones might be relevant to your research. Web sites, especially those maintained for academic purposes, also often include bibliographies.

Indexes

Indexes provide continually updated lists of articles published in newspapers and magazines and in academic and professional journals. Depending on the index, you can get citations, abstracts, or full-text articles.

- **Citations:** Indexes such as the *Readers' Guide to Periodical Literature* give you citations to a broad range of magazines. Most major newspapers, such as the *New York Times, Washington Post,* and *Wall Street Journal* maintain up-to-date indexes. The online source ArticleFirst indexes over 13,500 journals in many fields, as does CARL Uncover, which indexes more than 17,000 journals.

- **Abstracts:** Some general online indexes such as Periodical Abstracts and Readers' Guide Abstracts provide abstracts (or summaries) of articles. Many specialized indexes in specific disciplines, such as Historical Abstracts, Chemistry Abstracts, and Sociofile, include abstracts as well. Abstracts are brief descriptions that can help you get a sense of the issues related to your research and how to plan further reading.

- **Full Text:** Some online indexes allow you to print the full text of an article. LEXIS/NEXIS Academic Universe, for example, offers full text of many newspapers, magazines, and documents of various sorts. JSTOR: The Scholarly Journal Archive provides the full text of articles in academic journals across many fields, and Expanded Academic ASAP has access to full-text versions of some of the articles in the 1,600 periodicals it indexes.

General Indexes

Readers' Guide to Periodical Literature
New York Times Index
Wall Street Journal Index
Washington Post Index
Editorials on File
Facts On File
Access: The Supplementary Index to Periodicals
Alternative Press Index
Left Index
Chicano Index
Index to Black Periodicals
Business Periodical Index
Biography Index
General Academic Index

Specialized Indexes

Education

Current Index to Journals in Education
Education Index

Humanities

America: History and Life
Art Index
Historical Abstracts
Humanities Index
Music Index
Philosopher's Index
Religion Index One: Periodicals

Science and Technology

Applied Science and Technology Index
Biological and Agricultural Index
Engineering Index
General Science Index
Index Medicus
Physics Abstracts
Science Abstracts

Social Sciences

American Statistics Index
Index to Legal Periodicals

PAIS (Public Affairs Information Service) International in Print
Psychological Abstracts
Social Sciences Index
Sociofile

FINDING A RESEARCH PATH

USING A GENERAL INDEX

Amira Patel decided to consult the *Readers' Guide to Periodical Literature* to find magazine articles on the English Only from the past ten years. She began with 1991 and worked ahead to 2001. Using the heading "English language," here is what Amira found in the 1995 volume.

> English Language
> *See also*
>> Booksellers and bookselling—English language literature
>> English as a second language
>> Sex discrimination in language

> The comeback of English. D. Seligman. il. *Fortune* v131 p141 Ap 3 '95
> One nation, one language? [English-only movement; cover story] S. Headden. il map *U.S. News & World Report* v119 p38-42 S 25 '95
> Open letter [G.O.P. must respond to court decision striking down Arizona's English-only law] *National Review* v47 p14+ N 6 '95
> Se habla ingles [debate over English as the national language] W. F. Buckley. *National Review* v47 p70-109 '95
> Speaking in tongues [opinions of S. Reinhardt and A. Kozinski in court decision striking down Arizona's English-only law] H. Johnson. il *National Review* v47 p28-30 N 6 '95
> Accents
> Let's talk southern [C. O. Hadley teaches southern accent to actors] C. Griffith-Roberts. il por *Southern Living* v30 p82 F '95

Using a Specialized Index

I had used the *Readers' Guide to Periodical Literature* in high school, but I had never used indexes for scholarly articles, so I asked a librarian to show me what to do. She gave me a list of the indexes in the social sciences available online at our library and explained that I could search more than one at a time.

The most promising index seemed to be Sociofile but I also included Criminal Justice Abstracts, PAIS International, and Social Work Abstracts in the search. As usual the big thing was finding the right keywords. First I tried "immigration" and "language" and got 323 references. I took a look at the first few and realized I needed more focus. So I decided to use "Language policy—United States" as keywords. It worked when I was searching the library catalog, and it worked again. I got 30 references—many of which are relevant. And I also got abstracts of each article (Figure 16.8).

WinSPIRS 2.0

Usage is subject to the terms and conditions of the subscription and License Agreement and the applicable Copyright and intellectual property protection as dictated by the appropriate laws of your country and/or International Convention.

No.	Records	Request
1	20442	LANGUAGE
2	137013	POLICY
3	257170	THE
4	173538	UNITED
5	186668	STATES
*6	30	LANGUAGE POLICY AND THE UNITED STATES

Record 1 of 30 - PAIS International 1972-1/98
AN: 91-0301338
TI: The "official English" movement and the symbolic politics of language <u>in the United States.</u>
AU: Citrin,-Jack
SO: Western-Political-Quarterly; 43:535-59 S 1990
PY: 1990
NT: Analyzes the role of feelings of national identity in the debate over <u>language policy.</u>
DE: United-States-Languages; United-States-Nationalism; Bilingualism-United-States
LA: E; English
IS: 0043-4078
SF: bibl (s) table (s)
PT: P; Periodical

Record 2 of 30 - Social Work Abstracts 1977-9/97
AN: 21739
TI: Effects of the English-only movement on bilingual education.
AU: Edwards-R-L; Curiel-H
AD: Mandel School of Applied Social Sciences, Case Western Reserve Univ., Cleveland, OH 44106
SO: Social-Work-in-Education. 12(1): 53-66, Oct. 1989.
PY: 1989
HC: 26(1), 1990, No. 306
AB: In recent years, we have witnessed in this country the emergence of a new social movement, called the English-only movement, that advocates the adoption of legislation making English the official language of our land. This movement focuses much of its attention on efforts to eliminate bilingual education. A study provides an overview of the evolution of the English-only movement in the <u>United States,</u> with particular attention paid to the relationship between that movement and bilingual education. The history of official U.S. involvement with <u>language policy</u> is reviewed, and the potential impact of the legislative agenda of English-only proponents is considered.
DE: Bilingual-programs; Education-
CC: 3230 Education-Schools

FIGURE 16.8 **Abstracts from Sociofile**   *(continued)*

Record 3 of 30 - sociofile 1/74-12/97
TI: The Hispanophobia of the Official English Movement in the <u>United States;</u> La hisponofobia del movimiento "Ingles oficial" en los Estados Unidos por la oficializacion del ingles
AU: Zentella,-Ana-Celia; Sepulveda,-Sandra
IN: City U New York, NY 10021
JN: Alteridades; 1995, 5, 10, 55-65
IS: 0188-7017
CO: ALTEFL
NT: Translated from English by Sandra Sepulveda.
DT: aja Abstract-of-Journal-Article
LA: Spanish
CP: Mexico
PY: 1995
AB: Recent attempts in the US to introduce various laws on state & federal levels sanctioning exclusive use of English in public communication & efforts to amend the country's constitution by recognizing English as the only official language of the land are interpreted as hispanophobic, discriminatory, & racist. The social & political causes are sought, & the arguments behind these initiatives are refuted. After some episodes of linguistic intolerance are related, results of a questionnaire conducted in 1988 & 1994 (N = 417 & 320, respectively) are reported. Informants of different ethnic origins were asked their opinions regarding the bilingualism of 911 operators, bilingual ballots, education, & advertising & official status of English. Changes between 1988 & 1994 are discussed, & ethnic origin is identified as the dominant variable affecting attitudes. Adapted from the source document. (Copyright 1997, Sociological Abstracts, Inc., all rights reserved.)
DE: *<u>Language-Policy</u> (D445500) ; *Nativism- (D550200) ; *Bilingualism- (D079500) ; *Hispanic-Americans (D360600) ; *Racism- (D690000) ; *Xenophobia- (D935200) ; *Whites- (D919800) ; *Social-Attitudes (D780300) ; *English-Language (D261600)

FIGURE 16.8   *(continued)*

Government Publications

The U.S. government publishes massive amounts of information annually, largely through the Government Printing Office (GPO). Some of the most commonly used publications are these:

Congressional Quarterly Almanac. Published annually, includes overview of legislation and policy, as well as important speeches and debates and some analysis.

Congressional Quarterly Weekly Report. Weekly news updates on legislative and executive actions, includes overviews of policy debates.

FINDING A RESEARCH PATH

USING GOVERNMENT DOCUMENTS
Here is Amira's account of how she found government documents relevant to her research.

As I got deeper into my research, I realized that the English Only movement emerged as immigration to the United States increased after the immigration law changed in 1965. I wanted to get some statistics on the patterns of immigration—where people came from, how many new immigrants there are, where they settled. I remembered that one of the Web sites I had browsed when I was getting started included a link to the U.S. Immigration and Naturalization Service (INS) home page, so I decided to check it out (see Figure 16.9). I found it contained lots of the information I was looking for.

Statistical Abstract of the United States. Annual report of the Bureau of the Census, includes a range of social, economic, and political statistics, with tables, graphs, charts, and references to other sources.

Many government documents are now available online:

"Keeping America Informed." The homepage of the GPO, provides online access to many publications:

Library of Congress. Offers access to an enormous range of government and library resources:

"Thomas: Legislative Information on the Internet." Developed by the Library of Congress, includes databases on Congress, current bills, public laws, committee information, online version of the *Congressional Record*, and historical documents: and many government agencies have their own Web sites, such as Bureau of the Census and the IRS Digital Daily on tax matters from the Treasury Department <www.irs.ustreas.gov/basic/cover.html>

Posting a Query

One of the main differences between print and online research is that the Internet is interactive. Not only can you find books and articles but also groups of people on academic and professional listservs who are actively discussing the issues in their fields. You can extend your research by posting a query to one or more listservs. You should have a specific question in mind. Before you post your query, check whether the list maintains a FAQs to make sure that your question is not already answered.

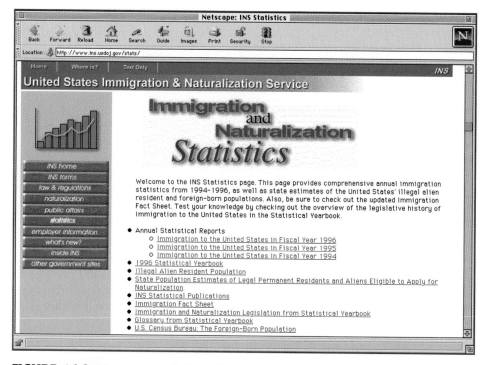

FIGURE 16.9 Homepage of the U.S. Immigration and Naturalization Service

FINDING A RESEARCH PATH

POSTING A QUERY

Amira decided she would check out listservs to see if there were ongoing discussions of language policy and English Only. One of the librarians showed her how to locate online discussion groups. Under the heading "languages and linguistics," Amira found a number of listservs, including Multi-L, maintained by the International Association of Applied Linguistics and devoted to "the exchange of information, news, and opinion about all aspects of minority language education."

Amira wrote a brief query, explaining her research project and requesting suggestions:

> Friends: I am an undergraduate doing research on the emergence of the English Only movement. One of the central claims of English Only supporters is that the United States needs an official language because many recent immigrants, especially Spanish speakers, resist learning English. Do you know of any studies that investigate the acquisition of English by immigrants? Any suggestions would be appreciated. A quick response would help me a lot. Thanks in advance.

Within a few days, Amira received six messages with information on recent studies of English acquisition, as well as notes of encouragement and further reading suggestions.

READING AND EVALUATING SOURCES

How you read depends on your purpose and where you are in the research process. As you have seen, preliminary research involves reading to develop a research question. At early stages in your research, you may well be doing a good deal of skimming just to get a sense of what the issues are.

Once you've decided on a research question and located sources, you can get down to the work of reading with a direction in mind. At this stage, you are probably reading to gather information and to understand what others have said about the question you're investigating.

As you read, you also need to start thinking about how you can use your sources in your research paper. It can be helpful to see the reading you do as part of planning your paper. Here are some of the ways researchers typically use source material in shaping research reports:

- To provide background information on the question

- To review previous research on the question

- To explain existing differences of analysis and interpretation of the question

- To offer supporting evidence for their position

- To present counterevidence that calls their position into question—evidence that must be accounted for

- To present opposing positions that require a response

Taking Notes

The way you take notes will depend on what you are reading and what use you might make of the material. For example, if it's fairly early on in your research, you may not be sure a particular source will be useful. In such cases, you can just write a short summary, noting what kinds of information the source contains. Later on, you can go back and take fuller notes if it makes sense to do so.

For material that provides background information, record the pertinent facts and data. In other cases, especially when you're reading about previous research or existing differences of interpretation, your notes should be more extensive. If your purpose is to answer an important question or solve a problem, you may want to indicate in your notes how the evidence you've turned up provides support for your interpretation or analysis. If you're planning to explain how your views relate to others' views or to argue a position where there are opposing views, make sure you summarize fully and fairly what others have said.

Perhaps the most important point to make about notes is that they need to be complete and accurate. You can avoid the last-minute hassle of running back to the library to check a fact or statistic by making sure you record it accurately in the first place. The same is true for quotations. Make sure you copy the writer's words exactly and that you put in quotation marks so you'll know where the quote begins and ends. And don't forget to note the number of the page on which the quotation appears.

People use different methods of taking notes. Some like note cards because they can arrange them according to the sections of their paper. Others worry that note cards will get lost and prefer to use spiral notebooks where they can keep all their notes in one place. Still others like to make photocopies to underline and annotate—and then quote or cite them directly. Finally, researchers are increasingly using computers to record and store notes. Computer programs can save you time by allowing you to search your notes for keywords and phrases and to cut and paste quotations.

Evaluating Sources

Evaluating sources is treated in detail in "Evaluating" in Chapter 2 and "Questions to Ask About Evidence" in Chapter 3. The following questions distill the main considerations you should take into account. Consult the relevant sections in Chapters 2 and 3 for a fuller discussion.

1. Does the source provide information that is relevant to your research question? Don't include a source just because it has interesting information or gives you another item for your Works Cited page.

2. Is the source up-to-date? Or, if it's an older source, is it acknowledged as important by recent writers in the field? After all, intellectual figures such as Darwin, Marx, Freud, and Max Weber are still important.

3. What credibility does the writer have? Is he or she recognized as an authority in the field?

4. What is the writer's point of view? What are his or her political or social allegiances? How do these allegiances influence what you have read?

5. Is the publication in which the source appears or the press that published it one of good reputation? What is its editorial slant?

Keeping an Open Mind

One of the main purposes of doing research is to learn new things and encounter new perspectives. It's helpful to imagine research not just as a matter of looking things up but of making new acquaintances and listening to what they have to say.

Research involves you in an ongoing conversation, and as in any conversation in which you participate, other speakers may well influence what you think and believe. Stay open to these influences. Don't let yourself get boxed in trying to prove something when the weight of the evidence runs against you. Be flexible. It's not unusual for researchers to modify their initial ideas in light of

FINDING A RESEARCH PATH

TAKING NOTES

Here are the notes Amira Patel took on an article she found in the *National Review*. Notice how she is careful first to record information and quotations fully and accurately from the article. Then she follows up with her own notes about how she might use this source and what further questions it raises for her research.

O'Beirne, Kate. "English as the Official Language of the U.S. and Bilingual Education." *National Review* 1 July 1996: 21.

Cites a number of opinion polls:
- In a 1996 Gallup poll, 82% favored making English the official language.
- A 1993 poll by the Tarrance Group found 78% of registered voters favored official-English laws, and over 60% favored it strongly.
- A 1993 poll by the San Francisco Chronicle found that 90% of Filipino, 78% of Chinese, and nearly 70% of Hispanic immigrants in California favored official English.

Gives details on the Republican Party position on official English and bilingual education, ballots, and health care. Argues that given popular support for official English and opposition to bilingualism, Republicans should take a stronger line.

Key quote:
"We must stop the practice of multilingual education as a means of instilling ethnic pride, or as a therapy for low self-esteem, or out of elitist guilt over a culture build on the traditions of the West." Bob Dole, in a speech to the American Legion.

Notes:
Check San Francisco Chronicle poll. I may need to explain such high support of official English among immigrant groups. My guess is it's a sign of the desire to assimilate and could be used to argue that official English is unnecessary.

English Only and bilingual education is caught up to some extent in party politics. But I'm not sure this helps explain it.

Quote from Dole may be useful in defining the English Only position.

what they find in their research. On the other hand, don't be bullied into abandoning your views. Just because someone you've read is an expert in the field doesn't necessarily mean that you should agree with his or her views or that you can't come up with persuasive alternative arguments.

A good way to keep an open mind during the process of research is to use exploratory writing periodically to reflect on what you've been reading. You might, for example, respond to the following questions to think about your research:

1. Given what you've read so far, what sources have made the strongest impression on you, whether you agree with them or not?

2. How have these and other sources influenced your thinking? Do you see your research question in the same way as when you started researching? What changes, if any, have occurred?

3. What new questions or perspectives have you encountered? How do you plan to deal with them?

PLANNING AND DRAFTING

There's always more to read, and it may seem that the research process could continue indefinitely. In certain respects, of course, this is true. Individuals have devoted their lives to research and never really reached the end of what they could learn. That's why deadlines are so useful—to remind writers that they need to emerge from the research process and start writing.

An important point here is that you need to make sure you're not using research to procrastinate and avoid writing. As already mentioned, when you're reading and evaluating your sources, you should also be making tentative plans about how to use these materials in your paper. Moreover, you can begin drafting well before you end your research. In fact, many researchers find that drafting helps them refine the focus of their research and directs them to issues they need to investigate further. To put it another way, you don't have to stop your research when you begin writing. But you do have to begin writing.

A CLOSING NOTE

As you can see from Amira Patel's sketch of her outline for her research paper on the English Only movement, she has listed topics and points of analysis that will be central to drafting her paper. Her task now is to begin writing so that she can see how the information and ideas from her research connect to each other.

You'll no doubt reach a similar point in your own research—when it's time to start writing. Remember that you know a lot by this point. You will have information, evidence, and arguments from others that may well not be widely available to your readers. So don't feel that just because you know something,

FINDING A RESEARCH PATH

MAKING AN OUTLINE

Once her research got into high gear, Amira Patel decided to sketch an outline of her paper. She realized that this was only a tentative plan, but it helped her see what kind of information and analysis she needed to start drafting.

Set up the issue of English Only
    background information on states with English Only laws
    public opinion polls
    emergence of U.S. English and English First
    present basic positions and arguments of English Only

State purpose of paper: to explain the emergence of English
    Only movement as "hispanophobia" resulting from new
    patterns of immigration and cultural anxiety

Historical background
    relation of language policy and nativism/Americanization
        Anti-Irish literacy requirements for voting (1850s)
        American Protective Association's campaign vs. German-language instruction
        in parochial schools (1880s)
        U.S. Bureau of Americanization (early 1900s)

    1965 Immigration Reform Act
        ended racial quotas
        "new immigration"
        demographic shifts[[emdash]]increase in Latino population

Analysis of English Only movement
    familiar sources of nativism
        economic stagnation (California)
        widening gap between rich and poor
        distrust of public institutions
        breakdown of community
    "hispanophobia" in California and the Southwest
        historical roots
        present manifestations
    explain focus on language as symbol of imagined lost community

everyone else must know it too. You're the authority who is immersed in the topic and issues of your research, and it's your job to explain how it all fits together. Keep in mind what your purpose is in writing your research paper: To what extent do you need to inform, explain, evaluate, or argue about the issues that have come up in your research? What sources are likely to persuade your readers to take your point of view seriously? How can you make the best use of what you've found in the research process?

In Chapter 18, you'll see how researchers incorporate the results of their research by paraphrasing, summarizing, and quoting.

CHAPTER SEVENTEEN

Field Research

Not all research is conducted in the library. In fact, the library may be just a starting point, providing you with an overview of your topic and the background information you need in order to undertake field research. Field research includes making observations, conducting interviews, using questionnaires, attending performances, and watching the media. In fact, researchers often combine two or more of these methods in a research project.

Researchers turn to these methods of inquiry when they have questions that can't be addressed solely on the basis of print or electronic sources. Here are some research questions that call for fieldwork:

- To determine whether a shopping mall in the area should enforce a curfew for teenagers, you observe the mall on weekend nights to see what danger or nuisance, if any, teenagers pose.

- To compare the personal experiences of Vietnam veterans to historians' accounts of the war, a student in an American history course decides to locate and interview five vets.

- To find out how much the undergraduates at their college drink each week, a group of students designs and administers an anonymous questionnaire.

- To write a paper in a literature course on the popularity of Poetry Slams, you attend a number of performances.

- To research the plots of soap operas, the role of the audience in daytime talk TV, or the films of Martin Scorsese, you spend a good deal of time watching footage.

As you can see from these examples, the kind of field research you do and how extensive it will be depend on the questions with which you begin, as well

ETHICS OF FIELDWORK

Researchers confront a number of ethical issues about their relationship to the people they are studying. Within the world of social science research, for example, there is considerable debate about how much researchers should tell participants about the study being conducted. Some argue that participants should know only the bare minimum about the study (such as that the researcher is interested in "the environment"). These social scientists assert that if participants know more about the study, the results are likely to be influenced or biased. Others, however, believe participants should know as much as possible (such as that the researcher is interested in "the differences between middle-class men and women in their attitudes toward the environment"). These researchers argue on ethical grounds that the fieldworker should explain the study as well as what will be done with the results.

There is also a debate about how much researchers should tell study participants about themselves. Some argue that fieldworkers should not be friends with participants or disclose personal information. They believe that clear lines between researchers and participants are needed to avoid complicating their relationship and potentially compromising results. Others, however, think the line between researcher and participants can be more fluid. They believe that revealing personal information and developing friendships with participants can strengthen results by giving researchers greater access to people's lives.

Researchers need to decide these issues for themselves. In some instances, researchers also need to have their fieldwork approved by Institutional Review Boards (IRBs), which research institutions such as universities and hospitals have created to oversee the risks to participants and the ethics involved in research design.

as the amount of time you have. Field research can be time-consuming, but it can also give you information and insights that you could not get in any other way.

In this chapter, we'll look at how researchers work in the field and three common methods they use—observation, interviews, and surveys. Then we'll look briefly at how to use performances, museums, and the media for research.

OBSERVATION

Observation has an important advantage over other research methods: It gives you direct access to people's behavior. Let's say you've done some background research on how men and women interact in conversations, and you want to test some of the findings in the published literature. You might decide to see whether students at your college follow the pattern described by Deborah Tannen in *You Just Don't Understand*—that men interrupt more during conversations and are less likely than women to use questions to elicit comments from others. Interviewing or surveying wouldn't give you very reliable information, because even if people were willing to be honest about how they behave in conversations, it's not likely that they could be accurate. In contrast, by going to the school dining hall over a period of several days, you could observe what men and women in fact do when they talk and what conversational patterns emerge.

The Process of Observation

Planning

The following questions can help guide your planning. You can use them to write a proposal that explains the role of observation in your research plan (see box below).

1. Why does the line of research you're pursuing call for observation? What research question or questions are you addressing?
2. How exactly can observations help you answer your research question?
3. What kinds of observations would be most useful? Who and what do you want to observe? What are the best times and places for these observations? How many observations should you do?
4. What should your observations focus on? What exactly do you want to record in your field notes? What method or methods will you use to record your observations?

You may need to request permission to observe, as well as permission to use any recording devices.

Conducting Observations

When you arrive at the place where you'll do your observation, look for a vantage point where you will be able to see what's going on and yet won't be obtrusive. Consider whether you want to move periodically from one spot to another to get a number of different perspectives on the activity or place you're observing. Make sure any equipment you've brought—camera or tape recorder—is ready to use.

WRITING PROPOSALS FOR FIELD RESEARCH

No matter what field-research method you're considering, writing a proposal can help you develop your research design. A proposal should explain:

- The main question or questions you're trying to answer
- Why the particular method you're planning to use is an appropriate research strategy for answering the question or questions
- How you plan to conduct the research
- What you think the results might be

Researchers typically develop their own system of taking field notes. Nonetheless, a few suggestions may be helpful. Begin by writing down the basic facts—the date, time, and place. Keep your notes on one side of the page. Depending on your research questions, here are some things to consider:

- **The setting:** Describe the overall size, shape, and layout. You may want to sketch it or draw a diagram. Note details—both what they are and how they are arranged. Pay attention to sounds and smells, as well as to what you can see.

- **The people:** Note the number of people. What are they doing? Describe their activities, movement, and behavior. What are they wearing? Note ages, race, nationality, and gender. How do they relate to one another? Record overheard conversation using quotation marks.

- **Your response:** As you observe, note anything that is surprising, puzzling, or unusual. Note also your own feelings and reactions, as well as any new ideas or questions that arise.

THREE CONSIDERATIONS TO TAKE INTO ACCOUNT WHEN YOU DO OBSERVATIONS

1. Recognize that you'll be observing a limited group and making a limited number of observations. Your findings may confirm or dispute what you've read, or they may suggest new questions and lines of research. Be aware, however, that while your results are valid for the group you observed, the group itself may not be representative of all the students at your college, not to mention all men and women. So when you generalize on the basis of your observations, acknowledge the scope of your research to ensure the claims you make, take these limits into account.

2. Take into account, too, the fact that your presence can have an effect on what you observe. People sometimes behave differently when they know they're being watched. They may clown around, try to make themselves look good, or otherwise act in relation to the observer. The best way to deal with this fact is to conduct multiple observations. In many cases, people being observed will get used to the presence of the observer over time.

3. Finally, be aware of the assumptions you bring to the observations—both when you are conducting the research and when you are analyzing the results. All researchers, of course, operate from a point of view, so there's no reason to think you can be a neutral bystander just recording what happens. For this reason, however, there is a very real danger that you will record in your observations only what you expected to see. Observers' assumptions can cause them to miss, ignore, or suppress important events. Being conscious of your own assumptions can help keep you open to things you had not anticipated.

Analyzing Your Notes

After you've finished your observation, read through your notes carefully and, if you want, type them up, adding related points that you remember. Then make sure you analyze your notes from the standpoint of your research questions:

1. What patterns emerge from your notes? What are your main findings? What, if anything, surprised you?

2. What research questions do your notes address? What issues remain to be addressed?

3. Do your observations confirm what you have read? How would you explain any discrepancies?

4. What should your next step be? Should you go back to the library? Should you conduct further observations? If further observations are needed, what form should they take?

FIELDWORK PRACTICE

After getting their permission, observe the dinnertime conversation and interaction of your family or a group of friends, taking notes of your observations. When you are finished, read through your notes, considering what they reveal about the patterns of interaction you observed. Then answer the following questions:

1. Do you think your presence as an observer had an effect on what people said and did?

2. How difficult is it to observe and keep notes? What, if anything, could you do to make the process easier?

3. What did you expect to happen at dinner? How did these assumptions influence your observations? Were some things you observed unexpected? Do you think your assumptions caused you to miss anything? Were there certain things you chose not to include in your notes? Why?

4. What tentative conclusions do you think are legitimate to draw from your observations?

WORKING TOGETHER

Evaluating Documentaries

Many documentary films and television shows are based on observation. These include National Geographic shows on animals in the wild; investigative reporting on *60 Minutes, 20/20,* and other news programs; and films such as Frederick Wiseman's acclaimed documentaries (*Titicut Follies, High School,* and others), *Don't Look Back* (on Bob Dylan), *Hoop Dreams,* and *Streetwise.* Locate a documentary television show or film that makes use of information obtained through observation. Work with two or three other students. Watch the documentary. Then see if you can reach a consensus on the following questions, even if the only consensus is to agree to disagree:

1. What kinds of information were obtained through observation? What procedures did the film- or videomaker use? What is the film- or videomaker's relationship to the subject of the documentary?

2. Describe what you see as the purpose of the documentary. How do the filmed observations relate to these purposes? What is their effect on you as a viewer?

3. Evaluate the selection of observations presented in the documentary. Why do you think the film- or videomaker chose what is shown in the documentary? What, if anything, seems to be left out? Do you think the film- or videomaker has made reasonable decisions concerning selection? Explain why or why not.

INTERVIEWS

As you saw in Chapter 7, "Profiles," interviews are often an essential part of capturing the personality and opinions of the person being profiled. Interviews, of course, are not limited to profiles; they have a range of uses. Here are three common situations in which researchers can make good use of interviews.

- **Interviews with experts:** Interviewing an expert on anorexia, the 1930s jazz scene in Kansas City, the current status of the cod fishing industry, or virtually any topic you're researching can provide you with up-to-date information and analysis, as well as a deepened understanding of the issues involved in these topics—and can make a significant contribution to a research project. In such cases, interviewing an expert offers a source of information that supplements print or electronic sources.

- **Interviews with key participants:** Interviews can do more than just supplement your research. In some cases, interviewing takes on a central role in a research project, especially in research on contemporary issues where it makes sense to talk to the people involved. Suppose you are planning to research the role of public libraries in relation to recent immigrants. You would certainly want to see what's been written about the topic, but you could also interview librarians at neighborhood branches who work with, say, Russian Jews, Southeast Asians, Haitians, or Latinos. In turn, these interviews could lead to further interviews with recent immigrants, as well as community organizations, to get their perspective on what libraries are doing and might do. The research paper you write will quite likely feature prominently the information you've gathered from these interviews as the main source of data, with print and electronic sources providing background and context for your research.

■ **Oral histories:** Interviews with people who participated in significant historical events can provide a useful focus for research. To understand the event from the perspective of a rank-and-file worker, you might interview a trade unionist who participated in a significant strike. Or to understand the origins of the New Right on college campuses in the early 1960s, you might interview someone who was involved in the founding of Young Americans for Freedom. To understand the Dust Bowl and Great Depression, you could interview your grandmother about her experience migrating from Oklahoma to California in the 1930s. Interviews such as these are often called oral histories because they are the spoken accounts of important historical moments based on people's memories of their lived experience. For this type of research, you need, of course, to look at what historians have said—both to generate questions before the interview and to relate the oral history to professional accounts after the interview as part of the written presentation of your research.

As you can see, the type of interviewing you do depends largely on the kind of research question you're raising and the sources it leads you to.

The Interview Process

Planning

The following considerations can help you get started on planning interviews. You can use these considerations to write a proposal that explains how the interviews fit into your research design (see the box in this chapter, "Writing Proposals for Field Research").

■ **Background research:** The first step, as in any research, is to get an overview and basic information about your topic. At this point, you are likely to be formulating questions to guide your research. Consider how interviewing can help you answer these questions. What do you hope to find out?

■ **Choosing interview subjects:** The nature of your research question should suggest appropriate subjects to interview. Does it make sense to interview an expert on the topic? Or does your research seem to call for interviews with people involved in the subject you're investigating? Are the people you're considering likely to provide the information you're looking for?

■ **Preparing interview questions.** Use the notes from your background research to prepare interview questions. Interviewers normally use open questions to get their subjects talking—phrasing questions so that the natural answer is a yes or a no generally leads to a dead end. How open, of course, depends on your research question and your subject. If you are interviewing an expert, your questions should be precise and seek specific information ("Estimates vary on the number of cod in the North Atlantic. Can you give me your view?"). For oral histories, on the other hand, questions often begin at a general level ("Tell me what it was like growing up in Oklahoma") but become more specific ("Do you recall when and why your family decided to migrate to California?"). When you have come up with a list of questions, organize them so that one question leads logically to the next.

■ **Considering the types of interviews**: The in-person, face-to-face interview is probably the best-known type of interview, but there are alternatives you may want or need to consider. The box summarizes four possibilities, their advantages and disadvantages.

Setting Up the Interview

Whether the person you plan to interview is a stranger, a friend, or a relative, you'll need to set up the interview. Generally this means writing a letter or making a telephone call, both to ask for permission and to set a time (or a deadline in the case of an interview by mail). Introduce yourself and your purpose. Be honest about what you are doing—many busy people are happy to help students with assignments. However, be prepared to be turned down. Sometimes busy people are just that—busy. If someone seems too busy to meet with you in person, ask whether you could interview him by telephone, mail, or e-mail—or whether he knows someone else you could interview. Above all, be polite. Be sure to schedule the interview far enough in advance of your due date to allow you to follow up with more questions or with further research if the interview leads to areas you had not previously considered. For in-person or telephone interviews that you want to record, ask at this point for permission to record. And, if it's appropriate, ask the person you're interviewing if there is anything you should read before the interview.

Conducting an In-Person or Telephone Interview

For in-person and telephone interviews, the interview itself is a crucial moment in your research. To get an in-person interview off on the right foot, arrive promptly. Make sure that you dress appropriately and that you bring your questions, tape recorder (if you have permission to record the interview), a pad and pens, and any other materials you might need. For telephone interviews, make sure you call at the time agreed upon.

Because in-person and telephone interviews are really conversations, the results you get will depend in part on your flexibility as a listener and a questioner. The person you're interviewing will be looking to you for guidance, and it is quite likely that you'll be faced with choices during the interview. Let's say you are interviewing someone about why she attends your college. She says, "I

FOUR TYPES OF INTERVIEWS

- **In-person interviews:** In-person interviews have some significant advantages over the other types. Often, when answering your question, the person you are interviewing may take the conversation in a new direction. Although at times this means you'll need to guide the conversation politely back to your topic, sometimes the new direction is one that you hadn't thought of and would like to explore. At other times you may realize that your questions aren't working and that to get the information you need, you'll have to revise and supplement them on the spur of the moment. But often, in-person interviews take on a life of their own—the person you are interviewing starts talking, and all you have to do is sit back and listen.

  Some researchers prefer to take handwritten notes during in-person interviews. Doing so, however, poses certain difficulties. Responses to your questions may be long, and you may not be able to write fast enough. And devoting all your attention to note taking makes it harder to think about what the person is saying and harder to guide the interview by choosing the next question or formulating a new one. For these reasons, many researchers use a tape recorder. But be flexible about using one. Most people don't mind, and the tape recorder will simply fade into the background. But some people are bothered by it and might not be as open as they would be if you took notes. If you feel the disadvantages of tape recording are outweighing the advantages, be prepared to change methods.

- **Telephone interviews:** Telephone interviews are similar to in-person interviews. Both enable you to be flexible in your questioning. Some people may feel telephone interviews a bit more difficult to manage because rapport may not emerge as easily as in an in-person interview. Others, though, find them liberating, as they don't have to deal with the added variables of the interview setting.

  A speakerphone is useful if you've been given permission to record the conversation. Even if you haven't, a speakerphone makes it easier for you to take notes.

- **Mail and e-mail interviews:** Sometimes you might prefer or may have to conduct your interview by mail or e-mail. You might, for example, want to interview someone who isn't willing or able to schedule an in-person or telephone interview but who has no objection to answering questions. One advantage of mail or e-mail interviews is that they provide you with a written record. Unlike in-person or telephone interviews, there's nothing that needs to be transcribed or that could be forgotten. On the other hand, it may be difficult to follow up on interesting ideas or to clarify points. Phrasing and organization of questions are especially crucial in mail or e-mail interviews because you can't adjust your line of questioning as you can in an in-person or telephone interview.

  If possible, use e-mail rather than traditional mail. With e-mail the process is considerably quicker. Moreover, with e-mail you can easily quote and respond to messages so that there is some conversational give and take.

- **On-line interviews:** Interviews can also be conducted online. Real-time synchronous communication sites, such as IRCs (Internet Relay Chat), MUDs (Multi User Domains), and MOOs (MUD Object Oriented), allow computer users from around
  (continued)

the world to "talk" to each other in writing in real time. Online interviews are especially useful if you're researching a topic related to cyberspace. For example, if you're writing about Internet censorship or the growing commercialization of the Web, you'll find many people online who are knowledgeable about this issue (though, for balance, you'd also want to get offline views as well).

Like mail and e-mail interviews, online interviews can help simplify note taking by recording the conversations. Make sure, however, that you are familiar with the technology necessary to record the interview—you don't want to lose all of your hard work.

came because they've got a really good computer science program, I got a good financial aid package, and I didn't want to go very far from home. You know what I mean?" Then she pauses, looking at you for direction. You've got a choice to make about which thread to follow—the student's academic interests, her financial situation, or her desire to stay near home.

After the Interview

Especially with in-person and telephone interviews, plan time immediately afterward to review the results of the interview and to make further notes. Transcribe your tape, if you recorded the interview, or print out hard copies of e-mail or on-line interviews. Make sure that you've noted direct quotations and that you've written down pertinent information about the interview (such as the time, date, and location).

Analyzing the Transcript

Material from an interview can be used in many different ways in a research project. It can be central to the final report or can provide supplementary quotations and statistics. The ideas you had ahead of time about how you would use the interview might be changed by the interview or by other aspects of your research process. To help you understand what use to make of the interview, write responses to these questions:

1. What are the most important things you learned? List what seem to be the main points.

2. What, if anything, surprised you? Why?

3. What does the interview contribute to your understanding of your research question? How does the information relate to what you've already learned about your topic? If information, opinion, or point of view differ, how do you account for this?

4. What questions does the interview raise for further research? What sources does it suggest you use?

A Final Note on Interviews

Be sure to thank the people you interview. (A note or e-mail message is a nice touch.) And, when you've finished your paper, send them a copy along with a letter or e-mail thanking them again.

FIELDWORK PRACTICE

Work with a partner. Interview him about why he decided to attend your college. Before the interview, think about the questions you want to ask, how you want to conduct the interview—in person, by telephone, on-line, or via e-mail—and how you want to keep track of what's said. Write a paragraph or two about the interview experience. What sorts of questions were most effective? Did any ideas and topics come up that you had not expected? What decisions did you make during the interview about threads to follow in the conversation? What were the advantages and disadvantages of the interview method you chose? What problems did you experience in recording information?

Compare your response to the interview process with those of classmates. What generalizations can you, as a class, draw about interviewing?

WORKING TOGETHER

Evaluating an Interview

Working with two or three other students, locate a print or televised interview. If it's in print, make sure it follows a question-and-answer format. (Weekly newsmagazines such as *Time* and *Newsweek* frequently feature question-and-answer interviews.) If it's televised, make sure it's an extended interview, such as those on *Oprah* or the *Larry King Show,* and not just a sound bite. Read or watch the interview. Then answer the following questions:

1. Why do you think the person interviewed was chosen? What makes the interview significant to readers or viewers?

2. Consider the interviewer's questioning strategy. What does he or she want to find out? Do the questions seem well-designed to provide this information? Do they follow a logical order?

3. What decisions does the interviewer seem to make during the course of the interview? What threads does the interviewer pursue along the way? Are there threads the interviewer seems to ignore?

4. How does the person interviewed respond? Is she more willing to talk about some questions than others? Does she dodge some topics? What does the interviewer do in such a case?

5. Do you think the interview is successful? If so, on what terms and for whom—the interviewer, the person interviewed, or both? If the interview seems less than a success, why do you think this is so and who is at fault—the interviewer or the person interviewed?

SURVEYS

Surveys are similar to interviews, except that they obtain responses from a sizeable group of people rather than from just a limited number. Surveys can target a particular group of people—to find out, for example, why students at your college have chosen to major in biomedical engineering, or why employees at a particular company do or don't participate in community service activities. Or they can examine the beliefs and opinions of the "general public," as is the case with those conducted by political pollsters and market researchers on everything from people's sexual habits to their religious beliefs to their product preferences.

While interview questions are generally open, surveys tend to use more "closed-ended" questions, such as true/false, yes/no, checklists, ranking, and preference scales. In this sense, they sacrifice the depth of information to be gotten about one person for the breadth of data about many people.

Deciding whether you should design and distribute a survey depends largely on what you're trying to find out. If, for example, you've read some research on the television viewing habits of college students and want to find out if students at your school fit the patterns described, it makes sense to survey many students about their habits rather than to interview three or four. The results you get are liable to give you a more accurate picture.

The Process of Designing and Conducting a Survey

If a survey seems appropriate to your research project, you'll need to decide whom you will survey, prepare a questionnaire, conduct your survey, and then compile and analyze the results. It can help to write a proposal that explains why a survey is an appropriate strategy for your research project (see the box in this chapter, "Writing Proposals for Field Research").

Getting Background Information

Designing a survey is similar to designing an interview. Namely, you'll begin by researching your topic to get an overview and background information. Then you'll determine whether a survey is the most appropriate method for addressing your research question: Does it make sense to gather information on the opinions and habits of a number of people instead of talking to a few in depth or doing another form of research? At this point, before you expend the time and effort it takes to design and conduct a survey, make sure that a survey is likely to provide you with the information you're seeking.

Selecting Participants

To be sure that they can generalize from the results of their surveys, professional researchers try to obtain responses from a representative sample of the population they're investigating. If, for example, you're surveying employees of a company or students who major in bioengineering, it should be easy enough to send questionnaires to all of them. In other cases, however, you may need to choose people within the population at random.

For example, if you're studying the students' opinions of a first-year writing program, you could get a random sample by surveying every tenth person on the class lists. But even in that case, make sure that your responses are representative of the actual population in the classes and reflect their demographic composition. You may need to modify the distribution of your survey to guarantee it reaches a representative sample—men, women, blacks, whites, Latinos, Asians.

If your results are to be meaningful, you'll also need to include enough participants in your survey to give it credibility. Keep in mind that regardless of how you conduct your survey, not everyone will participate. In fact, as pollsters are well aware, it's generally necessary to survey many more people than you expect to receive responses from. Often as few as 10 percent of the surveys mailed out will be returned. A good rule of thumb is to aim for 40 percent and, if you don't get it the first time, do multiple distributions.

When you write up your findings, any generalizations based on your survey should be limited to the population your survey represents (you should not, for example, generalize about American voters as a whole based on a survey of students at your college). Be sure to discuss any potentially relevant information on survey participants, such as information on age, gender, or occupation.

Designing the Survey

The results of your survey will depend to a large extent on the questions you ask. Here are some considerations to take into account in designing a survey:

1. Include a short introduction that explains the purpose of the survey and what you will do with the results. Point out that survey participants' opinions are important. Ask them to complete the survey, and give them an estimate of the time it will take to do so.

2. Make sure the questions you ask are focused on the information you need for your research. It's tempting to ask all sorts of things you're curious about. The results can be interesting, to be sure, but asking more questions than you actually need can reduce your response rate. In general, keep the survey brief in order to maximize returns.

3. Design the survey so that it is easy to read. The visual design should suggest that it won't take long to fill out. Don't crowd questions together to save space. And leave plenty of space for open questions, reminding survey respondents that they can write on the back.

4. At the end of the survey, write a thank-you and explain where or to whom the survey should be returned.

Types of Questions

Questions can take the form of checklists, yes/no questions, categories, ranking scales, and open questions. Each type of question works somewhat differently from the others. Usually you will want to combine several types to give you the particular information you need. You will also need to consider the most effective and logical order to present the questions. Surveys typically begin with the least complicated or most general questions and end with open-ended questions.

Here are examples of the most common types of questions designed for a research project investigating whether the political attitudes and involvement of students at the researcher's college support or refute claims in the published literature that students today are generally apathetic when it comes to politics.

Checklist

Which of these political activities have you participated in? Please check all that apply.

_____ voted in national election
_____ voted in state or local election
_____ campaigned for a candidate
_____ worked for a political party
_____ attended a political rally or demonstration
_____ belonged to a political organization or advocacy group
_____ other (specify): _____

Yes/No Questions

Are you a registered voter?

_____ Yes
_____ No

Categories

How would you describe your political views?

_____ left-wing
_____ liberal
_____ moderate
_____ conservative
_____ right-wing
_____ none of the above/don't know

Ranking Scales

Please rank the following items according to their importance as national priorities. (Use 1 for the highest priority, 7 for the lowest.)

_____ strengthening the economy
_____ reducing crime
_____ balancing the budget

_____ improving education
_____ improving the health care system
_____ improving race relations
_____ reducing poverty

Lickert Scale

[Lickert scale questionnaire items gauge the degree of agreement with particular statements of opinion. Researchers typically design a sequence of such items.]

Please indicate the degree to which you agree or disagree with the following statements. Enter the number that best expresses your view on each item.

1—Strongly agree
2—Agree
3—Not Sure
4—Disagree
5—Strongly Disagree

_____ It is important to be well-informed about current political events.
_____ There's no point in getting involved in politics because individuals can have little influence.
_____ Voting in elections is a responsibility, not just a right.
_____ The political system is controlled by politicians and lobbyists.

Open-Ended Questions

[Open-ended questions call for brief responses. Such questions are more time-consuming and difficult to tabulate than closed questions, but they can often yield information that other types of questions will not.]

What, if anything, has motivated you to be interested in political affairs?

_____

_____

_____

What, if anything, has posed obstacles to your being interested in political affairs?

_____

_____

_____

After you've prepared your questionnaire, try it out on a few people. Do their answers tell you what you wanted to know? Based on these answers, have you covered all the issues and have you phrased your questions well? If you see any problems, revise your questionnaire. Now is the time to get it right—before you administer it to a lot of people.

Conducting the Survey

Your survey can be distributed in various ways—in person, by mail, by telephone, or online through listservs, newsgroups, or Web sites. Your choice of how to conduct the survey will depend on your choice of a sample population, on your deadline, and on your resources (mail surveys, for example, can be quite expensive because you'll need to provide stamped self-addressed envelopes).

Compiling, Analyzing, and Presenting Results

Compiling results amounts to tallying up the answers to each question. This is a fairly straightforward procedure for closed questions such as checklist, yes/no, multiple-choice, and ranking and Lickert scale items. For open questions, you might write down key words or phrases that emerge in the responses and tally the number of times these (or similar) words or phrases occur. Keep a list of answers that seem of special interest to use in your research report as quotations.

Researchers present the results of closed questions in the form of percentages in the text of their reports. In addition, you may want to design tables or other visual displays of your results to complement the written report.

Remember that your results do not speak for themselves. You need to analyze and explain how they are significant to your research project. The following questions can help you begin such an analysis:

1. What patterns emerge from responses to individual questions? What patterns emerge from responses across questions?

2. How would you explain these patterns? Try to think of two or more explanations, even if they appear to be contradictory or mutually exclusive.

3. What is the significance of these explanations for your research? If the explanations seem contradictory, can you think of ways to reconcile them? If not, on what grounds would you choose one or the other?

4. What tentative claims might you make based on your analysis of the results? How would you justify such claims?

FIELDWORK PRACTICE

Work together in a group of three or four. Your task is to design a pilot survey to determine student opinion about some aspect of the academic program or student services at your college. You could focus on, say, advising, orientation for new students, required first-year courses, tutoring, or anything else that interests you. Begin by listing the kind of information that you want to get from the survey. Then write five to ten questions that seem likely to give you this

ETHICS OF RESEARCH

LOADED QUESTIONS

Public opinion polls are a fixture in American politics. Most political candidates, the two major political parties, and many other political organizations and advocacy groups use opinion polls to understand the public's mood and to shape policy. In fact, at times political polls can go beyond simply providing information that will play an active role in the formation of public policy. In political debates, the results of opinion polls are often used to buttress the position of one side or the other. Because opinion polls have become such an important part of political life, there is the temptation to use them in a partisan way.

Take, for example, a poll conducted by advocates of casino gambling in Rhode Island to determine the degree of public support. The main question in the poll—"Would you approve a casino if it would reduce your property taxes and improve education?"—is clearly a loaded one because it stacks the deck with casino proponents' arguments. As political pollster Darrell West noted, the "corollary question from an anti-gambling perspective" might read, "Would you support a casino if you thought it would raise crime rates and increase the level of gambling addiction?"

Not surprisingly, a majority of people polled favored casino gambling when the question was framed in terms of casino revenues reducing taxes and improving education. However, when the question was posed in an unbiased way—"Do you favor or oppose the construction of a gambling casino?"—the results were quite different. Fifty-three percent opposed the casino, 42 percent supported it, and 5 percent had no opinion.

information. Test your survey by administering it to ten to fifteen classmates. Once you've gotten their responses, evaluate your survey:

1. Did you get the information you were looking for?
2. Is each of the questions worded in such a way that it provides the information you anticipated?
3. Should you word any of the questions differently to obtain the information you're seeking? Should you delete any of the questions or add new ones?
4. Explain your answers.
5. Compare your group's experience to that of other groups. What conclusions can you draw about survey design?

PERFORMANCES, MUSEUMS, AND THE MEDIA

Attending performances such as lectures, seminars, readings, plays, and concerts; visiting museums; and watching films, videos, and television or listening to the radio and recorded music can all be important forms of research. Depending on the nature of your research, these activities can provide information and perspectives to supplement your work with print and electronic sources. Or they can be the main focus of your research. This section briefly explains what performances, museums, and the media offer to researchers.

Performances

Your college may sponsor lectures, readings, or seminars that bring noted speakers to campus. Attending such events can provide you with information that you couldn't find elsewhere and give you the opportunity to question the speaker. In addition, college or local theaters and music and dance companies may stage plays and concerts related to your research. Attending such live performances can deepen your understanding, say, of a Shakespeare play, a Verdi opera, or a style of jazz, folk, or popular music—and offer a useful supplement to reading about the topic or listening to recordings. In all these instances, taking notes is probably the most appropriate research strategy.

On the other hand, performances may themselves provide the focus for your research. You might, for example, want to research what takes place at a Metallica concert or a poetry reading in a local bookstore. In cases such as these, you'll likely draw on observation and perhaps interviews, as well as reading pertinent sources or listening to recordings.

Museums

Visiting art, science, natural history, and history museums can provide you with a wealth of information to enhance your research. Depending on your topic, you can see in person paintings, sculpture, or photographs pertinent to your research; artifacts and displays from a historical period you're investigating; or scientific exhibits. Some museums, as well as historical societies, have special collections and archives that offer research sources unavailable elsewhere. Again, note taking is probably the research strategy you'll use.

Museums can also be the focus of a research project. Museum studies is a relatively new field that covers the subject of who visits museums, why, and what they do. By reading some of the literature in this field, you can frame questions to answer with field research methods—observation, interviews, and questionnaires.

Media

As you're probably aware, documentary films, television and radio programs, and music and spoken-word recordings can be good sources of information to add to the print and electronic sources you're using. Research in such cases is likely to be a matter of taking notes.

At the same time, films, television, radio, or recorded music can also be valuable sources for studying the media and mass communication. For example, if you want to investigate the issue of violence in children's television shows, you may want to watch a variety of children's programs in order to count the incidences of violence and identify the types of violence depicted. Or you could analyze television commercials to see how men and women are depicted and what, if any, gender stereotypes are perpetuated. In this type of research, it can be quite helpful to tape television or radio programs so that you can return to them in the course of your inquiry.

FIELDWORK PRACTICE

Working together with two or three classmates, think of three research questions that investigate some aspect of the media—film, television, radio, or music. What sources would you use to answer each question? What information would they offer? How easy or difficult would it be to gain access to these sources? After you've answered these questions, evaluate the original three research questions. Are they all equally feasible or does one or more seem to offer a better option for research? Explain your answer.

PART FIVE

Presenting Your Work

INTRODUCTION:
COMMUNICATING WITH YOUR READERS

The struggle to get your ideas down on paper may make manuscript preparation and document design seem like an afterthought, something you attend to after the real work of drafting is done. Finishing a writing task, however, involves more than just printing out what you've written. Written texts, after all, do not transmit thoughts directly from the writer's mind to the reader's. Like other forms of communication (telephone, radio, television, or film), writing uses particular media such as the printed page and the computer screen to record and transmit messages. Looked at in this way, manuscript preparation and document design become central to the activity of writing: They call attention to the material form and visual appearance writing takes on to present your ideas to readers.

There are three main reasons to learn more about manuscript preparation and visual design:

■ **To establish credibility with your readers:** The reader's first impression of your writing is likely to be influenced by its visual appearance. A sloppy manuscript, a research paper that doesn't use the proper conventions of citation, or a lab report that fails to present the standard pattern of organization will raise doubts in the reader's mind about the credibility of the person who prepared it. Obviously this can undermine the rhetorical effectiveness of the writing, no matter how interesting or insightful the contents may be. To put it another way, manuscript preparation and document design are means of establishing the writer's ethos—of presenting the writer as a credible and authoritative person.

■ **To enhance readability:** One of the marks of effective writing is that readers find it easy to follow. When they don't have to struggle to read the written text, they can concentrate on what the writer is trying to say and they will be more likely to give your ideas a fair hearing. As you've seen throughout this book, writers strive in various ways to emphasize main points and connect them to supporting evidence. There are many visual resources writers can draw on that cue readers to the important information and line of reasoning in a written text—everything from paragraph breaks to bulleted lists to section headings to graphic display of facts and data. Learning how to use these visual resources is an important way to enhance readability.

■ **To assist you in planning and drafting:** Think of writing not just as getting ideas down on paper but as designing the visual appearance of a manuscript or document. This can, in many writing tasks, actually help you plan and draft. Many of the genres you've studied in this book—fund-raising letters, certain public documents, various types of reports, proposals for grant funding—use standard forms or variations of them. Each of these genres—as well as memos, resumés, newsletters, flyers, and brochures—have a typical "look" on the page. Not only does the look of the page enable readers to identify easily what they are reading but the visual appearance of these forms of writing also provides a kind of scaffolding that can help writers organize their material.

As you have seen, there have already been discussions of the visual appearance of written texts at various points in this book—particularly in the treatment of some of the genres and the "Visual Design" readings in Part Two. In the following chapters, you'll find more information on how to prepare manuscripts and design documents. Chapter 18, "Research Papers," explains how to present the results of research based on the guidelines of the Modern Language Association (MLA) and the American Psychological Association (APA). Chapter 19, "Visual Design," explores some of the purposes of visual communication and offers suggestions about such familiar documents as flyers, newsletters, brochures, and Web sites. Chapter 20, "Essay Exams," offers suggestions about how you can most effectively present your work when you are writing under pressure. Chapter 21, "Writing Portfolios," shows how you can design a portfolio of writing that presents and comments on the work you have done in your writing course.

CHAPTER EIGHTEEN

Research Projects: Using MLA and APA Styles

As a college student, you are likely to be called on in some of your courses to do research and present the results in written form. The research papers you're asked to write may be short ones that rely on only a few sources, or they may be longer term papers based on much more extensive research. In either case, your task as a writer is to present your research by integrating the sources of information, analysis, and argument you've found into a paper of your own design. This chapter explains how to integrate your research materials and how to cite your sources appropriately.

Most documentation systems use in-text citations with a list of works cited at the end of a paper. There are two main styles of citation in academic research:

- **Modern Language Association (MLA) style,** which uses an author- and page-number system common to the arts and humanities.

- **American Psychological Association (APA) style,** which uses an author- and-year system common to the social and natural sciences.

Check with your instructor if you're not certain about which style to use or whether you should use another system.

This chapter presents information on how to integrate your source material into a research paper and on the basic features of MLA and APA.

USING SOURCES IN ACADEMIC WRITING

Academic writing does more than simply present the results of research. More important, it shows how the writer's research grows out of issues and problems in a particular field of study, and explains the significance of the research to this ongoing discussion. Integrating and citing sources in a research paper lets your readers know how your work fits into a larger conversation.

584

Students sometimes think that using sources weakens their writing—that readers will think the important ideas in a paper come from others instead of from them. In college, however, readers expect writers to use and acknowledge sources. Readers want to understand what others have said about the issue you've researched, who has influenced your thinking, and how you stand in relation to the analyses, interpretations, and arguments others have offered.

Plagiarism and the Ethics of Acknowledging Your Sources

The purpose of acknowledging your sources is to provide readers with the grounds to understand and evaluate the research you've done and the significance you claim for it. Readers should be able to trust that the work you're presenting is your own and that it clearly distinguishes between your ideas and those of your sources. In this sense, acknowledging your sources properly is not simply to avoid plagiarism but to establish a relationship of honesty and good faith with your readers. Accordingly, the ethical problem of plagiarism—to take the words or ideas of someone else and present them as your own—is not just that it amounts to stealing another person's work but that it breaks the bonds of trust between writer and reader that are necessary for the genuine communication and exchange of ideas to take place. In short, plagiarism threatens the principles of academic, professional, and civic honesty required for people to reason together.

Sometimes plagiarism is an ethical lapse that amounts to stealing and cheating—for example, when students buy research papers, turn in work that someone else has done for them, or copy passages out of books or articles to present as their own. Often, however, plagiarism is unintentional, resulting from a misunderstanding of how to use and cite sources properly. For this reason, to avoid plagiarism, you need to be aware of the conventions of citation and the various options you have in integrating sources into your own writing.

Integrating Sources

The three basic methods of integrating sources into a research paper are paraphrasing, summarizing, and quoting. Each method has its own distinct function.

Paraphrasing

Paraphrasing means to restate in your own words. A paraphrase is typically the same length as the original. It's normally used when you want to present in your own words all the information in a passage. Because paraphrase reproduces in your words the details in the original, it is usually used for brief passages that you want to explain thoroughly.

Summarizing

Summarizing means to select main ideas from the original and to present them in your own words. Unlike a paraphrase, which is approximately the same length as the original, a summary condenses the material. Depending on your purposes, you can summarize all or a portion of the source that is pertinent to your research. (If you do summarize selectively, make sure you don't distort the meaning of the original.) Summaries can range from a sentence to a paragraph or more in length, depending on the amount of detail you need. Summaries are typically used to define a problem, explain a controversy, support an interpretation, and present and refute an opposing view.

Quoting

Quoting means duplicating the exact words as they appear in the original. In general you should use direct quotations sparingly. Quotations are best suited when you want to capture something in the tone of the original that you'd lose by paraphrasing, or when a direct quotation from a respected expert will lend authority to your writing. Short quotations, even a key phrase, taken from the original and worked into a sentence of your own construction, are often more effective than longer ones.

Sample Paraphrase and Summary

The following passage is from Alan M. Kraut's chapter "Plagues and Prejudice: Nativism's Construction of Disease in Nineteenth- and Twentieth-Century New York City" that appears in *Hives of Sickness: Public Health and Epidemics in New York City.* It's fairly representative of the kinds of sources you're likely to be working with.

> *Original:*
>
> As early as the 1830s, Irish immigrants who lived in rundown shanties and tenements along New York's rivers were being blamed for importing the cholera epidemic (from which they suffered disproportionately). Fear of cholera, especially after the epidemic of 1832, stimulated public demand for inspection of emigrants prior to departure. Soon, those who left from western European ports began to receive an exam from a physician employed by the country of departure, lest shiploads of emigrants be annihilated by cholera during the voyage.
>
> (Alan M. Kraut, "Plagues and Prejudice," p. 67)
>
> *Paraphrase:*
>
> According to Alan M. Kraut, during the 1830s, there was widespread concern about the danger of cholera being brought to the U.S. by immigrants. Prime suspects were Irish immigrants, who lived in substandard housing near the rivers of New York City and suffered a high rate of cholera. Following the cholera epidemic of 1832, public pressure mounted to examine

emigrants before they left Europe. In order to prevent devastating outbreaks of disease onboard the ships, physicians hired by the European countries inspected departing passengers (67).

Summary:

During the 1830s, in Alan M. Kraut's view, the fear that immigrants were bringing cholera with them to the U.S. led to health inspections of departing passengers in the European ports (67).

WORKING WITH QUOTATIONS

Depending on your purposes, you can integrate material into your writing through short or long quotations. Short quotations use a word, a phrase, or a sentence, while longer quotations present extended passages from a source. Short quotations are inserted into your sentences and identified by quotation marks. Long quotations are set off from the rest of the text in block form and don't use quotation marks (except for any quotation marks that may appear in the original). MLA style identifies long quotations as any passage of more than four lines in length, while APA style considers any passage of more than forty words to be a long quotation. (The examples that follow use MLA style.)

Short Quotations

Words

Writers typically quote single words to emphasize important points and represent key concepts in their discussion. Often the quoted word is a term that someone has coined for analytical purposes, as in these two instances:

> The ceremonial suspension of normal identities by World Wrestling Federation stars offers spectators a way to participate in what Victor Turner calls a "liminal" moment, when ordinary time and everyday human affairs come briefly to a halt and the extraordinary takes over.

> Stuart Hall's notion of "encoding/decoding" in media communication enables us to see how messages are transformed as they circulate from production to reception.

Notice in these two examples that the key terms "liminal" and "encoding/decoding" appear in quotes and that in each case the author is noted. There are no page numbers, however, because the terms appear throughout the original sources, which are then acknowledged in Works Cited.

Phrases

You can integrate phrases as elements in sentences of your own construction:

> Alan M. Kraut explains how the growing fear that immigrants were bringing cholera to the U.S. "stimulated public demand for inspection of emigrants prior to departure" from Europe (67).

Sentences

Or you can use a complete sentence or two from your source:

> According to Alan M. Kraut, "[f]ear of cholera, especially after the epidemic of 1832, stimulated public demand for inspection of emigrants prior to departure" (67).

Long Quotations

For long quotations, indent one inch (or ten spaces) from the left margin if you are using MLA style or a half-inch (or five spaces) from the left margin if you are using APA style, and in both cases double-space the passage. Using this block form tells readers that the material is quoted directly from the original, so you don't need quotation marks. The page citation goes in parentheses two spaces after the punctuation at the end of the quote. The example below uses MLA style—ten spaces to form the block. For single paragraphs or portions of a paragraph, do not indent the first line. If you quote two or more paragraphs, indent five spaces at the beginning of each paragraph.

> Public health historian Alan M. Kraut points out how Americans have long viewed immigrants as carriers of disease:
>
> > As early as the 1830s, Irish immigrants who lived in rundown shanties and tenements along New York's rivers were being blamed for importing the cholera epidemic (from which they suffered disproportionately). Fear of cholera, especially after the epidemic of 1832, stimulated public demand for inspection of emigrants prior to departure. Soon, those who left from western European ports began to receive an exam from a physician employed by the country of departure, lest shiploads of emigrants be annihilated by cholera during the voyage. (67)

Citing the Author

As you can see from the examples of paraphrases, summaries, and short and long quotations, citing the author at the beginning of the quote and including an in-text citation at the end enables you to mark clearly the presentation of material from your sources so that readers can distinguish it easily from your own ideas. Phrases such as "according to Kraut," "in Kraut's view," "Kraut claims," and "Kraut points out" are common identifying tags. The citation that appears in parentheses—(67)—shows readers where the quote ends and provides the page number in the original for readers who want to find the passage. Identifying tags, quotation marks, and in-text citations serve, in effect, as on-and-off switches that tell readers when you are presenting sources.

To achieve sentence variety, you can shift the placement of these source markers. For example, in a short quotation, you can cite the author not only in the beginning but also in the middle of the sentence:

> In the 1830s, "Irish immigrants who lived in rundown shanties and tenements along New York's rivers," Alan M. Kraut notes, "were being blamed for importing the cholera epidemic" (67).

Or at the end:

> "Fear of cholera, especially after the epidemic of 1832, stimulated public demand for inspection of emigrants prior to departure," Alan M. Kraut claims (67).

AVOIDING PLAGIARISM

The basic guideline for avoiding plagiarism is simple: Acknowledge your sources clearly and accurately. Notice that the following paraphrase fails to acknowledge either the author or the quoted words (which are underlined):

> During the 1830s, there was widespread concern about the danger of cholera being brought to the U.S. by immigrants. Prime suspects were Irish immigrants, <u>who lived in rundown shanties and tenements along New York's rivers</u> and who suffered a high rate of cholera. Following the cholera epidemic of 1832, public pressure mounted to examine emigrants before they left Europe. Physicians hired by the European countries inspected departing passengers, <u>lest shiploads of emigrants be annihilated by cholera during the voyage.</u>

To correct this, the italicized changes first cite the author (switching the source on), next put Kraut's phrases in quotes, and then give an in-text citation at the end (switching the source off):

> *According to Alan M. Kraut,* during the 1830s, there was widespread concern the danger of cholera being brought to the U.S. by immigrants. Prime suspects were Irish immigrants, "*who lived in rundown shanties and*

tenements along New York's rivers" and who suffered a high rate of cholera. Following the cholera epidemic of 1832, public pressure mounted to examine emigrants before they left Europe. Physicians hired by the European countries inspected departing passengers, "lest shiploads of emigrants be annihilated by cholera during the voyage" (67).

FITTING QUOTATIONS TO YOUR SENTENCES

Under certain circumstances, you may modify the material you're quoting. The two basic techniques for modifying the original passage are ellipses and brackets. You use ellipses to omit something in the original and brackets to add or change something. Here are examples of typical uses of each.

Ellipses

Ellipses are a set of three periods with a space before and after each (...). Use ellipses when you want to omit part of the original passage.

> "As early as the 1830s," Alan M. Kraut notes, "Irish immigrants . . . were being blamed for importing the cholera epidemic" (67).

When you quote single words or phrases, you don't need to use ellipses because readers can see you're quoting only part of a passage. Notice that the example (page 588) under "Phrases" doesn't use ellipses.

If the material you're omitting occurs between sentences, add a fourth period .... to mark the end of the first sentence.

> Alan M. Kraut notes similarities between the official response to cholera, polio, and tuberculosis in the nineteenth and early twentieth centuries and to AIDS in the 1990s:
>> In the early 1990s, the federal government continued to pursue institutional means of epidemic control to stop AIDS at the border, a means that stigmatizes immigrants of all nationalities . . . .
>> As in earlier crises, the federal government had sought to use exclusion to control the epidemic; immigrants were subjected to mandatory testing for no clear epidemiological reason other than foreign birth. (83)

Brackets

Brackets are used to make small changes in the original passage so that it fits grammatically into your sentences.

According to Alan M. Kraut, the federal government's use of mandatory AIDS testing repeats a pattern that can be found in earlier public health crises, "stigmatiz[ing] immigrants of all nationalities" (83).

Brackets can also be used to change capitalization and add clarifying material.

Original:

Wealthy New York City merchants and uptown landowners, who in the early 1850s proposed the creation of Central Park, hoped to create a refined setting for their own socializing. But seeking to establish the public value of their project, they also invoked the language of the English sanitary reformers and claimed the park would improve the health and morals of the city's working people.

(Alan M. Kraut, "Plagues and Prejudice," p. 57)

Use of Brackets:

Alan M. Kraut shows how the proposal to create Central Park drew on themes from the public health movement. "[S]eeking to establish the public value of their project, they [wealthy New York City merchants and uptown landowners] also invoked the language of the English sanitary reformers and claimed the park would improve the health and morals of the city's working people" (57).

Quotations within Quotations

The passage you want to quote may at times contain quoted material. If the passage is long enough to use block form, then keep the quotation marks as they are in the original. If, however, you are going to incorporate a quotation that includes a quotation into your own sentence, then change the double quotation marks (") in the original into single quotation marks (').

Original:

Against this backdrop of economic depression, the physician and city inspector John Griscom launched a new phase of sanitary reform in his 1842 report when he singled out "the crowded conditions, with insufficient ventilation" of dwellings as "first among the most serious causes of disordered public health."

(Alan M. Kraut, "Plagues and Prejudice," p. 54)

Quotations within a Quotation:

Alan M. Kraut claims that "John Griscom launched a new phase of sanitary reform in his 1842 report when he singled out 'the crowded conditions, with insufficient ventilation' of dwellings as 'first among the most serious causes of disordered public health'" (54).

REVISING SOME COMMON PROBLEMS IN WORKING WITH SOURCES

The following questions offer further guidelines to read your work and make needed revisions:

Do You Need the Quote?

Quoted material should be chosen carefully to advance the line of thinking in a research project. It should emphasize main ideas, not just be used decoratively or as proof that you've read a number of sources. Notice that the quoted material in the following sentence does not really convey a main idea but instead seems to be used just for the sake of adding another quote:

> The plot of *Wuthering Heights* puts the death of the heroine in the middle of the novel. Although she has died in childbirth, Catherine Earnshaw relentlessly haunts Heathcliff until eighteen years later he too finally rests by her side in a grave "on the edge of the churchyard" (Frank 219).

The quoted phrase does not really contain an idea that matters to the discussion. Quotes like this one should be scrutinized closely to see if they are needed.

Is It Clear Where Sources Start and Stop?

As mentioned already, one of the keys to avoiding plagiarism is marking clearly where quoted material starts and stops. Notice how the first two quotes—the underlined sentence and phrase—seem to be "floating" in the paragraph—and how the in-text citation (219) confusingly appears before the writer has finished quoting from the source.

> *Wuthering Heights* uses subtle psychological portrayals of its main characters, Catherine Earnshaw and Heathcliff, to turn them into mythic figures. "They are driven, tormented, violent lovers, and there are no wedding bells for them in the final chapter." In the grip of a titanic passion, their love can only be realized in death. Before his death, Heathcliff arranges to have the sides of his and Catherine's adjoining coffins dismantled "so that in death they might finally achieve the consummation of their love" (219). This is the "perfect and irrevocable union," Katherine Frank says, "which had tormented and eluded them when they were alive."

All the quoted material is from Katherine Frank's book *A Chainless Soul,* but readers will have to guess the source of the first two quotes. This problem can easily be fixed, as you can see by the italicized revisions:

> *Wuthering Heights* uses subtle psychological portrayals of its main characters, Catherine Earnshaw and Heathcliff, to turn them into mythic figures. "They are driven, tormented, violent lovers," *Katherine Frank says,* "and there are no wedding bells for them in the final chapter." In the grip of a titanic passion, their love can only be realized in death. Before his death, Heathcliff arranges to have the sides of his and Catherine's adjoining coffins dismantled "so that in death they might finally achieve the consummation of their love." *According to Frank,* this is the "perfect and irrevocable union—which had tormented and eluded them when they were alive" (219).

Are Sources Used Purposefully or Just Strung Together?

Make sure your sources are set up so that readers will see how each quoted and paraphrased idea fits into your writing. Sources that are strung together, as in the following example, resemble research notes transcribed directly into a paper. As you can see, the writing seems to ramble from quote to quote without any sense of purposeful direction:

> The musical label "soul" is associated with Motown and Memphis in the 1960s, but the term has been in use much longer. According to gospel singer Mahalia Jackson, "What some people call the 'blues singing feeling' is expressed by the Church of God in Christ…. The basic thing is soul feeling. The same in blues as in spirituals. And also with gospel music. It is soul music" (qtd. in Ricks 139). "Soul assumes a shared experience, a relationship with the listener…where the singer confirms and works out the feelings of the audience. In this sense, it remains sacramental" (qtd. in Guralnick 3). "As professions, blues singing and preaching seem to be closely linked in both the rural or small town settings and in the urban ghettos" (Keil 143). Nonetheless, "Ray Charles's transformation of dignified gospel standards into cries of secular ecstasy came in for a good deal of criticism at first, mostly from the pulpit" (Guralnick 2).

A revision of this paragraph would require unpacking each quote by explaining the ideas and connecting them to the main points in the paper. Each quote may need its own paragraph, or the writer might combine two or more quotes in a paragraph. In any case, the quotes need space to breathe.

Do You Provide Commentary Where It Is Needed?

Quoted material is, of course, central to a research paper. But quotes don't speak for themselves. As you've just seen in the example with the string of quotes, you need to connect your sources to the main points in your paper so that readers can see how and why the sources are significant. Your commentary is crucial to making these connections explicit. In the following example, notice how the quote leaves us hanging because it is not followed up by commentary from the writer:

> *Wuthering Heights* is partially based on the Gothic tradition, a quasi-horror writing that features haunting imagery, desolate landscapes, and supernatural encounters. Bronte draws on the Gothic to turn her main characters, Catherine Earnshaw and Heathcliff, into mythic figures in the grip of a titanic passion. Catherine marries Edgar Linton, and Heathcliff marries Edgar's sister Isabella, but these marriages have no impact on Catherine and Heathcliff's passionate love. Nor does death. Although she dies in childbirth in the middle of the novel, Catherine relentlessly haunts Heathcliff until eighteen years later he too finally rests by her side. As Katherine Frank explains:
>
>> Before he dies, Heathcliff makes a ghoulish arrangement with the sexton to knock out the adjoining sides of his own and Catherine's coffins so that in death they might finally achieve the consummation of their love—a perfect and irrevocable union—which had tormented and eluded them when they were alive. (219)
>
> In earlier Gothic novels, the central narrative is often approached by way of a frame tale that uses diaries, letters, and other documents, which are transcribed or edited by the narrator. Similarly, the reader approaches the narrative of *Wuthering Heights* via an outsider, Lockwood....

A few lines of commentary from the writer would not only consolidate the point in the paragraph but also set up a smoother transition into the next paragraph.

>> ...the consummation of their love—a perfect and irrevocable union—which had tormented and eluded them when they were alive (219).
>
> In true Gothic style, Bronte blurs the line between life and death to create an imaginary world of haunted and uncontrollable passions.
>
> This imaginary world is typically both verified and kept at a mysterious distance in Gothic novels by a frame tale that uses diaries, letters, and other documents, which are transcribed or....

IN-TEXT CITATIONS

Documenting your sources is a crucial aspect of presenting your work in a research paper. A reliable rule of thumb is that you should cite the source of any information, analysis, interpretation, or argument that is not common knowledge (for example, William Shakespeare was a British playwright in Elizabethan England, the earth travels around the sun, Darwin formulated the theory of natural selection).

Until recently researchers generally used footnotes or endnotes to cite the work of others. Today, however, the two main styles of citation—MLA and APA—use parenthetical citations instead. Information about the source is included in the text and keyed to a list of works cited at the end of the paper. The information called for by MLA and APA in the parenthetical citation differs somewhat. MLA uses author and page, while APA uses author, year, and page.

The following list shows how MLA and APA styles set up parenthetical citations for many types of sources. For further information, ask your teacher or consult *MLA Style Manual and Guide to Scholarly Publishing* (2nd ed., 1998) and *Publication Manual of the American Psychological Association* (5th ed., 2001).

Sources with One Author

In many instances, you'll be citing the author in the sentence that uses the source material.

MLA

According to Daniel J. Czitrom, following the Civil War, there appeared the "first rush of literature on the pathology of mass communication, with which we are so familiar today" (19).

Note that you do not repeat the author's name when you give the page number at the end of the quotation.

APA

According to Daniel J. Czitrom (1982), following the Civil War, there appeared the "first rush of literature on the pathology of mass communication, with which we are so familiar today" (p. 19).

Note that in APA style the date of publication appears immediately after the author's name.

If you don't cite the author in the sentence, then use these forms:

MLA

Following the Civil War, there appeared the "first rush of literature on the pathology of mass communication, with which we are so familiar today" (Czitrom 19).

MLA style notes the author and the page number, with no punctuation in between or "p." before the page.

APA

Following the Civil War, there appeared the "first rush of literature on the pathology of mass communication, with which we are so familiar today" (Czitrom, 1982, p. 19).

APA style includes the author's name, the date of publication, and the page number, with commas in between and "p." before the page number.

Notice that for both MLA and APA styles the final period comes after the citation.

If you have used two or more sources by the same author:

MLA

Following the Civil War, there appeared the "first rush of literature on the pathology of mass communication, with which we are so familiar today" (Czitrom, *Media* 19).

When you have more than one source by an author, MLA style uses the author's name, a shortened version of the title (the full title is *Media and the American Mind: From Morse to McLuhan*), and the page number.

APA

Following the Civil War, there appeared the "first rush of literature on the pathology of mass communication, with which we are so familiar today" (Czitrom, 1982, p. 19).

APA style remains the same because the work is already noted by the year. However, if you are citing in APA style more than one work published by an author in the same year, add a letter to the date (1982a, 1982b) and key these to your references at the end of the paper. For example, if you cited a second work Czitrom published in 1982, the first work would be cited as:

(Czitrom, 1982a, p. 19)

and the second would look like this:

(Czitrom, 1982b, p. 43)

Sources with Multiple Authors

MLA and APA use different systems to cite sources having more than one author.

MLA

If the work has two or three authors, cite all:

> Despite the claims made for it, literacy "is not in itself a panacea for social inequity" (Lunsford, Moglen, and Slevin 2).

If the work has more than three authors, use the first author's name followed by "et al."

> What we know of Indian cultures prior to 1700 has mostly been gleaned from the evidence of various artifacts, such as pottery, weapons, and stories passed down from generation to generation (Lauter et al. 5).

APA

If the source you are citing has two authors, include both last names in the reference, separated by an ampersand (&).

> An infusion of IT (Information Technology) will result in a "net employment reduction for the institution" (Massey & Zemsky, 1995, p. 245).

For sources with three to five authors, list all of the authors' last names the first time you cite the source, separating each name by a comma and putting an ampersand before the final name.

> Despite the claims made for it, literacy "is not in itself a panacea for social inequity" (Lunsford, Moglen, & Slevin, 1990, p. 2).

For subsequent citations, include simply the last name of the first author followed by "et al." and the year and the page. If sources have six or more authors, use the last name of the first author and "et al." in every citation:

> Despite the claims made for it, literacy "is not in itself a panacea for social inequity" (Lunsford et al., 1990, p. 2).

Sources with No Author Listed

If no author is listed on the work, both MLA and APA use a shortened version of the title.

MLA

> A recent study found that men who frequent prostitutes or have many sexual partners may increase their wives' risk of cervical cancer ("Man's Sex Life").

Note that if your source appears on a single page, MLA does not require you to list the page number.

APA

A recent study found that men who frequent prostitutes or have many sexual partners may increase their wives' risk of cervical cancer ("Man's Sex Life," 1996, p. 15).

The MLA and APA citations use a shortened version of the title of the article, "Man's Sex Life and Cancer in Wife Linked."

Quotations from Secondary Sources

Whenever possible, you should cite the source where a quotation appeared originally. There may be times, however, when you need to cite a quotation within someone else's work. You can do so by using "qtd. in" (MLA) or "cited in" (APA). In the following two examples, the writer is quoting the blues musician Son House from an interview that appeared originally in Pete Welding's book *The Living Blues.* Unable to locate Welding's book, the writer cites the interview as it is quoted in Greil Marcus's book *Mystery Train.*

MLA

"He sold his soul to the devil to get to play like that," House told blues historian Pete Welding (qtd. in Marcus 32).

APA

"He sold his soul to the devil to get to play like that," House told blues historian Pete Welding (cited in Marcus, 1975, p. 32).

WORKS CITED (MLA) AND REFERENCES (APA)

Every source that appears in the text should be included in a list on a separate page at the end of your paper. Don't include works that you read but did not cite. MLA calls the list "Works Cited," while APA uses "References." Both systems alphabetize by author's last name or the first word in the title of a work with no author.

Books

Here is the basic format for MLA and APA. Notice how they differ.

MLA

Gardner, Howard. *Multiple Intelligence: The Theory in Practice.* New York: Basic, 1993.

MLA style uses the complete first name of the author, capitalizes throughout the title, lists the date at the end of the citation, and indents the second line five spaces. Notice that the period following the book title is not underlined or italicized. In MLA style, use the abbreviation "UP" for university presses: Boston: Northeastern UP.

APA

Gardner, H. (1993). *Multiple intelligence: The theory in practice.* New York: Basic Books.

APA style uses the author's first initial, lists the date right after the author's name, capitalizes only the first word in the title and after a colon (plus any proper nouns), and indents the second line five spaces. In APA style, the period following the book title is underlined or italicized.

Both systems double-space throughout.

Notice in the examples that the place of publication is well-known. In these cases, don't add the state. In other instances, where the place of publication is not well known, do add the state:

Thousand Oaks, CA: Sage

Two Listings by One Author
MLA

Gardner, Howard. *Extraordinary Minds: Portraits of Exceptional Individuals and an Examination of Our Extraordinariness.* New York: Basic, 1997.

---. *Multiple Intelligence: The Theory in Practice.* New York: Basic, 1993.

When you're listing two or more works by the same author, use alphabetical order according to title. For the second title, type three hyphens and a period in place of the author's name.

APA

Gardner, H. (1997). *Extraordinary minds: Portraits of exceptional individuals and an examination of our extraordinariness.* New York: Basic Books.

Gardner, H. (1993). *Multiple intelligence: The theory in practice.* New York: Basic Books.

Gould, S. J. (1977a). *Ontogeny and phylogeny.* Cambridge: Cambridge University Press.

Gould, S. J. (1977b). Sociobiology: The art of storytelling. *New Scientist, 80,* 530–533.

APA style uses chronological order to list works. When an author has more than one work published in the same year, list them in alphabetical order by title and add lowercase letters to the year—1977a, 1977b.

Books with Multiple Authors

MLA

For two or three authors, list them in the order in which they appear. Invert only the first author's name.

> Current, Richard Nelson, Marcia Ewing Current, and Loie Fuller. *Goddess of Light*. Boston: Northeastern UP, 1997.

If there are more than three authors, you may list them all or list only the first author followed by "et al."

> Anderson, Daniel, Bret Benjamin, Christopher Busiel, and Bill Parades-Holt. *Teaching On-Line: Internet Research, Conversation, and Composition*. New York: HarperCollins, 1996.

or

> Anderson, Daniel, et al. *Teaching On-Line: Internet Research, Conversation, and Composition*. New York: HarperCollins, 1996.

APA

For works with two to six authors, list the authors in the order in which they appear on the title page, using last name and initials. Use an ampersand before the last author's name.

> Anderson, D., Benjamin, B., Busiel, C., & Parades-Holt, B. (1996). *Teaching online: Internet research, conversation, and composition*. New York: HarperCollins.

Books by a Corporate Author or Organization

If no individual is named as author, give the name of the corporate or organizational author as it appears on the title page.

MLA

> NOW Legal Defense and Educational Fund. *Facts on Reproductive Rights: A Resource Manual*. New York: The Fund, 1989.

APA

NOW Legal Defense and Educational Fund. (1989). *Facts on reproductive rights: A resource manual.* New York: The Fund.

Books by an Anonymous Author

In MLA style, if no author is listed or the author is anonymous, begin with the title of the publication.

MLA

Primary Colors: A Novel of Politics. New York: Random, 1996.

APA

Primary colors: A novel of politics. (1996). New York: Random House.

In APA style, begin the entry with the title if no author is listed. If a work's author is designated as "Anonymous," however, use the word "Anonymous" at the beginning of the entry.

An Edition of an Original Work
MLA

Melville, Herman. *Moby-Dick.* 1851. Ed. Alfred Kazin. Boston: Houghton, 1956.

APA

Melville, H. (1956). *Moby-Dick.* (A. Kazin, Ed.). Boston: Houghton Mifflin. (Original work published 1851)

An Introduction, Preface, Foreword, or Afterword
MLA

Kazin, Alfred. Introduction. *Moby-Dick.* By Herman Melville. Ed. Alfred Kazin. Boston: Houghton, 1956. v–xiv.

APA

Kazin, A. (1956). Introduction. In H. Melville, *Moby-Dick.* (A. Kazin, Ed.). (pp. v–xiv). Boston: Houghton Mifflin.

Edited Collections
MLA

Grumet, Robert S., ed. *Northeastern Indian Lives.* Amherst: U of Massachusetts P, 1996.

APA

Grumet, R. S. (Ed.). (1996). *Northeastern Indian lives.* Amherst, MA: University of Massachusetts Press.

Works in Collections and Anthologies
MLA

Ochs, Donovan J. "Cicero's Rhetorical Theory." *A Synoptic History of Classical Rhetoric.* Ed. James J. Murphy. Davis: Hermagoras, 1983. 90–150.

Fitzgerald, F. Scott. "Bernice Bobs Her Hair." *The Short Stories of F. Scott Fitzgerald: A New Collection.* Ed. Matthew J. Bruccoli. New York: Scribner, 1989. 25–47.

APA

Ochs, D. J. (1983). Cicero's rhetorical theory. In J. J. Murphy (Ed.), *A synoptic history of classical rhetoric* (pp. 90–150). Davis, CA: Hermagoras.

Fitzgerald, F. (1989). Bernice bobs her hair. In Matthew J. Bruccoli (Ed.), *The short stories of F. Scott Fitzgerald: A new collection* (pp. 25–47). New York: Scribner.

Translations
MLA

Sartre, Jean Paul. *The Age of Reason.* Trans. Eric Sutton. New York: Bantam, 1959.

APA

Sartre, J. P. (1959). *The age of reason.* (E. Sutton, Trans.). New York: Bantam Books.

Book in a Later Edition
MLA

Woloch, Nancy. *Women and the American Experience.* 2nd ed. New York: McGraw, 1994.

APA

Woloch, N. (1994). *Women and the American experience* (2nd ed.). New York: McGraw-Hill.

Dictionary Entries and Encyclopedia Articles

MLA

"Freeze-etching." *Merriam-Webster's Collegiate Dictionary.* 10th ed. 1996.

"Australia." *The Concise Columbia Encyclopedia.* 3rd ed. 1994.

Jolliffe, David A. "Genre." *Encyclopedia of Rhetoric and Composition.* Ed. Theresa Enos. New York: Garland, 1996.

In MLA style, for familiar reference works such as *Merriam-Webster's Collegiate Dictionary* and *The Concise Columbia Encyclopedia,* you can omit listing the editors and publication information. For less familiar or more specialized sources, however, you should include all the information. Page numbers are not needed as long as the work is arranged alphabetically.

APA

Freeze-etching. (1996) *Merriam-Webster's collegiate dictionary* (10th ed.). Springfield, MA: Merriam Webster.

Australia. (1994). *The concise Columbia encyclopedia* (3rd ed.). New York: Columbia University Press.

Jolliffe, D. A. (1996). Genre. In Theresa Enos (Ed.), *Encyclopedia of rhetoric and composition.* New York: Garland Publishing.

Government Documents

MLA

United States. Department of Commerce, International Trade Administration. *A Guide to Financing Exports.* Washington: GPO, 1985.

APA

Department of Commerce, International Trade Administration. (1985). *A guide to financing exports.* (Monthly Catalog No. 85024488). Washington, DC: U.S. Government Printing Office.

APA includes the catalog number of the publication.

Unpublished Doctoral Dissertations

MLA

Herzong, Mary Lucinda. "Living and Dying: Accommodating AIDS into Autobiography (Immune Deficiency)." Diss. U of California, 1995.

APA

Herzong, M. L. (1995). *Living and dying: Accommodating AIDS into auto-biography (immune deficiency)*. Unpublished doctoral dissertation, University of California, Berkeley.

Articles in Periodicals

Here are examples of the basic MLA and APA formats for listing articles that appear in periodicals such as scholarly journals, magazines, and newspapers.

MLA

Eldred, Janet Carey. "The Technology of Voice." *College Composition and Communication* 48 (1997): 334–47.

MLA style uses the author's full name, marks article titles by using quotation marks and capitalization, and shortens the number of the last page (334–47).

APA

Eldred, J. C. (1997). The technology of voice. *College Composition and Communication, 48,* 334–347.

APA style uses abbreviations for first and middle names, and the date follows the author's name. APA does not use quotation marks or capitalization for articles (except for the first word of the title). In APA style, the name of the journal, the volume number (48), and the comma that follows it are all underlined or italicized. APA style includes "the" capitalized in the titles of newspapers and magazines such as *The New York Times* or *The Nation*, but MLA style does not. APA style lists full page numbers (334–347).

Scholarly Journals with Continuous Pagination

Notice in the examples that the only number given is the volume number (48). This is because the journal paginates continuously from issue to issue over the course of the volume. In such cases, simply list the volume number in the appropriate place. You don't need to include the issue number.

Scholarly Journals that Page Each Issue Separately

If every issue of the journal begins with page 1, include the issue number along with the volume number.

MLA

Ebert, Theresa. "Writing in the Political: Resistance (Post)modernism." *Legal Studies Forum* 15.4 (1991): 291–303.

APA

Ebert, T. (1991). Writing in the political: Resistance (post)modernism. *Legal Studies Forum,* 15(4), 291–303.

Magazine Articles

The first two examples show how to list magazines that appear monthly or bimonthly and weekly or biweekly. The third example is an article without an author listed.

MLA

Wahl, K.U. "Chinese Wind-Driven Kite Flutes." *Experimental Musical Instruments* Sept. 1997: 26–30.

Pollitt, Katha. "The Other L Word." *Nation* 8 Sept. 1997: 10.

"Pleas from Prison." *Newsweek* 24 Nov. 1997:44.

APA

Wahl, K.U. (1997, September). Chinese wind-driven kite flutes. *Experimental Musical Instruments,* pp. 26–30.

Pollitt, K. (1997, September 8). The other L word. *The Nation,* p. 10.

Pleas from prison. (1997, November 24). *Newsweek,* p. 44.

Newspaper Articles

MLA

Morrow, David J. "Attention Disorder Is Found in Growing Number of Adults." *New York Times* 2 Sept. 1997:A1.

"AMA Plans Seal of Approval for Physicians." *Providence Journal-Bulletin* 19 November 1997:A5.

APA

Morrow, D. J. (1997, September 2). Attention disorder is found in growing number of adults. *The New York Times,* p. A1.

AMA plans seal of approval for physicians. (1997, November 19). *The Providence Journal-Bulletin,* p. A5.

Editorial

MLA

"The Bludgeoning of Taiwan." Editorial. *New York Times* 8 Mar. 1996:A30.

APA

The bludgeoning of Taiwan. (1996, March 8). [Editorial]. *The New York Times,* p. A30.

Review
MLA

Ewald, Paul W. "Pedigree of a Retrovirus." Rev. of *Viral Sex: The Nature of AIDS*, by Jaap Goudsmit. *Natural History* June 1997: 8–9.

APA

Ewald, P. W. (1997, June). Pedigree of a retrovirus [Review of the book *Viral Sex: The Nature of AIDS*]. *Natural History*, 8–9.

If there is no author listed for the review, begin with the title of the review. If there is no title, use "Rev. of *Title*" for MLA format and "[Review of the book *Title*]" for APA. In this case, alphabetize under the title of the book being reviewed.

Letter to the Editor
MLA

Daniels, John. Letter. *New York Times* 8 Mar. 1996:A30.

APA

Daniels, J. (1996, March 8). [Letter to the editor]. *The New York Times*, p. A30.

Miscellaneous Sources

Films and Videocassettes
MLA

Citizen Kane. Screenplay by Orson Welles. Dir. Orson Welles. RKO, 1941.
Star Wars. Dir. George Lucas. Perf. Mark Hamill, Harrison Ford, Carrie Fisher, and Alec Guiness. Videocassette. CBS Fox, 1992.

APA

Welles, O. (Writer and Director). (1941). *Citizen Kane* [Film]. Hollywood: RKO.
Lucas, G. (Director). (1992). *Star wars* [Videocassette]. Hollywood: CBS Fox.

The amount of information to include about films and videocassettes depends on how you have used the source. In addition to title and director, you may cite the writer and performers as well.

Television and Radio Programs
MLA

"Tuskegee Experiment." *Nova.* WGBH, Boston. 4 April 1995.

APA

Tuskegee experiment. (1995, April 4). *Nova*. Boston: WGBH.

Records, Tapes, and CDs

MLA

Ellington, Duke. *The Far East Suite*. Bluebird, 1995.
Springsteen, Bruce. "Youngstown." *The Ghost of Tom Joad*. Columbia, 1995.
Verdi, Giuseppe. *La Traviata*. London Symphony Orchestra. Cond. Carlo Rizzi. Teldec, 1992.

APA

Ellington, Duke. (Composer). (1995). *The far east suite* [Record]. New York: Bluebird.

Springsteen, B. (Singer and Composer). (1995). Youngstown. *The ghost of Tom Joad* [cassette]. New York: Columbia Records.

Verdi, G. (Composer). (1992). *La Traviata*. [With C. Rizzi conducting the London Symphony Orchestra]. [CD]. New York: Teldec.

Interviews

MLA

"Interview with Barbara Kingsolver." By Anita Amirault. *The Progressive* 20 Mar. 1998:30–34.
Haraway, Donna. "Writing, Literacy, and Technology: Toward a Cyborg Literature." By Gary A. Olson. *Women Writing Culture*. Ed. Gary A. Olson and Elaine Hirsch. Albany: SUNY, 1995. 45–77.
Kenny, Maurice. Personal interview. 27 April 1997.

MLA cites interviews by listing the person being interviewed first and then the interviewer. Note that the first two interviews are published and the third is unpublished.

APA

Amirault, A. (1998, March 20). Interview with Barbara Kingsolver. *The Progressive,* pp. 30–34.

Olson, G. A. (1995). Writing, literacy, and technology: Toward a cyborg literature. [Interview with Donna Haraway]. In G. A. Olson & E. Hirsch (Eds.), *Women writing culture* (pp. 45–77). Albany: State University of New York.

APA lists the name of the interviewer first and then puts information on the interview in brackets. APA does not list unpublished interviews in references but cites them only in parenthetical citations in the text: (M. Kenny, personal interview, April 27, 1997).

Lecture or Speech

MLA

Kern, David. "Recent Trends in Occupational Medicine." Memorial Hospital, Pawtucket, RI. 2 Oct. 1997.

APA

Kern, D. (1997, October 2). Recent trends in occupational medicine. Lecture presented at Memorial Hospital, Pawtucket, RI.

Online and Electronic Sources

The dramatic increase of information available through the Internet and electronic sources is changing the way people do research—and simultaneously raises the problem for researchers of how to cite Web sites, e-mail, listservs, newsgroups, and databases. In this section we look at the guidelines provided by the MLA and the APA.

For online sources, MLA and APA guidelines call for much of the same information you use for print sources, such as document title and author's name (if it is available). In addition, MLA and APA also call for two special items of information:

- **Date of posting and retrieval:** Online sources can change quickly, so you need to provide dates that identify which version of a source you are citing. If it is available, provide the date of publication or update when the source you consulted was posted online. You can always give the date you retrieved the source.

- **Uniform resource locator (URL):** So readers can find online sources, give each source's exact and complete electronic address or URL. The easiest way to make sure the URL is accurate is to copy it from your browser's address window and paste it in your paper. If you have to break up an address at the end of a line, do not use a hyphen. Make the break only after a slash (/).

Web Sites: Basic Format for Professional and Personal Sites

MLA

Crawford, James. *Language Policy Web Site & Emporium.* 8 Feb. 2001 <http://ourworld.compuserve.com/homepages/jwcrawford>.

U.S. English Only. Home Page. 1 Jan. 2001. U.S. English Only. 8 Feb. 2001 <http://www.us-english.org>.

The order of information for MLA: Name of author, creator, or site owner, if available; title of document, if named; date of last posting, if available; name of any institution or organization associated with the date; date of retrieval; URL enclosed in angle brackets < >.

In the first example, no posting date is given, only the date of retrieval. The second example includes both posting and retrieval dates. Notice in the U.S. English Only example, where the Web site is not titled, you add the description "home page" without underlining, italicizing, or putting it in quotes.

APA

Upstate Economic Development Council. (2000, March 15). *Prospects for rural revitalization.: New crops and new markets.* Retrieved July 7, 2001, from http:www.upecodev. gov/html

Crawford, J. *Language policy web site & emporium.* (n.d.). Retrieved February 8, 2001, from http://ourworld.compuserve.com/homepages/jwcrawford

The order of information for APA: Name of author, creator, or site owner, if available; date of last posting; title of document, if named; date of retrieval and URL in one sentence, without using angle brackets or a period at the end.

As is true with print sources, APA uses an initial for an author's first and middle names and capitalizes only the first word in a document title and the first word following a colon. Notice in the second example that you use "n.d." (no date) if there is no date of posting available.

Web Sites: Scholarly Projects and Databases

MLA

Kheel Center for Labor-Management Documentation and Archives. 2001. Cornell University School of Industrial and Labor Relations. 14 July 2001 <www.ilr.cornell.edu/library/kheelcenter/default.html?page+home>.

History of "Race" in Science, Medicine, and Technology. Ed. Evelynn Hammonds and Michelle Murphy. Feb. 2001. Massachusetts Institute of Technology. 5 May 2001 <http://www.mit.edu/ his.race.html>.

For scholarly Web sites and databases, include editors' names, if any, and sponsoring organization.

APA

Kheel Center for labor-management documentation and archives. (2001.) Retrieved July 14, 2001, from Cornell University School of Industrial and Labor Relations Web site: http://www.ilr.cornell.edu/library/kheelcenter/default.html?page+home

Hammonds, E. & Murphy, M. (Eds.). *History of "race" in science, medicine, and technology.* (2001, February). Retrieved May 5, 2001, from Massachusetts Institute of Technology Web site: http://www.mit.edu/his.race.html

Web Sites: Secondary Pages
MLA

Stone, Eric J. "What Would the Founding Fathers Think About Official English?" 30 Dec. 1997. U.S. English Only. 8 Feb. 2001 <http://www.us-english.org/stone.html>.

"The Triangle Factory Fire." *Kheel Center for Labor-Management Documentation and Archives.* 24 Mar. 2001. Cornell University School of Industrial and Labor Relations. 14 July 2001 <http://www.ilr.cornell.edu/trianglefire/>.

Notice that the URL links to the Web page cited, not to the U.S. English Only home page or the Kheel Center.

APA

Stone, E. J. (1997, December 30). What would the Founding Fathers think about official English? Retrieved February 8, 2001, from the U.S. English Only Web site: http://www.us-english.org/stone.html

The triangle factory factory fire. (2001, March 24). Retrieved May 1, 2001, from Cornell University of Industrial and Labor Relations, Kheel Center for Labor-Management Documentation and Archives Web site: http://www.ilr.cornell.edu/trianglefire/

Notice that the U.S. English Only and the Kheel Center Web sites are included in the retrieval statement.

Online Books and Reports
MLA

Ginsburg, Allen. *Howl and Other Poems.* San Francisco: City Lights, 1956. 14 Sept. 2001 <http://php.indiana.edu/~avigdor/poetry/ginsburg.html>.

APA

Harrison Rips Foundation. (2000). *Creating underdevelopment: Capital flight and the case for debt reduction in South Africa.* Retrieved August 5, 2001, from http://www.ripsfoundation.org/southafrica.report.html

Online Scholarly Articles
MLA

Poole, Jason. "On Borrowed Ground: Free African-American Life in Charlestown, South Carolina 1810–61." *Essays in History,* 36 (1994): 112–145. 10 Mar. 1999 <http://www.lib.virginia.edu/journals/EH//EH36/poole.html>.

Warren, William. "Allergies and Spatio-Temporal Disorders." *Modern Psychology* 6.3 (1997): 15 pars. 13 Nov. 2000 <http://www..liasu.edu/ modpsy/ warren6(3).html>.

Foster, George. "Language Policy in Namibia*." Southern Africa Review* 7 (2001). 18 June 2001 <http://www.soafricarev.org/foster7.01>.

Online journals may give page numbers (as in the first example); number paragraphs (as in the second example); or not use numbers at all (as in the third example).

APA

Poole, J. (1994). On borrowed ground: Free African-American life in Charlestown, South Carolina 1810–61. *Essays in History,* 36, 112–145. Retrieved November 13, 2000, from http://www.lib.virginia.edu/ journals/EH/EH36/poole.html

Warren, W. (1997). Allergies and spatio-temporal disorders. *Modern Psychology,* 6 (3). Retrieved November 13, 2000, from http://www..liasu .edu/modpsy/warren6(3).html

Online Magazine or Newsletter Article

MLA

Shapiro, Bruce. "Dead Reckoning." *Nation* 6 Aug. 2001. 10 Aug. 2001 <http://www.thenation.com/doc.mhtml/?i=20010806&s=shapiro>.

Rimington, Eleanor. "Court Case Challenges Microsoft." *WinNews Electronic Newsletter* 8 Mar. 1998: 15 May 2001 <http://www.winnews.com/ yr1998/mar/rimington_8768.html>.

APA

Shapiro, B. (2001, August 6). Dead reckoning. *The Nation.* Retrieved August 10, 2001, from http://www.thenation.com/doc.mhtml/ ?i=20010806&s=shapiro

Rimington, E. (1998, March 8). Court case challenges Microsoft. *WinNews Electronic Newsletter.* Retrieved May 15, 2001, from <http://www .winnews.com/yr1998/mar/rimington_8768.html>.

Online Newspaper Articles

MLA

Morrow, David J. "Attention Disorder Is Found in Growing Number of Adults." *New York Times* 2 Sept. 1997. 15 Oct. 2000 <http://archives .nytimes.com/archives/search/fastweb?search>

APA

Morrow, D. J. (1997, September 2). Attention disorder is found in growing number of adults. *The New York Times.* [Newspaper, article in archive.] Retrieved October 15, 2000, from http://www.nytimes.com/ archives/search/fastweb?search

Notice that source information can be added in brackets.

Online Posting to Electronic Forum
MLA

Marshall, Richard. "The Political Economy of Cancer Research." 21 Apr. 1997 Online posting. H-Net List on the History of Science, Medicine, and Technology. 28 Sept. 1999 <h-sci-med-tech@h-net.msu.edu>.

Lopez, Arsenio. "Globalization or Imperialism as the Highest Stage of Capitalism?" 18 November 2000 Online posting. Black Flag Forum. 31 June 2001 <http://www.blackflag.org/openforum/mail-archive111800>.

Murphy, Christian. "Irish FAQ: The Famine." 5 Apr. 1998. Online posting. 1 May 1998 <news:soc.culture.irish/Irish_FAQ_The_Famine>.

Notice that for Usenet news groups, as in the third example, the name of the news group appears in the URL.

APA

Lopez, A. (2000, November 18). "Globalization or imperialism as the highest stage of capitalism?" Message posted to Black Flag Forum, archived at http://www.blackflag.org/openforum/mail-archive111800

In general, only cite in References those postings that have been archived and thus can be retrieved. See note on APA in next section.

E-Mail
MLA

Fox, Tom. E-mail to the author. 25 Feb. 2001.
Braun, Lundy. "Re: Myth of Killer Viruses." E-mail to the author. 4 May 2000.

For e-mail, list the title (if there is one) from the e-mail's subject heading.

APA

APA style treats e-mail, as well as any nonarchived postings on electronic forums, as a nonretrievable source. Cite e-mails and other nonretrievable sources in the text as personal communications, but do not list them on the References page. For example:

Medical historians have challenged Elaine Showalter's view of chronic fatigue syndrome (L. Braun, personal communication, February 25, 1999).

SAMPLE MLA AND APA RESEARCH PAPERS

The following two research papers are good examples of MLA and APA styles. Brion Keagle's "Blues Song and Devil's Music" (MLA format) was written for a term paper assignment in an African-American literature and culture course. Jenny Chen's "Defining Disease: The Case of Chronic Fatigue Syndrome" (APA format) was written in response to a research assignment in a science writing course.

Before we present the papers, it may be useful to note manuscript preparation features common to MLA and APA and features that are distinct.

Checklist of Manuscript Preparation for MLA- and APA-Style Research Papers

Features Common to Both MLA and APA Style

- Manuscript should be double-spaced, including block quotations and Works Cited and References pages.

- Format a one-inch margin all around, top and bottom, left and right.

- Indent five spaces to begin a paragraph.

- Number pages consecutively, including Works Cited and References pages.

Special Features Called for by MLA Style

- Unless your teacher tells you to, do not include a separate cover sheet. Type the following information, double-spaced, at the top left corner of the manuscript, in this order: your name, your professor's name, course number, and date. Double-space and center the title of your paper. Follow conventional rules of capitalizing words in a title. Don't use boldface, underlining, all capitals, or showy fonts. Double-space and begin the text.

- Insert page numbers in the upper right corner, flush with the right margin, one-half inch from the top of the page. Precede the page number with your last name. Begin the text one inch from the top.

- Put your bibliography on a separate page, titled "Works Cited." Center the title one inch from the top, without any quotation marks, underlining, boldface, or italics. Include in the Works Cited only those works you have cited in the text of the paper. It is not a comprehensive bibliography (you may have used other works which are not cited).

Special Features Called for by APA Style

- Use a separate cover page. Center your title approximately one-third from the top of the page. Type the title double-spaced if it has more than one line. Follow usual capitalization conventions. Don't use all caps, boldface, quotation marks, underlining, or italics. Center and double-space your name. Double-space again and type the course number, and then following another double space, type the date.

- On the page immediately following the cover sheet, include a 100- to 150-word "Abstract" that summarizes the contents of your paper.

- Begin the text on the third page. Don't repeat the title. Number all the pages, beginning with the cover sheet as page 1 and the "Abstract" as page 2. Type a running head (shortened version of the title) before the page number.

- APA style research papers are much more likely than MLA style papers to use section headings. Some research papers will use the conventional headings—"Introduction," "Methods," "Results," and "Discussion"—but others will use headings based on the content of the paper. Notice the section headings Jenny Chen uses in her paper.

- Your bibliography or References should begin on a separate page, following the text. Center the word "References" one inch from the top, without any underlining, italics, quotes, boldface, or other special treatment.

Brion Keagle

Dr. Trimbur

English 1XX

2 May 19XX

BLUES SONGS AND THE DEVIL'S MUSIC

In the 1930s, Son House and Charlie Patton were names to remember in the Mississippi Delta. Two of the most popular blues singers on the circuit, they did not have the time or interest to show a newcomer named Robert Johnson the ropes. Trying unsuccessfully to hang out with the older, more accomplished musicians, Johnson could not play the guitar to save his life and was often an object of ridicule. Eventually he disappeared and was promptly forgotten. Two years later, however, he appeared again, still looking to be heard. His elders tried to put him off, but he persisted. Finally, they let him play during a break and left him alone with the tables and chairs. Outside, taking the air, House and others heard a loud, devastating music of a purity and brilliance beyond anything in the memory of the Mississippi Delta. "He sold his soul to the devil to get to play like that," House told blues historian Pete Welding (qtd. in Marcus 32).

Thus was born the legend of Robert Johnson. He had sold his soul to the devil to play the blues. As Jon Spencer puts it, "The ambitious, daring, or desperate individual who wanted to learn the so-called 'black art' of playing the blues was believed to have gone to the crossroads at midnight where and when he 'took up' his instrument from the devil" (27). Opinion is divided on whether Johnson actually did sell his soul to the devil. There are,

Keagle 2

on one hand, the "bluesmen who knew [Johnson] and believed he made a pact with the devil" and, on the other, the "folklorists who don't" (Finn 210). In the minds of Johnson's contemporaries one thing was certain: no one could get so good so fast without some kind of supernatural intervention.

The compositions that resulted from the supposed deal were so intricately woven and suffused with the dark, the satanic, the evil, and the terrible as to be almost supernatural themselves. As music critic Greil Marcus says, "There were demons in his songs—blues that walked like a man, the devil, or the two in league with each other" (24). The terror in Johnson's "Cross Road Blues" can be seen, for example, on a literal level, as part of a "tragic" song about a "homeless man adrift on the highways of America" (Yurchenco 452), trying to flag a ride as the sun goes down. For a lone black man in the 1930s, the crossroads could be a dangerous place. But, as Robert Palmer says, Johnson is not afraid simply of the white sheriff or passing rednecks. The terror in "Cross Road Blues" is also "metaphysical" (126). In the first verse, Johnson sings, "Went down to the crossroads, fell down on my knees/Asked the Lord above, have mercy, save poor Bob if you please" (Johnson).

To say that Johnson's blues are haunted is to understate the sense of evil pursuing him. In "Hellhound on My Trail," Johnson seems to feel the devil closing in on him, perhaps to exact his part of the bargain:

> I got to keep moving
>
> Blues falling down like hail
>
> Ummmm

Blues falling down like hail

And the days keep on worrying me

There's a hellhound on my trail.

It could be, as Julio Finn argues, that when Johnson went away for two years, he was initiated into a voodoo cult by a Root Doctor deep in the bayous of the Mississippi Delta (215). Whether an actual initiation is the source of Johnson's legendary deal with the devil, the story of Robert Johnson reveals a deep-seated association of the blues with evil. In the words of blues singer Rosa Lee Hill, "The blues...is for the bad man and the church songs for the Lord" (qtd. in Mitchell 66). The elder of a church congregation warned an aging blues singer: "You better quit singing them blues. You ain't too old for the devil to get you" (qtd. in Mitchell 133).

Clearly there is a profound mistrust of the blues where the fate of one's soul is concerned. For many, the word "blues" has a negative, ungodly connotation, while gospel, first cousin to the blues, is considered righteous, pious, and acceptable in the eyes of God. In *Blues People*, Leroi Jones (Amiri Baraka), says that with "the legal end of slavery, there was now proposed...a much fuller life outside the church. There came to be more and more backsliders and more of the devil's music was heard" (40). To understand how the blues and gospel polarized as forms of musical and cultural expression, we need to examine both African and American culture and the process of acculturation that translated African values and beliefs to life in North America.

Musically speaking, blues and gospel share the same components. Most of the musical elements have their antecedents

Keagle 4

in West African tradition. Key ingredients are the use of polyrhythms (generally with the off beat emphasized), "blue notes" (rising emotions are associated with a falling pitch), and a variety of vocal techniques to color the melody and give it identity and expressiveness (Barlow 4). Good musicians use their instruments as they would their voices, to emulate the sounds of human speech. Notes are bent or flattened, and special attention is paid to volume. Ending the description here, however, would be to neglect the most crucial, elemental aspect of both the blues and gospel, the component which avid listeners never fail to discern and the property which makes or breaks performers depending on how they use it and how much of it they possess. This most prominent aspect of the blues and gospel is called soul. If one were to mention it in the right circles, an entire dancehall or church full of people would comprehend it instantly but remain almost entirely unable to define it.

The term "soul" is such an elusive one that it rarely appears in the index of books on African American music. As a musical label, soul music refers to the Motown and Memphis sounds of the 1960s. But the term has been in use much longer, as the gospel singer Mahalia Jackson explains:

> What some people call the "blues singing feeling" is expressed by the Church of God in Christ. Songs like "The Lord Followed Me" became so emotional...[they] almost led to panic. But the blues was here before they called it the blues. This kind of song came after spirituals. The old folk prayed to God because they were in an oppressed condition.

While in slavery they got a different kind of blues. Take these later songs like "Summertime," it's the same as "Sometimes I Feel Like a Motherless Child" ...which had the blue note in it. The basic thing is soul feeling. The same in blues as in spirituals. And also with gospel music. It is soul music (qtd. in Ricks 139).

Soul, as the British writer Clive Anderson puts it, "is made by black Americans and elevates 'feeling' above all else....Soul assumes a shared experience, a relationship with the listener...where the singer confirms and works out the feelings of the audience. In this sense it remains sacramental" (qtd. in Guralnick, *Sweet Soul* 3). Soul, in other words, means empathy, solidarity, and what Richard Wright called an "other worldly yearning" (128) for a better time and an end to oppression. Rooted in the spirituals of slavery, soul is a spiritual and emotional force that binds performer and audience together in the blues and gospel alike.

From a musical standpoint, there are more similarities than differences between blues and gospel. Both embrace the concept of soul and a technical vocabulary of blue notes, dynamic vocal displays, polyrhythms, semitones, and bent or slurred notes. Nonetheless, despite the common property of soul, the blues are marked as secular and gospel as sacred. According to Charles Keil, a "transgressing" bluesman must give up his evil ways once and for all to answer the call of the church. "The transition," Keil says, "from blues role to preacher role is unidirectional" (*Urban Blues* 148). For most of the history of the blues and gospel, the line between the two has been a fixed one. One was in the blues camp or the gospel camp. For this reason, when Guitar Slim recorded the eight bar ballad "Feelin' Sad" in 1952, his use of heart wrenching gospel cries and moans over horn and piano accompaniment was viewed as blasphemous and disrespectful. The idea of "unadulterated backcountry gospel with secular lyrics" was, as Robert Palmer notes, a matter of "using the Lord's music to do the Devil's work" (248). Similarly, "Ray Charles's transformation of dignified gospel standards into cries of secular ecstasy came in for a good deal of criticism at first, mostly from the pulpit" (Guralnick, Searching 2).

The schism between blues and gospel, secular and sacred music in the African American tradition evolved out of the lived experience of the Africans brought to North America as slaves. African values held by the earliest slaves had to be adapted to fit into a Christian culture, while traditional folkloristic and religious figures had to assume new guises in order to survive in the New World. For our purposes, the transformation of Legba, the Yoruban trickster, is particularly illuminating.

Jon Spencer suggests that of all the African trickster-gods, Legba "best personified the blues....He is both malevolent and benevolent, disruptive and reconciliatory, profane and sacred, and yet the predominant attitude toward him is affection rather than fear" (11). Legba intervenes between humans and the gods. He is the guardian who opens the door for other supernatural powers. He is considered the only entirely unpredictable god in the Yoruban pantheon. Thriving on chaos and confusion, he is not summonable by the ordinary means used to call on the other gods. Instead, he is encountered at the crossroads in his role as the "ultimate master of potentiality" with the power "to make all things happen" (Thompson 18).

In the figure of Legba, there is no separation of good and evil, the sacred and the secular. Legba stands for the integration of all the contradictory forces of life. According to Julio Finn, it is not the devil Robert Johnson encountered at the crossroads but Legba the trickster who meets him at midnight, tunes his guitar, and gives him the power of the blues song (215–17). The story of Robert Johnson selling his soul to the devil comes from a reinterpretation of the Legba figure that turns him from Yoruban trickster to Christian devil. The life forces that coexist in the African Legba polarize into good and evil under the pressure of Christianity. In the Christian faith, God represents all that is good, Satan is the ultimate agent of evil, and there remains no room in between for a trickster deity like Legba.

The Yoruban trickster turns from a unification of opposites into a polarized figure—with the emphasis on his evil and frightful side. Similarly, African American music polarized as well. As a polytheistic people oriented themselves to the monotheistic world of Christianity, good and evil separated. The concurrent development of gospel and blues is a direct result of this process. From their common sources in slave songs, gospel became the African American's devotional music, while the blues became the sinful counterpart. There was no middle ground.

This theme of polarization is readily apparent in the relation of the preacher to the bluesman. It has often been said that the two roles are similar. "As professions," Keil says, "blues singing and preaching seem to be closely linked in both the rural or small town settings and in the urban ghettos" (*Urban Blues* 143). Both employ the same call and response pattern of performance. The difference is that in gospel praise is directed toward God. In blues, the acclaim is for the benefit of the performer. For this reason, no one can be a bluesman and preacher simultaneously. The social roles are mutually exclusive. There are many instances of bluesmen becoming preachers, or preachers backsliding into the blues. But there are virtually no examples of individuals serving both masters at the same time. In his youth, blues singer Big Bill Broonzy alternated back and forth between roles and was told categorically by his father to stop "straddling the fence" (Keil, *Urban Blues* 145).

The separation of the sacred and secular is also evident in the comparison of the church and the juke joint. Charles Keil refers to a "Saturday night and Sunday morning pattern" of African American weekends (*Urban Blues* 164). Saturday night was often spent at the juke joint where blues musicians provided the entertainment by engaging the audience in such participatory actions as hand clapping, dance, and call and response rituals where the bluesman asks "Did you ever love a woman who didn't love you?" Sunday morning was occupied in a similar way. In church the hand clapping, dance, and call and response pattern are just as apparent, only the preacher asks "Have you got good religion?"

Keagle 9

Bluesmen like Robert Johnson and Peetie Wheatstraw used this polarization of the sacred and the secular to their advantage in constructing an image for themselves. As Keil says, "In most things connected with the blues, there is a pattern of African American culture and at the same time there is a commercial aspect to it in terms of what will sell. The aura sold records" (personal interview). As Finn notes, the fact that bluesmen vouched for the credibility of Robert Johnson's deal with the devil is in part a marketing strategy that "adds to the charm of this blues life—and it sells records" (210).

The history of the blues is filled with musicians playing with names and personas, inventing a reputation for themselves. Peetie Wheatstraw, the self-proclaimed "High Sheriff from Hell," is a classic example. Robert Johnson bought the image. Tommy Johnson may have invented it. He advised his fellow bluesmen: "you take your guitar and go to...where a crossroad is....A big black man will walk up there and take your guitar, and he'll tune it. And then he'll play a piece and hand it back to you. That's the way I learned to play anything I want" (qtd. in Guralnick, *Searching*). These men knew the appeal of the transgressive side of human nature and the power that the "devil's music" seems to hold. They knew that the power of the crossroads, black cat bones, and conjuring were more immediate and tangible than any promise Heaven could make.

Paul Oliver says the blues are the songs of people who have turned their back on religion. There is certainly some truth to this statement, but it relies too much on the polarization of sacred and secular traced in this paper. In many respects, the notion of the blues as a gift from Legba, the black man at the crossroads, is not a turn away from religion as much as it is a turn back to an older religion, an African one without the severe polarization of good and evil, god and devil, heaven and earth of Christianity. As Jon Spencer notes, the reason some blues musicians might have sold their souls to the devil is that they "were seemingly not that frightened of him" (31). If not a source of "good," in the dualistic Christian sense, the devil was more like a conjure man than a satanic anti-Christ, a source of power in this world.

Keagle 11

WORKS CITED

Finn, Julio. *The Bluesman: The Musical Heritage of Black Men and Women in the Americas.* New York: Interlink, 1992.

Guralnick, Peter. *Searching for Robert Johnson.* New York: Harper, 1982. 14 Oct. 1998 <http://www.thebluehighway.com/tbh1.html>.

---. *Sweet Soul Music: Rhythm and Blues and the Southern Dream of Freedom.* New York: Harper, 1986.

Johnson, Robert. *Robert Johnson: King of the Delta Blues Singers.* Columbia, PCT 1654, 1985.

Jones, Leroi (Amiri Baraka). *Blues People.* New York: Morrow, 1963.

Keil, Charles. Personal interview. 15 April 1997.

---. *Urban Blues.* Chicago: U of Chicago P, 1969.

Marcus, Greil. *Mystery Train.* New York: Dutton, 1975.

Mitchell, George. *Blow My Blues Away.* Baton Rouge: Louisiana State UP, 1971.

Oliver, Paul. *Blues Fell This Morning: Meaning in the Blues*, 2nd ed. Cambridge: Cambridge UP, 1990.

Palmer, Robert. *Deep Blues.* New York: Viking, 1981.

Ricks, George Robinson. *Some Aspects of the Religious Music of the United States Negro: An Ethnomusicological Study with Special Emphasis on the Gospel Tradition.* New York: Arno, 1977.

Spencer, Jon Michael. *Blues and Evil.* Knoxville: U of Tennessee P, 1993.

Thompson, Robert Farris. *Flash of the Spirit.* New York: Vintage, 1983.

Wright, Richard. *12 Million Black Voices: A Folk History of the Negro in the United States.* New York: Viking, 1941.

Yurchenco, Henrietta. "'Blues Fallin' Down like Hail': Recorded Blues, 1920s–1940s." *American Music* 13.4 (1995): 448–69.

DEFINING DISEASE:
THE CASE OF CHRONIC FATIGUE SYNDROME

Jenny Chen

English 1XX

November 20, 19XX

ABSTRACT

The current controversy about whether chronic fatigue syndrome (CFS) is an illness with an organic basis or an imaginary condition poses important questions about how the medical profession defines disease and contains important consequences for treatment. CFS affects predominantly white, middle-class women. Literary critic Elaine Showalter has recently argued that CFS is a contemporary version of nineteenth-century neurasthenia or nervous exhaustion and should be treated by psychotherapy. Others argue that treating CFS as a psychological disorder stigmatizes CFS patients and causes conflicts between patients and doctors. Recently some physicians have proposed that the biomedical model of disease is too rigid and that the medical profession and the public need to understand how the physical and psychological operate simultaneously in patients' illness.

Defining Disease 2

The publication of Elaine Showalter's *Hystories: Hysterical Epidemics and Modern Media* (1997) has intensified the debate over chronic fatigue syndrome (CFS) and how it should be defined as a medical condition. According to a recent report (Reyes & Luciano, 1997), CFS has been recognized since the early 1980s as an illness whose cause is unknown and for which no diagnostic tests have been developed. CFS patients are predominantly white middle-class women. The "illness is diagnosed primarily on the basis of symptoms and signs reported by the patient and exclusion of other possible causes of prolonged, debilitating fatigue" (Reyes & Luciano, p. 2).

In Showalter's view, CFS is a psychogenic condition, a modern day form of nineteenth-century neurasthenia or nervous exhaustion. For Showalter, CFS has no physical basis but results from repressed and unarticulated psychological conflicts that manifest themselves in such flu-like symptoms as sore throat, tired and achy feeling, low-grade fever, and swollen lymph nodes. The appropriate treatment is psychotherapy.

One of the things that makes Showalter's book so controversial is that she groups CFS, as well as gulf war syndrome and multiple personality syndrome, with other contemporary "hysterical epidemics" such as alien abductions, satanic ritual abuse, and recovered memory. In Showalter's account, people "learn" the symptoms of these disorders from the media, telecommunications, and e-mail: "Infectious epidemics of hysteria spread by stories circulated through self-help books, articles in newspapers and magazines, TV talk shows and series, films, the Internet, and even literary criticism" (p. 5). For her critics, however, lumping illnesses such as CFS and gulf war syndrome together with UFOs and satanic cults trivializes real suffering. By defining "illness as a story instead of a physical condition (with the CFS sufferer acting out, say, the narrative of the bored and frustrated housewife), Showalter diverts our attention from real suffering" (Marcie Richardson, Re: Showalter as medical historian, E-mail to the author, April 15, 1997).

The controversy over Showalter's new book is not just an academic one. CFS presents an interesting and important case study of how medical conditions are categorized and how they acquire legitimacy. Skepticism concerning CFS is not limited to literary critics such as Showalter. It is also widespread within the medical profession. Whether CFS is an illness with an organic basis or an imaginary condition is a question that carries important implications for treatment. Should CFS be treated by a physician or a psychiatrist? Answers to this question depend on assumptions about how illness is defined.

BACKGROUND ON CFS

Chronic fatigue syndrome began to draw national attention in the early 1980s. In 1984, the outbreak of a mysterious illness in Incline Village, a small town of 6,000 inhabitants near Lake Tahoe, manifested a number of symptoms subsequently associated with CFS—dizziness, sore throats, headaches, diarrhea, shortness of breath, rapid heartbeat, and overall weakness. Within a year, there were over one hundred cases reported, and the Center for Disease Control (CDC) sent a team to investigate. CDC officials concluded that the Epstein-Barr virus, suspected at the time of being the source of chronic fatigue symptoms, could not be established as the cause of the mysterious illness (Johnson, 1996, pp. 33–51).

The Lake Tahoe outbreak is emblematic in many respects of the state of knowledge about CFS. For one thing, many of the patients were affluent young professionals, and their condition became known in the media in the 1980s as "Yuppie Flu." At the time, some physicians believed the cause of fatigue might be stress or overwork.

Second, physicians and researchers noted that patient conditions included immunological and neurological dysfunction. Nonetheless, no causal agent could be established. Lake Tahoe patients were no more likely than the general population to show evidence of infection with Epstein-Barr virus, and subsequent studies have eliminated Epstein-Barr as a candidate (Reyes & Luciano, 1997, p. 2). Other studies have eliminated a host of chemicals, bacteria, and viruses as suspected causes (Showalter, 1997, p. 125). At present, the etiology of CFS is unknown. The condition remains elusive to researchers.

Third, while there is no established cause, there are nonetheless a cluster of symptoms that seem to be associated. The persistence of these symptoms led CDC in 1988 to classify chronic fatigue as a syndrome and publish a case definition of CFS. According to CDC guidelines, the diagnosis of CFS depends on two major criteria, namely the exclusion of other clinical conditions (such as cancer, AIDS, or multiple sclerosis) and the

Defining Disease 5

persistence of symptoms over a period of six months or more. Then patients must show at least six of the following eleven symptoms: mild fever, sore throat, painful lymph nodes, muscle aches, excessive fatigue after normal activity, headaches, joint pain, impaired mental functioning (forgetfulness, excessive irritability, confusion, inability to concentrate, and so on), sleep disorders, and rapid onset of symptoms.

To put it in other words, the CDC classification of chronic fatigue as a syndrome establishes CFS as a medical condition that can be diagnosed as a cause of illness. CFS does not have the status of disease. Instead, it is considered to be a syndrome, or cluster of associated symptoms whose causes are unknown.

A recent report from CDC (Reyes & Luciano, 1997) summarizes a good deal of available information about the demographics of CFS. It confirms earlier studies that set the mean age of CFS patients at the time of onset at 30 years. It notes that the reported prevalence of CFS ranges from 3.8 to 9.6 cases per 100,000. And it indicates that the vast majority of CFS patients are white (96%) and female (85%), with median household income of $40,000.

DEFINING ILLNESS

As Simon Wessely (1994) says,

> Worrying about whether or not CFS exists...is hardly the issue. It exists in the real world....What lies behind CFS is neither a virus, nor psychiatry, but our idea of what constitutes a real illness, what doesn't, and what we do to make something real. (p. 29)

Although Showalter argues that people should not be ashamed of hysteria, there is nonetheless a strong stigma attached to imaginary illnesses. As Arthur Kleinman and Stephen Straus (1993) write, "In much of biomedicine, only a tangible or laboratory abnormality justifies the imprimatur of a 'real' disease" (p. 3).

Often if the organic cause of an illness is not known, the illness is dismissed as a "real" disease and the sufferer is not entitled to sympathy from doctors or society. Charles Rosenburg (1992) says that "[f]or many Americans, the meaning of disease is the mechanism that defines it" (p. 312). For patients with cancer, tuberculosis, multiple sclerosis, and other diseases with established etiologies, an identity and a social role are available to patients based on diagnosis by the medical profession. Naming a patient's disease in effect gives him or her "permission" to be sick and offers validation to the patient's complaints.

Such diagnosis, as Hans Selye writes, can have direct benefit to the patient: "It is well-established that the mere fact of knowing what hurts you has an inherent curative value" (cited in Berne, 1995, p. 53). Rosenburg makes a similar point when he says that even "a bad prognosis can be better than no prognosis at all; even a dangerous disease, if it is made familiar and understandable, can be emotionally more manageable than a mysterious and unpredictable one" (p. 310).

Moreover, there are very real legal and financial consequences to the diagnosis of disease. Health benefits from insurance companies normally cover only those medical conditions that are considered to be legitimate and well established. Similarly eligibility for disability benefits and other social services is based on medical diagnosis. Employers' policies concerning medical leave, job responsibilities, special accommodations, and so on likewise depend on definitions of illness and disease.

DEFINING AND TREATING CFS

The popular press and medical journals discuss CFS in very different terms. According to a study of all the articles published in the British scientific, medical, and popular press between 1980 and 1994, only 31% of articles in medical journals believed the cause of CFS to be organic rather than psychological, while 69% of the articles in newspapers and magazines held to an organic explanation for the illness (MacLean & Wessely, 1994). This division between journalism and biomedicine is a troubling one because it points to divisions between patients and physicians concerning the origins and treatment of CFS.

In newspapers and magazines, CFS is often portrayed as a mystery disease which has yet to be conquered by modern medicine. The idea that the cause of CFS is out there to be found is reassuring to CFS patients, in part because it tells the familiar story of the march of scientific progress and its victories over disease. In this sense, CFS patients have their own stake in desiring that the causes of CFS are organic. Such a view of causation, where a pathogenic agent causes a pathological effect, is the basis for a potential cure in store—the magic bullet that can knock out the illness.

Defining Disease 8

An organic cause of the illness not only makes CFS more treatable. It would also lift feelings of guilt and stigma from patients and clear them of charges of laziness, malingering, depression, and deceit. As David Bell (1995) writes, "Patients are angry and frustrated, interpreting the debate over emotions as trivializations of their illness and as the explanation for why so little is done for them" (p. 53). In many of the magazine articles, especially in personal accounts of CFS, patients express deep and abiding anger that physicians routinely describe their illness as psychological in origin. Part of the conflict between patients and doctors stems from the fact that defining CFS as a psychological syndrome, as most physicians do, appears to disqualify the patient's experience as a proper illness and portray it as a moral failing instead.

The most sympathetic physicians, on the other hand, respond that patients and the public at large need to recognize that psychological illness is just as real as illness that has a somatic basis. Anthony Komaroff (1994) says that CFS "may become a paradigmatic illness that leads us away from being trapped in the rigidity of the conventional biomedical model and leads us toward a fuller understanding of suffering" (52). Komaroff's sentiments are important ones, and there seems in principle to be growing agreement, in the words of the British Royal College of Physicians, Psychiatrists, and General Practitioners, that "CFS cannot be considered either 'physical' or 'psychological'—both need to be considered simultaneously to understand the syndrome" (cited in Brody, 1996, p. C14).

Nonetheless, the paradigm shift that Komaroff talks about has yet to take place, and the world of medicine continues to hold to a traditional biomedical model of illness in which patients with organic illness are treated by physicians and patients with psychological problems are treated by psychiatrists. So the basic problem of legitimate and illegitimate illness remains, marked by the presence or absence of organic causes. Perhaps the best solution, as Kleinman (1993) suggests, is to have physicians, not psychiatrists, treat CFS patients:

> One can affirm the illness experience without affirming the attribution for it; in other words, we can work within a 'somatic' language and do all the interventions...from the psychosocial side, but in such a way to spare patients the...delegitimization of their experience. (p. 329)

REFERENCES

Bell, D. S. (1995). *The doctor's guide to chronic fatigue syndrome.* Boston: Addison-Wesley.

Berne, K. H. (1995). *Running on empty: A complete guide to chronic fatigue syndrome.* Alameda, CA: Hunter House.

Brody, J. E. (1996, October 9). Battling an elusive foe: Fatigue syndrome. *The New York Times,* p. C14.

Johnson, H. (1996). *Osler's web.* New York: Crown Books.

Kleinman, A. (1993). CFS and the illness narrative. In A. Kleinman & S. Straus (Eds.), *Chronic fatigue syndrome* (pp. 318–332). London: Wiley.

Kleinman, A., & Straus, S. (1993). Introduction. In A. Kleinman & S. Straus (Eds.), *Chronic fatigue syndrome* (pp. 3–25). London: Wiley.

Komaroff, A. K. (1994). Clinical presentation and evaluation of fatigue in CFS. In S. Straus (Ed.), *Chronic fatigue syndrome* (pp. 47–64). New York: Marcel Dekker.

MacLean, G., & Wessely, S. (1994). Professional and popular views of chronic fatigue syndrome. *British Medical Journal, 308*, 773–786.

Reyes, M., Simons, L., & Luciano, P. (1997, February 21). Surveillance for chronic fatigue syndrome: Four U.S. cities, September 1989 through August 1993. *Morbidity and Mortality Weekly Report, 46* (SS–2), 1–13.

Rosenburg, C. (1992). *Explaining epidemics and other studies in the history of medicine.* New York: Cambridge University Press.

Showalter, E. (1997). *Hystories: Hysterical epidemics and modern media.* New York: Columbia University Press.

Wessely, S. (1994). The history of chronic fatigue syndrome. In S. Straus (Ed.), *Chronic fatigue syndrome* (pp. 11–34). New York: Marcel Dekker.

CHAPTER NINETEEN

Visual Design

Why does visual design belong in a writing class? There are two main reasons. First, visual communication is playing an increasingly important role in everyday life, in the workplace, in the public sphere, and in academic settings. Accordingly, the ability to read and evaluate visual messages—whether they come through the mass media, printed texts, or computer screens—has become a central part of what it means to be literate.

Second, visual design belongs in a writing class because writing itself is a visual form of communication, and learning to write in part means learning how to produce well-designed print and digital texts—everything from academic papers, reports, and resumés to flyers, brochures, newsletters, posters, and Web sites. Throughout this book, we've talked about what makes written texts persuasive and easy to follow. At this point, we need to examine the visual dimension of writing and how the design of the page can contribute to readability and persuasion.

We start by considering how visual communication is used for purposes of identification, information, and persuasion. Next, we will see how you can create effective page designs and use type to enhance your message. Finally, we will look at such common visual design projects as flyers, newsletters, brochures, and Web sites.

The goal of the chapter is to enable you to understand some of the basic principles of visual design so that you can produce documents that fit the situation, that help readers navigate the page, and that influence your readers in the ways you intend.

HOW VISUAL DESIGN EMBODIES PURPOSE

In Chapter 14, "The Form of Nonfiction Prose," we looked at how written forms embody writers' purposes. In this section, we will do something similar by considering how visual forms embody designers' purposes.

Identification

One of the primary functions of visual design is to identify things, places, publications, and organizations. Street and building signs, flags, logos, trademarks, letterheads, package labels, and mastheads on newspapers and magazines are just some of the typical visual forms used for purposes of identification. For example, the sign system developed in 1974 for the U.S. Department of Transportation by the Amer-

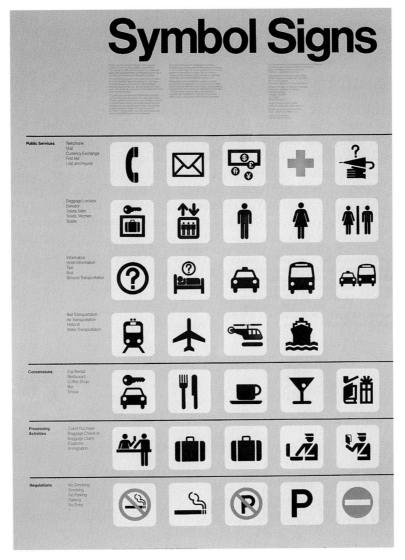

Transportation Symbols

ican Institute of Graphic Arts (signs and poster designed by Roger Cook and Don Shanosky of Cook and Shanosky Associates, Inc.) provides a wordless set of symbols to help passengers, drivers, and pedestrians orient themselves in airports and on highways. On the other hand, mastheads on newspapers and magazines use words themselves as visual symbols, to send a message about the publication's identity and attitude—for example, the fashionable elegance of *Vogue* or *Architectural Digest,* the high-tech look of *Wired,* or the hip iconoclasm of *Interview.*

Analyzing Logos and Trademarks

Logos and trademarks identify a broad range of organizations—corporations such as IBM, hip stores such as Vertigo, nonprofits such as United Way, and political movements such as Solidarity in Poland. Notice how each of the logos included here projects a strong sense of the organization's identity.

For example, the noted graphic designer Paul Rand uses bold, square capital letters to give the IBM logo a powerful and conservative look, while April Greiman mixes typefaces to project a playful "new wave" look for the clothing and gift store Vertigo. On the other hand, notice that Saul Bass's logo for the United Way uses no words at all but instead the visual metaphor of an open hand enclosing a small figure within half circles to create an image of a supportive community that takes care of its needy members. The logo for Solidarity, the Polish trade union that helped end one-party Communist rule in 1989, uses letters as visual forms to suggest both a sense of massed strength and of collective movement.

Logos

1. Quaker Oats was one of the earliest food products to be packaged in visually attractive containers instead of shipped in bulk. Since the late nineteenth century, the symbol of the Quaker has been a familiar one to
   consumers. (There is no actual connection between Quakers and the
   American Cereal Company, which first marketed Quaker Oats; the figure was chosen because Quaker merchants were associated in the popular mind with honesty and trustworthiness.)
   You can see how the visual design depicting the Quaker has changed
   from the full figure that originally appeared on Quaker Oats packages in
   the nineteenth century, replaced in 1946 by the designer Jim Nash's
   image of the Quaker face and, more recently, by the full-color realistic
   portrait that is now the main image on Quaker Oats boxes.

c. 1900

Corporate logo 1946

Corporate logo 1970

c. 2000

Quaker Oats Logos

2. Bring a Quaker Oats box to class. Notice that in addition to the picture
   of the Quaker man on the front, at the bottom on the side there is also
   a small logo of the Quaker, a more abstract and schematic version

developed in 1970 by Saul Bass as a corporate trademark. Compare Bass's corporate logo to the image of the Quaker on the front of the package. How does each project a different image to readers? Why is the realistic image appropriate for shoppers and the more abstract logo appropriate to identify the corporation that produces Quaker Oats?

3. Sometimes designers hit the wrong note, as is the case with the original Apple Computer logo—which was replaced by Apple's now well-known apple logo. Consider Apple's original logo. How does the apple and Isaac Newton connect to Apple Computer? Do the lettering and banner of Apple Computer Co. seem to fit the company? Do you think designers created an effective alternative in the current logo? Explain your answer.

4. Imagine that you have been commissioned to create a logo for a particular company, organization, or institution. What image and identity will you want to project? What graphics, typeface, or combination could you use to create this identity? Sketch one or more logos. Explain your design decisions.

Source: Apple and the Apple logo are trademarks of Apple Computer, Inc., registered in the U.S. and other countries, used with permission.

Information

With scanners and desktop publishing programs, writers can readily integrate informational graphics into their texts. For writers, the point of adding graphics is not simply to add visual interest to documents that are primarily verbal but to use visual display to help readers visualize important processes, trends, and relationships.

The visual display of information can be divided into three categories: textual, representational, and numerical.

Textual Graphics

Textual graphics organize and display words, phrases, sentences, or paragraphs either within or separate from the main text. Textual graphics are normally used to emphasize key points.

Bulleted lists use phrases or sentences to highlight main ideas in an easy-to-read format. "The WPA Outcomes Statement for First-Year Composition" in Chapter 6, for example, lists abilities students should have acquired after taking a first-year writing course.

Pull quotes, such as the one in "The Success Taboo," pull out a key phrase or sentence from the main text to display the writer's main ideas.

The Success Taboo
By Bob Herbert

Somehow over the past two or three decades a lot of black kids absorbed the message that academic achievement was something to be shunned. Excellence in sports or the various entertainment fields was one thing, a good thing, but high marks and academic honors were something else. Academic achievement, according to this mind-bogglingly destructive way of thinking, was a white thing, and thus in some sense contemptible. The tragic result has been that in many schools across the country black kids who apply themselves to their studies are often ridiculed and at times ostracized.

A black teacher in the Bronx told me in a despairing tone that she has male students who would rather be paraded in handcuffs before television cameras than be caught reading a book. I've had many students tell me in interviews that they are afraid to raise their hands in the classroom because they don't want to repeat the experience of being laughed at for giving the correct answer.

A black 17-year-old girl who worked part time at a mall in Marietta, Ga., was taunted recently by high school classmates who showed up at her job to express their resentment at the high marks she was getting.

Now, and not a moment too soon, comes Hugh Price, president of the National Urban League, with an ambitious first step toward turning this madness around.

"We haven't surrounded our young people with enough opportunities to excel academically and to be recognized for excelling," said Mr. Price. "We haven't had the rituals in our own community that reward young people for doing well."

The Urban League has drawn together 20 national black organizations, including the Congress of National Black Churches, for what it calls the Campaign for African-American Achievement. The idea is to improve the academic standing of black youngsters by encouraging and rewarding excellence in the classroom, and by improving the quality of the education that is offered to black youngsters in the public schools.

A statement announcing the campaign said: "We have to reverse the increasing gap in academic achievement between African-American and other children. We have to increase the low rates of enrollment of African-American youngsters in college preparatory courses and attack the inequitable allocation of resources for public education."

There is an urgency in Mr. Price's manner as he talks about this effort. He and his colleagues recognize that black men and women will have to be substantially better prepared educationally if they are to survive economically as we move into the 21st century. Employers, as Mr. Price noted, "expect much more in the way of academic preparation than ever before." And affirmative action, however one feels about it, is almost certain to continue its fade from the scene.

The achievement campaign will try in a variety of ways to generate enthusiasm among students and parents for the hard work that is necessary to succeed academically. This will not be easy in environments that are plagued by poverty, broken families, drug abuse, violence and the widespread notion that what is taught in the classroom is not relevant to the lives of the students.

The campaign will establish an honor society, called the National Achievers Society, to focus attention on black youngsters who excel academically. The first induction ceremony, to be presided over by Gen. Colin Powell, will be held next spring.

When black students excel.

September has been designated Achievement Month by the campaign. The plan is to have Urban League affiliates, black churches and other organizations conduct a month-long series of high-profile events each year celebrating the efforts of black youngsters who are doing well in school.

Meanwhile, leaders of the campaign are working with professional organizations and universities around the country to determine where improvements in the public schools need to be made and what specific kinds of academic help are needed for under-achieving students.

This is not a perfect plan. Much of it will be modified and some of it will fail. But it does send the crucial message that academic achievement is as important for black people as anyone else. It's a message that somehow has escaped the consciousness of too many black children.

Pull quote

Tables, such as "The Medical Bottom Line," organize and display information that enables readers to make comparisons—in this case between marijuana treatment and conventional treatment of a number of medical conditions.

Charts, such as the "Chemical Engineering Suggested Course Sequence," show processes, relationships, and functions.

Time lines, such as "A Growing Arsenal Against HIV," list events on a horizontal axis to enable the reader to visualize change over time.

Representational Graphics

Representational graphics use pictures to orient readers in time and space and to illustrate processes, relationships, and events.

Photographs, such as those in Chapter 7 in the profile of Dr. Susan Love and in the ads from Pfizer and the Service Employees International Union, enable readers to visualize a person.

SOURCE: NORML

■ States with medical-marijuana laws

The Medical Bottom Line

Though largely illegal since 1937, marijuana may prove an effective alternative to more commonly prescribed drugs for some diseases. California, Arizona and Massachusetts are leading the fight to make marijuana more readily available. They aren't alone: 26 states and the District of Columbia have passed various laws and resolutions establishing therapeutic-research programs, allowing doctors to prescribe marijuana, or asking the federal government to lift the ban on medical use.

CONDITION	MARIJUANA TREATMENT	CONVENTIONAL TREATMENT
Cancer chemotherapy Often causes extreme nausea and vomiting	● Active ingredient THC reduces vomiting and nausea, alleviates pretreatment anxiety	● Marinol (synthetic THC): Commonly used but can cause intoxication. Pill form only, hard to swallow if you're vomiting. ● Serotonin antagonists such as Zofran (ondansetron): Can be taken intravenously but more expensive than Marinol.
AIDS-related wasting Low appetite, loss of lean (muscle) mass	● Improves appetite	● Marinol: Boosts appetite, but smokable marijuana allows better dose control. ● Megase (megestrol acetate): Stimulates appetite and may reduce nausea. Currently being compared to Marinol for cancer patients.
Pain and muscle spasms Associated with epilepsy and multiple sclerosis	● Reduces muscle spasms; may ease incontinence of bladder and bowel and relieve depression	● Dantrium (dantrolene sodium): Capsules or injection can relax nerves and muscles to calm spasms. Can cause liver damage. ● Lioresal (bactofen): Tablet alleviates spasticity but also causes sedation. Sudden withdrawal can cause hallucinations and seizures.
Glaucoma A progressive form of blindness due to increased pressure inside the eyeball	● When smoked, it reduces pressure within the eye. But it may also reduce blood flow to the optic nerve, exacerbating the loss of vision.	● Xalatan (latanoprost): Once-a-day eye drop. Low rate of side effects. Changes eye color in some users. ● Beta-blocker eye drops: Can cause lethargy and trigger asthma attacks. ● Miotic eye drops: Allow eye to drain faster but constrict the pupil, dimming vision. ● Carbonic anhydrase inhibitors: Decrease production of fluid in the eye, but can cause numbness and weight loss.

Table

CHEMICAL ENGINEERING SUGGESTED COURSE SEQUENCE

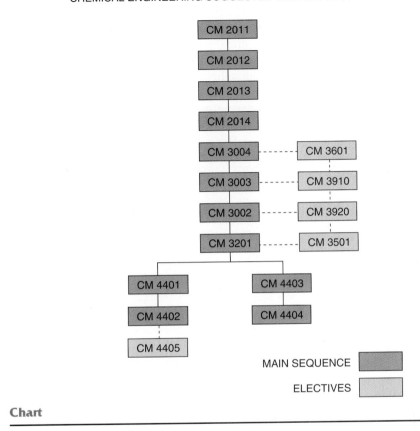

MAIN SEQUENCE

ELECTIVES

Chart

A Growing Arsenal Against HIV

Over the past decade the FDA has approved nine drugs—six RT inhibitors and three protease inhibitors—to combat the AIDS virus. None of them is very effective by itself, but researchers are finding that certain three-drug combinations can shackle HIV for long periods.

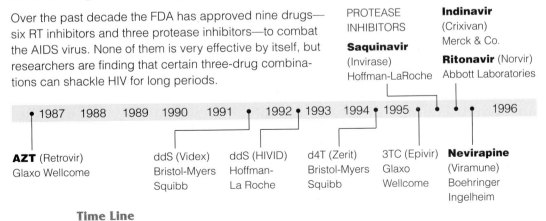

Time Line

Maps, such as that of Vieques Island, off the coast of Puerto Rico, where protestors have opposed the U.S. Navy's practice bombings, help readers visualize the location of events. Notice in this case how the second map locates Vieques in a larger geographical perspective.

Diagrams, such as "Anatomy of a Concussion," use simplified representations to help readers visualize how processes take place.

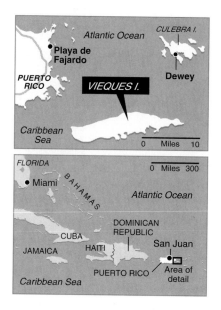

Map

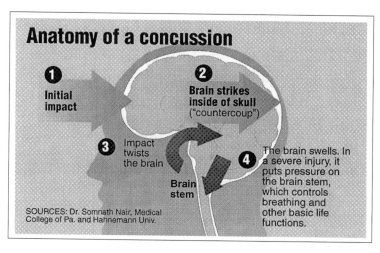

Diagram

Numerical Graphics

Numerical graphics put the primary focus on quantitative data instead of words or diagrams. Numerical graphics enable writers to analyze the data they are working with and to represent trends and relationships.

Tables, such as "Red Sox Statistics," are probably the simplest form of numerical graphics. They display numbers and words in rows and columns, enabling readers to see relationships. While tables have the lowest visual interest of numerical graphics, they are useful when you have large amounts of information you want to organize and display in a logical and orderly way.

Line graphs, such as those in "Bad Air Days," are used to show variation in the quantity of something over a period of time, in this case the percentage of late departures, canceled flights, and late arrivals of all airline flights between 1995 and 2000. By charting the number of cases on the vertical, or y, axis and the period of time on the horizontal, or x, axis, writers can establish trends.

RED SOX STATISTICS (Through Friday)

BATTERS	AVG	OBA	AB	R	H	2B	3B	HR	RBI	BB	SO	SB	CS	E
Ramirez	.389	.461	113	18	44	6	0	9	34	14	32	0	0	0
Hillenbrand	.325	.336	114	14	37	9	1	3	13	1	13	0	1	4
Bichette	.314	.351	35	4	11	1	0	1	3	2	7	0	0	0
Offerman	.287	.376	87	14	25	6	0	1	6	13	18	0	0	2
Everett	.286	.375	112	22	32	5	2	4	18	12	29	3	1	1
Varitek	.280	.366	82	6	23	6	0	0	7	11	13	0	0	2
Nixon	.262	.364	84	16	22	8	0	2	11	11	12	1	1	2
Lansing	.250	.283	56	7	14	2	0	1	4	3	4	0	0	0
Daubach	.241	.306	87	16	21	6	1	7	19	8	26	0	0	1
Lewis	.233	.250	43	5	10	3	1	1	4	1	6	0	0	0
Stynes	.233	.233	43	7	10	2	0	0	0	0	5	1	0	1
O'Leary	.209	.233	86	7	18	2	1	1	9	3	17	0	1	1
Hatteberg	.152	.222	33	4	5	2	0	1	5	2	7	0	0	2
Grebeck	.053	.100	38	1	2	1	0	0	2	2	9	0	0	0
Totals	.273	.332	1029	143	281	61	6	31	137	83	199	6	4	18

PITCHERS	W	L	ERA	G	GS	SV	IP	H	R	ER	HR	BB	SO
Arrojo	1	0	0.00	9	0	4	15.1	9	0	0	0	5	13
Martinez	3	0	1.47	6	6	0	43.0	31	8	7	0	12	66
Beck	0	1	2.12	13	0	1	17.0	15	7	4	1	5	14
Schourek	0	1	2.13	10	0	0	12.2	5	3	3	2	7	7
Wakefield	1	0	2.61	7	0	2	20.2	23	7	6	2	3	17
Ohka	2	1	2.67	6	6	0	30.1	32	13	9	1	10	20
Nomo	3	2	3.00	6	6	0	36.0	15	13	12	3	20	36
Garces	1	0	3.14	10	0	0	14.1	6	5	5	1	5	14
Castillo	3	2	4.50	6	6	0	30.0	32	15	15	3	7	20
Crawford	2	0	4.50	5	5	0	26.0	27	13	13	2	8	20
Lowe	1	5	7.41	11	0	3	17.0	24	14	14	4	7	13
Totals	17	12	3.02	29	29	10	262.1	219	98	88	19	89	237

Table

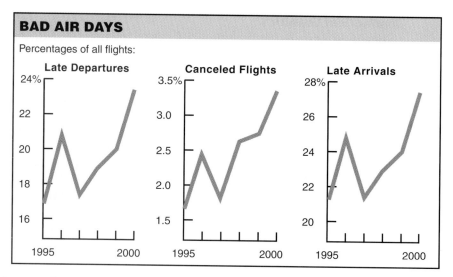

Line graphs

Bar charts, such as "Race and Capital Punishment," enable writers to compare data and to emphasize contrasts among two or more items over time. Bar charts run along the horizontal axis from left to right. Column charts serve the same function as bar charts but run along the vertical axis, from down to up.

Pie charts, such as the "Percent Distribution of 1993 State Lottery Proceeds," divide the whole of something into its parts, displaying the individual items that make up 100 percent of the whole. Notice that the size of each slice is proportional to its share of the total. This helps readers see the relative weight or importance of each slice in relation to the others. And for this reason most graphic designers agree that to ensure readability, pie charts should use five or fewer slices. More slices make the pie too cluttered and hard to read.

Analyzing Visual Patterns of Meaning

In effective visual display of information, the facts don't just speak for themselves. The task of visual design is to highlight patterns of meaning—whether key points, comparisons, relationships, trends, or processes—that enable readers to make sense of the available information.

One of the most famous—and tragic—cases where the visual design of information did not clearly highlight a key relationship was the Challenger

RACE AND CAPITAL PUNISHMENT

In North Carolina homicide cases in which the defendant is eligible
for the death penalty, a nonwhite defendant is much more likely to
receive it for killing a white victim than a nonwhite victim.

RACE OF DEFENDANT	RACE OF VICTIM	NUMBER OF CASES	PERCENTAGE SENTENCED TO DEATH, 1993-1997
Nonwhite	White	284	11.6%
White	White	541	6.1%
White	Nonwhite	80	5.0%
Nonwhite	Nonwhite	616	4.7%

SOURCES: THE COMMON SENSE FOUNDATION; NORTH CAROLINA COUNCIL OF CHURCHES

Bar chart

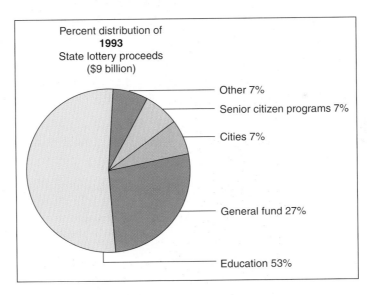

Percent distribution of
1993
State lottery proceeds
($9 billion)

Other 7%

Senior citizen programs 7%

Cities 7%

General fund 27%

Education 53%

Pie chart

Shuttle disaster in 1986. Morton Thiokol engineers warned that evidence from earlier flights suggested cold temperatures could cause the O-rings in the Challenger's rockets to erode and not seal properly. The engineers, however, were not able to design a clear visual representation of the relationship between low temperature and O-ring damage. Notice, for example, how the engineers' chart shows the history of O-ring damage on earlier flights, thereby establishing a potential problem. But the chart does not establish a pattern of meaning to highlight the key relationship in question—between damage and temperature. Nor was the engineers' chart of the history of O-ring temperatures able to visualize this relationship.

Notice how a simple scatterplot of all flights, graphing temperature against damage could have provided a visual pattern of meaning. Whether such a visual

HISTORY OF O-RING DAMAGE ON SRM FIELD JOINTS

| | SRM No. | Cross Sectional View | | | Top View | | Clocking Location (deg) |
		Erosion Depth (in.)	Perimeter Affected (deg)	Nominal Dia. (in.)	Length Of Max Erosion (in.)	Total Heat Affected Length (in.)	
61A LH Center Field**	22A	None	None	0.280	None	None	36°–66°
61A LH Aft Field**	22A	None	None	0.280	None	None	338°–18°
5IC LH Forward Field**	15A	0.010	154.0	0.280	4.25	5.25	163
51C RH Center Field (prim)***	158	0.038	130.0	0.280	12.50	58.75	354
51C RH Center Field (sec)***	158	None	45.0	0.280	None	29.50	354
41D RH Forward Field	13B	0.028	110.0	0.280	3.00	None	275
41C LH Aft Field*	11A	None	None	0.280	None	None	--
418 LH Forward Field	10A	0.040	217.0	0.280	3.00	14.50	351
STS-2 RH Aft Field	2B	0.053	116.0	0.280	--	--	90

(handwritten margin notes: Oct. 30, 1985 ; Jan. 85 ; July)

*Hot gas path detected in putty. Indication of heat on O-ring, but no damage.

**Soot behind primary O-ring.

*** Soot behind primary O-ring, heat affected secondary O-ring.

Clocking location of leak check port-0 deg.

OTHER SRM-15 FIELD JOINTS HAD NO BLOWHOLES IN PUTTY AND NO SOOT NEAR OR BEYOND THE PRIMARY O-RING.

SRM-22 FORWARD FIELD JOINT HAD PUTTY PATH TO PRIMARY O-RING, BUT NO O-RING EROSION AND NO SOOT BLOWBY. OTHER SRM-22 FIELD JOINTS HAD NO BLOWHOLES IN PUTTY.

Chart that shows a potential problem on the Challenger

display would have influenced the final decision to launch can only be a guess. All we can say for sure is that unfortunately the launch did take place. Temperatures were in the 20s, the O-rings did not seal properly, and the Challenger exploded.

		HISTORY OF O-RING TEMPERATURES (DEGREES–F)		
MOTOR	MBT	AMB	O-RING	WIND
DM-4	68	36	47	10 MPH
DM-2	76	45	52	10 MPH
QM-3	72.5	40	48	10 MPH
QM-4	76	48	51	10 MPH
SRM-15	52	64	53	10 MPH
SRM-22	77	78	75	10 MPH
SSRM-25	55	26	29	10 MPH
			27	25 MPH

Chart of the history of 0-ring damage

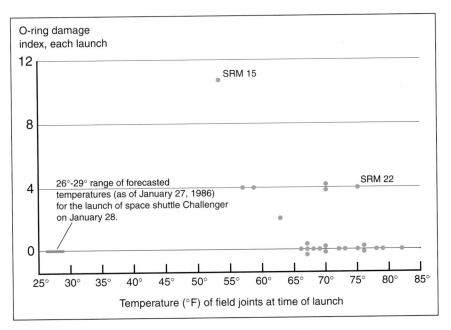

Scatterplot of all flights, designed by Edward R. Tufte

ETHICS OF INFORMATION DESIGN

People often say you can prove anything with numbers. This may sound cynical, but there is good reason to be suspicious of the visual display of quantitative information. The problem is not so much that information designers outright lie as that inadvertently or intentionally, they introduce distortion into their designs by trying to add visual interest. The information design expert Edward R. Tufte says that inept and misleading graphics are widespread in part because visual designers believe that statistical data is boring to readers and in need of jazzing up. As Tufte shows, however, instead of making the data more lively, graphic effects often misrepresent or exaggerate their meaning.

Notice, for example, that the numerical increase in "Fuel Economy Standards for Autos" from 1978 to 1985 is 53 percent—from 18 to 27.5 miles per gallon. As visualized, however, the increase from the line representing 1978 standards, which is 0.6 inches, to the line representing 1985 standards, which is 5.3 inches, amounts to 783 percent—a huge distortion of the facts. Moreover, by departing from the usual order of listing dates on an axis—either bottom to top or left to right—the

(continued)

FUEL ECONOMY STANDARDS FOR AUTOS

Set by Congress and supplemented by the Transportation Department. In miles per gallon.

This line, representing 18 miles per gallon in 1978, is 0.5 inches long

This line, representing 27.5 miles per gallon in 1985, is 4.5 inches long

ETHICS OF INFORMATION DESIGN

(continued)

new standards seem to be surging directly at us, exaggerating their effect. Tufte redesigned this display of information with a simple graph so that the size of the graphic matched the size of the data. As you can see, instead of the dramatic, ever-increasing change visualized on the original, Tufte's redesign shows that the new standards start gradually, double the rate between 1980 and 1983, and then flatten out—a pattern disguised in the original display. Notice, finally, how the redesign includes a simple comparison of the expected average mileage of all cars on the road to the new-car standards, another clarifying item of information missing from the original.

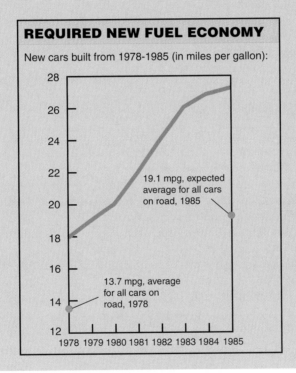

REQUIRED NEW FUEL ECONOMY

New cars built from 1978-1985 (in miles per gallon):

19.1 mpg, expected average for all cars on road, 1985

13.7 mpg, average for all cars on road, 1978

EXERCISES

1. Look through some recent issues of magazines and newspapers and find three examples of the visual display of information to bring to class. Be prepared to explain how (or whether) your examples organize and display information in a way that complements the written text. Does the size of the graphic match the size of the data? If not, what is the effect?

2. The following situations present clusters of information that can be represented in visual form. In each case, decide whether a line graph, a bar

chart, or a pie chart is the best choice to convey the information to readers. Make a sketch of your choice to display this information.

a. You are preparing the annual report for a community service organization at your college. Part of your task is to explain how the organization has spent the annual budget of $7,500 it receives from the college. Expenditures are the following: $1,500 for printing leaflets, brochures, and the quarterly newsletter; $1,000 for speakers' fees; $500 for a workshop for members; $2,500 to send five members to a national conference on community service; $1,750 for donations to local community organizations; $250 for refreshments at meetings.

b. Biology classes at your college are in high demand. No new faculty have been hired, nor have any new courses been offered in the past ten years. With the rapid increase of biology majors, classes are overenrolled. In some cases, even majors can't register for the courses they need. You want to make the case that your college needs to hire more biology faculty and offer more courses. Here are the numbers of biology majors in the past ten years: 1991—125; 1992—132; 1993—114; 1994—154; 1995—158; 1996—176; 1997—212; 1998—256; 1999—301; 2000—333.

c. You are working for your college's office of alumni affairs and you are involved in a campaign to increase alumni donations. No one has ever researched whether donations vary depending on the majors of the alumni. To help plan the campaign, you are asked to find out how donations differ according to the majors of the alumni. You decide to look first at alumni who graduated between 1965 and 1974 and have established their careers. Here are the numbers of alumni who graduated in the ten–year period and the donations they gave in 1997 arranged by type of major: social sciences, 1,300 graduates—$158,000; humanities, 1,680 graduates—$98,000; business, 2,180 graduates—$326,000; engineering, 940 graduates—$126,000; sciences, 1,020 graduates—$112,00; fine arts, 720 graduates—$48,000; nursing and allied health, 680 graduates—$54,000.

3. In "Since When Did *USA Today* Become the National Design Ideal," Michael Rock argues that the "infographics" in many magazines, newspapers, and textbooks are draining information of "its significance in the name of accessibility." (The essay appears in Chapter 8.) Test Rock's claim by looking at a week or more of *USA Today*.

4. In a group with two or three other students, choose one of the reading selections that appear in another chapter. Design a visual display of information to emphasize a main point, trend, relationship, or process in the reading. Be prepared to explain your design.

Persuasion

You don't have to look very far to see how visual design is used for purposes of persuasion. Advertising, public service announcements, and advocacy campaigns of all kinds contend for our visual attention—on television, printed pages, posters, billboards, and Web sites.

Persuasion can address its readers in a number of ways. The famous Uncle Sam army recruitment poster of World War I, for example, took a direct approach to readers, staring them straight in the eye to deliver its command message "I Want You," while a British recruitment poster from the same era took a more indirect approach, putting readers in the role of spectators looking into a living room after the war where children ask their father "Daddy, what did YOU do in the Great War?" The difference between direct and indirect approaches is still apparent today, in the contrast, say, between the direct command of "just say no" antidrug, antisex, and antismoking messages and a more indirect approach where we are spectators witnessing, say, the effects of heroin addiction on someone's life, successful struggles to kick the habit, or some combination of the two.

Because the contemporary landscape is so cluttered by images, persuasion depends in part on simply getting the viewer's attention in the first place. To make its message stand out, visual design draws on the use of sight in two distinct but related ways—seeing images and reading text. Effective design engages viewer-readers in putting pictures and words together to form meaningful messages. In some cases, such as Jean Carlu's poster promoting production during

Persuasive messages

World War II, viewer-readers can take in at a single glance the powerful visual symbol of industrial mobilization that Carlu designed. Here reading and seeing are interlocked, just as the image and text create one figure. Notice, on the other hand, how the billboard promoting reading classes uses images and letters that viewer-readers must first see and convert into words in order to form and read sequentially the sentence "Can you read?" Finally, the ad from Physicians Against Land Mines involves viewer-readers in completing the image by reading the text that fills the space where the girl's leg is missing.

Analyzing the Visual Design of a Persuasive Symbol

In 1998, proponents of the peace accord in Northern Ireland began a campaign to persuade voters to approve a power-sharing treaty between Catholics and Protestants. Neither Catholics nor Protestants had any illusions that the treaty would immediately end the long-standing conflict or the violence that had plagued Northern Ireland for generations. The most advocates of the treaty could say is that approval of the political settlement could be a step toward peace. For these reasons, when the London advertising agency Saatchi & Saatchi showed prospective voters three possible logos for the campaign to approve the peace

accord—a dove, an olive branch, and children—the prospective voters rejected all three, saying such symbols of love and peace were too upbeat and "sappy," given the circumstances. Instead, the designers ultimately used familiar road signs as logos to fashion the campaign—both the arrow for "Vote Yes. It's the Way Ahead" (see page 656) and another with the sign for a no-through road and a warning that a vote against the treaty is a "dead-end street."

EXERCISES

1. Find a number of advertisements, public service announcements, or other forms of publicity that integrate words and images into a visual design. Try to get as wide a range as possible, and bring five or six to class. Working with two or three other students, pay attention to how each visual design addresses you as viewer-readers. Does it address you directly so that you feel someone is talking to you, or does it position you in the role of a spectator? Consider how the approaches—direct and indirect—embody the designer's purposes and the persuasive effects of the designs.

VOTE YES. IT'S THE WAY AHEAD.

Printed and Published by the "YES" campaign, PO Box 833, Belfast BT1 1E2.

2. Using the same group of materials, this time analyze how seeing and reading work together and separately in the way you make sense of the message. What images do you see? What words do you read? How do they go together to form a message?

3. The Guerrilla Girls are activists in the art world who protest discrimination against women and minority artists. The poster we feature here draws on all three purposes of visual design—identification, information,

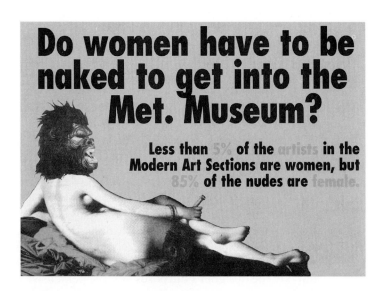

and persuasion. In terms of identification, the gorilla masks have become the Guerrilla Girls' logo (and a means of disguising their identities). In addition, people in the art world will identify the nude figure as the nineteenth-century painting *Odalisque* by Jean Auguste Dominique Ingres. How does the poster combine these two items of identification? How does it use information to make its persuasive point? How does it put text and image together to form a message?

VISUAL DESIGN: FOUR BASIC PRINCIPLES

In this section, we look at four basic principles that apply to virtually any document you may be called on to design. As you will see, each principle emphasizes a particular aspect of design, but finally all four overlap and mutually reinforce each other.

Group Similar Items Together

Grouping similar items creates visual units of attention on the page and thereby helps readers to organize and remember information. Notice in the original version of NBA player ratings how the items on the list are so close together and so undifferentiated from each other that readers have a hard time seeing how the list is organized.

NBA PLAYER RATINGS (ORIGINAL)

Centers
Shaquille O'Neal, Lakers
David Robinson, Spurs
Theo Ratliff, 76ers
Antonio Davis, Raptors
Forwards
Chris Webber, Kings
Kevin Garnett, Timberwolves
Antonio McDyess, Nuggets
Tim Duncan, Spurs
Guards
Kobe Bryant, Lakers
Allen Iverson, 76ers
Jerry Stackhouse, Pistons
Gary Payton, Sonics

Clearly the list needs to be broken up visually, with similar items grouped together, so readers can see at a glance what the categories are. In the first redesign, the three rating lists appear as separate units but the headings—centers, forwards, guards—seem unconnected, with too much white space "trapped" between visual elements that go together.

NBA PLAYER RATINGS (REDESIGN #1)

Centers

Shaquille O'Neal, Lakers
David Robinson, Spurs
Theo Ratliff, 76ers
Antonio Davis, Raptors

Forwards

Chris Webber, Kings
Kevin Garnett, Timberwolves
Antonio McDyess, Nuggets
Tim Duncan, Spurs

Guards

Kobe Bryant, Lakers
Allen Iverson, 76ers
Jerry Stackhouse, Pistons
Gary Payton, Sonics

Notice in the final redesign the way the groupings have been tightened into single visual units and how the use of bold type emphasizes the visual categories.

NBA PLAYER RATINGS (REDESIGN #2)

Centers
Shaquille O'Neal, Lakers
David Robinson, Spurs
Theo Ratliff, 76ers
Antonio Davis, Raptors

Forwards
Chris Webber, Kings
Kevin Garnett, Timberwolves
Antonio McDyess, Nuggets
Tim Duncan, Spurs

Guards
Kobe Bryant, Lakers
Allen Iverson, 76ers
Jerry Stackhouse, Pistons
Gary Payton, Sonics

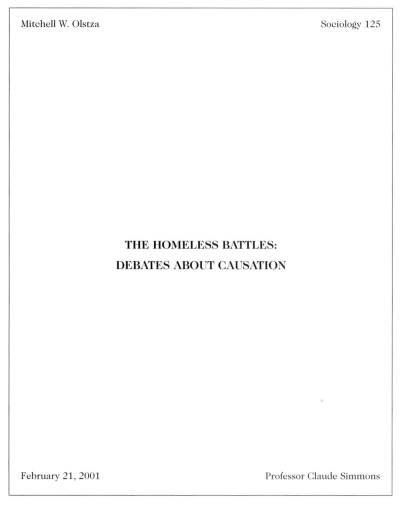

Title page (original)

The same idea of grouping similar items applies to the design of a whole page. Notice how the information on the following title page seems to float around without establishing a clear pattern. The reader's eye tends to wander because the page lacks emphasis.

In the following page redesign, information is no longer scattered along the border but concentrated into two groupings—title and author's name occupy the top third of the page, while course information comes at the bottom. Notice also how the redesign shifts from all capitals to lower case for easier readability and has enlarged the type size in the title and author's name for emphasis.

The Homeless Battles:
Debates About Causation

Mitchell W. Olstza

Sociology 125
Professor Claude Simmons
February 21, 2001

Title page (redesign #1)

Align Visual Elements

Alignment refers to the placement of visual elements on the page—whether you center them or align them flush left or flush right. Notice how the title page takes on a striking and sophisticated look when it is aligned flush right.

Alignment gives page layouts a clean and crisp look. Notice how the photo scanned onto the page from "The Homeless Battles" is out of alignment with

The Homeless Battles
Debates About Causation

Mitchell W. Olstza

Sociology 125
Professor Claude Simmons
February 21, 2001

Title page (redesign #2)

the text. It traps white space in a distracting way, and the caption underneath the photo competes with the text for the reader's attention.

Aligning the photo with the lines of text and moving the caption flush left reduces the trapped white space. Putting the caption in italics helps to separate it more distinctly from the main text.

Olszta 2

instead of a game of craps, it's the game of life. Sometimes you're up but often your down. There is no home at all, and work consists of begging. What money you do have is not just for anything, but only for the essentials. The latter is the life of a homeless person, one that has no permanent residence or simply, a home.

A home offers a sense of security, of permanence of ones own space. Fortunately, most Americans will not have to face the ordeal of losing their personal space. The psychological repercussions of losing a home are permanent and very damaging to pride and moral. It is easy for those that do not experience

Sleeping on The Streets tough times to easily dismiss the real problems faced by the homeless. An attempt to realize the smaller complexities of being homeless is never sought.

Many people such as elected officials and successful citizens quickly point out that the reason of homelessness can be explained by some simple relationship. There is a lot of research on these reasons, and yet, very little discussion can be found regarding the everyday challenges of homelessness that creates a barrier to getting out of a homeless status. The simple explanations are either homelessness is invoked by the lack of affordable housing, substance abuse, or having a mental disability.

The federal definition of affordable housing is housing that costs 30% or less of a persons income. Between 1991 and 1995, median rental costs paid by low-income renters rose 21%, and during this same period the number of low-income renters

Page from "The Homeless Battles" (original)

Olszta 2

instead of a game of craps, it's the game of life. Sometimes you're up but often your down. There is no home at all, and work consists of begging. What money you do have is not just for anything, but only for the essentials. The latter is the life of a homeless person, one that has no permanent residence or simply, a home.

A home offers a sense of security, of permanence of ones own space. Fortunately, most Americans will not have to face the ordeal

Photo aligned with lines of text

 of losing their personal space. The psychological repercussions of losing a home are permanent and very damaging to pride and moral. It is easy for those that do not experience tough

Caption aligned with left margin and lines of text

Sleeping on The Streets times to easily dismiss the real problems faced by the homeless. An attempt to realize the smaller complexities of being homeless is never sought.

Many people such as elected officials and successful citizens quickly point out that the reason of homelessness can be explained by some simple relationship. There is a lot of research on these reasons, and yet, very little discussion can be found regarding the everyday challenges of homelessness that creates a barrier to getting out of a homeless status. The simple explanations are either homelessness is invoked by the lack of affordable housing, substance abuse, or having a mental disability.

The federal definition of affordable housing is housing that costs 30% or less of a persons income. Between 1991 and 1995, median rental costs paid by low-income renters rose 21%, and during this same period the number of low-income renters

Page from "The Homeless Battles" (redesign)

Alignment becomes especially important when you work with columns, such as in newsletters and brochures. Notice the lack of alignment on the original newsletter page and how the design is tightened and aligned in the redesigned version.

Too much white space trapped between articles

Too much white space between columns

Hole left at bottom right

Newsletter (original)

Aligned issue and number

Aligned title and headings flush left

Moved photo and aligned with title

Tightened spacing between articles and columns

Moved Table of Contents to fill hole

Newsletter (redesigned)

Use Repetition and Contrast to Create Consistent Visual Patterns

Repetition means repeating a visual element—a bold font, a bullet, spacing—to create a consistent visual pattern on the page. Repetition unifies the disparate visual parts and cues readers to where they can expect certain types of information to appear. *Contrast,* on the other hand, is a way to emphasize certain visual elements—to make them stand out.

Martha Smith
143 Oakland Avenue
Philadelphia, PA 19122
(215) 555-2000

Education

Bachelor of Arts in English
Temple University, 1999

Experience

Journalism internship—*Philadelphia Inquirer*
1998–1999
    Covered and wrote by-lined articles on school board meetings
    Researched sex education K-12 for special report
    Assisted editor in preparing special education supplement

Public Relations Assistant—Trinity Repertory Theater, Camden, NJ
1997–1998
    Wrote advertising copy and designed promotional brochures
    Conducted focus groups
    Prepared instructional materials for Theater in the Schools

Writing Center Tutor—Temple University
1996–1999
    Tutored students on wide range of writing assignments
    Worked with international students
    Trained new tutors

Entertainment Editor—*Temple Daily News*
1997–1998
    Planned and assigned music, art, drama, and film reviews
    Edited reviews
    Led staff meetings

Related Skills
    Written and spoken fluency in Spanish, reading ability in French
    Feature Writing, Graphic Design, Editing, Photojournalism

Achievements/ Activities:
    Dean's list (every semester)
    Member of Sigma Tau Delta, International English Honor Society
    Secretary of Amnesty International, Temple University chapter
    Varsity cross-country and indoor and outdoor track

References: Available upon request

Resumé (original)

Notice, for example, how your eye wanders as you read the original version of Martha Smith's resumé. She has grouped similar items, but she doesn't use a consistent design to present them—some of the headings are centered and some are flush left, and the indented items of information don't line up. Moreover, there's little contrast beyond the use of white space.

In the redesigned resumé, Martha Smith uses repetition to create a consistent visual pattern. All the headings are now aligned, and a repetitive visual scheme of bullets has been added to mark items. The consistent movement from bold to light typeface produces a clear pattern of emphasis.

Martha Smith
143 Oakland Avenue
Philadelphia, PA 19122
(215) 555-2000

Education
Bachelor of Arts in English
Temple University, 1999

Experience
Journalism internship—*Philadelphia Inquirer*
1998–1999
- Covered and wrote by-lined articles on school board meetings
- Researched sex education K-12 for special report
- Assisted editor in preparing special education supplement

Public Relations Assistant—Trinity Repertory Theater, Camden, NJ
1997–1998
- Wrote advertising copy and designed promotional brochures
- Conducted focus groups
- Prepared instructional materials for Theater in the Schools

Writing Center Tutor—Temple University
1996–1999
- Tutored students on wide range of writing assignments
- Worked with international students
- Trained new tutors

Entertainment Editor—*Temple Daily News*
1997–1998
- Planned and assigned music, art, drama, and film reviews
- Edited reviews
- Led staff meetings

Related Skills
- Written and spoken fluency in Spanish, reading ability in French
- Feature Writing, Graphic Design, Editing, Photojournalism

Achievements/ Activities:
- Dean's list (every semester)
- Member of Sigma Tau Delta, International English Honor Society
- Secretary of Amnesty International, Temple University chapter
- Varsity cross-country and indoor and outdoor track

References: Available upon request

Resumé (redesign #1)

Add Visual Interest

Visual design can follow the first three principles and still be a bit boring. Adding visual interest will not only make readers more likely to pay attention to your message. It also increases your credibility as someone who knows how to make a sophisticated and stylish presentation.

Martha Smith's redesigned resumé is certainly serviceable. It's clear and easy to follow. Notice what a flair for visual interest can do for her page.

MARTHA SMITH

143 Oakland Avenue
Philadelphia, PA 19122
(215) 555-2000

Education

1999   **Bachelor of Arts in English**
              Temple University

Experience

1998–1999   **Journalism internship** at *Philadelphia Inquirer*. Covered and
              wrote by-lined articles on school board meetings. Researched sex
              education K-12 for special report. Assisted editor in preparing
              special education supplement.

1997–1998   **Public Relations Assistant** at Trinity Repertory Theater, Camden,
              NJ. Wrote advertising copy and designed promotional brochures.
              Conducted focus groups. Prepared instructional materials for
              Theater in the Schools.

1996–1999   **Writing Center Tutor** at Temple University. Tutored students on
              wide range of writing assignments. Worked with international
              students. Trained new tutors.

1997–1998   **Entertainment Editor** at *Temple Daily News*. Planned and
              assigned music, art, drama, and film reviews. Edited reviews.
              Led staff meetings.

Related Skills

              Written and spoken fluency in Spanish, reading ability in French.
              Coursework in feature writing, graphic design, editing, and
              photojournalism.

Achievements/Activities

              Dean's list (every semester)
              Member of Sigma Tau Delta, International English Honor Society
              Secretary of Amnesty International, Temple University chapter
              Varsity cross-country and indoor and outdoor track

References available upon request

Resumé (redesign #2)

Notice the design features that have been added in this redesign—the rules (horizontal lines) that divide sections, bold sans-serif headings combined with light typeface, and a layout that uses more of the page and adds more white space.

NEWSLETTER

Contents

Use reverse lettering and screens for emphasis and to "color" black and white pages

NEWSLETTER

This Week's Headline

Heading

Use vertical director and combine single and double column layouts

You are Invited

50th Anniversary
George & Martha

Saturday
March 17, 1776

Use ornaments and clip art for visual themes

The Latest News

Number 1

Number 3

Number 2

Number 4

Use rules (horizontal and vertical lines) to separate items and emphasize layout design

Design Features: Adding Visual Interest

WORKING WITH TYPE

Type refers to standardized forms of letters and characters. Until quite recently, it was largely graphic designers in printing companies who knew about the various styles of type and determined which ones to use for a particular document. In the age of the personal computer, writers now have access to hundreds of type fonts and can change their size and underline, italicize, or make them boldface with the click of a mouse.

However the vast range of possibilities now available can be overwhelming. Writers need to understand what their options are in using type, and what kinds of effects their design decisions are likely to have on readers.

Type and White Space

In visual design, *white space* does not refer simply to the empty places on a page where no writing or illustrations appear. White space plays an active role in setting off type, adding to visual interest and breaking up the monotony of solid text. Here are two reductions of the sections you've just read. Notice how the absence of white space makes the page dense and forbidding in the first reduction.

First reduction:

WORKING WITH TYPE Type refers to standardized forms of letters and characters. Until quite recently, it was largely graphic designers in printing companies who knew about the various styles of type and determined which ones to use for a particular document. In the age of the personal computer, this has changed dramatically. Now writers have access to hundreds of type fonts and can change their size and underline, italicize, or make them boldface with the click of a mouse. The vast range of possibilities now available, however, can be overwhelming. Writers need to understand what their options are in using type, and what kind of effect their design decisions are likely to have on readers. **Type and White Space** In document design, white space is not simply the empty places on a page where no writing or illustrations appear. White space plays an active role in framing text, adding to visual interest, and breaking up the monotony of solid type. As you have seen in the section on headings, the surrounding white space makes headings more or less prominent.

Second reduction:

WORKING WITH TYPE

Type refers to standardized forms of letters and characters. Until quite recently, it was largely graphic designers in printing companies who knew about the various styles of type and determined which ones to use for a particular document. In the age of the personal computer, this has changed dramatically. Now writers have access to hundreds of type fonts and can change their size and underline, italicize, or make them boldface with the click of a mouse.

The vast range of possibilities now available, however, can be overwhelming. Writers need to understand what their options are in using type, and what kinds of effect their design decisions are likely to have on readers.

Type and White Space

In document design, white space is not simply the empty places on a page where no writing or illustrations appear. White space plays an active role in framing text, adding to visual interest, and breaking up the monotony of solid type. As you have seen in the section on headings, the surrounding white space makes headings more or less prominent.

When you encounter a page that looks like the first version, one of two things is likely to be true: there is a need to get as much information as possible on each page (as in many reference books), or someone doesn't really want to make the information accessible (notice the fine print in advertisements, credit card statements, contracts, and so on). In the second version, at least you can find your way around.

Assuming you aren't trying to hide anything, here are some guidelines about making type readable.

Use White Space to Emphasize Paragraph Divisions

In the second reduction, the white space enables readers to identify paragraphs and to treat each as a separate unit of meaning. White space contributes to the openness of the page by breaking up large expanses of type.

Use Upper- and Lowercase Letters

In general, the combination of upper- and lowercase letters is easier to read than all uppercase letters. This is because uppercase (or capital) letters are uniform in size, making them more difficult to recognize than lowercase letters. The combination of upper- and lowercase uses more white space and therefore produces more visual variety. Notice the difference between these two paragraphs:

USE UPPER- AND LOWERCASE LETTERS. IN GENERAL, THE COMBINATION IS EASIER TO READ THAN ALL UPPERCASE. THIS IS BECAUSE UPPERCASE (OR CAPITAL) LETTERS ARE UNIFORM IN SIZE, MAKING THEM MORE DIFFICULT TO RECOGNIZE THAN LOWERCASE LETTERS, WHERE THERE IS MORE WHITE SPACE AND THEREFORE MORE VISUAL VARIETY. NOTICE THE DIFFERENCE:

Use upper- and lower letters. In general, the combination is easier to read than all uppercase. this is because uppercase (or capital) letters are uniform in size, making them more difficult to recognize than lowercase letters, where there is more white space and therefore more visual variety. Notice the difference:

Use Leading Appropriately

Leading is the typographer's term for the white space that appears above and below a line of type. Leading is what makes a printed page look more or less "gray." The grayer the page, the denser the type and the harder it is to read.

The basic guideline is that you need more leading, or space above and below type, when lines of print are long, less when they're short.

Compare the readability of these two paragraphs:

Long lines of type are easier to read when they have more leading. This is particularly true if the type itself is small. Compare the readability of these two passages of 9-point type. This passage is single-spaced. The extra leading in the second passage helps direct readers' eyes, so they don't skip a line or return to the one they've just read.

Long lines of type are easier to read when they have more leading. This is particularly true if the type itself is small. Compare the readability of these two passages of 9-point type. This passage is single-spaced. The extra leading in the second passage helps direct readers' eyes, so they don't skip a line or return to the one they've just read.

For shorter lines, as in newsletters and other documents with columns, use less leading. If there's too much white space, reader's eyes can drift when they leave one line and look for the start of the next. Notice the difference between Column A and B:

Column A

For shorter lines, as in newsletters and other documents with columns, use less leading. If there's too much white space, readers' eyes can drift when they leave one line and look for the start of the next.

Column B

For shorter lines, as in newsletters and other documents with columns, use less leading. If there's too much white space, readers' eyes can drift when they leave one line and look for the start of the next.

On the other hand, titles are easier to read when the leading is tighter, integrating the words into one visual block. Notice the difference:

Entertaining Satan:
Witchcraft and the Culture
of Early New England

Entertaining Satan:
Witchcraft and the Culture
of Early New England

Use Alignment Appropriately

In general, use flush-left/ragged right alignment for lines of type. That way all lines start in the same place at the left margin, and readers' eyes can return easily to the same spot when they finish reading a line. *Ragged-right alignment* creates an open, informal feeling by providing variable amounts of white space at the end of a line. This variability enables readers to see the difference between the lines, making it easier for them to move from line to line and thereby avoid inadvertently skipping a line.

Type that is *justified* (or aligned uniformly on the right margin) normally creates a darker, denser-looking page. Justified type can often be more difficult to read because more words are hyphenated and gaps can appear between words. Notice the difference in the two columns:

Flush Left/Justified Right:

Type is easier to read if it is aligned along the left margin. That way all lines start in the same place, and readers' eyes can return easily to the same spot when they finish reading a line. On the other hand, type that is justified (or aligned on both left and right margins) is often more difficult to read. This is . . . .

Flush Left/Ragged Right:

Type is easier to read if it is aligned along the left margin. That way all lines start in the same place, and readers' eyes can return easily to the same spot when they finish reading a line. On the other hand, type that is justified (or aligned on both left and right margins) is often more difficult to read. This is . . . .

TYPEFACE

Typeface refers to the design of letters, numbers, and other characters. There are thousands of typefaces available. The visual appearance of typeface contributes to the personality or character of your document. Part of working with type is choosing the typeface that creates the right image and thereby sends the appropriate message to your readers.

Serif and Sans Serif Typefaces

Typefaces are normally divided into two groups—serif and sans serif. *Serif* typefaces include horizontal lines—or serifs—added to the major strokes of a letter or a character such as a number. *Sans serif* typefaces, by contrast, do not have serifs. Notice the difference:

Serif	*Sans serif*
Clarendon	Arial
Palatino	Gill Sans
Times	Helvetica

The typical use and stylistic impact of typefaces vary considerably. Serif typefaces are more traditional, conservative, and formal in appearance. By contrast, sans serif typefaces offer a more contemporary, progressive, and informal look. Accordingly, serif is often used for longer pieces of writing, such as novels and textbooks. It is also the best bet for college papers. The horizontal lines make serif easier to read, especially in dense passages, because they guide the reader's eyes from left to right across the page. On the other hand, technical writers often use sans serif for user's manuals and other documents because it evokes a more modern, "high-tech" look.

Typefaces also differ in *weight*—or the thickness of the letters. A heavier, blacker type will darken your page, making your message appear more serious and substantial. A lighter type will show more white space and create a more spacious, informal mood. With bold, italic, and underline functions on a word processor, you can make further alterations.

Heavier type:	**Times Bold**
Lighter type:	Helvetica

Display or Decorative Typefaces

Display or decorative typefaces offer many options for creating the look you want in newsletter nameplates, organizational logos, invitations, posters, signs, advertisements, and other documents. Display typefaces can project the mood and image that's appropriate for an organization or occasion. The trick, of course, is finding the style that's right—that conveys the message you want to readers.

Notice the different images display type creates for Jetstream Printers. This type projects a sleek and contemporary look:

Jetstream

The following typeface, however, is probably too staid and conservative, more appropriate, say, for a bank, stock brokerage company, or law firm:

JETSTREAM

On the other hand, this type is too light-hearted and informal. It's better suited for a restaurant or fashion boutique:

Jetstream

By the same token, notice how the "alternative" style of type in the following announcement doesn't match the occasion.

The Office of the President

at

Worcester Polytechnic Institute

invites you

to a

Reception and Banquet

in honor

of

Retiring Professor of Mechanical Engineering

Aldous Smiley

If you received such an invitation, you might well feel, perhaps without fully realizing why, that something is off—the delivery or packaging of the message doesn't fit the occasion. On the other hand, if the typeface had been more formal, you probably would not have even noticed it. Appropriate type sometimes does its work by not calling attention to itself.

Mixing Typefaces

In some cases, combining different typefaces can enhance document design. Newsletters, for example, often use sans serif type for headlines and serif for text. Make sure, however, that combinations of typefaces project a consistent image and that the styles used are compatible. Notice the sense of chaos mixed styles can create:

The Office of the President

of

Worcester Polytechnic Institute

invites you

to a

Reception and Banquet

in honor

of

Retiring Professor of Mechanical Engineering

Aldous Smiley

Use the design principles we've just looked at to redesign this ad for the fall film series at Warehouse State.

Warehouse State

FALL FILM SERIES

Classic Film Noir

All showings in Harrington Hall at 8:00 pm

Wednesday, September 14, 2001
Double Indemnity (1944)
Directed by Billy Wilder
With Fred MacMurray and Barbara Stanwyck

Wednesday, October 17, 2001
The Asphalt Jungle (1950)
Directed by John Huston
With Sterling Hayden and Marilyn Monroe

Wednesday, November 30, 2001
Touch of Evil (1958)
Directed by Orson Welles
With Orson Welles, Charlton Heston, and Janet Leigh

VISUAL DESIGN PROJECTS

This section looks at some of the considerations writers typically take into account when they design and produce documents such as flyers, newsletters, brochures, and Web homepages.

Preliminary Considerations

Like other writing tasks, design projects begin with a call to write—the felt need to send a message from an individual, group, or organization to prospective readers. Developing the design of a particular document will depend on answering questions such as these:

1. What is the occasion that calls on you to design a document? What kind of document is most appropriate given the circumstances (a flyer, leaflet, letter, brochure, or other format)? What is its purpose? Whose interests are involved? What is your relationship to the people who want the document produced and to those who will read it? What image should the document project?

2. Who are your readers? What use will they make of the document? What do you want them to do after they have read it? What tone and style are likely to be effective?

3. What information will you be working with? How much of the document will be written text? What graphics do you have to use? How many sections do you foresee? In what order will they appear? Will you be doing all the writing? Some? Who else is involved?

4. What technology do you have to work with? What does it enable you to do? What constraints does it put on the document?

5. Are there any financial or time constraints you need to be aware of? Who will pay for the printing? When does the document need to be finished? Is this a realistic time frame?

By answering these questions, you can begin to make some basic decisions about the layout and other design features of your document. In particular, you will need to decide on the materials you will use in the document—color, type and color of ink, type and color of paper, whether you plan to scan in illustrations or photos, and clip art.

Working Sketches

The next step is to sketch a preliminary layout for the document. At this point, document designers often sketch a number of different arrangements. Such working sketches can help you identify potential problems.

The working sketches for a newsletter and brochure might look like the following. Notice how each sketch uses a frame within which the page components are arranged. In the first two instances the document designer is working with columns and sketching where features such as headlines, headings, and boxes will go. For brochures, you'll need to pay attention to how the panels will work when the brochure is folded.

Newsletter sketch

Brochure sketch (inside)

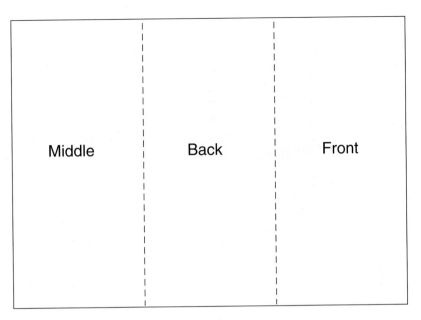

Brochure sketch (outside)

From Sketch to Document: Some Examples

The following sections contain examples of four types of common documents—flyers, newsletters, brochures, and Web pages.

Flyers

Flyers are really small posters that can be passed out or posted on bulletin boards. They may announce upcoming meetings, events, and performances; advertise sales and other limited-time promotions; or urge people to do something. To be effective, flyers need to convey all the pertinent information at a glance. To do so, successful flyers combine seeing and reading with:

- Large headlines
- A minimum of text in the body
- Attention-getting visuals and/or design features

Newsletters

Newsletters are used by companies and organizations to communicate within their own groups and to the public. They run from a single page to eight pages

This flyer was designed for the Rhode Island Department of Health to urge parents to immunize their children. The headline is the word immunization in Khmer, the national language of Cambodia. Notice how the word in its English, Khmer, Lao, Hmong, Spanish, and Portuguese versions creates a strong border to frame the flyer. The flyer uses an attention-getting photo and concise text.

or so, depending on their purpose and frequency. In many respects, they are like newspapers or little magazines. Key elements of a successful newsletter include:

- A distinctive nameplate and logo that identifies the newsletter
- Clear identification of the sponsoring organization
- Volume and/or issue number and date

- A table of contents—on front or back cover
- Consistent design that maintains the identity of the newsletter from one issue to the next
- Use of design features such as sidebars, boxes, pull quotes, photos, and illustrations to break up the text and add visual interest

FOOD BANK news

SUMMER 1999

KEEPING "RHODE ISLANDERS FOR A HUNGER-FREE STATE" TUNED IN

One Family's Struggle to Survive

I am from Cambodia and traditionally vegetables and rice are our meal. But most food pantries don't have fresh vegetables to give us. I can't afford to buy food after I pay rent for the month, so we eat what we get from the pantries," said Jennifer Prak, speaking to our executive director Bernie Beaudreau at the West End Community Center in Providence where she is a client.

"I am 28 years old and I have six children," she continued. "My husband Hak works full time and makes $12.00/hour, but that only pays the rent and bills, with none left over for food. We get some food stamps but when Hak works overtime they take our food stamps away. We can't get ahead."

Jennifer came to America from Cambodia in 1980 when she was just eight years old, herself a middle child of eight brothers and sisters. "When she told me she and her mother were the only survivors of Pol Pot's reign of terror in Cambodia, it became clear why she has six children of her own," says Bernie. Jennifer once wrote a long story about her memories of the Khmer Rouge genocide when she was in high school. Now, she told Bernie sadly, "I try to forget."

Cultural differences between herself and her Americanized children make the daunting task of feeding six hungry mouths even more formidable. "It's a big job to feed my family," Jennifer says. "My children now like American food but my husband and I want Cambodian food. Sometimes I cook two meals."

While some people attempt to cheat the welfare system to receive more assistance, Jennifer says she will not lie. "I am called stupid for telling the truth, but I'll be honest," she said firmly.

Jennifer asked Bernie for help getting into

Jennifer Prak, with sons Felix, 1, and Allex, 4, must rely on food pantries to feed her family of 8.

a GED program so she could get her high school diploma, go on to college and get a degree and a job that would help her family get out of the hole they are stuck in. She wants desperately to move to a nicer apartment in a safer neighborhood. "Where we are now there are gangs and drugs and guns. I am afraid to let my children play outside." Her primary concern is making sure her children survive the streets of her neighborhood.

With all that Jennifer and her family have gone through over the years and the challenges they face going forward, the Food Bank's services are able to make more food available to her, with dignity and generosity. It's what the Food Bank and our network of food pantries and soup kitchens does best—helping families get the assistance they need to break the cycle of poverty and hunger.

How The Food Bank Works

The Rhode Island Community Food Bank works as a conduit of resources between the food industry and our network of 470 member agencies who assist hungry people. We accept, inspect, and sort large bulk food donations from stores like Stop & Shop and Shaw's, food producers, industry wholesalers, local farmers, and food drives. We then distribute the donated food to our member agencies, who provide it directly to families and individuals in need throughout Rhode Island and southeastern Massachusetts. In 1999, we will distribute over five million pounds of food to an average of 35,000 people per month.

A Summit to Address Child Poverty

When the Rhode Island Public Expenditure Council released a February 15 report on education in Rhode Island it contained shocking new data about a dramatic increase in childhood poverty. The front page of *The Providence Journal* declared the news—that nearly one in three Rhode Island school children were in or near poverty. Perhaps out of shock or disbelief, it produced no immediate response, either from the public or state leaders.

Behind the initial silence, the Boards of the Food Bank and the George Wiley Center planned a response. We sent letters calling for a summit on childhood poverty to the Governor and legislative leadership. We held a February 24 rally at the State House to garner support for the summit. Senator Tom Izzo and Representative Tom Slater were there to lend their words of support, along with 25 other community advocates.

It took a great deal of convincing that such a summit was needed and that it could be a bi-partisan, community effort. We formed a coalition of major philanthropic, religious, business, advocacy and service organizations and generated hundreds of phone calls to the Governor's office, employing the membership of Rhode Islanders for a Hunger-Free State. In early May we orchestrated "Child

Poverty Awareness Week" beginning with the Letter Carrier's Food Drive, involving over 150 people in a 39-hour Fast for Rhode Island's Children in Poverty, and ending with Taste of the Nation.

Finally, in mid-May, we received word from the Governor and Senate and House leaders that they would personally attend a two-hour Child Poverty Summit on June 4. To have these leaders spend two hours on child poverty was a victory in itself. Twenty five leaders from various sectors attended, and nearly everyone concurred that it accomplished its intended objectives: to have leaders recognize the problem and commit to creation of a plan for addressing it. The Governor suggested the formation of a Children's Economic Policy Council. The group committed to a day-long summit in October where many more leaders will participate in forming a plan.

We are grateful to Governor Almond, Senator Kelly, House Leader Martineau and others for their leadership in this effort. The work we must do for the thousands of Rhode Island children in poverty is vitally important. With a community effort where all become shareholders in the resulting plans, we can indeed turn back the child poverty trend in our state.

Bernard J. Beaudreau

Bernard J. Beaudreau, *Executive Director*

New Board Member

The Food Bank welcomes Charles S. Fradin to the Board of Directors. Charles is president of Copley Distributors, a Rhode Island company that imports and distributes alcoholic and non-alcoholic beverages. He joins 19 other area professionals and business leaders on the board.

A long-time supporter of the Food Bank, Charles has also served other community organizations, including the Jewish Federation, the Center for Family Business, and the Wine and Spirits Wholesalers Association of America.

Charles holds a B.A. from Skidmore College and an M.B.A. from the Weatherhead School at Case Western Reserve University. He resides in Providence with his wife and two children.

Garden Tours

For a donation of $8 per person to the Food Bank, Ms. Sydney Tynan of Little Compton will open her four acres of beautiful gardens and meadow paths to the public for use as a site for meetings, picnics, or just relaxation! A large deck can accommodate groups. Call (401) 635-2117 for reservations and directions.

Food Bank Agencies Wish List

The following items are needed by our member agencies:
- Freezers
- Refrigerators
- Shelving
- Office cubicle dividers

Call Erica Franco at (401) 826-3073 x224 to make a donation. Thank you!

The first two pages of the Rhode Island Community Foodbank's newsletter Food Bank News *show some typical design features—the identifying logo (repeated at the bottom of page 2), photographs, the use of a screen to highlight "How the Foodbank Works," a sidebar listing the board of directors, message from the executive director, and a panel of short items on page 2.*

Brochures

Companies and organizations use brochures for promotional and informational purposes. Brochures usually include three or four panels. (See, for example the brochures in Chapter 8, "You Can Make a Difference" and "Ashcroft: Ghost Town.")

Here are some considerations to take into account when you're designing a brochure:

1. Make the purpose of the brochure easy to identify. The front cover headline should cue readers to the subject and purpose.

2. The brochure should be easy to use. The outside panels—front, back, and middle—are often designed to be read separately. The inside panels should be designed as a continuous space.

3. Make sure the brochure has all the information readers need—names, addresses, and phone numbers of organizations; maps showing how to get to a store, museum, or historic district; bibliography; steps readers can take; answers to frequently asked questions; basic facts.

Web Sites

Web sites expand dramatically the design options available to you, enabling the use of multimedia features such as graphics, video, and sound. Web sites also present a different way of thinking about and using documents. Instead of organizing information in a linear way, from start to finish, Web sites provide links within the document and to external Web sites so that readers can decide on their own path.

Depending on your interest and technical skill, you can draw on the multimedia capabilities of the Web or you can keep it simple. Remember, though, that while Web sites offer multimedia design features, written text is still their key element. Graphics, video, and sound are exciting features of Web site design—but they also take more time to download than text does. For this reason, use these features carefully. If it takes too long to download, readers may become impatient and leave your site. And remember, some people browse the Web with their graphics capacity turned off. So make sure your message will come across in the text. Use clearly identifiable, concise units of text. Keep in mind that it's harder to read text on the screen than on the page. Provide links for readers to obtain more details.

Here are some of the basic considerations designers take into account when constructing Web sites:

- A home page should give an overview of the Web site—identifying the purpose of the site, summarizing the information it contains, and providing the means to navigate the site. The homepage should also send a visual message about the site. What logo, images, background color, and font best match your purposes? How formal or informal, conservative or casual, intimate or distant do you want the site to be?

- The navigational tools should be easy to find and indicate the main subjects of your site. You can use a menu, icons, or words to do this. Keep your navigational tools consistent throughout the site. Visitors should always know where they are and be able to get back to the homepage without clicking the back button on the browser.

ENDANGERED SPECIES ENDANGERED SPECIES ENDANGERED SPECIES ENDANGERED SPECIES ENDANGERED SPECIES EN

What can you do? It's simple.

Watch your step. Stay on the bedrock trails when hiking on the alpine summits.

Please stay on the marked trails!

Do the rock walk! When you are on a summit, walk on the bedrock and step over crevices and small pockets or depressions with any hint of soil or water. Remember, you can track away centuries of nature's work with a single misplaced step.

The soil at high altitudes is often saturated by atmospheric moisture. A small pocket of water or black muck is one indicator of potential plant habitat. So, it makes sense to avoid disturbing any such area.

Please spread the word about our endangered alpine plants. Tell your friends to make every effort to minimize off-trail trampling. Tell them to stay on the trail. Tell them to be careful, or our fragile alpine meadows will be lost forever.

Summit Steward Program

What is a Summit Steward?

The Summit Steward Program began in 1990 as a cooperative program between The Nature Conservancy, Adirondack Mountain Club, and New York State Department of Environmental Conservation. The Stewards provide an educational presence on the summits of the very peaks that are so threatened by hiker trampling. The program is based on the belief that hikers are unaware of the destruction they are causing by walking off the trails and hard rock surfaces.

PARTNERS IN LAND PROTECTION
P.O. Box 65
Keene Valley, NY 12943

(518) 576-2082

Printed on recycled paper

Each year hikers stray off the bedrock trails in the Adirondack Mountains...

Lapland Rosebay

and without realizing it they trample plants as rare and endangered as those found in the tropical rainforests...

Summit Steward Program

ENDANGERED SPECIES ENDANGERED SPECIES ENDANGERED SPECIES ENDANGERED SPECIES ENDANGERED SPECIES

Are there really endangered and threatened species here in the Adirondacks?

Save the whales...the spotted owl...the bald eagle...the manatee. The list of endangered species goes on and on. Their causes are celebrated on t-shirts, with direct mail campaigns, in newspaper articles throughout the world. Yet...

In our lifetime, and in our corner of the world, species of alpine plants have already been lost.

In our lifetime, other species, now on the verge of extinction, could disappear from the alpine summits of the Adirondack Mountains in New York State — **gone forever.**

These rare, threatened and endangered plants have survived since the last ice age. That's more than 10,000 winters of the severest conditions known. While these plants can survive harsh, frigid winters and dry, sunscorched summers, they can't survive the conditions under a hiker's foot.

It takes thousands of years for enough soil to accumulate to support this plant life. Yet in seconds, the foot of a misguided hiker can destroy this mini-habitat and the plants that grow here.

Why are alpine meadows endangered?

New York has fewer than 80 acres of arctic alpine plant communities all within the High Peaks Region of the Adirondack Mountains. These plants, such as the Lapland Rosebay, exist only in the extreme conditions on the summits of the state's highest peaks. Although the plants are hardy, they are sensitive to erosion caused by the wind and water and by the physical contact of hikers' boots.

Each year hikers stray off the bedrock trails in the High Peaks of the Adirondack Mountains and trample plants as rare and endangered as those found in the tropical rainforests.

This brochure from the Summit Steward Program uses a line drawing to unify the three inside panels.

- As in other kinds of visual design, repetition and consistency are critical factors. You could, for example, repeat an identifying logo or header on each page, background color, and the placement of navigational tools to create a consistent visual theme.

- Headings, frames, and rules break up the page. But in using them, be sure not to clutter up your page.

- Web sites are interactive. Provide feedback forms so that readers can respond to your site.

Notice how the homepage of Global Exchange uses color, seemingly handwritten fonts, and illustrations to emphasize its focus on campaigns for global justice.

CHAPTER TWENTY

Essay Exams

Essay examinations are certainly among the most challenging writing situations you face in college. The reason is pretty straightforward. Whether the exam consists of identification items, short-answer questions, full-length essays, or a combination, you have to write under pressure. First, there is the pressure to finish all the parts of an exam within the allotted time. Then, there is the pressure of writing on demand, when someone else—namely, your instructor—chooses the topics and asks the questions. There is also the pressure of writing for evaluation, to demonstrate to your instructor that you understand the course material and can work with it in meaningful ways. And finally, there is the pressure of writing without having available the usual resources, such as notes, textbooks, articles, or dictionary—a pressure that calls on you to write from recall.

As many students can attest (and many teachers remember from their days as students), these pressures can be anxiety-provoking. Small wonder. After all, something real is on the line; you can't know in advance exactly what will appear on the exam and you have to produce on the spot, often by juggling multiple parts of a test. At the same time, writing under pressure can push you to new insights and unforeseen connections—when the course material seems to jell in ways you had not quite imagined. Exams indeed call on you to perform for a grade, but successful students realize that exams can also be important learning experiences, in which you clarify for yourself the main themes and key concepts in a course. In fact, grades often depend on this kind of clarification, as it takes place in response to the questions on an exam.

The writing task you face on essay exams can be stated quite simply: You need to produce a good first draft in the time you're given. To do this, you'll need to develop an overall approach to writing essay exams. Developing a systematic strategy is your best bet for dealing with the pressures of an essay exam and to maximize your performance. In the following sections, we'll look at the four basic steps of successful exam writing:

1. Preparing for essay exams
2. Analyzing the format and questions of an exam
3. Planning an answer
4. Writing the essay exam

PREPARING FOR ESSAY EXAMS

Your preparation for an essay exam should begin at the very start of the course. Going to class, taking good notes, keeping up with the readings, doing the assignments, and participating in discussion sections are all ways to prepare for exams—and are generally more successful than cramming at the last minute. But this is no doubt advice you've heard before. Assuming that you're keeping up, the real question is how you can get the most out of studying the material in the course.

Students sometimes equate studying with simply memorizing bodies of information. Now certainly, in some courses, where the exams consist of multiple-choice, true/false, matching, and fill-in-the-blank items, test taking may rely heavily on the recall of memorized information. Make sure you understand how you will be tested. It's perfectly reasonable to ask your instructor, a teaching assistant, or a student who has already taken the course about the types of exams you can expect so that you can plan your study accordingly.

For courses with essay exams, you'll need to recall information, but largely to show what you can do with it: how you can relate facts, details, examples, and terms to the main themes and key concepts of the course. In such courses, instructors are not likely to hold you responsible for every item of information covered in the class. Instead, they want to see whether you can identify the central issues of the course and explain how information fits together in meaningful patterns. The danger of relying exclusively on memorization is that it can cause you to stuff your head full of separate items of information and fail to see the big picture.

In this sense, preparing for essay exams amounts to finding the big picture—the main ideas, terminology, controversies, explanations, and conceptual frameworks in a course. You can do this in part by paying attention to chapter headings, summaries, and highlighted terms in your textbook and by noticing what your instructor emphasizes in lectures, writes on the board, or includes in review sheets distributed before exams. Teachers and textbooks alike will often mark key points: "The two most important criticisms of sociobiology are…" or "The three main factors that led to the construction of the Ringstrasse in 19th century Vienna are…."

Pay attention to how the material in the course is divided. If it is organized chronologically, look for distinct periods (such as Reconstruction or the Great Depression) and the emergence of artistic, intellectual, and political trends (such as the Harlem Renaissance, Freudian psychoanalysis, or McCarthyism). If the course is organized thematically, look for connections between readings and the central themes. If the course presents an introduction to a broad field of study, keep track of the topics that form the separate sections. You may want to meet regularly with a small study group of classmates to review course material and discuss the most important themes and concepts.

As exams approach, you (and your study group) can prepare by trying to anticipate questions your instructor might ask and what an effective answer might be. Remember, an essay exam is likely to call on you to work with the course material—not just to recall information but to analyze key themes, explain their significance, make an interpretation, defend a position, criticize a theory, or recommend a path of action.

WORKING TOGETHER

Preparing for Exams

Working with two or three other students, read a chapter from a textbook in a course one or more of you are taking. As a group, identify key ideas, terms, concepts, theories, controversies in the chapter. Write two essay questions based on the chapter. Present the questions to your class, explaining why you think they capture the chapter's central issues.

ANALYZING EXAMS

You can save yourself a lot of problems by paying close attention to the overall format of the exam and by reading each question carefully.

Surveying the Format

Before you start writing answers to exam questions, take time to survey the format of the exam. Notice how many questions there are, how many points each one carries, and any directions about how long an answer should be or how much space the exam allots to it.

Use this information to divide your time so that you'll be able to answer each question. Careful time management can keep you from running out of time.

As you survey the exam, make some tentative decisions about which questions to answer when choices are offered and the order you will follow. You don't have to take the exam from start to finish; students often find they do their best when they begin with the questions that seem the easiest to them. That way you can build some confidence before tackling questions you find more difficult. But if you do decide to answer questions out of their order, make sure you don't inadvertently skip a question altogether.

Analyzing Exam Questions

Analyzing exam questions is really a matter of recognizing the type of question and then clarifying what the question is calling on you to do.

The three most common types of questions that call for written answers are identification items (often called IDs), short-answer questions, and essays. They differ in the length of writing called for and in the points they carry. Usually you can tell the type of question at a glance, according to its format, the directions it gives, and the amount of space provided for an answer.

Identification Items (IDs)

Identification items normally call for short statements that identify or define material from the course. There will frequently be a series of items, and usually each item will carry only a few points.

SAMPLE ID ITEMS (FROM MEDIA AND MASS COMMUNICATION)

Define each term in a sentence or two (2 points each).

    a. Cognitive dissonance
    b. Agenda setting
    c. Technological determinism
    d. Hot and cool media
    e. Gatekeepers

ID items such as these call on you to define course topics clearly and concisely. Most often, you'll have only a few minutes to spend on each item. For example:

A. COGNITIVE DISSONANCE

Cognitive dissonance is a state of psychological discomfort that occurs when information a person receives is inconsistent with the person's already-held attitudes.

GUIDELINES FOR ANALYZING EXAM QUESTIONS

The following guidelines can help you analyze any exam question that calls for a written answer.

1. Look for key terms in the exam questions. Some key terms—such as *describe, summarize, explain, analyze,* and *evaluate*—provide directions. Other key terms are topics from course material. Take, for example, the exam question, "Describe the Monroe Doctrine and give two examples of when it was used." The key term *Monroe Doctrine* refers to a topic from lectures and reading, while *describe* and *give two examples* provide directions. Putting directions and topics together will help you understand the purpose of the question and clarify how you should treat course material in your answer.

2. Notice whether the question has more than one part. If so, make sure you understand what each part calls on you to do. The question on the Monroe Doctrine, for example, contains two parts—first to describe it and then to give two examples.

3. Consider what information you need to answer the question. Draw on course material from lectures, readings, and discussions.

4. Determine the amount of time you can spend on each answer. Use these questions to determine how long it should be: How many points does the question carry? How much time do you have to answer it? How much space is provided on the exam?

Short-Answer Questions

Short-answer questions call for answers that can range from a sentence or two to a mini-essay. Typically short answers are a paragraph or two in length. Depending on the question, you'll have anywhere from a few minutes to ten minutes or so to write your answer.

SAMPLE SHORT-ANSWER QUESTIONS (FROM GENERAL CHEMISTRY)

Answer each question in a sentence or two (5 points each).

1. Contrast *mass* and *weight*.
2. Define the word *molecule*.
3. Explain the relationships among the number of protons, neutrons, and electrons in an atom.
4. Compare physical processes with chemical processes.
5. Describe how a percent yield is calculated for a chemical reaction.

Note that a key term in each question—*contrast, define, explain, compare,* and *describe*—gives directions about what to do with course topics such as "mass," "weight," and "molecule."

Sample Short-Answer Questions (from Early American History):

Write a paragraph or two on each of the following items. Define the term and explain why it is significant (10 points each).

1. The Glorious Revolution
2. The Middle Passage
3. Virgin Soil Epidemics

Note that the key terms in this question call first for the recall of information about a particular course topic (*define*) and second for an elaboration of its significance (*explain*). For example:

1. The Glorious Revolution

In 1688, James II baptized his first son a Catholic, thereby perpetuating a Catholic monarchy in England. Fed up with James' arbitrary rule, parliamentary leaders responded by inviting James' Protestant daughter Mary and her husband William of Orange to take over as king and queen. James fled to France, and this bloodless change in the monarchy became known as the Glorious Revolution.

The Glorious Revolution had significant effects on the colonies. Colonists in Boston arrested the royal governor Sir Edward Andros and restored the colonial assembly he had tried to abolish. The Bill of Rights and Toleration Act passed by parliament in 1689 limited the power of rulers and guaranteed a degree of religious freedom. More important, the Glorious Revolution set a precedent for revolution against the king. John Locke's defense of the Glorious Revolution, Two Treatises on Government (1690), profoundly influenced political thinking in the colonies by arguing that when rulers violated the people's natural rights, they had the right to overthrow their government.

Essay Questions

Essay questions are usually allotted more time and more points on an exam than ID items and short-answer questions. You'll have more time to plan and write your response. Typically essay questions will give you anywhere from 20 minutes to an hour.

As is true of ID items and short-answer questions, the secret to writing effective essay exams is recognizing what the question calls on you to do. The box on pages 689–690 presents some of the most common writing tasks you'll encounter on essay exams.

SOME COMMON ESSAY EXAM QUESTIONS

■ **Summarize main ideas:** You are asked to recall main ideas and present them clearly and accurately. Example from an anthropology course:

> In their article "The Consequences of Literacy," Ian Watt and Jack Goody trace changes that occur with the rise of literacy. What do they see as the main differences between oral and literate cultures? In their view, what are the main consequences of literacy?

■ **Explain significance:** You are asked to explain the importance of course material by giving reasons and examples. Example from a history of science course:

> Watson's and Crick's discovery in 1953 of the double helical structure of DNA ushered in the "molecular revolution." What exactly did they discover? Explain the significance of their discovery to the field of biology. Give examples to illustrate the "molecular revolution" they initiated.

■ **Apply concepts:** You are asked to apply concepts to works studied in the course or from your own experience. Example from an African-American literature course:

> The theme of "passing" as white appears in a number of important African-American novels. Analyze the theme of "passing" in at least three of the following novels we've read: Frances E. W. Harper's *Iola Leroy*, James P. Johnson's *Autobiog-*

raphy of an Ex-Coloured Man, Jessie Faucett's *Plum Bun*, Nella Larsen's *Passing*. What do you see as the main differences and similarities in the treatment of this theme?

Example from a sociology course:

> Define Erving Goffman's notion of "underlife" behavior. Explain how and why it takes place and in what contexts. Use the notion of "underlife" to explain behavior you have observed or read about.

■ **Discuss a quotation:** You are asked to comment on a quotation you are seeing for the first time. Often written by your instructor, these quotations will typically raise a controversial point to discuss. Example from an American history course:

> "The coming of the Civil War and the failures of Reconstruction have been seen by historians and others as failures of morality. This is wrong. The problems were actually political. Smarter politicians could have resolved these problems easily." How would you respond to this argument?

■ **Compare and contrast:** You are asked to analyze similarities and differences between two works or ideas. Example from a Latin American literature course:

> Julia Alvarez's *How the Garcia Girls Lost Their Accents* and Cristina Garcia's *Dreaming in Cuban* both treat issues of immigration and acculturation. Compare and contrast the two novels' exploration of cultural identity and change. *(continued)*

(continued)

- **Analyze causes:** You are asked to explain why and how something happened. Example from a film course:

   Explain the emergence of film noir in Hollywood films of the 1940s and 1950s. What values, beliefs, and ideologies of the time do these films embody?

   Example from a Russian history course:

   What factors led to Stalin's consolidation of control in the Soviet Union?

- **Evaluate:** You are asked to make a judgment about the strengths and weaknesses of one or more works or concepts. Example from a mass communication course:

   Evaluate the debate between Walter Lippmann in *The Phantom Public* and John Dewey in *The Public and Its Problems*. Explain the respective positions each thinker takes on the role of the public in political life. What do you see as the strengths and weaknesses of their arguments? Where do you stand in the debate?

- **Propose a course of action:** You are asked to analyze a problem and propose your own solution. Example from an education course:

   Briefly summarize the arguments for and against bilingual education. Then explain what you think should be done. Be specific in describing the kinds of programs you think can be successful.

- **Synthesize a number of sources:** You are asked to develop a coherent framework to pull together ideas and information from a number of sources. Example from a management course:

   You have read case studies of managerial strategies in a number of major companies—IBM, Nike, Harley Davidson, Apple, and General Motors. Based on these readings, explain what you see as the major challenges currently facing management. Use information from the case studies to illustrate your points.

- **Creative questions:** Occasionally instructors will ask students to take on the identity of a historical or literary character, to write dialogue, or to make other types of creative responses. Example from a colonial Latin American history course:

   The year is 1808, and Spanish Americans are reeling from the news that Napoleon has invaded Spain and deposed the king. Two Creoles meet in a tavern, and their conversation soon turns to the political future of the colonies. Create a dialogue in which one argues for independence while the other urges continued loyalty to Spain.

WORKING TOGETHER

Analyzing Essay Questions

Working with two or three classmates, analyze the essay questions listed in the box. What key terms are given?—identify directions and topics. What information would you need in order to answer the question successfully? What does each question call on you to do?

PLANNING YOUR ANSWER

How you plan your answer depends largely on the type of question and the time and points allotted to it. Answering ID items, for example, should take you just a few seconds to recall the key information you need. For short-answer questions that call for a paragraph or two, you may want to underline key terms or write down a few quick notes to help you organize your answer. (Note in the sample short answer on the Glorious Revolution how the writer uses a key term in the directions to focus each of the two paragraphs: first she "defines" the event and then "explains" why it was significant to the American colonies.)

Full-length essays, of course, require more planning time. In fact, it's not unusual to spend a quarter of the allotted time to planning an answer. Here are some guidelines for planning:

1. Read the question carefully, noting key terms to clarify what your purpose should be. What kind of answer is the question calling for? What is the topic of the question? Are you being asked simply to define, describe, or summarize? To what extent are you asked to analyze, interpret, evaluate, or argue according to your own understanding of the material?

2. See if the question offers any organizational cues. If the question has multiple parts, consider whether these parts offer a possible scheme for arranging your answer. Often the parts consist of questions that lead logically from one to another.

3. Write a brief outline of key points. Begin with the main point—the response that answers the main question being asked. Then decide how to arrange supporting reasons, details, and examples.

4. Before you start writing, double-check your outline to make sure it answers what the question asks—not what you want it to say.

Notice how the brief outline below uses the essay question to organize an answer.

Essay Question

You have read arguments for and against legislation to make English the official language of the United States. Write an essay that explains why this has become such a controversial issue. What is at stake for each side in the debate? Explain your own position, citing evidence to support it.

Brief Outline

Main point: Demographic changes in the U.S. and the "new immigration" from Latin America and Asia have called national identity into question.

Pro: Desire for national unity
Anxiety about immigration
Belief that "old immigrants" (1890–1920) assimilated and learned English quickly

Con: U.S. as nation of immigrants
   Value of many languages in global economy
   Belief in multiculturalism
My position: Against English Only legislation
   For increased language classes for recent immigrants

WRITING A GOOD ANSWER

Writing a good answer on an essay exam amounts to producing a good first draft. You can make additions and corrections, but you won't have the time to do thorough revisions. Here are some suggestions to help you write an effective answer:

1. State the main answer to the question in the opening paragraph. Essay exams don't need introductions to set up the main point. One good strategy is to use the question (or main question when there is a series) as the basis of your opening sentence. Answer the question as clearly as you can. First impressions on essay exams count. Your opening paragraph should encapsulate the main line of your thinking and forecast what's to come.

2. Provide supporting evidence, reasons, details, and examples in the paragraphs that follow. Draw on material from lectures and readings, but don't pad with extraneous material. You don't need to show off how much you can recall. Instead, you need to show how you can relate supporting evidence to your main answer.

3. Highlight your understanding of the course material. Demonstrate how you can work with the information, ideas, and themes in the course. Make sure, however, that you're not just presenting personal opinions for their own sake. Link your insights, evaluations, and proposals to the course material.

4. Write an ending, even if you're running out of time. A sentence or two can tie together main points at the end.

5. Make additions neatly. New ideas may occur to you as you're writing, and you should incorporate them if they fit into the main line of your thinking. You can add a sentence or two by writing neatly in the margins and using an arrow to show where they go in your answer.

6. Write legibly, and proofread when you've finished. You can make corrections by crossing out and replacing words and phrases. Do so as neatly as you can. A messy exam is hard to read and creates a negative impression.

7. Watch the clock. If you're running out of time or need to go on to another question, it's best to list points from your outline. This way you can show where your essay is going, even if you can't finish it.

SAMPLE ESSAY ANSWERS

The following two essays were written in a colonial Latin American history course in response to this question:

> "Latin America's ruling elites maintained their position largely through ideological domination. Witness their ability to make patriarchy an unchallenged social assumption. Aside from such exceptional figures as Sor Juana, women at every level of society readily accepted their inferior status, along with the rigid gender conventions that called for female passivity, obedience, and sexual modesty." Discuss.

As you can see, the essay question is a quotation that takes a position on issues in the course, along with the direction "discuss." The key term *discuss* doesn't seem to provide a lot of guidance, but experienced students know that *discuss* really calls on them to offer their own interpretation of the quotation, along with reasons and supporting evidence from readings and lecture.

The first essay is annotated. You can use the second one to sharpen your own sense of an effective essay answer.

ANSWER A

Connects key terms in essay question to establish main focus of the answer.

Although Latin American elites frequently used a policy of coercion to govern indigenous and African populations, they also used consent to maintain their position in colonial society through ideological domination. Colonial society was based on a hierarchical system of authority and dependence, in which the ruling elite established strong ties with the ruled through a shared ideology. Patriarchy, the social assumption that men were responsible for controlling the lives of women, was central to this shared ideology.

Explains key term "patriarchal ideology."

The colonial elite based its political and moral authority on the patriarchal ideology of men's superiority, masculinity, and honor and women's inferiority, modesty, and submission. Dignified men acquired their authority by controlling and protecting their dependents—women, servants, workers, and slaves. Women, on the other hand, were socialized to be modest and obedient and were regarded as dangerous and likely to succumb to temptations, instincts, and desires unless controlled by fathers and husbands.

Illustrates key term with details and an example.

From father to husband, men had power over a woman's sexuality. Marriage was used by fathers to improve their status and make alliances with other families. Little consideration was given to a woman's own preferences. Once married, a woman was subordinate to her husband. The crime of rape, for example, was seen not as a crime against the woman but rather an assault on the honor of her father or husband. In cases of rape, fathers or husbands would publicly profess their shame, humiliation, and lack of honor for failing to protect a daughter or wife.

Notes exceptions and gives examples of exceptions.

There were certain groups that posed exceptions to this gender ideology of male control and female dependence. Heiresses, nuns, and widows negotiated a certain amount of autonomy in specific circumstances. For example, the Condessa de Santiago inherited a fortune and became a powerful economic and political force—until she married and her power ended. Nuns such as Sor Juana found a limited space for self-expression in the convent, as demonstrated by the numerous literary works produced by nuns. Widows were the largest group of autonomous women. By law, dowries reverted to widows when their husbands died. However, women without husbands, especially widows, were suspected of immoral acts. The legend of La Florona, the "weeping widow," illustrates how autonomous women were seen as uncontrolled and threatening.

Analyzes role of patriarchal ideology among plebeian women.

In the lower classes, there was a significant gap between the theory and practice of patriarchal ideology. Plebeian women were in the public sphere much more than elite women not because of their greater autonomy but because of financial necessity. The labor these women did as vendors, seamstresses, and domestic servants was hardly empowering, and they were often subjected to verbal, physical, and sexual abuse. In this way, they still adhered to the system of patriarchy and remained the dependents of their male employers.

Analyzes role of patriarchal ideology among plebeian men.

For men, masculinity, honor, and social superiority were achieved by controlling dependents. By accepting such a patriarchal ideology, male plebeians, servants, and slaves were constantly reminded of their own position as dependents, with little economic or political authority over their lives. Lower-class and slave men could not exercise the type of patriarchal control and protect their women as the upper classes did. But because the lower classes believed in patriarchal control, they in effect consented to the moral and political leadership of the upper classes.

Ending ties key terms together.

Morality, dignity, and honor, thus, were identified with the ruling elite in colonial society. This gender ideology reinforced the power of the ruling elite as both women and plebeian men consented to its patriarchal assumptions.

ANSWER B

Depending on the circumstances, the ruling elite in colonial Latin America used force or consent to govern. For example, they routinely used military power against the Indian population and to suppress slave revolts. In addition, the Inquisition in Latin America used physical force, including torture to eliminate dissent.

Ideological domination was an important tool of the ruling elite, and patriarchy became one of the unchallenged social assumptions that reinforced the authority of the upper classes. The view was widely held by members of colonial society that men were the natural rulers and that women should be controlled by men. Men were considered authoritative, while women were supposed to be obedient.

Thus women in colonial society were excluded from both economic and political power. Excluded from the priesthood, higher education, and the professions, women were forced to remain in the home. This dependence reinforced male authority and kept women powerless and unable to challenge dominant social assumptions. Because women were the socializers of the family, they transferred this gender ideology to their children and thereby further reproduced the system.

If a woman misbehaved, she would dishonor her father or husband and her household. A stain on a woman's reputation tainted the reputation of her entire family. It was therefore a man's responsibility to control a woman and protect her against herself and keep her in the domestic sphere. Fathers decided the person a woman would marry or if she should become a nun. An unmarried woman in the presence of unmarried men was always accompanied by a chaperone to guard her virtue. Husbands controlled their wives and protected them. By engraining women with the dominant ideology of patriarchy, the elite were able to rule without opposition.

This gender ideology, however, did not transfer completely to the lower classes in colonial society because in order to be proper, women had to come from wealthy families. Single lower-class women often worked before they married, and this was considered threatening to their morals. Still, plebeian women did view males as authority figures. Once they married, they were subordinated to their husbands and restricted to the home. Women were considered devious and threatening and therefore needed to be protected and controlled by male authority.

Lower-class men, however, never achieved total patriarchal power and were in no position to challenge authority figures or social assumptions. While they accepted the rigid gender conventions of the dominant ideology, plebeian men remained dependents in relation to the upper classes. Due to their servile and economically insecure position in society, plebeians could not fully protect their women, which was one of the prerequisites of full manhood as colonial society understood it.

Nuns, heiresses, and widows were able in limited ways to evade patriarchal control. Except for priests, men were basically excluded from convents, and so to some extent the nuns could organize their own affairs. Heiresses might achieve a measure of autonomy by inheriting money, and widows received their dowries if their husbands died.

Overall, though, the gender ideology of patriarchy in colonial Latin America was very unfair to women in general and was used to keep lower-class men in their place.

WORKING TOGETHER

Analyzing an Essay Answer

Working with two or three other students, follow these steps:

1. Look again at the essay question that appears at the beginning of this section. What exactly does it call on students to do? Clarify for your-selves what seems to be the main writing task facing students who are taking this exam in colonial Latin American history.

2. Read the first essay answer and annotations. How well do you think it handles the writing task?

3. Read and analyze the second essay answer. Given your sense of what the writing task calls for and how well the first essay answer handles the task, what do you see as the strengths and weaknesses of the second answer? Be specific. What particular features of the essay work well or not so well?

CHAPTER TWENTY-ONE

Writing Portfolios

Portfolios are often used by painters, graphic designers, architects, photographers, and other visual artists to present their work to teachers, prospective clients, museum officials, gallery owners, or fellowship selection committees. Portfolios enable artists to select a representative sample of their best work and to display it in an organized form. The same is true for writing portfolios. In a writing portfolio, students choose a sample of their work to present as the culminating project of a writing class.

Writing portfolios offer students a number of benefits. They allow students to decide on the writing they want to present to the teacher for evaluation. Students typically select from among their various writing assignments a limited number to revise for their portfolios. In this way, they can show teachers how they have handled different kinds of writing tasks. Portfolios also provide students with the opportunity to reflect on how they have developed as writers and to explain what the writing they've done means to them as students, learners, and people.

Writing portfolios have benefits for teachers too. A portfolio provides teachers with a range of writing to evaluate instead of single papers. One of the premises of writing portfolios is that teachers can make fairer and more accurate appraisals of student writing if they can read various types of writing, written for various purposes, in various forms, for various audiences.

How portfolios are graded varies. In some writing programs, portfolios are evaluated by one or more other teachers who do blind readings—that is, students' names are removed. In other cases, portfolios are submitted to and graded by the student's teacher. The weight assigned to the portfolio grade varies too. If your teacher asks you to prepare a portfolio, she will tell you how much it counts toward your final grade.

WHAT SHOULD YOU INCLUDE IN A PORTFOLIO?

To put together a final portfolio, you will need to include samples of various kinds of writing. Your teacher will give you further directions. Some teachers are quite specific about what to include, while others will offer students more room for planning the contents of their portfolios.

Amount of Writing to Include

Part of designing a portfolio is making decisions about what best represents you as a writer. If you include most of the writing you've done, you defeat the purpose. Many teachers ask for only four or five pieces of writing. Others ask for more or leave the number open to student choice.

Types of Writing to Include

In designing a portfolio you are asked to select not only a limited number but also a range of writing that represents the different types of work you've done. If you include only personal narratives or informative writing or argumentative essays, you won't give readers enough sense of this range, and your portfolio will seem too one-dimensional. Your teacher may tell you exactly what types to include, or you may be given more room to decide.

SOME OPTIONS FOR A WRITING PORTFOLIO

Here are some types of writing often included in portfolios:

A Reflective Letter

Almost all writing portfolios begin with a letter of reflection that introduces you and your portfolio. The purpose of such a letter is to persuade your instructor (or any other readers) that you have accomplished the goals of the course.

A reflective letter might discuss the choices you have made in designing your portfolio, explain your development as a writer and the role of writing in your life, evaluate strengths and weaknesses in your writing, and discuss your experience as a writer and person in your writing class. The letter should provide readers with a sense of who you are. And it might also indicate where you see yourself going next in developing your writing.

The writing you have done in response to the "Literacy Events" assignment in Chapter 1 and "Reflecting on Your Writing" throughout the book can provide you with material for your reflective letter.

Jennifer Principe

Dear Professor Trimbur:

Writing has always been an important form of expression for me. I have always had a hard time expressing myself verbally, and I feel that writing gives me a control over my words that I can't find anywhere else. Writing has almost become a form of medication for me, an objective ear always willing to listen. For as long as I can remember, I have kept a journal that I write in whenever there is something I want to straighten out in my life. My journal is one of the best ways I know to explore my thoughts and decide on a course of action to take. Writing forces me to slow down and really consider how I feel about something. It also creates a permanent record that I can go back to at any time.

Although I enjoy and rely on this sort of informal writing, I have felt for a long time that the formal writing I do in my courses could use improvement, and English 101 has definitely helped me to grow as a formal writer. In high school, my English teachers told me I had good ideas but that my writing was wordy and unfocused. I understood what they were saying, but unfortunately they never explained what I should do about my problem. This made writing a very frustrating experience for me.

In English 101, I think the most important thing I learned is that when I start writing I usually don't have a definite idea of where I am going. What I have found through the writing assignments and the peer commentaries is that my main ideas are often unclear at first, but as I get to the end of a draft they become much clearer. As I write more, I begin to focus on an idea and my essay begins to make more sense. In many cases, I could take ideas from the end of a draft and bring them up to my introduction to give me focus.

The writing samples included in my portfolio were chosen with several criteria in mind. First, I chose writing that I had strong personal feelings about because when I believe in a topic my writing tends to be more passionate and heartfelt, and thus more effective. For this reason, the writing samples that are included in this portfolio are strongly rooted in my personal beliefs. Second, I chose different kinds of writing so readers could see how I approached various writing assignments.

I chose to include the peer commentary I wrote for Joe Scherpa. I don't think this was necessarily the best commentary I did, but I was particularly happy about Joe's reaction to it. A week or so after I completed the commentary, Joe told me that my commentary helped him do a complete revision on that assignment. He seemed grateful for my suggestions and happy with the revised version of his work. Although I realize that my commentary was not the sole motivation for his revisions, I was happy to see that he felt it had made a difference in his writing.

In conclusion, I feel this class has been quite beneficial in my growth as a writer. I got lots of practice in different kinds of writing. I'm planning to major in chemical engineering, and I know that writing will be an important part of my upcoming career, as well as in my personal life. For my career, writing will be a tool that I will often need to get my point across. I feel that I need to work on knowing when to put personal opinions into my writing and when I should be more objective. Sometimes I get carried away by my feelings about a topic. This class has helped me to understand different writing situations, and I think I am now better able to see when the personal side is appropriate and when it's not.

Revised Writing Assignments

Portfolios usually include revised writing assignments. This gives you the opportunity to review the work you have done over the course of a term and to decide which writings you want to bring to final form and which best represent your abilities. It's a good idea to select a range of purposes and a range of genres. Your teacher will tell you how many to include.

A Case Study

Some teachers ask students to include a case study of one of the writing assignments—with working draft, peer commentary, and the final version, as well as your own explanation of how you worked on the piece of writing. Case studies look in detail at how you planned, drafted, and revised one particular piece of writing. They offer you the opportunity to analyze the choices you made. Be specific by examining how you drafted and revised a key passage or two.

SAMPLE CASE STUDY

Matt Axt

INTRODUCTION

I decided to present my essay "Citizens X" as a case study because it is the paper I revised the most and the one I got the most helpful peer commentary on. I have included the working draft of the essay, the two peer commentaries I received, and the final draft.

The two peer commentaries made me realize a couple of things about my first draft. Both seemed to agree that my position wasn't as clear as it should be and that the ideas in paragraph three didn't connect to my main idea very well. I agreed with this right away. I thought the draft had a good opening and was going along fine until the end of paragraph two. At that point, I lost interest in what I was doing. Maybe I just lost track of what I wanted to do. Anyway, paragraph three is basically filled up with a bunch of ideas that I don't really think explain my generation but that other people often bring out. It started to dawn on me that if I wanted to use these ideas I'd need to make sure readers didn't see them as mine.

The other main consideration I had to deal with comes up in the second peer commentary. This was written by a kid I'm pretty good friends with, and at first I was a little irritated about him trying to tell me what I think. And I had no idea what he meant about not being so nice. I thought we were supposed to use a reasonable tone. I put this one away and tried to forget about the paper for a day or two.

When I re-read the draft and the feedback after two days, I started to agree with my friend that I needed to work on how I stated my position but that there was also a bigger problem concerning what the purpose of the essay was. When I wrote the working draft, I thought I was simply explaining why my generation is so apathetic—that it had to do with our childhood and current social problems. After thinking about it more, however, I realized I really wanted to defend my generation—not to claim a lot of us aren't apathetic, burned out, and cynical about politics but to say that the apathy isn't exclusively our fault and that the media shouldn't blame us. I particularly liked what my friend said about how the media is run by a bunch of baby boomers trying to blame us for their own failures. So my friend gave me a little more heart to get back to the draft and say what was really on my mind. This can be seen in the way I revised my main point at the end of paragraph one, changing the sentence "I believe the conditions and attitudes present during our childhood have caused this 'decline'" to the much more forceful "We're taking the blame for the failures of previous generations."

WORKING DRAFT

CITIZENS X

I'm a member of Generation X, and believe me, it's not that much fun. The generation I belong to has been under fire for the last few years. As the media and journalists portray us, we're disinterested in politics, obsessed by personal success, and stressed out by everyday life. In the United States, young people are supposed to be the hope of the future, but if you read the popular press, you might well conclude that there is no future. No generation in the recent past has been as vilified as my generation has. We're pictured as a generation in decline, an ominous sign of the bankruptcy of the American Dream. But what has caused the so-called decline of youth over the past twenty years or so? I believe the conditions and attitudes present during our childhood have caused this "decline."

The political atmosphere of the late sixties and early seventies has caused an apathetic attitude toward politics. The resignation of President Richard Nixon, following the Watergate scandal, seems to exemplify politics for people my age. The illegal activities committed by the head of state caused negative attitudes to develop toward politics and politicians. Growing up in the shadow of Watergate, people my age developed a distrust in politics. As a result, the youth of today have much less interest in government and politics than young people had in the past. My generation was preceded by the Movement and the furor of Vietnam War protests. The energy that the youth of the Vietnam War era invested in changing the political system was phenomenal. Following this period of political activism should come a lull, and I believe we are it.

Social problems such as the AIDS epidemic, drug abuse, homelessness and poverty, and the decline of America as an economic power are contributing factors to the decline of youth. Faced with a terrible disease like AIDS, young people have realized that we are not invincible. Drugs offer an escape from reality, but only intensify the condescending attitude of our elders. How can one have an optimistic attitude toward the future when our economy has slowed down, our national debt has skyrocketed, and the baby boomers already have all the good jobs? Growing up with these problems has caused pessimism and fear about the future.

PEER COMMENTARY #1

Matt,

I think you've got a great idea for an essay here. Your opening paragraph sets out the issues well, but I wasn't altogether sure what position you're taking. At first, I thought you were going to explain why and how "conditions and attitudes present during our childhood has caused this 'decline.'" But as I read on, I wasn't sure. I think my uncertainty has to do with how the reasons you give in paragraphs two and three are connected to the position you state in the last sentence of paragraph one.

The first reason—that political scandals such as Watergate have caused cynicism—is pretty clear, but toward the end of the paragraph, when you talk about the Movement of the sixties, you make it sound like it's a natural progression to go from an activist generation to a disinterested or passive one.

The third paragraph opens with a bunch of social problems. I agree they're all problems that affect us, but they're not from our childhood. They're all happening right now, so to raise them doesn't really seem to support the position you've stated in your opening.

Basically I agree with a lot of what you're saying. My problem with the essay so far has to do with how the third paragraph connects to your position. It seems you're just throwing in a lot of ideas and then the essay just seems to run out of steam and stop. I'm not sure what to suggest. Somehow you need to connect the two paragraphs to your position statement more clearly and then give a stronger ending.

I think this draft positions readers in a confusing way. At first it seems you're going to defend our generation against charges that we're apathetic, materialistic, and stressed out. But then it seems that you agree that there has been a decline. So I couldn't really figure out whether your position was one of defending us against the media or explaining why we're in "decline." Plus, I'm not sure what you mean by decline.

PEER COMMENTARY #2

Dear Matt,

Your essay starts out by saying that you "believe the conditions and attitudes present during our childhood have caused this 'decline.'" OK, paragraph two sort of explains how that has happened, but I don't exactly see how all the social problems in the third paragraph give reasons.

I'm going out on a limb here (we're pretty good friends) and read between the lines. If you want my opinion (here it comes), you're not really saying what I sense is your real position. I think you want to defend our generation to some extent by saying hey, it may be true that we appear to be apathetic in comparison to other generations, like anti-war activists during the Vietnam War, but that it's not our fault. We didn't make this mess. We inherited it, and the media (mostly burned out baby-boomers, by the way) are trying to blame us. They're the ones who can't face reality. We're the nightmare they created—apathetic voidoids with pierced body parts and tattoos.

So my advice is don't be so nice. You seem to want to finesse it, and maybe your real feelings aren't coming out as strongly as they could.

FINAL DRAFT

CITIZENS X

I'm a member of Generation X, perhaps the most vilified generation in recent American history. My generation has been under fire for the last five years or so. As the media and journalists portray us, we're apathetic about politics, obsessed by personal success, and stressed out by everyday life. In the United States, young people are supposed to be the hope of the future, but if you read the popular press, you might well think the future is a nightmare of body-pierced, tattooed young people hooked on drugs, MTV, and *Beverly Hills 90210*. We're pictured as a generation in decline, an ominous sign of the bankruptcy of the American

Dream. And in many ways, we like to act the part. We're the busters, the slackers, the affectless voidoid generation. But beneath this pose is a real problem that has not been fully addressed by either the media images or youth culture styles. Why has this generation been so vilified? We're taking the blame for the failures of previous generations.

The media would like to represent my generation as a symbol of everything that has gone wrong in America over the past twenty years. We're presented as the product of divorce, broken homes, and single parents. Even if our parents stayed married—and statistically speaking, about half of them did—they both went to work, leaving us alone at home, latch-key kids raised by afternoon television. In the face of a declining economy, a skyrocketing national debt, downsizing, and lay-offs, the media has labeled us materialistic and careerist, when in fact the baby-boomers have already bagged all the good jobs. Compared to the political activists in the civil rights, anti-war, and feminist movements of the sixties and early seventies, our generation is portrayed as passive, apathetic, cynical—without a galvanizing issue to give it a cause and a sense of mission.

These portrayals of my generation are not altogether wrong. They each help describe what the older generation seems to see as the particularly disturbing mood of young people today. But they don't go very far toward explaining this mood. People forget that the shaping political experiences of my generation begin with Watergate and the resignation of President Richard Nixon, with scandal and illegal activities in high places. Growing up in the shadow of Watergate, people my age developed a distrust in politics and politicians, and nothing has come along on the political scene to give us much hope for an attitude adjustment. Despite our support for Bill Clinton, the country's first MTV presidential candidate, his presidency seems bogged down, ineffective, and wavering on issues like gays in the military and universal health care.

Apathy does indeed run deep through my generation. If anything, it's become a dominant style. Acting cool, distanced, and nonchalant is all part of the image. But to blame us for this apathy is another matter. While we may fail the political activism test when we're compared to the protesters and organizers of the sixties and early seventies, the comparison itself is self-serving because it fails to ask what the activists accomplished. It's precisely this generation of baby boomers who are now running the country and shaping public opinion. Blaming young people my age for the country's current social problems is a convenient way to evade responsibility for the world they have built but don't like the looks of.

Peer Commentary

If you have written peer commentaries, you may want to include a representative one, prefaced with an explanation of what you learned through the peer commentaries and what it was like for you to do them.

SAMPLE INTRODUCTION TO PEER COMMENTARY

Margaret King

At first, it was difficult to criticize a classmate's work for fear of being too harsh and possibly offending them. But as the term progressed, it became easier because I learned what to look for and how to make helpful suggestions. I realized that as a writer I wanted my classmates to give me honest feedback and that the best peer commentaries I got didn't try to judge my working draft but to give me suggestions about what to do with it. I tried to apply these ideas to the peer commentaries I wrote. I think the peer commentaries gave me insight as a writer and helped me to learn to read more critically and make choices in the revision process.

Commentary on Collaborative Writing

If you were involved in a collaborative writing project, you might write a short commentary about your experience. What role did you play in the group's work? How does collaborative writing differ from individual writing? What is gained? What, if anything, is lost? Explain your thoughts and feelings about your involvement in producing a group-written project.

SAMPLE INTRODUCTION TO COLLABORATIVE WRITING

David Sanchez

To me, group projects have both good and bad points. Luckily, however, I believe the good points outweigh the bad points. In my opinion, the worst part about doing a group project is setting up meetings. With an abundant amount of other work, finding a time that everyone can meet sometimes becomes difficult. In addition, when the group finally meets, you usually end up talking about other things and basically just hanging out. It seems that for every hour or so of a meeting, only about thirty minutes of work is done.

On a good note, however, the actual project usually produces an interesting result. By having more than one person work on a project, especially a written one, a better result will usually come out. Each person adds a different view and also finds mistakes others have missed.

As we have seen through our writing assignments, no one can write a perfect paper the first time. Through each peer commentary, many possible areas of improvement come to light and therefore a better final paper. The same is true of writing a paper with other people.

An additional drawback to writing a group paper, however, is that since it is written by more than one person, more than one idea is conveyed. Yes, as I said before, this is good in a way, but it also makes it harder to write a creative paper. Each person ends up having to modify their view in order to go along with everyone else.

Another bad thing, which can arise from some group projects, occurs when one or more people in the group do not do their parts. When this happens, the other people in the group end up doing too much work and get frustrated. I was happy to find that both John and Joe were willing to do the work. We first met a couple of times to decide on a topic for the project and to begin work. Next we all contributed to the collection of data for the survey. We then divided the paper into three sections, and each wrote one. Finally we had a meeting in order to bring the three parts together and to write an introduction and a conclusion.

Overall, I enjoyed doing the group project with John and Joe. Prior to doing it, I had not known either of them very well. Through this project, I can say that I have become friends with both of them. We all worked together quite well and produced a project I was happy with.

Samples of Exploratory Writing

If you have done exploratory writing, you could include a few samples that, for whatever reason, you like the most. Write an introduction that explains what it was like for you to do exploratory writing, what you learned, how this kind of writing differs from other writing assignments, the benefits you see, and so on.

SAMPLE INTRODUCTION TO EXPLORATORY WRITING

John Hogan

Exploratory writing was one of my favorite things in this course. When doing this type of writing, I felt free to say what I wanted, any way I wanted. All of this freedom allowed me to put down on paper exactly what I was thinking. Usually when writing a more formal paper, I find that as I am writing I spend too much time making sure everything is structurally and grammatically correct. Many times I lose sight of some of my new ideas, as I try to perfect the previous ones. Here, there was no pattern or structure that had to be followed. When doing exploratory writing I simply wrote and did not worry about grammar, spelling, unity, or coherence.

Miscellaneous

Depending on your teacher's directions, you may include a miscellany of writing done in or out of class—letters, notes, e-mail, newsgroup dialog, poetry, fiction, posters, leaflets, and flyers. Introduce these writings and explain what called on you to write them and how they differ from the other writing in your portfolio.

ON-LINE PORTFOLIOS

People usually think of portfolios as a sequence of printed documents that readers go through from start to finish. If your teacher agrees, you could design an on-line portfolio on the Web. You would need, of course, to include all the required components of a print portfolio. A challenging part of designing such an on-line portfolio is making it easy for readers to understand how the parts are linked together.

Credits

TEXT CREDITS

CHAPTER 1: 12 "NIKE Code of Conduct," WWW.NIKE.COM. Reprinted by permission of NIKE, Inc.; 14 "Hazardous Waste Storage Area" ad reprinted by permission of the Office of Risk Management at Brown University; 16 From the South Providence Neighborhood Ministries Newsletter, Spring 1988. Reprinted by permission; 18 From "Ejercito Zapatista de Liberacion Nacional," http://www.ezln.org. Reprinted by permission; 18 From "The Zapatistas, Chiapas and the Irish Mexico Group," http://flag.blackened.net/revolt/mexico.html; 25 From *Narrative of the Life of Frederick Douglass* by Frederick Douglass, 1863; 26 Reprinted by permission of the publisher from *One Writer's Beginnings* by Eudora Welty, Cambridge, Mass.: Harvard University Press, Copyright © 1983, 1984 by Eudora Welty; 27 Reprinted by permission of the publisher from Margaret Finders, *Just Girls* (New York: Teachers College Press, © 1997 by Teachers College, Columbia University. All rights reserved.), pp. 41–45.

CHAPTER 2: 35 "The Hereditarian Theory of IQ: An American Invention," from *The Mismeasure of Man,* Revised and Expanded Edition by Stephen Jay Gould. Copyright © 1996, 1981 by Stephen Jay Gould. Used by permission of W. W. Norton & Company, Inc.; 39 From "Distancing the Homeless" by Jonathan Kozol From *Rachel and Her Children,* Crown, 1988. Reprinted by permission; 54 From "Historical Collections at the New York Academy of Medicine," website: http://www.nyam.org/library/history/seminars.html. Reprinted by permission of the New York Academy of Medicine; 54 "Drudge Report," http://www.drudgereport.com; 56 Jason DeParle, "Learning Poverty First Hand," *New York Times Magazine,* April 27, 1997; 58 "My Culture at the Crossroads." *Newsweek,* October 9. Copyright © 2000, Newsweek, Inc. All rights reserved. Reprinted by permission.

CHAPTER 3: 66 "Two Letters Regarding a Readiness to Learn Family Learning Center." Copyright © 1995 by *Harper's Magazine.* All rights reserved. Reproduced from the July issue by special permission; 77 From MALCOLM X SPEAKS. Copyright © 1965, 1989 by Betty Shabazz and Pathfinder Press. Reprinted by permission; 97 "Abortion Is Too Complex to Feel All One Way About" by Anna Quindlen. Copyright © 1986 by The New York Times Co. Reprinted by Permission. 101 "*New York Times* Ad Campaign," September 1999. Reprinted by permission of Quixote Center, http://www.quixote.org; 102 "Call for a Moratorium on Executions," Fall 1999. Reprinted by permission of Quixote Center, http://www.quixote.org.

CHAPTER 4: 113 December 12, 1965 letter, as submitted, from *The Letters of Pfc Richard E. Marks, USMC* by Richard E. Marks. Copyright © 1967 by Gloria D. Kramer, executrix of the Estate of Richard E. Marks. Reprinted by permission of HarperCollins Publishers; 114 "An Ellen Viewer to Her Mother" from *Letters of the Century: America 1900–1999.* Edited by Lisa Grunwald & Stephen J. Adler, Oct. 1999; 116 "Letter to the Editor" by Kristin Tardiff, *Providence Journal-Bulletin,* May 3, 1994. Reprinted by permission of the author; 117 "Commit a Crime, Suffer the Consequences" by Mark Patinkin. Copyright © 1994 *Providence Journal-Bulletin;* 118 From "Letter to the Editor" by John R. Taylor, Jr., *Providence Journal-Bulletin.* Reprinted by permission of the author; 121 "Crossing the Bikini Line" — Galen Sherwin and Ingrid Newkirk letters. Copyright © 2000 by *Harper's Magazine.* All rights reserved. Reproduced from the April issue by special permission; 123 "My Dungeon Shook: Letter to My Nephew on the One Hundredth Anniversary of the Emancipation" c 1962, 1963 by James Baldwin was originally published in The Progressive. Collected in *The Fire Next Time,* published by Vin-

CHAPTER 19: 641 "The Success Taboo" by Bob Herbert. Copyright © 1997 by The New York Times Co. Reprinted by permission; 642 "The Medical Bottom Line." *Newsweek*, February 3. Copyright ©1997, Newsweek, Inc. All rights reserved. Reprinted by permission; 643 "A Growing Arsenal Against HIV." *Newsweek*, December 2. Copyright © 1996, Newsweek, Inc. All rights reserved. Reprinted by permission; 645 Red Sox Statistics from the Providence Journal, Providence, Rhode Island, April 6, 2001. Reprinted with permission of The Associated Press; 647 "State Lottery Proceeds." U.S. Bureau of the Census, *Statistical Abstract of the United States: 1995* (115th edition.) Washington, DC, 1995; 650 Required Fuel Economy Standards: New Cars Built from 1978 to 1985 by Edward Tufte, from *The Visual Display of Quantitative Information*, 1983, p. 58; 679 Food Bank *news* from the Rhode Island Community Food Bank, Summer 1999. Courtesy of the Rhode Island Community Food Bank; 681 From the "Summit Steward Program" brochure by The Adirondack Chapter of The Nature Conservancy and The Adirondack Land Trust; 682 Global Exchange at http://www.globalexchange.org. Reprinted by permission.

CHAPTER 21: 699 Jennifer Principe, Reflective letter. Reprinted by permission of the author; 700 Matt Axt, Introduction, draft, and "Citizens X." Reprinted by permission of the author; 705 Margaret King, Introduction to peer commentary. Reprinted by permission of the author; 705 David Sanchez, Commentary on collaborative writing. Reprinted by permission of the author; 706 John Hogan, Introduction to exploratory writing. Reprinted by permission of the author.

PHOTO CREDITS

Photo research by Photosearch, Inc.; Cover *Metropolitan Life* by Victor Arnauoff. Detail/Coit Tower, San Francisco, CA. Don Beatty Photo ©1981; 1 *California Industrial* by John Langley Howard. Detail/Coit Tower, San Francisco, CA. Don Beatty Photo ©1981; 7 *California Industrial* by John Langley Howard. Detail/Coit Tower, San Francisco, CA. Don Beatty Photo ©1981; 9, R Courtesy of The Adirondack Museum, Blue Mountain Lake, N.Y. Photo by Jim Swedberg, Photography; 11 ©1991, *The Washington Post*. Photo by Lucian Perkins. Reprinted with permission; 12 From the book *Graffito* by Michael Walsh; 17, T Cruz, Manuel. *Signs from the Heart*, "Untitled (Homeboy)," detail. Approx. 161 x 201. Ramona Gardens Housing Project, East Los Angeles; 17, B Courtesy of the Teamsters Union; 18, BR Photograph of protest: Courtesy of Revolt; 32 *California Industrial* by John Langley Howard. Detail/Coit Tower, San Francisco, CA. Don Beatty Photo ©1981; 50, T Globe Editorial, Inc.; 50, B Reprinted by permission of *The Wall Street Journal*, ©2002 Dow Jones & Co., Inc. All Rights Reserved Worldwide; 58 Guy Aroch/Corbis Outline; 63 *California Industrial* by John Langley Howard. Detail/Coit Tower, San Francisco, CA. Don Beatty Photo ©1981; 92 Courtesy of UNITE; 107 *City Life* by Victor Arnauoff. Detail/Coit Tower, San Francisco, CA. Don Beatty Photo ©1981; 111 *City Life* by Victor Arnauoff. Detail/Coit Tower, San Francisco, CA. Don Beatty Photo ©1981; 117 *The Providence Journal*; 145 *City Life* by Victor Arnauoff. Detail/Coit Tower, San Francisco, CA. Don Beatty Photo ©1981; 182 *City Life* by Victor Arnauoff. Detail/Coit Tower, San Francisco, CA. Don Beatty Photo ©1981; 206 NYT Permissions/NYT Pictures; 222 *City Life* by Victor Arnauoff. Detail/Coit Tower, San Francisco, CA. Don Beatty Photo ©1981; 225 Steve Goldstein; 238 Courtesy of Pfizer. Photo by Noren Trotman/NBA Photos; 239 Coutesy of Service Employees International Union. AFL-CIO.CLC.; 256 *City Life* by Victor Arnauoff. Detail/Coit Tower, San Francisco, CA. Don Beatty Photo ©1981; 259 Patrick Bonz/Habitat for Humanity International; 261 Kim MacDonald/Habitat for Humanity International; 269 Hulton Archive/Getty Images; 270 Photofest; 274 *Mary Wollstonecraft Shelley* (detail) by Richard Rothwell. Courtesy of the National Portrait Gallery, London; 275 *Mary Wollstonecraft Shelley* by Richard Rothwell. Courtesy of the National Portrait Gallery, London; 276 *Mary Wollstonecraft*. British School/ Board of Trustees of the National Museums and Galleries on Merseyside (Walker Art Gallery Liverpool); 277 *William Godwin* by Henry William Pickersgill. Courtesy of the National Portrait Gallery, London; 278 *Percy Bysshe Shelley* by Amelia Curran. Courtesy of the National Portrait Gallery, London; 279 *Frankenstein* (frontispiece) by Chevalier after Holst, 1831. Courtesy of the National Portrait Gallery, London; 280 Reproduction of cover of *Frankenstein, Creation and Monstrosity*, edited by Stephen Bann (Reaktion Books, London, 1994). Cover illustration: Marc Solomon Dennis, Coyote Hand, etching, 1993; 289, T William Gottlieb/Retna Ltd.; 289, B Frank Driggs Collection; 290, T Aram Avakian/Sony Records/Woodfin Camp & Associates; 290, B William Gottlieb/Retna Ltd.; 307 *City Life* by Victor Arnauoff. Detail/Coit Tower, San Francisco, CA. Don Beatty Photo ©1981; 325 J. Gordon/NYT Pictures; 326 Image courtesy of www.adbusters.org; 344 *City Life* by Victor Arnauoff. Detail/Coit Tower, San Francisco, CA. Don Beatty Photo ©1981; 367 Photograph courtesy of the Office of the President, National Urban League, Inc.; 368 Courtesy of U.S. ENGLISH Foundation, Inc.; 386 *City*

Life by Victor Arnauoff. Detail/Coit Tower, San Francisco, CA. Don Beatty Photo ©1981; 403 V. Laforet/NYT Pictures; 421 *California Industrial* by John Langley Howard. Detail/Coit Tower, San Francisco, CA. Don Beatty Photo ©1981; 428 *California Industrial* by John Langley Howard. Detail/Coit Tower, San Francisco, CA. Don Beatty Photo ©1981; 431 ©1985 Quantity Postcards; 447 *California Industrial* by John Langley Howard. Detail/Coit Tower, San Francisco, CA. Don Beatty Photo ©1981; 461 *California Industrial* by John Langley Howard. Detail/Coit Tower, San Francisco, CA. Don Beatty Photo ©1981; 492 *California Industrial* by John Langley Howard. Detail/Coit Tower, San Francisco, CA. Don Beatty Photo ©1981; 519 *Library* by Bernard B. Zakheim. Detail/Coit Tower, San Francisco, CA. Don Beatty Photo ©1981; 527 *Library* by Bernard B. Zakheim. Detail/Coit Tower, San Francisco, CA. Don Beatty Photo ©1981; 561 *Library* by Bernard B. Zakheim. Detail/Coit Tower, San Francisco, CA. Don Beatty Photo ©1981; 581 *Newsgathering* by Suzanne Scheuer. Detail/Coit Tower, San Francisco, CA. Don Beatty Photo ©1981; 584 *Newsgathering* by Suzanne Scheuer. Detail/Coit Tower, San Francisco, CA. Don Beatty Photo ©1981; 636 *Newsgathering* by Suzanne Scheuer. Detail/Coit Tower, San Francisco, CA. Don Beatty Photo ©1981; 637 Design by Roger Cook and Donald Shanosky. Courtesy of Cook and Shanosky Associates, Inc.; 638 IBM and the IBM logotype are registered trademarks of International Business Machines Corporation; 638 ® Registered trademark of United Way of America; 638 Courtesy of the Polish Cultural Institute in NY; 638 Courtesy of April Greiman/Pentagram; 639 Courtesy of The Quaker Oats Company; 640 Apple and the Apple Logo are trademarks of Apple Computer, Inc., registered in the U.S. and other countries, used with permission; 640 Apple and the Apple Logo are trademarks of Apple Computer, Inc., registered in the U.S. and other countries, used with permission; 642 Newsweek. ©February 3, 1997, Newsweek, Inc. All rights reserved. Reprinted by permission; 644 NYT Graphics/NYT Pictures; 644 Reprinted with permission of Knight-Ridder/Tribune Information Services; 646 Courtesy of the Bureau of Transportation Statistics; 647 NYT Graphics/NYT Pictures; 650 NYT Graphics/NYT Pictures; 653 Library of Congress; 653 Savile Lumley, *Daddy, what did YOU do in the Great War?*/Imperial War Museum, London; 654 Library of Congress; 654 *Can You Read?* Billboard. Diane Cain, designer, Brooklyn Seven Design Group. Courtesy of Sheila Levrant de Brettville; 655 Leo Burnett/Physicians Against Land Mines; 656 Courtesy of Stratagem NI.; 656 © 1995 by the Guerilla Girls; 662 Angel Franco/*New York Times*/Getty Images; 678 Courtesy of POON & GIANNINI Advertising; 679 Bob Thayer/*The Providence Journal;* 679 Courtesy of the Rhode Island Community Food Bank; 681 Courtesy of the Adirondack Chapter of The Nature Conservancy & the Adirondack Land Trust; 683 *Newsgathering* by Suzanne Scheuer. Detail/Coit Tower, San Francisco, CA. Don Beatty Photo ©1981; 697 *Newsgathering* by Suzanne Scheuer. Detail/Coit Tower, San Francisco, CA. Don Beatty Photo ©1981.

Index

Page numbers followed by *f* indicate figures.

GUIDE TO READING SELECTIONS

The reading selections in *The Call to Write* come from a wide variety of sources. The following list shows where you can find academic, popular, and professional writing, as well as examples of student writing.

ACADEMIC, POPULAR, AND PROFESSIONAL WRITING